STONEWALL IN THE VALLEY

STONEWALL IN THE VALLEY

Thomas J. "Stonewall" Jackson's Shenandoah Valley Campaign Spring 1862

Robert G. Tanner

STACKPOLE BOOKS

Published by
STACKPOLE BOOKS
5067 Ritter Road
Mechanicsburg, PA 17055

Printed in the United States of America

First Stackpole edition (updated and revised)

10 9 8 7 6 5 4 3 2 1

Previously published in 1976 by Doubleday & Company, Inc.

Grateful acknowledgment is made to the following for permission to use previously copyrighted material:

David McKay Company, Inc.—*Destruction and Reconstruction* by Richard Taylor, copyright © 1955 by Richard Taylor. Published by Longmans Green and Company. *Stonewall Jackson and the Civil War* by G. F. R. Henderson, copyright © 1961 by Longmans Green and Co. Published 1936 by Longmans Green and Co. Reprinted by permission of David McKay Company, Inc.

University of North Carolina Press—*The Valley of Virginia in the American Revolution* by Freeman H. Hart and *Notes on the State of Virginia* edited by William Peden. Published for the Institute of Early American History and Culture.

University of Pittsburgh Press—*A Borderland Confederate* by William L. Wilson, copyright © 1962 by the University of Pittsburgh Press. Reprinted by permission.

Library of Congress Cataloging-in-Publication Data

Tanner, Robert G.

Stonewall in the valley : Thomas J. "Stonewall" Jackson's Shenandoah Valley campaign, spring 1862 / Robert G. Tanner. — 1st Stackpole ed., updated and rev.

p. cm.

Previously published: Doubleday & Co., 1976.

Includes bibliographical references (p.) and index.

ISBN 0-8117-1708-9 (hard)

1. Shenandoah Valley Campaign, 1862. 2. Jackson, Stonewall, 1824-1863. I. Title.

E473.74.T36 1996

973.7'32—dc20

95-37571

CIP

Still for my parents

CONTENTS

LIST OF ILLUSTRATIONS

Photographs (all following page 236)

Maps

INTRODUCTION

Two decades ago, in the Introduction to the first edition of this work, I wrote of the "South's largely unknown Valley Campaign of 1862." I argued that the Shenandoah Valley Campaign led by Major General Thomas J. "Stonewall" Jackson had not been presented without serious misconceptions—indeed had been obscured by a romantic haze that blurred the reality of one of the most interesting episodes of the War Between the States. The book undertook to correct that problem by recounting in depth the campaign from the Confederate viewpoint, a task last undertaken in the 1880s by a man who saw the action firsthand as a member of Jackson's staff, William Allan. The research was accomplished by 1972, and with publication in 1976, I assumed that the project was finished. That assumption must now be seen as optimistic. Temerity has had its punishment, and accuracy compels an admission that in some significant respects the campaign remains unknown, or at best incompletely described. Hence this volume.

A new study was made desirable, in the first instance, by the increasing body of information and analysis about the war in the Shenandoah Valley. The corpus of material emerging since the early 1970s includes many original sources. The personal diary of Brigadier General Charles Winder, third-ranking officer of the Valley Army, has surfaced, with valuable details on movements of the Stonewall Brigade. The brigade's service is also chronicled by a particularly fine set of letters by and other papers not heretofore available pertaining to Captain S. J. C. Moore of the 2d Virginia. Diaries and letter collections of many other soldiers in the ranks, including Watkins Kearns, Joseph Shaner, William T. Kinzer, and A. S. Wade, give additional insight into the operations of the Stonewall Brigade during the Valley Campaign. Greater attention to Brigadier General Turner Ashby's Valley cavalry was possible through a set of Ashby papers recently deposited with the Virginia Historical Society. The diary of Major Frank Jones, who served as Jackson's special aide at the Battle of Kernstown, has come to light and combined with existing sources to clarify much about that battle. The archives of the Virginia Military Institute have in recent years become better organized under the direction of Ms. Diane Jacob, allowing discovery of a number of items relating to V.M.I. cadets who served in the campaign.

Important new materials have been identified by regimental historians. For a work dealing with a Virginia campaign waged principally by Virginia troops, the *Virginia Regimental Histories Series,* which is nearing completion after more than a decade of scholarship, is very helpful. The series offers separate volumes on each regiment and battery raised in the Old Dominion. With a focus narrowed to one unit, each author has been able to examine his or her subject in rich detail and has brought to light unknown or overlooked first-person accounts. Important work has been done as well on units from beyond Virginia, especially the splendid regiments of Richard Taylor's Louisiana Brigade. The want of more first-hand accounts from those commands was something I regretted when writing the first edition. Happily, that gap has been filled with some very interesting material concerning Louisiana infantrymen; much of this has become known through the efforts of Terry L. Jones and T. Michael Parrish. The authors of all these unit histories have shared their discoveries, and it is a pleasure to thank them for their aid.

The current emphasis on tactical studies also enhances knowledge of the Valley Campaign. Monographs have appeared on Jackson's Romney Campaign and the Battles of McDowell, Winchester, Cross Keys, and Port Republic. The indefatigable Robert Krick, Chief Historian of the Fredericksburg-Spotsylvania National Military Park, is currently reconstructing the Battles of Cross Keys and Port Republic, and doubtless his study will answer every question on those encounters. If such a position as National Answer Man for the War Between the States should ever be created, Mr. Krick inevitably will be appointed. Beyond his keen insight into all aspects of the war, he generously shared many diaries and letter collections unearthed through his efforts as well as those of the park staff, and his assistance is much appreciated.

Biographies of those at or near the top echelons of Southern command during the Valley Campaign have appeared since the mid-1970s (or are shortly to be released). These include lives of Jackson, Jefferson Davis (rendered even more valuable by an ongoing and very comprehensive edition of his papers, which as of 1995 has reached the year 1862), Robert E. Lee, Joseph E. Johnston, Richard S. Ewell, Richard Taylor, Turner Ashby, Campbell Brown, and Jedediah Hotchkiss (two studies). Much of the foregoing is first-rate work and has furthered understanding of 1862 operations in the Valley. Also, some contemporary views of both terrain and participants of the campaign have been discovered in photographic archives.

New materials have prompted reevaluation of documents previously available but not fully utilized or simply unappreciated. In this category are several original sources. First are the papers of Jedediah Hotchkiss. The vast repository of Hotchkiss items in the Library of Congress long has been mined, but since the mid-1970s the library has reorganized this collection while transferring it to microfilm. It was especially enjoyable to find through this new scheme Hotchkiss's actual field diary for the campaign. Additionally, the New York Historical Society maintains Hotchkiss's handwritten "Memoranda—Valley Campaign of 1862"; this represents a postwar effort to summarize the campaign and supplements the several versions of Hotchkiss's diary. It has not apparently been widely examined.

Among other items of interest formerly overlooked are the papers of Brigadier General L. O'Bryan Branch. Apparently these files have not been read in connection with the Valley Campaign. Although Branch's role in the Shenandoah was tangential, the unpublished letters to Branch from Richard Ewell helped clarify Confederate planning during the decisive phase of the Valley offensive; indeed they led to a new view of Jackson's intentions as he readied his assault on Banks during May 1862. (That view is summarized in Appendix A.) Of great value from a private's vantage point of the campaign are the writings of Lancelot Minor Blackford of the Rockbridge Artillery. Although these letters have been known in part from a long-out-of-print work, the full letters located at the University of Virginia are unmatched in both quantity and precision of comment on the battles of and life in the Valley Army. The papers of Robert L. Dabney yielded the answer to a minor mystery of the war, the question of what response Jackson received from a May 20 telegram hurriedly sent to Robert E. Lee in effect asking him to overrule Joseph E. Johnston's orders as to further operations in the Shenandoah. Finally, an obscure column in the June 16, 1862, New York *Herald* has provided fresh information on Confederate planning after the Battle of Winchester.

The variety of new information on the war as a whole is reflected in several miscellaneous aspects of the Valley Campaign to receive attention in the last two decades. The creation of the C & O National Park has helped clarify understanding of Jackson's late 1861 operations against that system. The remarkable coincidence of three classmates from West Point's class of 1846 (McClellan, Jackson, and George Gordon) interacting directly and indirectly during the Campaign has been related in a fascinating study, John Waugh's *The Class of 1846.* Even the modern experience of farming fields where once the Valley armies contended has been described, by Peter Svenson in *Battlefield.* Margaretta Barton Colt's *Defend the Valley* offers a gripping account of four years in the Shenandoah seen through the lives of one extended family; this fine work makes readily available significant material on the 1862 campaign.

There are, in short, ample fresh resources to prompt another look at the Shenandoah Valley Campaign of 1862, and such an examination is undertaken here. Although this book builds on the first edition of *Stonewall in the Valley* and duplicates with only minor changes its first two chapters and Appendixes A to D (now B to E), all subsequent chapters are substantially different, embodying much new insight on central aspects of the campaign. Jackson's remarkable council of war in March 1862 is examined in minute detail to essay the wisdom of his plan to launch a predawn surprise attack against overwhelming Union numbers rather than retreat before them. The long-standing assumption that Stonewall intended in late April to depart the Valley and return via the Virginia Central Railroad is rejected; this is a plan he apparently never made but one for which he has received much praise. The operations of Richard S. Ewell while Jackson was fighting in the Alleghenies come into sharper focus, giving additional support for a new understanding of Jackson's preferred but unexecuted plans for defeating his nemesis, Nathaniel Banks. The mystery of Jackson's appeal to Lee to countermand Johnston's orders in May 1862 is resolved, and the role of Johnston in prompting Jackson's apparently risky drive toward Harpers Ferry in late May is revealed for the first time. Jackson's grueling retreat from Harpers Ferry to Port Republic is described in depth, as is the remarkable skirmish that erupted in the streets of Port Republic at the end of that retreat. The end-of-campaign debate within the Confederate high command as to the Valley Army's next mission is reconstructed and evaluated. Finally, the various battles of the campaign are covered in fair detail to round out the story.

The analysis of these insights takes place within a new conceptual framework. Since the 1970s, the method long prevailing in American circles of presenting military campaigns as an interaction of strategy (meaning roughly the combination of battles and wide maneuvers employed to achieve the overall war aim) and tactics (the conduct of combat on the battlefield) has given way to a multi-layered scheme. Though this book does not strive in any way to be a treatise on military science or art, it is worthwhile to outline this framework, at least insofar as it will be utilized from time to time. The term "strategy" is now used to define the overall war goals of a nation as articulated for action in a theater of operations. "Tactics" remains the direct fighting of battles. The intermediate level is termed the "operational art," which stands between strategy and tactics. It has been defined as follows: "The planning level of war that constructs campaigns and major operations in order to accomplish the theater goals articulated at the strategy planning level."[1] The operational art of war is typically a maneuver conducted by corps-sized or greater forces and involves speed, selective engagement, and deep penetration of high-value enemy terrain—exactly what Jackson was doing in the Shenandoah. The development of this matrix of analysis has been traced elsewhere[2] and need not be repeated here. It is appropriate to note that the method has been employed increasingly in recent years to discuss campaigns of the War Between the States.[3] My hope is that some reference to this method will make the narrative more meaningful for current military history students.

For all the discussion of military theory, however, this book remains principally a Civil War history. It relates to the Valley Campaign primarily from the Confederate point of view and with a focus on the Valley Army as a developing entity. Given the mass of new Southern sources noted above, this is both necessary and desirable. The Valley Army's story is an intensely interesting human drama. That story is told wherever possible in the contemporary words of the men who fought with Stonewall in what one of them called "the most exciting campaign of this war."

Many people helped bring this history to completion. In addition to those individuals already acknowledged, it is a pleasure to list with sincere thanks these others who have corresponded with the author or sources and/or provided research assistance: Joseph H. Carpenter, Covington, Virginia; Randall S. Gooden, West Virginia University; James

Mann, Beaverdam, Virginia; Timothy Kearney, Raleigh, North Carolina; Juanita G. Grant, Averett College, Danville, Virginia; Keith Bohannon; Glen L. McMullen, Blacksburg, Virginia; Lewis Leigh, Fairfax, Virginia; Richard B. Kleese, Strasburg, Virginia; H. E. Howard, Lynchburg, Virginia; Margaret M. O'Bryant, Albemarle County Historical Society, Charlottesville, Virginia; J. Harvey Bailey, Charlottesville, Virginia; Virginia Ann Heyerdahl, Cumberland, Maryland; Susan Riggs, College of William and Mary, Williamsburg, Virginia: Vesta Lee Gordon, Charlottesville, Virginia; Dora S. Tylor, Winchester, Virginia; Richard J. Sommers, Carlisle Barracks, Pennsylvania; Wilbur Meneray, New Orleans, Louisiana; Ted Alexander, Sharpsburg, Maryland; William Erwin, Jr., Durham, North Carolina; Claire McCann, Lexington, Kentucky; Mr. John Hennessy, Frederick, Maryland; Mrs. Anita Cummins, Port Republic, Virginia; Mr. Ben Ritter, Winchester, Virginia; and Mr. Lee Wallace, Jr., Falls Church, Virginia. Special thanks are owed Dr. Charles F. Bryan, Jr., Director, Virginia Historical Society and a "Brother Rat," who made use of the society's great resources, sometimes via long distance, possible as well as easy; to Richard L. Armstrong, author of several works touching the Valley Campaign who took many an afternoon from his own writing to share information; to Professor Brandon H. Beck, Director, Civil War Institute, Shenandoah University, Winchester, Virginia, for aid with original material on the battle of May 25, 1862; and to Don Pfanz of Fredericksburg, Virginia, who, while working on a new biography of Ewell, located some rare material on Ewell's role in the Valley Campaign and generously shared it.

For superb technical and research assistance I wish to thank Ms. Amelia Hutchens, Ms. Sharon Kelly, Ms. Carolyn Keeling, and Ms. Lisa Fountain, and for excellent editorial guidance I am indebted to Mr. Jack Davis and Ms. Sylvia Frank.

With the help of these friends, I have amassed a sufficient database to recount a full military history of the South's Valley Campaign of 1862. If that is not now finally done, the fault is mine alone.

PROLOGUE

The Stonewall Brigade was going home. Sergeants were in the camp already, bellowing to strike tents. That guaranteed it. The brigade was leaving the Confederate Army at Centreville, Virginia, and going home to the Shenandoah Valley. Private John Opie of the 5th Virginia Infantry began to imagine a furlough; the rowdy E Company Irishmen of the 33d Virginia celebrated with a barrel of stolen whiskey. Rarely did the entire brigade agree on anything, but every man was happy about this shift. The transfer to Winchester, Virginia, would get them out of General Joseph E. Johnston's soggy camps and back to the headquarters of their former commander, "Stonewall" Jackson.

On November 9, 1861, a rebel swarm in the guise of an infantry brigade descended on the depot at Manassas Junction, Virginia. An assortment of wheezing locomotives waited to transport them to the Valley. Cars to accommodate five regiments had been ordered; enough for only three had come. Forced to await space on the return trains, the 4th and 33d Virginia shuffled aside, grunting about army boondoggles. The 2d, 5th, and 27th Virginia tossed their gear onto the open-burden flatcars and packed in around it.

A slow journey bounced these Virginians to Manassas Gap in the Blue Ridge Mountains, where steam yielded to muscle. Several grades were too steep for the gorged trains, so everyone walked, creating a scene that was vintage Confederacy: hundreds of foulmouthed infantry tramping up dust and flinging bits of gravel at the lumbering cars beside them. Eventually they gained the summit, reboarded, and entered the Shenandoah Valley. Wags such as Private Jim Frazier of the 5th Virginia warned that the couplings between an engine and its cars could snap on the downgrade. The show that followed—with the locomotive straining to keep clear of the butting cars—was spectacular, said the comics. Suddenly uneasy men enjoyed the ride less until the tracks leveled off to run westward across the Valley floor to Strasburg, which was reached after dark. The troops were hungry, parched, and ready for a bung knocking. They plunged off the trains and made for town in roaring good spirits.

Next morning, November 10, many men were too drunk to make reveille. Roll callers tallied scores absent. In the 27th Virginia only Captain James Edmondson's Company H answered all present, and it numbered fully a third of the regiment. As the rebels marched off beneath a cold rain, Edmondson's company was detailed to herd forward stragglers, who fell from ranks by the dozen. Many were still wild with drink and had to be battered to the ground with muskets before they would move.[1]

In the 2d Virginia things were the same. Some of its officers, "being too much of parlor soldiers to march at their posts," wrote Lieutenant Sam Moore to his wife, hired coaches to hurry ahead into Winchester so they could claim the best hotel rooms. They passed their commands quite grandly on the road, thought Moore, who watched his own company shrink around him. "Our company behaved abominably on the march, as indeed did nearly all the companies in the regiment—most of our men went home, leaving me not more than 30," he admitted.[2]

John Opie was thinking about granting himself a furlough from the ranks of the 5th Virginia, but he heard a rumor that kept him in place. Winchester's citizens were said to have volunteered to shelter the regiments. This was welcome news: tents had been left at Strasburg because there were no wagons to haul them, so the men could look forward to nothing more than sleeping on wet ground in the woods. Now a real bed in a warm house beckoned. The rebel pace quickened even as the rain poured down in thicker streams.

The northward route of march toward Winchester passed over land on which many of these rebels would bleed and die during the next three years. A mile from Strasburg they crossed a swift-flowing creek banked with cedars. Here in 1864, some of them would almost annihilate a Federal army, summoning Union General Philip Sheridan to his famous "Ride," before being destroyed in turn. Beyond Cedar Creek they entered the beautiful farming hamlet of Middletown; the stone-bordered road they followed now would six months hence be filled with slaughtered Union cavalry, "a shrieking, struggling mass of men and horses, crushed, wounded and dying," a man in ranks today would describe it.[3] More miles carried the troops through a tiny village called Kernstown; west of it, on a low ridge, these men would wage a desperate fight in March 1862, and more than a few would fall there.

A mile from Winchester and near hills where yet others would die, the column halted abruptly, stood silent in the furious rain, then exploded with profanity as orders rippled back to countermarch several miles to an unsheltered bivouac. Stonewall Jackson knew his soldiers would carouse all night once inside Winchester and was determined to keep them out. The general's rock-ribbed discipline—"He would have a man shot at the drop of a hat, and drop it himself," grumbled one Confederate after the war[4]—would not permit a single night's relaxation. He had belted Winchester with local militia under instructions that no one was to be admitted without a pass signed by him.

The Stonewall Brigade nearly mutinied as a result. When Colonel William Harman of the 5th Virginia motioned to about-face, his own brother, captain of the lead company, refused. A lieutenant and then a sergeant balked, until the irate colonel charged toward the sergeant threatening to saber him. At that, Captain Harman drew his sword and promised revenge. The brothers glared at each other for long, wet minutes before, slowly, orders prevailed.[5]

Or so it seemed. In fact, the indomitable Stonewall was about to be outflanked and overrun. As John Opie's company sloshed away, Opie broke ranks and announced that anyone who wanted to go into town could follow him. Three men did and they darted off, part of a mob that included officers and enlisted men alike. Lieutenant Moore of the 2d Virginia reached the campground as one of only six officers still with the regiment, which had shrunk to one fifth its size.[6] The road to Winchester was full of soldiers heading to town, and the militia guards never had a chance to stop them. Forged passes abounded. When John Opie's group was stopped, the men weighed the alternative of returning to a tentless camp in the rain and found it unacceptable. Opie and friends blared that "Jackson and all hell" could not keep them out of Winchester, fixed bayonets, and charged. The startled militiamen fled.[7] Another pack of invaders chased a militia detail into the center of town before letting it escape.[8]

The 5th Virginia's Jim Frazier masterminded the most ingenious break-in that evening. He collected fifty or sixty truants and marched them to a guard post. Halting his "command," Frazier stepped forward with an explanation that General Jackson had summoned him to Winchester with his company to arrest unauthorized men there. The militia promptly opened the way. A few hundred yards down the road, the "company" disbanded, and each man found friends and a warm bed. "I think it safe," chuckled one of Frazier's company, "to say that fully half the brigade visited Winchester that night."[9]

The men in ranks had had their way: theirs was a homecoming even Stonewall Jackson could not deny.

Part I

1

THE SHENANDOAH

We spent ye best part of ye
Day in admiring ye Trees and
richness of ye land.

—GEORGE WASHINGTON

Between the river-laced Piedmont Region and the matted Allegheny Mountains of the Middle Atlantic states there is a corridor. That corridor, in Virginia, is the Shenandoah Valley. The Valley runs southwestward from the Potomac River more than 150 miles to the James. It is flanked on the east by the Blue Ridge and on the west by the Alleghenies, but the passage between these boundaries is a generally smooth path of clover and blue grass. Indian tribes that followed migrating herds up and down this corridor did not realize that it was one of the great early highways of the New World; they were content to regard it simply as a gift of the stars.

The Valley spans geologic time as well. The northern fringes touch or are near two eastward-flowing rivers that are among the oldest of North America, the Potomac and the Susquehanna. From the Valley's southern fringes it is a short journey to the New and Kanawha rivers, younger streams that flow westward to the Ohio River Valley. Many who traveled between the Atlantic Ocean and the Ohio followed the east water routes that curled around the Shenandoah, and for them this Valley was more portage than corridor.

It was at the same time a sally port, a staging area for those who had no patience or no time for river detours and chose instead to strike due west to the heartland of the Ohio River Valley. The western margin of the Shenandoah was little more than one hundred miles from the Ohio Valley, but the way was treacherous. It was walled by the highest mountains east of the Mississippi and by forests of tangled hardwoods. Dead trees lay like abatis among the living; the forest floor, where air never stirred, was spiked with brambles that could shred a man's flesh. Yet there were wind passes and streambeds through this wilderness. With his pack filled from the abundant game that grazed in the Shenandoah, a hardy man could survive a trek across the high mountains.

Corridor, portage, and sally port, the Shenandoah touched many sections of America, and its early history was the clash of people in motion.

The Indians warred here first. Delawares paddled up the Susquehanna, then traveled south to the Valley on foot. Ferocious and arrogant Shawnees were hardened by the march over the Alleghenies from the west. Cherokees pushed northward from Tennessee, and Catawbas from the banks of their river homeland in the Carolinas. Why they warred is not known; there were buffalo and elk and red-tailed deer for all, and still the Indians clashed.[1]

Every fall, when hunters stalked their game in the Valley, the war arrows also flew. The Catawbas and Delawares were the most bitter rivals. Though neither tribe claimed the region, neither could tolerate the other in it. They skirmished continually, and there were outbreaks of full-scale carnage, as when a Delaware war party snatched some prisoners deep within the Catawba homeland. A vengeful Catawba band tracked them for two hundred miles, eventually overtaking the raiders just west of the Shenandoah at the Hanging Rock, a jutting limestone cliff that left only a narrow ledge between it and a stream. The Delawares had foolishly halted on this ledge. The Catawbas flung themselves across the stream and behind their prey. Years later, a visitor identified a seventy-yard trench of Delaware graves near the battleground.[2]

Who the first white man was to enter the Valley is a matter of debate. As early as 1670 German John Lederer was poking around some passes of the Blue Ridge. "A pretty scholar" according to one contemporary, Lederer wrote an account of travels to the Valley in Latin, but the truth of some statements is doubtful: his imagination probably exceeded his skill in Latin.[3] An expedition led by Thomas Batts and Robert Fallam may have traversed the southern Shenandoah during 1671. Batts and Fallam certainly reached the New River and claimed it and the unknown river into which it fed, the Ohio, for England, thereby lodging Britain's foot in the trans-Allegheny door.[4]

Royal Governor Alexander Spotswood's popularly accepted claim to discovery of the Shenandoah probably rests more on his skill as a host and a promoter than on his prowess as an explorer. Spotswood came to the New World as governor of Virginia Colony in 1710. He whetted a thirst for expansion with good rum and fast talk and drove the frontier steadily westward toward the Blue Ridge. Superstitious colonists dreaded that barrier as a haunt of sundry monsters; Spotswood had an idea that the Great Lakes, discovered the previous century, were on the other side. In 1716 he persuaded thirty of the local gentry to join him in an expedition to find the answer.

Spotswood's answer was the Valley, a land of great charm with its smooth vistas, supple contours, and gentle name: Shenandoah, daughter of the stars. Spotswood first saw it from the crown of the Blue Ridge on September 7, 1716, and the governor marked the occasion royally, ordering his wine steward to unstrap saddlebags bulging with champagne and other suitable potions. Spotswood claimed the Valley for King George I of England and led a toast to his sovereign's health with champagne. The explorers fired a volley and pledged the health of the Princess Royal with burgundy. Another volley, and Spotswood led a salute to the remainder of the royal family with claret. A ragged volley followed. Next came a toast to the governor, by which time no one recalled what beverage was sampled. Before dark, a comely little stream meandering across the Valley had grown grand enough to be styled the Euphrates.[5]

For all Spotswood's bibulous enthusiasm to entice Virginians beyond the Blue Ridge, it was the Pennsylvania Germans and the Dutch who pioneered this frontier. Eager to increase its population at the expense of other colonies, Virginia retained professional promoters. By 1730 the colony had granted John and Isaac Van Meter a tract of forty thousand Valley acres on condition that they settle one non-Virginia family per thousand acres on it. The Van Meters had two years in which to satisfy this requirement, a condition imposed with most subsequent large grants. The result was a frantic pace in early Valley settlement. One promoter, threatened with forfeit of his land for insufficient population, supposedly met his quota by representing every cow of his herd as a family head.[6] Germans and Dutch from Pennsylvania were recruited for the Valley before they were in any way inured to the hardships of frontier life, and particularly to frontier warfare.[7] Sometimes pathetically unarmed, they moved south from counties like Lancaster, Lebanon, and Berks, forded the Potomac, and raised villages in the northern Shenandoah, including Mecklenburg (later Shepherdstown), Stephensburg (Newtown), Staufferstadt (Strasburg), and Muellerstadt (Woodstock).

Behind the Germans and Dutch came Scotch-Irish pioneers, who first nestled between them and the Potomac. The outcome of this arrangement was recorded by an early historian:

> The national prejudices which existed between the Dutch and Irish produced much disorder and many riots. It was customary for the Dutch on St. Patrick's Day to exhibit the effigy of the saint, with a string of Irish potatoes around his neck, and his wife Sheeley with her apron loaded also with potatoes. This was always followed by a riot. The Irish resented the indignity to their saint and his holy spouse, and a battle followed. On St. Michael's Day the Irish would retort and exhibit the saint with a rope of sour krout [*sic*] about his neck. Then the Dutch, like the Yankee, "felt chock full of fight" and at it they went pell-mell.[8]

The Scotch-Irish trekked on into the southern Shenandoah, where they were reinforced by Englishmen migrating from east of the Blue Ridge. Counties named Rockbridge and Botetout and villages named Lexington and Fincastle sprang up to rival the unpronounceable German communities.

These hamlet toeholds were possible only because the Indians initially ignored the whites to pursue tribal wars. But by the mid-1700s this had changed. Braves of all tribes saw their game preserve vanishing, as farms, many laid out by a teenage surveyor named George Washington, cluttered the bison trails. Indians saw the passing of their world and began to fear the white farmers as the true enemy.

Indian fears were exploited by France, which at that time embodied the very devil to the English-speaking world. France and England asserted conflicting titles to much of the North American continent west of the Shenandoah. England had chartered Virginia Colony to extend from the Atlantic to the Pacific, and the claim this charter gave to the Ohio River Valley was buttressed by Batts and Fallam's discovery of the New River. As early as 1745 Virginia was granting tracts of land located along the Ohio River. France claimed the same region by reason of Sieur de La Salle's explorations and, more practically, by occupation. French trappers and traders based in Canada carried the fleur-de-lis throughout the Ohio River region, but their sway was tenuous and would snap if fence-loving English farmers penetrated the Alleghenies. It thus became urgent to dam the westward spread of English colonies, and in this struggle, aroused Indians became France's major weapon.

Vicious Indian raids began to threaten the colonies from New York to the Carolinas. Virginia's long and open frontier along the Shenandoah made it especially vulnerable, and the massacre of George Painter's family near Muellerstadt was typical of the violence that engulfed the Valley in the 1750s. Painter and his wife were ambushed and killed and their bodies thrown into the burning house. His babies were strapped to branches for target practice; rescuers found four riddled corpses swaying in the wind. White captives were herded to Indian villages, where drunken savages jabbed blazing pine needles into their prisoners' eyes or poured gunpowder into gaping wounds and touched off the powder.[9]

Virginia's royal governor at this time, Robert Dinwiddie, was not slow to link these atrocities to French possession of the Ohio Valley. The French had to be driven out, and the governor selected surveyor George Washington to convey the message. Born as the first whites were settling the Shenandoah, Washington spent his youth surveying the Valley. He had pocketed enough from his frugal dealings to purchase 1,459 acres of Valley real estate before his nineteenth birthday, and that purchase sealed his commitment to a region he found surpassingly beautiful. He did not hesitate to serve as Dinwiddie's courier. The French were certain to reject the governor's demand, but diplomacy required that it be delivered anyway; Washington understood that the task was a necessary first step in halting Indian depredations. He made an arduous journey that carried him almost to Lake Erie in midwinter and brought back to Williamsburg an unequivocal "No."

Washington's reward was command of a small body of troops on the Shenandoah frontier. Displaying a sure grasp of military geography, he attempted to shield the Valley by fortifying a strategic river junction *west* of the Alleghenies. The conception was foresighted, but Washington was denied adequate support. The attempt ended with his Virginians being thrown back into the Valley, where they learned they had ignited a conflict known in America as the French and Indian War and in Europe as the Seven Years' War.

King George II of England, who had succeeded his father in 1727, dispatched professionals to fight this war in the New World. 1755 saw the arrival of Major General Edward Braddock, who wisely attached Washington to his otherwise ill-starred expedition. Unfortunately, Braddock ignored Washington's advice. Marshaling his army in the northern Shenandoah, Braddock bored through the Alleghenies toward Fort

Duquesne, at the confluence of the Allegheny and Monongahela rivers, where marauding Indians swapped Valley scalps for French rum and gunpowder. Braddock's Redcoats methodically widened a trail all the way to Duquesne to accommodate wagons and heavy artillery. Washington protested this blind application of textbook tactics to forest warfare—Braddock halted "to level every Mole Hill," he fumed[10]—and augured the disaster that came. The British were annihilated within sight of their objective by an outnumbered band of Indian warriors and French soldiers employing surprise and good cover. Washington, who extracted the survivors almost single-handedly, was left to contend with two immediate consequences of defeat: the Shenandoah was stripped of army protection and the Indians had won a new highway into the Valley.

Slaughter of colonists in the Valley peaked with sudden fury, and twenty-three-year-old Washington was promoted to commander of Virginia's entire armed establishment and charged with defense of the Shenandoah. It was not a promising assignment. Washington reconnoitered the Valley frontier, to discover farms whose owners had fled, leaving dishes on the table and livestock straying in the field. He also related stumbling across the grave of one man killed by Indians, hastily buried by neighbors, then dug up and gnawed by wolves.[11]

At this stage of his career, Washington lacked both the magnetism to restore public confidence with a grand gesture and the means to end Indian depredations through action. As a result, he was criticized mercilessly. Foreshadowing his behavior during the colonies' struggle for independence from England, Washington replied with silence. He established headquarters in the northern Shenandoah town of Winchester and fortified it as best he could. He shuffled his ragged militia companies from one stopgap post to another, and he continued to urge the project that had sparked this war, a system of frontier defenses *west* of the Valley. Washington realized the impossibility of garrisoning every mile of this elongated frontier. He knew, on the other hand, that the Shenandoah was a natural sally port, that it was possible to recruit and provision here, to rest, refit, and prepare expeditions into the defiles of the Alleghenies, and Washington believed active garrisons in those defiles could protect the Valley.

Washington was heeded, and Governor Dinwiddie entrusted him with construction of bristling defenses from the Potomac to the James. Strongpoints were planned in the gaps and along streams plunging out of the Alleghenies. These defenses generally were of three types: two-story log cabins with the second story projecting over the first, palisaded stockades, and large, rectangular forts capable of sheltering several hundred men.[12] Washington devoted the year 1756 to these fortifications, beginning work at the northern and southern ends of his line and hammering toward the middle. He mastered every conceivable difficulty to construct twenty-two strongpoints, only to realize that their completion aggravated another problem. He had never intended that log ramparts would replace vigilance; he had envisioned the Shenandoah's forward redoubts as shelters for active garrisons. He thus was appalled to discover his Valley militiamen adopting the sedentary theory of garrison duty. Washington toured the line during November and confided to Dinwiddie:

> I found them [the garrisons] very weak for want of men, but more so by indolence and irregularity. None I saw in a posture of defense, and few that might not be surprised with the greatest of ease. An instance of this appeared at Dickinson's Fort, where the Indians ran down, caught several children playing under the walls, and had got to the gate before they were discovered. . . . They [the militia garrisons] keep no guard, but just when the enemy is about; and are under fearful apprehensions of them; nor even stir out of the forts.[13]

Until Valley militiamen could be taught to stalk, ambush, and harry the Indians, Washington's line remained a partial barrier. Such lessons took time, time that meant the loss of Valley lives. Late in 1757, after Washington had contemplated forcing all Valley families to group themselves permanently near the largest forts, he wrote Dinwiddie that unless more powerful garrisons were mustered or a major expedition mounted against Fort Duquesne, there would hardly be "one soul living on this side of the Blue Ridge the ensuing autumn."[14]

Again displaying a sure grasp of military reality, Washington had realized that the key to the war was Fort Duquesne. George II's advisers had similar ideas and in 1758 sent General John Forbes to take it. Forbes assembled a large expedition, followed a wiser route to Duquesne than had Braddock, and succeeded in almost anticlimactic fashion. The French razed their fortress and fled as Forbes approached. England's prize was control of the Ohio River Valley. Washington's prize, after treating the electorate to almost a half gallon of spirits per man,[15] was a seat from the Shenandoah in Virginia's House of Burgesses.

Throughout most of the world, the Seven Years' War sputtered to a conclusion in 1763 with the Treaty of Paris, by which France ceded its Ohio Valley possessions to England. And though peace ostensibly returned to North America, the Shenandoah remained in a state of turmoil. Whites were now eager to settle the newly won land beyond the Alleghenies. Indians, having been swept back onto those lands, resisted all the more fiercely. During the summer of 1763 the fabled Chief Pontiac assembled an Indian confederacy to continue the war without the French. Chief Cornstalk and his Shawnee braves pledged to carry this war to the Shenandoah.[16] Atrocities on both sides spawned revenge and greater horrors: soon Indians and whites alike fattened their dogs with the flesh of their prisoners.

New massacres finally jolted the Valley into the strong defensive posture Washington had advocated. His chain of Allegheny forts was strengthened, and Valley militiamen began to harry the Indians from those forts with increasing might. The frontier was never sealed, but breakthroughs became rarer and more costly for the Indians. By 1774 the Shenandoah was able to spearhead an awesome counterattack. An army drawn from the southern Shenandoah knifed westward into Shawnee territory via the Kanawha River that autumn, and Shawnee scouts reeled back with word that the indolent militia of earlier years was no more. Now came a compact, mobile striking force. Protected in the column's center were five hundred pack horses carrying thousands of pounds of fresh provisions; the marching column itself was surrounded by a swarm of skirmishers. Officers were able and the men were superbly armed. All in all, it was probably the best-planned and best-led American expedition ever fielded to that time. At the junction of the Kanawha and Ohio rivers, the Valley army found its enemy.

One of the great pitched battles of the American West ensued. Each side numbered approximately one thousand, including, under the leadership of Chief Cornstalk, Shawnees, Delawares, Mingoes, and Ottawas. The Valley army was encamped on a peninsula between the Kanawha and the Ohio. Before dawn on October 9, 1774, Cornstalk led his braves across the Ohio to this peninsula and advanced toward the white camp through a wooded bottom entangled with vines and creepers. Other braves waited on the far banks of the Ohio and the Kanawha to slaughter whites who attempted to swim the rivers. The ambush was nearly complete when Cornstalk's scouts foolishly sprang at two Shenandoah men foraging for wild turkeys. One of these foragers escaped to report "five acres of ground covered with Indians as thick as they [can] stand one beside another."[17]

Valley men probed outside their camp and found Cornstalk in the tangled bottomland, where the battle exploded. Both sides fought from behind trees, rocks, or whatever cover they could find. The lines often surged to within twenty paces of each other, and every Valley army field officer was soon killed or wounded. The fight lasted six to eight hours, until Valley frontiersmen repulsed an Indian flank attack and pursued to gain commanding ground on the Indian flank. The stampede that followed broke the Shawnees forever, and Cornstalk begged for peace before year's end.[18]

The struggle for American independence erupted within another year, and in this war the Shenandoah proved a vital corridor linking northern and southern colonies. The Continental Congress's first troop requisition from Virginia was filled by two companies of Shenandoah marksmen,[19] who march northeastward along the Valley, crossed the Potomac, and continued through to Philadelphia and Boston. These marksmen were followed along the Shenandoah corridor by hundreds more. The corridor led southward as well, and Valley men moved that way in 1776 to help repel a British landing at Charleston, South Carolina. Their equipment—long rifles, tomahawks, and scalping knives—bore witness to the Valley's readiness for war. Major General Charles Lee is reported to have said of the Valley regiment that joined him at Charleston: "[It] was not only the most complete of the province, but, I believe, of the whole continent. It was not only the most complete in number, but the best armed, clothed and equipped for immediate service. Its soldiers were alert, zealous and spirited."[20]

At home, the Valley successfully fielded its militia reserves against Indians, who were now sponsored by the English rather than the French. The reserves held. The Valley's western bulwarks were too strong to be breached, its garrisons too alert to be bypassed. The very existence of these outworks had nudged the frontier into the Alleghenies, and the new frontier in turn flung its garrisons farther west; Virginia's defenses soon rested on the Ohio River. The frontier struggle would grind on under its own bloody momentum throughout the Revolution and for a decade thereafter, but it would grind toward an outcome made inevitable by Washington's first bold step into the Alleghenies.

When the man who had spent his youth surveying the Shenandoah and his early manhood defending it took his first presidential oath, the Valley, after two generations of war, had conquered peace on its own terms.

II

The seven decades between Washington's first inauguration in 1789 and John Brown's raid on Harpers Ferry in 1859 witnessed enormous material and economic progress throughout the Shenandoah. Valley men and women of this period fervently believed that the blessings of peace, resown throughout the land, would prove longlasting,[21] but that was not to be: these decades of growth actually molded the Shenandoah into a region that neither Union nor Confederacy could ignore during the stark years 1861–65.

Near the northern edge of this vast battleground was Winchester, first city of the Valley. Winchester was founded in 1743 by one of the earliest Englishmen to pioneer the Shenandoah, and British influence adhered in many ways, including street names such as Piccadilly, Loudoun, Kent, and Cork. As British tradition dictated, Winchester also boasted a courthouse complete with whipping post and ducking stool. The latter was a broad plank balanced on a pivot; offenders were strapped on the plank and dunked into a murky stone-lined pit. Unruly females and town drunks kept the stool busy during frontier days.[22]

During the era of ducking stools and Indian raids, Winchester remained a crossroads village of sixty log cabins lining streets that, despite tidy English names, were mires.[23] Only with the close of the Revolution and the dawn of sustained peace did Winchester come of age. The easiest route to market for much of the Shenandoah's crops and manufactured goods was northeastward along the Valley corridor to Winchester, thence to Washington, Baltimore, or Pennsylvania. Economically, the Valley was tied as closely to the North as to Tidewater Virginia, and Winchester was a conduit for much of a rapidly expanding trade.

Tavern keepers were first to tap the new wealth. On the corner of Loudoun and Cork streets, Peter Lauck raised the sign of his Red Lion Inn. William Van Horne announced fine accommodations on the corner of Loudoun and Fairfax; Henry Marsh was in competition across the street. Stables, wagon yards, and warehouses sprouted to accommodate the traffic such inns attracted.[24]

Local entrepreneurs joined the boom. Charles Welch and George Legg established a mill on Market Street and shipped their flour northward. George Barnhard opened a coach factory. George Ginn manufactured stoves, plows, and mill machinery and amassed, in the quaint phrase of an early writer, "a snug property."[25]

The log courthouse on Loudoun Street grew into an imposing courthouse square with a plastered court building crowned by a town clock. Taverns were within walking distance of the square, and on their way down Loudoun Street to refresh themselves, city fathers watched the construction of a new jail, market house, tobacco warehouse, and fire station. In the laissez-faire spirit of the age, the fire station was a private enterprise operated by the Star Fire Company. Some things, however, do not change: court days found the public vying with judges for room at hitching posts on the square, and soon new posts appeared marked JUDGES' HORSES ONLY.[26]

By the 1840s Winchester was thriving. The city welcomed a medical school and installed gas streetlights along raised sidewalks that replaced boards strewn atop the mud. The population was affluent enough to support three drama societies, a library, and a corset factory.[27] There were numerous private schools. Some, like Miss Marie Smith's Dresden Embroidery School and Lucinda Morrow's Girls' School—the latter charged a regal tuition of three dollars per quarter—polished the city's young ladies. Others, like Winchester Academy, honed its young men with classes in chemistry, civil engineering, higher mathematics, Italian, German, and Hebrew.[28] Graduates of Winchester's schools officered the banks, newspapers, courts, and churches that flourished in this community of comfortable red brick homes.

South of Winchester stood the villages of Staufferstadt and Muellerstadt, which bowed to popular desire after the Revolution and substituted the more euphonious names of Strasburg and Woodstock respectively. But some elements of German tradition lingered. Strasburg had a German-language weekly well into the 1800s. Enriched by limestone strata, the pastures around these villages provided lush grazing, and Valley men of German and Dutch extraction displayed their ancestral talent for breeding livestock. The Valley had sustained Washington's army at the siege of Yorktown with five hundred thousand pounds of dressed beef and large herds on the hoof[29]—this at a time when the Shenandoah was supplying its own militia forces as well—and by the mid-1800s, Valley dairies and ranches were among America's best.

As a prime horse and mule region, the Valley was rivaled only by middle Tennessee and Kentucky. Horses especially were a mania in the Shenandoah. The Valley's young men searched the bloodlines of their steeds as reverently as their elders traced family genealogies, and, finding too little challenge on the hunt, they revived the medieval-style tournament they had read of in Sir Walter Scott's novels. Youths presented themselves at these spectacles as plumed and armored knights. Lances at the ready, they charged toward a target of three rings spaced thirty yards apart. The rings dangled from bars by thin wires and decreased in diameter from two inches to a barely visible half-inch, but many a rider was steady enough of seat and hand to collect all three on his lance during a single charge.[30]

Most Valley riders were carried on the rolls of Virginia's militia, yet tournaments were the most martial exercises they knew. All able-bodied Virginians between the ages of eighteen and forty-five were supposedly enrolled in militia units from their counties of residence. In 1861 a 140,000-man paper army of five infantry divisions and five regiments each of cavalry and artillery existed; Shenandoah counties were assigned to provide one infantry division and much of the cavalry.[31] A general staff, chaplains, surgeons, and even musicians were also authorized, but, in truth, this militia had atrophied following the Revolution. Poor muster rolls left at least 60,000 men unaccounted for. Senior militia commanders tended to be prominent citizens with proper statehouse connections but without military experience. Equipment was inadequate or nonexistent: as late as 1861 none of Virginia's cavalry regiments were armed.[32] Quarterly militia drills were required by law[33] but rarely took place that frequently. When held, these drills mingled the atmosphere of county fair, family reunion, and revival meeting, and in the Shenandoah, they were the only social events to rival the tournament.

This neglect of military matters was perhaps explained by the fact that many Valley men had little time to spare from their fields. Between 1800 and 1820, the iron plow replaced the wooden plow, and fertilizers came into widespread use in the Shenandoah, with accompanying increased yields of barley, flax, beans, and root crops. Orchards of bright-flowering apple trees began to grace the land. Corn, oats, rye, and above all wheat burgeoned into major industries. Wheat yields of twelve bushels per acre, nearly twice the average from other sections of Virginia, were common during the 1830s; the Valley average was fifteen bushels by the 1850s. Careful harvesters gleaned crops of thirty and even forty bushels per acre, and all Valley farmers were overworked with the bounty of their fields.[34]

It was not by chance, then, that the first mechanical reaper, Cyrus McCormick's "Virginia Reaper," was wired together in the Valley. McCormick, Rockbridge County born, came to manhood watching a sea of grain toss around him. He toiled long hours with a scythe, and the ache of his arms prompted an idea. In 1831 he demonstrated the first machine to incorporate the principal components of the modern grain harvester: straight reciprocating knife, guards, platform, main wheel, side-moving cutter, and divider at the outer end of the cutter bar. This product of a Valley man's imagination revolutionized world agriculture and made possible the endless grain fields of America's Midwest.

McCormick's reaper also highlighted the Shenandoah as one of the more industrial regions of the South. Iron forges had been glowing here since the Revolution and had given impetus to other industries. Woolen factories and flour and lumber mills abounded. J. Meixell and Company began production of a sophisticated threshing machine at its Harrisonburg plant by 1839; C. S. Weaver was in competition by 1844. Nine years later Henry Miller of Harrisonburg patented a corn harvester. Miller's neighbor, J. G. Sprinkle, patented a novel steam engine, and by 1861 his engines were powering the presses of the *Rockingham Register.*[35]

During their early years, towns like Harrisonburg and Staunton, which lay in the southern Valley and were not convenient to Winchester by road, shipped their goods to market by river, which explains names such as Port Republic among the inland hamlets of the southern Shenandoah. There were few roads worthy of the name between those hamlets and Northern markets, so gundalows, or barges, measuring nine by ninety feet funneled Valley flour and pig iron down the Shenandoah to the Potomac.[36] River trade even became dominant enough to shape the Valley's language with a curious idiom. Shenandoah streams drain generally northward to the Potomac, and to go *downstream* is thus to go *northward,* to go *upstream* is to go *southward.* The Valley's *northern* region accordingly became known as the *lower* Shenandoah and the *southern* region as the *upper.* Similarly, to travel *northward* is to go *down* the Valley, while to travel *southward* is to go *up* it. When turnpikes and railroads supplanted river highways, this seemingly backward terminology* persisted. The idiom remains common usage in the Shenandoah today, and it is observed throughout this work.

Water transport was so much a part of early life around the Shenandoah that when its rivers could no longer bear the expanding commerce the solution was a better river. The same era that saw New York's Erie Canal saw two major waterways projected across the Valley's northern and southern fringes. The most important was the Chesapeake & Ohio (C & O) Canal, which was to link the Atlantic with the Ohio River Valley. Though never completed, the canal was nevertheless an outstanding achievement of its time. By 1850 it had pushed its sixty-foot-wide channel along Maryland's Potomac shore from Washington as far as Cumberland. Barges of one hundred tons' burden plied its waters, and it steadily grew into a major artery for Allegheny coal fueling the East Coast. The mirror image of the C & O was the James River Canal; its promoters hoped to mingle the waters of the James and the Kanawha. Financial difficulties stopped work on it near Buchanan, in the upper Shenandoah, where, despite disappointment for the backers, it opened Valley commerce to Richmond and eastern Virginia on a truly competitive basis.

Between these canals flowed the Shenandoah River, which was unsuited to canalization. The middle Valley therefore faced potential isolation by poor roads and crowded rivers, and its solution was a superhighway for the horse and wagon. In 1834 the Virginia legislature chartered the Valley Turnpike Company to lay a road from Winchester south to Staunton. Engineers of the Valley Turnpike—or simply the Pike as it was known locally—made a then uncommon effort to keep the right-of-way straight, so that travelers were sometimes astonished by a clear view ahead for two or even three miles. The Pike was bedded with cement and buttressed on either side with limestone shoulders; its smooth surface was supported by layers of compacted gravel piled atop the cement bed.[37]

---

*In normal usage, because the top of a map always represents the northernmost portion of the area depicted, to go *up* is to go *north,* and, conversely, because the bottom of a map represents the southernmost portion of the area depicted, to go *down* is to go *south.*

The Pike, completed by 1840, was a superb paved (or macadamized) highway, resistant to storms, which could dissolve some Valley roads into muddy troughs. This trunkline encouraged other parallel and intersecting pikes, a few also paved, but the typical Shenandoah road of the 1860s remained rough going indeed. Moreover, only the main roads had bridges over the region's major streams; many Shenandoah rivers were crossed by ferry operations or, more frequently, at fords in use since Indian times.

Increasing transportation demands brought railroads into the Valley during the 1840s and '50s. The Baltimore & Ohio (B & O) Railroad came first with a right-of-way stretching from Baltimore to Harpers Ferry, Virginia. There the line bridged the Potomac and hurried through the lower Valley. It entered Martinsburg, veered north to hug the Potomac's south bank until it crossed the river to Cumberland, Maryland, and ran from there southwestward to the Ohio River Valley, a route that capitalized on the Valley's central location in the eastern states. The line both tapped Shenandoah resources for the Atlantic seaboard and utilized its best routes to and through the Alleghenies to the Ohio heartland. Harpers Ferry and Martinsburg became thriving depot towns as the line made the Valley's lower exits more attractive to Northern merchants. Winchester quickly ran a thirty-two-mile spur to Harpers Ferry to link itself with the B & O and retain its position as the transportation hub of the southern Valley.

The B & O was one of America's major railroads by the 1860s. It was also one of the longest, totaling 513 miles of track exclusive of numerous sidings. Its assets reached the then staggering sum of $30 million and included 236 locomotives and more than 3,400 freight cars. Both sides would claim the B & O when war came, but it was the Union that acted first to secure its terminals in Baltimore, Maryland, and Wheeling, Virginia (now West Virginia). Thereafter the Confederacy sought to cripple it, and the South would damage this line more frequently and more extensively than any other.[38]

Impressive as were B & O facilities, the prewar Valley required even additional rail outlets. Had the Shenandoah been a garrison state like Prussia, it would have planned these new lines according to military contingencies, but here economic factors governed. The Valley's second right-of-way was surveyed in the 1850s from Strasburg to Manassas Junction, thirty miles southwest of Washington, where the route could join an existing roadbed leading north into Washington and south to Gordonsville and eventually to Richmond. A Prussian would have been disgusted, because if a conflict did arise the new line inevitably would be severed as Northern forces advanced to protect Washington by occupying Manassas Junction. Nevertheless, work commenced and progressed rapidly. The Manassas Gap Railroad built westward across Piedmont, Virginia, climbed the Blue Ridge at the gap that shares its name, and descended to span the Shenandoah River by an impressive 450-foot wooden trestle at Front Royal. From Strasburg, the line swung south and into trouble. Stage owners, wagoneers, and bargemen opposed it, as did one prominent farmer who feared the iron horse would frighten his "milch cows."[39]

Adverse interests could not throttle the Manassas Gap Railroad, although they did delay it. By 1861 the railhead lay at the village of Mount Jackson, and a forty-mile gap yawned between it and the Virginia Central Railroad. That line extended west from Richmond to Gordonsville, thence across the Blue Ridge and upper Shenandoah. Its principal Valley depot was Staunton. To travel by rail from Strasburg to Staunton it was necessary to follow a two-hundred-mile semicircle east through Manassas Junction, south to Gordonsville, and west across the Blue Ridge again. And there was still another gap in the Valley's rail net: a projected track between Strasburg and Winchester was not even surveyed by 1861.

Nor did the two Virginia lines serving the Shenandoah match the capabilities of the B & O. The Manassas Gap was a mere seventy-seven miles long, and it was so deficient in sidings that for many hours each day it was a one-way railroad. The Virginia Central owned only 27 locomotives and 188 boxcars and flatcars. Its only repair shops were located in Richmond and were so small that maintenance had to be performed outdoors.[40] If there was any single area in which the Valley was at a decided disadvantage as civil war neared, it was in its rail net.

In the field of education, on the other hand, the Valley surpassed many areas, North and South. The Shenandoah's college tradition began when George Washington richly endowed a promising academy in the late 1700s. This institution thereafter renamed itself Washington College (today, Washington and Lee University) and moved to Lexington in the upper Valley. Seeking to prepare its students for peace with a curriculum of ancient and modern languages, mathematics, and philosophy,

Washington College actually groomed a generation of warrior historians prior to the 1860s. When war came to the Shenandoah, hundreds of the college's students and alumni joined the South, among them Alexander "Sandie" Pendleton, Hugh White, Edward Moore, John Apperson, and James Langhorne. These were bright young men who observed as well as fought the war, and their observations, contained in lucid diaries and letters, are an invaluable source on the Valley Campaign of 1862.

Lexington became a two-college town with the founding of the Virginia Military Institute in 1839. Conceived by a distinguished group of educators and soldiers, including a veteran of Napoleon's 1812 Russian campaign, V.M.I. evolved during the next two decades into an incomparable Southern tradition: a college modeled on West Point but designed to prepare young men for civilian as well as military life. The appeal of that goal was quickly demonstrated. President Zachary Taylor personally supervised additions to the Institute's arsenal, the state of Virginia expanded its barracks, and the original faculty of West Pointers was strengthened by V.M.I. graduates. Those instructors coupled scientific and military education with rigorous discipline, and on the eve of war, the V.M.I. alumni and Corps of Cadets provided the South with an invaluable reserve of officers. Throughout the Valley Campaign of 1862, V.M.I. was well represented: at various times the Confederate cavalry and many Southern batteries and infantry regiments were commanded by V.M.I. men.

For those aspiring to college, there were numerous Shenandoah preparatory academies, such as the institutions of Winchester. Also typical of both the number and excellence of Valley schools were those clustered around Martinsburg, where no less than a dozen educational ventures prospered in a county of only a few thousand inhabitants. As was true of Valley colleges, these academies trained many who, though they were little more than boys, left eloquent accounts of their wartime experiences. John Opie and John Casler were outstanding among this number.

Valley academies were the personal achievements of no-nonsense schoolmasters such as New York–born Jedediah Hotchkiss. Hotchkiss came to love the Shenandoah on a walking tour in 1847, and it became his home for the next fifty years. He achieved such initial success with a variety of tutoring jobs that Augusta County farmers subscribed his Mossy Creek Academy, near Staunton. A few years later he founded a second school. Both ventures flourished, probably because Hotchkiss typified his adopted neighbors. He was a sincere Christian, a family man, serious, and thrifty. Even his hobby, mapmaking, distinguished him as a solid and sensible citizen. He was self-taught as a mapmaker, but he became a recognized expert, and his hobby was to serve the Confederacy well.

Hotchkiss was representative of the Shenandoah in two other respects: he abhorred slavery and stoutly opposed secession. Slavery had long been declining throughout the Valley, and what few slaves remained were among the best treated of the South. Concerning disruption of the Union, the Shenandoah consistently opposed it. When the Union began to fragment, the people of Staunton pledged their loyalty to it en masse.[41] Every county of the Valley rejected disunion with a majority of votes for the Southern moderates John C. Breckinridge or John Bell in the presidential election of 1860. Even so, the Valley never doubted that it belonged to Virginia, and Virginia, to the South. The South, commented the Winchester *Virginian,* was "one family . . . , and if South Carolina secedes, and thus inaugurates a final issue with the North, we are necessarily forced to stand in defense of our homes, interests and people."[42]

Valley residents nodded in anguished agreement with that comment, all the while hoping that a war that grew more certain with increasingly strident debate over slavery might somehow spare them. But this was a pipe dream. The Shenandoah's very location, combined with an abundance of almost all things, made it a battlefield in the years 1861 to 1865. The Valley was a natural corridor between North and South. Its farms could both sustain armies and swell their ranks with literate recruits. Here were iron foundries, machine shops, and textile mills. Here was a military academy already renowned as the West Point of the South. And here was an arsenal, the United States Arsenal at Harpers Ferry.

At the northeast corner of the Valley, the Shenandoah and Potomac rivers converge in turbulent splendor. Thomas Jefferson described the scene as a "riot and tumult roaring" and wrote, "You stand on a very high point of land. On your right comes up the Shenandoah, having ranged along the foot of the [Blue Ridge] mountain a hundred miles to seek a vent. On your left approaches the Potomac, in quest of a passage also. In the moment of their junction they rush together against the mountain, rend it asunder, and pass off to the sea. . . . This scene is worth a voyage across the Atlantic."[43]

This mighty rush of rivers swept the town of Harpers Ferry into existence. In 1747 Robert Harper, an English architect commissioned to design a meetinghouse for Winchester's Quakers, passed this way. Like Jefferson later, he was awed by the natural beauty here. With an architect's practical eye, he also saw need for a ferry, and Harpers Ferry was born.

Years later, a fledgling United States government harnessed the waters at Harpers Ferry to power an arms factory. The quality and variety of weapons produced in this armory grew, and a storage place became necessary. A government complex arose at the Virginia end of the B & O's Potomac bridge. Two storage buildings were built for an arsenal near the bridge; located west of the arsenal, across the intersection of Potomac and Shenandoah streets, was a sturdy brick fire-engine house. The armory itself lay west of the fire station. It was within a walled enclosure, although it was by no means well secured: its low walls were manned at night only by one watchman.

It was this complex that John Brown, "Osawatomie" Brown of Bleeding Kansas, coveted. In Brown's fanatic mind the key to ending slavery was guns. If he could provide even a few thousand arms, he had no doubt that slaves across the South would explode in bloody revolt. And it made no matter to Brown that there were few slaves in the Valley to be armed—the Lord, he must have believed, would raise up an army somehow for the holy work of butchering slaveholders.[44]

On the evening of Sunday, October 16, 1859, after several months spent making furtive reconnaissances of the Harpers Ferry area from his headquarters in an old farmhouse across the Potomac in Maryland, Brown launched his now famous raid. His "army" consisted of a handful of followers. Beneath the cover of a hard rainstorm, he slashed all telegraph wires into Harpers Ferry and stationed several men to obstruct the B & O bridge. Things continued to go according to plan when Brown approached the armory. The night watchman refused him entrance, but he easily broke inside the walls. Brown's eyes blazed with a wilder light as he saw rows of newly made muskets, and he immediately dispatched runners to spread the work of liberation among local slaves.

Harpers Ferry discovered itself at war the next morning. Workers reporting for the armory's morning shift were herded inside its walls under leveled rifles. Raiders opened fire on the town, and several townspeople, including the mayor, a grocer, and a Negro porter, fell.

A snarling posse of Harpers Ferry men and county militia, many of them the worse for drink, counterattacked that afternoon. They first shattered the detail on the B & O bridge. One abolitionist there tried to escape by swimming the Potomac but was wounded and drifted to a rock; Valley men swarmed over the rock and knifed him to death. The mob flung its one prisoner off the bridge and used him for target practice as he bobbed helplessly down the Potomac.

Brown, meanwhile, concentrated his men in the brick engine house on Potomac Street, and the fighting continued throughout the day and night. The abolitionists had provisioned themselves well; townspeople helped themselves from the arsenal across the street from Brown's fort, and the gunfire grew deafening. There were more dead and wounded on both sides.

Mercifully, this slaughter was ended on Tuesday morning. Eighty Marines under the command of United States Army Colonel Robert E. Lee arrived to quell the insurrection. Lee deployed his troops and demanded Brown's surrender; when the crazed man hollered "No," the Marines finished the affair. They battered their way inside the engine house and disarmed Brown, who lay wounded on the floor with his bleeding sons. Only then did Brown have time to consider that not a slave had joined him.[45]

During Brown's subsequent trial on charges of treason and conspiracy to commit murder, numerous affidavits were offered to support the defense contention that Brown was insane,[46] but the prosecution prevailed. On December 2, 1859, he was hanged amid extraordinary precautions. Two thousand Valley militia, buttressed by the Virginia Military Institute Corps of Cadets, formed a square around Brown's gallows. Loaded howitzers studded the array to devastate an oft-rumored rescue attempt that never came. Before thousands of relieved onlookers, John Brown kicked out the final seconds of his life.[47]

For the Valley, the terror at Harpers Ferry kindled bitter memories. Save that white had preyed on white, John Brown's raid was little different from Indian strikes of a century earlier: the surprise attack, the killing, and the counterattack had all unfolded in a hideously familiar sequence.

For the nation, Brown's raid was the omen of horrors never known before, or since, in America. Events moved rapidly after October 16, 1859: Abraham Lincoln was elected president within one year; South Carolina seceded from the Union within fourteen months. Fort Sumter was bombarded into submission in another four months. Lincoln mobilized seventy-five thousand volunteers in April 1861 to suppress the rebellion, and the Shenandoah confronted a new war.

2

A NEW WAR

The exposed condition of the Virginia frontier between the Blue Ridge and the Allegheny Mountains has excited the deepest solicitude of the government.

—JUDAH P. BENJAMIN

The Shenandoah's most savage conflict began as a romp. Valley volunteers and militia by the hundreds mustered in Winchester as Virginia's Secession Convention met. Bombardment of Fort Sumter on April 12–13, 1861, made the outcome of this convention certain, and the majority of Virginians were ready to embrace the Southern cause. Most Valley men were in accord. And Shenandoah men knew they could not demonstrate their loyalty better than by securing the Harpers Ferry arsenal. They waited fitfully for word of a secession vote and crowed about easy victories they would win. Since Harpers Ferry was guarded by only fifty Federal troops, this was safe talk; there was heady assurance in the companionship of overwhelming numbers.

When Virginia voted itself out of the Union on April 17, the novice army fidgeting in Winchester instinctively swarmed northward. Captain John Imboden's men trundled along hauling a horseless battery of six cannons. As the guns seemed to gain weight with every mile, Imboden stopped to hire some horses. The farmer he approached, however, thought the rebel horde a poor risk and refused, whereupon Imboden took the animals he needed by force. As Imboden moved on, the red-faced farmer shook his clenched fist and promised an indictment from the next county grand jury.[1]

On the evening of April 18 the rebel mob swarmed into Harpers Ferry. Some men had been here before to snipe at John Brown and led the surge along High Street, glowing with the thrill of a short-lived chase. The arsenal in front of them suddenly erupted, and the streets were flayed with whizzing triggers, bolts, and stocks. The defenders had fled, igniting powder trains that sparked into the warehouse. The attackers, now a fire brigade, swerved into the armory enclosure. They saved the priceless arms-making machinery there by working through the night without regard for repeated explosions from the crackling arsenal, which was just dangerous enough to spice this first conquest. War, the rebels decided, was exhilarating.

Other Virginians were frantic to join this advance guard, because Harpers Ferry lay far enough north to generate hope that it might see at least one gallant battle before the Yankees surrendered. It was the front, and men who would fight to reach Winchester in November did not tarry there for food or shelter in April. Striking heroic poses, they disdained the comforts of Winchester and scampered off like boys on a spring outing who, distracted by a scuffle, desert the picnic table. "As we marched out of town the brass bands were playing, the drums beating, colors flying, and the fair ladies waving their handkerchiefs and cheering us on to 'victory or death.' Oh! how nice to be a soldier," wrote one.[2]

As if by order, each new arrival at Harpers Ferry placed himself on full alert. His days passed in relentless vigilance demanded by the conviction that a Northern army would attack momentarily. If one man was detailed as night sentry, his entire company was apt to join him voluntarily. Since officers supposed the Federals planned to storm the town by train and debark at the depot, many sentinels spent hours faithfully staring at B & O track.[3] Even the enemy's refusal to deliver such a shrewd blow did not dampen Confederate zeal.

The Yankees, after all, were to be thrashed with ease. One grand victory should finish the war, and it would not do to miss any of this romantic adventure. Nor should one attend in less than immaculate dress. Many Valley men reported for duty wearing garish buff and yellow uniforms.[4] Captain Jim Edmondson sent home from Harpers Ferry for striped calico shirts; white ones dirty too fast. He also required a pair of pants in a shade he specified as blue caramel.[5] One rebel wrote: "Many of the privates brought with them their personal servants, while the officers were equipped with all that was necessary for elaborate entertainment."[6] John Imboden believed the "fuss and feathers" displayed around Harpers Ferry could match the Champs Élysées on a pleasant afternoon.[7] It was a splendid frolic and confirmed the universal opinion that the soldier's whole duty was to posture heroically.

On April 30 a colonel of Virginia volunteers arrived to correct that opinion. He was Thomas J. Jackson, an obscure retired U.S. Army brevet major whose advent went unnoticed because, according to notions of the day, he hardly looked like a soldier. He wore a plain, ill-fitting U.S. Army uniform. He was cursed with absurdly big feet and hands, and his speech was as ungainly as his movements. The only notable thing about him was the lemon he sucked incessantly; his expressionless look struck some as "wooden,"[8] some as "sleepy,"[9] and no one as inspiring. After meeting Jackson one group of officers despaired, "there must be some mistake about him; if he was an able man he showed it less than any of us had ever seen."[10]

But Jackson was an able man, and he had instructions from Governor John Letcher of Virginia to take command at Harpers Ferry. His first care was to sort out the troops thronging his camps. These he found to be of two types. One consisted of the burgeoning Virginia volunteer force, of which Jackson was an officer; the other was the militia. Volunteers were enrolling in newly authorized statewide units that would soon join regiments from sister states in a true Confederate army. The county-based militiamen, on the other hand, were local defense forces entangled by politics and of little value on the battlefield. The perfectionist Jackson had no use for this militia system and lured the militiamen into the volunteer forces whenever possible.

Volunteers were obliged to enlist either for a one-year term or for the duration of the war.[11] The majority of gallants at Harpers Ferry assumed one year was ample time to whip the North. Jackson was less certain and encouraged enlistment "for the duration," but there were few men willing to commit themselves to such an indefinite future. Most signed on only for twelve months. (In the spring of 1862 Confederate armies almost disappeared as a consequence.)

Volunteer or militiamen, enrolled for the duration or not, all of Jackson's men were sent to drill, target practice, guard duty, and more drill. Reveille blared at 5 A.M. every day,[12] and Jackson kept his men busy for the next seventeen hours. Much of that time was spent evacuating captured arms-making machinery, all of which found its way to Richmond or Columbia, South Carolina.[13] To arm his own troops,

Jackson offered to purchase private weapons at a tempting $5 apiece.[14] When that did not work, he took the responsibility of ordering one thousand flintlocks from the state arsenal at Lexington.[15] There were no horses to pull his wagons, so Jackson dispatched his quartermasters to buy them on credit. When credit was refused, he simply impressed the animals.[16] Artillerist Imboden, who had left Harpers Ferry prior to Jackson's arrival, returned a few days later: "What a revolution three or four days had wrought! I could scarcely realize the change. . . . The presence of a mastermind was visible in the changed conditions of the camp."[17]

Imboden also returned in time to see Jackson swing into action on another front. By some unwritten détente, the Baltimore & Ohio Railroad had been allowed to continue its service across the Valley's tip to the Allegheny coal fields. The railroad was shuttling coal to Washington at capacity along this route, and Jackson decided to stop it. From Point of Rocks, some miles east of Harpers Ferry on Maryland's Potomac shore, to Martinsburg, the B & O was double tracked; that is, it had separate lines allowing traffic to pass in opposite directions. Both tracks crossed the Potomac at Harpers Ferry. Jackson, making a veiled threat, warned company officials that racket from the never-ending trains disturbed his camps and must cease. The railroad agreed to his demand to funnel its traffic through Harpers Ferry between 11 A.M. and 1 P.M. When the B & O timetable was readjusted to give the town the busiest railroad in America two hours a day, Jackson pounced. At 11 A.M. he began barricading the eastbound lane at Point of Rocks while permitting westerly traffic as usual. He had the reverse done at Martinsburg. At 1 P.M. Jackson tore up all ends of the double tracks and stranded more than four hundred locomotives and cars.[18]

This man Jackson got things done. In three weeks he had hammered a mob into the rudiments of an army and hoodwinked one of the Union's major railroads out of the war. He soon gave his volunteers something else to scrawl home. Anticipating the upcoming transfer of forces raised by Virginia to Confederate command, the Confederate government dispatched Brigadier General Joseph E. Johnston to take control at Harpers Ferry. Johnston arrived before Jackson received official notice of his mission, and the latter declined to turn over command until he was shown proper authorization. Jackson knew Johnston at least by reputation, and he knew it would serve Virginia's best interest to integrate her forces as speedily as possible into the Confederate army.

Nevertheless, he required the necessary paperwork and would have arrested Johnston had he insisted on taking charge without it. Before he assumed command, Johnston had to dig through his saddlebags until he found a letter that established his authority.[19]

Few other colonels, especially those who knew something of Joe Johnston, would have sent him back to his saddlebags for orders. An autocratic, petulant man, Johnston did not tolerate any trespass on his authority. He regarded civilian as well as military superiors with a certain mistrust and tended to be curt in his dealings with them. Johnston was the highest-ranking former U.S. Army officer to join the South, and he would become one of its five full generals—only to take offense at the fact that he ranked fourth in seniority. He was, however, a generous superior—his men came to know him simply as "Old Joe"—and because he treasured his own prerogatives, he respected the correctness of Jackson's stand. He also was impressed by Jackson's groundwork: militia who had refused to volunteer had been weeded out; those who had volunteered had been grouped into Virginia regiments that in turn were ready to come under Confederate authority. Jackson's reward was promotion to brigadier general in the Confederate army and command of one of three infantry brigades Johnston organized at Harpers Ferry.[20]

The new brigade consisted of the 2d, 4th, 5th, 27th, and 33d Virginia regiments. Every man was a volunteer. They were drawn largely from the Shenandoah, and a contingent of Allegheny and Blue Ridge mountaineers added strength. Jackson thought it a "promising" unit and went to work on it.[21] He saw that each man got a musket and drilled them until they could barely hobble. Extraordinary attention to every paragraph in the manual of arms won him the respect of his soldiers and Johnston's greater confidence.

Jackson hoped to bloody his brigade quickly. In this he differed from Johnston, who was to prove himself an apostle of strategic retreat. Before the war's end Johnston would back to the gates of the South's two most important cities, Richmond and Atlanta. His premise was that territory lost could be regained, but the casualties of a great battle could not.

Accordingly, when a Union army forded the Potomac upstream from Harpers Ferry on June 15 Johnston withdrew to Winchester, and his troops had their first lesson in massive destruction as they evacuated Harpers Ferry. B & O bridges over the Potomac were blown up;

captured locomotives were derailed into the river. At other points across the lower Valley, water towers were destroyed, bridges blown up, a hundred miles of telegraph wire torn down, and captured trains, loot from Jackson's great train robbery, put to the torch. Many of the cars burned were twenty-ton coal gondolas with full loads; they glowed for weeks.[22]

A month of sporadic skirmishing occupied the Valley, until, on July 18, the news every volunteer craved reached Winchester. A Federal army from Washington, under the command of Brigadier General Irvin McDowell, was advancing on Manassas Junction and the Southern army of Brigadier General Pierre Beauregard, conqueror of Fort Sumter and the Confederacy's earliest folk hero. The battle everyone assumed would decide the war was at hand, and Johnston was summoned to evade the enemy opposite him and reinforce Beauregard. When the destination was announced, Jackson's Brigade bolted forward into a sprint. Equally jubilant citizens packed the sidewalks when the rebels paraded through Winchester, and everyone beamed with the knowledge that war was a glorious, romantic adventure. It was magnificent, wrote Mrs. Cornelia McDonald, "the Confederate banners waving, the bands playing, and the bayonets gleaming in the sun. . . . Many of the companies were made up of mere boys, but their earnest and joyous faces were fully as reassuring as the martial music was inspiriting."[23]

The ensuing Southern victory at the First Battle of Manassas (known in the North as the First Battle of Bull Run) was a classic bit of Americana. Johnston eluded the Federal army facing him and reached Manassas Junction at the eleventh hour. Jackson's Brigade entered the fight swiftly and withstood a fierce artillery barrage and fiercer infantry attacks to win itself and its general the title "Stonewall." Those who cherish a romantic tale insist the name was given by Brigadier General Barnard Bee, who, with his own brigade shattered and fleeing, spotted Jackson's firm lines and called to his men, "There is Jackson standing like a stone wall! Rally behind the Virginians!" Revisionists might claim Bee was hollering in disgust over Jackson's refusal to advance to the more exposed position Bee held,[24] but in the rosy glow of victory, connotations of the name "Stonewall" were only good. From that day on Jackson was known as "Stonewall" and his men were the "Stonewall Brigade."

Jackson, normally silent to the point of rudeness,[25] boasted that his brigade was to the Southern army what the Imperial Guard had been to

Napoleon.[26] He wrote to his wife that his command "was the first to meet and pass our retreating forces—to push on with no other aid than the smiles of God; to boldly take its position with the artillery that was under my command—to arrest the victorious foe in his onward progress—to hold him in check until reinforcements arrived—and finally to charge bayonets, and, thus advancing, pierce the enemy's center." In reply to her anger at the small mention of him in newspaper accounts of the triumph, Jackson added a thought that disclosed a crack in his Christian armor—ambition: "I am thankful to my ever kind Heavenly Father that he makes me content to await His own good time and pleasure for commendation."[27] Jackson did not even consider that commendation might not come at all; it was, he seemed to assert, cached in heaven anticipating efforts he would not fail to give.

With the battle that swept Jackson to write of Napoleon's Imperial Guard and inspired his men to don the title "Stonewall," the spirit of romantic adventure crested. The next weeks showed Valley volunteers some less exhilarating facets of army life. The rebel victors were as disorganized by their success as the vanquished, and they remained near the battlefield to regroup. The only stream through the Stonewall Brigade's camp tasted of decaying corpses.[28] Southern railroads faltered under the burden of supplying the army at Manassas Junction and by August the rebels knew hunger. To alleviate the situation, a great camp was established at Centreville, but autumn came early with chilling rains. Even Jackson could not drill in ankle-deep mud, and his troops were left to cope with an escalating boredom.[29]

Jackson was likewise frustrated by inaction, in particular by the failure of the Confederacy to follow up victory at Manassas. As the weeks passed he dreamed of an offensive, of a drive to take the war across the Potomac—and beyond. A fellow officer described Jackson outlining his theory of how to prosecute this war: Stonewall would "destroy industrial establishments wherever we found them, break up the lines of interior commercial intercourse, close the coal mines, seize and, if necessary, destroy the manufactories and commerce of Philadelphia and of other large cites within our reach . . . subsist mainly on the country we traverse, and making unrelenting war amidst their homes, force the people of the North to understand what it will cost them to hold the South in the Union."[30]

Instead of the ruthless offensive Jackson longed for, there was only inaction, by which the Southern position in Virginia slowly eroded. Stories of dissension in the high command were carried like a serial by Richmond newspapers. General Beauregard fell into an embarrassing wrangle with Confederate President Jefferson Davis over his plans at Manassas. Eventually the former was shunted off to Tennessee with his reputation as a folk hero beclouded. Standing ahead only of Beauregard when the Confederacy promoted five men to the rank of full general, Johnston griped about seniority bitterly enough to poison his relations with President Davis.

Northwest of Staunton, Union columns stabbed deep into the Alleghenies. Newly appointed General Robert E. Lee was sent to rally a small force, known as the Army of the Northwest, defending this area, but first-rate men were betrayed by weather and poor equipment. Faulty logistics slashed rations to four biscuits per day per rebel;[31] lack of medical support left some regiments at one-quarter strength.[32] Wrote one Confederate:

> When we came here we had to lie on the frozen ground without any fire. We have now built a fireplace in our tent, but we have no straw, and a continual vapor is rising from the frozen but now thawing ground. . . . Many times the mud has been shoe-top deep in and out of our tents. . . . It is evidently a condition in which God never intended any human being to be placed.[33]

The Confederate drive to free the Alleghenies was a failure that buried Lee in the public mind for a year. It also cost Virginia fifty of her doggedly antislavery mountain counties, which, on October 24, voted to secede from the Old Dominion and begin to organize the new state of West Virginia.

By autumn of 1861, Virginia was awakening to the reality that it had slipped back a hundred years. The Shenandoah was once again Virginia's frontier, and beyond the Valley the Alleghenies were suddenly alien, infested with an enemy more powerful than even the Shawnees.

II

Union strikes against the fringes of the Shenandoah grew more serious throughout the autumn. Federals were particularly active among the many

Union sympathizers of the fertile South Branch Valley (in what is now West Virginia), to the west of Winchester, and there were persistent rumors of an impending effort to capture Romney. That village dominated the South Branch Valley (named for the South Branch River, a tributary of the Potomac) and lay only two days' march from Winchester.

As had been the case when Washington headquartered in Winchester a century earlier, the Shenandoah Valley was virtually undefended. Three brigades of quibbling militia, perhaps fifteen hundred men, were in the field.[34] These men bore ancient flintlocks for which there was insufficient ammunition, or none at all.[35] Although militia ranks had thinned as many men volunteered, militia officers remained plentiful. These peacocks refused to vacate their ceremonial posts or to combine their understrength units, so that brigadier generals headed regiments, colonels headed companies, and captains led squads.[36] The two pieces of heavy artillery in the Shenandoah could not be used because no one knew how to load them.[37] The Valley's only cavalry was a semiguerrilla outfit headed by sixty-year-old Colonel Angus McDonald and a younger but wholly inexperienced Lieutenant Colonel Turner Ashby.

Shenandoah defenses were crumbling by October. The enemy struck swiftly and in force against Romney, capturing the village, three hundred rifles, and one hundred horses and mules of Colonel McDonald's command.[38] As the Confederate grasp west of the Valley faltered, B & O crews pushed reconstruction on segments of the line destroyed earlier by rebel raiders; after the fall of Romney, Northern crews were free to concentrate on the important Big Cacapon River bridge thirty miles northeast of the village. On the Valley's opposite flank, Federals seized Harpers Ferry and rifled local wheat bins for a week before Turner Ashby could muster three hundred militia with their antiquated muskets, some cavalry companies, and a light cannon mounted on a converted wagon. A ragtag skirmish ensued, during which Ashby's cannon collapsed and the enemy safely recrossed the Potomac while militia officers tried to pull rank on Ashby, who had been the only real fighter on the field.[39]

Word of these debacles reached the Confederate capital at Richmond more quickly by agitated letters from prominent Valley citizens than through official channels. James L. Ranson depicted conditions near Harpers Ferry directly to President Davis: "Last night a lady swam the Shenandoah to let us know that the enemy were being re-enforced, and the first aim would be to destroy our woolen factories along the Shenandoah; also our large flouring mill. . . . This done, our whole county must be devastated, and, to say nothing of our mills, slaves and other valuable property, all the grain in stock or garner will be burned up."[40] The Valley's representative in the Confederate Congress, Alexander R. Boteler, warned the secretary of state: "The condition of our border is becoming more alarming every day. No night passes without some infamous outrage upon our loyal citizens."[41] Another prominent Virginian, Andrew Hunter, pleaded the problem as one of command to Secretary of War Benjamin: "The feeling is becoming very general among our people that while we have men ready and willing to protect the border against these incursions of the enemy, yet that we are suffering needlessly for want of competent officers. . . . I beg leave to submit whether it be not practical and expedient to send here . . . some competent regular or experienced officer of the army to take charge of and direct the whole military operations of this quarter . . ."[42]

Such recommendations heightened the fears of President Davis and War Secretary Benjamin and committed them to providing the Shenandoah with at least a competent commander. They recognized Virginia's great valley as the salient geographic feature of the eastern theater of war—the entire region east of the Alleghenies—and knew it must be held. In terms of military geography, the Valley was thrust between North and South like a giant spear—a spear whetted at each end. At its northern tip the Shenandoah plunged deep into the Union. Rebels on the Potomac stood 30 miles behind Washington and 150 miles north of enemy lines in Kentucky and Illinois. Those Federal wings could best be linked by the Baltimore & Ohio Railroad and Chesapeake & Ohio Canal, but as Jackson had demonstrated, these routes were vulnerable in the Shenandoah, constraining the Yankees to a lengthy detour through Pennsylvania and Ohio. A similar problem loomed for the Confederacy across the Valley's southern tip, near which the Virginia & Tennessee Railroad linked Richmond with its western armies. Union conquest of the upper Valley could sever that link and necessitate a rail circuit through the Carolinas and Georgia. Such a conquest could also cut the flow of Valley grain to Richmond via the James River Canal.

Also strategic were the Valley's eastern and western boundaries; here too the Shenandoah divided Union from Confederacy. To the west Union divisions dominated the Alleghenies. To the east was the lair of the Confederate army protecting Richmond. Good roads traversed the

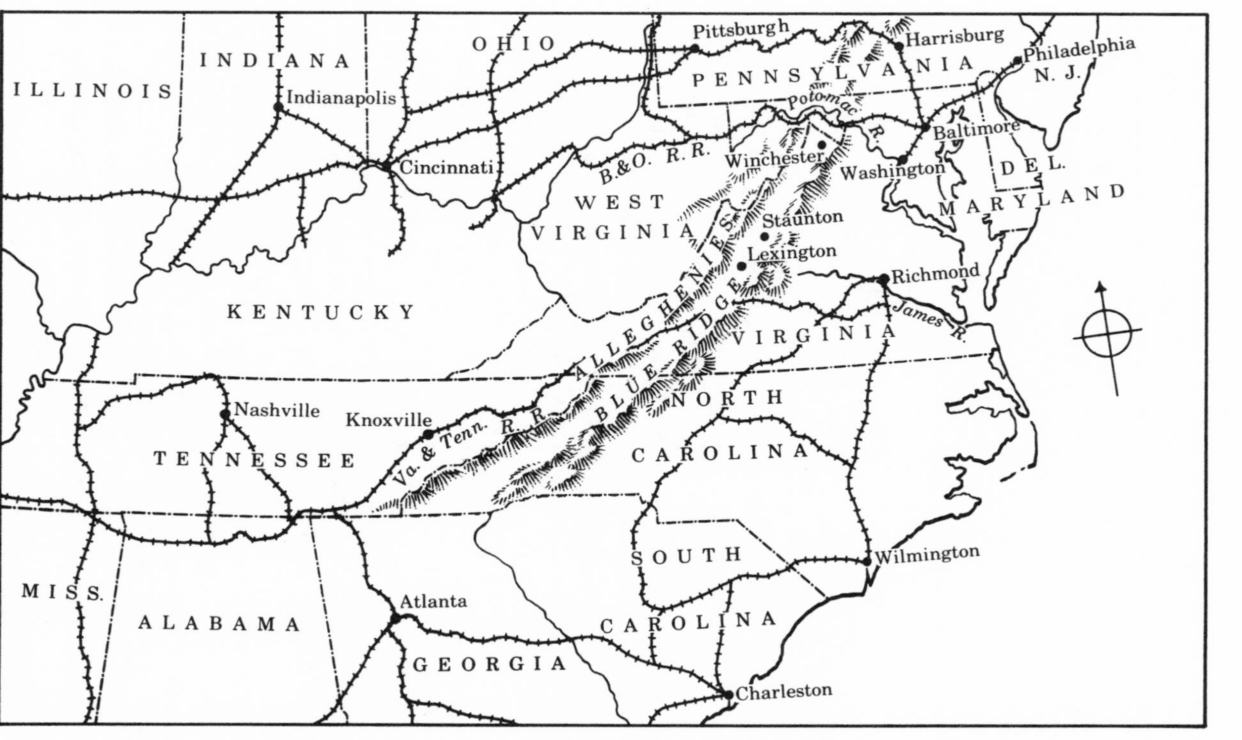

1. The Shenandoah Corridor

Note especially the strategic rail routes crossing the Valley's northern and southern reaches.

Valley from the Alleghenies to the Blue Ridge, through which no fewer than eleven gaps opened onto the alluvial plains of central Virginia. Through each of these gaps a Federal column could lunge behind Confederates located north of the James River, and the danger worsened the farther north a Confederate army maneuvered. An enemy force at Staunton, in the upper Valley, would stand one hundred miles from Richmond; an enemy force at Winchester, in the lower Valley, would be half that distance from the rear of Johnston's army at Centreville. The Shenandoah thus formed the strategic left flank of any Southern defensive line in Virginia. Jackson, perhaps the Confederacy's ablest student of military geography, firmly believed that "if this Valley is lost, Virginia is lost."[43]

The reverse was also true: so long as the South controlled the Valley, it could maintain a war in Virginia. An army inferior in numbers must exploit secrecy and surprise, and the forested Blue Ridge passes offered the rebels excellent opportunities for cloaked maneuver. The Shenandoah remained the corridor that Valley men reinforcing George Washington during the Revolution had shown it to be. Lee invaded Pennsylvania in 1863 behind the cover of the Blue Ridge. The Confederate raider Lieutenant General Jubal Early came this way during 1864 to threaten Washington, and rebel guerrilla John Mosby fought for months using the byways of the Valley.

Further, a poor army with at best just sufficient transportation, like the rebels defending the Old Dominion, required ready rations in any area of extended operations, and the Shenandoah was one long wheat field. Its farms alone could sustain Confederate armies in Virginia for many months. "[The Shenandoah] is a perfect stomachic Elysium," marveled one rebel. "Hot batter cakes and good coffee, butter and molasses, eggs, two sorts of preserves, milk, hot loaf bread, mush, boiled ham was the bill of fare this morning. . . . For dinner we have canned tomatoes and corn and beans, and everything in as great abundance as at breakfast, only more so."[44] Not until 1864 did the North see that the rebels continued to sally from the Shenandoah because they could eat as they marched there, and then Major General Philip Sheridan was loosed with fifty thousand men to ravage Valley farms. In the process he annihilated the Confederates who opposed him, though he might have spared himself this effort. Once Sheridan scorched the Valley's agricultural base, no sizable Confederate force could ever operate there again.

But Sheridan was three years away and would not descend upon the

Valley until the North grasped its total significance. In 1861 Federal concern focused on the lower Valley between the Manassas Gap Railroad and the Potomac. Two things made this sector of immediate importance. First, the lower Shenandoah flanked Washington. Anywhere north of Strasburg was north of Washington, and anywhere north of Martinsburg was north of Baltimore. The headquarters of Confederate Valley forces at Winchester was a scant sixty miles northwest of the Union capital. Also critical were the B & O and C & O links between Washington and the Midwest. Despite Union progress in rebuilding the B & O's Allegheny trackage, full east-west service was impossible because of destruction of the Potomac bridges at Harpers Ferry, while the C & O Canal was subject to harassment by Turner Ashby's cavalrymen. President Davis and Secretary Benjamin knew all of this, and when they spun their map around to study the Valley from the viewpoint of their Northern counterparts, they feared that it was only a matter of time until the enemy moved against it in force. Clearly the Union could not permit the Shenandoah to prick at Washington and cut its vital communications much longer.

So Davis and Benjamin marked Union progress toward the Valley like a slow blue stain on their war map and decided they must act. Though they had no troops to spare, they could provide the leader that Valley citizens had requested. They hoped at the same time to end turmoil in the Southern command structure. Their solution was the creation, on October 22, of a department of war embracing Virginia north of the Rappahannock River; General Johnston was entrusted with overall command.[45] The Shenandoah was designated a separate district within Johnston's department. The Valley District was bounded by the Blue Ridge and Alleghenies and extended south from the Potomac to the vicinity of Staunton, an area of roughly five thousand square miles. The district was to have its own army and its own commander. On October 21 Benjamin notified Jackson that he had been selected, a choice dictated not only by solid performance at the head of his brigade but also by his popularity in and knowledge of the region. In retrospect the choice seems inevitable, but it was not. First suggested for the post was Brigadier General Henry R. Jackson, who had served without distinction in Lee's Allegheny campaign. Nor did the government simply have its Jacksons confused: Major General E. Kirby-Smith would be considered for Valley commander before Thomas J. Jackson finally was appointed.

Jackson's appointment brought with it the rank of major general and full powers to act in all matters relating to the defense of his district and to all military operations therein.[46] Under the new organization Johnston continued as Jackson's superior and would synchronize Valley operations with those of the main army at Centreville. He would not, however, be providing any troops. Secretary Benjamin bluntly cautioned Jackson that his initial force would be small, mostly the militia already in the field, and that he could not necessarily expect reinforcements soon. In the meantime, Richmond hoped Jackson's fame in the area might stimulate an outpouring of volunteers.[47]

The Confederacy waged much of the war by fielding commanders without armies; such posts connoted either desperation or confidence. In this case the government expressed its faith in Jackson, yet he was a little disappointed. Ironically, he wanted less to go to the Valley, the scene of his greatest triumphs, than to the Alleghenies, mountains that had frustrated no less a man than Robert E. Lee. Western Virginia was Jackson's boyhood home, and he was troubled by Union advances there. As early as his tour of duty at Harpers Ferry, he had lobbied for an Allegheny command.[48] He realized, as had Washington before him, that Virginia's best defense against attack from the west was the occupation of those mountains. Jackson nonetheless accepted the Valley assignment without pressing his personal desires, and he was to defend it so tenaciously no one could have imagined he ever thought of another command. One of his officers eventually would write: "Jackson is the very man to be put in the Valley of Virginia, for he believes altogether in its importance, & it would be hard to convince him that the axis of the world does not stick out somewhere between Winchester & Lexington."[49]

False rumors of an enemy advance caused Johnston to retain Jackson with his old brigade for a few days in late October, and it was November 4, 1861, before the general departed to the Valley. He was accompanied only by a staff of three men. One was Colonel J. T. L. Preston, a founder of the Virginia Military Institute and once a partner of Jackson's in tannery and real estate ventures. Preston would be a principal assistant in his capacity as adjutant general, although he would soon vacate this post to return to the Institute. The other two men would remain with Jackson until his death. Major Wells J. Hawks served as commissary officer; his was the all-important task of keeping soldiers fed. Jackson fundamentally comprehended the adage that "amateurs talk about strategy while professionals talk about logistics," and he relied greatly upon Hawks's careful work for the underpinning of victory. At least once a week Jackson would receive reports from Hawks on the status of foodstuffs, reports he studied with care. It was not chance that, as he lay dying, the last name Jackson called was that of Major Hawks.

The third aide was Lieutenant Alexander Pendleton, known to his friends as Sandie. Sandie was the son of Brigadier General William N. Pendleton, a West Pointer who had left the U.S. Army and become rector of the Episcopal church in Lexington; with the outbreak of war he had returned to active duty and would soon be Robert E. Lee's artillery chief. Jackson had a tendency to choose sons of clergy as his assistants; perhaps he thought serious upbringing made for accurate staff work, and if this was his theory he proved it with this extraordinary twenty-one-year-old. Sandie had entered Washington College at age thirteen and instructed some classes before graduation. Thereafter he assisted his father as a teacher at a boys school in Lexington and went on to graduate work at the University of Virginia. A man of boundless intelligence and much good humor, he served as assistant adjutant general and aide de camp to Jackson, posts in which he handled all assignments in a way satisfactory even to Stonewall.

The little command party had reached only Strasburg by dark, but Jackson was determined to gain his post on the fourth. Lieutenant Pendleton was sent to find horses or a coach for Winchester while Jackson reviewed papers in the depot. Townspeople began to collect to see their protector, and one drunk staggered in to inquire, "Are you General Jackson?" He seemed not to comprehend the affirmative reply and stood muttering, "Are you the stone, stone, the stone, are you Stone Fence Jackson?" The drunk eventually retired in a nearby chair and fell asleep while Jackson led his staff on to Winchester.[50]

There Jackson's first task was to locate the foe, and one thing was readily apparent: the Shenandoah was threatened on two fronts. To the west an estimated four thousand Union troops around Romney were stripping the South Branch Valley, and those Federals were just two days west of Winchester by an all but undefended road.[51] The Valley's western border was equally exposed for fifty miles south of Winchester, and, for the present at least, Jackson was most concerned with this front. The Union divisions of Major General N. P. Banks dominated western Maryland to form the northern front. Banks massed a heavier force to the north, but, excepting the foray against Harpers Ferry, he had remained relatively inert and had made little effort to coordinate activity on his front with Allegheny-based operations.

If the enemy fronts did converge on the Valley, Jackson could guess how they would come. He foresaw one Northern column driving east from Romney to Martinsburg, another column sweeping south from Maryland to Martinsburg, and the two forces uniting there to advance on Winchester. If that happened, there would be nothing Jackson could do; the combined Union host would outnumber him beyond hope. Fortunately, the Federals were divided by command as well as geography. Those to the west belonged to the Department of Western Virginia, which was headquartered in the Allegheny wilderness at a flyspeck called Camp Gauley Mountain. Banks's command belonged to the Army of the Potomac, which was headquartered at Washington. Cooperation between separate military commands would be difficult, giving Jackson that much aid from his opponents. Nevertheless, Jackson had drawn one of the most difficult tasks Richmond had to allot that autumn—defense of a long frontier exposed from not one direction but two. From the first, he understood that his Valley Army must play a desperate game: operate between larger enemy concentrations so as to keep them apart.

If his Army failed in this game, it could not expect rescue. A demidivision of infantry, the closest Southern forces, faced heavy odds forty miles east of Winchester at Leesburg. Johnston was farther away, at Centreville. To complicate matters, there was no direct steam communication between Centreville and Winchester. The Manassas Gap Railroad, it will be recalled, swung south at Strasburg. From that city a trip to Winchester would have to be completed over the macadamized Valley Pike.

The Pike ran up the Shenandoah from Winchester to Staunton, and the line of that highway on his map beckoned Jackson's eye to the southwest. Here his thoughts lingered. He knew Robert E. Lee's Army of the Northwest was recovering near Huntersville, West Virginia, from its unsuccessful Allegheny offensive. Lee had been transferred to defend the Confederacy's Atlantic seaboard, leaving Brigadier General William W. Loring in charge at Huntersville. Brigadier General Edward Johnson (not to be confused with General Joseph E. Johnston, who commanded at Centreville) screened Allegheny passes northwest of Staunton with part of his army, but the bulk of it was idle. As boredom was the worst sequel to the punishment these men had endured, Stonewall determined to offer them a taste of victory.

Before his first day at Winchester had ended, Jackson dispatched Colonel Preston to Richmond with a candid message that the Valley was "defenseless" and that part or all of Loring's army must be redeployed to it. The need was great: "It is very important that disciplined troops not only of infantry, but also of artillery and cavalry be ordered here. It appears to me that there should be at least twenty pieces of field artillery, with their complement of horses, harness, implements, etc., assigned to this command."[52] Richmond had nothing like those reinforcements on hand, but the dismal state of Valley District defenses, worse now (because of Romney's fall) than when the District was created, compelled War Department action. Probably before Colonel Preston arrived, Secretary Benjamin had decided to shift the Stonewall Brigade and Captain William McLaughlin's first-rate Rockbridge Artillery back to the Valley from Joe Johnston's army at Centreville.[53] He realized Jackson needed more, and the secretary hinted that Loring's command might be made available.[54]

Johnston howled so loudly about losing the Stonewall Brigade that Benjamin had to placate Old Joe with double its numbers in replacements, explaining, "The Valley District is entirely defenseless and will fall into the hands of the enemy unless General Jackson has troops sent to him immediately."[55] Excited by rumors of a transfer, Jackson's former command leaped when it got the word. The 2d, 5th, and 27th Virginia swarmed ahead by train to make a surprise visit to Winchester on the evening of November 10. The 4th and 33d Virginia waited behind at Manassas Junction for the return trains. Since no one knew when these trains would return, the men were not permitted to pitch their tents, even after a steady rain began, and Private John Casler of the 33d recollected, "We had a glorious night in the rain and mud."[56] Casler, however, was squatting in the wrong mudhole. The E Company Irishmen of his regiment swilled a barrel of whiskey and grew so jolly their last officer deserted the Army in despair.[57] A long night followed before the trains appeared and the last of the Stonewall Brigade bounced home to the Shenandoah.

3

THE MANNER OF MEN

I burned fencerails when cold, stole when hungry, drank when thirsty, swore when angry, and was oftentimes insubordinate.

—John Opie

Mrs. Cornelia McDonald, who depicted the "joyous" boys parading through Winchester on their way to Manassas in July, wrote of those who returned in November: "All the glory seemed to have departed from the eager and enthusiastic army of the summer before."[1] It was true. The rebels now felt much as they looked: patience, like boot leather, was thinning, and thoughts of war's romance were as faded as their uniforms. Conditions around Winchester did not brighten this outlook. The autumn was unusually severe. Storms screamed down from the Alleghenies, bringing days of rains. Frigid winds slashed the cotton tents of the Stonewall Brigade; rebels sometimes battled for hours merely to hold tent poles in place. Mumps, fever, and diphtheria swept the ranks.[2]

The boys longed for home and rest, but they found neither in Jackson's army. The morning after the Stonewall Brigade stormed Winchester, Jackson's patrols were out to arrest officers who had left their posts. Lieutenant Moore of the 2d Virginia found himself replacing one of the truants as I Company commander. A serious thirty-five-year-old, a prewar attorney with a young wife and small children, Moore realized that to be in Stonewall's army meant giving up thoughts of seeing his family, though they were only twelve miles away in Berryville. Instead he focused earnestly on his new task. "My plan," he wrote his wife in the first of many letters to chronicle his service in the Valley, "is to treat the men with kindness and consideration in my personal intercourse with them, to attend to their wants and comforts as far as possible, to extend to such as deserve it all reasonable and proper indulgences, but at the same time, in my official character to be firm and decided, condemning all improper conduct and punishing without fear or affection where punishment is deserved."[3] Moore found much to correct, and within a week he had a sizable percentage of his company in the guardhouse for fighting or unofficial absence.[4] Those not under arrest went back to basics with daily company drills, but the new captain feared he would have to act even more sternly before some men resolved to do their duty.

Moore was right. The rebels were distracted from thoughts of the war, often by thoughts of Winchester's female population. Wrote twenty-four-year-old Private Lanty Blackford of the Rockbridge Artillery: "I am actually pining for some ladies society, and being near to it as I am here makes me wish to seek it stronger than ever," an amazing confession for the very devout Blackford, as he was writing to his mother.[5] A recent graduate of the University of Virginia, Blackford possessed a fine classical education. He enjoyed writing and early in the war decided to forgo a diary in favor of long, precise letters home. The letters remained secure with his family and ultimately formed an invaluable account from the private's viewpoint of the struggles of the Valley Army both on and off the battlefield. As to the question of girls, most boys shared Blackford's pining, for they were in such a state that many of them saw "every woman" as a beauty who deserved attention accordingly.[6] Jackson, of course, sought to restrain such unmilitary endeavors. Declaring Winchester off limits, he isolated the Stonewall Brigade in a camp four miles north of the city, but this only challenged the ingenuity of his men. Jackson's old regiments also considered the new camp unfair, since the militia remained near Winchester to guard it. Volunteers harbored a collective grudge against the "melish," whose sole function appeared to be blocking their fun. They supposed the militiamen enjoyed an easy life in the city while they languished in rural exile, and, with no hope of furloughs, the volunteers could not be denied escapes to clean, warm Winchester.

Private John Opie of the 5th Virginia devised a three-stage plan for outwitting the "melish." He first learned their password by eavesdropping on a militia post barring the road to Winchester. Next, he used chalk to decorate his jacket with officer's shoulder straps that were indistinguishable at night from the real item. Finally, he "obtained" a sword, and when darkness fell, "there was a full fledged lieutenant—sword, shoulder straps and countersign. The objective point, Winchester; the attraction, the beautiful girls of the town."[7]

Private George Baylor of the 2d Virginia resorted to impersonation of another sort. He decamped with three friends and headed for the nearest checkpoint, with one truant howling like a madman. The others pretended to be his escort to Winchester's mental ward. When the militia hesitated to pass them, the "lunatic" flung himself at the guards, and the way was immediately opened.[8]

Winchester was a reward worth such imaginative efforts. A favorite pastime there was eating, and every family welcomed soldiers to the table. One girl remembered that the table was never set at her house "without a large addition to the family circle. This is always prepared for, morning, noon and night, as it is a matter of course that soldiers will be brought in just at the right time and so cordially received that they feel they have perfect right to come again whenever it is convenient to them."[9] These meals were a prelude to what rebels called the "social campaign of Winchester."[10] There were frequent dances. Bees were organized, in which girls knitted for soldiers while the soldiers entertained them. The fun was splendid, although the knitting accomplished by thirty girls at one bee was assessed by Private Lanty Blackford of the Rockbridge Artillery as insufficient to put a single Confederate in socks.[11] In some cases the fun went too far, and militia doctor Abraham Miller would soon diagnose "a number of girls in the different neighborhoods in an interesting way, so the war has done something for the increase of the army."[12]

The troops also waged a campaign against Jackson's ban on liquor. At Stonewall's order, spirits were authorized to soldiers for medical purposes only. Local taverns were supposed to sell only to the bearer of a prescription signed by a surgeon, endorsed by the colonel of his regiment, and endorsed again by his brigade commander, but this was a simple obstacle for the thirsty to hurdle. Three tipplers forged the appropriate names on a bogus prescription and sent another to Winchester in the guise of hospital orderly, who inevitably returned with a fifth of pain killer.[13]

Officers too broke the prohibition. Captain Albert Pendleton of the 4th Virginia received a package from home containing liquid refreshment. He shared his good fortune at lunch one day, and his fellow officers departed to conduct afternoon drill in a haze of joyous anticipation.[14] The L Company officers of the 5th Virginia received three kegs of rye from home and invited other officers of the regiment to join them. Private Opie was not included, which he regarded as an oversight to be corrected:

> Securing two tin buckets, we left for the rear of the tent, which was crowded with officers who were compelled to stand up for the want of space. We pulled up two or three tent pins, rolled out a keg, filled our two buckets with the old rye, and then rolled back the keg and replaced the tent pins. We then made a campfire that resembled Vesuvius and raised Cain; but as the officers of the regiment were engaged in the same meritorious business, we escaped punishment. The next morning the regimental colors were found lashed to the tallest tree in the camp.[15]

Opie did not relate, probably could not remember, whether officers or enlisted men raised the colors.

While lashed above the 5th Virginia's camp, the regimental battle flag meant that the troops had won a round in an unceasing clash between themselves and Stonewall. Jackson always sought to pound his men into the mold of the thoroughly obedient professional soldier, but he never succeeded. An assertive independence was virtually built into the Valley Army. Its companies were drawn from neighborhoods of a few hundred, sometimes a few dozen, families, and privates found it difficult to accept a cousin or boyhood friend as a superior. Further, the Confederate practice of selecting company officers by company election tended to exclude strict disciplinarians from positions of command.

Straggling (leaving the marching column without permission) was the most common means by which Jackson's soldiers ignored discipline. Men were constantly leaving ranks for a hot meal or a comfortable place to rest for the night. They were often tempted to drop out by well-meaning Southern women who inevitably had food ready for passing troops or were forced to straggle when they outran their wagons and had nothing to eat. Jackson's relentless marches worsened the problem by literally walking the boots off his men. The barefooted drifted to the rear, where, with the exhausted and the malingerers, their numbers were sometimes considerable. Jackson's columns were never the compact surging mass portrayed by his admirers; they tended to be, rather, a weary corps surrounded by hundreds of roving panhandlers.

Marches led eventually to battlefields, and there too an ingrained individuality marked these men. They could not be arrayed in the shoulder-to-shoulder formations prescribed by military textbooks of the day. They were quick-witted and self-reliant, "more of a freelance than a machine," said one of their generals.[16] In attack, each rebel aligned on himself, dodging forward and firing as he saw fit. In defense, each judged the strength of his position for himself and left when he thought it useless to remain. John Opie was to state later, without a twinge of guilt, "In war, I ran when it was necessary, fought when there was a fighting chance."[17]

But the most persistent obstacle to rigid discipline in the Valley Army proved to be its very youth. John Casler, who was destined to become one of the Army's best anecdoters, was hardly beyond his twenty-first year when the war started. Typical also was John Opie, who was seventeen on the eve of the war and welcomed it as salvation from his classes in analytical geometry. Junior officers were scarcely older. Thirty-seven-year-old Jackson was an antique to these youngsters, who called him "Old Jack" as often as they did "Stonewall" and who did not appreciate his regulations any more than youth enjoys restrictions of any kind. "The truth is," asserted one of these young warriors, "we were soldier boys, and the boy was sometimes more in evidence than the soldier."[18]

The commander of these soldier boys was of different, more rigid stuff. Major General Thomas J. Jackson was utterly serious in all things. The early death of both parents and a hard youth in the mountains of western Virginia had already made him a humorless young man when he entered the United States Military Academy at West Point in 1842. Ill-prepared academically, Jackson had to devote more time to his studies than most of his classmates. He did so without complaint and stood seventeenth in a graduating class of forty-two. He earned two promotions for gallantry during the Mexican War and rose to the rank of brevet major before he left the U.S. Army in 1851, after, portentously, a bitter feud with a fellow officer.

During the next ten years, Jackson taught at the Virginia Military Institute, where he worked as diligently as ever, but received little appreciation. When cadets gathered to laugh and gossip about their teachers, they came down hardest on him. He became the butt of the roughest cadet humor. Upperclassmen once strapped a gagged "rat" (the V.M.I.

term for a freshman) to a chair, tilted it against Jackson's door, and disappeared. When Jackson opened the door, the helpless rat plopped at his feet.[19]

Despite harassment, Jackson slowly garnered a measure of respect. He became the man at V.M.I. who got the call where there was serious work to be done. He commanded the V.M.I. detachment at John Brown's execution, and he marched the Corps of Cadets to Richmond to serve as drill instructors when the war began. After a brief scare by an assignment to the mapmaking department, Jackson secured his first command at Harpers Ferry.

In his personal habits Jackson was a strange man. He impressed many as incapable of laughter; jokes seemed a mystery to him. He sat bolt upright at his desk and never touched the back of his chair. When thinking, Jackson stared ahead fixedly, totally absorbed by his business.[20] He often rode beside his marching columns, raising alternate arms heavenward. Some said Jackson was praying, others claimed that Jackson supposed this peculiar practice relieved weight in the hand by draining blood back to the heart. Such oddities of behavior, coupled with his religious fervor, gave rise to talk that Jackson was insane.

This talk of lunacy was a recurring irritant in Jackson's life, especially until the talkers grew accustomed to him. Many V.M.I. cadets found that three or four years were insufficient to adjust and dismissed him as a "hell of a fool." During the spring of 1862, when their commands merged with the Valley Army, Generals Taylor, Ewell, and Whiting all questioned Jackson's sanity, doubts that gave way to admiration as victories followed. According to the measure of victories gained, Jackson was sane enough.

One measure of Jackson's sanity was his silence. He never shared his thoughts if there was an alternative, and if there was no other way, he said no more than absolutely essential. "If silence be golden, he was a 'bonanza,'" reflected one observer.[21] This silence implemented Jackson's desire to "mystify, mislead, and surprise," not only the enemy but his own forces as well.[22] His marching orders, for example, sometimes specified a move "in the direction of" a place that was not the goal. He veiled his intentions so consistently that Major General Richard Ewell, who came to admire Stonewall, nevertheless admitted that he never received a message from Jackson without dreading orders to march on the North Pole.[23]

Like his speech, Jackson strove to make his discipline the tightest in the Confederacy. He had a mania for enforcement of regulations, and he probably court-martialed more offenders than any other officer of the Confederate army. In July 1862 Jackson unquestionably set some sort of record by keeping every general of his command busy with court-martial duty.[24] He expected everyone to follow orders without delay, question, or comment. "Arrest," he tersely instructed the commander of one disorderly regiment, "any man who leaves his post, and prefer charges and specifications against him that he may be Court-martialed. It will not do to say that your men cannot be induced to perform their duty. They *must be made to do it*" (italics Jackson's).[25]

Enormous ambition fueled this devotion to duty. When Dr. Hunter McGuire, a member of his staff, asked Jackson about his emotions the first time he came under enemy fire during the Mexican War, the general confided he was afraid the battle would not be severe enough to allow him to win distinction. McGuire thereafter observed an intense earthly ambition in his chief: "Ambition? Yes, far beyond what ordinary men possess."[26] Nothing less than the conquest of a continent could slake that ambition. Jackson once visited Quebec, and there he stood before the Wolfe Memorial on the Plains of Abraham and read aloud Wolfe's last words, "I die content." In a rare show of emotion, Jackson exclaimed, "To die as he died, who would not die content."[27]

A craving for distinction, for the delayed commendation Jackson wrote of to his wife after the First Battle of Manassas, flowed in the blood of this man. It conflicted mightily with a genuine Christian humility. The vigor with which Jackson practiced Christian discipleship—before the war he would neither read nor write a letter on Sunday—sprang partially from this conflict, but he never quieted his ambition. Shrewd Brigadier General Richard Taylor once glimpsed this compulsion: "It was but a glimpse. The curtain closed, and he was absorbed in prayer. Yet in that moment I saw an ambition as boundless as Cromwell's and as merciless. . . . His ambition was vast, all absorbing. Like the unhappy wretch from whose shoulders sprang the foul serpent, he loathed it, perhaps feared it; but he could not escape it—it was himself."[28]

Once, when he was unable to obtain sufficient rifles for his command, Jackson requested twelve-foot pikes as substitutes.[29] The requisition has appeared comical over the years, but Jackson meant no jest.

Stonewall intended that all those so armed would fight until he gave the word to stop, and he would have court-martialed the shirkers. Jackson gave his best effort under every circumstance and demanded no less from others. One perceptive rebel touched the essence of Jackson when he wrote, "In truth the great soldier was an altogether earnest man."[30]

In his earnest way, Jackson did not see the boy in any of his soldiers, and he reacted sternly to their escapades around Winchester. Many of those who broke into town on the evening of November 10 were promptly arrested, and Old Jack's restrictions grew harsher as his troops continued to evade them. When he discovered that visiting relatives were smuggling liquor to his men, he ordered searches of every civilian vehicle entering his camps. Any spirits found were poured on the ground, and the wagon and team were confiscated.[31] Stonewall issued orders requiring all officers to obtain passes from his office before they left their camps.[32] One soldier was executed by firing squad for assaulting an officer.[33]

Despite such efforts, Old Jack never forged a professional army. His troops became unbelievably tough fighters, but professional obedience he could not instill. Declared one of Jackson's rebels: "The Confederate soldier was peculiar in that he was ever ready to fight, but never ready to submit to the routine duty and discipline of the camp or the march. The soldiers were determined to be soldiers after their own notion and do their duty for the love of it, as they thought best. The officers saw the necessity for doing otherwise, and so the conflict was commenced and maintained to the end."[34]

From this clash of volunteers and a rigid professional soldier emerged an immortal compromise, Jackson's "Foot Cavalry."

II

Even more pressing than Jackson's concern with discipline during November and December 1861 was the weakness of the Army of the Valley District (already called simply the Valley Army), and Jackson sought reinforcements with a special urgency. He reminded Secretary Benjamin that the Army needed Loring's command. He ordered his militia commanders, Brigadier Generals Boggs, J. H. Carson, and G. S. Meem, to concentrate their brigades at Winchester, and he assembled and armed all other militia units from the northern Shenandoah.[35]

The Valley Army's first reinforcement came in the person of one man, Brigadier General Richard B. Garnett, a new commander for the Stonewall Brigade. Garnett bore the name of a distinguished family that had already given an able son (Brigadier General Robert Garnett) to the Confederate cause. A West Pointer, Richard Garnett had seen twenty years' duty on the western frontier. He had battled Indians from Texas to the Dakotas and served in California in the raucous days after gold was discovered on John Sutter's land. His trim, agile appearance bespoke a strenuous life in the open, and he was browned until he resembled the rancheros of California. Brooding eyes set in a narrow, almost pinched face added something of the conquistador image.

Despite his qualifications, Garnett reached the Shenandoah with two handicaps: he was replacing the brigade's first and very successful commander, Jackson, and Jackson did not want him. The Stonewall Brigade eyed Garnett skeptically when, at Jackson's order, Colonel Preston rode out and introduced him to his new command, but Garnett overcame that challenge within a few weeks. He was as direct and unpretentious as Jackson, and unlike the latter, he was willing to hear grievances. Excepting Jackson, Garnett proved the most popular of the brigade's seven commanders, and it became as much Garnett's Brigade as it was the Stonewall Brigade.* The second problem he could not master. Jackson believed Garnett's assignment to the Valley was due to political influence, which immediately tainted Garnett in Jackson's opinion. When his discipline proved milder than Jackson's, the latter's doubts mounted.[36]

Old Jack was better pleased by his own efforts to organize artillery batteries for the Army. His U.S. Army career had been with the artillery, and he appreciated the uses of cannon. Fortunately, the Army had many excellent gunners, many of whom had learned gunnery from Jackson on the V.M.I. drill field. The general found an idle section (two guns) and assigned it to a former student, Lieutenant W. E. Cutshaw. To man his guns, Cutshaw got the Irishmen of the 33d Virginia, whose antics had driven their last officer to desert from the Manassas Junction

* Traditionally, Civil War brigades, both North and South, were identified simply by the surname of their commanders. A nickname such as Stonewall was an exception resulting from unusual unit courage. Hence, Jackson's original command was known both as the Stonewall Brigade and as Garnett's—later Winder's—Brigade.

while the regiment awaited its return to the Valley. The section grew mildly proficient in a few days, and Jackson planted it at Hanging Rock,[37] a strongpoint on the road to Romney that had once witnessed a massacre of Delaware Indians.

The governor of Virginia scraped together five guns for the Valley District. They were odd-looking things—"alleged cannons," someone quipped[38]—but they could do good work under an efficient officer. Jackson thought of dependable Joe Carpenter, who captained Company A of the 27th Virginia. Like Cutshaw, Carpenter had been one of Jackson's promising gunnery pupils, and the student now received a new task from his former professor. Jackson transferred Carpenter to lead the new battery; the infantrymen of Company A went along to become cannoneers.[39] A similar transfer converted Captain James Waters's Company L of the 5th Virginia to Waters's West Augusta battery.

The finest battery in the Shenandoah, and one of the very best of the Confederacy, was Captain William McLaughlin's Rockbridge Artillery. Its ranks were crowded with well-educated young men: twenty-eight college graduates, twenty-five theology students, and seven men with master's degrees.[40] From its rosters rose leaders such as Sandie Pendleton's famous father, Brigadier General William N. Pendleton. These gunners hailed from the Lexington area, and Jackson knew many of them by name. He was therefore especially concerned to hear that some had picked up the Stonewall Brigade's drinking habits. The battery's march to Winchester from Centreville had included an unscheduled halt at a wayside distillery, after which it ingloriously entered Winchester with a wagonload of dead-drunk gunners.[41]

Another battery emerged from the cavalry operating around the Valley. Three young cavalrymen, all of them Jackson's students six months earlier, had ventured beyond their lessons. Captain Robert Chew, nineteen, and Lieutenants Milton Rose, seventeen, and Jamie Thomson, eighteen, sold Turner Ashby and Secretary Benjamin the idea of a battery of horse artillery. Unlike conventional artillery units in which gunners trailed the cannons on foot, each of Chew's men would ride his own mount. The battery would go where the cavalry went, as fast as it went. The idea stressed mobility; guns must be lightweight and a large contingent of spare horses was essential. Secretary Benjamin was particularly enthusiastic about the concept and provided the first horse artillery in America since the Mexican War with a flexible complement of three guns: a stubby twelve-pounder howitzer deadly at short range, a medium-range three-inch rifled piece, and a long-range English Blakely gun.[42]

As important as the guns were the gunners. The prospect of excitement with Chew lured many good men to his battery, among them a twenty-two-year-old former apprentice painter from the New Market area, George Neese. Neese, originally a member of the militia, had commenced his service a few days after Jackson reached the Shenandoah; Neese's first tour of duty was guarding one of the large siege guns around Winchester, to which there was no immediate threat. Neese had little formal education, but he had a quick mind and a sense of humor, and it did not take him long to realize that life with Chew could be much more interesting. In early December he joined the battery, and at about the same time he began recording daily entries in his diary, a work that was to be of great historical value.

Chew's command was to serve under Lieutenant Colonel Turner Ashby, a man born for combat. Three generations of Ashby's forebears had fought America's battles. A great-grandfather had served through the French and Indian War; a grandfather was wounded when George Washington attempted to surprise the British at Germantown, Pennsylvania. His father, John Ashby, was a Virginia hero of the War of 1812, and Turner Ashby was worthy of his stock. He had been in the saddle since his boyhood in Fauquier County, east of the Blue Ridge, and he could do anything on a horse. At thirty-four years of age, he was a paladin, respected by all he met as a natural leader. When rowdy construction gangs were pushing the Manassas Gap Railroad through Fauquier during the 1850s, Turner had organized a company of mounted citizens and enforced order. Upon hearing of John Brown's raid at Harpers Ferry, Turner gathered his company for action. He arrived too late to see Brown captured, but for the next eight weeks his riders patrolled the Potomac to blunt any abolitionist effort to free Brown.

After Virginia seceded in April 1861 Turner Ashby's company resumed its Potomac patrols near Harpers Ferry, where tragedy struck. His younger brother fell in an ambush, and there were rumors he was sabered without mercy after begging to surrender. Those close to Turner felt he believed the story and became obsessed with revenge.[43] He ambushed and harassed the Federals constantly. He temporarily shut down the B & O by expertly blasting a boulder onto its tracks.[44] He borrowed a farmer's homespun suit and swayback plow horse and ambled across the Potomac, passing himself off as a horse doctor. The disguise made him welcome in Northern camps all the way to Pennsylvania, and he returned with valuable information.[45]

Such intense energy made Ashby the ideal company commander; only later, when his fame attracted too many riders to his command for him to manage, did his command deteriorate. In the beginning he won much praise. An inspector general from Richmond visited Harpers Ferry in May, found Ashby to be "an excellent officer,"[46] and added, "I am quite confident that, with the vigilance which is exercised by Captain Ashby, no enemy can pass the point which he is directed to observe."[47] Even perfectionist Jackson felt secure at Harpers Ferry with Ashby on patrol.[48]

By the time Colonel Angus McDonald organized a regiment of Shenandoah cavalry, Ashby was the unquestioned choice for his second in command, as lieutenant colonel,[49] and it was a wise choice. Ashby's already growing reputation helped attract some excellent companies led by captains like John Winfield, John Fletcher, and George Sheetz. These men were not soldiers by profession, but they were resolved to do their duty. Sheetz, for example, was seen squinting over *The Cavalry Officer's Manual* at many a fireside.[50] McDonald's regiment provided most of what defense the Valley had from July to November 1861. Sixty years old, McDonald was unable to meet the strain of active campaigning for long, and when Jackson assumed command of the Valley District, Ashby headed the Shenandoah cavalry. He had deployed his men in a picket line that stretched eighty miles, from Harpers Ferry west to Moorefield.

Ashby galloped between these outposts on a magnificent white horse that accented his swarthy complexion and beard. He was short but very strong; his endurance seemed eternal. One rebel pictured him thusly: "Imagine a man with thick coal black hair, heavy black beard, dark skin, large black eyes, sleepy looking except when the Yankees are in sight, then they do flash fire." The soldier went on to describe Ashby as approximately five feet, eight inches and about 130 pounds, and called him the "best and most graceful rider in the Confederacy."[51] He was a soldier's officer: Private Lanty Blackford of the Rockbridge Artillery had pleasant chats with him more than once and found nothing of the hauteur that sometimes accompanied high rank; he was the kind of officer a private felt at liberty to question about the events of the day.[52] Unfortunately, his correspondence, both official and private, was sketchy, so it is difficult today to know more of the man behind that long, black beard.

One thing is certain: Ashby did not evidence fear. He seemed to have no regard for the danger of enemy bullets[53]—indeed, he found in them a useful foil for his style of leadership, because he believed a commander should be in front of his riders and take risks in order to inspire them. His displays of iron nerve heartened ordinary men to follow wherever he rode, and as word of his exploits grew with the telling and retelling, hundreds refused to volunteer without assurance they could ride with Ashby.[54]

Yet courage was often counterbalanced by another Ashby trait, his lack of concern with (or his inability to achieve) anything approaching normal organization and discipline. Ashby's command did not function like a regular military unit, a problem exemplified in the late summer of 1861 when Harry Gilmor, a young Marylander, decided to join the cavalry. On August 31 he slipped over the Potomac and rode south until he met some of Ashby's pickets. They took him to their chieftain, whom he found at camp lying on the grass surrounded by troopers. Gilmor was assigned to Captain Frank Mason's company and that night rode out on his first mission. Gilmor and one other raider snuck into the streets of Harpers Ferry. They drew shots from Federals who had lain in ambush, and Ashby, who had concealed two of his companies nearby, returned fire and scattered the enemy. "We had one man killed. The enemy had two killed and several wounded. Thus ended my first day of war," Gilmor recalled.[55]

Without drill or even inspection of his equipment—if he had any—Gilmor had ridden off and started fighting. It was exciting, but it was not building a true cavalry arm. A farmer, Ashby had little formal and no military education, and he did not share the passion of men like Jackson for drill. He perhaps naively saw the patriotism of his men as a substitute for strict regulations. His lifelong riders were perfect shots. Their tall, blooded mounts were superb. What more was necessary to make a cavalryman, Ashby wondered.

That question foreshadowed problems. Romantic visions had stirred the thoughts of those who became the Valley cavalry long before the war, and it was for this reason that the region's social highlight had been the medieval-style tournament copied from the novels of Sir Walter Scott. Ashby was a frequent contestant in these affairs.[56] And now a "band of brothers" mentality did more than the enemy to hamper Ashby's regiment. It remained deficient in organization, training, and discipline. It had only one other field-grade officer, Major Oliver Funsten, a physician and state legislator before the war. Funsten was a giant of a man who rode a horse bigger than Ashby's and carried an oversized saber; doubtless he looked the part of a cavalryman, but he had no military experience.[57] Companies sometimes lacked any officers.[58] With a roll of extra clothes dangling from their saddles, boys like Gilmor trotted off to join Ashby's cavalry. When they got tired or the weather turned nasty, the boys strayed home. "Every private was a general and needed no guidance or direction from his officer," vowed one trooper.[59] Without benefit of discipline, Ashby's troopers, and some of his officers, greeted the war as a jolly new tournament.

Lack of clear-cut jurisdiction obliged Jackson to tolerate such conditions, for Ashby's regiment enjoyed a vague autonomy that sheltered it from Stonewall's direct control. The Valley cavalry was recruited under special War Department authorization and reported to Richmond, not Winchester.[60] Likewise, authorization and equipment for Chew's Battery came from Secretary Benjamin, not Jackson. Ashby was eager to cooperate with Stonewall for the most part, but on matters such as discipline he showed little promise.

There came a time when Ashby did not know how many men he could field, but in November he told Jackson he had 34 officers and 508 men. Stonewall listed those figures with his first monthly report. He also showed 4,000 effective infantry and artillerymen. There were 20 pieces in his batteries and roughly 1,000 militia in his training camps.[61] It would have pleased Jackson to learn that news of better discipline among the militia had already reached Richmond.[62]

At the headquarters of this little host, Jackson was collecting a staff that matched his own devotion to hard work. He was so determined to have capable aides that he investigated prospects to the point of discovering whether they rose early, a mark of diligence Jackson esteemed.[63] A particularly important addition was Major John A. Harman, who served as Army quartermaster. At age thirty-seven Harman was a contemporary of Jackson, and like him, he had seen service in the Mexican War. He tried farming after that war before entering the stage business, in which he and his brothers dominated ground transportation in the Shenandoah. In 1859 his vehicles moved the cadet detachment from V.M.I. to stand guard at John Brown's execution; the detachment was commanded by then Major Thomas J. Jackson. The impression of either man on the other is unknown, but there was no recorded friction such as would occur often between them after 1861. Harman had no fear of Stonewall, wrote of him as "crack-brained," and did not hesitate to resign if he felt misused, which he often did given the work he was asked to perform. Everything from organizing couriers to minding a big iron safe for the Army's payrolls fell to his department. He secured for the Valley Army the best wagons Jackson saw in the war, and he was to display an awesome talent at moving those trains over difficult terrain. Several stern lectures from the general failed to break Harman of his incredibly profane language, and it became a standard saying in the Army that, when the trains were in a dangerous place, "Never mind, the old Major will bring them out all right if hard work and swearing can do it."[64]

What Harman was to the Army's wagon train Dr. Hunter H. McGuire, Valley District Medical Director, was to its health. Son of a physician and an inspired student, McGuire graduated from medical college and was teaching surgery in Philadelphia at age twenty-three. Angered by anti-Southern bias after the John Brown raid, McGuire helped start an exodus of Southern medical students from the City of Brotherly Love to Richmond. He was practicing in Winchester when the war began and was assigned to duty as medical director at Harpers Ferry during Jackson's first weeks there. Once he had determined the quality of this young man, Jackson never let him go. McGuire was graced with an innovative mind, and he assembled an ambulance corps and the Confederacy's first system of reserve hospitals for the Valley Army.[65]

To guard Headquarters, Jackson chose Captain Harry Morrison's Company I, the Liberty Hall Volunteers of the 4th Virginia. This remarkable company was initially recruited from Washington College, and it ranked among the best-educated units of the war, North or South. One fourth of its men had been preparing for the ministry. The unusual concentration of intelligence and devotion attracted Jackson, although he never favored his guard. The Volunteers were often in the front rank of the regiment during battles. Quieter times saw these rebels stationed near Headquarters with four sentries at the general's door, where they learned to step lightly. "Not that he was cross," recalled Lieutenant John

Lyle, "but anywhere in his neighborhood was a proper place to put on your dignity." Only once did that dignity falter. Late one evening a sentry started a whistling bee, and things grew happy until Jackson stepped from his office and "squelched it."[66]

III

Throughout November and December, Jackson continued to arrange his district. Work went forward on fortifications around Winchester; crews were taught to serve the several pieces of heavy artillery near town. Work parties went to the northern tip of the Valley to uproot and haul off Baltimore & Ohio tracks for use on Confederate lines; by December practically all the rails between Harpers Ferry and Martinsburg had been removed. The pace at Headquarters was such that Colonel Preston described to his wife a slack day's activities as follows: "We started a section of artillery this morning, and made arrangements for receiving a regiment of militia, sent out to arrest a suspected man, released a number of prisoners from the guardhouse, and received and attended to several couriers with dispatches."[67]

On November 20, barely two weeks after taking his post, Jackson offered General Johnston and Secretary Benjamin his first essay in strategy. Given the views he had expressed a few weeks earlier on how he would invade and lay waste the Union if only Johnston's army would cross the Potomac, his strategy was predictably offensive in nature. It was, however, grounded in the realities of his district and called for a defensive-offense, a policy similar to that urged by George Washington a century earlier. Jackson argued in essence that the Valley must be defended from its western frontier; the Shenandoah could best serve as a sally port from which to catapult an aggressive garrison into the Alleghenies at Romney. If reinforced by Loring's Army of the Northwest at once, Jackson wrote, he would attempt to surprise the Federals and recapture this strategic town.

Jackson believed the chance for success was good because a strike from the recently defenseless Valley would not be expected, and the fruits of victory would be significant. The unlooked-for surrender of Federals at Romney would be a demonstration of Southern power to the many Union sympathizers in the fertile South Branch Valley. Several good roads crossed this valley toward the Shenandoah; a vigilant garrison at Romney could deny the enemy these passages and thus prevent the junction of Union fronts around Martinsburg. Indeed, the most important reason to Jackson for plunging into the Alleghenies was that territory taken there would become a buffer between enemy fronts to the north and west of Winchester. Jackson did not divulge particulars as to how the Yankees at Romney were to be trapped, but he stressed the need for surprise and capture. He visualized a swoop, not a gradual buildup culminating with a Braddocklike advance. Care had to be taken to conceal Confederate intentions.

Jackson packaged something for everyone in his letter. He knew Johnston anticipated an attack at Centreville, so he argued that the Romney thrust would give the impression that Johnston had weakened his army. This should precipitate a Northern offensive; if it did not, nothing could, and Johnston could stop worrying about Centreville. Jackson promised to reach Johnston in time to help if the enemy did advance. He also knew Loring was worried about Union moves toward Staunton if he left the upper Valley. For him, Jackson noted that any such advance would expose the enemy rear to Confederates at Romney. For Secretary of War Benjamin, Jackson suggested that capture of the Romney garrison would enable the Valley Army to guard the Shenandoah without additional reinforcements. But speed leading to capture of the enemy garrison was essential; let Loring come at once, Jackson concluded.[68]

Conceived in urgency, Jackson's offensive materialized slowly. Johnston did not welcome the prospect of Jackson drawing enemy attention toward Centreville.[69] Benjamin merely informed Loring of the plan and allowed him to elect to join it.[70] Loring waited almost until December to agree to the effort, and promised his men would cheerfully endure every hardship, though he also pleaded the necessity of delaying his march for Winchester until transportation could be assembled to move a large baggage train. This might take two or even three weeks. Nor was all of Loring's force committed to the operation. Elements of the Army of the Northwest under Brigadier General Edward Johnson were to remain on station west of Staunton. Loring would bring only three brigades totaling approximately six thousand men to the Valley District.[71]

Jackson had premised his operation upon immediate action with every available man, and he was disappointed by Loring's response. By mid-December, despite rumors of growing Union strength in Romney, only one of Loring's brigades was encamped at Winchester. The other two dawdled with supplies around Staunton. Jackson implored Benjamin to get Loring moving, but nothing happened.[72]

Unable to strike at his preferred target, Stonewall resolved to go after the nearest target, the C & O Canal, which followed the Potomac River along the Shenandoah's northern rim. With the B & O Railroad in Confederate possession from Harpers Ferry to beyond Martinsburg, the Union was making maximum use of the canal to mass coal reserves in Washington. The canal was filled from a series of ingenious river dams built of stout timber "cribs" holding quarried stone. The Potomac flowed over the dams but left enough slack water behind them to permit drainage as needed through locks into the canal. One of these river dams, No. 5, supplied a long portion of canal directly north of Winchester (below Martinsburg); Jackson already had failed to break it with two small raids, and in December he determined upon an assault in force. His target selection was doubtless influenced by knowledge that even before the war Dam No. 5 had proven weak in places (so that it leaked badly) and that construction to replace the old structure with a better masonry dam was not far advanced.[73]

Carson's militia, Garnett's Brigade, and the Rockbridge Artillery prepared to march. The orders typically were silent about destination. Lieutenant Jim Langhorne of the Headquarters Guard wrote his father, "We as usual do not know . . . which direction we are to go. . . . No one but Old Jack himself knows where, or for what purpose we are going."[74]

Reveille blared at 4 A.M. on December 16. Rebels downed as much breakfast as they could get and lined up; before dawn they were headed toward the Potomac.[75] The fatiguing march was enlivened by speculation about some flatboats being hauled along; perhaps Old Jack was going to invade Maryland.[76] On the seventeenth the column reached Martinsburg, where soldiers could see for themselves what remained of the B & O rolling stock they had torched the previous summer as they evacuated the lower Valley. One private of the Rockbridge Artillery "saw about 30 . . . burnt locomotives standing where they were burnt." He added that Jackson's scavengers were busy stripping anything usable from the wrecks.[77]

Joined by most of Ashby's cavalry at Martinsburg, the column pressed forward to Dam No. 5. Darkness was falling as the Confederates approached undetected by Union pickets on the far bank. A large, square log crib anchoring the dam on the Virginia shore was directly ahead. If the timbers could be cut away and the stones inside scattered, the weakened dam ought to give way, leaving the lock on the opposite side of the Potomac dry. Since ammunition shortages prevented simply bombarding the dam with artillery, the work had to be carried out with ax and crowbar.[78] Jackson enjoined absolute silence on his regiments, banned campfires,[79] and gathered details from several companies of the Stonewall Brigade. The troops moved to the south bank, where they found heavy tools—and a barrel of whiskey. For once the spirits were authorized; there were rumors that Old Jack even ladled out a tinful to each worker. Thus fortified, the men started their task by erecting a brush screen, behind which they could attack the timber cribbing with less exposure to Federal muskets.[80]

Those muskets were active by dawn, making it too dangerous to continue the work. Skirmishers bickered all day, but that night another fatigue party renewed the project, grumbling all the time that it was a "dam detail."[81]

Northern artillery arrived on the Maryland shore by the nineteenth and targeted Confederate infantry posted in a mill near the dam. Jackson took a single cannon across a field to return fire at a barn filled with Yankees on the opposite shore; as an old gunnery instructor, he could not have been impressed when only two of fifteen shots managed to find the target.[82] Meanwhile, Captains McLaughlin and Chew each rolled out a gun and scattered some Federal sharpshooters. The rebels were jeering at the sight when concealed Union guns returned fire with frightening accuracy. McLaughlin yelled for everyone to take cover in trees fifty yards to the right and sent Lieutenant William Poague to bring up the rest of the Rockbridge Artillery.

Poague never forgot the scene that greeted his return. Officers and men alike were snake-dancing from one side of a big pine tree to the other as Yankee shells burst nearby. Jackson was there, standing in the open, trying to talk the gunners back to their pieces. No one was responding, and even Jackson was seen to duck an occasional incoming shell. There was only one man who did not bow his head. Arms folded across his chest, Turner Ashby strolled quietly around the cannons.

Poague decided right there that Ashby was the bravest man he had ever seen, a thought that Poague admitted came to him while he was hunched as low in his saddle as the pommel would allow. As fresh Confederate guns arrived, the enemy ceased firing, and the Southerners did not reopen.[83]

Nightfall brought a new problem. The mill shelled earlier on the Virginia shore was now in flames, burning so brightly that it was unduly risky for work parties to approach the dam. The night was lost,[84] and Stonewall had to worry that the enemy would make torches of other buildings. Jackson's solution was a ruse as simple as it proved effective: he feinted an invasion. On the twentieth Carson's militia took the flatboats and marched up the Potomac with orders to be as obvious as possible. When the enemy hurried upstream as expected, Captains Frederick Holliday of the 33d Virginia and Henry Robinson of the 27th Virginia led volunteers to finish dismantling the dam's support on the Virginia shore.[85] Sam Moore got the first idea he was progressing with training his company of the 2d Virginia when it was tasked to provide skirmishers to cover this work.[86] The breach could be completed only by men standing in the river itself, so some Confederates endured numbing hours before they weakened the dam enough to hear a great crack followed by the sound of rushing water. As the dam emptied, this segment of the canal was left useless.

The breach was small. The canal would resume operations soon, but there was no more time for this enterprise, and the rebels marched for Winchester on the twenty-first. The pace was interrupted by only one incident, an escapade involving none other than Jackson himself. His staff relished this tale:

> After riding along some distance, the General spied a tree hanging heavy with persimmons, a peculiar fruit of which he was very fond. Dismounting, he was in a short time seated aloft in abundance. He ate in silence and when satisfied started to descend, but found that it was not so easy as the ascent had been. Attempting to swing himself from a limb to the main fork of the tree, he got so completely entangled that he could move neither up nor down and was compelled to call for help. He remained suspended in that attitude until his staff, convulsed with laughter, brought some rails from a fence near by and made a pair of skids to slide him to the earth.[87]

Once back in their camps, the Southerners thought of Christmas, and homesickness reached epidemic proportions. On Christmas Day the troops flocked to surrogate families in Winchester, but this only heightened the longing for home. Captain Sam Moore found he had not gained as much ground as he had thought in making serious soldiers of his men and complained to his wife, "The men of our entire regiment have behaved shamefully during the holidays; the companies have all been so much reduced by the men going home without leave that we could not turn out more than one-fourth upon any emergency. I am in despair about this thing."[88] Jim Langhorne was awash in melancholy as he wrote home: "How different will be the year approaching . . . to those of the few years of my short life. Instead of being at home with those I love so dearly, exchanging bright hopes for the future . . . I will be on a hostile march against those who at this time last year I called 'brothers, countrymen and friends.'"[89]

Other rebels found more satisfactory remedies against their homesickness. Harry Gilmor of Ashby's Cavalry, already promoted to sergeant, spent Christmas at Shepherdstown on the Potomac. There he got so intoxicated he began setting off fireworks and taking potshots at Federal pickets across the river; he eventually annoyed an enemy battery into opening fire in his direction, and shells landed in the town. Jackson heard of it and demanded Ashby investigate and report. No record of the report exists, but Gilmor was none the worse for whatever was done—in three more months he was a captain.[90]

Jackson, meanwhile, was not thinking of Christmas. By his return to Winchester he learned that Loring's command still had not arrived. Worse, fresh intelligence from Romney numbered the enemy there at ten thousand men, with additional reinforcements en route.[91] Nonetheless, Jackson was determined to move on Romney, believing that not to do so was tantamount to surrendering the lower Shenandoah. By December 16 the B & O bridge on the Big Cacapon River northeast of Romney was repaired, making the line operational except across the Valley. That alone would draw Union attention to the area. Federals west and north of Winchester eventually must realize the superiority of their position and unite around Martinsburg. Jackson emphasized this danger in a Christmas Eve letter to Johnston: "Our true policy is to attack the enemy in his present position [Romney] before he receives additional re-enforcements, and especially never to permit a junction of their forces at or near Martinsburg." The delay in undertaking this operation caused Jackson to substitute the word "attack" for "capture," but he did not think the mission a forlorn one. When joined by Loring's command the Valley Army would number 7,500 volunteers, 2,200 militia, and 650 cavalry, a force equal to the enemy in Romney. Jackson closed his message with a promise to march against Romney at the "earliest practicable moment."[92]

This moment depended on Loring, and that did not promise an early start. Loring had delayed his redeployment to Winchester until December while he assembled stores and baggage, and as he moved, the first severe storm of the winter broke around Huntersville. The Army of the Northwest slid out of the Alleghenies along gullies of snow and mud, and much of its equipment was lost. "The wagoneers were forced to throw out tents, blankets, etc., all of which were burnt; they also abandoned broken wagons and horses who would stop off the road and roll many feet down the mountain," wrote Lieutenant Lavender Ray of the 1st Georgia.[93] This trek sparked hopeful rumors that the Northwesterners were heading for comfortable winter quarters at Winchester, and some jubilant men threw away their weapons.[94]

Loring's column was delayed in part because Shenandoah civilians proved as generous as the rumors indicated. The passing regiments were fed and fed again. Lieutenant Ray recalled slogging into the little village of Bridgewater during a snowstorm to be welcomed by smiling women with milk, bread, and other good things.[95] Sergeant Ham Chamberlayne met one Valley man passing out invitations to soldiers to join him for supper; after the meal the host insisted Chamberlayne drop in at his brother-in-law's home, where he was entertained so royally he forgot to rejoin his regiment. Next morning, Chamberlayne escorted his host's three daughters to watch the column move off, then returned with them for still another meal. "Our march thro [*sic*] the Valley will be altogether one of the pleasant remembrances of my life," he wrote.[96] This sort of attention did not encourage haste, and Loring's force was not completely assembled at Winchester until the day after Christmas.[97]

The Army of the Northwest—Loring's command was to retain its separate identity while serving with Jackson—added three brigades to the Valley Army. The first to reach Winchester was that of Colonel William B. Taliaferro and consisted of the 1st Georgia, 3d Arkansas, and 23d and

37th Virginia regiments. Scion of a prominent Tidewater family, Taliaferro was commissioned an infantry captain during the Mexican War and mustered out a major. He served afterward in the Virginia legislature, and in the 1850s was president of V.M.I.'s Board of Visitors, where no doubt he heard for the first time of Thomas J. Jackson. By the time of John Brown's raid he commanded the Virginia militia, and he had entered active service soon after Fort Sumter; still, as Jackson would soon discover, Taliaferro had not lost the habit of bringing political clout to bear on military decisions. At the same time, Taliaferro's severe leadership style had roused talk among his men that the enemy would be spared the trouble of shooting him. One Georgian had gotten drunk on the march to Winchester and assaulted Taliaferro, then vanished from the guardhouse the night before his court-martial.[98]

Conditions in Loring's other units were comparable. Like Jackson's, Loring's men had grown tired of war and intended to find what pleasure they could regardless of officers. The second of Loring's units was commanded by Brigadier General S. R. Anderson, a self-made man who had seen service in the Mexican War as lieutenant colonel of the 1st Tennessee Volunteers. 1861 began Anderson's second war at the head of Tennesseans; his brigade was composed exclusively of infantry regiments from the Volunteer State: the 1st, 7th, and 14th Tennessee regiments. Christmas Day found the Volunteers camped around Strasburg, where, like the Stonewall Brigade, they went on a spree. When orders came to hurry immediately to Winchester, the Tennesseans balked until they finished their fortified eggnog, and some of them soon passed out on the highway.[99] Colonel William Gilham commanded the third of Loring's brigades, consisting of the 21st, 42d, and 48th Virginia regiments and lst Regular Battalion. Gilham was a West Pointer (he graduated one place above William T. Sherman in the class of 1840) who had taught there and seen action in some of the bloodiest battles of the Mexican War before coming to the Virginia Military Institute as a professor and eventually commandant of cadets. As such he was Jackson's prewar superior. Immediately prior to the war he had published a drill manual for all arms, hundreds of pages of elaborate and careful maneuvers that Jackson would utilize for the Valley Army. Finally, two good batteries came with Loring, Captain Lindsay M. Shumaker's Danville Light Artillery and Captain Lawrence S. Marye's Hampden Light Artillery, with four guns each.

As commander of these units, General Loring was now also second in command of the Valley Army. Loring had done a man's work while still a boy during the Seminole War in Florida during the 1830s; he had lost an arm in the Mexican War at the battle of Chapultepec. Despite this wound, Loring had remained in the U.S. Army to fight Indians on the frontier and gain a colonelcy by 1856, making him the youngest line colonel of the old army. There was no question of his courage, yet he had displayed little aptitude for high command. His redeployment to Winchester had been inexcusably slow. Worse, he seemed powerless to prevent his troops, who had admittedly suffered severely in the Alleghenies, from slipping close to demoralization.

Eager or disillusioned, the Northwesterners were all going on Jackson's expedition to Romney, as was every other man he could muster. He armed the last of his militia units. All furlough requests were rejected. On Christmas eve Jackson dispatched Colonel Preston back to Richmond with a final appeal for more men.[100] Preston was rebuffed, but word came from another source that some Choctaw Indians might be available; send them at once, Jackson replied.[101]

The weather moderated as year's end approached. By December 31 three mild days convinced Jackson the "earliest practicable moment" for his offensive was at hand, and he moved. Several companies of Garnett's Brigade joined Ashby in a new raid against Dam No. 5.[102] Artillery batteries filled their limber chests. All units were ordered to march at 6 A.M. the next day, January 1, 1862.[103]

The destination, as usual, was kept secret from the troops, which prompted the inevitable speculation. Hospital orderly John Apperson of the 4th Virginia noted in his diary that some men assumed they would move toward Romney, some thought toward Hanging Rock, and others, he wryly added, hoped they would shift into more comfortable quarters.[104] Lieutenant Langhorne assessed the bits of information he gathered during his sentry duties at Headquarters and concluded the Army would make another comparatively easy strike at the C & O Canal.[105] A wiser Captain John Graybill of the 33d Virginia ventured no guesses, reflecting in his diary only that Jackson's orders "indicated something more than a march."[106]

4

THE ROMNEY WINTER

In all the war I never . . . endured such physical and mental suffering.

—William T. Poague

January 1, 1862, began a winter ordeal for the Valley Army. From Winchester Confederate units followed a highway northwestward toward the hamlet of Pughtown. The morning was unseasonably warm, tempting hundreds of men to ignore orders and stuff greatcoats into company wagons—then temperatures dropped. The wind whipped down from the north with freezing cold, but the wagons lagged and soldiers could not retrieve their overcoats.[1]

The Valley Army's trains were in trouble from the outset. Major Harman was sick, hospitalized with a throat inflammation his assistant called "quinsy,"[2] and his profane energy was missed. It fell to his assistant, Captain Garbar, and others to push 160 wagon loads of provisions and stores over high hills and through deep ravines, and before the first nightfall some wagons were broken or overturned, further retarding the column.[3] By evening the vanguard had trudged only eight miles to Pughtown, but the trains were far to the rear.

Rebels were compelled to improvise against the cold that night. Messmates pooled blankets and bedded down en masse—"hog fashion," John Casler called it.[4] Some men risked breaching the Army's most inflexible standing regulation, which banned the use of fence rails from surrounding fields for firewood, to be punished by icy gusts that sprayed them with sparks. At the camp of the Rockbridge Artillery, flames jumped into dry grass and raced the gunners for their cannons; only at the last minute were the pieces saved.[5]

Jackson too was a victim of the confusion that bedeviled the Army.

That morning a Valley citizen had presented Stonewall a bottle of fine, rare whiskey. Jackson expressed his thanks hurriedly, imagined he saw a decanter of wine, and set it aside for safekeeping. The afternoon's cold prompted a drink, and Jackson quaffed several fingers' worth of his present. If the "wine" tasted strong to him, he said nothing of it as he passed the flask to his staff, which, emboldened by the general's example, emptied it. Shortly the brew's true nature became apparent. Old Jack began to talk freely, ranging over a variety of topics. He complained of the heat and unbuttoned his overcoat. "The truth is," wrote one of the staffers, "General Jackson was incipiently tight."[6]

Though he spoke of many things that evening, Jackson let no hint of the destination escape him. The first day's march had led the Army off the direct highway from Winchester to Romney and northwestward toward mountainous Morgan County, West Virginia, and the Potomac; no one knew why. Silent again by morning, Jackson led deeper into the Alleghenies. The weather deteriorated all day. The wagon ruts that served as a road kept the supply trains spread out for miles.[7] Breakdowns repeatedly stalled the trains and kept them far behind the infantry. The column began to cross a half-frozen bog about dusk, and here most of Loring's regiments became completely entangled with each other.[8] Many men had exhausted their rations and had begun to scavenge as the Army halted a scant eight miles beyond Pughtown, at Unger's Store.[9]

If this camp offered any comfort, it was to those few who were more concerned with guessing their mission than eating. They noted that Carson's militia brigade and several cavalry companies reached Unger's Store from Martinsburg that evening.[10] (Ashby with some of his riders was still opposite Dam No. 5, where he could decoy the enemy about rebel intentions and again hit the dam, a project Jackson would not give up. He rejoined the Army on January 5.) Jackson had now concentrated every available man, which meant serious work awaited, and where this work lay would be revealed by the route taken the next day. If the Army marched due north tomorrow, it would move on the resort village of Bath and, six miles beyond it, the town of Hancock, Maryland, on the Potomac's far bank. Or, the Army might follow a westward road from Unger's Store through Bloomery Gap to Romney.

When Old Jack motioned to push northward on January 3, many saw his goal but few his purpose. A Union force of fourteen hundred held Bath. This bridgehead could be expanded from across the Potomac and thus endangered the right flank of any Confederate advance on Romney. Jackson intended to wipe out the Federal bridgehead, cross the Potomac, and destroy valuable supply depots around Hancock. Rail and telegraph links between Union forces in western Maryland and at Romney also passed through this area, and Jackson wished to disrupt them to render concerted enemy action more difficult when he did descend upon Romney.

The first thing was to take Bath. Jackson quizzed soldiers who lived thereabouts and learned that the village stood at the eastern foot of a ridge called Warm Spring Mountain. The road by which the Army was traveling paralleled the eastern base of this ridge through Bath and continued straight on to the Potomac. Another road traversed the ridge from Bath to join a route at the mountain's western base. This combined highway led northward to a depot on the Baltimore & Ohio Railroad, thence through a gorge to the Potomac. To shut this potential escape route, Stonewall planned for his militia to cross the mountain some miles south of Bath and push along its western fringe. Simultaneously, Loring was to storm directly into Bath on the main road east of Warm Spring Mountain and herd the enemy northward toward the Potomac or westward into the militia. Though it would require a strenuous march, Jackson planned to fight this action on January 3 and demanded haste of his officers.[11]

The plan was simple but realistic, and only Confederate dawdling on the third defeated it. Taliaferro's Brigade started the march by backtracking to its wagons through the bog it had painfully traversed the previous night. By the time his men had struggled across that swamp and eaten, Taliaferro was forced to rest them for two hours.[12] When its wagons overtook the Stonewall Brigade during the day, Garnett allowed his famished men to prepare a meal. Jackson soon encountered the Stonewall Brigade and demanded an explanation.

"I have halted to let the men cook their rations," offered Garnett.

Stonewall glowered, "There is no time for that."

"But it is impossible for the men to march farther without them," the brigadier objected.

Stonewall repeated his orders and growled, "I never found anything impossible with this brigade."[13]

It moved immediately, and Jackson spurred on, angry that his men would think it more important to eat than march.

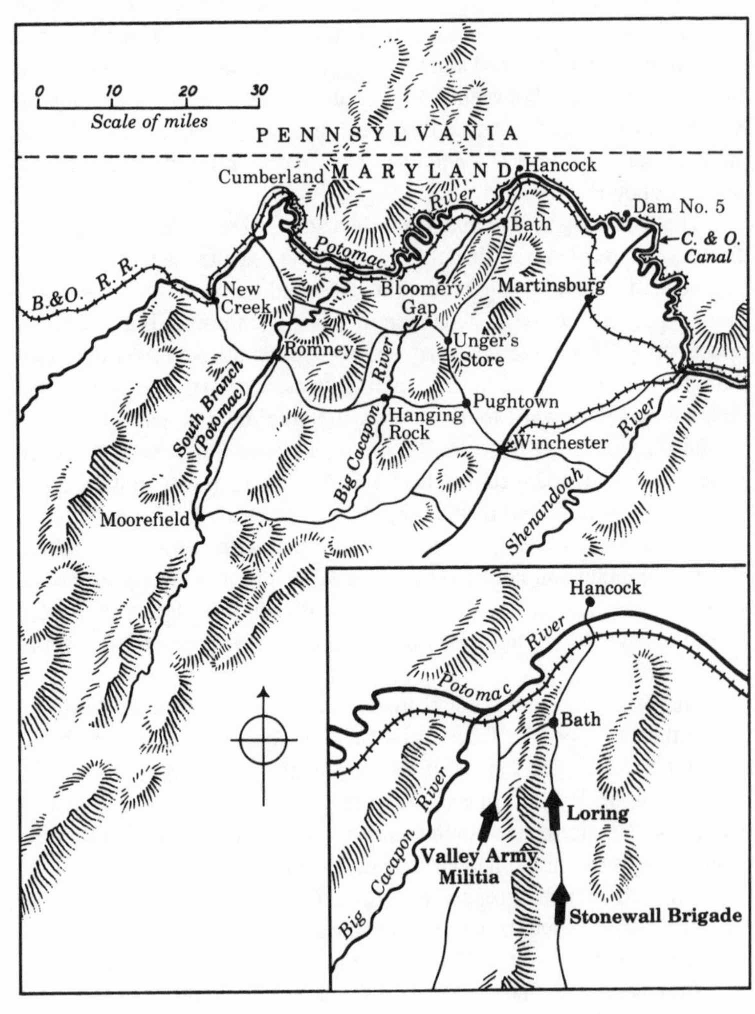

2. Area of Operations against Romney in January 1862
Inset: Action of January 4

The expedition neared Bath at dusk with its collective mind someplace else. The militia column moving west of Warm Spring Mountain gave up when it found the road obstructed with a few trees felled by the enemy.[14] Colonel Gilham, at the head of Loring's infantry, stumbled into Federal pickets; Gilham erroneously supposed he was screened by cavalry and was surprised at the firing. He deployed cautiously and began an inconclusive skirmish. Jackson sent Colonel Preston to bring up additional units, but Preston found nothing close enough to make a difference, so Jackson directed Gilham to charge into Bath with the men at hand. Gilham had commenced the movement when Loring appeared, countermanded the order, and instructed him to bivouac. It was now dark, with a snowstorm coming, but Jackson wanted to push ahead; Loring opposed the idea, and "unpleasant words" sparked between them before Jackson relinquished the attack.[15]

The incident worsened already cool relations between Loring and Jackson. Six years Jackson's senior, with vastly more command experience in the old army, Loring doubtless had anticipated some part in mapping the offensive he was now pursuing. Instead, he was asked and told nothing,[16] and his attitude soured. Handed a dispatch from Jackson to keep moving on the third, Loring reportedly exploded with words to this effect: "By God, this is the damnest outrage ever perpetrated in the annals of history, keeping my men here in the cold without food."[17]

Cold and hunger were exactly what the rebels faced as dark fell and the trains remained in the rear, stretched out along a road that was so narrow they could hardly move. And there were other painful lessons that night. A rapid snowfall commenced. Captain Sam Mullins of the 42d Virginia noted in his diary that his men had no tents and could only cover with their blankets. At 3 A.M. he roused his company to take it forward a mile to stand picket. "It was intensely cold and still snowing," he wrote. "Then came some of the realities of war: No Fire."[18]

January 4 was worse as the rebels pressed forward over ground deep with snow. The militia west of Warm Spring Mountain was halted by Federal musket fire; attempting to sideslip this obstacle, the militia was again surprised and several regiments panicked, neutralizing the entire force.[19] What transpired with the main column east of the mountain is uncertain. Gilham believed he was under orders to advance cautiously and did just that, often losing contact with enemy skirmishers;[20] Jackson was furious at the pace. Within a half-mile of Bath Gilham stopped when he found Federals atop heights commanding the road. Jackson and Loring conferred, and the 1st Tennessee was started up the mountain to dislodge them. Loring claimed the Tennesseans were then halted by Jackson to await reinforcements. Jackson claimed Loring lost so much time that it became necessary for him to throw other regiments into the attack lest the Army spend another night outside Bath.[21]

It is clear today only that the Yankees were ready to run before the attack unfolded. At the head of the Army Jackson saw the enemy begin to pull back and ordered Gilham to charge. Gilham's regiments double-timed through Bath and met the Tennesseans near the mountain's crown, only to spot one Federal column streaming northward to the Potomac while another disappeared to the west. The escape for those fleeing westward had been allowed by the earlier repulse of the militia.

There was no time for Jackson to join in as his men loosed obscenities on the militia. He instructed Gilham to overtake the Federals retiring west of Warm Spring Mountain. He dispatched the 3d Arkansas farther west to demolish the newly rebuilt B & O trestle over the Big Cacapon River. The balance of Loring's command was to follow several companies of cavalry, which had already thundered down the main highway toward the Potomac. Garnett was to occupy Bath and stand ready to support these missions. Hoping to salvage something from the day, Jackson dashed for Hancock.[22]

Nothing came of this pursuit. Gilham trailed the enemy into a narrow defile. Here the Union rear guard took a blocking position that he found unassailable, and Gilham abandoned the chase. Without bothering to inform Jackson, he camped for the night.[23] The Arkansas detachment moving on Big Cacapon River met determined resistance and was unable to reach its target. Approaching the Potomac, Jackson was nearly trampled by cavalrymen fleeting an ambush. Somehow he rallied them and thrust almost to Hancock before a second ambush stalled his advance. He hustled up two guns, blasted out the enemy, and prodded his riders forward again. The rebels finally reined on a bluff overlooking Maryland, but twilight made it impossible to ford the Potomac. Perhaps as a gesture of defiance to a day in which nothing went right, Jackson had his gunners lob several shells across the river.[24]

Had other officers and men shown Jackson's energy, they might have won warm quarters and abundant rations in Hancock. As it was, only Garnett's Brigade shared the meager stores remaining at Bath.[25]

Loring's men, spread over the countryside on an arctic night, suffered terribly.[26]

The following days saw the expedition's first solid achievements. The Arkansans burned the Big Cacapon railroad bridge and tore up miles of track and telegraph wire.[27] Under fire from enemy sharpshooters, cavalrymen dodged into a bulging B & O warehouse. They seized everything they could carry and burned the rest.[28] Jackson dispatched Ashby, who was just in from Dam No. 5, across the river under a flag of truce with a message for Hancock's commandant: surrender or he would attack with overwhelming numbers. When the enemy refused, Jackson began work on a bridge while Southern artillery opened on Federal positions in Hancock. The bombardment was in retaliation for past Northern shellings along Virginia's Potomac shore.[29]

Union batteries replied, but the deadliest hazard during these operations came from the weather. Mountain folk spoke of this as the cruelest winter in decades.[30] Snow fell again on January 5, deepening the layer in which the Confederates huddled to six inches.[31] It was too bitter even to cut firewood, and Jackson actually suspended regulations and allowed his men to burn fence rails—it was the only way to keep them alive. Pickets were not allowed fires and were literally near death after a few hours on duty.[32] Recalled one: "If I should use the army parlance and say [I] stood picket . . . I should have missed it. I ran picket for hours around and around a big tree; I had to do it to keep from freezing."[33]

Northern reinforcements, meanwhile, massed around Hancock, forcing Jackson to abandon any idea of crossing the Potomac. The alluring Union warehouses on the far bank had to be forgotten. Yet Jackson was not entirely dissatisfied with progress to date. Communications between the Alleghenies and the Potomac were severed, and the Federals were probably misled as to the true Southern objective. The Army had achieved everything it could along the Potomac; on January 7, it marched southward.[34]

Jackson's hope of now reaching Romney seemed to die with the anguish of the next days. Beneath dark, somber skies the temperature plunged below zero; one estimate claimed twenty degrees below.[35] Pulling his overcoat tighter, Lieutenant Henry Douglas saw ice frozen into the matted beards of his comrades. He made these observations in glances, because the road was caked with an unbroken sheet of ice and it was dangerous to take eyes off it for long. Despite careful stepping,

Douglas sat down three times "with emphasis."[36] John Lyle remembered the roar of men's rumps "hitting the road with a thud like that of a pile driver."[37] Legs were broken as men went down and bowled over those around them.[38] Loring's attitude was not improved when his horse fell and rolled over on him.[39]

The plight of the supply train was appalling. Overturned wagons littered the road. The horses had not been roughshod prior to leaving Winchester and could barely stand, so four infantrymen were detailed to assist each wagon. John Casler of the 33d Virginia toiled in one of these fatigue parties. Every time his vehicle rounded a curve, Casler and friends strained mightily to keep the horses upright and the wheels on the road. Casler once glanced up to see Old Jack throw his shoulder into a stalled wagon as hard as any private.

Ahead lay a hillock that tore Casler's attention from the general. Slight inclines were tedious work, and this knoll proved an agony. Casler's animals repeatedly smashed to the ground. At least one horse was on its side or belly throughout the upward shove. No sooner could that one be coaxed up than another slammed down, and sometimes all four collapsed at once.[40] Not far away Private Clem Fishburne of the Rockbridge Artillery was struggling with his gun. Descents were Fishburne's greatest trial. Brakes were useless on icy slopes, and the heavy cannon behind the team often lurched out of control and rammed the horses into a thrashing heap. Icicles of blood dangling from their knees almost to the ground bore silent testimony to the torment of these animals.[41]

The greatcoated Confederates lumbered on through a wilderness of snow. Eddying blasts swirled round them on every side. Their twisting and climbing road disappeared in places; at others, the wind had scooped and piled snow to bar the way. Men survived by filching raw corn from the horses or by gnawing roots of sassafras plants.[42] Pneumonia and yellow jaundice disabled hundreds.[43] Many were severely frostbitten and the flesh on their feet and hands peeled off like onion skin.[44] Jackson continued to permit the use of fence rails for fires,[45] around which his men packed until their uniforms smoked.[46] Fearful of what new ventures awaited, the Valley Army crept southward.

In the rebel camp at Unger's Store, a brawny officer squatted in the deep snow fumbling with pen and paper on January 10. He was Major Elisha

Paxton of the 27th Virginia, a man whose immense strength had won him the nickname "Bull." His hand numb, Bull could manage only a few lines to his wife, including this observation: "I take it for granted the General will come to the conclusion from this experiment that a winter campaign won't pay and will put us into winter quarters."[47] Though Paxton did not know it, Jackson had been forced to think of winter quarters—or worse.

On January 7 Jackson had received news that sent slivers of ice through him: Federals had surprised and routed the outpost at Hanging Rock, the only rebel strongpoint on the direct road from Romney to Winchester. It was there that Lieutenant Cutshaw's rowdy Irish gunners had been deployed, but they had lost both their pieces during the melee without a chance to fire.[48] For the next forty-eight hours, while his brigades staggered into Unger's Store, Jackson worried about this raid. His latest intelligence estimated there were as many as eighteen thousand Federals in Romney.[49] If the Hanging Rock attack indicated Union fronts from west and north were preparing to move toward each other, the rebels might be trapped in a fatal position halfway between Winchester and Romney. The only precaution Stonewall could take against this danger was to stitch together a few hundred infantry and hurry them south to watch the enemy at Hanging Rock.[50] The Yankees then mysteriously abandoned their incursion and withdrew to Romney as those rebels approached.

Jackson did not pursue. Thankful for a reprieve, he dispatched Meem's militia brigade to Moorefield, forty miles southwest of Winchester, and ordered Carson's militia brigade to reoccupy Bath. These shifts stripped eight hundred men from the main column[51] and meant but one thing: the Valley Army was going to postpone, and perhaps abandon, the march on Romney. Jackson had culled the Shenandoah to bring every possible man into ranks before he left Winchester; scattering them now would have been unthinkable if he was about to attack eighteen thousand Federals at Romney.[52]

Indeed, Jackson had little choice about halting. Wearily hospital orderly John Apperson noted in his diary that the Army was being crippled from sickness.[53] One of Loring's brigades carried three hundred men on its sick list, another, more than five hundred.[54] Dr. McGuire had thirteen hundred sick in Winchester. (Compared with the sick, the four killed and twenty-eight wounded the Army had suffered in combat seemed trifling.)[55] The sick overflowed Winchester's hospitals and had to be carted to other cities.[56] Subtracting hospitalized and redeployed men, the Valley Army near Unger's Store numbered at best seven thousand effectives.

Jackson's offensive had ground to a halt; at this point he could not have planned realistically to do more than refit and plan his next move.[57] In the meantime, he organized an essential cleanup. He put every farrier in the Army to work roughshodding the horses. Huge kettles were brought to a boil and the troops were ordered to bathe. Few of them had washed since December, and now they uncovered booming colonies of lice in their flannel underwear. It was a grisly experience for Jackson's teenagers; the snow hissed by their fires, pools of slush crept under their feet, and they stood naked in the cold to pick the "graybacks" off one another.[58]

In the midst of this cleanup, startling news arrived from Ashby. The Yankees had evacuated Romney![59] They had fled suddenly, leaving tents standing and precious medical supplies untouched. Ashby's scouts were already in the abandoned city. To Jackson it seemed a miracle, a blessing from the Almighty. Less devout men correctly surmised the Romney garrison had not been as strong as Southern sources indicated. The force that had first ousted the rebels during October was twenty-five hundred,[60] and this force had increased only to five thousand or six thousand by January.[61] The raid on Hanging Rock had been a sham designed to draw the rebels from the Potomac, where the Union dreaded a major operation.[62] The enemy had never planned to defend Romney against Jackson, whose strength they had overestimated as much as he had theirs,[63] and had left the place after receiving a false report that the rebels were approaching.[64] The enemy had handed Jackson his prize without a battle.

Stonewall's response was good news to every soldier of the Army: he began signing a ream of furlough petitions. Several high-ranking officers, including Colonel Gilham, were permitted to return to teaching duties at the Virginia Military Institute.[65] Jackson might as well have announced by general orders that the expedition's hard work had ended. The rebels now needed only to occupy Romney and secure the blessing of the Almighty. The Army resumed its march on January 13. Garnett headed the column so that no further time would be squandered by Loring's indifferent marchers.[66]

When the Confederates broke camp at Unger's the sun was actually shining.[67] It seemed a good omen, until a thaw made slush of the road. Garnett's Brigade outpaced its trains and suffered through another night without canvas.[68] Loring's regiments were hopelessly mixed with their trains. The 21st Virginia was held to a day's march of two hundred yards by wagons ahead of it. The wind quickened during the afternoon, and the sun vanished behind slate-colored clouds.[69] That night it snowed two inches.[70] The next day alternated rain and sleet.[71] The fifteenth was among the most miserable days ever known in the Alleghenies; sleet fell for hours, covering everyone with ice.[72] Loring's command floundered beneath this inclement pounding. One regiment inched five hundred yards and counted it a triumph.[73] Taught in a sterner school, Garnett's Brigade slogged into Romney by dark on the fifteenth. Jim Langhorne reported home with obvious pride, ". . . our brigade can beat them [Loring's brigades] marching badly."[74]

The distance separating Garnett's and Loring's brigades was more than the result of swift movement. Unused to Jackson's demands, Loring's men could not believe he had not retreated to Winchester days ago. Like most newcomers to Jackson's command, they equated his tenacity with insanity. They talked mutiny and swore to follow Jackson no longer. They booed and hissed him when he passed. "Lunatic," they shouted.[75] The resentful, disorganized Northwesterners did not begin filtering into Romney until January 17.[76]

By then, Jackson was advocating virtually a new expedition. His scouts reported that the Maryland village of Cumberland, twenty miles northwest of Romney, contained valuable enemy stores. Strategic B & O bridges were close by. Jackson asked Secretary of War Benjamin to dispatch him four thousand additional infantrymen for an attempt to capture the Federal garrison and depots at Cumberland and to hit the B & O again.[77] The reinforcements were not available, which nullified all prospect for a successful advance. But possession of Romney had aroused Old Jack's ambition, and he drew up another plan for the men he did have. He decided to strike the gigantic New Creek railroad bridge west of Cumberland. Jackson calculated that its destruction would sharply cut the flow of supplies into Cumberland. The enemy force there should wither like poison ivy snipped at the root, leaving Romney that much more secure. Stonewall alerted the first two brigades to enter Romney, Garnett's and Taliaferro's, to prepare for another march.[78]

These orders were probably the worst Jackson ever issued, particularly considering the many furloughs already granted. Jackson had reports that Cumberland was girded with twelve thousand Federal troops,[79] yet he planned to march into their vicinity with two shrunken brigades. The Stonewall Brigade was now in effect a reinforced regiment. Its 4th Virginia was led by two captains and a handful of lieutenants; John Apperson thought two thirds of his regiment was either on furlough or on the sick list, now grimly called the "broken book."[80] No more than one third of the brigade appeared fit for action to Jim Langhorne.[81] Taliaferro's command was decimated. His 23d Virginia Regiment was smaller than a company; its Company C had fifteen men able to walk.[82] Jackson's newest orders required too much, and Taliaferro's Brigade seethed on the edge of open rebellion. Stonewall quickly saw in its attitude that hope of a renewed advance was fanciful. He abandoned the Cumberland raid.[83]

The Valley Army now moved into winter quarters to guard the Shenandoah. Carson's militia brigade concentrated at Bath; Meem's militia brigade held Moorefield.[84] Boggs's militia picketed the environs of Romney, and Loring's command held the village itself. Garnett's Stonewall Brigade, which had proven the most dependable marching unit of the Army, was to take station at Winchester, where it would be within supporting distance of all fronts. Ashby's cavalry would rove the frontier and provide early warning of Union threats.[85] In taking these positions, the Army was repeating the forward defensive strategy employed by George Washington a century earlier.

The focal point of these dispositions was the garrison at Romney, the post of greatest danger. The Federals were only twenty miles away at Cumberland, and the South Branch Valley road system offered several routes by which they could launch a surprise attack. Jackson feared such a strike above all else. To lessen this danger, he deployed squads of relay couriers, sought extra cavalry, and commenced a telegraph line to Winchester.[86] Like Washington, he also expected his men to defend their western bulwark actively. They would need to reconnoiter, ambush, and harry the enemy, and these mountain battles would hold the Valley.[87]

Unfortunately, conditions at Romney thwarted vigilance from the start. "Of all the miserable holes in creation, Romney takes the lead . . . a hog pen . . . ," protested Private Ted Barclay of the Headquarters Guard.[88] It rained daily. Every street was an open sewer thanks to indiscriminate dumping by the Yankees, who had also left the courthouse building stacked high with rotten meat.[89] The streets decayed into slimy pools so deep even horses could hardly move.[90] Some regiments were quartered in cotton tents amid this muck; others lived in such poor buildings as had survived Yankee conquest. Private Dick Waldrop of the 21st Virginia, a young Richmonder who learned on this trip how much he missed his home in a proper city, lodged in a room with glassless windows on three sides and almost no wall on the fourth: "Altogether, it is so uncomfortable that *loafers* can't be prevailed upon to come near us."[91]

Hallelujahs erupted from Garnett's Brigade when it was ordered out of Romney.[92] As it departed for Winchester, it was watched by a surly Army of the Northwest. "Jackson's Lambs," screamed some, thinking Jackson showed favoritism to his old command with a comfortable assignment near Winchester. The Stonewall Brigade hurled obscenities back and left a garrison smoldering with resentment.[93]

Garnett's march to Winchester took three days along a road lined for miles by gutted houses; they were the result of the Northern raid on Hanging Rock. The Yankees had looted and slaughtered freely; cows, hogs, and even chickens lay decomposing along the way. For men who did not know it yet, this carnage was a blunt definition of "civil war." Garnett's men entered Winchester on January 25 and slumped exhausted and disillusioned around their campfires.[94] Bull Paxton's first letter home might have been written for all of them: "I think I am dirtier than I ever was before, and may be lousy besides. I have not changed clothes for two weeks, and my pants have a hole in each leg nearly big enough for a dog to creep through. . . . I am afraid the dirt is striking in, as I am somewhat afflicted with the baby's complaint—a pain under the apron."[95]

Jackson had sloshed ahead of Garnett to reach Winchester on the evening of January 23. It was an entry more gratifying than that of almost three months ago. On November 4, 1861, he had arrived with three men to assume a defenseless command. He had quickly identified the probable enemy threat and fashioned a reasonable plan to counteract it.[96] Admittedly, that plan had not succeeded completely. The enemy had suffered few casualties, and Confederate ranks were severely thinned from illness, although when Jackson returned to Winchester patients were leaving the hospitals there at a rate of thirty to one hundred men per day.[97] But more important, Jackson had achieved what he had set out to achieve with his winter expedition. Romney was again Southern, and

Union fronts to the west and north had been shoved farther apart. Some needed stores had been captured and additional damage inflicted on the Baltimore & Ohio Railroad. With earnest hard work, Jackson had dragged the Valley Army through its first offensive.

II

Within a week the Valley Army was stripped of its achievements. The flinty prospect of finishing the winter at Romney whipped Loring's men into an insubordinate frenzy. Officers of one regiment refused to leave their quarters during foul weather.[98] Soldiers of all ranks utilized a new grant of furloughs to hasten to Richmond. There they manufactured tales of Jackson's insanity and besieged government officials with demands to evacuate Romney.[99]

In Romney, Loring did little to quiet the discontent. Eleven brigade and regimental officers signed and handed a petition to Loring condemning the occupation of Romney:

> Instead of finding, as expected, a little repose during midwinter, we are ordered to remain at this place. Our position at and near Romney is one of the most disagreeable and unfavorable that could well be imagined. We can only get an encampment upon the worst of wet, spouty land, much of which when it rains is naught but one sheet of water and a consequent corresponding depth of mud, and this, too, without the advantage of sufficient wood, the men having to drag that indispensable article down from high up on the mountain side.
>
> Another consideration we would endeavor to impress upon your mind: All must be profoundly impressed with the paramount importance of raising an army for the next summer's campaign. When we left Winchester, a very large proportion of your army, with the benefit of a short furlough, would have enlisted for the war, but now, with the present prospect before them, we doubt if one single man would re-enlist. But if they are yet removed to a position where their spirits could be revived, many, we think, will go for the war.

The petition concluded by urging Loring to appeal to the War Department, if necessary, to secure relief. Endorsing the petition as expressing "the united feeling of the army," Loring dispatched it to

Secretary Benjamin by way of Jackson. The latter sent it on with a four-word comment: "Respectfully forwarded, but disapproved."[100]

Colonel Samuel Fulkerson of Loring's 37th Virginia sought the support of a friend in the Confederate Congress with this description of Romney:

> This place is of no importance in a strategic point of view; the country around it has been exhausted by the enemy, and its proximity to the enemy and the Baltimore and Ohio Railroad will wear us away (already greatly reduced) by heavy picket and guard duty. Besides this, there is no suitable ground and not sufficient wood here upon and by which men can be made comfortable. We have not been in as uncomfortable a place since we entered the service.
>
> With the benefit of a short furlough for the men, I am satisfied that at Winchester I could have enlisted 500 of my regiment for the war. With the present prospect before them, I do not know that I could get a single man.[101]

Colonel Taliaferro saw this letter and added a malevolent postscript: "The best army I ever saw of its strength has been destroyed by bad marches and bad management. . . . Not one [man] will re-enlist, not one of the whole army. It will be suicidal for the Government to keep the command here."[102]

Not content with this, Taliaferro skulked to Richmond and lobbied among his political friends for Loring's withdrawal. Taliaferro later claimed President Davis gave him a friendly hearing and concluded that Jackson had made a mistake.[103]

The horror stories from Romney converged on Richmond with rumors of an enemy stab into the lower Shenandoah. From his post at Leesburg, Brigadier General Daniel H. Hill spied increased activity across the Potomac and relayed word of it to Johnston.[104] The latter agreed that the Valley Army might be in trouble if the Federals were moving on Harpers Ferry or Winchester.[105] Warnings of such a thrust reached Stonewall from Secretary Benjamin on January 24.[106] Two days later an alarmed President Davis suggested that Benjamin have Jackson review the Valley's defenses.[107]

Rumor moved more swiftly than Johnston. On January 29 he had his inspector general en route to the Valley,[108] but Richmond was already stirred up by additional speculation that Northern forces were closing in on Loring.[109] The substance of these rumors has not survived, but they evidently forecast a Union advance into the area between Romney and Winchester.[110] At any rate, the stories were accepted. "It will be necessary to act promptly," Davis wrote Benjamin on the twenty-ninth.[111] Action came the next day. Without awaiting Johnston's evaluation or consulting either him or Jackson, Davis approved a withdrawal and instructed Benjamin to send the following telegram to Jackson: "Our news indicates that a movement is being made to cut off General Loring's command. Order him back to Winchester immediately."[112]

That order both ignored Jackson's authority and questioned his ability. Jackson attributed any unusual enemy activity north of the Potomac to B & O rebuilding efforts near Hancock,[113] and he was correct in this judgment. Benjamin's order demanded that he act on a different explanation, a precedent that rendered Jackson a puppet to tabletop strategists in Richmond. Neither the supposedly imminent Federal attack nor the adverse conditions complained of by Loring's army justified such an intrusion into Jackson's sphere of command. There was, in fact, no Union drive under way against Romney, and even had there been, to sacrifice Jackson's positions at the first enemy threat implied a fatal want of confidence in him. It also left Richmond looking foolish, because the government had tacitly approved defense of Romney when it sent Loring to join the Valley Army in order to take the place.

Jackson immediately issued the necessary orders for Loring's withdrawal to Winchester, a move that forced Jackson to abandon most of the positions held by his militia in the South Branch Valley as well. Three months of planning and hard work ruined, Jackson then sent a taciturn message by way of Johnston to Benjamin:

Headquarters Valley District
Winchester, Va. January 31, 1862

Hon. J. P. Benjamin, Secretary of War:

Sir: Your order requiring me to direct General Loring to return with his command to Winchester immediately has been received and promptly complied with.

With such interference in my command I cannot expect to be of much service in the field, and accordingly respectfully request to be ordered to report for duty to the superintendent of the Virginia Military Institute at Lexington, as has been done in the case of other professors. Should this application not be granted, I respectfully request that the President will accept my resignation from the Army.

I am, sir, very respectfully, your obedient servant,

T. J. Jackson
Major-General, P.A.C.S.[114]

Stonewall had quit the Valley Army, perhaps the war.

Jackson had not quit working. He knew that his resignation would require some days for approval, and during that interval Jackson tried energetically to salvage something for whoever succeeded him. He assured Johnston there was no Union drive under way against Romney and urged him to prevent Loring's withdrawal.[115] (This Johnston could not do.) Davis was ultimately responsible for the evacuation order, but Jackson cannily refrained from attacking the president while he made his point. He told his own political friends, among them Virginia's Governor Letcher, that his action was a protest against the secretary of war's interference with a command in the field. He grew almost eloquent in his rationale of this point: "If the Secretary persists in the ruinous policy complained of, I feel that no officer can serve his country better than by making his strongest possible protest against it, which, in my opinion, is done by tendering his resignation, rather than be a willing instrument in prosecuting the war upon a ruinous principle."[116]

The consequences of Jackson's noisy protest worked back up the Confederate chain of command. General Johnston imagined his own army at Centreville had been meddled with by Richmond, and he understood Jackson's frustration. He delayed Jackson's letter of resignation and made a friendly appeal to him suggesting that they join to reason with the government on the practice and, failing a satisfactory outcome, that both ask to be relieved. Johnston complained bitterly about the secretary of war to Davis, who replied with an equally caustic letter about Johnston.[117] All of this produced much unwanted notice for the Valley District, and the more Richmond looked at the Romney effort, the less it liked anything about it. "Utterly incompetent," was the reported comment of President Davis when he studied the operation.[118]

Despite the undesirable attention, Jackson found it difficult to leave the Valley Army. Friends throughout the Shenandoah and across the state implored him not to do so. Governor Letcher sent Congressman Alexander R. Boteler to Winchester. Boteler was a Princeton graduate and distinguished citizen of the lower Shenandoah who recently had served in the U.S. Congress and who now represented the Valley in the Confederate Congress; he brought a personal letter from the governor hammering on the theme of duty. Letcher's letter and a long talk with Boteler finally changed Jackson's mind. Jackson yielded slowly, but in the process he cemented a good relationship with the politically well connected Boteler, who during the coming months would become an unofficial lobbyist for Jackson at the capitol. On February 15 Letcher received Jackson's authorization to withdraw the resignation, which he promptly retrieved and returned to the Valley.[119]

This trouble was followed by other unhappy incidents. The Army of the Northwest, which evacuated Romney at a pace never known on the march toward it, was elated by the first rumors of Jackson's resignation and intended to celebrate by pummeling the Stonewall Brigade. A huge riot loomed as the Northwesterners staggered into Winchester. Though they were more a collection of individuals than fighting units,[120] and though complaining of a hard march, Loring's men possessed energy enough for brawls wherever they collided with Jackson's Lambs.[121]

Jackson, for his part, took a written jab of his own: he prepared court-martial charges against Gilham and Loring. Gilham was cited for failing to act aggressively outside Sir John's Run on January 4;[122] Loring received Jackson's special attention in two charges stating seven examples of neglect of duty and conduct subversive of good order and military discipline. Jackson submitted the charges to General Johnston for approval. What Johnston knew of conditions in Loring's units convinced him a trial was necessary. Unfortunately, he had so many officers absent he was unable to appoint a tribunal of sufficiently high-ranking men to hear the case, and so he asked Richmond for help.[123]

A tribunal was never assembled and the case was never tried, but the very act of preferring charges spoke volumes about Jackson. Gilham had been Jackson's prewar colleague at V.M.I. and had rendered invaluable service early in the war training thousands of recruits around Richmond. His education, writings, and Mexican War service constitute a distinguished career. Loring had won even more renown in Mexico and had been trusted after that war with command of the Department of Oregon during the days of the great gold rush; he had studied military science in Europe and returned to command the Department of New Mexico in 1860. Yet these men had not moved decisively in the presence of the Federals, and that Jackson would not accept.

In filing his charges Jackson achieved the questionable distinction of being the first Confederate to seek to court-martial a fellow general. Soon President Davis intervened personally, deciding that there would be no court-martial but that Loring and his command must be separated from the Shenandoah.[124] Observing every link in the chain of command, Secretary Benjamin informed Johnston that Davis wanted Loring's Virginia regiments and batteries transferred to his army at Centreville; all other regiments were to reinforce collapsing Southern defenses in Tennessee. Gilham departed the Valley Army in January for V.M.I. For reasons unknown, Richmond decided that Loring's service merited promotion to a major generalship. The orders were issued, and Loring was dispatched to Norfolk, the first of many subsequent posts he filled without distinction. After the fall of Norfolk he commanded the Army of Southwestern Virginia; he accomplished little there before being sent to the Deep South, where an evil star pursued him. John C. Pemberton blamed him for the Southern defeat at the Battle of Champion's Hill, which opened the door for the loss of Vicksburg. Loring led a division and briefly a corps during the apocalyptic struggle for Atlanta in 1864, and he was with the Army of Tennessee at its destruction outside Nashville late in the same year.

Johnston allowed Jackson to manage the redeployment of Loring's regiments. (Jackson had won this point, and no one ever interfered with the internal workings of his district again.) By the third week of February Jackson had most of Loring's non-Virginia units on their way out of the Shenandoah. The movements left the District almost as naked as it had been the previous November. After three months of hard work, Jackson was back to his start point.

There were many reasons for this reversal, and not the least of them was a muddled Confederate chain of command. Loring's army never had been formally a part of Jackson's; indeed, as Loring viewed the situation his was a separate force that had only come to Winchester upon "invitation" of Jackson to operate against the enemy. As late as February Loring wondered if even General Johnston had authority over him.[125] Within the still evolving Confederate command scheme, district and department commanders had not yet determined their exact relationships. And the problem was compounded by the tendency of those commanders to communicate directly with Richmond. Jackson was correct to resist intervention in his conduct of field operations, yet, in fairness, it should be recalled that he had often dealt with Richmond without going through General Johnston. This may not have been improper under existing practice, but it also opened the door for instructions in return. Jackson, in short, probably had overreacted. Surely one thing was clear: the Confederate high command was as yet imperfectly organized, a problem Jackson would meet again in the Shenandoah.

And there were other causes for the failure of January. Poor roads, supply train breakdowns, and awful weather occasioned much of the misery on the expedition against Romney. Exposure to the cruel weather was a product of Loring's dawdling. Had Loring assembled his forces at Winchester by the end of the three-week estimate he gave on November 29—that is, by December 20—Jackson could have held Romney before the snows fell. Yet these were all the superficial causes, and analysis would disclose more fundamental explanations for the failure of the Valley Army to achieve better results.

III

If Jackson analyzed his conduct of the winter expedition, he could not have concluded that he met his own rigid standards. His generalship was uneven, his leadership wavering from good to less than adequate, his decisions sometimes deftly gauging the limits of the possible and sometimes sweeping far beyond them—illustrating that even great generals have formative periods. Jackson obviously had not mastered every detail of the leap from brigade to army commander.

Jackson marched from Winchester with a grossly exaggerated impression of Union strength. This was initially the fault of his intelligence sources but ultimately the fault of Jackson for believing those sources. Even with his erroneous information, however, Jackson was correct to launch his offensive. Notwithstanding the risk of a Union surprise attack and the somewhat scattered deployment necessitated by a rebel garrison in the South Branch Valley, Romney's occupation was wise and showed that Stonewall was alert to possibilities the enemy overlooked or had yet to exploit. Jackson lay between two Northern fronts, and every mile he could wedge between them lessened the opportunity for enemy cooperation and increased the Valley Army's chance—its only chance—to deal separately with each Union front.

Jackson's decision to march on Romney via Bath was also sound. The Bath attack disrupted vital communications and masked the true Southern objective. And an incidental benefit of the attack should have become clear to Jackson on the way to Bath: capture of its garrison would have done much to reenergize Loring's faltering brigades. But clumsy tactics squandered this opportunity. Stonewall entrusted the critical task of blocking the western escape route from Bath on July 3 and 4 to his inexperienced militia, and he was disappointed. One of the militia regiments that panicked and allowed the enemy to escape Bath on the fourth was seeing its first action. It had been issued muskets less than two weeks earlier.[126] There seems no reason why more reliable units were not assigned the kingpin position given the militia.

Faulty deployment might have been corrected by pushing Loring into Bath early on the morning of January 4. By that time Jackson was aware of Loring's slowness. Why then did Stonewall himself not prod the Army of the Northwest forward at first light? Gilham's Brigade spent the night of January 3 barely two miles outside Bath but did not enter it until approximately 2 P.M. the next day. The records do not explain why Jackson permitted the morning hours to be lost, thus giving him an uncomfortable share of responsibility for at least part of the Union garrison's escape.[127]

By his retreat from Bath and his halt at Unger's Store on the ninth, Jackson indicated that he knew when to halt; reported Northern strength in both instances made it unwise to continue. And he was flexible enough to occupy Romney when the enemy handed it to him. Jackson erred when he issued orders to launch what was in effect a new expedition against Cumberland after reinforcements were denied him. That strike would have offered three thousand exhausted rebels as prey to twelve thousand enemy. Federals were on the alert for Confederate thrusts from Romney, and bad roads and weather were at work to prevent a quick Southern retreat. It is more than likely that Jackson's raiding column would have been trounced, leaving only two of Loring's unhappy brigades and the militia to defend the Shenandoah. With his plan for this raid, Jackson highlighted one of his major flaws as a commander: ambition sometimes clouded his objectivity.

Two more Jackson traits emerged during the Romney winter, and each would mark him until his death. First, in everything he did, from massing troops to throwing his shoulder into a stalled wagon, Old Jack showed a formidable drive; "go-aheaditiveness," General Taliaferro would later call it. Few men could have pushed the Valley Army as far as the Potomac, but Jackson had pushed on from there, had freed large areas from the enemy and established workable defenses with grumbling troops pounded by savage weather. It was a magnificent personal achievement displaying sustained energy. Yet within a week this success was undone because of a second trait, Jackson's inability to work skillfully with his fellow officers and soldiers. He might, for example, have told Loring a little of his plans; he might have explained to Loring's regiments the purpose in holding Romney. Such gestures could have helped preserve the gains made, but they were beyond Jackson. From his soldiers he did not expect and probably did not want understanding of orders—what he wanted was unquestioning obedience. The Romney winter revealed Jackson was without sympathy for the confusion or low spirits of others, and this gruffness, which seemed so harsh to his citizen soldiers, only grew coarser as the war progressed.

If Old Jack's inexperience hurt the Valley Army, the attitude of its rank and file was equally damaging. When those boys had crowded Southern recruiting camps during April 1861, they had imagined war as a pageant of heroic deeds performed on spotless battlefields. Eight months of army life had blunted that illusion and turned thoughts to home and mother.

Instead of furloughs, the Valley Army was given a lesson in the school of the soldier more terrible than anything it had encountered.[128] That lesson taught Private John Green of the 21st Virginia what it meant to march sixteen hours a day through gales of sleet, bed down in a snowstorm, and push on the next morning with nothing to eat. Green admitted, "I had read something of the suffering of our forefathers [in 1776] but never realized them until we came on this tour."[129] Private George Harlow of the 23d Virginia found that war was a comrade dreading whether he would lose two toes or his entire foot from frostbite.[130] Lieutenant Henry Douglas of the 2d Virginia recognized war for what it was as he watched ambulances packed with human wreckage file into Winchester: "Sentimentalists who imagine there is no way to die in war would be shocked at the sight of those who are expiring without a wound."[131] No, there were no spotless battlefields in war. "Ma," wrote Lieutenant Jim Langhorne of the Headquarters Guard, "the romance of the thing is entirely worn off, not only with myself but with the whole army."[132]

The Valley Army had needed men who were alert and resolved on the march against Romney, not boys dazed by lost illusions. Soon these rebels would master hunger and cold, but on this march they had buckled under the shock of hard lessons. Many had merely shuffled along with little interest in the outcome; theirs was a mood of men in whom the eagerness of volunteers was spent and the endurance of veterans unforged. These soldiers had discovered that war, no matter how brightly begun, really means little bands of gaunt men toiling over roads that have no end. They had grasped what it meant to be a soldier, but they had yet to adjust their lives to that stark realization. The Romney winter produced a short-lived and too-expensive Confederate success; given the mood and inexperience of the Southern soldiers and their general, it could hardly have been otherwise.

The immediate result of the Romney expedition was to intensify the longing of "Loring men" and "Jackson men" alike to escape the army, and letters from Winchester now reflected an ominous clock watching. "If I live this twelve months out, I intend to try mighty hard to keep out of [the army]. . . . I don't think I could stand it out another year," wailed George Harlow.[133] Private John Garibaldi of the 27th Virginia determined not to volunteer again: "I shall belong to the militia myself, for I see that the militia don't have so much hardship to go thru [*sic*] as the volunteers have, and they are getting the same wages and the same kind of rations, and they have more liberty than us," was Garibaldi's straightforward analysis.[134] But the militiamen too were weary. Militia surgeon Abraham Miller explained in a letter to his wife: "I am getting tired of soldiering. . . . I will hold on to my commission until after the draft, and then I will resign and try it at home for a while."[135]

The draft Dr. Miller wrote of was Virginia's answer to the most serious problem facing the South. The initial one-year enlistment of virtually the entire Confederate army would be expiring soon, and Southern soldiers were not disposed to reenlist. The Virginia legislature therefore ratified, on February 8, a bill under which all Virginia males between ages eighteen and forty-five not serving with the army would be entered in a militia pool from which they could be conscripted to fill state "volunteer" units.[136]

A plan enacted by the Confederate Congress the previous December offered Virginia volunteers temporary escape from both the Confederate army and the Old Dominion's draft. Designed to insure reenlistment of volunteers already in ranks, the law granted a generous bounty and a sixty-day furlough to all volunteer privates and noncommissioned officers who signed on for the duration of the war. In addition, reenlistees were guaranteed the right to reorganize themselves into new companies, elect new officers, and even change their branch of service.[137]

This well-intentioned law, known as the Furlough and Bounty Act, nearly wiped out the Valley Army. Hundreds of men signed their reenlistment papers and vanished on leave. As February drifted toward March, regiments waned into companies, companies into squads. On February 28 Captain Graybill of the 33d rostered forty-one men present in his company; by March 17 Graybill listed twenty-four.[138] It was not that men in the Shenandoah were unpatriotic: Surgeon Miller would serve through some of the war's heaviest fighting to be surrendered at Appomattox; captured in March 1862, John Garibaldi was exchanged and returned to fight until captured again at Spotsylvania in 1864. But for now they were frazzled from their introduction to war and wanted a break.

And if there could be no rest, they felt they deserved at least a change. Bull Paxton would rise to command the Stonewall Brigade and die leading it at Chancellorsville, yet disgruntled at not getting a furlough in January 1862 he tendered his resignation (later withdrawn).[139] Captain Sam Moore was severely wounded at Second Manassas and again in the Wilderness in 1864 but continued the fight. He ended the war as chief of staff to Jubal Early, Jackson's successor with what then remained of the Valley Army, yet in January Moore was trying to escape the infantry by recruiting a battery.[140] Lanty Blackford fought with the Rockbridge Artillery until discharged from service for illness only to return to do staff work until war's end, yet in January, as he contemplated his future, he had learned, "The annoyances of the life of a private are manifold . . . ; I believe I mind none now as much as guard duty these cold nights." To his family he inquired about the chances of a staff appointment with some rising brigadier general.[141]

Many in the Valley Army were seeking escape to the cavalry. "I think I will not volunteer next summer but join an independent guerilla party to scout around through Western Va. We will be in active employment during the summer and not subject to Genl. So and so, who grants 'no furloughs,'" wrote one infantryman.[142] This preoccupation with cavalry extended to Jackson's own doorstep, where his Headquarters Guard was aching to form a mounted outfit.[143]

Tales of the carefree life with Ashby's cavalry were especially delicious after the Romney ordeal. Private George Baylor joined the cavalry and happily recalled, "On horseback I felt like a new man and contemplated the war from a much more favorable standpoint."[144] As if to invite a rush, Secretary Benjamin authorized Ashby during February to add ten companies to the ten already under his command.[145] The cavalry chief reported the muster of eight new companies in less than a month.[146] To supervise this horde there were only Ashby, Major Funsten, and five or six novice staff officers.[147]

But even service under Ashby was not sufficient lure for some men. Dick Waldrop's company of the 21st Virginia was canvassed and not a man said he would reenlist; one of Waldrop's comrades muttered that the entire regiment had "gone to the dogs and will soon go to pieces."[148] Other difficulties arose: Colonel Preston left Jackson's staff to return to the Virginia Military Institute; the Federals renewed their onslaughts along the Valley frontier; the militia deserted by scores.[149] On the last day of February the Valley Army boasted a paper strength of 13,759, of whom only 5,400 were present and effective,[150] and that remnant was shrinking by several hundred per week. Listening one afternoon to the rain that promised spring, hospital orderly Apperson admitted in his diary that the Southern cause was getting "dark and doubtful."[151]

Part II

5

MARCH 1862

It requires a vast amount of faith
to be cheerful amid the general gloom.

—Harry Morrison

In Winchester, diarist John Apperson wrote of "dark and doubtful" Southern hopes. In Richmond, President Jefferson Davis, unopposed during a recent election to select a permanent Confederate president, echoed Apperson's fears in his February inaugural address. "Disasters" was the word Davis chose to review the war's recent months: "At the darkest hour of our struggle, the Provisional gives place to the Permanent Government. After a series of successes and victories . . . , we have recently met with serious disasters."[1]

It was true. On the North Carolina coast Union Major General Ambrose E. Burnside captured Roanoke Island, thirty cannons, and twenty-five hundred prisoners two weeks before Davis spoke. Burnside's victory primed him for forays into the Tarheel State's interior, buoyed Union sympathizers in the state, and threw open a backdoor approach to Richmond. Soon after Burnside struck, the Confederacy's hopes for its ironclad *Virginia* faded with the news of its drawn battle against the Union's ironclad *Monitor*.

West of the Alleghenies, Southern armies were retreating along a four-hundred-mile front. The Confederates had been routed at the battle of Mill Springs, Kentucky, during January. In Tennessee, Forts Henry and Donelson had surrendered to Union Major General Ulysses S. Grant by mid-February, and the defense of Tennessee collapsed with the loss of fourteen thousand prisoners. Irreplaceable foundries and rolling mills fell with Nashville to Union Brigadier General Don Carlos Buell. Missouri and northern Arkansas were lost forever when a Confederate army was mauled at the Battle of Pea Ridge in early March.

The situation in Virginia was critical. Effective communication between General Johnston and Richmond had ceased, partly as a result of caustic letters exchanged during the crises over Jackson's resignation. Faced by overpowering enemy numbers, Johnston began to withdraw on March 5 from the Manassas-Centreville area without even informing President Davis. The evacuation was badly managed in other respects as well. Some heavy guns in working order were left for the enemy. Unable to empty an army packing plant, Johnston consigned a million pounds of beef to the flames, and his ill-fed retreating columns were tormented by the aroma of sizzling steak.[2] The Federals seized Manassas Junction, and Johnston could not field a corporal's guard to harass them. "This army," he warned on February 16, "is far weaker now than it has ever been since July 20, 1861. . . . The law granting furloughs and bounty for reenlistment has done much to disorganize it, and [other] furloughs given under the orders of the War Department have greatly reduced its numerical strength."[3] He added a few days later, "The army is crippled and its discipline greatly impaired by the want of general officers; . . . a division of five brigades is without generals; and at least half the field officers are absent—generally sick."[4]

At winter's end, many people, in both North and South, looked for one final Union victory in Virginia to end the faltering Confederacy.

North of the Potomac, sprawled around Washington and across Maryland, lay the presumed victor of that coming Armageddon, the Army of the Potomac. It numbered more than 150,000 fresh volunteers. For months these men had been drilled and polished by the approved European textbooks. They paraded like professionals. They were superbly equipped by the factories of the North, and anything not available at home was purchased abroad in prodigal quantities. "There never was an army in the world that began to be supplied as well as ours," huffed one Union general. "The amount of waste is fearful. . . . I have seen loaves of bread thrown away that had not even been broken open. Our men will not use it if it is a little stale."[5]

The leader of this well-appointed colossus was hailed as the savior of his country, as a "Young Napoleon," and his dossier was outstanding. Major General George B. McClellan had matriculated at West Point by special permission at age fifteen and graduated in 1846 far ahead of his struggling Virginian classmate Thomas Jackson. He had been promoted twice during the Mexican War, had instructed at West Point, and had served as official United States observer during the Crimean War. He had directed the Union's drive across Virginia's Allegheny frontier in the spring of 1861, and though success lost nothing by his telling, he had demonstrated undeniable skill. After the Union's Manassas debacle, McClellan was given command of the Department of the Potomac, an area of operations including Washington, northern Virginia, and parts of Maryland (including Banks's command). McClellan proceeded to hammer these far-flung fragments into the magnificent Army of the Potomac, and by March 1862 he was prepared to lead that host to war.

McClellan intended to march on Richmond. Only one hundred miles from Washington, Richmond housed some of the most valuable munitions and industrial works remaining to the Confederacy. Here were boiler factories, mills, and shipyards. Richmond was the hub of Virginia's rail and canal net. It was the seat of the Confederate government, and the spirit of a fledgling nation could not survive the loss of such a symbol. McClellan believed that if he lunged toward Richmond, Johnston would be compelled to interpose, which would, he hoped, position Johnston's army to receive the final blow.

McClellan's problem was how to approach Richmond. The direct way was a march south from Washington through Manassas Junction and Fredericksburg, but McClellan had misgivings about this route. He had watched British divisions erode before Russian defenses during the Crimean conflict, and he knew the Russian positions were ditches compared to the rivers that barred the one hundred miles between his army and Richmond. McClellan esteemed Johnston as a master of defense warfare who would wait in deadly traps behind those rivers. McClellan also realized that the farther he pushed from Washington over the miserable roads of eastern Virginia, the more dependent he became for supplies on the bridge-studded Richmond, Fredericksburg & Potomac Railroad—an open invitation for rebel cavalry to strand him with one well-directed raid. Long before March, the Young Napoleon had begun to seek an alternate route.

McClellan's search for another way ended with one of the most ingenious amphibious proposals of military history. Instead of tramping overland from Washington to Richmond, McClellan decided to skirt Johnston by sailing his 150,000 men down Chesapeake Bay from Washington to Fortress Monroe. Already firmly garrisoned by Northern troops, Fortress Monroe dominated the tip of a peninsula formed by the York and James rivers (which gave McClellan's operation its name, the Peninsula Campaign). Richmond stood only sixty miles to the west. The Union bastion and a powerful navy guaranteed McClellan's communications and freed him to sweep westward toward the Confederate capital. On the way he expected to fight Johnston on his own terms. McClellan envisioned a frantic rebel effort to redeploy Johnston from northern Virginia to the Peninsula. He foresaw Southern units losing cohesion along jammed roadways, batteries streaming onto the Peninsula without ammunition, brigades arriving without commanders, the enemy driven to sacrifice divisions in costly stopgap attacks, and, ultimately, abandonment of Richmond by a shattered opponent.

McClellan's vast and in many ways admirable scheme eventually was submitted to the scrutiny of United States Secretary of War Edwin L. Stanton. With an outstanding career as a courtroom lawyer behind him, Stanton tended to direct the Union's war effort much like a barrister prosecuting his client's case. True to form, he decided that before McClellan sailed for the Peninsula to try the main issue, he should resolve a pending matter: the lower Shenandoah must be secured for the Baltimore & Ohio Railroad. McClellan amiably consented to this, for it did not require much reshuffling of his plan. The Young Napoleon contemplated shifting the right wing of his army, General Banks's corps in western Maryland, to cover the Washington area while the Army of the Potomac was on the Peninsula, but there was no reason Banks could not first clear the lower Valley. McClellan launched him into the Shenandoah during the last week of February with orders to oust the Confederates from Winchester, to plant a small garrison there for the protection of rail and canal communications, and to shift the majority of his command eastward to Manassas Junction. Explaining that pacification of the Shenandoah would set in motion the Peninsula Campaign, McClellan assigned Banks the overall task of securing the Washington area.[6]

Strategically, McClellan's Peninsula Campaign was grounded on two assumptions: one, that the rebels would mass around Richmond rather than counterattack Washington while the Army of the Potomac was steaming down Chesapeake Bay; and, two, that if the enemy did counterattack, Banks could handle it after he reached Manassas. Thinking only in military terms, McClellan accepted these assumptions as facts and assured everyone that Washington faced no danger; Johnston was certain to concentrate on the Peninsula, he said. Should the rebels do the unexpected, the capital was well fortified, and there were thousands of militia in Pennsylvania and New York to succor the city. McClellan insisted that a standing force of thirty thousand men was ample shield for the capital and its environs.

McClellan convinced many that his plan was sound, even brilliant. There remained, however, one doubter—President Abraham Lincoln. And Lincoln, with final control over Union strategy, was the one man who had to be satisfied about the Peninsula offensive. McClellan never devoted the time he should have to convincing Lincoln about his plan, perhaps because the latter had so far wielded his constitutional powers as commander in chief sparingly. But if McClellan had any question about Lincoln's willingness to intervene and plot the course of armies, when he thought it necessary, the general was destined for a shock.

Lincoln approved the goal of seizing Richmond, but he preferred a march against it by way of Manassas and Fredericksburg so as to keep McClellan between the rebels and Washington. Lincoln's ambassadors had doubtless cautioned him that Europeans might equate surrender of the national capital with the collapse of the Union; if Washington fell, foreign recognition of the Confederacy was a likely result. The loss of Washington would also shatter morale on the home front. Lincoln, in short, did not like McClellan's plan.

McClellan, however, clung to his turning movement, and in March Lincoln finally acquiesced in return for a promise, or at least what he thought was a promise. The president demanded that Washington be left entirely secure when the Army of the Potomac sailed, and Lincoln ordered McClellan and his corps commanders to determine the force necessary to provide this security,[7] an indirect means of requiring that McClellan's subordinates approve his dispositions. McClellan would have been justified in resigning over those demeaning orders (Jackson had done so for less cause) but instead chose the less forthright approach of acquiescing to the results of Lincoln's intrusion while secretly resolving to maintain his overall strategic view by any means. At a proper council of war a majority of corps commanders decided that complete security for Washington translated into twenty-five thousand men at Manassas Junction and thirty thousand within the city itself.[8] McClellan could agree to this because he was still counting on Banks's forces from the lower Valley to provide an ample garrison for Manassas, but it would shortly become evident that McClellan regarded this commitment as one to be met if all went according to plan and not, as Lincoln conceived it, as a precondition to the Peninsula offense. A still uneasy Lincoln ordered Secretary Stanton to emphasize that he would hold McClellan to this pledge: "The President, having considered the plan of operations agreed upon by yourself and the commanders of army corps, makes no objection to the same, but gives the following direction as to its execution: 1st. Leave such force at Manassas Junction as shall make it entirely certain that the enemy shall not repossess himself of that position and line of communication. 2nd. Leave Washington entirely secure."[9]

Lincoln thus had what he regarded as a promise of Washington's absolute security, while McClellan had what he regarded as a warranty of freedom from interference with his Peninsula Campaign; neither man actually understood the other's assumption, the worst possible circumstance under which to conduct a difficult sea-land offensive.

Lincoln and McClellan might have discovered and perhaps resolved their differences given time, but they had run out of time in March 1862. Banks had entered Winchester by midmonth. Even before this news, four hundred ships had begun embarkation of McClellan's lead divisions. It was a glorious sight, the largest army ever arrayed on the American continent boarding the largest fleet ever seen in these waters. The Army of the Potomac exceeded 150,000 men, with fifteen thousand horses and mules, eleven hundred wagons, sixty batteries of field artillery, and every accouterment of modern warfare: stupendous siege artillery, field telegraphs, even hydrogen balloons for aerial reconnaissance.[10] European observers were impressed with the power and efficiency of the army, a fact not overlooked by the peacockish McClellan. "Rely upon it," he wrote Secretary Stanton jauntily; "I will carry this thing through handsomely."[11]

II

Under the widening pall of McClellan's vast numbers, the Shenandoah reverted to a sideshow. McClellan urged his Valley commanders to retake Romney in early February yet warned them about his West Point classmate: "If you gain Romney look out for return of Jackson, whom

I know to be a man of vigor & nerve, as well as a good soldier."[12] Beyond that initial task, neutralization of the Winchester region was the Union's principal spring objective for the Valley.

General Johnston had no goals so ambitious as a return to Romney for the Valley Army. Instead, on March 1, he outlined what he wanted, and he seemed to rule out even a prolonged defense of Winchester. Johnston expected the Army of the Potomac to march overland directly south from Washington and planned to retire before it. The Valley Army must fall back on line with the main army, protect its flank, secure the Blue Ridge passes, and slow or stop enemy progress up the Shenandoah. Johnston especially needed Jackson to prevent Banks from reinforcing McClellan, who, Johnston knew, already substantially outnumbered him.[13]

Johnston's instructions typified his preference for retreating to preserve strength and allowing a diversionary detachment only to immobilize large enemy forces. The Valley Army was a sideshow in that retreat—if it was equal even to this minor task. Johnston had authorized Jackson to retain the Virginia regiments and batteries of Loring's command previously ordered to Centreville; the Army of the Northwest had ceased to exist (with the exception of a remnant under Brigadier General Edward Johnson west of Staunton). Yet even so the Valley Army mustered only eleven skeleton regiments and its militia.

Indeed, the term "Valley Army" was almost a misnomer for a body that numbered thirty-six hundred infantry in ranks by mid-March. Most of the regiments fielded only two or three hundred men; the entire Army did not exceed forty-six hundred present for duty, including cavalry. And there was no hope of aid. President Davis had advised General Johnston on February 28, in response to Jackson's requests for a specific force to allow him to confront Banks: "I have not the force to send & have no other hope of his reinforcement than by the militia of the Valley."[14] The Valley Army was on its own.

Compounding the problem of small numbers was a lack of experienced officers. There was no replacement available for Colonel Gilham, so Colonel Jesse Burks took his brigade. Burks was an 1844 graduate of V.M.I., but he had passed his adult life as a farmer and had no active military service before becoming commander of the 42d Virginia early in the war.[15] Colonel William Taliaferro had not returned to his brigade from his lobbying effort during the Loring controversy; this was not surprising given his role in that fiasco, but it meant that Colonel Samuel V. Fulkerson of the 37th Virginia commanded the brigade. Fulkerson was a self-made man who had risen to become a lawyer and a judge prior to the war; his military history was limited to the first lieutenancy of a regiment that had seen virtually no action in the Mexican War and later appointment to V.M.I.'s Board of Visitors. Fulkerson, like Burks, served without serious error in the 1861 campaigns in western Virginia.[16] Both Burks and Fulkerson had blundered by signing the petition condemning the occupation of Romney, which must have made them suspect to Jackson, though both eventually won his good regard.

Garnett's command, the 1st (Stonewall) Brigade, remained the backbone of the Army, with the 2d, 4th, 5th, 27th, and 33d Virginia Infantry regiments. Attached to it were McLaughlin's Rockbridge Artillery, Carpenter's Allegheny Light Artillery (of "alleged cannon" fame) and James Waters's West Augusta Artillery. Burks's 2d Brigade consisted of the 21st, 42d, and 48th Virginia and 1st Regular Battalion (nicknamed the Irish Battalion); attached was Captain Marye's Hampden Light Artillery. Fulkerson had only the 23d and 37th Virginia and Captain Shumaker's Danville Light Artillery in the 3d Brigade. The total artillery muster was twenty-seven guns, including Captain Chew's mounted battery. Valley militia regiments were too weak to be useful on the battlefield and were assigned sentry and picket missions. Ashby's cavalry carried out similar duties with a paper strength of six hundred riders, though that number was rarely in the field at any one time. In early March Ashby was promoted to full colonel, news Jackson passed along with a friendly note.[17]

Just as its army matched the weakness of Confederate units everywhere, so the Valley District had its portion of the disasters rocking the South. Federals had reoccupied Romney on February 7. Five days later they drove Shenandoah militia from Moorefield. Southern units guarding Bloomery Gap were routed with the loss of seventeen officers and fifty enlisted men on the fourteenth. Union Brigadier General James Shields was amassing twelve thousand men at Paw Paw, a scant ten miles west of Bloomery Gap. On the northern front, Banks's twenty-eight thousand men spilled over the Potomac into Harpers Ferry on February 24. By March 6 Banks held Bunker Hill, only twelve miles north of Winchester,[18] and Jackson directed Quartermaster Harman to evacuate all Army stores.[19]

Scenes played out around Winchester mirrored events in many Southern cities. The town was abruptly sealed off; movement in and out was thereafter allowed only by permit. Families secured passes and hurried away in pitiful refugee caravans. The bankers fled; inflation spiraled; rumors abounded. Near the courthouse square, carpenters completed a symbolic project: Winchester's Union Hotel, which with a burst of early wartime enthusiasm had shortened its name to "Ion," restored the "Un."[20]

In the camps of the Valley Army there was a different mood. The steady Federal approach demonstrated to these men their foe's immense strength, and this realization snapped the Romney winter's malaise. Most rebels found themselves eager to meet the enemy. Loring's former troops were even willing to follow Jackson. One rebel who enlisted at this time recalled years later, "The war fever, which had been hot upon us all the time, flamed out again as the Spring approached and it began to look as if in the change of hostile lines the army would draw back from Winchester."[21] Private Dick Waldrop displayed the same spirit: "I begin to feel as if it would be almost a disgrace for me to go home when my time expired, unless the tide of success should change and we win some important victories."[22]

A grim resolve began to supplant the vanished illusion of war as romance. Private Hugh White of the Headquarters Guard put aside his hopes of attending divinity school and wrote his parents that he had decided to reenlist: "I need not say how very important it is for the preservation of our army that as many of us as possible should stand firm in our places. . . . In doing this, every one must sacrifice a great deal."[23] This blunt affirmation was echoed throughout the Army's camps. The enemy was doing what furloughs and reenlistment drives could not—reviving the Valley Army's determination. Sam Moore heard the news all Confederates dreaded, that his hometown had been occupied and his wife and children were now behind Federal lines, but he repressed a desire to run to them and simply wrote his wife, as a soldier must, "I have concluded to stand to my post; in fact, there is no means of telling how soon an attack may be made upon us, in which event it would not do for me to be absent."[24]

Stonewall shared this fighting mood. Old Jack responded to Banks's seizure of Harpers Ferry by ordering Ashby to scout the town and determine the chance of capturing the Federals there.[25] Jackson concentrated the Army at Winchester and alerted all units to stand ready.[26] Ashby contracted his cavalry in a tough screen north of Winchester.

Jackson's hope was that Banks might expose a detachment upon which he could pounce; such a reverse surely would keep Banks fully concentrated in the Shenandoah. When General Hill withdrew his garrison from Leesburg as part of the overall withdrawal from Centreville, Jackson requested permission from Johnston for Hill to join him: "I greatly need such an officer, one who can be sent off as occasion may offer against an exposed detachment of the enemy for the purpose of capturing it. . . . The very idea of reinforcements coming to Winchester would I think be a damper on the enemy, in addition to the fine effect that would be produced on our own troops, who are already in fine spirits." He added an earnest conclusion: "If we cannot be successful in defeating the enemy should he advance, a kind Providence may enable us to inflict a terrible wound and effect a safe retreat in the event of having to fall back."[27]

From an officer whose force was so badly outnumbered this letter may have seemed fantastic to Johnston, who did not reply. Hill joined the main Confederate army south of the Rappahannock River near Culpeper, and the Valley Army was more isolated than ever before. It was sixty miles from Winchester to the nearest of Johnston's forces and ninety miles to the remnant of the Army of the Northwest under Brigadier General Edward Johnson. Yet Jackson refused to publish an appeal for all Valley men to join the Army lest the enemy learn its weakness. Stonewall did, however, explain something of his intentions to Alexander Boteler, his confidant during the Romney flap: "My plan is to put on as bold a front as possible and use every means in my power to prevent [Banks's] advance whilst our reorganization is going on. . . . What I desire is to hold the country as far as practicable until we are in a condition to advance, and then with God's blessing, let us [make] thorough work of it."[28]

Events quickly pressed the Valley Army to throw out its bold front. On March 7 Banks rattled southward into Ashby's pickets. A furious skirmish ensued.[29] Jackson double-timed his infantrymen out to form a brave but thin line of battle two miles north of Winchester.[30] Throughout the afternoon a bitter wind brought them the sound of Ashby's fight, which finally faded as he drove the enemy off the field. The infantry brigades remained in line until night, then slept in place.[31]

The next three days were anxious ones around Winchester. Rebels deepened trenches, sandbagged their redoubts, and cleared lanes of fire.[32] Major John Harman crated the last of the Army's stores. His responsibilities required him to maintain contact with the Army's supply base at Staunton, where his brother, Colonel Asher Harman, commanded, and as Banks closed on Winchester, John Harman jotted short bulletins to his brother. Often written with pencil and on small scraps of paper, these uninhibited personal notes caught the anxiety of a white-knuckled Valley Army:

> March 7: I have just had an order from Gen'l Jackson to send his wagon to headquarters; this looks like we are about to be off. . . . What is to become of us God only knows.
>
> March 8 [Here Harman referred to the alarm of the seventh]: At last the crisis is upon us. Everything is packed and ready for a move. Jackson will certainly make a stand if he can do it without the risk being too great.
>
> March 9, 12:30 P.M.: . . . still here. I do not know how long we shall be here. It is a terrible state of uneasiness to be in, I can assure you.
>
> March 10, 10 A.M.: I was to see the Gen'l this morning, and he talks as though he meant to fight. . . . There is no government property here that I know of, and all the wagons are loaded and horses harnessed and ready to move.[33]

The enemy continued to press. Federals along the District's western fringe were moving. General Shields's Division, destined to become a part of Banks's command, had inched from Paw Paw to the vicinity of Bath by March 6. On the eleventh Shields occupied Martinsburg and established liaison with Banks.[34] The enemy fronts from west and north had finally joined by advancing against Winchester, much as Jackson had augured. He was outnumbered ten to one by the nearly forty thousand Northern troops arrayed in the lower Shenandoah.

The Union host was in motion on the eleventh. Dawn brought rumors of an advance from the east via the Berryville road, and elements of Burks's Brigade hustled out in that direction.[35] Burks found nothing, but shortly after noon the Yankees came in sight north of Winchester, and Jackson concentrated all units to oppose them there.[36]

Stationed on a fortified hillock called Fort Alabama, Captain Morrison's Headquarters Guard company watched the armies squaring off. His men saw the enemy probing southward, first cavalry and skirmishers, then massive infantry formations. They picked out Ashby thundering into action—he was easy to spot on his tall white horse—and watched as he shattered the head of the Union column. More Federals darted forward, and a Southern brigade advanced against them in a ragged line. When the evening sun lit bayonets on the plain below, battle had not been joined, and the enemy drew off toward the north. Soon their campfires could be seen around Stephenson's Depot, a way station near which the railroad from Winchester to Harpers Ferry swung sharply to the east from a course parallel with the Valley Pike.[37]

About dark Old Jack passed instructions for the Army to march south to its wagons, cook rations, and wait. Only a handful of guards were left to stoke what the enemy should believe to be campfires.[38] It was the classic ruse of a retreating army, although nothing had yet been said about retreat. As usual, orders cloaked the next move. Captain Morrison led his company back to Headquarters, where Jackson inquired what he had observed from Fort Alabama; he was particularly interested in knowing whether any Federals were approaching from the west, along the route taken by the Valley Army toward Pughtown and Bath in January. Morrison had seen none, but a few minutes later he learned that one of his sharper-eyed men had spotted Federals sliding from the Pike to the Pughtown road. Morrison returned to report this fact, whereupon he was told to billet for the night in a house across the street. As he left, Morrison noted the Army's ranking officers reporting to Headquarters. He supposed they were coming to receive orders for the next day's action.[39]

The meeting was more extraordinary than Morrison could have guessed. Jackson had summoned his brigade and regimental officers to a council of war, his first. And it met to weigh a course so startling even Stonewall felt the need for approval. No firsthand account exists, but clues about the meeting come from a few contemporaries, and certain things can be surmised from the very nature of a council of war, which typically would review the strategic and tactical situation, hear the commander's proposal, and offer some comment upon it.

Jackson would not have known the exact position of Johnston's army as of that day, but Johnston's evacuation of Manassas was expected by all. Jackson correctly could point to that factor as justifying his decision to cling to Winchester. As long as Confederates held the city there could be no quick Union lunge against Johnston from the Valley, no Manassas in reverse. The brave show of force served a valid purpose, although the Valley Army was not called upon to sacrifice itself. Johnston had made it clear he did not want Jackson to hazard loss of his command.[40] There had been enough Confederate defeats of late, yet defending Winchester now bordered on what Johnston prohibited. Clearly Banks was strongly posted around Stephenson's Depot. Captain Morrison's intelligence about Federals on the Pughtown road indicated the enemy was to the west as well. The Yanks had occupied Berryville (twelve miles east of Winchester and connected to it by a good road) the day before; the reports that caused some of Burks's men to be sent toward Berryville were of at least five Union regiments advancing from that direction.[41] The speculation among Jackson's staff was that the Confederates would face a simultaneous advance from north and east,[42] a possibility that was surely discussed. Moreover, from Berryville Federal forces threatened the remaining roads to the Blue Ridge; the last safe retreat route was directly south via the Valley Pike.

This was the general situation, all of which was known at the time of Jackson's council and presumably provided a common basis for discussion. (It was also a generally correct understanding of Union dispositions. Banks actually had three large divisions operating in the lower Shenandoah: one at Berryville, one camped around Stephenson's, and the division of James Shields located some miles farther back around Martinsburg.)[43] Every officer in the room must have realized it would be self-slaughter to await attack at Winchester. Southern fortifications were incomplete, covering primarily the western and northern sides of town. Even unfinished the lines stretched two and a half miles, too long for the few defenders, and they had already been pronounced almost worthless by the Army's newly arrived engineer, Lieutenant J. K. Boswell.[44] The heavy artillery had been evacuated, along with almost all other property.[45] There was nothing left to sustain the rebels. The logical response to the Union noose in which the Army found itself was retreat.

Yet Jackson tonight was thinking neither of avoiding nor awaiting the enemy. He proposed instead a predawn surprise attack! And he had a target, the center of Banks's army at Stephenson's Depot.[46] Let the Army finish supper, rest a few hours, then strike before daylight, he proposed.

The commander of the Valley Army never lost his offensive mind-set, even if he had to resort to guile and bluff. Only two weeks later, when contemplating operations for a narrower region of the Shenandoah, Jackson would suggest to Johnston a plan for reinforcements to reach him in such a way that they could obstruct the Federal rear while he did the same in their front; Jackson predicted that panic would ensue with destruction of the Union army at little Southern cost.[47] Old Jack was urging the same sort of expedient tonight. A rebel sortie would find Federals unnerved by the past few days of skirmishing, the first combat most of them had seen. Darkness, surprise, and Confederate élan could stampede the enemy.

Stonewall's plan reduced the awesome odds against the Southerners by taking advantage of the wide separation between Banks's forces. The Federals at Berryville were ten miles from Stephenson's by air, and half again that distance by back roads. Jackson's intelligence was that Banks could be much reinforced by morning,[48] which suggests he suspected Shields would advance quickly from Martinsburg.[49] The general saw a chance to send part of Banks's army scuttling before others intervened.

For an outnumbered force to storm the enemy camp at dawn is an ancient and sometimes successful tactic; there were men in the Valley Army that night who in October 1864 would collapse whole divisions of veteran Yankees with precisely such a surprise a few miles outside Winchester at the Battle of Cedar Creek. This was essentially the proposal Jackson put before his officers, but they balked. The effort entailed a foray in relatively open country four miles north of Winchester; if the enemy did not panic, or if Shields arrived from Martinsburg, the tired Confederates would be beyond whatever protection their breastworks offered with abundant daylight for a Union counterattack (exactly what undid the initial Confederate success at Cedar Creek two years later). Worse, the Valley Army would have a city behind it and possibly enemy forces to cut off escape from both the left and right flanks. There would be little chance to use Southern artillery, since it could not fire with safety in the dark and thrusting it so far forward would be extremely dangerous. Logical arguments such as these doubtless were raised against the offensive. It is unknown whether Ashby was present, but anyone might have observed that his small cavalry force could not help scare away the enemy; it would be hard-pressed to do more than patrol the flanks east and west and protect the trains parked south of town.

It was on the position of the wagon train that the council discovered a major problem. Jackson had assumed that his wagons were packed relatively close to Winchester and that the infantry was close to them, but he discovered during the council that the train actually was parked five to seven miles south of the city. Knowing nothing of Jackson's plans, as usual, the regiments had marched, as ordered, until they found the wagons; indeed, some units could only be reaching their vehicles as the meeting was in progress. The entire Army was nine to eleven miles from where the general wanted to attack.[50]

That someone was not court-martialed for this apparent blunder has been a minor mystery, but Jackson may have seen his own handiwork. Two days earlier he had told Major Harman "to force all the baggage to the rear on the Strasburg road" if the enemy advanced; he added that the front would be the most exposed.[51] Harman admitted some confusion from Jackson's cryptic order, and he kept the wagons in a state of constant readiness. When the Federals advanced during the afternoon of the eleventh, Jackson deployed in hopes of being attacked;[52] it is not probable he at that point had thought of a dawn surprise or communicated anything about it to Harman. The likelihood rather is that Harman, seeing the Army going to the front and having heard nothing different from Jackson, merely followed his instructions and "forced" his wagons away from the exposed area, stopping when he thought he had a safe cushion.

By now it was approximately 9 P.M.; no more than eight hours remained until Jackson wanted to strike. A vigorous debate followed, with Jackson persisting that it could be done. The Army could do without rest! Let it begin its march to battle at once! His subordinates united in opposition. Their view was that troops who had done one hard day's soldiering could not make a long night march without rest or food and rout several times their strength at dawn. According to Sandie Pendleton, the location of the trains, plus undeniably inferior numbers, decided the question in the negative.[53]

The council ended before 10 P.M.[54] Captain Morrison was called back to Headquarters and told to take his command in the direction of Strasburg. Ashby relieved his fire guards outside town, and Sandie Pendleton went to order the brigade commanders to retire at daylight.[55] The march would be south along the Valley Pike to Strasburg, and as far south from there as necessary. The Shenandoah Valley Campaign of 1862 would begin with retreat.

Jackson left town about midnight accompanied by Dr. McGuire. The pair rode silently a short time, then paused to peer back at the city. McGuire took a sad look toward his home, then found himself staring at Jackson. The general was gripped by a rage born of frustrated ambition. On the large war maps in Richmond this withdrawal would be charted as a minor incident, another small column plodding south. For Jackson it was much more: an opportunity to damage the enemy missed. Suddenly he blared, "That is the last council of war I will ever hold."[56]

A calmer Jackson might have thanked his officers. There was no guarantee that sleepless, hungry rebels would have approached the Union camps undetected, or that only Yankees would have become confused and fled in the dawn fighting, or that the Federal column at Berryville would not have marched directly into the Confederate rear—a disaster Jackson hardly could have survived. There was certainly no guarantee that the Federals would not anticipate a surprise attack—indeed at least one Union brigade was under arms by 4 A.M. on the twelfth.[57] Winchester in fact was impossible to defend without greatly superior strength; outnumbered Union forces were crushed in May 1862, June 1863, and July 1864 attempting to cover the city, and a similar fate befell the Confederacy in September 1864. Given the odds against him, Jackson was going to lose Winchester, and the benefit of rolling the enemy away from it temporarily and perhaps slowing the flow of Northerners to confront Johnston was not sufficient to risk wrecking the Valley Army. Jackson apparently concluded as much before leaving the town, telling a friend that a battle would cost too many lives and he must "wait for a better time."[58]

What fault Stonewall found with the council's advice is therefore unknown, but to his pledge he was true. He had held his last council of war. Jackson settled deeper into the saddle, turned his horse, and trailed the Valley Army into a springtime of little hope.

6

KERNSTOWN

The most terrific fight of musketry
that can be well conceived.

—S. J. C. Moore

By the morning of March 12, the last Confederates in Winchester were cavalry, which meant Turner Ashby was about, waiting for the enemy. He would have looked, as always, the ideal equestrian: rein and forearm a straight line from bit to elbow, weight deep in the saddle, seat perfect. When Ashby confirmed the Yanks were coming in force, he turned and trotted out of town. Rumor had it that before he reached Winchester's outskirts two Union riders suddenly blocked his way. Ashby charged, dropped one Federal with a shot through the heart, jerked the other out of his saddle, and carried him by the throat to the nearest Southern outpost.[1]

Much exaggerated, the story perhaps grew out of a skirmish that flashed five miles south of Winchester around the hamlet of Barton's Mill. Private George Neese of Chew's Battery noted in his diary how the rear guard had fallen back past the village when the Yankees hit and caused a brief panic among some Confederate wagons. With a force of unknown size, Neese wrote, "Ashby made a desperate charge through town and drove them back beyond Kernstown."[2] That was a chase of at least two miles, a feat of which Confederate cavalrymen realistically could boast, yet it was the sensational rumor about disposing of two Yanks that became part of Ashby's lore.

This tale highlighted something ingrained in Ashby's boys: they believed their leader and themselves capable of such derring-do. And if Ashby displayed bravado, then others must as well. Cavalryman Harry Gilmor would later relate a tale that began with himself and a handful of riders sitting in front of a Winchester hotel that morning. He recalled

Ashby riding by and saying he had better retire because the enemy was in the north end of town. Gilmor instead went to the saloon (to write letters, he claimed). When he came out only two horsemen remained, and a short distance away was the head of the blue column. Gilmor and his soldiers moved off, stopping on the way to say farewell to some young ladies and accept a piece of cake. Gunshots rang out, and in the ensuing scurry around town Gilmor and his compeers were cornered in a lot with high stone walls on three sides and Federals surging forward on the other. Gilmor and another rebel cleared the wall under a brisk fire, but the last man was hurled over it as his stallion, rising to the jump, took a bullet. The unhorsed rebel sprang up, grabbed Gilmor's foot, and swung himself onto the croup of his mount to escape.[3]

It was a typical Southern cavalry romance, perhaps true to an extent, and also understandable, for the Yankee cavalry against whom they jousted so far had proven inept. Operations against them were a lark. "We thought no more of riding through the enemy's bivouacs than of riding around our fathers' farms," scoffed one rebel who was nineteen when the war ended.[4] Boys who had played knight-errant in the antebellum Valley tournaments had seen their fantasies come true, and if Winchester had to be evacuated, it could at least be given up with a few good adventures.

This attitude worried Jackson. Had he known about Gilmor's style of leaving Winchester, he could have been counted upon to spoil the fun by pointing out that Gilmor had no business staying after Ashby told him to move on, and that the thrilling chase wasted a perfectly good horse. Certainly, as the retreat down the Valley began Jackson realized it was more important than ever for Ashby to tighten discipline. Ashby was no longer only picketing the frontier; he now commanded the Valley Army's rear guard, and its vedettes had to be in place and alert. Perhaps betraying his concern, Jackson either picked or allowed Ashby to select four elite companies from the Stonewall Brigade to support the rear guard.[5] With the enemy within striking distance, the Army could ill afford a mounted arm entranced with notions of gallantry, a fact that posed a grim question for Jackson: could the cavalry operate effectively with him in the field?

The bitter answer to that question would not come for two months. For now the Federals pursued the retreating Valley Army at a distance, and

Ashby's rear guard had only an occasional skirmish for amusement. This feeble Northern showing bespoke the military temperament of Major General Nathaniel P. Banks. A politician by trade, one-time member of Congress, and influential member of the Republican party, Banks owed his command of Union troops in the Valley to political rather than military skill. Of the former he had much. During only his second term as a congressman, Banks won the longest struggle on record for speaker of the U.S. House of Representatives; when South Carolina seceded, he was retiring from the governor's mansion of Massachusetts. Political clout brought him Lincoln's nomination to a major generalship, for which he was otherwise uniquely unqualified. He had no prior military service. To his credit, Banks had worked up from the poverty of a New England mill town, knowing there hardships as tough as many soldiers, but he was no general.

Banks's timidity permitted the Valley Army an unhurried retreat from Winchester. It retired slowly through Strasburg and then southward along the Valley Pike; it did not reach Woodstock until March 15. On March 20 the Army was only twelve miles farther south at Mount Jackson, where it halted. Ashby's cavalry stiffened by Chew's Battery and the little elite corps from the Stonewall Brigade put up a stout covering fight. Meanwhile, a wagon train heaped with every item of conceivable military value from Winchester moved with the Army up the Valley Pike.[6] Paralleling the Army, Manassas Gap locomotives shuttled all rolling stock left in the District to the railhead at Mount Jackson. To ensure that none of this equipment reached the enemy now holding Manassas Junction, Jackson detailed his Headquarters Guard to burn several bridges along the line. Lieutenant Sandie Pendleton of Jackson's staff saw his friends from Washington College marching off and got permission to join their expedition. He recorded the destruction of two large structures outside of Front Royal as follows:

> The burning bridges presented one of the grandest spectacles I ever beheld. One bridge of considerable length was covered and drew like a funnel. A strong wind was blowing, and as soon as the fire was kindled at the east end of the bridge, it swept through and over it, catching the dry planks like tinder [and] made a mass of fire. It burned for some fifteen minutes, when the whole gave a crash and down went the brilliant, blazing structure; a splash and a column of steam and smoke rose up from the water below.

Pendleton closed his description with a sober reflection: "We were left in the darkness on the edge of a yawning gulf, to contemplate the destruction we had wrought."[7] More and more, the Army was coming to realize what war meant.

All of Virginia was learning this lesson. In response to a Confederate War Department requisition, the Old Dominion had called out forty thousand militia from her recent canvass of the state's male population, and twelve thousand of them were slated for the Valley.[8] Jackson had no illusion about twelve thousand men actually reporting for duty; he would have to work to get a fraction of that total. He was authorized to go get them when, on March 12, Governor Letcher issued an executive order empowering Confederate commanders in Virginia to rally every militiaman within the boundaries of their districts.[9]

Jackson mobilized the entire Valley militia at once. The response was good and included a bonus in the person of Jedediah Hotchkiss, the prewar Shenandoah schoolmaster who was also an accomplished mapmaker. Hotchkiss had taught himself the art of topography during holidays before the war, and he was uniquely talented in that subject. Robert E. Lee had employed him in the Alleghenies in the fall of 1861, until typhoid forced Hotchkiss to return home. Oddly enough, Hotchkiss's initial application for commission had not been acted upon, which meant he was still a civilian and would remain so throughout the Valley Campaign. Nevertheless, Hotchkiss resolved to tender his services to Jackson and joined the militia heading for the Valley Army.

His observations at this time are revealing. At Staunton on Monday morning, March 17, he found three militia regiments from the upper Valley. Since many militia had volunteered already, the regiments were exceedingly thin; when Company A of one regiment was ordered into line, a solitary figure strolled forward. Those present at Staunton were ready to do their duty, and others joined them on the march north to Mount Jackson, filtering in by twos or threes. Hotchkiss noted that morale was high. Even the flotsam of the Army's retreat—wagons of military stores and refugee carriages piled high with furniture and wailing children—did not depress the militiamen, and they covered a respectable sixteen miles in one day. Stonewall's induction officers at Mount Jackson matched this swift pace. The militia were given a recruiting lecture and advised to volunteer and secure the benefit of choosing the regiment in which they would serve. Many did so. The remainder were organized into a special battalion and put to drill.[10]

Hotchkiss rode over to Headquarters to report the militia's arrival and to renew contact with Will Baylor, an old friend serving as inspector general on Jackson's staff. Baylor thought Jackson would be interested in Hotchkiss and arranged an interview. Stonewall pumped Hotchkiss thoroughly about the militia and conditions in the upper Valley. The answers obviously impressed Jackson, and on March 26 he posted Hotchkiss to staff duties and gave him his first assignment—all with three sentences: "I want you to make me a map of the Valley from Harper's Ferry to Lexington, showing all the points of defense and offense between those points. Mr. Pendleton will give you orders for whatever outfit you want. Good morning, Sir."[11] With those terse orders, the ablest topographer of the war went to work for the Valley Army; his maps were to contribute greatly to the speed and precision of its movements. Hotchkiss also began a diary that, supplemented by elaborate postwar research, became the most valuable source of information about the Valley Campaign.

As Hotchkiss began his new assignment, Jackson turned to a task that had been occupying a good deal of his time recently. Johnston wished the Valley Army to keep Banks too busy to support McClellan, and to this end Jackson was giving himself a thorough lesson in Shenandoah geography. Unfolding his maps, Stonewall traced the rebel retreat up the Valley Pike through Strasburg and Woodstock to Mount Jackson. South of this point, the Pike led through Rude's Hill, New Market, Harrisonburg, and Staunton, where the Virginia Central Railroad tied the Valley with Richmond. With the destruction of the Manassas Gap bridge at Front Royal, the Virginia Central was the only rail link open to the Army. And since this latter line lacked a spur to Mount Jackson from Staunton, the Army's supplies were piling up there. Staunton thus became Jackson's main warehouse, and its defense became a major factor in his maneuvers.

Nature gave Jackson a second problem. East of Strasburg a huge interlocking system of ridges called Massanutten Mountain (or simply the Massanutten) rose precipitously and surged up the Valley for fifty miles. For this distance the Shenandoah corridor was actually two corridors, the Luray Valley between Massanutten Mountain and the Blue

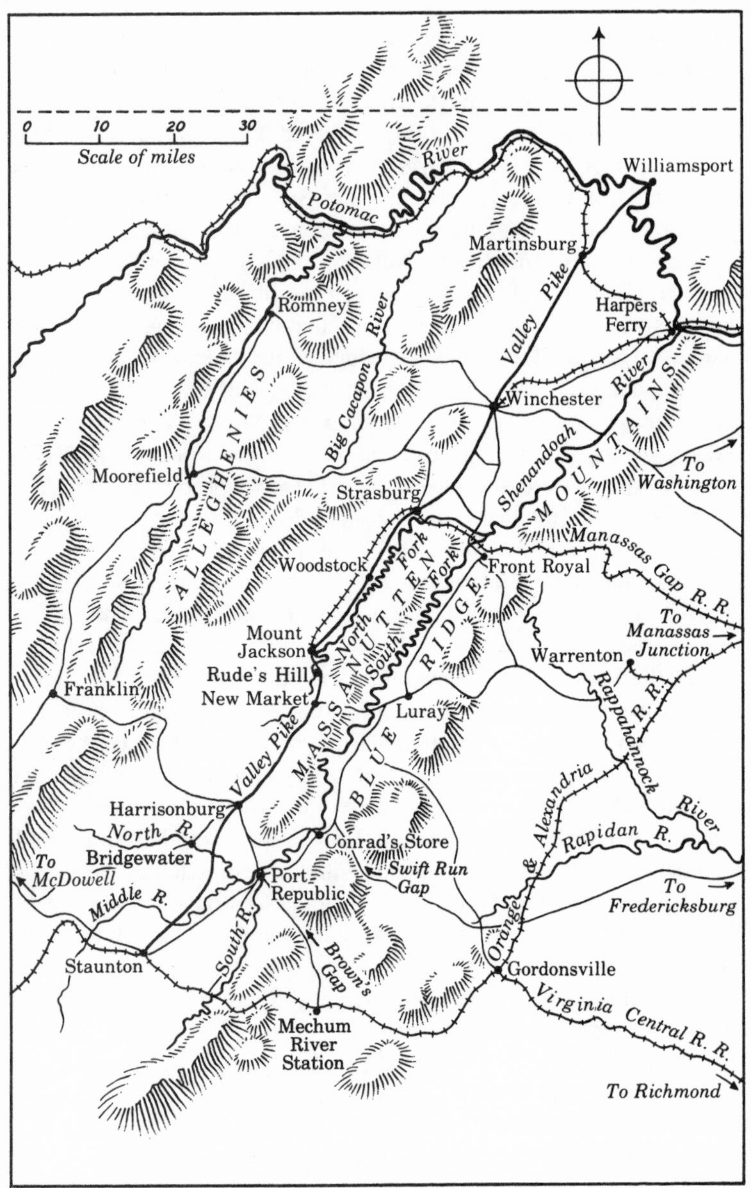

0
10
20
30
Scale of miles
Potomac
River
Williamsport
Martinsburg
Romney
River
Big Cacapon
Valley Pike
Harpers Ferry
Winchester
River
Shenandoah
MOUNTAINS
ALLEGHENIES
To Washington
Moorefield
Strasburg
Manassas Gap R. R.
Woodstock
Front Royal
North Fork
South Fork
MASSANUTTEN
BLUE RIDGE
To Manassas Junction
Mount Jackson
Rude's Hill
New Market
Warrenton
Franklin
Luray
Rappahannock R. R.
Valley Pike
Orange & Alexandria
Rappahannock
River
Harrisonburg
North R.
Conrad's Store
Rapidan R.
To McDowell
Bridgewater
Swift Run Gap
Port Republic
Middle R.
To Fredericksburg
South R.
Brown's Gap
Staunton
Gordonsville
Virginia Central R. R.
Mechum River Station
To Richmond

3. THE VALLEY

Ridge and the Shenandoah Valley between the Massanutten and the Alleghenies. This mountain divider was the salient geographic feature of Jackson's district, and he could never leave it out of his plans. It was always there to trouble him, a tangled green wall with but one way across: between New Market, in the Shenandoah, and the village of Luray, in the Luray Valley, was Massanutten Gap, the only viable pass in the rugged mountain for fifty miles. The difficulties posed by this barrier were endless. Jackson could not simultaneously retreat up both the corridors it formed. Had he retired into the Luray Valley from Winchester, he would have surrendered the richer Shenandoah, exposed Staunton, abandoned the Valley Pike to the enemy, and confined his forces to the muddy trails around Luray. On the other hand, retreat along the Pike left the Luray region unguarded and endangered Jackson's communications with Johnston. A Federal force east of the Massanutten could easily deny Jackson the Blue Ridge passes he might need to join Johnston if the latter called him.[12]

This was a risk Jackson had to take. Mobility was the essential factor in the Valley Army's future, and Jackson knew that the roads east of the Massanutten could not support swift operations.[13] Jackson accordingly withdrew his army west of the Massanutten toward Mount Jackson, thereby securing several advantages. He had the Valley Pike for movement north or south. He could cross Massanutten Gap to pursue an enemy column moving east over the Blue Ridge. At Rude's Hill (three miles south of Mount Jackson but well north of the road from New Market to Massanutten Gap) there were also formidable natural obstacles in the path of continued Union progress up the Shenandoah. Rude's Hill was a ridge more than one hundred feet above the Valley floor. Near it, the North Fork of the Shenandoah made two ninety-degree turns: the first turn wrenched its bed from north to east; the second, from east to north again. The result of these abrupt jerks was a forty-foot moat about a mile in front of Rude's. A single wooden bridge spanned this moat, and its destruction would slam the gates of a natural citadel. Nevertheless, Jackson was taking chances by remaining west of the Massanutten: Blue Ridge passes were open to the enemy, Confederate movements over them would not be without risk, and Jackson was poorly positioned to shield Johnston's left flank. Heavily outnumbered, Stonewall could not eliminate these risks, but he at least had retained freedom of motion by retiring to Mount Jackson.

As carefully as he reviewed mountains and passes, Jackson traced the courses of the Valley's several major rivers. More than once he ran his finger down the line of the North Fork of the Shenandoah as it twisted around Rude's Hill and followed a course roughly paralleling the Valley Pike to Strasburg. Here the river curled around the Massanutten and flowed to Front Royal. The Luray Valley was drained by the Shenandoah's South Fork, which began at the village of Port Republic. From the Port, as local residents called Port Republic, the South Fork ran directly to Front Royal to join the North Fork and form the Shenandoah River proper, which then flowed to the Potomac at Harpers Ferry.

Valley rivers would be swollen with spring rains during the coming months, giving their infrequent bridges special importance. Jackson's Headquarters Guard already had burned the Manassas Gap trestle over the South Fork at Front Royal. They also had burned the South Fork highway bridge in order to retard Federal movement into the Luray Valley. A second highway bridge over the North Fork at Front Royal was useless without its counterpart over the South Fork and was left intact. Jackson's own ability to enter the Luray Valley from Rude's Hill depended on possession of at least one of three bridges crossing the South Fork near Luray, and he doubtless told Ashby to watch them. Two other bridges, one over the South Fork near Conrad's Store and another over the North River (a tributary of the South Fork) at Port Republic, carried routes exiting the Valley to the east via Swift Run Gap and Brown's Gap, respectively. On the North Fork there was only one bridge, the structure near Rude's Hill.

The complexities raised by this skein of passes, streams, and bridges were compounded by unknown enemy intentions and uncertain Southern reactions. The Valley Army's predicament would change not only with each movement Banks made but also with those of McClellan and Johnston. Shifts by the main armies far beyond the Blue Ridge could make dead ends of passes across it, could sacrifice the Army's remaining rail line, or even open roads leading into its deep rear. And Jackson could not neglect the second front he faced directly to the west. Shields had joined Banks from the Alleghenies, and thousands of additional Federals were there within range to do the same. To summarize, every troop movement in Virginia meant that Jackson had to rethink his position as he searched for some way to keep two enemy fronts separated and at the same time to answer Johnston's need to keep Banks in the Valley.

II

Jackson's reflection yielded to action on Friday, March 21. By that day a dispatch from General Johnston dated March 19 would have been received, and therein Johnston let Jackson know he did not think the Valley Army was staying close enough to the Federals to keep them in the Shenandoah. Johnston had reached the Rappahannock River on his withdrawal from Manassas, and his assumption was that McClellan would follow. Aware that the Valley Army's retreat to the vicinity of Mount Jackson placed it forty miles south of Winchester, Johnston inquired, "Would not your presence with your troops nearer Winchester prevent the enemy from diminishing his force there? I think it certain that it would. It is important to keep that army in the Valley, and that it should not reinforce McClellan. Do try to prevent it by getting and keeping as near as prudence will permit."[14]

Jackson had clung to Winchester in the face of immense odds to accomplish what Johnston desired, but it appeared that the high command had not noticed. Old Jack must have been questioning how with his tiny force he could prudently get nearer Banks when another dispatch arrived, this one from Ashby near Strasburg. The cavalryman wrote that the enemy, who had not pushed vigorously south of Strasburg, had withdrawn toward Winchester. Ashby had only one company with him when he detected this retreat, but he had gone after the enemy with those few men and Chew's Battery, sending word for other cavalry units to join him.[15] That news, in light of Johnston's words, meant that the Valley Army should go northward immediately. Stonewall's need for haste was such that he did not pause to ready the new militia battalion for action. There was time only to alert the experienced brigades: cook rations and move in the morning.

It was a grueling march. There had been a fast, thick snow on the morning of the 21st,[16] and wet and cold persisted as the Confederates learned Jackson wanted them to reach Cedar Creek that day. "Can scarcely believe it possible as the distance is 21 miles," Sergeant Watkins Kearns of the 27th Virginia wrote in his diary. Kearns, like hundreds of others, did not make it: "Had to leave ranks near Edenburgh but do not catch up any more but still hear of the brigade advancing towards Strasburg. Night came on and they are still marching. . . . Reach Strasburg thoroughly exhausted."[17] Even wild rumors of riots in Maryland and Yanks fleeing Winchester—of being able to walk into the city—did not keep many soldiers in ranks.[18] The movement was the longest and fastest in months, and it was a much-thinned Valley Army that camped within sight of Cedar Creek.

As rebel infantry slumped around their fires they may have heard cannon fire to the north. It was Ashby. He had trailed weak Federal opposition to the outskirts of Winchester; there he spurred forward to skirmish with the few Yankees he could see. Recording the scene in his diary was gunner George Neese of Chew's Battery: "We went to within a mile and a half of the edge of [Winchester] and got a position for our pieces and fired at some infantry that was at the edge of town. Still there seemed not to be many troops there and we thought no artillery at all. A few companies of Ashby's cavalry charged to go to town, but just before they got to town one whole regiment rose from behind a fence and fired on them and drove them back, but fortunately none of them were touched. We still fired on their infantry and we were still under the impression that the enemy had no artillery but they satisfied us as regards the impression pretty soon . . . for in less than twenty minutes they had a battery planted on a hill west of town to rake the road and position which we occupied. They opened their battery on us which drove us from our position immediately in consequence of their having the best position. They also had eight pieces and we only had three."[19] The skirmish boiled until sunset, when Ashby drew back to consider what he had learned. His skirmishers spent the night on the south side of a little village called Kernstown located three miles from Winchester; Federal vedettes lay on the other end of the village.[20]

Despite the artillery, Ashby did not see any significant infantry force: perhaps no more than four regiments were present. There was also word from scouts that even this force was under orders to move in the direction of Harpers Ferry.[21] This news went to Jackson along with a suggestion from Ashby that he might have stormed into Winchester if aided by a single infantry regiment.[22]

The news demanded that Jackson maintain pressure. If only four regiments remained in Winchester, Banks was departing the Valley; that must be stopped. The exposed Union remainder might be destroyed with limited risk to the Valley Army, and such a defeat could keep Banks in the Shenandoah as Johnston desired. At early dawn of the twenty-third Old Jack hustled forward the elite infantry force of four companies that had been operating with Ashby. Captain John Nadenbousch commanded.[23] In the detail was Sam Moore's company of the 2d Virginia, which was beginning a habit of turning up when things got hot. Moore's solid training and attention to detail were paying off; his men had attracted the attention of both Ashby and Jackson during the winter fighting,[24] and now they were on their way to even more serious duty.

Nadenbousch's party overtook Ashby around midmorning on the twenty-third as the cavalry probed beyond Kernstown. Ashby already had sent scouts east to search for Federals departing Winchester, and he had Chew's Battery blasting away at Union skirmishers posted in a stand of timber a mile north of Kernstown.[25] Ashby lost no time throwing forward the infantry; Moore's company and one other raced across fields toward the treeline. The Confederates drove off the enemy and scoured the woods to discover a Federal battleline about one hundred yards ahead. Moore and his men opened fire and saw the enemy hesitate, then bring up more strength and move to the attack. Nadenbousch brought his other two companies into a severe skirmish. The Confederates stood well against impossible odds but took about a dozen casualties, sizable losses since the number involved in the skirmish was small.[26] Ashby was there watching and concluded Northern forces were increasing.[27] (In fact there was more than a brigade of Federals ranged against Ashby, with ample artillery.) Ashby saw what he described to Nadenbousch as "heavy columns" behind the Federal lines and told him to withdraw.[28] By early afternoon the Confederate vanguard was on high ground a little south of Kernstown. Ashby's line was anchored west of the Pike near Opequon Church and stretched east a few hundred yards with Chew's guns astride the Pike in the center.

This was the situation when, between 1 P.M. and 2 P.M., Jackson came up; as he approached he was advised by a source he thought remarkably reliable that the Union force did not exceed four regiments.[29] Jackson did not name Ashby as the source, and his report implies that it was not the cavalryman. The intelligence may have come from Winchester civilians, among whom Jackson had more than a few spies.[30] Based on the firefight of the morning, Ashby might have given a less optimistic report, but it seems Jackson and Ashby did not actually speak on the twenty-third.[31] Jackson felt the pressure of time that day, and he later admitted that he did not think he had time to delay for "making much reconnaissance."[32] Perhaps he should have taken time to confer with Ashby, but Ashby should have made sure Jackson fully understood that the field was not necessarily as it had been twelve hours earlier. It is possible that better communication might have avoided the battle that was threatening to explode.

Yet it was a Sunday, and that alone might prevent a fight; Jackson was loath to break the Lord's peace. Moreover, the thirty-five to forty miles marched by the Army in scarcely more than thirty hours had thinned Southern ranks; there would be no more than three thousand winded infantry to challenge whatever lay ahead. And Jackson could not have any illusion about what would happen if his cold, hungry men chased the enemy through Winchester that evening: many troops would disappear to the homes of their friends and relatives. If the enemy counterattacked in the morning Stonewall might not have a corporal's guard to oppose them. It seemed wiser to let the troops bivouac where they now were, a mile or two south of Kernstown, and orders were passed accordingly. Rebels were turned into woods west of the Pike and allowed to rest.[33]

In the end, though, Stonewall could not avoid a fight. If Banks was leaving the Shenandoah the departure might continue while the rebels rested, a result unacceptable under Johnston's instructions. And if Banks used the night to countermarch his divisions, the odds now apparently in favor of the Valley Army would be reversed. Indeed, Jackson realized as he prowled the front that the Federals might be tempted to just such a concentration. From the ground lost during Ashby's morning skirmish, particularly from a knob about a half-mile west of the Pike called Pritchard's Hill, the Yankees could count Southern regiments along the Pike. With the enemy probably observing how thin were Confederate ranks, Jackson deemed it necessary to force an engagement.[34]

The terrain before Jackson was typical of the Shenandoah: pastures surrounded by stone walls or fence rails, rolling wheat fields and clumps of timber spread out on either side of the Valley Pike as it stretched off toward Winchester. Roughly a mile north of the cavalry around Opequon Church was Pritchard's Hill, an excellent position from which Union guns might decimate any Confederate advance down the Pike. The enemy was already pounding at Ashby from that post. The infantry Ashby had battled all morning were arrayed east of the Pike, and to move against them would likewise expose the rebels to artillery fire from Pritchard's. Better ground was on the left. Parallel and two miles west of the Pike was a low, partially wooded elevation called locally

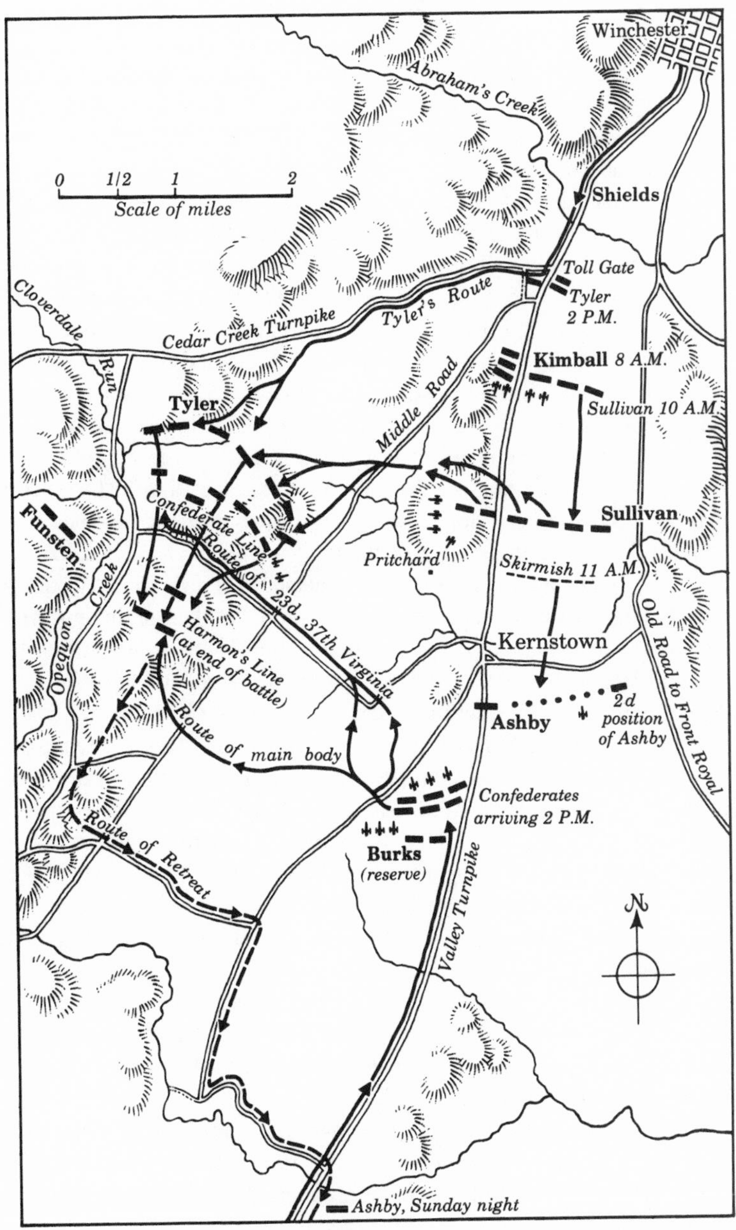

4. Battle of Kernstown, March 23, 1862

Redrawing of a map prepared under the direction of Jedediah Hotchkiss for William Allan's *History of the Campaign of General T. J. (Stonewall) Jackson in the Shenandoah Valley.*

Sandy Ridge. If Jackson could secure it he could challenge the Union position on Pritchard's or even pivot around the Federal right to wedge between them and Winchester. There was time for nothing more elaborate, and Jackson resolved to move to the left.

The first thing was to ensure that the approach to Sandy Ridge was open. Jackson found Fulkerson's little brigade in woods a half-mile west of the Pike; quickly he sent them farther to the west to scour another stand of timber. Perhaps because Fulkerson's command was so small—only 557 men present—Garnett was directed (or he thought he was directed) to add a regiment to this scout. Garnett deployed Colonel John Allen's 2d Virginia in support.[35] Captain Carpenter was tasked to send two guns as well.[36] Jackson scratched up 20 volunteers from the 2d Virginia and sent them out to watch for Yanks on the far left of the Army.[37] He also summoned Major Frank Jones of the 2d for special duty as a staff officer.[38] Jones was a Kernstown resident who knew the countryside; he could look across the Pike and see his front porch.

Other preparations were speedily finished. The four infantry companies that had fought under Ashby were returned to their regiments.[39] The cavalry chief was directed to send four mounted companies to the left to cooperate with Jackson and hurried them off under Major Funsten. Ashby remained with Chew's Battery and perhaps 150 riders to threaten the enemy along and east of the Pike.[40] In a field near a stone fence perpendicular to the Pike, Jackson arrayed his artillery. There it could cover the infantry lunge to the west and as well support Ashby's efforts to distract Federals east of the Pike. Colonel Burks's Brigade was stationed in rear of the guns to protect them and serve as Army reserve.[41] Word came from Fulkerson that he had found nothing in the woods between the rebels and Sandy Ridge,[42] and Jackson rode that way to start the offensive.

It was approximately 3:15 P.M. when Jackson reached Fulkerson's Brigade about a thousand yards west of the Pike. Probably on the way he halted to watch the two-gun detachment from Carpenter's Battery range in on Federal skirmishers in an old barn. The first shot arched gracefully through the barn door, scattering the enemy. "Good, good!" the gunners heard Jackson shout.[43] A few more shells caused what Carpenter estimated to be three Federal regiments, with cavalry, to retire to the north.[44] This was good shooting, and it was also one of several clues that Banks had more than four regiments on the field. Anyone from

Ashby to Sam Moore could have confirmed that the Yankees engaged that morning were serious fighters; the guns on Pritchard's Hill showed no sign of departing and in fact were directing their fire toward Fulkerson's command when Jackson rode up.[45] Such a powerful battery would not lack solid infantry support, which was apparently what Carpenter's two guns were shelling. Jackson might well have suspected a trap and retired; Confederate activity since midmorning was enough to worry Banks, all that was required of the Valley Army by Johnston.

Still, there had been sources believed by past experience to be reliable who reported that the enemy was weak, and not to storm ahead was to take counsel of fear. That Jackson did not do. Instead he attacked. Almost directly north and distant about a mile from where he found Fulkerson was Pritchard's Hill; a little more than a mile to the west of Fulkerson lay Sandy Ridge. Fulkerson heard Jackson say he wanted him to "turn a battery"—surely the guns on Pritchard's Hill—and that he would be "supported" by Garnett's Brigade.[46] Jackson then dashed to locate the cavalry on this wing. Major Funsten was in the area with 140 horses under spur; the general directed him to hold his command in readiness to charge if the Federals were driven off.[47] Jackson also took personal control of the Army's artillery. As the most experienced gunner on the field, Jackson decided he would give special attention to the cannons that day.[48] He sent Sandie Pendleton to instruct Fulkerson not to take his battery when he advanced, and a similar message went to Garnett.[49]

Some of Jackson's instructions were unclear to the men who received them, and they remain so today. The question of exactly what Fulkerson was ordered to do is an example. Later, after Fulkerson was dead, Jackson could not recall his precise instructions and would state under oath only that they were to the effect that Fulkerson's command "should lead in getting around the enemy's right flank."[50] In his written report Jackson revealed that his overall plan at the outset of the fight was to secure "a commanding position on the enemy's right, and thus, turning him by that flank, force him back from his strong position in front";[51] the document nowhere makes explicit that this was what Fulkerson was told. Fulkerson wrote in his report simply that he was told by Jackson to "turn a battery," a broad order properly allowing some discretion to the officer who must execute the mission; nonetheless, for Jackson to tell Fulkerson, a man with limited combat experience, to "turn" a powerful battery with five hundred soldiers was not necessarily the same thing as to send him to flank the enemy out of Winchester.

Comparably, Garnett did not understand Jackson's intentions. Garnett initially believed he was merely to detach one regiment to aid Fulkerson's push,[52] which he had done by sending over the 2d Virginia to help scout through the woods just west of the Pike. Jackson later denied such command, but he acknowledged that he failed to tell Garnett his plan before (or during) the battle and as well did not share with him his orders to Fulkerson.[53] Garnett also thought he was ordered to leave another regiment as an additional reserve with Burks near the first position of the artillery; he picked the 5th Virginia of Colonel William Harman.[54] Jackson recalled no such order, which certainly would have been totally inconsistent with the idea of bolstering Fulkerson for a successful turning movement.

Confusion was evident as Fulkerson formed lines pointing not west toward Sandy Ridge but northward toward Pritchard's Hill. He threw out skirmishers to tear down a plank fence barring the way and, sitting on his horse at the head of the column and lifting his hat, bellowed, "Men, follow me!"[55] The rebels raced into open fields directly in front of Pritchard's Hill, from which a galling fire was instantly opened. After pushing forward some distance Fulkerson swung to the left, with the right side of his column sweeping the Federal position. The rebels followed descending ground into meadows soft from the damp weather, and soggy ground and more fences slowed the advance while Union guns maintained a brisk fire. Fulkerson spotted a copse west of Pritchard's; he thought it might shelter his troops and altered his course to put trees between his men and the Union artillery. But he no sooner reached that point than another enemy battery standing in an open field beyond the copse opened a terrific fire. Fulkerson hurried his men still farther to the left, reaching woods on the foot of Sandy Ridge, only to have the enemy target this point as well. The men of the 23d and 37th would endure the bombardment for at least thirty minutes.[56] (This was another indication that Fulkerson had not understood he was to strike along the ridge; no commander would have remained under such punishing fire if he had specific orders to continue his drive.)

Garnett, who was ignorant of Fulkerson's mission, received Jackson's order "to support Fulkerson's command."[57] To Garnett it appeared Fulkerson was charging Pritchard's Hill, and he sprinted to deploy the three regiments still with him.[58] Colonel Ronald of the 4th and Cummings of the 33d[59] both were ordered into line of battle in the fields south of Pritchard's Hill; Cummings recalled advancing in line a short distance "immediately in the direction of the enemy's batteries."[60] As the 4th unfolded it was in advance of the 2d, and Garnett sent word for the 2d to break away from Fulkerson and join the Stonewall Brigade's advance.[61]

Maneuvering to threaten the enemy for Fulkerson's benefit, Garnett glimpsed what he took to be a strong column of infantry near the Union guns. He was not therefore surprised when Fulkerson veered westward instead of charging the guns; his assumption was that Fulkerson had decided a charge was impossible.[62] Garnett correspondingly shifted west with the 33d, expecting his other units would follow. To escape the deadly Union artillery Garnett deflected the 33d obliquely from Fulkerson's route, and by the change it found protection from a small rise partially blocking Federal fire. Garnett was several hundred yards distant from and to the south of Fulkerson's Brigade as he climbed Sandy Ridge; to gain protection from the enemy artillery he hustled the 33d over the crest. As he did, he lost sight of Fulkerson, and as Garnett looked around he realized as well his other units were not behind him; the last three regiments had not gotten the idea to follow.[63]

Unfortunately for Garnett, Jackson saw those three regiments in the open fields where he did not want them, and he dispatched Major Jones to lead them to Sandy Ridge.[64] Unable to find Garnett, Jones passed orders to the colonels, and the 2d, 4th, and 27th formed from battleline into columns and moved west after the 33d. Even on the ridge, however, the lack of precise orders thwarted action. Jones obviously knew nothing more to relate and rode back to the general. Colonel Allen sheltered his 2d Virginia in a safe place and went to find Garnett for orders.[65] The 4th Virginia was subjected to a fearful barrage as it climbed Sandy Ridge; Lieutenant Colonel Ronald was thrown and badly injured when his horse ran away with him. Time was lost while Major A. G. Pendleton assumed command and determined what to do.[66] The 27th happened to reach the ridge near a rock fence; Colonel Echols saw Carpenter's Battery approaching and set his men to pulling down the fence so the guns could pass. Jackson came trotting up and assumed this was Garnett's lead regiment. Stonewall was angered that Garnett was not with it and gave orders directly to Echols to cover Carpenter's Battery, which moved northward.[67] Jackson's loose orders and Garnett's failure to keep track of three of his regiments had combined to bring the Southerners to Sandy Ridge in no condition to sweep around the enemy flank. During the thirty minutes that Fulkerson was being hammered by Union artillery, the Stonewall Brigade was fragmenting.

Confederate artillery, on the other hand, remained a powerful and compact force. There were more than twenty Southern cannons available, and Jackson was determined to get them into action. Stonewall personally directed Captain McLaughlin to lead his eight-gun Rockbridge Artillery to the left with no delay.[68] Carpenter's and Waters's batteries rolled also. As the guns rumbled across the meadows to Sandy Ridge Federal artillery found the range, and Southern cannoneers knew they would have a battle. There would be no easy walk into Winchester today.

Faces stiffened and breath grew shorter. Gamblers flung aside well-worn decks and fumbled with neglected Bibles. Double-timing along with the Rockbridge Artillery was a broad-shouldered nineteen-year-old, Edward Moore, who had joined the battery the previous Monday. He came from Washington College, where his father had tried to shelter him while his older brothers fought. Moore had tolerated this haven for as long as he could, found he was paying no attention, and won permission to enlist. He had been delighted with his first few days; the camaraderie of the battery was wonderful. Now he saw another side of army life. The concussion from an enemy shell battered Moore to his knees: "We began to feel that we were 'going in,'" Moore wrote, "and a most weakening effect it had on the stomach."[69]

Stomachs calm or trembling, the Rockbridge Artillery was quickly "in." The marshy ground slowed the tired battery horses, giving the guns on Pritchard's Hill a rich target. Lanty Blackford was running through that shelling: "I can form no idea of the number of shells that fell around us while crossing that terrible field," he wrote four days later. "I, with the rest, was too busy trying to get out of the way of them to count or notice their number much."[70] As the battery started up through woods toward the crest of Sandy Ridge the enemy found the exact range. One gun was disabled, and then a shell ripped into the horses pulling Moore's gun. The off-wheel horse was blown to atoms; the saddle horse was badly mangled and the driver's leg cut off. A man walking beside the gun lost a foot. "A white horse working in the lead looked more like a bay after the catastrophe. To one who had been in the army but five days and but five minutes under fire, this seemed an awful introduction," Moore recalled.[71]

While Moore and his companions worked to clear the mess and hitch up new horses, McLaughlin wheeled his six serviceable guns to the brow of the ridge and bombarded Pritchard's Hill. Jackson, probably having just started the 27th Virginia forward after Carpenter, rode to the sound of McLaughlin's guns. Unhappy that he could not see all Garnett's regiments surging toward the Federal rear, he dispatched Sandie Pendleton to locate Garnett,[72] then renewed his special attention to the artillery. At one point he was directly behind a howitzer of the Rockbridge Artillery. The piece was commanded by Sergeant Clem Fishburne, who could see plainly that the rounds from his little gun were not reaching the Yanks. Accomplishing nothing, Fishburne's crew pleaded to be allowed to get behind a close-by wall. Fishburne allowed it and found himself justifying an idle cannon to Stonewall Jackson. Keep firing, the general growled; let the enemy "know we are about."[73] Before Fishburne could reopen a round slammed into the battery, badly mangling driver John Wallace. As Wallace was carried to a field hospital Ed Moore's gun crew on its way forward passed him, "horribly torn by a shell but still alive."[74]

The Rockbridge Artillery finally had seven guns on ground equally as commanding as Pritchard's Hill. Waters's four-gun battery reached the area to add its weight, and enemy fire seemed to falter.[75] Southern gunners also started to drop shells among Union infantry that would be seen to the east. To protect the batteries Jackson brought up the 21st Virginia from Burks's reserve brigade. Sandy Ridge was occupied and the enemy "turned," but they were not running. The Confederate offensive must continue, so Jackson spurred to check the progress of the infantry he wanted to find charging for Winchester.

Instead of a charge, Jackson found only Joe Carpenter's combative little battery and the 27th Virginia, and both were stalled. Carpenter had reached Sandy Ridge without casualties and without infantry support. The Irish Battalion was supposed to accompany him, but somehow it broke apart, with the larger fragment taking position close to McLaughlin's guns.[76] Displaying some of the best offensive spirit that day, Carpenter tracked onward. A few hundred yards along the crest he found Federals and at once raked them. This flushed out more Union guns, but two or three rounds from only one of Carpenter's "alleged cannons" drove them off. Carpenter then directed his fire to chase away some enemy infantry and cavalry.[77] Close by was the 27th Virginia, which had pushed beyond Carpenter only to stir up what the skirmishers thought were five or six Northern regiments. Colonel Echols slipped his men back behind a stone wall just in time to repulse a Union counterattack, but the Federals kept up a steady fire, and for at least twenty minutes the 27th fought alone.[78] At about this time Sandie Pendleton found Jackson to report he had been unable to locate Garnett, although he had spoken to some of the regimental commanders.[79] A very angry general now grabbed Major Jones and told him to search the fields he knew from boyhood until he discovered Garnett and got him moving.[80]

Garnett would have welcomed those orders. After reaching Sandy Ridge with only the 33d Virginia and still without orders to do more than "support Fulkerson," Garnett galloped ahead to find him. He found the former judge bringing his men over the crest to the western slopes that sheltered the 33d. Garnett was ready to offer support, but Fulkerson was uncertain what to do. He had been dispatched to "turn" a battery, which he had done, only to be so roughly handled that he had retired to the same side of the ridge as Garnett. To charge the guns with his little command was manifestly suicide. He had reported his position to Jackson and was, according to Garnett, awaiting orders.[81] (If totally true, such statement confirms Fulkerson never understood that his mission was to advance along the ridge around the enemy and deepens the mystery of exactly what Jackson told him to do.)

Had Garnett been advised that the ultimate objective was to sweep along the ridge, he might have joined Fulkerson now to do it, but his conduct establishes that he had no such understanding. Garnett in fact felt he was serving no useful purpose where he was and told Fulkerson he was thinking of marching the 33d back to where he had last seen the bulk of his brigade. What prevented that shift was catching sight of some of McLaughlin's cannons going into action. Soon McLaughlin spied what he thought was an enemy column advancing toward the Pike, and he sent word to Garnett of this emergency.[82] At almost the same moment, Lieutenant Colonel Grigsby of the 27th found him. Grigsby had been sent by an alert Colonel Echols when Jackson personally ordered forward his regiment;[83] probably Echols assumed Garnett was out of touch and needed to know Jackson had tasked the 27th to support a battery. This was the first knowledge Garnett had of that assignment,[84] and it may have caused him to believe his regiments were now to support the artillery in its growing duel. Garnett in any event went to the Rockbridge Artillery, no doubt arriving while Jackson was on a different part of the field.[85] Garnett still was assessing the situation and reestablishing contact with his regiments when, at last, Jackson's peremptory orders to advance the Stonewall Brigade were brought by Major Jones. About 4:30 P.M., the main Confederate body began to thrust in the direction of Carpenter's Battery and the 27th Virginia.

The rebels quickly collided with Yanks plunging southward in awesome numbers. Colonel Fulkerson with his two regiments was moving through thick woods left of where Carpenter and the 27th were blasting away when the 37th spotted a Union regiment on the far side of a clearing. Opposing units both sprang for a stone wall in the middle of the field. The 37th won that race and delivered a point-blank volley. Private George C. Pile remembered the slaughter: "We were armed with the old smoothbore musket loaded with ball and three buckshot. The Yankees had now reached within fifty yards of the fence when we opened fire, and it appeared like every shot took effect and what was left of them retreated to the wood from which they came. As there was only a space between us of 200 yards the ground looked like it was covered with the dead and wounded."[86] The rebels reloaded and Fulkerson hunkered down to hold the far left of the position.

Garnett's regiments came on to establish the center of the Confederate battleline. The 4th Virginia aligned generally to the left of the 27th;[87] the 33d aligned right of the 27th, with the 2d Virginia to the right of the 33d.[88] Sam Moore found himself facing musketry for the second time that day as the 2d advanced: "We marched up to within 25 paces of [the enemy] line and planted ourselves, drove the enemy from before us and held our position," he boasted to his wife. In the ensuing minutes he twice cheated death as a minié ball blew his cap off and another ball fired from the side slammed into his back, nicking the backbone and perhaps leaving a fragment.[89] Moore stayed at his post and earned his colonel's commendation.[90]

The ball that injured Moore's back could have been fired by Federals below Pritchard's Hill, who would have been aiming into the sun toward the right flank of the Stonewall Brigade. That flank was in advance a hundred yards or so of the knob held by the Rockbridge

Artillery, the 21st Virginia, and the Irish Battalion (the right flank of the entire rebel position). In the gap was an open field littered with straw stacks; Garnett thought the ground dangerous and squeezed his regiments into cedars farther to the left for cover. Here the woods were thicker, and the units become intermingled.[91]

If Garnett's men were under fire from two directions the enemy assuredly was present in far greater numbers than four regiments, and the raging, swelling howl of the battle warned Jackson something was wrong. He dispatched Sandie Pendleton to reconnoiter. The lieutenant found a high point and estimated that Union numbers must exceed ten thousand—the Confederates had fallen into a trap. "Say nothing about it," came Stonewall's reply; "we are in for it."[92] Victory was impossible; Jackson had to worry about saving the Valley Army. The only chance was to hold out until dark, perhaps an hour away, then retreat under cover of night. There were still two regiments near the Pike, the 5th Virginia and the 42d Virginia from Burks's command; Burks's other regiment, the 48th Virginia, had been left with the wagon train some distance up the road, but it might join the fight if it moved quickly. Urgently Jackson moved to bring up his reserves.

On the firing line the Confederates were indeed "in for it" as men fought and ducked and died. The 2d Virginia's color bearer was killed: Lieutenant J. B. Davis clutched the flag and went down; Lieutenant R. H. Lee hoisted it and was struck.[93] Colonel Echols of the 27th was badly wounded. Colonel Burks, his uniform riddled, had a horse blasted from under him.[94]

From the guns of the Rockbridge Artillery on the right to Fulkerson's little command clinging to its stone wall on the far left, the battle seethed. The Federals were repulsed but came on again and again, lapping closer like the incoming tide. As they did, they tended to slow down and bunch together; George Baylor thought they were in ranks twenty deep.[95] John Casler of the 33d saw Yankees standing "so thick a bullet could hardly miss them if aimed low enough."[96] Along a fence that partially shielded John Worsham's company of the 21st Virginia men forgot to kneel and fought standing; soon they were straddling the fence to take better aim.[97]

The furious combat raged for more than an hour of appalling smoke and din. Many survivors would remark about the sheer noise of the battle, and Jackson himself wrote a few days later, "I do not recollect of ever having heard such a roar of musketry."[98] The rapid fire exhausted Southern ammunition. Rebels borrowed from wounded comrades or frisked the dead for cartridges, yet their volleys began to slacken. Toward 6 P.M. the pressure of the Union attacks became unstoppable.

Or so Richard Garnett believed. His men shot away their last rounds; Northern cavalry began to appear, and Garnett faced the worst choice of a commander: whether to abandon a battle that seemed lost, though he had no orders to do so, or to stand and die awaiting instructions or help. Jackson had gone to hurry up the reserves and could not be reached; nor were the reserves in sight. Just at dusk Garnett made his lonely decision and pulled the Stonewall Brigade to the rear. "Had I not done so," he later wrote, "we would have run imminent risk of being routed by superiority of numbers, which would have resulted probably in the loss of part of our artillery and also endangered our transportation."[99] In this belief he may very well have been correct.

Jackson too knew that the Army was in danger. Only minutes before the infantry fell back Jackson found Major Funsten with his small cavalry flank guard and ordered him to a position from whence he could charge if the line cracked.[100] The Rockbridge Artillery turned its fire to support the main infantry fight and protect the flank should the enemy try to turn it.[101] Preparing for the worst, however, Jackson still hoped for a miracle. He had sent Major Jones to guide the 5th Virginia to the front. It was the largest of the Army's regiments. With the 42d Virginia and perhaps the 48th, nearly one thousand muskets could yet enter the fight to buy time for an orderly retreat. Another five minutes would bring them into action. And then the 5th appeared! Gunner Clem Fishburne saw Jackson waving his cap and shouting, "Cheer the reinforcements!" as the first panting troops came into view.[102] Colonel Harman cantered up requesting orders. "Reinforce the infantry engaged!" exclaimed the general.[103]

But now there was no front to brace. Garnett's retirement compelled Fulkerson on his left and Burks on his right to withdraw. Fulkerson's men stumbled in the near dark over fences and around a millpond, partially losing cohesion while enemy cavalry began to snap up prisoners.[104] The retreat could not be stopped. Unaware that the fallback had been authorized, Jackson discovered Garnett moving to the rear with his regiments, cornered his subordinate, and rasped, "Why have you not rallied your men? Halt and rally."[105] Stonewall collared a drummer boy and made him beat the rally.[106] "Go back and give them the bayonet," he yelled to men who complained they had no ammunition.[107]

It was impossible to halt the Confederates amid the noise and night. Although most units managed to preserve their organization, the retreat accelerated. The Liberty Hall Volunteers streamed off the ridge with Lieutenant John Lyle sure at least a thousand Yankees were using him for target practice.[108] Union cavalry slipped around Major Funsten's little party and poured onto the field to scoop up prisoners.[109] Federal infantry snuck through the shadows to within a short distance of Waters's Battery and gave it a volley. The gunners limbered up and started to roll off; as they did one cannon overturned when a Yankee bullet killed a horse. Sergeant Charles Arnell strained to upright the wreck until Federals were fifty paces away, then cut the traces and whipped the rest of the team to safety.[110]

The Rockbridge Artillery was almost cut off. McLaughlin saw two or three Northern regiments maneuvering to the right to separate him from the Pike and opened a barrage of canister that sent the enemy reeling.[111] New Federal regiments stormed from the field of straw stacks to his front and musket balls began to pepper his gunners. McLaughlin dragged several of his pieces into line and loosed canister at 150 yards' distance, slaughtering numbers of the foe.[112] Still they charged on, dropping rebel gunners until there were not enough men around one piece to move it, and McLaughlin yelled to flee. Sergeant Fishburne's caisson did not get far before a wheel horse was hit. In a dying panic it dragged the team and carriage across a stump, flipping the piece over. Within seconds a Union regiment was shooting point-blank while Fishburne cut the team loose and headed for the Pike.[113]

Into this hell came the last fresh Confederates. After hearing Jackson's order to reinforce the engaged troops, Colonel Harman marched several hundred yards toward the sound of the fight. Major Jones rode ahead to relay the arrival of the 5th Virginia to Garnett. He encountered the brigadier, who muttered that there was little the regiment could do.[114] Jones evidently heard something that sounded like an order, because he returned to Harman and stated he should move to the left to occupy some wooded terrain. At this moment the vanguard of the 5th was beyond the edge of the woods, and Harman feared that a countermarch might be taken by the troops as a sign of retreat. Accordingly, he ordered the lead company to "file left" then "file left" again, which brought the column smoothly into the woods.[115] Sadly for Garnett, Jackson happened by and to him the maneuver looked like retreat. He located Harman and told him to hold his ground, a message promptly and independently reinforced by Garnett, who instructed Harman to hold and help cover the retreat.[116] It was never proven that Garnett instructed Harman to retreat. Harman denied it, but Jackson thought he had seen it, and at that instant Garnett's fate was sealed.

Harman was squarely athwart the enemy's path, and blue regiments were massing around him. The 42d Virginia came up and aligned on his right; the 48th never made it to the field, so no more than seven hundred muskets were loaded and ready when the blue tide smashed against them. Five, six, and sometimes seven Union battle flags billowed before the Southern line. The Virginians fought, withdrew, were raked in a cross fire, reformed, and fought again. They sacrificed almost 20 percent of their strength in as many minutes, but they gained the needed time.[117] The enemy halted when night fell, and Harman slipped behind Ashby's skirmishers.

The cavalry chief also had fought well. He had kept Chew's Battery in constant action, annoying the enemy infantry east of the Valley Pike while sometimes gaining ground. And as always with the cavalry, there was even a bit of sport. Lieutenant Thad Thrasher was galloping over the field when he scared up a fox; the creature darted toward the Union lines, but one of Ashby's men was not to be denied a good hunt. Thrasher chased the fox almost into enemy ranks, drawing a cheer from Federals who held their fire in salute.[118] But today the spirit of romantic adventure collided with reality. Ashby determined to drive in the extreme left of the enemy line, and Thrasher volunteered to join the dash since he had just been over the ground. The charge pushed the Yankee skirmishers in on their main supports, but Thad Thrasher died in the fray.[119] Ashby so harried the enemy on his front that afternoon that they made no serious attempt to turn the Confederate right flank or seize the trains. Last from the field, Ashby and Chew blasted away while the Southern infantry completed their escape. Editing his diary for publication years later, Private George Neese perhaps remembered his feeling at that hour and wrote, "Mother, Home, Heaven are all sweet words, but the grandest sentence I ever heard from mortal lips was uttered this evening by Captain Chew when he said, 'Boys, the battle is over.'"[120]

III

The Valley Army staggered back up the Pike marveling at the day's events. "It was a harder fight than Manassas," thought Sandie Pendleton;[121] "the most desperate time I ever was in," wrote George Harlow;[122] "the most terrific battle yet!" exclaimed Jim Edmondson.[123] The two hours of incessant musketry known as the Battle of Kernstown had cost the Confederates 455 dead and wounded and 263 captured, total losses of one quarter of those actively engaged.[124] (On a percent scale, the losses rivaled Southern casualties at Gettysburg.) Two guns were left on the field. Bull Paxton admitted to his wife, "We have had a severe fight today and were pretty badly whipped."[125]

Wandering through the darkness, one of Ashby's cavalrymen paused by a small fire and found himself warming hands next to Old Jack. The boy mustered his courage to speak: "The Yankees don't seem willing to quit Winchester, General."

"Winchester is a very pleasant place to stay in, sir," came the curt answer.

The trooper continued: "It was reported that they were retreating, but I guess they are retreating after us."

Jackson replied only, "I think I may say I am satisfied, sir."[126]

That satisfaction, amid the wreckage of a badly trounced army, might have been augury, except that it reflected a commonsense grasp of what had happened that day. Despite the unexpected enemy strength at Winchester, Jackson knew Union troops had been leaving the Valley. He had struck a very hard blow against the remaining Federals, and although his own force was battered, he believed the enemy had suffered more.[127] This battle could not be ignored, and it was logical to assume it would delay and perhaps prevent additional enemy departures from the Shenandoah. This was what Jackson had been ordered to do, and here lay the cause for his satisfaction.

History would show that Old Jack's estimate of the situation was essentially correct. Banks had been redeploying as called for by McClellan's Peninsula plan. One division of eleven thousand men (Major General John Sedgwick's, which was on loan to Banks only for the advance on Winchester[128]) had already rejoined McClellan, and other units were taking up positions along the Manassas Gap Railroad east of the Blue Ridge. Another division, Brigadier General Alpheus S.

Williams's, had left Winchester for Manassas Junction on March 22, and Banks had departed for Washington about noon on the day of the battle.

The last Federal unit at Winchester was Shields's Division of ten thousand. Ashby had overlooked it on March 22 because Shields had kept most of it well hidden and had craftily uncovered only a token force to meet the rebel cavalry. Shields, a doughty Irish immigrant from County Tyrone, was everything Banks was not. He had learned the business of a general well at the head of an infantry brigade during the Mexican War. Shields's troops were Midwestern farm boys who knew how to bide their time and how to complement an able general with tenacious fighting. Northern losses at Kernstown were 568 killed and wounded,[129] fewer than Jackson imagined. Shields, however, knew the Valley Army was sixty miles from Johnston and did not believe it would have ventured a battle without large reinforcements. Moreover, he had been impressed by the Valley Army's fighting spirit. He estimated the Confederates had flung eleven thousand men at him and called them the "flower of the Southern army."[130] Fearing a new attack in the morning, Shields sent couriers after Williams's Division with orders to turn around and march all night to reach Winchester by dawn of March 24.[131] Banks returned immediately.

McClellan wired approval of Williams's recall, for his Peninsula Campaign was supposed to be prefaced by pacification of the Shenandoah: "Push Jackson hard and drive him well beyond Strasburg, pursuing at least as far as Woodstock, and, if possible, with cavalry to Mount Jackson."[132] Unfortunately, Banks could not push Jackson as hard or as fast as McClellan needed, compelling McClellan to vastly expand his plans for the Shenandoah. On April 1 McClellan informed his Valley deputy:

> The change in affairs in the valley of the Shenandoah has rendered necessary a corresponding departure—temporarily at least—from the plan we some days since agreed upon [Banks's redeployment to Manassas]. . . . The most important thing at present is to throw Jackson well back, and then to assume such a position as to enable you to prevent his return. As soon as the railway communications are reestablished it will be probably important and advisable to move on Staunton, but this would require secure communications and a force of from 25,000 to 30,000 for active operations. It should also be nearly coincident with

> my own move on Richmond; at all events, not so long before it as to enable the rebels to concentrate on you and then return on me.[133]

McClellan had originally contemplated stationing only a few regiments along and north of the Manassas Gap Railroad. That territory was to serve as a buffer zone between Confederate partisans and vital Union communications along the Potomac. But now the "flower of the Southern army" was in the middle of that zone and McClellan was directing Banks to press one hundred miles to Staunton with twenty-five thousand men. Kernstown thus lured the Union to undertake an extended Shenandoah campaign; it transformed a buffer zone into an active, and unexpected, sector of operations. McClellan did not want and could not afford such a sector, because it entailed a two-pronged invasion of Virginia. Neither McClellan on the Peninsula nor Banks in the Valley could readily support the other, and the rebels, as McClellan was already noting warily, now had the opportunity to mass against either Union prong.

But a more immediate problem for McClellan was that of how to garrison Washington. He had a promise to keep to Mr. Lincoln that the city would be entirely secure when he left it, and Kernstown derailed the orderly flow of troops from the Shenandoah upon which he depended to keep his pledge. Some of what was about to be revealed would have come regardless of Kernstown, because McClellan had started to decrease the forces detailed for Washington almost as soon as his corps commanders settled on the number, but the failure to get Banks's divisions to Manassas drove McClellan from any pretense of compliance with the dispositions that his corps commanders had voted as necessary for the city's defense. On April 1 he gave Secretary of War Stanton a list indicating that 73,456 men were deployed in a long arc covering the capital. That figure was comfortably above the number approved by the corps commanders; unfortunately, the location of these men bore no relation to what was agreed upon—at least, to what Lincoln thought was agreed upon—in March. McClellan tallied 10,000 men for the covering detachment at Manassas, a detachment that was supposed to comprise 25,000. And it was evident from the list that virtually none of the men McClellan placed at Manassas on paper were there. Part of the force was to come from troops McClellan suggested the government bring down from Pennsylvania! The garrison in Washington, which was to be

30,000 men, counted less than 20,000. McClellan added detachments that were in fact spread over all of northern Virginia, including Banks's command, to reach his assuring total, but he could not camouflage the weakness of the units actually present around the capital.[134]

McClellan could not end these numerical machinations. To supply a token force at Manassas, he ordered four thousand men from the Washington garrison to that point on April 1. The next day the commander of the capital's defenses complained to Secretary Stanton that McClellan also had called on him to ready several of his best regiments for the Peninsula.[135] Without these units there would remain perhaps thirteen thousand or fourteen thousand enlisted men to hold the thirty miles of fortifications that ringed Washington. Stanton investigated and stumbled onto some incredible facts. There was not a single field battery in the city fit for service; the city's heavy artillery was manned by ill-trained infantry—the gunners had been shipped to the Peninsula; few cavalrymen in the District of Columbia had horses.[136] McClellan, it appeared, had used the requirement to garrison Washington as an opportunity to dump the sweepings of his army, untrained or half-equipped regiments he could not trust in the field. Stanton buttonholed the first generals he found and posed one question: Was Washington entirely secure? Their answer came back promptly: No.[137]

Lincoln's response to the information Stanton fed him shackled Union operations during the coming months. The president began to seek some means to establish the conditions under which the Peninsula Campaign was supposed to have begun—that is, fifty-five thousand men posted in and around Washington. Contrary to what Jackson's most enthusiastic admirers might assert, there is no evidence that Lincoln was concerned about the Valley Army at this time or, indeed, that he saw any immediate threat to Washington from any quarter. Lincoln simply was aware that his capital was not "entirely secure." The president wished to correct this, and he found the means in General Irvin McDowell's thirty-thousand-man corps.

Bad luck seemed to plague Irvin McDowell. He had been compelled by politicians to lead the Union army to Manassas and fight a battle he knew it was not ready to fight in July 1861. In 1862 McClellan had scheduled him to embark for the Peninsula last. McDowell was still waiting around Washington to board his transports two weeks after Kernstown, and Lincoln decided he would not go at all. The president severed him from McClellan's command for garrison duty around Manassas. McClellan went to his grave believing McDowell conspired to arrange this, which was not true but which poisoned relations between the men now commanding the two largest concentrations of Union troops in Virginia.

Concerning McDowell's detachment, McClellan protested frantically, but the president would not relent: "I do not forget," he wrote McClellan, "that I was satisfied with your arrangement to leave Banks at Manassas, but when that arrangement was broken up and nothing was substituted for it, of course I was not satisfied. I was constrained to substitute something for it myself." Lincoln added a pointed inquiry: "Do you really think I should permit the line from Richmond via Manassas Junction to this city to be entirely open, except what resistance could be presented by less than 20,000 unorganized troops?"[138]

Next, Lincoln stripped McClellan of command over Federal forces in northern Virginia and the Valley, and, by not appointing a successor, the president kept the job for himself. Lincoln narrowed McClellan's authority to the Army of the Potomac and its drive toward Richmond. McDowell and Banks, whose corps heretofore had acted directly under McClellan, were made independent of the Young Napoleon. Lincoln created an autonomous military department extending from Washington east to the Blue Ridge and south toward Richmond for McDowell. His immediate task was to garrison Manassas Junction, from whence he would eventually advance south to Fredericksburg. The Shenandoah was designated a separate department for Banks. His mission was to beat back Jackson.[139]

On March 11 Lincoln had carved out another independent department in Virginia. This one superseded the Department of Western Virginia in the Alleghenies and was known as the Mountain Department. Major General John C. Frémont, the famous "Pathfinder" who led America's 1848 expansion through the Rocky Mountains to California, was given command here,[140] largely because he had sold Lincoln the idea of a three-hundred-mile push through the Alleghenies to an important Confederate rail junction at Knoxville, Tennessee. (Frémont would quickly abandon his idea of trudging through the mountains in favor of an advance southward along the Shenandoah corridor, so that the Valley Army's second front, which had been relatively quiet since Shields had joined Banks, was about to come alive once more.) Frémont wanted reinforcements for his Knoxville adventure, and Lincoln provided them by detaching Brigadier General Louis Blenker's Division from McClellan; this transfer cost the Army of the Potomac another ten thousand men.[141]

No longer authorized to command his former subordinates McDowell, Banks, and Frémont, McClellan had reason to be concerned when he landed on the Peninsula in early April, and Kernstown was the source of his woes. That tiny battle had two immense results: it lured the Union to open and sustain a new sector of operations, and (an unexpected bonus for the South) it disarranged Washington's defense, setting the stage for Lincoln's crippling remedy. McClellan had hoped to clear the lower Shenandoah, get Banks to Manassas, and strike on the Peninsula with a united Army of the Potomac. But as of April 4 his Peninsula Campaign master plan was abandoned. It had been replaced with four separate Federal armies operating in four tight little compartments toward four different objectives. All four would be coordinated, if at all, by Lincoln and Stanton, men lacking any military experience.

Jackson, of course, could know nothing of the contortions into which the Union high command would twist itself as he stood by a campfire on the night of March 23 and batted away the questions of an annoying cavalryman. He never claimed that McDowell's delay around Washington was a result of Kernstown. Jackson after all was attempting to keep Banks in the Valley, the battle's first result, not to cause detachments from McClellan's army, the second result. Though generals are sometimes credited with power to divine such things, they often do not understand how their efforts interact with other influences to produce enemy reactions. It is thus proper to credit Stonewall with no more than he had done—which was a great deal: he moved swiftly and decisively to seize what could be an excellent opportunity to accomplish his assignment of retaining Banks in the Valley. Initiating the battle despite Confederate weakness and exhaustion following a hard march was a difficult command decision complicated by imperfect knowledge of the opponent's strength, but such a dilemma is normal in war. Jackson was correct to take the risk because it lay within a wider context that meant even defeat had fair expectation to accomplish the mission—which is what happened on March 23, 1862. Kernstown was among the most productive battles the South ever waged.

A victory in the largest sense, Kernstown as a battle was a tactical disappointment. The Valley Army was not well fought, and the fault in the first instance lay with Jackson. It should have been a straightforward matter to dispatch a turning wing of only six small regiments with three batteries. The bulk of the force was the Stonewall Brigade, which Jackson had maneuvered successfully for months. At Manassas the brigade numbered in excess of twenty-five hundred men; it is unlikely that the forces started on the flanking drive at Kernstown numbered more than two thousand. The difference in March 1862 was that Jackson was not merely a brigade commander; he now commanded an army and as such had many other duties—the flanks had to be guarded, the cavalry posted, the trains located, and a reserve created. He acted as well that day as his own chief of artillery.

In his rush to supervise an army, Stonewall failed to take time to make his intentions clear, a major mistake because his brigade commanders were not seasoned battle leaders. Moreover, many field officers of the regiments were absent, and brigade commanders would of necessity be challenged in supervising their units. The Army needed precise instructions, but Jackson jumbled the operation with orders that did not fully describe the mission for the brigade leaders to whom it was entrusted. To send nonveteran commanders with unclear orders to attack what proved to be three times their strength was to invite a predictable result. Whether Confederates moving compactly along Sandy Ridge thirty minutes earlier just might have driven the enemy into a hasty retreat is questionable, but the only chance Jackson had to attain anything close to this result was lost by muddled orders. Plainly Jackson had not mastered all the details of the leap from brigade to army command on March 23.

Others made mistakes as well. Jackson could attach no blame to Ashby for his erroneous information on Union strength; Shields had fooled other observers also. Yet it was troubling that Ashby apparently did not communicate enemy strength as it was developed in the morning combat of the 23d. Major Funsten's operation to guard the retreat late in the battle had not gone well, which enabled Union cavalry to reach the field unopposed. And, with at least six hundred men under his command,[142] Ashby had fewer than three hundred in action on March 23. When Jackson pressed this point Ashby admitted the absence of many men: he had supposed there would be no engagement until the next day and had ordered his companies to assemble accordingly. He also cited the poor physical condition of his men and horses because of insufficient food and rest during the preceding week of active skirmishing.[143]

Jackson had no criticism of Fulkerson; indeed, Fulkerson's command won Old Jack's special praise.[144] But apparently every time Jackson saw that brigade it was advancing, and this was usually sufficient for Stonewall's commendation. Questions could be raised why Fulkerson did not communicate with Garnett before he opened his drive. Nothing in army regulations prevented Fulkerson from coordinating with Garnett, and if time was a limitation Fulkerson could have sent by courier to the commander of the Stonewall Brigade (on whom he would have to rely for support) word of what he intended to do when he moved toward Pritchard's Hill. Moreover, it is a mystery why Fulkerson initially ran directly at the enemy guns. He could have used the same sheltering ridge that Garnett found for the 33d Virginia to approach Sandy Ridge and then work around Pritchard's in comparative safety; to choose instead to storm toward the enemy and then run across their front is a strange way to "turn" a battery. The murderous fire to which Fulkerson's men were subject on their charge several times broke the column, and while it is impossible to tabulate which casualties fell at any given stage of the battle, Fulkerson's lead regiment (the 37th Virginia) suffered the highest number of killed and wounded of any Southern unit.[145] A more experienced commander might have taken a different approach and spared some of those lives.

Garnett was equally unimpressive at times. He could, and did, justifiably complain that Jackson's secrecy confused the mission; considering what he was told—and not told—to do, Garnett probably reacted logically in setting out to support Fulkerson as he did. However, the four regiments he eventually gathered on Sandy Ridge numbered fewer than one thousand men, merely a good-sized regiment at the beginning of the war. It was not unreasonable to expect him to keep track of them, yet somehow he lost sight of three. And once on Sandy Ridge he had failed to march to the sound of the guns. Observance of that maxim could cover a multitude of errors in Jackson's army, but Garnett by his own admission thought of turning back.

Stonewall had shown with Loring and Gilham an intolerance of unaggressive subordinates. But Garnett had, in Jackson's view, been even more derelict: after all else he had retired at the climax of an engagement and then impeded the flow of reinforcements. Jackson brooded for a week over Garnett's unauthorized withdrawal of the Stonewall Brigade, then he gave Sandie Pendleton an order. Wrote Pendleton: "General Jackson directed me to go and arrest [Garnett] and relieve him from command for 'neglect of duty'"[146] This was the first hint of Jackson's attitude, and the news tore through the Valley Army like an exploding hand grenade.

Jackson's specifications of neglect were such as to, in Garnett's words, "blast my character both as a soldier and a man."[147] The brigadier was not even allowed to stay with the Army; Jackson sent him to the rear. Court-martial papers followed citing seven examples of Garnett's supposed neglect of duty: (1) that Garnett initially advanced after Fulkerson with four regiments, then left three behind and continued with only one, and then notified Fulkerson that it would be withdrawn; (2) that Garnett separated himself from his command so that Major Jones was unable to find him to convey orders; (3) that Garnett was not with his leading regiment as it entered battle; (4) that he did not have a regiment in supporting distance of his leading regiment as it entered battle; (5) that he allowed his regiments to become intermingled during the fight; (6) that "Garnett gave the order to fall back, when he should have encouraged his command to hold its position"; and (7) that as the 5th Virginia entered the fight pursuant to Jackson's orders Garnett ordered it to retreat.[148]

The gravamen of Jackson's complaint lay in the sixth specification, Garnett's unauthorized retreat. Jackson expected subordinates to follow orders, and a retreat during battle without specific direction was intolerable. Stonewall was livid about that, and anger may have caused him to include some questionable charges. There was, for example, no regulation that required Garnett to escort his lead regiment into battle. The first and fourth specifications reflect as much Jackson's unclear orders as anything about Garnett, while the intermingling of the troops was probably unavoidable from the terrain. Colonel Harman flatly denied that he was ordered by Garnett to retire.[149]

Whether Garnett was correct to retreat cannot be answered today. The reserves Jackson marshaled did successfully retard the enemy after the front collapsed; if Garnett had waited for them, the Confederates might have held on until night and retired under its cover with significantly fewer men lost as prisoners. Perhaps the two guns lost in the retreat could have been saved. On the other hand, Garnett's troops were out of ammunition when he pulled them to the rear. His regimental commanders unanimously asserted that he thereby saved not only the Stonewall Brigade but the whole Army, that if he had waited any longer the entire rebel line would have been overrun. The only criticism of Garnett from the rank and file who bore the weight of the Union onslaught was that he did not retire soon enough.[150] These considerations escaped Stonewall. Jackson thought Garnett had pampered the Stonewall Brigade during the past months, and now he saw Garnett as the cause of the Army's collapse. When Richmond suggested reinstating Garnett almost a month later, Jackson angrily replied, "I regard General Garnett as so incompetent a Brigade commander that, instead of building up a Brigade, a good one, if turned over to him, would actually deteriorate under the command."[151] This sort of invective was unusual for Jackson and explains why he was unwilling to give his subordinate the benefit of any doubt. Indeed, Jackson did not even conduct a complete investigation before he acted. Only the day after Garnett's arrest did the general summon Major Jones, a key witness, and grill him about his recollection of the battle.[152]

Garnett was fundamentally a good soldier and a brave man. No issue of his personal courage was ever raised. He was not as stern a disciplinarian as Jackson, but he had handled the Stonewall Brigade respectably for a number of months. It had not fallen apart as had other units during the Romney march. Garnett was certainly an unlucky man; Jackson seemed to be on the spot every time something went wrong. And he did retreat on his own at the height of a battle. A military hierarchy must react severely to such initiative, especially when it is not indisputably correct; such is the nature of any system dependent upon obedience. Garnett, a West Pointer, knew he risked the wrath of that system when he gave his unauthorized order to retire.

The affair proved the sorriest in the history of the Valley Army. At first the reason for the arrest was unknown, and the Stonewall Brigade reacted bitterly. For weeks Jackson was greeted by an icy silence whenever he encountered his old regiments.[153] And the military justice system of the Confederacy proceeded slowly. Garnett's requests for a speedy trial could not be met as the spring campaign prevented gathering a panel of sufficiently high ranking officers; on May 6 Garnett offered to waive all considerations of rank on the court, but nothing happened.[154] Meanwhile important witnesses (such as Colonel Fulkerson and Major Jones) were being killed off, and Garnett began to compile sworn statements from those who knew the facts in case of their death. A trial scheduled in July was postponed by operations, and it was August before a court convened. Jackson and Pendleton were subjected to harsh cross examination by Garnett himself, who scribbled on a transcript more than once the word "Lie" by Jackson's testimony. Further proceedings were interrupted by another clash with Banks (the Battle of Cedar Mountain), and soon the Confederates were on their way to Second Manassas. The trial was never resumed. Garnett eventually was given by Robert E. Lee command of a brigade in Longstreet's Corp. He died in front of Union cannons in Pickett's Charge at Gettysburg. A few weeks earlier he had been a pallbearer at Jackson's funeral.[155]

The Valley Army would see other days as desperate as Kernstown, but no one would think of retreat; this was the one positive legacy of Garnett's removal. By it, Jackson made explicit what he demanded on the battlefield. He assigned positions to be held regardless of the danger and regardless of the price. To pull back when the situation seems hopeless is a natural instinct; Jackson demanded that his officers suppress it.

With the same earnest spirit, Jackson did all he could against the immediate consequences of defeat on the night after Kernstown. He summoned the recently organized militia battalion forward from Mount Jackson. Dr. McGuire was told to take whatever army wagons he required to evacuate the wounded. A few hours later the surgeon reported he had been unable to locate sufficient transportation and some wounded might have to be abandoned. The general's answer was to impress civilian carriages.

"That requires time," McGuire warned.

"Make yourself easy about that," Jackson said. "This army stays here until the last wounded man is removed. Before I will leave them to the enemy, I will lose many more men."[156] The Valley Army would learn to do its duty under every circumstance.

7

RETREAT, REORGANIZATION, AND A QUESTION

I have cleaned my gun
and am ready to take another pull at the Yanks
when opportunity occurs.

—DICK WALDROP

By the morning of March 24 the Army had learned Jackson's lesson. The troops re-formed their regiments while wounded men fit to travel were evacuated; those unsafe to move were left with local civilians, and Dr. McGuire's fears that many would have to be abandoned were relieved.[1] Shortly after 10 A.M., the Army began its retreat in good order. The deep boom of artillery rolled out behind as Ashby and Chew challenged the advancing enemy, who could be seen from high spots along the Pike.[2] Ahead lay Cedar Creek, where the road was interrupted by a cold stream of shoulder depth. The bridge had been burned on the retreat from Winchester, and there was only a poor ford; infantrymen picked their way across planks set between charred timbers of the bridge while wagons, ambulances, and artillery muddied the ford, then the retreat seemed secure. Cavalry stayed north of the creek as Chew's Battery set up on a low hill half a mile south of the bridge, and rebels broke ranks for the first meal most had eaten in twenty-four hours.[3]

Tents and other gear were tossed out of vehicles to get at pots, and cooking fires soon dotted the area. The men were too hungry to worry about elevations north of the creek that dominated the lower ground on which stood their wagons; they needed food. Major Jones had just gotten a slab of bread and meat when he noticed Southern cavalry galloping his way; Private Ed Moore and his new messmates of the Rockbridge Artillery were wolfing down plates of beans when a Federal shell tore into their hillside. Both men could see that the enemy had hurled Ashby over Cedar Creek and unlimbered long-range guns on the high ground. Union cavalry was deploying as well.[4]

What followed could have dwarfed the losses suffered in yesterday's battle. Panic erupted among rebel teamsters, who sped off, some with steam whirling from camp kettles swinging wildly about their wagons. They jammed the Valley Pike and stalled the cannons that tried to follow. Chew's pieces could not match the Yanks, and two long-range guns of the Rockbridge Artillery were ordered to return fire. Watkins Kearns of the 27th Virginia was writing in his diary as it happened: "The enemy get our range and throw shell at us with fearful effect. Two or three burst in our regiment killing Sgt. Robertson . . . and others in other companies and wounding several. All is confusion. Our batteries are replying with what effect we know not."[5]

Infantry sprinted for the rear by a sheltered trail, but Union guns bombarded them as well: "The 2d and 5th moved to the right and wound around amongst the hills, but our direction was seen and afforded a fine target for the enemy. . . . The 27th was cut in two and 6 men killed, or reported so, left . . . on the field as there was no time to recover them," recorded Major Jones.[6] The Rockbridge Artillery probably saved the day by drawing enemy fire; one man had his horse blown to bits as shells came screaming at him. Ed Moore's gun dropped a round into Union cavalry and then fled; he remembered passing several horribly mangled soldiers, one with clothes still aflame.[7]

With the sure instinct of a man whose survival depends on the work of others, Lanty Blackford thought, "There was criminal neglect somewhere in not letting us know sooner of the close advance of the enemy. We ran imminent risk of losing all our baggage and artillery, it seemed to me, owing to nothing in the world but the neglect of the proper authorities to give us orders to move sooner." Slowed by the wagon train ahead, Blackford kept thinking of the massed Union riders: "Few things are more painful to anticipate than being cut to pieces by cavalry for no reason but the carelessness of one or two men. . . . At one time I was almost confident we were done for and the general feeling among officers and men about me was for a half an hour one of calm desperation."[8] A spirited Federal drive could have inflicted serious casualties, but the enemy did not exploit the near panic, and the Army reached safety another six miles up the Pike.

This incident was one of the few in the Valley Army's history for which there is no record of Jackson's whereabouts, but he must have learned of it, and it could only have increased his doubts about the cavalry's effectiveness. It was the cavalry's role to provide a proper cushion between the Union advance and the Army's rear, and in this Ashby failed. The lapse could not be blamed on losses at Kernstown since only seven riders were killed or wounded there. And that there were problems with the cavalry could not be denied. Much trouble lay in a want of basic equipment. A few days before Kernstown one trooper had carried the spirit of knightly adventure to its illogical extreme by charging the enemy bareback armed with a club. Ashby inquired about weapons for his unarmed boys after this escapade, though he did not press his requests.[9] Certainly his role as a combat leader provided little time to grapple with requisitions, although more probably Ashby did not comprehend enough of military bureaucracy to know he must pursue them tirelessly. Whatever the cause, Ashby's regiment was not getting any better, and around this time Jackson felt it necessary to ask other commanders if they could spare some cavalry.[10]

Looking beyond the problems with the cavalry, Jackson discovered solid support for gratification over the outcome of Kernstown. The enemy was keeping strong forces arrayed against him. In his report of Kernstown to Johnston, which omitted mention of the ragged Southern retreat, Jackson stressed this concentration: "Though Winchester was not recovered, yet the more important object for the present, that of calling back troops that were leaving the valley, and thus preventing a junction of Banks' command with other forces, was accomplished."[11] There was even brief hope of reinforcement for Jackson: after learning of Kernstown Johnston started 5,000 men toward the Shenandoah. (Increasing demands for his attention elsewhere caused Johnston to cancel the redeployment before it was well begun.) Jackson could, however, note with pride that the Confederate Congress voted a resolution of thanks to the Valley Army for its "gallant and meritorious service in the successful engagement with a greatly superior force of enemy, near Kernstown."[12] The Valley Army was running an uncommonly good sideshow.

On March 26 the Federal pursuit column retired a few miles, and Jackson leaped after it.[13] He was told by informers fresh from across the lines that the enemy was under the impression his army was retreating to Staunton preparatory to joining Johnston. "I will try and correct this error," Jackson assured Johnston.[14] Of course, Old Jack knew he could only correct it for the present with bluster, because the ravaged Valley Army could not risk another stand-up battle now. It was in fact inevitably due for a long retreat. Its hope was that bluster would win time for a slow retreat during which to mobilize the Shenandoah.

Ashby rendered valuable help in the quest for time by developing an effective scheme to hinder Banks. Ashby stationed Chew's horse battery on a commanding hilltop to challenge the Federals whenever they advanced. The cavalry waited nearby to pounce on any enemy mounted detachment, which cowed the Federals into deploying their cumbersome infantry. When that slow process was nearing completion, Chew galloped off to another hill—and there were hundreds of hillocks in the Valley—for a repetition. Not until April 1 did Banks lurch beyond Woodstock. Ashby jumped him at once and played with the Union vanguard all day. This skirmish eventually ended at Stony Creek, where Chew furiously shelled the Yanks, Ashby's riders merrily burned a bridge over the creek, and the Federals came on too slowly to save it.[15]

The day before, Jed Hotchkiss had surveyed Stony Creek as part of the mapmaking project Jackson had assigned him and found it to be an excellent position from which to delay Banks.[16] The stream was deep and wide, and a quarter-mile to the south were wooded hills offering rebel snipers good concealment. It was a comfortable seven miles north of Mount Jackson and ten miles north of Rude's Hill. Jackson concurred with Hotchkiss. He delegated the defense of this line to Ashby and sent an infantry brigade to assist. The balance of the Army was planted on the crest of Rude's Hill, so that the Confederates were formidably positioned. Ashby was well placed along Stony Creek to keep the enemy out of Mount Jackson for some days. Should the Federals push into Mount Jackson, Stonewall hoped to slow them again by destroying the bridge over the moatlike North Fork of the Shenandoah. And between the river and the Southern lines atop Rude's the ground lay as flat as a Midwestern prairie, completely exposed to rebel artillery. Banks ground to a halt in front of these lines and gave Jackson more precious time.

Jackson had a use for every hour Banks allowed him: his militia needed time for drill; his skeleton regiments needed time to rest and refit; his quartermaster required time to concentrate the Army's stores at Staunton, out of the enemy's path.

Among the most important equipment hurried south now was a

giant Baltimore & Ohio locomotive, the 199. With other B & O rolling stock, some of it captured in Jackson's great haul at Harpers Ferry, the 199 had found its way to Mount Jackson. Stonewall wanted to get this valuable engine to Staunton, and the only way was up the Valley Pike. Squads of scavenger machinists went to work. They hoisted the locomotive with jacks, stripped everything removable except the rear driver wheels, swung it around, and lowered it onto the Pike. The strongest teams in the Valley were hitched to the engine by means of an ingenious rigging of front wheels and a chain with harnesses of forty horses. These stood more than one hundred feet ahead of the locomotive in ten rows of four animals abreast. A teamster mounted every fourth horse, and the chief engineer gave them a signal to start.

The 199 screeched a few hundred yards along the Valley Pike to the brink of its first obstacle, a sharp descent just south of Mount Jackson. With whatever brakes it had left squealing, the iron behemoth slid down that slope and came to rest upright and headed in the proper direction. By the time the lathered horses had dragged it a quarter-mile farther, fully onto the Shenandoah's North Fork bridge, that structure threatened to collapse and save Jackson the trouble of burning it. But his engineers threw together some pulleys and settled the 199 once again on the Valley Pike. Here it cracked the macadam surface and listed into the dirt beneath, to be reclaimed by the indefatigable engineers with jacks and timbers. Next came the pull up the thirty-degree incline of Rude's Hill, where hundreds of soldiers and civilians alike were impressed to man drag ropes.

After many long hours the 199 gained the summit of Rude's Hill, having come a total distance of two miles; ahead lay forty more miles of rolling hills. The crew was greeted along the way by open-mouthed children, frantic dogs, and old men who told them that a locomotive could not be dragged cross-country. The gainsayers seemed vindicated at the last moment, when the 199 broke loose and overturned only two blocks from its destination in Staunton. It lay mired in spongy earth like some prehistoric monster caught in a tar pit, but it was to be freed in a matter of days and put to work on Confederate lines; it would in fact survive the war and remain in service for many years.[17]

Wiser after their first effort, rebels whisked other rolling stock south from Mount Jackson, and the equivalent of several trains eventually were hauled up the Pike. Southerners even developed a certain flair for this kind of work, and soon no one marveled at it. Sandie Pendleton noted casually in a letter one day: "As I looked out of the window just now, I saw a railroad car traveling up the turnpike, showing what war can do."[18]

The Army's April rebuilding also brought an overhaul of its brigade commanders. General Johnston ironically picked this juncture to return to the Valley William Taliaferro, the politically influential colonel who had railed bitterly about the occupation of Romney, with the stars of a brigadier general on his collar and orders to reassume the 3d Brigade, which Colonel Fulkerson was rendering efficient. It was now Jackson's turn to protest, and he even went outside normal channels to do so. He objected directly to General Samuel Cooper, adjutant general of all Confederate armies, and sent the same statement via Johnston.[19] It did no good. Richmond insisted Taliaferro resume his former command. Fortunately, Taliaferro's attitude had improved, and he would demonstrate that the Romney spirit was gone. Jackson also sought a replacement for Colonel Burks, who had departed the 2d Brigade on extended sick leave, but he got no action and so left the brigade under its senior colonel, John Campbell of the 48th Virginia. Campbell was an 1844 graduate of V.M.I. who like so many others had found advancement through the law rather than the military. He studied law at the University of Virginia and had become a judge before the war. Of military service he had none prior to 1861, but he had campaigned in western Virginia before coming to the Army with Loring.[20]

Burks's Brigade might have been assigned to a new officer, Brigadier General Charles S. Winder, who reached the Army on April 1, except that Jackson utilized his arrival to be rid of Garnett. Winder reported to Headquarters that morning, almost simultaneously with word from Ashby of the skirmishing that ended with his cavalry defending Stony Creek.[21] For a time a serious engagement threatened; the Stonewall Brigade was ordered to succor Ashby, and Jackson wanted Garnett gone before any new battle. He dispatched Sandie Pendleton to arrest the latter and told Winder to lead the Stonewall Brigade to Ashby.[22]

A West Pointer, Winder had earned a captaincy in the prewar army at the early age of twenty-six, had fought Indians in Washington territory, and was regarded as something of a martinet. The regiment he led before reporting to the Valley, the 6th South Carolina, was among the

Confederacy's best. Tall and broad shouldered, with a high forehead, Winder was as good an officer as Jackson could have wished. He especially shared Stonewall's mania for discipline. What Winder's new commander and his new soldiers would never have imagined is how terribly he missed his family; his diary was filled with sorrow at separation from his children, whom he lovingly referred to as his "pets."

No battle erupted on Winder's first day, but the sudden arrest of Garnett hit the Stonewall Brigade like a thunderbolt. Regimental officers hurried to Garnett's tent to voice support and express their astonishment.[23] Garnett's popularity meant that Winder took command of troops that were in a foul mood. Jackson had laid the groundwork for more tension a few days earlier by reducing the Army's wagon trains. Despite Major Harman's excellent work, Jackson was adamant about increasing the Army's mobility by reducing its transportation. To do that meant all tents and much other personal baggage could no longer be carried and had to go, and Winder caught the resentment. When he passed the 33d Virginia Winder was hooted by John Casler and some comrades: "More baggage, more baggage."[24] On another occasion Winder was openly hissed. He ignored the malcontents and found their colonel. Should such incidents continue, Winder said, he would be held responsible.[25] The disturbances ceased. Winder went on to demand absolute enforcement of regulations, even to the point of classifying those who overstayed furloughs as deserters.[26]

Similar reforms were occurring throughout the Army. The troops muttered about new and harsher regulations, but their grumblings could not mask a growing will to prevail. His back still painful from his Kernstown wound, Sam Moore took little time to recover, marched out with his company when Ashby needed it to bolster his picket lines, and decided he would not be distracted from duty even to write home unless he was guaranteed a delivery. Instead, he wrote to his wife, he would focus solely on the war: "I shall throw away all idle dreamings, and set my face firmly to the discharge of my duties to my country, and shall march straight forward on the battlefield as one whose hopes of this world have passed away and who now only looks to that world which is to come for the reward of faith."[27]

Such were the thoughts of veterans. Observant Bull Paxton wrote of his regiment: "The soldiers . . . seem to exhibit the appearance of contentment and happiness. A mode of life which once seemed so strange and unnatural, habit has made familiar to us, and if peace ever comes many of them will be disqualified for a life of industry."[28] Captain John Graybill obtained a discharge from the service on April 23 and was writing within five days: "I have found the world more monotonous than I supposed. However, I am in fine spirits and hope to soon take the field again."[29] Shortly he did, joining the cavalry.

Life with Ashby was ever more attractive during the spring of 1862. The paladin learned he could sneak cannons and skirmishers though woods below Stony Creek and drop shells among Federals on the other bank, and he made it a frequent practice to do so.[30] Old Jack rotated one brigade with artillery support to the front every three days to back such operations. The entire Army thus got training in close-range picket work and, more dramatically, had a chance to watch Ashby.

John Worsham's company of the 21st Virginia was easing into the forward sentry posts one afternoon when the chieftain cantered by and instructed them not to fire unless Federals advanced. Accompanied only by a youthful courier, he rode out to reconnoiter and drew hostile fire. His aide's mount was shot dead. Ashby calmly told the boy to loosen the girth and carry away his tack. Ashby sat motionless under a hot fire until the task was finished, then turned and went back in a leisurely fashion to Southern lines.[31] On another occasion Ashby remained under enemy fire with absolute indifference while he munched his breakfast. When cautioned, he merely replied, "Never mind that . . . I am very hungry."[32] Ashby's example had the expected effect on his men, who were generally fearless under his direct command, although they tended not to repeat his example when he was elsewhere.

Ashby's style was well suited to impeding Union progress up the Valley, but even he could not retard Banks forever, and Jackson continued to think about the future. He summarized the Valley sector for Major General James Longstreet (who temporarily commanded Johnston's army when the latter was called to confer with President Davis in early April) as follows: Banks was spread along the Valley Pike from Winchester to Stony Creek, where both sides held strong positions.[33] With his present force Jackson could not hope to do more than draw Banks farther on, but given reinforcements—Jackson requested an impossible seventeen thousand men from Longstreet—Jackson thought he could strike Banks's rear. If only he had the manpower, Jackson wrote, "I could so threaten the enemy's rear as to induce him to fall back and thus enable me to attack him whilst retreating. . . . But, if the number asked for is not available, any that you send will, under Providence, have my best efforts expended upon it, and no stone shall be left unturned to give us success." To this crisp summary of his intentions Jackson added a significant cap: "If Banks is defeated it may greatly retard McClellan's movements."[34]

It is unclear whether Jackson here referenced the evolutions of McDowell's forces around Manassas or something much more dangerous. For a time McDowell's forces gave the appearance of a full pursuit of Johnston, but on the morning after Kernstown Federal steamers began to disgorge McClellan's army at the tip of the Peninsula, and Confederate attention turned to that region. All doubt of Union intentions was removed on April 4, when McClellan lurched up the Peninsula toward Richmond. That brought an urgent summons from Richmond for Johnston to combine his forces with those already opposing McClellan between the York and James rivers. Sequestered in the Valley, Jackson heard little of these events save what Longstreet shared with him, and Stonewall must have awaited eagerly a message to specify exactly what the high command now wanted him to accomplish.

The answer to that question would shift several times during the coming weeks; but the first version almost caused the loss of the Shenandoah. In early April, just as Banks ground to a halt before the Confederates' Stony Creek lines, Johnston ordered Jackson to leave the Valley and move east of the Blue Ridge if the enemy continued to press him.[35] Had Banks pushed just a little longer, the rebels might have completely abandoned his area, but Banks stopped, so Jackson stayed. By the second week in April Johnston was thinking about the Valley again and, before departing for the Peninsula, he dispatched new instructions. What must be done now was to preserve the agricultural riches of the Shenandoah and central Virginia for the main army. The Commissary Department, for example, calculated that ten thousand head of cattle could be gleaned from the Valley and the counties east of it. Johnston intended to station Major General Richard S. Ewell's Division to cover the region east of the Valley; Ewell would be posted along the Rapidan River near the town of Orange. Johnston's orders for the Valley Army contemplated slowing Banks in order to shield Staunton and the Virginia Central Railroad, one of the capital's principal supply conduits. Should Banks press onward vigorously, Jackson was to retire to Swift Run Gap (in the Blue Ridge twenty miles east of Harrisonburg); there he was empowered to summon Ewell and offer battle so as to keep the rail lines open and also to prevent Union forces from redeploying to other fronts.[36]

Several days later Johnston was on the Peninsula, and Jackson initiated his working relationship with General Ewell. On April 10 he penned the first of many notes to Ewell to inform him the Shenandoah was quiet but that he expected to fall back if Banks showed any initiative.[37] Jackson and Ewell began corresponding over the complexities of Shenandoah geography two days later. The also pooled their intelligence on a new Union force, Blenker's Division, which appeared to be en route to Banks from the Manassas region.[38]

These letters were interrupted by a burst of Federal activity. A Union detachment boldly forded the upper reaches of Stony Creek on April 16. Near a foundry called Columbia Furnace they snared virtually all of a sleeping rebel cavalry company. Ashby's troopers had not posted pickets and were completely surprised; fifty men, their horses, and equipment were lost.[39] Afraid this sudden Northern bravado signaled the arrival of Blenker's ten thousand men, Jackson retired his advanced infantry and artillery to the main line at Rude's Hill. He alerted Ashby to give up Stony Creek if pressed, and Major Harman prepared remaining rail assets at Mount Jackson for destruction.[40]

Before dawn on April 17 massed battalions of Federal infantry stormed Ashby's defenses, and the troopers galloped for Rude's, stopping only to chuck torches into the railcars. Union cavalry was close enough behind them to save several engines,[41] and the Federals stormed onward.

The North Fork of the Shenandoah was the last barrier between Banks and Rude's Hill, and it would not be a barrier unless the bridge over it was demolished. Ashby had entrusted this mission to Captain John Winfield, who paced nervously among twelve of his men at the bridge's southern end and watched smoke billowing from the railyard to the north. Chew's guns and the last gray cavalry clattered over the bridge. Winfield's detail hastily tore some flooring; Ashby stirred a torch into a pile of kindling. As flames slowly grew the rebels formed a line across the mouth of the bridge.

"Hold your fire," Winfield shouted.

At the last second: "Boys, pick your man like a squirrel in a tree, and FIRE!"[42]

Yanks fell on the far edge of the span, but they were too many to stop. Union riders swarmed across the bridge, stamped out the flames, and pounced on Ashby's troopers. Desperate hand-to-hand fighting followed. George Neese's crew unlimbered half a mile away but dared not fire as the opposing forces were completely tangled. Ashby was charged by four Yanks; one of their bullets hit his horse in the lungs and threw it into a death panic. The chieftain was almost taken while he struggled to regain control, but a dismounted rebel ran out of the swirling dust and smoke to drop one assailant. Captain G. W. Koontz and Private Harry Hatcher each picked off another Yank; the fourth disappeared.[43]

More Union squadrons dashed across the smoldering bridge, and the rebels were flung back upon Rude's. Captain Winfield swore the Yankees were not more than a saber's length away as he ran. Neese heard the metallic rattle of their scabbards above the rumble of his sprinting cannon.[44] Ashby fell behind them all; to those watching from the Confederate lines he appeared to be leading the Union attack. No other horseman could have escaped on a dying mount, but Ashby did it. He was the last man to enter the range of Southern guns on Rude's, which opened fire and blunted the Union onslaught. Dappled with sweat and blood, the magnificent charger carried Ashby by the roaring cannons and dropped. The cavalryman gave it a quick end, then sent for a huge black beast that few others could even mount. By nightfall souvenir hunters plucked the dead steed's mane bare.[45] "Thus," remembered one Southerner, "the most splendid horseman I ever saw lost the most beautiful war-horse I ever saw."[46]

It was a sad encounter for Jackson too. A vital crossing had been lost, and within hours a long-range Federal battery was pounding Rude's. If such unusual aggressiveness indicated that Blenker's command had swollen Banks's army to over thirty thousand men, the Valley Army was outnumbered five or more to one. Even the advantage of high ground would not compensate for this, and Jackson decided the time had come to head for the Blue Ridge in anticipation of uniting with Ewell's force. At 2:50 P.M. Jackson directed Ewell to move for Swift Run Gap, to which the Valley Army was already retiring.[47]

It was a ragged withdrawal: "it looks more like a rout than an army," growled Major Harman about the retiring column.[48] There was superfluous baggage everywhere, and Jackson personally superintended a division of the trains. All unnecessary items were directed to Staunton, and as soon as that convoy passed the North River, which flowed between Harrisonburg and Staunton, bridges offering easy access to the latter were torched. The remaining trains lurched eastward toward Swift Run Gap under a heavy rainstorm. One of Ashby's troopers got wildly drunk and tried to break into a civilian's home; the owner shot him dead.[49] A dejected column of infantry, dismayed at leaving their homes, progressed only a few miles from New Market.

The retreat resumed in the morning; fortunately Banks did not pursue. Nonetheless, Gunner Ed Moore would remember this march more often than any other of the war. It was almost surreal, for the shower had dampened the earth so that the marchers, and even artillery wheels, made little sound. "Our road lay along the edge of a forest occasionally winding in and out of it," Moore wrote. "At the more open places we could see the Blue Ridge in the near distance. . . . Here and there on the roadside was the home of a soldier, in which he had just passed probably his last night. I distinctly recall now the sobs of a wife or mother as she moved about, preparing a meal for her husband or son, and the thoughts it gave rise to."[50] The Army made its campfires on the evening of April 19 in Swift Run Gap near the hamlet of Conrad's Store.

The new position exceeded Rude's Hill in natural strength. The Confederates lay between spurs of the Blue Ridge that were pathless and gave the Army secure flanks. The rebels' camp was on the east side of the South Fork River, and there was only one bridge over that stream, a wooden structure around which Conrad's Store had grown up. Jackson did not anticipate that Banks would steel himself to attack such a position.[51] He also thought he would check Banks's drive toward Staunton from this base, since the cautious Yankee would not want to expose his rear to the Valley Army at Swift Run Gap by moving south from Harrisonburg. A month-long retreat of almost one hundred miles had taken the Army to a haven where, for a little while, it would be safe.

II

If the strength of the new position could be relied upon, early warning if Banks approached could not. Despite Ashby's heroics, the Valley cavalry daily was becoming less useful for tasks normally assigned to the mounted arm, and that in turn compelled Jackson to supervise its work. On April 19 Jackson for the first time dispatched one of his staff officers to direct the cavalry on an important mission. North of Conrad's Store lay a series of bridges on the South Fork of the Shenandoah: closest was a wooden structure known from its bright paint as the Red Bridge; near a crossroads called Honeyville six miles farther north was Columbia Bridge; and beyond it opposite the village of Luray was the so-called White House Bridge, named for a small stone house that had stood nearby for generations. Jackson wanted to raze these spans to keep Banks out of the Luray Valley and ordered Hotchkiss to do the work. This was not the sort of thing a mapmaker routinely handled, but Jackson trusted Hotchkiss. He told him he could employ all Southern cavalry in the Luray Valley for the raid, although he would have to find them first since Jackson had no idea where they were.

Hotchkiss eventually located the companies of Captains George Sheetz and Macon Jordon in an old foundry, where Jordon and most of his boys were guzzling applejack. With more than the usual hoopla the riders responded to Hotchkiss's orders and wove off toward the Red Bridge. There a detail separated to prepare the span for burning while the rest of the column proceeded downstream. Hotchkiss sensed trouble near Honeyville, concealed his men, and explained the need for a careful scout. The troopers soon loped back with assurances that the enemy was nowhere around. Hotchkiss sent Sheetz to burn Columbia Bridge and told Jordon to sober up his company.

Unfortunately there was no time to sober up. The scouts had overlooked a Union task force of infantry, artillery, and cavalry. Federal dragoons surprised Sheetz on the span and flung him back upon the main body. Hotchkiss had only enough warning to tell Jordon to get his company into line while he rode out to count the enemy. Instead of forming his men, the besotted Jordon trotted after Hotchkiss. Federals swept up the road, caught the rebels unprepared, and drove them off in a panic. "Our men broke at once except some 3 or 4, and a perfect stampede of them took place; the enemy pursu[ed] for 3 miles; every attempt to rally was unavailing, some men actually throwing away their guns, many their coats, blankets. . . . I never saw a more disgraceful affair—all owing no doubt to the state of intoxication of some of the men, and to the want of discipline," wrote Hotchkiss. Some drunks were so terrified they scampered over the Blue Ridge and did not rejoin the Army for days. Hotchkiss managed to outrun the Federals and burn Red Bridge as he retraced his steps to Swift Run Gap, but the two other structures were untouched. Hotchkiss complained to his wife in a letter that evening: "When Ashby's men are with him they behave gallantly, but when they are away they lack the inspiration of his presence, and being undisciplined, they often fail to do any good."[52]

The mapmaker's report of this fiasco to Jackson was as blunt as his letter home, and it was nearly concurrent with receipt by the general of an inquiry from Richmond. The assistant adjutant general wanted to know if Ashby really had twenty-one companies and only one other field-grade officer. He pointed out that if the men were to be well drilled there must be sufficient officers; Jackson's early attention to the matter was "desired."[53] The cavalry's indiscipline was beginning to attract unwelcome scrutiny, and on April 24 Jackson sought to correct the situation with this order:

> The General Commanding hereby orders Companies (A–K) of Ashby's cavalry to report to Brigadier-General Taliaferro, and to be attached to his command; the other companies of the same command will report to Brigadier-General Winder, to be attached to his command. Colonel Turner Ashby will command the advance-guard of the Army of the Valley when on an advance, and the rear-guard when in retreat, applying to Generals Taliaferro and Winder for troops whenever they may be needed.[54]

In effect, Ashby was stripped of his regiment. Winder and Taliaferro would see to the supply and training of the riders, while Ashby was left to borrow his men when needed.

Jackson's decision was as unexpected as the snowstorm that hit the Valley that same day,[55] and as well again revealed his inability to work skillfully with subordinates. There is no evidence that Jackson offered explanation or even advance notice of his action to Ashby, and the result was the expected one. The enraged cavalryman stormed into his own headquarters, kicked some shavings onto the fire, and slumped before it in a black mood. Hotchkiss found him in this mood and listened as Ashby complained about Stonewall mistreating him by ordering that the cavalry be drilled. "He seemed to think," recorded Hotchkiss, "that although he had so many companies he could easily manage them all himself and that it was [unnecessary] to have them drilled."[56] Ashby was bitter and seethed that his command was organized under special permission from the War Department and that Jackson could not legally interfere. Ashby's regimental surgeon tramped in from the cold to hear Ashby pouting that if he were of equal rank with Jackson he would challenge him to a duel.[57] That, of course, was impossible, but Ashby did strike a blow: he sent General Winder his resignation to be forwarded to Jackson. With it went the resignation of Major Funsten.

This news traveled fast. John Harman revealed his sympathies as he informed his brother in Staunton, "A great calamity has befallen us; there is a rupture between Ashby and Jackson. . . . Ashby will not submit, and we are in great danger from our cracked-brained Genl."[58] Tired of brooding by evening, Ashby spurred to see Jackson.[59]

Two men from different worlds confronted each other at Headquarters. Ashby was a courageous loner. His was a world in which freeholders banded together in times of peril, drove off their foemen, and trotted home—just as Ashby did when rowdy railroad workers menaced his neighborhood during the 1850s. Jackson the West Pointer was imbued with the traditions of the professional army, in which obedience and regularity were core values. Ashby was at heart a cavalier. He rejoiced at acts of courage and admired them in an opponent. Never was his concept of a leader better expressed than when he advised his surgeon that a commander "should go to the front and take risks in order to keep his men up to the mark."[60] Jackson was more pragmatic. He once heard a rebel officer regret that his men had shot a gallant Federal who was doing just what Ashby prescribed. Jackson instantly rebuked the Confederate: "Shoot them all, I do not want [the enemy] to be brave."[61] Jackson the flint-eyed disciplinarian made his infantry as solid as any in the Confederacy; Ashby the cavalier stunted his riders at a tournament mentality.

Ashby's was a dying tradition, but it was to survive a little longer. The meeting with Jackson did not resolve their problem, and the cavalier stomped from Headquarters amid talk of quitting the Valley Army and organizing a new, totally separate command. This prospect stirred General Winder to intervene. Winder gave himself a headache on the twenty-fifth shuttling between Army Headquarters and Ashby, doubtless providing the latter a chance to talk out his anger. Winder got something like a promise from Ashby to drill his troopers,[62] and Jackson agreed to "detail" the cavalry back to Ashby. Jackson thus saved face, since the cavalry technically continued under his direction, but Ashby in fact resumed unfettered command. As he had no concern with paper organization anyway, his dignity was assuaged. There was actually little else Jackson could do. Every Valley trooper would want to follow Ashby if he left, and if denied they would be too demoralized to do any good. Ashby withdrew his resignation (as did Major Funsten) and the impasse was settled, Major Harman chuckled, "by Gen'l. Jackson backing square down."[63]

New problems emerged as the Army reorganized itself under the provisos of Southern draft laws. The inevitable disorder in such a reshuffling was compounded by conflicting laws from the Confederate and Virginia governments. The South was attempting a general conscription, the first such experiment in American history, and it was a confusing process. During the preceding weeks, Virginia had canvassed its male population; on March 10 Virginia had drafted forty thousand of these militia to fill "volunteer" units. The result of these moves was to bring the militia into the volunteer army. Volunteers had the option to either reenlist or wait out their terms, at which time they were mustered out of the army and rostered with the militia. But since militiamen were being siphoned off to fill depleted volunteer units, a mustering out was followed by a mustering back in, frequently back into the same company and for the duration of the war.[64] The earlier plan of the Confederate Congress, the Furlough and Bounty Act, also applied to Virginians. It granted reenlistees furloughs, bounties, and the right to change their branch of service. Many of those who stayed with the Valley Army through Kernstown did so seeking some loophole in the Virginia law or waiting to switch their branch. At virtually the last moment, April 21, the Confederate Congress dashed these hopes by enacting national conscription of all males without the transfer privilege but with the right to elect company and regimental officers.[65]

This rolling barrage of legislation hit everyone, even Jackson's Headquarters Guard. It had taken such heavy losses that it needed a large infusion of militia draftees. Thirty-three conscripts joined one day, with more slated to arrive the next. The original volunteers learned that the new men, who would have a majority by morning, planned a block vote for their own candidates in the election of company officers. The volunteers howled to their regimental commander, Colonel Charles Ronald, and got swift relief. Ronald scheduled the election that night, and after he managed to have all sentries released from Headquarters duty, the volunteers fielded a majority of two.[66] Those two votes swung the election for captain to a veteran, devout Hugh White. White, whose ambition was to attend divinity school, accepted the job with serious qualms. He found many things about army life "irksome."[67] He had no formal military education and assumed his duties with only the preparation of his months of service with the regiment and a willingness to learn the work of a captain. Not all units chose even this well; some proven officers were defeated and a few unfit men elevated.

Elections were only one of the difficulties created by the spring regrouping of Southern armies. Many men joining the ranks came without equipment, posing new burdens for quartermasters such as Major Harman. Equally often the new soldiers arrived overburdened by well-meaning relatives who actually had provided little of use. One veteran described in later years how his father, who should have known better after long years of service in the United States Army, allowed parental feelings to overrule judgment as he collected a kit for his son: "He took great pains in getting what was necessary for me. The baggage of a private . . . was not extensive. How little was needed my father, even at that time, did not know, for though he was very careful in providing me with the least amount he thought necessary, I soon found by experience that he had given me a great deal too much."[68]

The caring father was Robert E. Lee, who a few days after Kernstown sent off his eighteen-year-old son Robert Jr. to the Rockbridge Artillery as a private. The superb reputation of the battery actually lured too many talented recruits. Dr. McGuire's brother joined, as did the son of Congressman Alexander Boteler. Soon there were too many men for the six remaining guns, so it was decided to convert the unit into an artillery battalion of three batteries. New companies were organized, captains were elected, and everything was arranged; then the additional cannons were not delivered. A second set of elections had to be conducted, and Lieutenant William Poague won the captaincy. "A strict, efficient, and gallant officer, and a polished and agreeable gentleman," was Private Blackford's opinion of his new commander.[69] A twenty-six-year-old graduate of Lexington's Washington College, Poague was a member of the bar of Saint Joseph, Missouri, when the war erupted. He had served with the battery from its early days, and he was the obvious choice to replace Captain McLaughlin, who declined reelection.

Poague's first challenge was to pare the battery down to 150 men; those not selected were transferred or detailed to guard prisoners.[70]

The reorganization was debilitating for Ashby's cavalry because the scramble to join persisted regardless of a ban on switching service branch written into the draft laws. On April 21, for example, almost an entire cavalry company was organized of former Stonewall Brigade infantrymen.[71] Men who showed initiative raising the new units tended to command, and so the venturesome, if inexperienced, Harry Gilmor, who had risen from private to sergeant in four months, was elected leader of a company he gathered; on March 27 he became one of Ashby's captains at age twenty-four.[72] Gilmor's unit was among the more than twenty companies of Ashby's regiment; the precise number cannot be determined, but estimates ranged at the time from twenty to twenty-six companies.[73] Whatever the total, it was at least twice normal regimental size and more than Ashby could discipline, train, equip, and lead in battle. Yet Ashby did not realize or would not admit that his command had grown beyond his ability to control.

The Army's reorganization extended over the next weeks, and lingering bitterness from aspects of it would occasionally hamper operations. No brigade ended April under the same officer who led it at Kernstown, and nearly half the regiments had new commanders. In some units the men simply voted out stern disciplinarians, but mostly they had the wisdom to retain good leaders. The always earnest Captain Sam Moore was given proof that his efforts to mold his company of the 2d Virginia Infantry were paying off; he was reelected without a dissenting vote.[74]

Many even tolerated the process with humor. In Chew's Battery George Neese found himself elected to the post of chief gunner. Years later, he recalled this as a good joke: "I know very little about gunnery, in fact, nothing except that a gun in good health never shoots backward." He resolved to learn but did not expect much success mastering the technical principles of artillery science: "I can plainly see that if I ever acquire any efficient knowledge of practical gunnery it will have to be gathered on the battlefield, a rather dangerous place to be experimenting with fireworks. . . . If any Yanks should happen to get hurt by my first attempt at gunnery, it will be their fault, not mine."[75]

There was humor, and there was hope. The Army was becoming ready for a campaign. Esprit de corps was rising; rather than being broken at Kernstown, morale was boosted, since the men believed they had fended off fifteen thousand to twenty thousand Yankees that day. Wrote Captain Moore: "Taking it all together it was a splendid affair on our side; instead of discouraging us it has given us fresh confidence in our ability to meet the invaders."[76] As word of Kernstown spread up the Valley, hundreds of furloughed men hastened to ranks. Offers of help arrived from as far away as Lexington, where Superintendent Francis H. Smith of the Virginia Military Institute tendered the service of the Corps of Cadets.[77] Another reinforcement, the 10th Virginia, came from Johnston's army. Recruited from the Valley, the 10th served through the winter with Johnston and agitated constantly to be returned to defense of its home. It finally won a transfer and on April 21 marched into Swift Run Gap to become part of Taliaferro's Brigade. The newcomers were swiftly assailed with dire yarns about life under Stonewall. The 10th would soon get enough of it, John Casler taunted: Old Jack would make them earn their bread.[78]

Though the cavalry was inefficient and some infantry were bitter about conscription, the Army's overall condition was better than might have been anticipated a month earlier. Men returning from furloughs, volunteers, and draftees brought its foot strength to roughly eighty-five hundred by the end of April,[79] and Ashby counted perhaps one thousand riders. The trains were lightened and mobility enhanced by discarding much cumbersome baggage. The troops had been toughened at Kernstown and during the retreat. Most important, the Shenandoah's citizen soldiers were ready for a real fight. The militia, which Jackson had distrusted since the beginning of the war, was integrated into regular units. The process of elections and luring volunteers to reenlist with furloughs was passing, and soon everyone would be in "for the duration."

Several notable additions to the staff complemented the reorganization. With strong recommendations from his friend Sandie Pendleton, Henry Douglas, a practicing lawyer before his twenty-first birthday and recently a lieutenant with the 2d Virginia, joined as special aide to the Army's inspector general. A "wide awake, smart young man" in the eyes of Hotchkiss,[80] Douglas was another of the sons of clergymen whom Jackson tended to choose for his assistants. Also called was Lieutenant Colonel Stapleton Crutchfield, who became chief of artillery. Perhaps Kernstown had convinced Jackson he needed someone to manage the Army's guns, the task now given to Crutchfield. Once a student under Jackson at V.M.I., Crutchfield subsequently served on the faculty with him there, and his abilities were so considerable that Stonewall even overlooked the fact that he liked to sleep late.[81]

The duties of adjutant general had been handled on a temporary basis since Colonel Preston's departure, and Jackson now filled this post. Equivalent to the modern chief of staff, the job exacted tedious yet vital attention to detail; not until late April did Jackson find his man, the Reverend Robert L. Dabney. Educated at Hampden-Sidney College, the University of Virginia, and Union Theological Seminary, Dabney was a brilliant theologian of national reputation who possessed no military experience save a brief stint as a regimental chaplain in the summer of 1861. He had returned to seminary only to have the war take most of his students, and Dabney was looking to be of service. Jackson heard of it and posted an offer to Dabney to be his adjutant. Dabney traveled to Swift Run Gap to dissuade Stonewall by admitting his ignorance of things military. Nonsense, said Jackson: "Rest today and study the Articles of War and begin tomorrow."[82] Only Major Harman could argue at Valley Army Headquarters, and Dabney took the assignment with the rank of major.

The appointment sparked a round of quipping by the Army's more irreverent soldiers. Among them was the new colonel of the 27th Virginia, Andrew Jackson Grigsby, who joked, "I concluded that Old Jack must be a fatalist sure enough when he put an Ironside Presbyterian parson as his chief of staff. But I have bright hopes of headquarters, seeing they are no longer omniscient."[83] A man of great intellect, Dabney tried hard, but his efforts were not always appreciated. Long after the war Douglas believed Sandie Pendleton accomplished most of the work and jotted in the margin of a book on Jackson that none of the staff knew what Dabney really did.[84]

Postwar jealousies aside, the staff Jackson assembled was one of the best of any army. These aides, like any staff, struggled with the paperwork Stonewall generated—an incessant toil of "'Publish a General Order to be ready to march at Dawn,' 'Send your pickets on the Luray road to watch the enemy,' 'Give Mr. Thingambob a pass,'" was how Sandie Pendleton described the office duty[85]—but they had other cares as well. Orders too important for the lighthearted messengers provided by Ashby were carried by Jackson's aides. They were often found helping steady the line in battle, and some staffers graduated to field command. Douglas carried a Union bullet from Gettysburg to the end of the war, at which time he commanded an infantry brigade. Colonel Crutchfield lost a leg at Chancellorsville, returned to the service, and hobbled along on the retreat to Appomattox; he died commanding a brigade four days before Lee surrendered.

Lacking a trained cadre of junior officers who could be trusted with major details away from the Army, Jackson often delegated these duties to his staff. This was becoming particularly true with Ashby's cavalry, and during the weeks ahead Jackson's staffers would often find themselves in front of a mounted column. Much more than paper monitors, Jackson's staff members were extensions of the general on and off the battlefield, and their zeal and competence helped immeasurably to take the reorganized Army intact and victorious through grim tests that awaited.

III

"My plan is to put on as bold a front as possible and to use every means in my power to prevent [Banks's] advance whilst our reorganization is going on. . . . What I desire is to hold the country as far as practicable until we are in a condition to advance, and then, with God's blessing, let us [make] thorough work of it."[86] Thus had Jackson outlined his vision to Alexander Boteler before leaving Winchester, and much had been done to fulfill the preliminaries. Yet as surely as the plan offered hope, it contained an insistent question: What next? The Valley Army was as ready to advance as could be hoped, but much of the Shenandoah had been surrendered. The Army's presence in the Valley amounted to a bridgehead across the South Fork opposite Conrad's Store, and rumors persisted that this toehold would be relinquished and the Army withdrawn toward Richmond. The rebels wondered, What next?

Even had Old Jack been disposed to answer such a question, he would have been without a reply when the Army arrived at Swift Run Gap, because more variables than ever before were then at play. In the first place, Jackson once again had to think, as when occupying Winchester, of the quandary posed by dual Union thrusts against a vital Southern asset, in this case the railhead at Staunton. Banks reached Harrisonburg by April 21, where he was only twenty-five miles north of Staunton. And in the Alleghenies Union troops commanded by Brigadier General R. H. Milroy were pressing toward Staunton from the west. (This was the lead element of the army of John C. Frémont, who wanted to begin his march up the Valley toward Knoxville, Tennessee, from Staunton.) Milroy was opposed by the remnant of the Army of the Northwest under Brigadier General Edward Johnson, known to his troops as "Allegheny" after his many months of service in that theater.

Banks's advance, which had forced Jackson to abandon Rude's Hill on the seventeenth, made cooperation with Edward Johnson vital, but it was slow to develop. Stonewall apparently did not alert Johnson of his retreat until the morning of the eighteenth,[87] at which time he asked Johnson to join him in Harrisonburg to coordinate operations.[88] Allegheny came on the nineteenth but found no Valley Army in Harrisonburg and rode on to meet Jackson at Swift Run Gap. He struck one rebel he passed as a "large and rather rough looking man,"[89] an accurate enough description, but no one questioned his abilities as a soldier. An 1838 graduate of West Point, Johnston had seen action in most of the major battles of the Mexican War and at posts from the Dakotas to California after it. His first assignment after secession was as colonel of the 12th Georgia Infantry, which he moved to the Alleghenies early in the war, and he had not left those mountains since. After Loring redeployed to Winchester, Johnson barred a Union approach to the Valley at a tough little battle in December 1861, soundly defeating Union General Milroy. Now the fruits of that victory were being lost, and under growing pressure Johnson was retreating upon Staunton. When he met Jackson on the evening of April 19, Johnson's three thousand men occupied fortifications atop Shenandoah Mountain some twenty-five miles west of Staunton.

Johnson's camp was between Banks to the north and Frémont to the west, a predicament Jackson and Johnson addressed in a lengthy conference.[90] They probably concluded that Banks was unlikely to drive on Staunton and thereby expose his lines of communication to Jackson at Swift Run Gap, but they could see other Union options. Banks might thrust far enough south to threaten Johnson's rear so that he would have to retire, handing Staunton to Frémont by default. (Unknown to the Southern generals, something very like that was happening even as they conferred.) Banks and Frémont could try to unite via a road that ran southwest from Harrisonburg (the Harrisonburg and Warm Springs

Turnpike); such a juncture could give them a force of almost forty thousand men. Jackson feared this move most, for the Valley Army could do little to protect either Johnson or Staunton against such a host. It was also conceivable that Frémont might defeat Johnson and take Staunton regardless of Banks or Jackson. There seemed no remedy against these permutations, and the meeting ended without a decision as to future operations.

Jackson got more bad news on April 21, news that compelled him to think beyond Banks and Frémont, Johnson and Staunton to a new situation developing east of the Shenandoah. On that day he learned that Federals were massing on the Rappahannock River opposite Fredericksburg. Five thousand of McDowell's men were there, and the bulk of his command was joining them overland from Manassas. Because Fredericksburg was less than sixty miles directly north of Richmond, the Confederate high command anticipated that McDowell would open a second front against the capital. A stopgap force under Brigadier General Charles Field had been assembled to resist McDowell, but it had already burned the Rappanahannock bridges and retired some distance south of the river.[91]

Profoundly disturbing, the letter that worried Stonewall with this information bore the signature of Robert E. Lee, and in this there was encouragement. Lee at the time was largely unknown beyond the borders of Virginia. The war thus far had been a succession of thankless tasks for him: a hectic mobilization of Virginia, a hopeless campaign in the Alleghenies (with some of the same regiments now under Stonewall), and a fight against impossible odds along the Atlantic seaboard. He recently had left the coast for Richmond and another lackluster assignment, Commanding General of Confederate Armies. Impressive in title only, the post tied him to a desk in Richmond bereft of clearly defined authority. The job at best made Lee an adviser to the president and a worst his military handmaiden, although as the position evolved Lee came—more by custom than specific authority—to supervise some forces remote from Richmond.[92]

It was not exciting duty, yet Lee gave it his best, and in fact he performed services of great value at this post. He had first begun to notice the Valley when Banks forced Jackson away from Rude's Hill. As a result Lee feared for a time that Banks would succeed in occupying Staunton,[93] and in seeking a solution to that and other problems Lee observed the dispersion of Confederate forces across central Virginia and the Valley. While Johnston retained overall command of this theater of operations, he was so ensnared on the Peninsula that he had not communicated with Jackson since early April and had written only once to Ewell.[94] With great skill, Lee moved to fill the vacuum. In his letter briefing Jackson on the Northern concentration opposite Fredericksburg, he advanced a basic goal for Stonewall. The threat to Richmond from Fredericksburg must be overcome.[95] The South could not stand an enemy onslaught from the Rappahannock, which would almost certainly bring the loss of Richmond and the destruction of Johnston's army. To avoid this, Southern forces in central Virginia must be united. Lee suggested that Jackson could join with Ewell's forces to reduce the pressure from Fredericksburg by routing Banks.[96] Lee reasoned, no doubt, that Banks's defeat would expose McDowell's deep flank behind the Rappahannock and thereby discourage any Union attempt to thrust southward from the river.

Jackson replied to Lee's letter of April 21 two days later, explaining that he did not think he could be much help. He pointed out the threat that Banks posed from the north to Staunton's rail link with Richmond; Jackson in turn menaced any direct move against Staunton by Banks, but Stonewall could not do much more than posture without Ewell. Jackson's intention remained to attack some exposed portion of Banks's army or, voicing a possibility that increasingly intrigued him, a maneuver into the Federal rear. Unfortunately, Banks afforded no opportunity at present for a blow, and Jackson offered Lee nothing better than hope the enemy would make a careless move. He added that his offensive notions violated the spirit of Johnston's orders of early April.[97] Later that day Jackson received more details of the daunting odds facing General Fields outside Fredericksburg. Seeing no chance of action in the Valley, Jackson wrote Lee again to suggest that Ewell might be used to best advantage with Fields.[98] Against the possibility of orders for Ewell to move eastward, Jackson already had halted Ewell's march to Swift Run Gap and told him to await instructions.[99]

These messages were uncharacteristically negative for the truculent Jackson. Lee was not able to disguise a note of disappointment in his next dispatch, dated April 25: "I have hoped in the present divided condition of the enemy's forces that a successful blow may be dealt them by a rapid combination of our troops before they [the enemy] can be strengthened themselves either in their position or by reinforcements." Lee left the chance for success of such a combination in the Valley to Jackson's estimate. He noted that Southern intelligence indicated the North had weakened its forces twenty-five miles northwest of Fredericksburg at Warrenton; Jackson and Ewell might lunge at this point. If this was not feasible, Ewell could join Field, for whom Lee was prying eight thousand men from other sectors, and deliver a surprise attack at Fredericksburg. Lee did not insist that Jackson choose any of these alternatives and emphasized that he only made suggestions as to how McDowell might be neutralized. But he concluded his letter in a manner than must have fired Jackson's imagination: "The blow, wherever struck, must, to be successful, be sudden and heavy. The troops used must be efficient and light."[100]

Jackson mulled over this letter, for it subtly yet significantly expanded his mission. Johnston's instructions of early April were defensive: protect lines of supply from the Shenandoah to Richmond, divert Banks, but give battle in the Blue Ridge where the chance of a severe defeat was lessened. Lee now proposed that Jackson strike, and strike beyond the Valley if necessary, two things Johnston had not explicitly authorized. Guided by Lee's vision Jackson would no longer endeavor just to retard enemy progress up the Valley; rather, he was to attack at a place of his own choosing as an integral part of Richmond's defense. What Lee urged might bring all Johnston desired, but it would be more dangerous than awaiting Banks atop the Blue Ridge and could put Jackson beyond the point where Johnston could reinforce him, or he Johnston.

But everything continued to change! Banks had inched his way into Harrisonburg by the time Jackson received Lee's letter of the twenty-fifth. In response, Jackson directed Ewell to resume his march toward the Blue Ridge.[101] Marking these changes, Jackson could summarize the overall situation as follows: two campaigns were under way in Virginia. One belonged to McClellan, who had established himself on the Peninsula and ground forward fifteen miles to Yorktown, site of the Revolutionary War siege. There he had been bluffed to a halt by a theatrical little rebel garrison that put on a facade of great strength. The delay enabled Johnston to arrive at Yorktown, and the main armies faced each other in siege lines fifty miles southeast of Richmond. McClellan's tortoiselike advance did not surprise Jackson; he remembered him from

West Point and told his staff, "McClellan lacks nerve."[102] This was true, but McClellan did have one hundred thousand men and dozens of heavy guns, muscle enough to dictate the pace at which his campaign would proceed. Johnston had about fifty-five thousand men and was seeking to stay out of McClellan's grasp; Johnston was already anticipating another retreat nearer the capital. McDowell's forces were rapidly mustering at Fredericksburg, preparing, Jackson supposed, to join McClellan by an overland descent upon Richmond from the north. McDowell's numbers would soon exceed thirty thousand; Field had fewer than twelve thousand, even after the reinforcements provided by Lee joined him.

The second campaign in the Old Dominion was that of the Valley Army, and unlike the first, it was at a rough equilibrium. Banks could not go on to Staunton with the rebels at Swift Run Gap; the rebels were too weak to drive Banks out of the Shenandoah. But the first side to maneuver wisely might upset this balance in its favor. Banks had twenty-two thousand men at Harrisonburg, and what he intended was unknown. Jackson was relieved to note, however, that Blenker's Division (which had been ordered to join Frémont) had passed through the Valley and had not joined Banks as Jackson had feared when the rebels retreated from Rude's Hill. Finally, Milroy's approximately three-thousand-man vanguard of Frémont's forces (about twenty thousand total when joined by Blenker) was pressing Edward Johnson back toward Staunton and threatening to upset the tenuous Valley balance.

Old Jack's calculations demonstrated that at least 160,000 Federals were ranged across Virginia; perhaps half that number of Confederates opposed them. Such odds could only be redressed by maneuver, and Jackson and Ewell led the only movable Southern columns. Johnston, Field, and Edward Johnson were each nailed in place by powerful Union forces. The war had unfolded so that, at this particular movement, only Jackson, with Ewell, was free to move. The Valley Campaign that Jackson had been waging since the evacuation of Winchester was the only offensive means available to stop McClellan's Peninsula Campaign. But the war continued to spread, and Stonewall had to act before Ewell was called to plug some new gash.[103]

Swift action in the Shenandoah was needed for still another reason. Since the Valley Army had evacuated Rude's Hill, Banks had been boasting that the rebels had fled the Valley. He reported to War Secre-

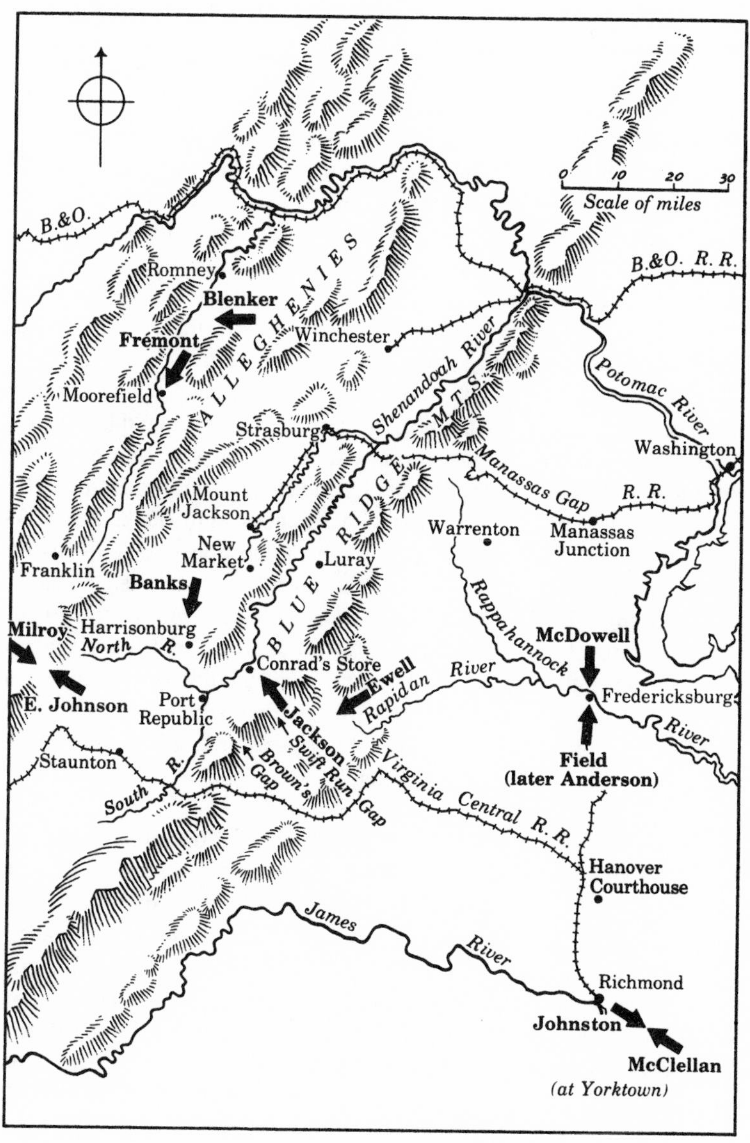

5. General Situation, April 30, 1862

tary Stanton on April 19: "I believe Jackson left this valley yesterday."[104] On April 22: "Jackson has abandoned the valley of Virginia permanently, *en route* for Gordonsville."[105] On April 24, Banks placed Jackson near Stanardsville, east of the Blue Ridge.[106] On April 30 he claimed, "Jackson is bound for Richmond. This is a fact, I have no doubt. . . . There is nothing to be done in this valley this side of fortifications on this side of Strasburg."[107] Banks overstated his case slightly, since Jackson was clinging to his Shenandoah toehold at Swift Run Gap, but there was no question that the Valley Army had been pushed well south. Union rail and canal communications across the lower Shenandoah were fully restored by the end of April, and all that was asked of Banks after Kernstown seemed accomplished.

Abraham Lincoln therefore reasoned that Banks's redeployment from the Shenandoah, contemplated before Kernstown, could be revived. Rather than leading to garrison duty around Manassas, however, this shift was to provide reinforcements for McClellan, who wailed daily for the return of McDowell's divisions. Assurances from Banks that Jackson had departed the Valley offered Lincoln an opportunity to answer McClellan's pleas, and on May 1 the president transferred Shields's Division from Banks to McDowell. Once he was joined by Shields (Shields's march would be by way of Front Royal and the Manassas Gap), McDowell, with forty thousand men, would push south from Fredericksburg to join McClellan in the final attack on Richmond. Banks was to retire to Strasburg with his gravely reduced force, entrench well, and police the Potomac frontier.[108]

Lincoln's new plan was exactly what Lee predicted from Fredericksburg in his letter of April 25, and it was the reason he kept prodding Jackson to strike somewhere in central Virginia or the Valley. Stonewall's blow would, it was hoped, dislocate whatever the North planned from Fredericksburg by stripping McDowell's flank and making it unsafe for him to cross the Rappahannock, and that in turn would relieve pressure on the Confederate capital. The Valley was becoming much more than a sideshow for both North and South: Shields had to disentangle from the Shenandoah and join McDowell for the pivotal march to Richmond; Jackson had to prevent just such a contingency.

There were several options available to Jackson at Swift Run Gap to block McDowell's advance. He could slip out the back door of the

Gap and maneuver northward along the eastern shoulders of the Blue Ridge to attack the Warrenton area. He might storm west through Massanutten Gap and isolate Banks at Harrisonburg. Further reflection made Jackson hesitant about this scheme, since Banks could wage a delaying action in Massanutten Gap that might enable him to get his main force to New Market in time to repel the thrust. Also interesting was a sprint down the Luray Valley toward Front Royal and the deep Federal rear around Winchester; such a raid would clear Banks out of the upper Valley and pose a danger to McDowell. Jackson outlined these courses to Lee on the twenty-ninth.[109]

Intriguing as were these maneuvers, Jackson's preference was another option, one for which he was awaiting a reconnaissance report from Hotchkiss. Jackson outlined in his April 29 letter a plan to join Johnson west of Staunton, thrash Frémont, and then turn on Banks. Indeed, that general course was almost demanded by events during the ten days since his meeting with Johnson. When Johnson came on the nineteenth it had been assumed—at least by the men Johnson left behind on Shenandoah Mountain—that the Valley Army would cover their rear by a stand somewhere in the vicinity of Harrisonburg. Within hours after Johnson departed, however, word came that Jackson had opened the Army of the Northwest's rear by heading for the Blue Ridge; those remaining in charge in the Alleghenies took no comfort in the fact that Jackson had burned the bridges over the North River, which separated them from Banks. Johnson's deputies decided to withdraw in response to this news, and even as Jackson and Johnson met, the latter's troops were pulling back to within sight of Staunton.[110] Johnson would not hear of it until returning to his command; by that time there was nothing to do but continue the retrograde, which exposed Staunton to Frémont's troops. Despite his desire to form a juncture with Ewell for action in the Shenandoah or somewhere east of it (which would deal directly with the threat from Fredericksburg), Jackson viewed Frémont's drive toward Staunton as a "special emergency"[111] he must resolve before addressing other fronts.

Jackson's response was to dash southwestward across the front of Banks's army from Swift Run Gap via the village of Port Republic to Staunton, whence he and Johnson could overrun Frémont's vanguard.[112] It was a familiar scheme for Jackson; the uniting of Confederate forces and swift descent upon the enemy to keep opposing forces divided was exactly what he had tried to do against Romney in December 1861. On this new march his flank would be covered from Swift Run Gap to Port Republic by the South Fork of the Shenandoah, and from there on by the North River. With luck he could reach Johnson before the enemy could react—the key was celerity and secrecy of movement. On the twenty-sixth the general sent Hotchkiss to Johnson to determine what strength he thought necessary for a successful campaign.[113] At the same time Hotchkiss could reconnoiter the roads that the Army must utilize on a march against Frémont.

Jackson had not awaited Hotchkiss's information to make ready his offensive. Since leaving Rude's Hill he had been drawing Ewell's command toward the Blue Ridge, and on the twenty-eighth Ewell came to Swift Run Gap in person. The conference of that day was in no respect a council of war. Though Ewell and Jackson were of equal rank and commanded comparable numbers, Jackson was dictating the course. He evidently showed little interest in Ewell's preference for the strike via Massanutten Gap into Banks's rear[114] and instead assigned Ewell a support role to his own offense. The Valley Army might be hit in open terrain if Banks somehow got across the rivers Jackson would use as flank cover on his march. Ewell could lessen that menace by occupying Swift Run Gap when Jackson started his drive; if Banks detected Jackson's course, Ewell's presence at the Gap still presented a threat against Banks's hitting the Valley Army en route to Staunton. Before the generals parted, Ewell understood the importance of his division remaining at Swift Run Gap until Jackson stopped Frémont. Although the evidence is circumstantial, Jackson probably indicated he could return before May 10 to meet Banks.[115]

The essence of Jackson's plan was contained in his April 29 letter to Lee; about the hour he finished writing Jackson received the last information he wanted. At 4 o'clock on a rainy, misty afternoon, Hotchkiss reappeared at Headquarters. He had found Johnson's army in camp around West View, which meant some units were within five miles of Staunton. The troops were ready for a fight, and Johnson had even discussed an opportunity to capture Federals to the west. The least encouraging part of the report dealt with road conditions: there had been much rain in past days, and the roads were muddy and badly cut up by Confederate supply convoys. Alone and well mounted it took Hotchkiss twelve hours to cover only thirty miles from Swift Run Gap to Staunton via Port Republic.[116]

That news was worrisome, since speed was crucial to the operation, but the Valley Army had learned to master worse than bad roads, and Stonewall ended his interrogation of Hotchkiss with orders for his third offensive since January. The first had been stopped by the snows of Romney, the second by superior numbers at Kernstown. Surely the third would succeed! Ewell was alerted to move into the Gap the next day. Hotchkiss was detailed to sneak up in the morning to the southern tip of the Massanutten Mountain, from which he could observe Banks's camps and movements around Harrisonburg. Ashby was assigned to demonstrate in the direction of Harrisonburg guided by Hotchkiss's signals.[117] Orders to be under way before the sun were Jackson's answer to the insistent question, What next?

8

McDOWELL

We are in hard looking
country now.

—JOHN APPERSON

In the early hours of April 30 Private Joe Kaufman of the 10th Virginia was roused by a fife and drum corps pounding through his camp. Kaufman and his regiment were newcomers to the Valley Army—they had arrived only nine days previously—but they guessed they were about to see combat with Stonewall. Kaufman was marching westward by 4 A.M., and with excitement he braced himself to go after Banks. The infantry crossed the Shenandoah's South Fork and assembled in a large wood while Ashby probed ahead with cavalry, Chew's Battery, and foot support to within five miles of Harrisonburg. Hotchkiss was at his station atop Massanutten Mountain watching for any response by Banks. But there was no Union reaction to signal to Ashby, and in the absence of Federal movement the cavalrymen drew back. After noon the infantry recrossed the river, assuming they would return to their starting point. In fact, they would have found their camps occupied by the division of Richard Ewell, which filled Swift Run Gap while the enemy was pressed well away, so there was no return to old campfires for Jackson's brigades. Instead the column turned right at the eastern mouth of the bridge and headed south. What next?

The only answer was a cloudburst, under which the mystified troops shuffled to a bivouac five miles from Swift Run Gap. There were no tents. Joe Kaufman drew a half pound of bacon, his only ration for the day, ate, and went to sleep beneath a spiteful rain that would outlast the night.[1]

The southward march resumed in the morning, and the heavy rain and plodding feet churned the road into a channel of mud. Joe Kaufman sank to his knees with each step. "The worst road I ever traveled over. Rained all the time. The mud has no bottom at all. Oh! will it never stop raining. We traveled about 8 or 10 miles today without anything to eat," Kaufman wrote in his diary.[2] Kaufman's officers agreed: Lieutenant Colonel E. T. H. Warren of the 10th wrote his wife: "The roads were the very worst I ever saw and the rain came down in torents [*sic*]."[3] Some who survived the expedition to Romney griped that this ordeal was worse.[4] The woodlands on either side were soggy and dotted with quicksand, but many Southerners abandoned the road to take their chances there; whole regiments lost cohesion as the Army wallowed along the bank of the Shenandoah's South Fork River.[5]

Shoving and sliding by his gun of the Rockbridge Artillery, Lanty Blackford could not believe what the Army was encountering. He wrote his mother, "It is impossible for me to give you an idea of the road; I never knew anything to be traversed by wheeled vehicles that was like it. . . . There were sometimes great sluices of water running along the road for hundreds of yards; at others pools 18 or 20 inches deep which could not be got around. There were places where the mud seemed fully a foot deep, and uneven so that in putting one foot before the other neither horse or man could tell how deep it would go down." Blackford added that his comrades were as exhausted as he had ever seen them.[6] Only the cursing heaped on Jackson from every quarter united these soldiers.[7]

Next morning, May 2, the sun came out. Hotchkiss took the entire 42d Virginia ahead to mend the road, "the worst," he groaned, "I ever saw in the Valley of Virginia."[8] Other staff members joined Old Jack as he lugged rocks to shore up chuckholes.[9] By force of habit and with much profanity the Army advanced to the vicinity of Port Republic by evening. (As they bivouacked, rebels could note menacing bluffs on the far side of the South Fork, but few would have believed that six weeks hence they would defend those bluffs against Federals trekking this same road from Swift Run Gap.) The Confederates had covered fifteen miles in two and a half days, a stern initiation to the Valley Army for newcomers like Joe Kaufman. His diary entry for the day read: "I begin to think Old Jack is a hard master from the way he is putting us thru [*sic*]. . . . My feet have given out but still I have to travel on. Oh, how I wish peace would be declared!"[10]

If not peace, a halt might have been nearer than Kaufman could have guessed, because the Valley Army's third offense had gotten into trouble as speedily as its earlier efforts. At Port Republic two streams formed the South Fork of the Shenandoah; Jackson would need to cross only one to gain a road to Staunton, but the stream was not bridged and the ford was so high that a man on horseback would have to swim his mount to cross.[11] Much time would be lost getting the infantry beyond that obstacle, if it could be done at all. Worse, the indefatigable Ashby—Ashby!—had fallen sick and was unable to do more than direct his scattered command by courier. The probe of the thirtieth was to be his last action for days.[12]

Ashby's absence must have been related to the fact that a strong Federal patrol came within a mile of Port Republic from Harrisonburg on May 2. Two rebel cavalry companies drove them off at the last moment, taking a few prisoners,[13] but the threat was serious enough that some infantry units spent hours under arms to repulse another attack.[14] It was probable that Banks already knew of the Confederate movement (which in fact he did[15]), presenting a real danger that Federals might seize high ground west of Port Republic while the Army was crossing the river there. That risk was unacceptable, particularly because there was no reason to expect that the thoroughfare from Port Republic on to Staunton was any better than the one just endured. On the day he ought to have been in Staunton, Jackson was mired down halfway there with his march probably discovered. Another man might have forsaken the enterprise; Joe Kaufman's "hard master" looked for another road.

A highway that was both safe and good was available. Southeast of Port Republic was Brown's Gap, in the Blue Ridge; the passage up and down the gap was graded and firm. A day and a half's march through the gap would carry Jackson to Mechum's River Station on the Virginia Central Railroad; from there a decent road paralleled the tracks westward to Staunton. The problem was that at Mechum's the Army would be almost as far from Staunton as it had been in Conrad's Store, and even if some trains could be found to speed the movement, it would be several days before the rebels fully assembled at their destination. Time was short, but no alternative to this detour existed. On May 3 Jackson started his infantry out of the Shenandoah while instructing Major Dabney to have Ashby deploy all available riders to screen the detour. Jackson asked only for two cavalry companies to serve as advance and rear guard, but such was his distrust of the cavalry that the general had Dabney emphasize that captains of the companies Ashby detailed must be "discreet, trustworthy and sober."[16]

The route of May 3 took the Army southeastward into Brown's Gap;[17] most units camped that night out of the mud on or at the summit of the Blue Ridge. The next day was Sunday, but Jackson ignored the Lord's peace. He had news from Allegheny Johnson that the Union vanguard was within sixteen miles of his position, which placed Federals nearer Staunton than the Valley Army. Johnson urged Jackson to "come up as soon as possible,"[18] and Stonewall's troops pressed on to Mechum's River Station. There the general gathered cars for the Army's sick and shoeless and forwarded them to Staunton.[19]

Over the next two days the balance of the Army followed, mostly on foot. The haste with which the Brown's Gap detour was arranged is reflected by how few miles and how little time the Virginia Central Railroad actually saved Jackson. Apparently only three or four trains were mobilized; in some baggage cars men were packed as tightly together as they could stand.[20] Of those detraining first in Staunton one civilian observed, "Many are ragged, quite a number are without shoes; a large proportion are dirty and apparently sickly," suggesting Jackson was able to move only those unable to march.[21] The wagons and artillery recrossed the Blue Ridge at Rockfish Gap by a road generally paralleling the tracks, and much of the way the infantry was with them. Many regiments were not picked up by the trains until they had marched almost half the way from Mechum's Station to Staunton,[22] and it was May 6 before the last rebels gained the city.[23]

There was not even room for Headquarters on the trains; Jackson and his staff came by horse to Staunton on the fourth. Once there, Jackson was busy taking stock of two fresh units with which he would operate.[24] The first was familiar, for Colonel Preston was in Staunton with almost the entire Virginia Military Institute, two hundred cadets.[25] Jackson considered Frémont's threat to Staunton of a magnitude sufficient to justify calling out everyone in the area, and he had accepted Superintendent Smith's offer to field the Corps. Many of the cadets were boys, but they had arms and knew how to use them, and Jackson did not overlook any source of aid. He was particularly pleased that with the Institute came Colonel T. H. Williamson, a faculty member widely regarded as one of the ablest engineers in Virginia.[26]

Jackson also met with Edward Johnson on the fourth,[27] finally consolidating the last two brigades of the Army of the Northwest with the Valley Army, something he had desired since 1861. The 12th Georgia and 25th and 31st Virginia composed the first brigade of Johnson's command; the second consisted of the 44th, 52d, and 58th Virginia Infantry regiments. Attached were three batteries commanded by Captains Charles Raine, John Lusk, and William Rice. The total strength was approximately three thousand men and twelve guns.[28]

In the fine quality of those men, and as well in a lack of sufficient numbers of experienced officers to command them, Johnson's brigades mirrored the Valley Army. There were no generals present besides Johnson; senior colonels, both men in their fifties with virtually no prewar military experience, commanded each brigade. Colonel Z. T. Conner of the 12th Georgia led the first brigade. Born in 1811, Conner had enlisted as a private in one of the first Georgia volunteer units. He later became lieutenant colonel of the forming 12th Georgia and took over as its colonel after Johnson was promoted to general. Two years older than Conner, Colonel William C. Scott of the 44th Virginia led the other brigade. Scott was a graduate of the University of Virginia and an attorney who fought his battles in the courtroom and Virginia legislature; he was without military experience prior to entering the Virginia militia early in the conflict.[29] He had limited service in the Alleghenies before going to Richmond to attend a convention that rewrote Virginia's state constitution in November; returning to his unit only briefly in January 1862, he was soon furloughed home because of illness and only recently had returned to his command. In the next month one man would prove himself while the other failed at a crucial moment; for now the two colonels would lead their little brigades as part of a demi-division under Johnson.

Johnson's soldiers had received a good foundation from their West Point–trained general. They had seen occasional sharp battles and much boredom in the mountains of western Virginia since the previous summer, and while for them the romance of war had long ago disappeared amid those dreary highlands, they were reacting like most Confederates with increasing determination to oppose ever deeper Union penetration of the Old Dominion. These men would do their duty—although, as always, it would be in their own style. They especially felt the absence of female company entailed by their long service in the mountains, and one soldier recalled how any time a girl passed he could see boys crawling from their tents just to look. General Johnson relearned this longing to his embarrassment when, shortly after falling back to Staunton, he gave a young lady a buggy tour of his camps. Related one soldier to his father: "The boys as [Johnson] passed all gave him a loud cheer. He took it all in a very good humor, but I think he was annoyed a little. . . . I expect you think we are very foolish, but when you remember that we have not seen a woman worth looking at for ten months I think we are perfectly excusable."[30]

Jackson could count almost ten thousand such young men in the environs of Staunton, an impressive force with the exception of the cavalry. On the fourth Jackson ordered Ashby's companies to rotate from Port Republic westward in the direction of Mount Sidney (ten miles north of Staunton on the Valley Pike) and establish contact with Johnson's pickets. With Ashby still on the sick list, Jackson was unable to determine who was in charge and directed his order to "the commander of the cavalry."[31] A few days earlier, on April 25, the general had not been able to provide Johnson any mounted assistance. He had written to Johnson that the "condition of my cavalry is such at present as to prevent keeping a company between the enemy [in Harrisonburg] and Staunton." With hundreds of cavalry supposedly available, Jackson was unable to offer Johnson's little command one company to safeguard its rear: "You will have to rely on your own resources," he warned.[32] Jackson was getting the answer to the question of the cavalry's ability to operate with him effectively in the field, and the answer was not encouraging. On May 6, in response to a trial balloon from Richmond concerning promotion for Ashby, Jackson reminded his friend Alexander Boteler that discipline and drill were essential to success in handling large masses of troops and confided that Ashby's want of those qualities was so basic that he would regard it as a "calamity to see him promoted."[33] During coming operations much of the cavalry would be left to protect Staunton against any advance from Harrisonburg; Jackson would trust only a few mounted companies under arguably Ashby's best captain, George Sheetz, to accompany him against Frémont.[34]

Unsatisfactory as the cavalry arm was, Jackson did not allow it or anything else to interfere with his strike against Frémont. He shuttled the last of his infantry into Staunton from beyond the Blue Ridge. He paired Hotchkiss with V.M.I.'s Colonel Williamson and tasked them to scout the way to Frémont's nearest units sixteen miles west of Staunton.[35] Word came in on the evening of the fifth that Banks had left Harrisonburg. Stonewall's first thought was that Banks had shifted to the southwest by the Harrisonburg and Warm Springs Turnpike to unite with Frémont; he sent a note to Ewell back at Swift Run Gap asking him to do anything he could to retard such a juncture.[36] By the sixth he had heard rumors that Banks was retiring northward along the Pike; Captain Winfield took some of Ashby's troopers to locate Banks but fell into a scrambling fight with Union cavalry outside Harrisonburg and therefore could not have reported anything certain.[37] (In fact, Banks was slipping into the fog of war insofar as Jackson was concerned, and often during the next three weeks he would not be sure where or in what strength Banks could be found.) There was more definite news from the other front that day when Williamson and Hotchkiss returned from their reconnaissance: Frémont's advance had withdrawn to the west.[38] That prompted immediate response. The general wrote again to Ewell suggesting that the latter might trail Banks from a safe distance so that Banks would know he was being watched; Jackson advised that he intended to pursue Frémont.[39]

General Johnson already had started westward on the afternoon of the sixth; units of his demidivision reached the crest of North Mountain (ten miles from Staunton) by evening.[40] Thus the Confederate vanguard was departing camps west of Staunton only a few hours after the Stonewall Brigade, last of Jackson's troops, approached it from the east. Jackson rushed the next day to close this gap. He penned a note to Ewell advising that he was leaving in haste and got Taliaferro's, Campbell's, and Winder's brigades (in that order) on the road after Johnson.[41]

The day was clear, and the column kept a good pace through the foothills of the Alleghenies and toward the bigger ranges beyond, until tiered ridges loomed above them. The Confederates leaned into the ascent and started to climb. "It is up one mountain and up another and so on for the whole road," wrote Sandie Pendleton.[42]

For those of the Valley Army who once had styled themselves "Loring men," this climb was familiar: most of them had sweated over these ridges on their first marches of the war. One of the V.M.I. cadets now trudging along with the Valley Army, B. A. Colonna, had been with the 21st Virginia when it marched west from Staunton in 1861. Catching sight of the 21st now, Colonna had to reflect on the transformation eleven months had produced. In June 1861 each company of the regiment was allotted four Conestogas to haul trunks and tents, and many companies hired additional vehicles for more personal baggage. Almost all men had started with hundred-pound packs full of "necessities"—items gradually thrown away as the owner realized what it meant to march like a pack mule. One rebel recalled of those early days:

> After we had trudged along some five miles in a sweltering sun, I tried to give my six-shooter away, but could not find any one to accept it, and over in the bushes I threw it. I then unbuckled my Damascus blade, made an offer of that, but was likewise refused, and it was thrown into the bushes. I then tried to give away a blanket, but no one would accept, so away it went. I thought, probably, the war would end before the winter. By the time we reached the summit of the mountain nearly all the men in the regiment had disposed of their extra appendages by leaving them in the bushes.[43]

Cadet Colonna had witnessed this eleven months earlier, but now everything he saw had a lean, strictly utilitarian look. There were no tents and no trunks. The entire 21st had only a few wagons. The soldiers carried no more than a musket, a light haversack, and one blanket. Colonna laughed: "I doubt whether the whole of Jackson's army had as much impedimenta as the 21st had on leaving Staunton in 1861."[44]

Southern uniforms, or the lack of them, also amused Colonna. The Army had grown shabby as a year of war tattered the bright attire of the previous spring. Comfort rather than style was now the criteria for apparel. Civilian clothes abounded. Stiff boots had given way to brogues with wide, thick bottoms and flat heels. The towering busbies and shakos that adorned the ranks—and blew off in a strong wind—during the early days had been replaced with slouch caps. Dick Waldrop of the 21st Virginia ambled along in a pair of pants at least six sizes too big and with legs the size of salt sacks; he loved them, for they afforded plenty of stretching room.[45]

Stragglers had grown wise with their ways too. A standard joke had it that an accomplished straggler could feign more misery, spin more tales of woe, and find more to eat than ten ordinary soldiers. Colonna recollected many stragglers along the way "looking unhappy."[46] And others ranged far beyond the roadside. Ed Moore and Clem Fishburne of the Rockbridge Artillery, for example, schemed to make a side trip to visit some lady friends when the Army left Staunton. Fishburne backed out at the last moment, and Moore went on alone. The attractive girls regaled him with food and drink, and he did not rejoin the Army until the close of its next battle.[47]

Such was the Army of the Valley as it clambered into the Alleghenies. The troops had changed the military to conform to their notions as fully as they were being molded by it. These rebels would never become professionals, but they were growing nonetheless into veterans to be feared.

II

The pursuit of Frémont's now retiring vanguard, under General Milroy, took the rebels into Highland County, rough country offering opportunity for, and danger of, ambush. General Johnson was thinking of ambush as he neared his former base on Shenandoah Mountain on the afternoon of May 7; he tried to waylay a Union force there but merely killed and wounded a few while the rest fled. He also bagged a prisoner who boasted that Milroy had six thousand men and was about to be reinforced by six thousand more. Johnson nonetheless chased up the mountain to regain his old fortifications and then plunged down the opposite slope. His troops watched the enemy retreating over the next ridge (known locally as Bull Pasture Mountain) and were eager to press on when the Federals opened with a hidden battery.[48] With Jackson's brigades still some distance to the rear,[49] Johnson wisely pulled back and waited until daylight to resume the hunt.

Early on the eighth, Johnson pushed down Shenandoah Mountain and over the Cow Pasture River amid groves of low sycamore, then started up Bull Pasture Mountain. This mountain rested on the eastern side of the Bull Pasture River; on its far bank, thirty-six miles from Staunton, lay the tiny crossroads community of McDowell. Milroy's forces were expected there. Johnson stopped his column on the slopes of Bull Pasture Mountain and rode forward to reconnoiter. Ahead were only a few rebel skirmishers already banging away at the enemy. Taking a party of thirty men and a few officers, Johnston left the road and climbed a high mountain spur called Sitlington's Hill, from which he

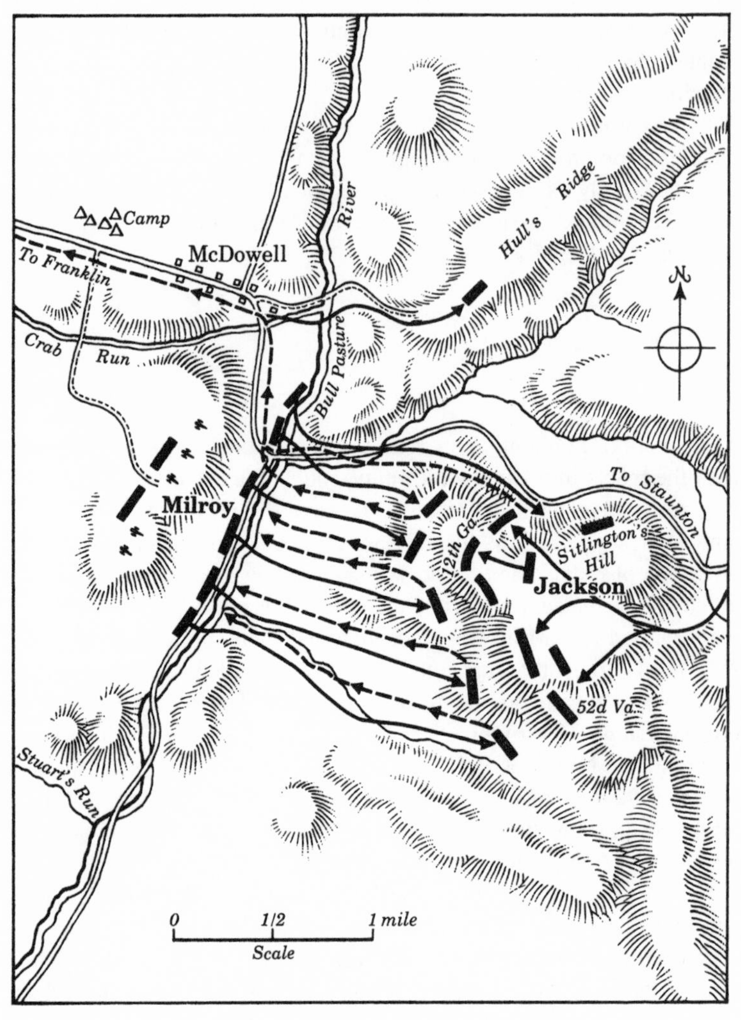

6. ACTION AT MCDOWELL, MAY 8, 1862

Redrawing of a map prepared under the direction of Jedediah Hotchkiss for William Allan's *History of the Campaign of General T. J. (Stonewall) Jackson in the Shenandoah Valley.*

overlooked the vicinity of McDowell. He had not been there long when he looked up to see Jackson and Hotchkiss riding up.[50]

Jackson had stirred early that morning. He dashed off another note at 5:10 A.M. to inform Ewell of the previous day's events and urge him to stay within striking distance of Banks,[51] then rode with Hotchkiss to catch Johnson's vanguard. They began to pass Johnson's halted regiments, which clogged the narrow road on the eastern slope of Bull Pasture Mountain, shortly after noon. A mile beyond this column Jackson and Hotchkiss found a rock outcropping from which the general could see Union encampments around McDowell while Hotchkiss penciled a sketch of the area. The pair next scrambled to the crest of Sitlington's Hill and located Johnson. The two generals, now effectively the Army's cavalry screen, rode so far forward they drew attention from Union skirmishers, who pumped a hot fire at them; the generals retired a short distance to decide the next move.[52]

The important terrain features were apparent. The road from Staunton ran, with twists and cutbacks, generally east-west down Bull Pasture Mountain to cross the Bull Pasture River by bridge; north of the road and roughly paralleling the river, to which it was close, was a ridge known as Hull's Hill. Federals were posted there, including some artillery, but heavier enemy forces were on the western bank of the river near where the bridge carried the road into McDowell. The hill on which the Confederates stood was south of the turnpike and farther from the river than Hull's Hill. It stretched for about a mile in the shape of a curve with its convexity toward the river. The ends were shaley and somewhat higher than the middle, which meant the middle ground was exposed to semicircular fire from below. There were many patches of forest and some ravines running up the five hundred feet from the valley floor to provide cover for a skilled foe, yet the climb was a laborious one, especially for men with musket and pack. Overall, Sitlington's Hill seemed thoroughly defensible.

Defense was not, however, under discussion on top of Sitlington's Hill. The Valley Army's objective was to hurt Frémont quickly, which could be achieved only by aggressive action. Two opportunities emerged. Confederate guns atop Sitlington's Hill could dominate Northern lines below;[53] the challenge would be to find a way to bring up cannons. The Confederates had gained the summit by a narrow, steep, and boulder-clogged ravine. Guns would never negotiate that gorge, although it might be possible to cut an alley for them at another point. The pieces would have to be dragged up by main strength, and they would be impossible to remove if battle went adversely. Second, there was something like a cow path behind Sitlington's Hill that wandered under several miles of thick forest cover to a point south of Milroy's lines. If the river could be forded there a march of five miles would place the flanking party athwart Milroy's only escape route. Scouts hinted that the lane was passable for rebel artillery, although taking guns into the Federal rear, if less exhausting than manhandling them to the summit of the Confederate position, would pose just as much risk of losing them in case of a Southern reverse.

The more daring tactic might be the safer. Milroy did not necessarily know that Johnson had received Jackson's reinforcements. If the Federal general were befogged, he might be captured by a sudden descent of unanticipated rebel strength into his rear. This was the sort of blow Stonewall longed to strike, and evidence suggests he was considering it strongly. But it was by now midafternoon, and the rear brigades were still some distance off. Battle could not be launched before dawn, so there was no need to commit to a plan.[54] Probably Jackson decided to weigh the alternatives further; it is certain only that he assumed there would be no battle that day. He dispatched word to the rear brigades to halt while ordering Johnson to secure the high ground. Federal skirmishers infested the lower slopes of the hill, and Union cannoneers had backed their gun carriages into V-shaped holes to gain elevation and fling an occasional shell at the Confederate crest,[55] so Johnson brought up all his force.

Johnson personally deployed his arriving regiments. His old command, the 12th Georgia, took the area of greatest exposure in the center; the 52d Virginia went to the far left and immediately fell in with enemy skirmishers. The 58th was stationed to the left in support of the 52d while Colonel Scott's 44th Virginia was posted on the right near a ravine. The Northern artillery fire continued with no great accuracy, but as a precaution Johnson arrayed his lines in two-man pairs with five yards between each pair. Around 5 P.M., as Johnson completed these arrangements and rode to scout beyond the right of the 44th, he heard skirmish fire growing fiercer.[56] Instinct took him back to the sound of the guns, and as he reached the 44th he saw Northern columns crossing the river and surging against his right flank. Milroy had not waited to be flanked.

The heaviest Federal assault was directed toward the Confederate right and center and inflicted significant losses. Almost from the first, the 12th Georgia suffered terribly in its assigned center position. Colonel Conner eventually gave orders to withdraw to a safer spot, but the Georgians shouted they would not run from Yankees. At one point Conner dragged a wing of the regiment back, only to see it sprint out again as he went to withdraw the other.[57] The attack on the right flank, against the 44th, was especially dangerous, and Johnson placed the 25th Virginia there as it reached the field. His final regiment was not in sight, but word came that Jackson, who was near the road at the base of Sitlington's Hill, had grabbed the 31st Virginia and stationed it to repel any Union advance along that route. Jackson elected to remain near the 31st to ensure a Southern escape route. He left to Johnson conduct of the battle, while sending up a courier to advise that he was bringing forward his three brigades.[58]

For the next hour the Valley Army would pay for Jackson's brigades not having been closer to the front when battle exploded. Although Confederate strength in the region exceeded Milroy's forces, the five Southern regiments initially defending Sitlington's Hill barely outgunned the five Union regiments Milroy threw at them.[59] As evening came on, shadows stretched out to veil Federals on the slopes while rebels were silhouetted against the lighter sky, and Confederate losses mounted. Colonel Scott of the 44th attempted to lessen the risk by ordering volley fire, a rotating drill whereby the front rank delivered its fire, retired a few paces, and lay on the ground to reload. That may have lessened casualties, but Scott watched with rising anger as the pauses to reload became longer and the distance some men retired greater. As the firing increased, some rebels slipped back farther and lay on their faces. Scott tried to rouse them with appeals to pride, then threats, and when all failed he began to ride over them, forcing the shirkers into line.[60]

By 6 P.M. the battle had become, in Johnson's words, "very terrific,"[61] with an intensity highlighted by an observation of one Confederate staff officer. The top of Sitlington's Hill was covered with white thorn bushes and small trees. Observing the battlefield from below the next day, the Southerner was startled to see it covered with blooming shrubs. Knowing it was too early in the season for blooms, he went to investigate, whereupon he discovered that what appeared a hilltop in blossom was really the white wood of branches and twigs splintered by Union bullets.[62] Another visitor found two acres on the summit almost mowed by gunfire; bushes six inches in diameter had been cut by bullets until they fell.[63] Hotchkiss visited the summit and saw "bushes, that were very thick in the field where our men were mainly posted during the engagement, cut into splinters by the bullets of the enemy."[64]

It was under such fire that Taliaferro's Brigade joined the fight. Taliaferro saw the left wing was holding and that the greatest threat was to the right and center. Johnson had already reinforced that wing with a few companies from other units, and Taliaferro bolstered it with his 23d and 37th Virginia. Minutes later a column of Federals sneaked up a dark bottom to within fifty yards of the Southerners and shattered them with a volley. The line splintered momentarily before Colonel Scott rallied his men.[65] Next up was the 10th Virginia, Private Joe Kaufman's regiment. Taliaferro ordered it toward the 12th Georgia, and Kaufman got his taste of action under Stonewall. "I could see the men falling in every direction as we were going in. I cannot tell or have any idea of the number killed or wounded," he wrote. His regimental commander, Colonel Gibbons, fell mortally wounded, then his captain was shot in the foot. "It was the hour to try men's souls, but we went into it cool and deliberate," noted Kaufman in his diary.[66]

By sundown the battle was general. There was much action at close quarters. Johnson handled the contest well, shuffling his troops to repulse every thrust, and he was at the front when a ball tore apart his ankle. Allegheny was carried from the field by stretcher; this wound was serious and would keep him out of action for months. As he was being placed in an ambulance, Jackson joined him. They spoke quickly, during which time Jackson could confirm that General Taliaferro was the highest-ranking officer on the Hill. Only two days earlier Jackson had written that Taliaferro, whom he regarded as incompetent, should never have been promoted from colonel;[67] now he was leading the fight. "Go up to Gen. Taliaferro and give him my compliments and tell him I am coming in person with the Stonewall Brigade and he must hold his position until I come," Jackson snapped to Hotchkiss.[68] About this same time the lead regiment of Campbell's Brigade, the 21st Virginia, came hustling down the McDowell road. Jackson found the commander, Lieutenant Colonel Cunningham, and told him to take the place of the 31st Virginia guarding the Army's escape route so the latter regiment could join the fight at the summit. "Tell your men they must hold the road!" Jackson shouted to Cunningham,[69] then spurred to hasten the Stonewall Brigade.

Hotchkiss, meanwhile, was riding up the clogged ravine past several more regiments of Campbell's Brigade. Unable to make headway through the jammed crowd, he dismounted and stumbled up on foot to find chaos in the near dark. Many units had lost cohesion. Hundreds of men were roving about shouting for comrades or tending their wounded. Those still on the line were mingled together like a swarm of bees. Hotchkiss gave his instructions to Taliaferro, who responded wisely by aligning Campbell's regiments to block any renewed effort to wrap around the right flank.[70] As dark fell the musket fire finally slackened.

It was only then that the Valley Army amassed overwhelming numerical superiority with arrival of the Stonewall Brigade and V.M.I.'s cadets, units that had given a full day's soldiering while ultimately achieving nothing. They had moved early and marched hard to reach Bull Pasture Mountain as Jackson and Johnson had been studying Union dispositions. Hearing skirmish fire (probably the sniping that had interrupted Jackson's reconnaissance), Winder had his men drop knapsacks and double-quick for the front, only to receive the order from Jackson to go into camp. Gunfire was clearly audible, but neither courier nor Winder could know it was developing into more than a skirmish, so Winder countermarched two miles to level ground beside the Cow Pasture River. About 8 P.M., as his men lit their cooking fires along the stream, Winder received new and peremptory orders to get to the battle. With profanity that can only be imagined, the troops retraced their steps west. On the way they met Jackson, who rode with them even as the tumult of battle declined.[71]

It was fully night as these rebels clawed their way to the top of Sitlington's Hill, their climb lit only by moonlight casting "a pale and sickly glow."[72] Jackson, not knowing if the enemy would attack once more, put Winder in reserve and set the V.M.I. cadets to the gruesome duty of collecting dead and wounded. The wounded had to be manhandled down the gorge on crude stretchers made of rifles and blankets; bounced and sometimes dropped, their shrieks were hideous.[73] "O, the dead! the dying! the screams of the wounded! I have never seen so much of it," wrote Major Jones of the 2d Virginia.[74] Jackson moved around the field, quietly supervising the aftermath of battle: "Gen. Jackson is here—cold—collected—impenetrable—saying but little—watchful—thoughtful," wrote Watkins Kearns in his diary.[75]

Jackson's foremost concern was preparation for the morrow. Confederates could see enemy campfires beneath them and had to prepare for renewal of the engagement. When at length it seemed certain the enemy would not return that night, Jackson began rotating brigades off the mountain to get some rest;[76] about 1 A.M. he sent the Stonewall Brigade back to camp. That march brought to thirty-five miles the distance covered since morning, a pace so grueling many in the brigade lacked energy even to cook. They slept instead, missing their chance to eat, for within two or three hours Jackson summoned them to the front again.[77] About 1 A.M. Jackson and a handful of his staff came back a few miles to Headquarters; they walked the distance, being actually too sleepy to ride. No sooner did the general reach Headquarters at 2 A.M. than he detailed Hotchkiss back to the battlefield to explore a byway for getting artillery to the crest of Sitlington's Hill and to report whether the enemy had departed McDowell.[78] Before dawn rebels were in place to renew the fight.

There was to be no more battle; daybreak disclosed that the Federals were gone. Jackson started to draft a report of this success but was not pleased with his words. He crumpled one piece of paper and then another before he found one sentence that said it all: "God blessed our arms with victory at McDowell yesterday."[79]

III

The Battle of McDowell was an affair of gnats compared with later engagements of this war; by 1864 it would not have been rated more than a skirmish. The Union assault on Sitlington's Hill was a spoiling attack designed to buy time until dark when the Federals could escape from what they understood was an untenable position before superior numbers. The attack was never intended to capture the heights; had that been contemplated, more of the available Union strength would have been engaged at the outset.[80] Even so the Yankee onslaught had been intense. Confederate losses were 532 killed and wounded. The bulk of the fighting had been done by eight regiments of Johnson's and Taliaferro's commands, which took all but 28 of the casualties. Fully a third of the total loss came from the 12th Georgia. Union dead and wounded were slightly less than half that total, a surprising figure since the Confederates possessed numerical superiority and the high ground. Probably 4,700 Confederates had been engaged out of 10,000 in the region; they fought 2,200 Federals out of approximately 3,200 within sight of the field.[81]

Practical considerations partially explain the unusual loss ratio. One Confederate officer attributed greater Southern losses to the fact that uphill aiming tended to be more accurate than downhill, which often overshoots by firing too high. At least one rebel confirmed this theory. Soon after the battle John Apperson of the 4th Virginia toured the field, noting like many others the severe damage to trees on the summit. He then slid down to the Federal positions as outlined by discarded cartridge papers. He could detect hardly any signs of damage to the trees there.[82]

Undoubtedly the time of day entered this equation as well, because Confederates on the crest were more visible than their opponents on the darker slopes. Still, for troops holding high ground to inflict half the casualties they took while repulsing less than an all-out assault by an outnumbered foe was not a brilliant success. The full explanation of heavy losses rested with the 12th Georgia, whose high casualties distorted the statistics. The savaging of the Georgians cannot be gainsaid: casualties among enlisted ranks were two, three, and even four times those in other regiments. The 12th lost nineteen captains and lieutenants killed or wounded; many companies had hardly any officers left after the battle.[83] Still, their position was critical to holding the entire line, and the regiment did what was expected in Jackson's army, which was to hold assigned positions regardless of loss.

The battle also was marred by a classic mistake on Jackson's part. He had not prepared for every eventuality; instead, he apparently had assumed the enemy would follow the obvious course. If the Federals knew of his juncture with Johnson, then retreat toward Frémont was manifestly the correct decision; and even if Milroy thought he faced only Johnson, for him to attack was extremely risky. Jackson overlooked the possibility that the enemy might have heard of the Confederate juncture and would feel so threatened they would view a spoiling attack as their best option. Stonewall decided there would be no battle on the eighth and disposed his rear brigades accordingly. He evidently expected the enemy to remain supine while he plotted their destruction; Milroy did the unexpected and played hob with the Valley Army, catching it spread out. In his development as army commander, Jackson had been given another lesson: he could not count on the enemy to do what made sense from his view of their situation.

Had all of the Army been near the field in compact formations about 5 P.M., Stonewall might have been able to deliver an early counterstroke. The left wing of the Confederate line was never greatly pressed, and Colonel M. G. Harman of the 52d Virginia was maneuvering to surprise the Union right flank when he was wounded. The counterattack stalled while attention turned to holding the Southern right.[84] If the Stonewall Brigade been able to join Harman's assault, the goal of the Allegheny offensive might have been achieved with one stroke. Certainly it could have inflicted heavier casualties on Milroy, and the failure to inflict them meant the Valley Army's return to the Shenandoah to confront Banks had to be postponed.

Notwithstanding such considerations, Jackson was gratified by what had been accomplished. He was especially pleased with Johnson. The two generals had conferred personally only three times since April 19, including the scout on May 8, and Stonewall's decision to remain near the McDowell road prevented him from witnessing the latter's conduct of the fight, but Stonewall still praised Johnson's combat leadership. Months later, when Johnson recovered enough for active duty, Jackson wanted him: "[He] was with me at McDowell and so distinguished himself as to make me very desirous of having him as one of my Division commanders," he wrote.[85]

Johnson doubtless benefited from contrast with the unfortunate Garnett, for memory of the latter still rankled Jackson. He wrote bitterly of Garnett in a private letter to Alexander Boteler on May 6, and Colonel Williamson of V.M.I. recalled his seeking the opinion of Colonel Grigsby during this time as to whether the Stonewall Brigade could have held out another five minutes at Kernstown. (Grigsby was certain it could not.)[86] The rebels had again been pressured at McDowell, but Johnson, unlike Garnett, kept the faces of his men toward the enemy. A resolute fighter could expect Jackson's approval, and approval from Stonewall was sufficient for Johnson's second star. Allegheny led a division of Valley Army veterans, including the Stonewall Brigade, to Gettysburg. Of Taliaferro, who had led the Army briefly at the crises of the battle, Jackson took no notice in his official report other than to acknowledge that after being hit Johnson "turned over the command to General Taliaferro."[87] Johnson was more generous, crediting Taliaferro with behaving "most gallantly."[88]

The high command in Richmond found satisfaction with the little victory primarily because they believed Jackson would now return to the

Shenandoah. Robert E. Lee read Jackson's report of the victory by May 14 and sent a complimentary dispatch. In it he once again urged Jackson to combine his forces with Ewell and drive Banks from the Valley.[89] Joseph E. Johnston heard of the fight by May 12 and hoped Edward Johnson's command could now hold Frémont while Jackson and Ewell combined against Banks.[90]

Stonewall had never been far from that intention. He notified Ewell on May 10 that he would trail Milroy's forces for a time and that he hoped this maneuver might bring opportunity to cleave into Banks's rear from the west. He of course wanted Ewell to join in if that happened.[91] But returning now to the Shenandoah to deal head-on with Banks seemed impossible. Although the rebels believed the Yankees had suffered heavier losses than was the case, the enemy had not been crippled. There had been few prisoners, and the retiring Federals had managed to destroy much valuable property before evacuating McDowell.[92] Plainly Milroy and behind him Frémont remained an intact fighting force still too close to Staunton. The Federals could regain lost territory if the Valley Army turned away too soon, so Frémont had to be further tested.

Before that challenge a day's work remained at McDowell. Jackson swept the area for Union stragglers while the Stonewall Brigade advanced a few miles to assure that the enemy was no longer nearby.[93] Burial parties were organized. "Near the scene of the battle we passed our men at work burying our dead. The graves were dug about 20 yards off the road in a thickly wooded spot, and the dead men ranged in rows along the road side awaiting interment," wrote Lanty Blackford. "That one glance, it seemed to me, was enough to cure any reflecting and reasonable man of the vanity of this thing called military glory."[94] The Army closed up around McDowell and was allowed to rest and cook. Major Harman explored the Union camps for supplies but could find only hard bread; this he issued to the troops passing through as an extra ration.[95] It was scant reward for a hard-won action.

That victory was half a year coming. The Stonewall Brigade had reached the Shenandoah to begin forming the Valley Army six months earlier, six months during which the Army knew almost nothing but frustration. It three times failed to disrupt permanently the C & O Canal. The expedition to Romney degenerated into an icy disaster. Before evacuating Winchester Jackson could not get his trains where he wanted them to allow his dawn attack, and when the Army did strike at

Kernstown it collided with unsuspected superior forces. Cavalry lapses wasted lives the day after Kernstown and led to repeated failures on independent missions. Army command was often in crises with Jackson's resignation; court-martial charges against Loring, Gilham, and Garnett; acrimonious objection to Taliaferro; and the standoff with Ashby. Even the relatively straightforward task of getting from Swift Run Gap to Staunton turned into a muddy ordeal. Had Jackson instead of Johnson taken a bullet at McDowell, Stonewall would have come down through the years in a much different light: one of the many eccentrics who crowd the war's history, a good brigadier promoted beyond his competence who ended up surrendering much of the Shenandoah before falling at a battle whose purpose was obscure.

From a different perspective, however, the last six months were a success. The creation and then reorganization of the Valley Army were themselves a victory. Few times in history has an army been formed while waging so active a contest. Merely to consider that in the middle of the campaign Jackson had to tolerate having his regimental officers submitted for election is to highlight the difficulty of only one aspect of his task. The key to ultimate success was that he never stopped trying, and by earnest hard work Jackson built an army. He gathered an excellent staff; he pulled together an artillery wing; he kept the confusion of the draft and reenlistment laws from dissolving his infantry; he never relaxed a stern discipline that was making soldiers of his boys. And he never stopped looking for reinforcements. First the Stonewall Brigade, then the militia of his district, and then the Army of the Northwest were absorbed. When D. H. Hill pulled out of Leesburg in March, Jackson tried to claim him. No source of manpower, from Choctaw Indians to V.M.I.'s little Cadet Corps, was rejected, and Jackson's ceaseless efforts were bringing results. In November 1861 the new major general came to the Shenandoah without an army; on May 9, 1862, Jackson (with Ewell's command at Swift Run Gap) could wield 17,500 men for further operations. That the Valley Army was poised to continue the war was a victory as meaningful as that won at McDowell.

And the next morning the Valley Army did continue the war. The dawn was bright, without clouds, and the day was warm. The Army set off after Milroy, the first of many retreating Union generals these Confederates would stalk. It was May 10, 1862. Jackson had exactly one year to live.

Part III

9

IN THE ALLEGHENIES

Gen. Jackson is hard on soldiers.

—SHEPHARD PRYOR

The Valley Army's pursuit of Milroy after McDowell was a continuation of the mission that led it out of Swift Run Gap: Staunton had to be made safe while preventing at all costs the juncture of Frémont and Banks. Scouts reported that Milroy had retreated toward the town of Franklin, thirty miles away, so the Army targeted that point. Six miles outside McDowell the Confederates turned into a narrow valley formed by one of the Potomac's headwaters and marched directly northward. The path was along the western side of a clear little river filled with trout.

Jackson's latest intelligence pinpointed Banks at New Market, nineteen miles north of Harrisonburg.[1] Between New Market and Harrisonburg three roads ran from the Valley Pike through river gaps to the neighborhood of Franklin. Banks could use these routes to succor Frémont unless the gap roads were closed. Brock's Gap, the northernmost pass that directly connected New Market and Franklin, was beyond Jackson's immediate reach, but he got word to local cavalry units to obstruct it.[2] The closer roads through North River and Dry River gaps were a task for an enterprising staff officer, upon which thought Jackson motioned Hotchkiss to follow him.

Old Jack had been running Hotchkiss up and down mountains for two weeks, and since he had done well Hotchkiss received still harder work. Jackson took him aside from the marching columns, away from all listeners, and gave him a new task. Shaking his long index finger like a schoolmaster, the general told Hotchkiss he wanted the two gap roads blockaded by dawn. The mapmaker was to use cavalry in the area for the work. "Take a squad of couriers," Jackson continued, "and send me back a messenger every hour telling me where you are and what you have done."[3]

Hotchkiss dug his spurs in and galloped off on a fifty-mile circuit through McDowell, back to the Shenandoah, and into the Alleghenies from the east. His assignment was formidable: first, corral some reliable cavalry—Jackson had mentioned one company, but Hotchkiss rejected it because he knew its commander was a drunkard, so Jackson said to use whoever he could find; second, locate some tools—the cavalry could not be counted on to have any; third, plug probable bottlenecks. And do it now. It was the kind of hard duty the Army was learning to expect and to master. His home was on the way, so Hotchkiss rode there to rest and feed his horse; en route he stumbled upon Captain Frank Sterrett's Churchville cavalry company, a local defense unit not part of Ashby's command.[4] Sounding more like a field officer than a mapmaker who had no official rank, Hotchkiss told Sterrett to meet him at his home by 3 A.M. The rebels were trotting into the North River Gap before dawn. They requisitioned axes and crowbars from trappers and set to work. They burned bridges, felled trees, and rolled boulders down onto the road. Daylight found the work progressing well, and Hotchkiss shifted by way of Emanuel Church and Ottobine Church to Dry River Gap and finished the job. At regular intervals he dispatched a progress report to Stonewall.[5]

Hotchkiss's couriers confirmed to Jackson that all possible had been done to maintain the separation of Banks and Frémont. The goal of protecting Staunton required a more direct confrontation with Frémont, which would not be easy in the twisting valley, rarely more than a quarter-mile wide, through which the Army marched. Men in ranks anticipated another fight but thought this bleak country would offer no hardships surpassing those already endured—then the forest ahead of them began to smolder. The Yankees had set the woods afire to cover their retreat. After a week or more without rain the timber burned readily, and the steep slopes on either side created an ideal catch basin for smoke. Soon the Confederate advance was clouded by a thick gray screen; at points visibility was reduced to two hundred yards.[6] "The valley was filled with dense smoke so that we could not make out what was in front of us, though occasionally the fog and smoke were opened by a shot or shell from the enemy fired to let us know that they still existed," remembered Clem Fishburne.[7]

There was a strange beauty in these fires. William Allan of Jackson's staff recalled long afterward how dead trees exploded into dramatic fireworks displays: "At night the light was exquisitely beautiful. These dead trees were columns of fire. Some were hollow and the fire came out through all the holes. In the case of others, the breaking of a limb would produce a shower of falling sparks from all parts of the tree, far more beautiful than any fireworks I ever saw."[8]

The flames also proved an effective deterrent. Jackson grumbled that the smoke made the advance as difficult as a night attack.[9] The few mounted companies with the Army seem to have disintegrated amid the smoke, and mounted couriers disappeared when fighting started. Jackson put the Stonewall Brigade in front and kept going. By the afternoon of May 11 General Winder led his men to within a few miles of Franklin.[10]

At a point where a thickly wooded hillside forced the road into a long rightward curve, Winder sent Colonel Ronald's 4th Virginia up the slopes to move parallel to it. The Liberty Hall Volunteers had rejoined its regiment from Jackson's Headquarters and was deployed as skirmishers in the sweep. Ted Barclay wrote home describing how their advance carried them through burning woods only to come within range of Federal artillery: "The place was now very dangerous so we fell back behind a ledge of rocks just in time to escape a shower of grape shot which certainly would have killed all of us if we had stood where we were. . . . Now was the time to endeavor to get off the hill, so we fell back two or three hundred yards where we met the burning mountain. You can imagine our dilemma, the enemy in front and a burning mountain in the rear."[11] The Volunteers managed to complete their escape as Federal guns shifted to other regiments Winder was deploying, and the rebel advance continued. The rebels picked their way through burning brush and past several camps where Federals had just been cooking. Winder was at the front, searching for a better view. Soon he ordered his aide, McHenry Howard, to carry word of the skirmish to Jackson; he told Howard to report also that his cavalry couriers had disappeared.

Howard located Stonewall, who looked around for someone to supply couriers and found Harry Gilmor, the dashing escapee from Winchester with his newly recruited company. Gilmor promised couriers who would not run away, but as Lieutenant Howard took them forward Old Jack rode along as well. Soon the general was at the front, where occasional Union shells were bursting over the trees just above him. Accompanied by Winder, Jackson climbed a slope to see that the road descended into a deep chasm with Yankees on the far end. Skirmishers were busy and Union artillery switched to rounds of canister, shots that hit no one but advertised what lay ahead. This line was too strong for direct assault. Winder recommended turning the enemy right flank, but it was nearly night, and with the smoke obscuring everything Jackson suspended operations.[12] His information now indicated that Milroy had been reinforced by Frémont's main body, and Jackson wanted a detailed reconnaissance.[13]

The Valley Army was up early on May 12 searching for an attack opportunity. Parts of Winder's and Taliaferro's brigades were deployed as skirmishers. The artillery of both sides boomed and growled.[14] Jackson's information convinced him the enemy would give battle if pressed, an option he pondered in light not only of the terrain but with a view toward the larger situation in the Shenandoah. That same morning he had a dispatch from Ewell, still in Swift Run Gap. Ewell reported that Banks was preparing rations at New Market with the evident intent of moving, where he could not guess.[15] Jackson suspected that Banks feared the Valley Army would drive another fifty miles through the Alleghenies to strike at Winchester from the west; Stonewall thought Banks was readying a pullback to Winchester to counter the stroke.[16]

The prospect that Banks would move from New Market was equally worrying to General Lee in Richmond. Lee relayed this concern to Jackson on May 8, and Jackson surely had the dispatch when he was outside Franklin. Lee surmised that Banks would leave the Valley to reinforce the Union host assembling under General McDowell at Fredericksburg; Lee advised Jackson he had suggested to Ewell that the latter should shift from Swift Run Gap to intercept Banks on such a march.[17] This recommendation—Lee had not yet ordered Ewell to do anything—gnawed at Stonewall because he did not want to lose Ewell and because he did not believe Banks would abandon the Valley. And even if Banks left the Shenandoah, to hurl Ewell upon him alone was to scatter the Southern forces Lee wisely had sought to unify. Obviously, at high levels there was tension about the inactivity of Ewell's Division,[18] and Jackson could not be sure how long Ewell would either choose to or be permitted to cooperate with him.

It was against this backdrop that Jackson had to decide whether a battle at Franklin could be won and won so as to influence to advantage events in the Shenandoah, and beyond. The strength of the Union position outside Franklin guaranteed a hard fight with high casualties, and even a success did not offer a practical chance to strike into Banks's rear from the Alleghenies. That ploy was weakened by Jackson's own efforts to block the river gaps. Jackson soon determined that the Valley Army had done all it could to protect Staunton. Frémont in Franklin was almost seventy miles from that point, a sufficient safety zone to allow operations against Banks. It was on the destruction of Banks that Southern attention needed to focus. There would be no further battles in the Alleghenies.

Since the Army would not fight on May 12, it could worship. Jackson issued an order congratulating the troops on victory at McDowell and inviting them to divine services. Major Dabney donned his robes to preach in a wide sward that rose gently to a wall of pines. His theme was the war as God's punishment for sin, a message punctuated by the roll of Northern artillery and the billowing pine smoke that surrounded the Army. Jackson attended this worship, and observers did not think he stirred an inch during Dabney's sermon.[19] Services concluded, the rebels were given a few hours' rest, and then the return to McDowell began. Only the thinnest of cavalry screens, under command of Captain Harry Gilmor, was left behind to keep burning the forests so far untouched and create the impression the infantry was still about. During the next several days there would be no report from these cavalrymen that Frémont had ventured out in pursuit. Stonewall could blow smoke too.[20]

II

On May 12, the day Jackson marched south from Franklin, Banks divided his command. Part of it left New Market for Strasburg with him, while Shields's Division, victors at Kernstown, traversed the Massanutten Mountain and headed northward in the direction of Manassas Gap and the road to Fredericksburg. What Lee had foreseen was coming to pass: the bulk of Banks's command was destined for Fredericksburg. And the force at Fredericksburg was targeting Richmond. At Fredericksburg, General McDowell had engineers across the Rappahannock and was rebuilding the bridges there.[21] From those bridges the road ran straight to the Confederate capital.

Southern pickets observed Shields's march via Massanutten Gap and promptly related word to Ewell. At 2 A.M. on May 13, Ewell wrote to Jackson of the redeployment and added that he would shift to face Shields directly or perhaps cross the Blue Ridge to intercept him via Gordonsville.[22] This message must have dispirited Jackson, for it betokened he had been too long in the mountains. The next courier from Ewell delivered a note dated 4 P.M., May 13, and indicated that Ewell remained at Swift Run Gap. "I am urged by strong reasons to get back to Gordonsville to oppose the advance from Fredericksburg," he wrote. Ewell did not want to desert his comrade, but he posed a blunt question: "Repeatedly called to return to Gordonsville as I have been by General Lee, the knowledge Richmond is threatened by . . . forces from Fredericksburg and the Peninsula, the uncertainty of your delay all make me feel very anxious. . . . Please answer as soon as possible and let me know how long you wish me to remain here."[23] This question Jackson did not answer, but Stonewall's correspondence took up a relentless theme: where was Banks?

Developments in the Shenandoah meant the return to it must be by forced march, and this march badly fatigued Confederate infantry. Private Jim Hall of the 31st Virginia wore through his shoes. There were no extra pairs, but in the Valley Army having no shoes was no excuse to stop. Hall had to keep marching: one day he limped eighteen miles barefoot.[24] The V.M.I. cadets were knotting their shoes together with twine.[25] Save what lucky anglers could catch, food became scarce. Some units, both men and horses, were marching on half rations.[26] "We have been living harder in respect of rations than we have ever done since I have been in the service," complained Lanty Blackford.[27]

Major Harman, the Army's quartermaster, was discovering his own version of hell in the Alleghenies. Only a month before he had had to rush home to support his family through an epidemic of scarlet fever; Jackson had given him forty-eight hours and rejected a plea for an extension despite the death of two Harman children.[28] Then at McDowell one of his brothers fell critically wounded leading the 52d Virginia.[29] Harman worked diligently through it all, but now, trying to transport food for an army the destination of which he never knew and attempting to prod a wagon train along a road that was sometimes little better than a buffalo trail, Harman's task was becoming impossible. Several times he ventured to ask the objective, which brought a stern rebuke from Stonewall. That was none of Harman's concern, groused the general, who handled the inquiry with characteristic want of tact. Instead of doing anything to ease Harman's load, the general crabbed that he was not working hard enough. Crusty John Harman thanked him for his candor and handed in his resignation; he wrote his brother, "I feel very much outraged and would not remain a day longer if I could help it. . . . I shall press the resignation if he disapproves it; I can no longer be comfortable with him."[30] At that Stonewall admitted much of the fault had been his; he subsequently became "quite friendly," Harman wrote, and the major joined Ashby as one of the few men ever to back Jackson "square down."[31]

Hunger was aggravated by a four-day rainstorm that began on the thirteenth. The torrents meant wet clothes and blankets, useless firewood, swollen creeks to ford, and dirty springs from which to drink—all that and the endless, bottomless mud.[32] The Liberty Hall Volunteers exploded with profane disgust when their company wagon lost a wheel and their mess gear clattered into the muck.[33] One rebel summarized the entire expedition when he wrote home, "We marched over more mountains than I ever imagined before, and had to camp at night on the side of some mountain without a sign of a tent and with it generally raining pitchforks—and as cold as Greenland without a thing to eat—as when it rained we could not make the fire burn well enough to cook anything. At one time we went without a morsel to eat for 36 hours."[34]

Jackson chose this time to impose a further strain with new march regulations. It was as if he thought his need for swift marching could be satisfied from a military textbook; the new requirements read as though they had been copied from Colonel Gilham's *Manual*.[35] Henceforth, each regiment would halt every hour, stack arms, and rest precisely ten minutes; at no other time could men leave ranks. Exactly one hour was allotted for lunch. Only tools, mess equipment, and officers' baggage were to be carried in wagons. Roll would be called immediately before leaving and immediately after reaching every camp. The regulations fill a page of tightly spaced fine print, of which one section read, "During marches men will be required not only to keep in ranks, but the proper distances must be preserved, as far as practicable, thus converting a march, as it should be, into an important drill, that of habituating the men to keep in ranks." Jackson's emphasis lay with the idea of keeping men in ranks—straggling must end. This order was headed, appropriately, "Headquarters, Valley District, Camp on the Road."[36]

Regulations, fatigue, rain, hunger, and lingering bitterness over the draft proved too great a torment for seventeen men of the 27th Virginia, and when the Army camped again near McDowell they turned defiant. Their original twelve-month enlistments had just expired, and they stacked arms and proclaimed themselves free men. What happened next was intense. The commander of the 27th, Colonel Grigsby, appealed to Winder for guidance. Winder forwarded the request to Headquarters.

Jackson exploded in paroxysms of rage when Grigsby's request reached him. Major Dabney witnessed it. "What is this but mutiny? Why does Colonel Grigsby refer to me to know what to do with a mutiny? He should shoot them where they stand," ranted Jackson. Dabney wrote quickly as the general dictated ruthless instructions: Grigsby was at once to assemble his other companies with loaded weapons, parade the unarmed mutineers before the regiment, briefly explain the nature of their misconduct, and offer opportunity to resume duty. All refusing would be shot within the minute. So that everyone would understand the consequences of defiance, Jackson issued his reply in the form of a general order circulated to all brigades.[37]

Authorized to deliver the ultimate punishment, Grigsby acted. Sergeant Watkins Kearns of the 27th was watching and recorded the outcome: "[The mutineers] were reported to Gen. Jackson who gave them their choice of taking up their arms or being instantly shot. They took arms."[38]

This abortive rebellion reflected, more than anything else, mental and physical exhaustion of the soldiers. Troops on the march with Jackson did not routinely reach camp until sundown. They then had to cook rations for dinner and the next day, a task that could not begin until the trains arrived. Cooking and eating then kept the men up for several more hours. With reveille at 3 A.M. so the march could start at an early hour, sleep was disappearing from their lives. Moreover, guard duty, which lessened rest by two to four hours per shift, was coming around more frequently as the ranks dwindled from battle casualties, sickness, and desertion.[39] Loss of sleep, coupled with hunger and constant physical effort, was a continuous reality now for the Valley Army.

Only with fatigue overcoming reason could any rebel have fancied Jackson might yield about anything; the mutiny produced no concessions and did not even break the pace. The Army slogged to the eastern fringes of the Alleghenies by May 15. Jim Hall hobbled another fifteen miles barefoot that day.[40] Joe Kaufman described the day in his diary thusly: "I feel very much worsted. It has begun to rain again. Very hungry."[41]

Ironically, the only men still excited to continue the drive, the V.M.I. cadets, departed the Army on May 15. The Board of Visitors had decreed that they must return to studies. Jackson wished to retain them and was as disappointed as the cadets. They headed for Lexington with long faces but not without an order from Jackson commending them for the "promptitude and efficiency with which they have assisted in the recent expedition."[42]

Ashby's cavalrymen, on the other hand, were still romping about the Shenandoah. Ashby had by this time resumed his duties, although he was much thinned from illness. His reappearance did not improve performance of the mounted arm. Jackson detailed some riders to drive captured cattle out of the Alleghenies. They did so, then turned the herd into a field and left it to scatter.[43] During this time trooper Bill Wilson, a nineteen-year-old transferee to the cavalry, recorded much jolly fun in his diary as many gallants took up racing to amuse themselves.[44] One company had not had a roll call in weeks, and a payroll did not exist, but no one seemed to worry.[45]

Friday, May 16, was officially proclaimed by President Davis as a day of fasting and prayer throughout the Confederacy. The Valley Army remained in camp in observance of this proclamation. Divine services were held, which hospital orderly John Apperson believed was a fine idea; prayer had been ignored recently by many, although he thought the Army already had been fasting for long enough.[46] Rain continued, and the troops had neither shelter from it nor protection from the spongy ground. Captain H. W. Wingfield of the 58th Virginia wrote in his diary that the camp was "so rainy and disagreeable . . . we are but little rested."[47] It occurred to Ted Barclay that he turned eighteen this day. He could not have imagined a year earlier that he would spend this birthday hunched beneath a downpour wearing a uniform he had been unable to wash for three weeks.[48]

Shared hardship united the Valley Army on one thought as it moved off on May 17. The direction now was northeastward, down the last slopes of the Alleghenies and toward the Shenandoah, home for most marchers. "Home! How sweet it sounds," wrote Joe Kaufman.[49] Kaufman probably would not have guessed that officers could share such feelings, but Charles Winder wrote in his diary that same day, "Oh, how

I've thought of my own [young] ones longing to see them. God bless them."[50] Both Kaufman and Winder might have been surprised to know that at about this time Jackson would find himself sitting in the open, writing on his knee for lack of a table, and confiding to his wife, "How I do desire to see our country free and at peace! It appears to me that I would appreciate home more than I have ever done before."[51]

Where to find and smash Banks, a frazzled, homesick Army, an unreliable cavalry—Jackson had these problems as he came down from the mountains on May 17, and as he would discover the next morning, he had others as well.

10

DICK EWELL'S DILEMMA

Gen. Jackson has stayed much longer than I anticipated.

—RICHARD S. EWELL

On April 30, 1862, Major General Richard S. Ewell's Division entered the Shenandoah to occupy the camps vacated by Jackson when he began his drive into the Alleghenies. Eager to meet the famous Stonewall, Ewell's boys paraded through Swift Run Gap with bands blaring.[1] Their introduction to Stonewall was to find him gone without a trace.

The neighborhood did, however, boast girls whose acquaintance Ewell's boys could make. Young Captain John Nesbit headed a company of mountaineers from a Georgia regiment. Sharing a common bond with the Blue Ridge people, the Georgians were quickly at ease: "It was so homelike," recollected Nesbit.[2] His mountain men found their way to many pretty girls, and any they missed were looked after by an Alabama regiment. To ensure high times at their nightly dances, the rebels also learned the whereabouts of local stills, and time passed as painlessly as they could desire.[3]

If these newcomers to the Shenandoah were typical Confederates, their commander, Richard Ewell, was truly unique. He habitually tilted his bald, bomb-shaped head (which brought him the nickname "Old Bald Head" from his men) to one side to talk, and when he spoke it was with an explosion of soldier's profanity—all uttered with a noticeable lisp. He was highly exacting. Ewell was particularly enraged to receive a "don't know" for an answer, and his couriers dreaded him more than the Yankees when they didn't know the answer to one of his questions. He spurned information from "reliable sources"; what his scouts had not themselves seen, Ewell did not want to hear.[4] His camps chuckled over the rumor that Ewell, a skillful man in the kitchen, restricted himself to a concoction called frumenty (hulled wheat boiled in milk with sugar, raisins, and egg yolk) in deference to a possibly imaginary ulcer, and by any calculation Old Bald Head merited front rank in the pantheon of Confederate eccentrics.

Grandson of a member of George Washington's first cabinet (Benjamin Stoddert, Secretary of the Navy), Ewell was a Virginian whose life had been dedicated to the profession of arms. Acceptance at West Point had been a boyhood dream. He did well there and graduated in 1840, a classmate of William T. Sherman. He saw much combat in the Mexican War and spent the next decade and a half as a cavalryman chasing Indians across the frontier. Ewell was good at it and liked to boast he had learned everything about leading fifty cavalrymen and forgotten everything else. "In this he did himself injustice," objected one of his admirers, who believed he possessed a fine tactical eye on the battlefield and maneuvered units as large as a division with skill.

Resigning from the U.S. Army at the start of the war, Ewell won rapid promotion in the Confederacy. He was commissioned a lieutenant colonel of cavalry in April 1861 and had a brigadier general's stars and an infantry brigade by June. His command protected a quiet sector at the Battle of Manassas and he saw no action there, but he handled his men well in all respects and found himself a major general with a full infantry division by January. That frightened him a little, for a year earlier he had only been a captain of the 1st U.S. Dragoons. He lay awake some nights wondering what to do with his division, and occasionally he demanded of his confidants, "What do you suppose President Davis made me a major general for?"[5]

Ewell's Division, like its general, had not had opportunity to prove itself during a frustratingly inactive winter with Johnston's army. Few of his regiments had seen action, but its mettle was sound. Brigadier General Isaac Trimble, an 1822 graduate of West Point who had served well in the U.S. Army and then as a Baltimore railroad executive, headed one of Ewell's brigades. At sixty years of age Trimble was a fragment of ancient history to his young soldiers, but he knew something about modern war. In April 1861, while others were prattling about the romance of war, the white-thatched Trimble commandeered a train and raced north from Baltimore burning bridges to delay Federal troops in transit to Washington. During Johnston's withdrawal from Manassas, Trimble had been assigned to manage train movements. Nor did age or hard work soften Trimble's disposition; during the division's recent reorganization, when an officer he deemed to be competent and brave was voted out, Trimble compelled a new election and made it clear who was to win.[6] His command was a representative collection of Deep South units: the 15th Alabama, 16 Mississippi, 21st Georgia, and 21st North Carolina.

Brigadier General Arnold Elzey, another Marylander, headed the smallest of Ewell's brigades. Elzey, a West Pointer, had served with distinction in almost every battle of the Mexican War and had led the decisive Southern counterattack at Manassas. His excellent record merited a larger force, but at present he commanded only the 13th Virginia and 1st Maryland, units known to Jackson from his early days in the war at Harpers Ferry. The 13th Virginia received its excellent initial training from an officer the war would make immortal, A. P. Hill. The regiment was currently under Colonel James Walker, who as a V.M.I. cadet won immortality at the Institute by challenging then Professor Jackson to a duel. The incident, which surely was recounted around the campfires of the thirteenth, began as Jackson was butchering a lecture one day. Cadet Walker elected to whisper on a more interesting topic. Jackson called for quiet, but chatter persisted, seemingly from Walker's side of the classroom. Jackson resorted to written disciplinary charges, to which Walker returned a disrespectful objection. A court-martial followed in which there was hostile testimony about whether Walker actually did all the talking. The hearing concluded after sixty-two pages of transcripts with an expelled Walker demanding satisfaction from Jackson on the field of honor. Superintendent Smith urged Walker's father to get the livid youth home before "serious difficulty" erupted. Fortunately, this was done; there was no duel, and Walker went on the University of Virginia Law School and a distinguished legal career.[7]

Elzey's other regiment was one he had headed as its first colonel, the 1st Maryland. The unit was now under Colonel Bradley Johnson. A Princeton graduate, lawyer, and former Maryland state's attorney, Johnson was something of an orator, a skill he would employ in the Valley. His troops were men who cared enough about the Confederacy to filter south to its armies, but upon reaching Swift Run Gap the regiment was racked by morale problems. A few of its companies had mustered in under conditions similar to those of Virginia troops, usually a twelve-month enlistment; in the enthusiastic early days, however, most Maryland companies had been mustered in for the duration of the conflict, a literal commitment to fight to the end. Those men now asserted that they had been deceived and that they could no longer be held in service, especially since their home state had not seceded and thus Confederate conscription law was inapplicable to them. The sophistry of camp lawyers aside, the real problem was that the Marylanders had seen enough of infantry life and wanted transfers to the cavalry. Richmond refused, and much bitterness ensued.[8]

Completing the infantry roster was Brigadier General Richard Taylor's Louisiana Brigade, the 6th, 7th, 8th, and 9th Louisiana and an attached infantry battalion. In his delightful recollections Taylor described these regiments in entertaining prose but with an often faulty memory. The 6th, for example, was according to Taylor recruited in New Orleans and composed of Irishmen, "turbulent in camp and requiring a strong hand." There was a preponderance of Irish, but there were hundreds of Southern natives and as well dozens of German-born immigrants among the 6th. Recollection served Taylor better about the 7th. He thought it a crack unit, perfectly capable of stopping a herd of elephants. While the majority of companies in each of Taylor's regiments had enlisted for the war, the entire 7th was mustered in on that basis. Commitment brought a high standard, and the 7th was the sort of polished military machine Jackson wanted to make of his Valley regiments. Taylor remembered the 8th as a regiment of French-speaking Acadians: happy men, born cooks, with a fine regimental band, they were likely to finish even the weariest day with a concert. Taylor recalled the music accurately, but only a handful of the 8th were Cajuns; most were born of Louisiana and other Southern Anglo-American parents, and there were Irish and Germans as well. Taylor romanticized the 9th into a regiment of planters or sons of planters from the privileged world of north Louisiana where large plantations graced the Mississippi. In reality most men of the 9th were small farmers; there were a few merchants, clerks, and laborers, but hardly a genteel planter among them.

Fact and fiction combined naturally in Taylor's last unit, Major Roberdeau Chatham Wheat's infantry battalion of so-called "Louisiana Tigers." One company was made up of soldiers of fortune. One particularly rowdy company with more than a few criminals in its ranks, the

Tiger Rifles, had lent its name to the entire command, which overall possessed such a bad reputation as cutthroats and drunks that no other regiment or brigade wanted it.[9] The Tigers were fierce in battle: at Manassas some threw away their muskets and charged with knives. They fleeced the dead of both armies under an absurd banner with the words "as gentle as" inscribed beneath a lamb, and only the iron hand of Major Wheat kept them in tolerable order. Six feet, four inches tall and 240 pounds, Wheat had learned to savor combat during the Mexican War, and afterward he emerged as a notable soldier of fortune in Cuba, Nicaragua, and with Garibaldi in Italy. It was said he had spent more time under fire than any man in North America.[10]

General Taylor was likewise a figure who commanded respect. When a band of intoxicated Tigers failed in an attempt to storm the brigade guardhouse to liberate some of their imprisoned fellows, Taylor had two of the ringleaders executed by a firing squad drawn from Wheat's Battalion. The entire division was marched out to witness it. Against the possibility that the Tigers would not fire, Taylor stationed a company of the 8th Louisiana with loaded weapons immediately behind the firing squad. The first execution in the Army of Northern Virginia took place on schedule, and after that even the Tigers were a little tamer.[11]

A man of considerable wealth, Taylor had an impressive educational background, having graduated from Yale and also studied at Harvard and Edinburgh, Scotland. Although he had had no military training, he had long been a student of military history, including the campaigns of his father, General and former President Zachary Taylor. He was brother-in-law to Jefferson Davis, and he worked as hard as his connections were good. His brigade's good march discipline, for instance, was the product of his strenuous effort. As Johnston withdrew from the Centreville area during March, Taylor was unhappy with the rampant straggling, a problem that infected his own command, and he began to root it out. He taught his men to bathe their feet at the end of the day, showed them how to heal sores, and gave advice on picking boots. The brigade's standard uniform was modified to include two pairs of boots per man. By riding at the rear of the column to encourage those who fell behind (sometimes he gave them rides as well), Taylor provided an example that his officers copied. The men responded with their best efforts and soon regarded straggling a disgrace.[12] Excepting a tenuous discipline among the Tigers, Taylor's was a model brigade. It totaled approximately three thousand men present for duty, and it was fated to become a workhorse in the Shenandoah.

Ewell's force included two artillery units: the Courtney Light Artillery, six guns, under Captain A. R. Courtney, and the Baltimore Light Artillery, four guns, of Captain John Brockenbrough.[13] Attached also were the 2d and 6th Virginia Cavalry regiments commanded respectively by Colonel Thomas Munford and Lieutenant Colonel Thomas Flournoy. Munford, a classmate of James Walker's in V.M.I.'s class of 1852, had worked closely as a cadet officer with Jackson when he first joined the Institute faculty; Munford did not challenge him to a duel and managed to graduate. Thereafter he was a planter, and like many of that background he joined the cavalry at the outset of the war. He led part of the cavalry pursuit following the victory at Manassas. Flournoy had been elected to Congress in 1846 (where he gained the friendship of another freshman representative, Abraham Lincoln) and later ran unsuccessfully for governor of the Old Dominion. There were still equipment shortages in both regiments, and Munford's in particular lacked sufficient ammunition and arms, but these horsemen had been schooled in regular army discipline and had the potential to be much better cavalry than the ragged bands led by Ashby.

Serving as Ewell's aide-de-camp was twenty-one-year-old Campbell Brown, a bright young man who possessed the extra advantage of a widowed mother by whom Ewell had been smitten. Ewell took on the son as a way to keep the attention of Widow Brown, and he got in the bargain an excellent assistant and future son-in-law. In later years Brown was to prove an invaluable source on the exploits of Ewell's splendid command. In the spring of 1862 that division had a total strength of approximately eighty-five hundred men,[14] men who wanted to get into the war. But as days and then weeks passed uneventfully in Swift Run Gap, the division began to question whether it would ever join Jackson's Valley Campaign.

Richard Ewell shared that concern. On the afternoon of April 30, as Ewell's men were pitching camp, Jackson returned to brief Ewell once again before he marched for Staunton. Hotchkiss reported on his observations of Banks's camps,[15] and surely Jackson emphasized that Ewell must not leave the Shenandoah until the Valley Army returned from the

Alleghenies. Perhaps by design, Campbell Brown found a copy of the court-martial charges against Garnett in Stonewall's headquarters that night.[16] So Ewell sat down to wait, and during the next days he watched the war unfold through Jackson's eyes. Old Jack regarded cooperation as so vital that he relaxed his secrecy enough to keep Ewell up-to-date on his movements. From his detour into Brown's Gap until he reached Franklin, Jackson sent Ewell a note each day save one. Of everyone in the Confederacy, Ewell alone had regular news of the Allegheny drive.[17]

Jackson's communications frequently included a repetition of the call to stay put, a simple assignment at first, but a task that became harder as Jackson went farther into the mountains on what seemed to Ewell a comparatively insignificant mission. Ewell saw other opportunities slipping away when Jackson pushed beyond McDowell, and his worry mounted until, when Colonel Walker of the 13th Virginia stopped by his office one day, he found an outlet.

"Colonel Walker," Ewell lisped, "did it ever occur to you that General Jackson is crazy?"

This was a tempting question, no doubt recalling to Walker his opinions about Jackson at V.M.I., but he replied with lawyerlike restraint, "I don't know, general. We used to call him 'Fool Tom' Jackson at the Virginia Military Institute, but I do not suppose he is really crazy."

That was not the answer Ewell wanted. "I tell you," he ranted, "he is as crazy as a March hare."[18]

Ewell's invective was fueled in part by his inability to react to the Union's evolving strategy as manifested by Banks's retirement from Harrisonburg and McDowell's increasing strength at Fredericksburg, both of which were clear by the first week of May. Robert E. Lee had linked these aspects of the equation and wanted action in central Virginia or the Valley to counteract any drive on Richmond from Fredericksburg. To achieve this goal Lee reinforced Ewell. Lee drained other fronts to free a brigade of North Carolinians under Brigadier General L. O'Bryan Branch and ordered it to Gordonsville, twenty-five miles southeast of Swift Run Gap, to act under Ewell's direction.[19] Branch's regiments were arriving in Gordonsville by May 7.[20] That same day Lee found the brigade of William Mahone en route from Norfolk to Richmond; he changed its destination to Gordonville as well.[21]

Two additional brigades would almost double Ewell's command to more than twelve thousand infantry. This was too large a force to be idle, and with increased manpower came prodding from Lee. Lee did not want the reinforcements drawn to Swift Run Gap unless emergency required. Instead, he desired these forces to form a column that could thrust beyond the Rappahannock to cut the Manassas Gap Railroad and relieve pressure at Fredericksburg.[22] Lee did not order Ewell to undertake this drive, although he several times hinted strongly that it should be done.[23] Lee's idea conflicted with Jackson's assignment to stay put, so Ewell found himself in a literal tug-of-war. Thus on the same date, May 6, Jackson instructed him, "Do not leave the valley so long as Banks is in it and I am on the expedition of which I spoke to you,"[24] while Lee wrote, "If enemy have withdrawn from Harrisonburg I see no necessity for your division at Swift Run Gap. Object may be concentration at Fredericksburg. Try and ascertain. Can you cut off party at Culpeper Court-House [east of the Blue Ridge]?"[25]

Ewell chafed over his dilemma. Should he operate east of the Blue Ridge in defiance of Jackson's plan or linger at Swift Run Gap and ignore Lee's call to action? Like any good subordinate, Ewell tried to resolve this puzzle in favor of the offensive already under way. He explained the importance Jackson attached to keeping his force at Swift Run Gap to Lee and secured Lee's approval to remain stationary so long as Banks stayed in the Valley or it was necesary for Jackson's purposes. Implicit in Ewell's mission at Swift Run Gap, however, was the idea that Banks's army would act as a single column,[26] an assumption smashed by the next development Ewell faced. By May 13 came word that a column under Banks was retiring from New Market to Strasburg along the Valley Pike. Another force under Shields likewise was moving, crossing from New Market over Massanutten Mountain into the narrow region between the Blue Ridge and the Massanutten called the Luray Valley. This information Ewell summarized and dispatched to Jackson. Shields's route would take him across the South Fork of the Shenandoah to the town of Luray; once there his logical destination was Fredericksburg, so that Banks's army was no longer operating as a single column. This was a scenario not covered by anyone's instructions for Ewell.

Old Bald Head had a combat soldier's instincts to attack. He summoned Colonel Munford and told him to move with his 2d Virginia Cavalry and part of the 6th to impede Shields's progress. "Ewell was crazy to attack Shields," recalled Munford.[27] Munford set off by daylight with his cavalry bolstered by several cannons.[28] Ewell waited frantically for news. A dispatch from Munford that he had intercepted Shields surely would have brought Ewell hurrying out of Swift Run Gap in support, but despite sending two couriers per day Munford was unable to deliver word of his whereabouts for several days.[29] The reason for the failure is unclear, but for Ewell it was as if Munford had disappeared, and lacking certainty on anything Ewell remained in place.

While passing these anxious hours, Ewell reviewed his dilemma in a sorrowful letter to his niece. The letter was an excellent summary of the coils by which he was entangled:

> I was ordered here to support General Jackson, pressed by Banks. But he [Jackson], immediately upon my arrival, started on a long chase after a body of the enemy far above Staunton. I have been keeping one eye on Banks, one on Jackson, all the time jogged up from Richmond, until I am sick and worn down. Jackson wants me to watch Banks. At Richmond, they want me everywhere and call me off, when, at the same time, I am compelled to remain until that enthusiastic fanatic comes to some conclusion. Now I ought to be en route to Gordonsville, at this place, and going to Jackson, all at the same time. That is, there is reason for all these movements and which one is taken makes it bad for the others. The fact is there seems no head here at all, though there is room for one or two. I have a bad headache, what with the bother and folly of things. I never suffered as much with dyspepsia in my life. As an Irishman would say, "I'm kilt entirely."[30]

The next day a horseman brought additional word from Jackson, dated May 13. Old Jack advised he was returning to the Valley, so Ewell knew the Allegheny offensive was ending. Jackson betrayed how much he was out of touch with events in the Valley by his view of Banks's movements. In essence Jackson wrote not to worry that Banks's command might head east of the Blue Ridge; he suspected that Banks aimed instead to unite with Frémont and possibly advance on Staunton. Jackson's final paragraph made better sense to Ewell: "If Banks goes down the valley I wish you to follow him, so that he may feel that if he leaves the Valley, not only will we reoccupy it, but that he will also be liable to be attacked as soon as he shall have sufficiently weakened his forces on this side of the Shenandoah."[31]

Jackson would not have received Ewell's note relating the split of Banks's force when he wrote on the thirteenth, so the letter Ewell read on the fourteenth did not fully apply to the existing situation, but Ewell had had enough war by courier. Jackson's letter he would construe as authority to chase Banks down the Valley, and he advised Lee he would do so.[32] Orders were issued for the division to start the next morning into the Luray Valley. The target would be the bridges over the Shenandoah's South Fork near Luray; with control of them Ewell could strike the nearest Federals.

Ewell summoned the detachment under General Branch at Gordonsville to join him at Luray via a march through Madison Court House. He cautioned Branch to travel light; in a dispatch ringing of the Stonewall style, he emphasized, "The road to glory cannot be followed with much baggage."[33]

Resolution appeared vindicated before nightfall. A message written by Jackson arrived at 7:20 A.M. that morning (the fourteenth); it acknowledged that a march by Banks to Fredericksburg was a contingency against which plans must be drawn. Jackson still did not accept the division of Banks's force, and he presumably thought Ewell confronted a united column, but he nonetheless urged offensive action by inquiring whether Ewell could use Ashby's cavalry to retard Banks until the Valley Army neared. Jackson promised he would be about forty miles from Harrisonburg that evening.[34] The aggressive tone of Jackson's letter was sufficient for Ewell to conclude that the time for sitting at Swift Run Gap had ended.

On the morning of May 15 Ewell marched out of Swift Run Gap looking for a fight. His division turned at Conrad's Store and pounded northward along the east bank of the Shenandoah's South Fork River toward the hamlet of Honeyville and the nearby Columbia Bridge (one of the structures Hotchkiss had been unable to burn in April because of intoxication among Ashby's riders); Elzey's Brigade secured the bridge by nightfall.[35] It rained heavily that day, and the road was bad, but the division covered fifteen or more miles, an excellent pace. It was a fine beginning to an offensive, and it proved to be the end of one, for as Old Bald Head rode along his regiments he was hailed by another courier. After weeks of messages from Lee and Jackson, Ewell could not have been surprised by one more courier, but this man bore a message with a signature Ewell had not seen since coming to the Valley—that of Joseph E. Johnston. What next?

II

As the month of May advanced, Johnston, like Lee, had been pondering what role the relatively large forces in central Virginia and the Shenandoah ought to play in Richmond's defense. This gave hope that the Valley commanders were to receive definitive word of what was desired of them, yet Johnston's efforts in this regard were hampered by a severe lack of information. He had received during the past weeks only sporadic reports on central Virginia, and on May 10 Johnston complained to Lee about being denied the requisite information to direct operations there.[36] On May 12 Johnston emphasized his authority over Ewell and Jackson in a letter to the latter, but he had to admit discovering only that day where Stonewall was: "I have just learned that your victory over Milroy was beyond Staunton," he wrote, adding that he now assumed Jackson could return to the Valley and his "observations of Banks." Johnston knew nothing of the enemy's strength, nor even that of Jackson, but thought Stonewall might attack Banks or "endeavour to prevent his leaving the valley by your positions. Should he move toward Fredericksburg before you return to the neighborhood of Harrisonburg, you and Gen. Ewell should make the corresponding movement as rapidly as possible."[37]

Thus Johnston wanted Banks attacked in the middle Valley or at least threatened sufficiently to keep him from departing that region. It was another version of the plan Lee had been urging, and there was to be more discussion of this offensive later that same day. Not long after he finished writing to Jackson on May 12, Johnston received at his headquarters a visit from Jefferson Davis and Robert E. Lee. By the time they finished rethinking the direct threat posed by McClellan the hour was late, so Davis and Lee stayed over, which offered the three West Pointers a chance to talk long into the night.

Lee and Johnston had been classmates in the West Point Class of 1829; Davis was one year ahead of them. It was as if Franklin D. Roosevelt, George C. Marshall, and Dwight D. Eisenhower all attended the same military institute together and met three decades later to plan the D Day invasion. With almost a century of military experience among them, the three men surely ranged over the entire war picture in Virginia. Unfortunately only a fragment of what must have been a fascinating conversation was recorded, but that fragment dealt with the Shenandoah. Davis suggested Ewell and Jackson could do more than watch Banks; they should drive him into the lower Shenandoah and crush him there. The results would be significant, and Davis urged the blow be delivered immediately. The response Davis received—probably from Johnston since only three days later Lee would be pressing the same move on Jackson—was that such an operation was impossible.[38]

Davis and Lee departed in the morning, but Johnston again wrote to the Valley. He sent a message to Ewell that evidenced a slightly more aggressive spirit than that conveyed to Stonewall the prior day: "I have written to Major General Jackson to return to the Valley near you, and, if your united force is strong enough, to attack General Banks. Should the latter cross the Blue Ridge to join General McDowell at Fredericksburg, General Jackson and yourself should move eastward rapidly to join either the army near Fredericksburg or this one. I must be kept informed of your movements and progress, that your instructions may be modified as circumstances change."[39] It was this message Ewell was handed as he marched down the Luray Valley on the fifteenth.

Despite Johnston's letter, Ewell did not move on the sixteenth. A hard rain continued, and Ewell's men needed rest and a chance to find something to eat after their excellent effort of the prior day. The best Ewell could do was to keep his scouts busy patrolling the Luray Valley, and from them he learned (at about this time) that Federal units in unknown but apparently not great strength had occupied the village of Front Royal thirty miles to the north. He also kept busy mulling over Johnston's latest instructions. Obviously Johnston, like Jackson and Lee, did not comprehend the separation of Banks and Shields, and absent from Johnston's order was language permitting any discretion in executing them.

Ewell probably had no idea where to march on the sixteenth when new dispatches arrived to further complicate the picture. In sequence impossible to establish, communications came from Jackson and Munford. Stonewall's two short notes were both dated May 15; one inquired what force Ewell could bring to an attack on Banks, and both spoke of a juncture with Ewell at Harrisonburg.[40] Those notes must have unleashed a severe bout of Ewell's dyspepsia. Jackson had authorized him to advance, and he had hurried down the Luray Valley, the quickest route to the enemy and one that allowed Branch's column to join the hunt.

Jackson now wanted to unite at Harrisonburg, on the other side of the Massanutten; had Ewell known that was what Jackson intended, he could have covered the same fifteen miles he made yesterday and been in Harrisonburg. Now Ewell was out of position. And Johnston directed them both to operate east of the Blue Ridge—Jackson was out of position for that.

That there must be combat beyond the Valley seemed assured by news from Colonel Munford. His messengers were now getting back with rumors that Shields had turned from Front Royal (at the top of the Luray Valley) and was traversing the Blue Ridge.[41] By 10 A.M. Ewell knew enough to compose a summary for Jackson. He copied a portion of Johnston's order and restated everything else he knew. Ewell pleaded for Jackson to finalize a plan: "On your course may depend the fate of Richmond," he stressed.[42]

Before long there was fresh intelligence from Munford, dated 7 P.M. of the fifteenth. Munford had encountered a sizable Federal column ten miles east of the Blue Ridge near Flint Hill on the afternoon of the fifteenth. He fanned out his riders and disputed the way in a skirmish more noisy and long than deadly. There were few casualties, but Munford compelled the enemy to deploy. "Think of a whole army drawn up in line of battle and kept so for six hours by two hundred and fifty half armed cavalry," he boasted.[43] The fight verified that the enemy was moving to Fredericksburg in force. (It also depleted Munford's ammunition, and with his command virtually defenseless he was called farther east toward Richmond to resupply. This removed most of his cavalry regiment from service in the Valley during the next week.[44])

As the hours passed Ewell was handed intelligence placing Shields's numbers at six thousand.[45] He hardly could keep up with the onslaught of words. During the day he stopped Branch's column on its march to Luray and then restarted it.[46] Within a few hours more he decided Johnston's orders demanded the pursuit of Shields. He penned a note warning Jackson that he would move accordingly[47] and hastened yet another rider to Branch telling him "to retrace your steps to Gordonsville with as much dispatch as you can."[48]

Ewell's profanity was the stuff of legend. He could swear, marveled Colonel Munford, "in a style that defies descripton,"[49] and on the morning of the seventeenth he must have been ignited by a fresh message from Jackson. Ashby had informed Jackson that neither Banks nor

Shields had left the Valley, but the cavalry chief had relayed an erroneous report about Union reinforcements streaming westward from Winchester to Frémont. Writing late on the sixteenth, Jackson therefore advised that Ashby could not join Ewell's advance. Instead, Ashby was to cut off communication between Banks and Jackson while the latter sprinted to Harrisonburg; from there Jackson wished to unite with Ewell "and strike a successful blow."[50]

Had Ewell not warned Colonel Walker that Jackson was crazy? If the "enthusiastic fanatic" insisted no Federals had left the Valley then he could stay to fight them! Cussing wildly, Ewell decided to march toward Fredericksburg in accordance with Johnston's orders. The head of the division, still Elzey's little brigade, climbed the Blue Ridge at Fischer's Gap on the seventeenth. That put the 1st Maryland and its morale problems in front. One of the twelve-month companies in fact was to be mustered out that day. Colonel Johnson assembled the company before the entire regiment and tried oratory to persuade them to stay.[51] He failed, and the company marched rearward while the balance of the regiment headed up the Blue Ridge in a surly mood. There was little regard for military regulations that afternoon when the Marylanders found a barrel of hard liquor at a wayside inn. "[It] was soon emptied," wrote Sergeant James Thomas.[52] The regiment ended the day on the crest of the Blue Ridge; the regiments of Trimble's Brigade camped on the slopes.[53]

Taylor's Brigade was not with them. Three diary sources specify that the Louisianans retraced their steps along the Shenandoah's South Fork in the direction of Swift Run Gap on the seventeenth. There is no official explanation, but the brigade by night reached Waverly, only five miles from Conrad's Store.[54] Possibly Ewell anticipated that Elzey's and Trimble's units would clog the mountain pass and thought Taylor might make better time by the longer route through Swift Run Gap. It is tempting to speculate that Old Bald Head simply felt uneasy leaving Jackson. Ewell shortly would unite with Branch; in numbers at least Branch could replace Taylor. Perhaps Jackson might encounter Banks somewhere around Harrisonburg after all, and Taylor's men could help. But if that were Ewell's motive he shortly became dissatisfied with it. In fact, he was unhappy with everything he had done.

The need was to strike somewhere now with a unified force. Ewell had worked to find a way, but Southern detachments were as dispersed as those of the enemy. Jackson was beyond Harrisonburg; Taylor was at

Waverly and the rest of Ewell's force straddled the Blue Ridge; Branch was backtracking to Gordonsville. Twenty thousand Confederates were accomplishing nothing within sixty miles of each other! They were so close that couriers leaving Jackson at dawn easily reached Ewell by evening, and soon such a rider appeared.

Jackson had written at 5 A.M. on May 17 after receipt of the communication from Ewell that included Colonel Munford's report of his skirmish with Shields near Flint Hill. Jackson again evidenced his blind spot regarding Shields; not looking beyond the Shenandoah, Jackson directed Ewell to have his division at New Market by May 21. "Let us," he wrote, "relying upon God for success, prepare for attacking Banks." Jackson repeated his opinion that Banks did not intend leaving the Valley. He did, however, at least recognize it as a possibility and suggested that in such event Ewell must hold him until Jackson could catch up, but, he concluded, "this cannot be determined upon until we know what the enemy is doing."[55]

Ewell by now challenged the limit of his profanity. He knew what the enemy was doing; he could not understand Jackson. What would that fanatic do when he realized the separation of Banks's army? Would he ever realize it? What must be done in the meantime? With Jackson at last writing of a general assault in the Valley, should Ewell march in the opposite direction after Shields?

These questions Ewell answered with a shout to halt. Every unit subject to his command was ordered to stop in place. General Branch was sent a note to stop, the fourth recasting of the North Carolinian's marching orders in thirty-six hours.[56] Ewell resolved he would do everything possible to secure definite orders. He personally briefed his aide, Campbell Brown, then started him for the telegraph office at Gordonsville to communicate to Lee the conflicts that rendered action impossible and seek clarification.[57] Another oath and Ewell demanded his horse. It was long past dark, but Dick Ewell bounced on and dug in his spurs. He was going to face Jackson and settle the course of this campaign.

11

DOWN THE VALLEY

God grant that we may be
enabled to make a good lick.

—John Harman

On the evening of Saturday, May 17, as Ewell resolved on personal action, the Valley Army reentered the Shenandoah from the Alleghenies. After those stark, smoldering mountains, the budding Valley was paradise. It was the first day in five without rain. Orchards were in magnificent bloom; fields were lush with clover—"how our weary horses did revel in it," wrote Ed Moore.[1] Camp was pitched that evening on the road from McDowell to Harrisonburg at Mount Solon, a crossroads twelve miles southwest of Harrisonburg. Prosperous farms surrounded the Army, and famished rebels spread across the countryside to visit them.

Ed Moore borrowed a horse to forage cavalry style and found abundant reward in a comfortable Dutch household. The family felt pity for the hungry Moore and sent him back to the Army with a ham wedged in the saddle with him, a bucket of butter dangling from one arm, and a box of pies from the other. His horse took a fall on the way, but the forager's instincts were true. He dropped the reins and balanced his treasures; when the animal recovered its feet, not a morsel had slipped an inch.[2]

General Ewell probably had been passing men such as Moore for hours when, early on May 18, he reached the camp at Mount Solon after a long night's ride. What he discovered must have prompted afresh the thought that Jackson was crazy. Every hour counted now, yet the Valley Army would not march. It was Sunday, and Jackson did not wish to break the Lord's peace with warlike activities. Thousands of troops were napping or cooking or washing their clothes;[3] worship services were slated for later in the day. Perhaps the hardest thing Ewell ever did was not to bolt for his divison and whisk it away from this "crazy fool" Jackson, but he had come this far, so he kept coming.

Ewell located Stonewall, and the two generals found privacy in an old mill.[4] Both men knew as they sat down that the Confederate war picture was darker now than during March. In April the Battle of Shiloh had been lost in Tennessee, with ten thousand Southern casualties. Strategic Island No. 10 in the Mississippi River had fallen to Union Major General John Pope the day after Shiloh. New Orleans had surrendered by the end of April, and from there Admiral Farragut steamed up the Mississippi River; he was unopposed with an oceangoing fleet in the heartland of the South. Baton Rouge surrendered to his warships on May 9, Natchez on May 12. Most of Tennessee was under Federal sway by then, and a one-hundred-thousand-man Union army was edging into northern Mississippi.

From the far West to the Atlantic coast the South knew only defeat. On March 28 the Confederacy lost the Battle of Gloriatta Pass, New Mexico, the Gettysburg of the West. Saint Augustine fell to Union naval forces in March, Apalachicola and Jacksonville in early April. Fort Pulaski on the Georgia coast fell on April 11, shutting Savannah to blockade runners. On May 9, as the Valley Army recovered from its battle at McDowell, the Southern naval base at Norfolk, Virginia, was abandoned, leaving the ironclad *Virginia* without a port and compelling the crew to scuttle her. From his base on Roanoke Island Union General Burnside had penetrated throughout the sounds of North Carolina; by May he wielded a powerful force that could operate against the Confederate capital from below or isolate it with a drive inland to cut Richmond's major rail link to the Deep South at Goldsboro, North Carolina.

On the Peninsula, Johnston withdrew from his Yorktown lines and started a retreat that would carry him to the gates of Richmond. A costly but inclusive battle outside Williamsburg on May 5 did nothing to retard McClellan's advance, and there was humiliation when four hundred Southern wounded had to be left behind as the retreat continued. The only Southern victory of note anywhere since the beginning of 1862 was McDowell, and amid so many disasters it did not seem to matter. When the victory became known in Richmond McClellan was thirty miles away with one hundred thousand men, and sidewalk strategists denounced the Valley Army's offensive as rash.[5]

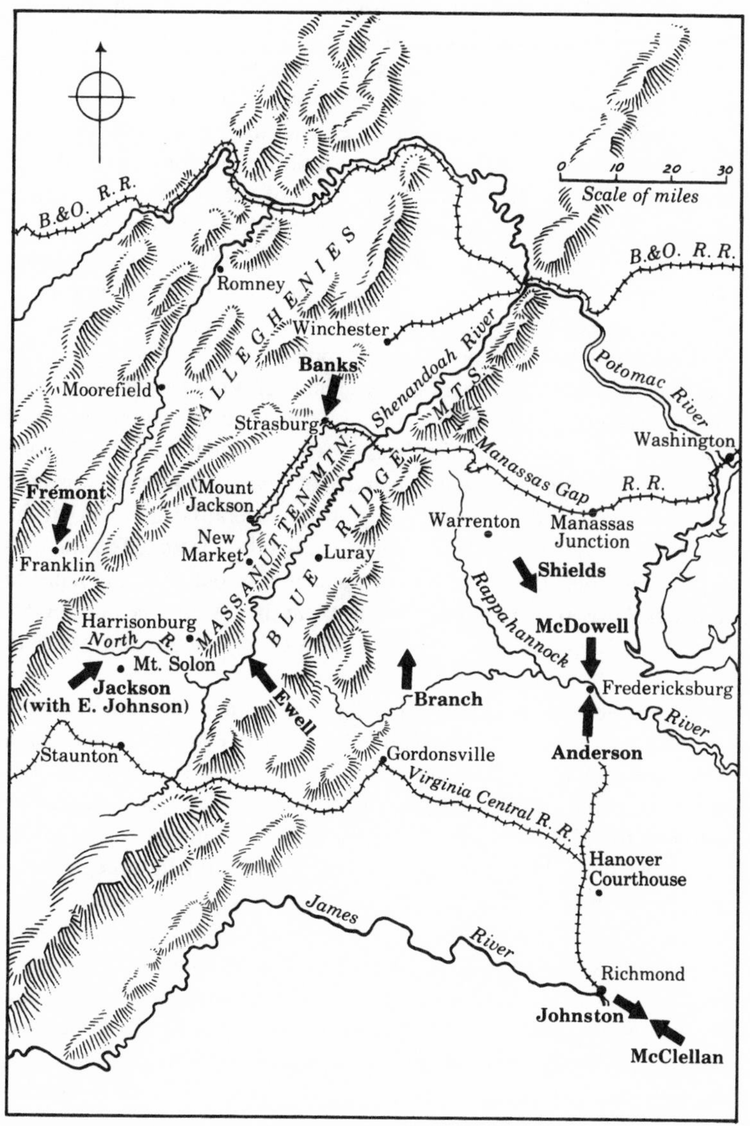

7. General Situation, May 18, 1862

Urgently, then, Jackson and Ewell considered what they might do against the flood tide of defeat. Few details of their meeting are recorded; Hotchkiss noted only that it was a long consultation.[6] Likely they spread out a map to recapitulate deployments across central Virginia, and together they would have known enough to plot correctly the location of Union and Confederate units as follows: Frémont was hunkered down at Franklin; the Union front west of the Valley briefly was neutralized. Banks was digging in his remaining forces at Strasburg; Shields had crossed the Blue Ridge with a reported six thousand infantry (actually the number was ten thousand). Shields was en route to Fredericksburg, where McDowell's large corps was waiting. From Franklin to Fredericksburg Northern armies were spread in an arc extending more than one hundred miles; it was a classic blunder. Luck or fate had placed the Shenandoah Valley in the interior of that arc. Jackson with all of Allegheny Johnson's command was at Mount Solon, Taylor's Brigade was near Conrad's Store, the remainder of Ewell's command was atop the Blue Ridge, and not many miles away General Branch was on the road from Gordonsville to the Valley. These rebels if united would outnumber Frémont, Banks, or Shields, and if they outpaced the latter to Fredericksburg to join Southern forces there they would face even odds against McDowell. Manifestly the issue was not whether but where to attack.

The generals doubtless pooled the correspondence each had from Richmond for guidance. The voluble Ewell surely explained his decision of the previous evening to halt and send Campbell Brown with a telegram requesting instructions from Lee. In that information Stonewall may have found irony, for he independently had taken the same action at almost the same hour. The night before, Jackson finally accepted that Shields was marching to Fredericksburg while Banks remained in the Valley. He thereupon posed the question of his and Ewell's assignment to Johnston; at about the same time Ewell was writing for clarification from Lee, Jackson was drafting a letter to Johnston. Stonewall wrote that Banks was fortifying at Strasburg, that he planned to unite with Ewell, crush Banks, and then menace Frémont's rear so as to prevent a renewed effort against Staunton by the Pathfinder. If Johnston wanted him to move east, he would do so; Stonewall asked only that Johnston give him specific orders by telegram.[7] There was no return message from Johnston by morning of the eighteenth.

There was in all likelihood another communiqué from Lee in Jackson's files by the morning of the eighteenth. Lee had written under pressure on May 16; on May 15, while Jackson was suppressing mutiny in the Stonewall Brigade, Federal gunboats had bombarded Confederate batteries at Drewry's Bluff only seven miles from Richmond. The enemy was repulsed, but the threat was serious enough that Lee diverted to Drewry's Bluff Mahone's Brigade (which he had started to Ewell after Branch's Brigade was ordered to central Virginia). Lee described the Union naval thrust and stressed again the importance of stopping what remained of the Union's Valley forces from reaching Fredericksburg, or possibly the Peninsula. Then came the heart of his message, a final call for action in which Lee must have echoed what he heard President Davis urge to Johnston during their meeting of May 12: "A successful blow struck at [Banks] would delay, if it does not prevent, his moving. . . . Whatever movement you make against Banks do it speedily and if successful, drive him back toward the Potomac, and create the impression, as far as practicable that you design threatening that line." These were electric words, yet Lee was constrained to remind Jackson that his operations must be viewed in light of the struggle of the main armies: "But you will not, in any demonstration you may make in that direction, lose sight of the fact that it may become necessary for you to come to the support of General Johnston, and hold yourself in readiness to do so if required."[8]

Strike in the Valley, yet be mindful of the situation at Richmond: Lee's message encapsulated the explicit and implicit conflicts under which Jackson had campaigned for the past month. Reduced to essentials, the instructions ran something like this:

1. In mid-April Johnston had directed Jackson to protect the Valley while retreating to Swift Run Gap, which Jackson had done.
2. In late April Lee had urged him to undertake an operational maneuver so as to hinder Union movements from Fredericksburg (thus relieving pressure on Richmond). Jackson had finished the groundwork for this strike by his victory at McDowell.
3. On May 12, unaware of the division of Banks's army, Johnston had ordered Jackson to pursue "Banks" if the latter crossed the Blue Ridge, which half of "Banks" now had done. Similar orders went to Ewell from Johnston on the thirteenth.

4. On May 16, aware of the division of Banks's army but apparently without knowledge of Johnston's letters, Lee had urged Jackson again to smash Banks in the Valley.
5. Conclusion: Jackson and Ewell faced a problem as old as warfare. The campaign was at a turning point that required immediate action. They had an abundance of orders, none of which corresponded to the actual situation as they knew it, and high command was too far away for quick communication. Efforts to clarify the mission might not be successful for days, during which time their commands ought not be idle. Should they follow what seemed to be Johnston's instructions to pursue Shields beyond the Blue Ridge, or Lee's to attack Banks in the Shenandoah?

Logic dictated that the objective must be Banks or Shields. Even Frémont's total destruction would not put at risk any crucial Union asset, and to engage all available Confederate strength against the Pathfinder would be to remove them from the strategic calculus that shortly must determine Richmond's future. A strike to Fredericksburg was impractical, because it would take many days for the Valley Army to reach that point, and time was limited. The nearest targets were the best, but it must be one or the other; to divide Southern forces to attack Banks and Shields would forfeit the advantage of superior numbers. Beyond such general observations, the two major generals were on their own.

Major Dabney, perhaps an observer at part of the discussion, implied that Ewell broke the impasse. His division was in the Valley, and he therefore was willing to follow Jackson's orders, not Johnston's. He stated that if Jackson would give the word, he would lunge down the Valley after Banks, not east after Shields.[9] Ewell's proposal strained to the limit any discretion permitted by Johnston's most recent message, but it also offered the surest chance of success. Shields was a moving target; his location would change daily, and bringing him to ground beyond the Blue Ridge required time. Banks was stationary and close. If the rebels moved the next morning, Monday, they could unite by Wednesday near New Market. From there a march of at most two days would take them to Banks at Strasburg.

Jackson did not hesitate. History would judge more harshly than Johnston if the present opportunity was lost. Jackson requested Ewell to prepare a statement of his dilemma, then composed a solution. Noting first that Ewell had received letters from Generals Lee and Johnston and himself requiring different actions, Jackson wrote out an order advising Ewell: "As you are in the Valley District you constitute part of my command. Should you receive orders different from those sent from these headquarters, please advise me of the same at as early a period as practicable." Having taken responsibility for keeping Ewell, Jackson then instructed him in writing to encamp on the Valley Pike between New Market and Mount Jackson by Wednesday night (May 21) "unless you receive orders from a superior officer and that of a date subsequent to the 16th instant."[10]

The operation embodied in the writing Jackson handed Ewell was straightforward: all Confederates in central Virginia were to converge on Banks, fortifications or not. Ewell was to reverse his direction, traverse Massanutten Gap to New Market, and press northward along the Valley Pike toward Mount Jackson. The brigades under Jackson would pursue a northeasterly course to Harrisonburg and come up to join Ewell at New Market by the twenty-first. The column under Branch would follow Ewell's route and should arrive in time for the decisive battle. It is speculation, but there might have been some further discussion concerning a route of march for the brigade of Louisianans camped at the southern exit of the Luray Valley. Rather than retracing his steps through the Luray Valley to Massanutten Gap, which would be filled with Ewell's and Branch's regiments, General Taylor could as easily proceed west to the Pike to meet Jackson near New Market, and this was ordered.

Such were the means by which the Southern convergence against Banks was to be achieved.* Ewell had found what he sought and more by his night's ride. Although he avowed an enthusiastic atheism, Old Bald Head was thankful enough to attend the Valley Army's worship with Jackson. He heard Major Dabney preach an excellent sermon to Conner's Brigade, then bounced onto his horse and thundered off to ready his division.[11]

---

* This portion of the narrative presents a reconstruction of events different than that of any previous work on the campaign, including the earlier work of this author. For this reason the question of exactly where Jackson originally planned to attack Banks, and when, is considered at length in Appendix A.

Jackson also got busy. He needed to move with rapidity and so attended after Dabney's sermon to the hurdle of the North River, a wide stream that intersected his route at Bridgewater. The town's namesake bridge had been burned in April when the Army retired into Swift Run Gap.[12] What had blocked Yankee cavalry passing over the stream to Staunton now barred Jackson's way to Harrisonburg. Close to the charred bridge was a ford, which received Old Jack's personal inspection, but deep water threatened time lost crossing there. The general turned for ideas to Hotchkiss, who lived thereabouts, and as usual the mapmaker had a thought. One of the units that had joined the Valley Army with Johnson's command was a remarkable platoon of Negro laborers, the "African Pioneers." These men were workers of skill and great practical ability who had been employed during the past months to maintain the road from Staunton to Johnson's mountain camps. They were led by Captain C. R. Mason, a redoubtable engineer who was to show himself capable during the war of some extraordinary building feats. This part of the Valley abounded with large hauling wagons, and Hotchkiss suggested Jackson let Mason cobble some of them into a bridge.[13] Jackson agreed, and the next day Mason had a row of large vehicles standing side by side across the river, tongues pointed upstream, with planks secured from one wagon to the next.[14]

There was time in the Shenandoah for nothing more elaborate than making bridges of wagons, for the calendar was now a principal opponent. Shields would billet at Fredericksburg before many days, and the Valley Army must strike before he could depart there. Discipline on the march must be tightened yet again. Orders boomed from Headquarters that the Army was to move automatically at 5 A.M. each day.[15]

That same day, as Jackson and Ewell agreed upon their onslaught, Shields was thirty miles from Fredericksburg.[16]

The Confederate sprint began on Monday, May 19, with Ewell relaying to General Branch Jackson's instructions that they should both be between New Market and Mount Jackson by the twenty-first and instructing Branch to resume his march toward New Market;[17] Branch approached the eastern foothills of the Blue Ridge only a day's march from Columbia Bridge by nightfall.[18] Elzey's and Trimble's brigades countermarched from the crest of the Blue Ridge to Columbia Bridge.[19] Taylor's Brigade hurried around the southern end of the Massanutten; it bivouacked near the village of McGaheysville about seven miles from Harrisonburg.[20]

From Taylor's camp it was but a half day's march to Jackson's vanguard, which had tested Captain Mason's wagon bridge outside Bridgewater on the morning of the nineteenth. The span was a crude expedient, but one that served. The first regiments, those of Johnson's old command, hustled through Harrisonburg and made a mile or two north along the Valley Pike.[21] Of necessity some time was lost filing over the wagon bridge, and the rear units did not get far beyond Bridgewater before dark.[22] There was thus a distance of seven or eight miles between the head and tail of Jackson's column, a gap he would not close for days, but Jackson was thinking only of the vanguard, now within a day's march of New Market. Toward evening the general sent Ewell a note asking a little more from him. Stonewall now wanted Ewell to camp beyond (north of) Mount Jackson by Wednesday the twenty-first; if possible Ewell should get his command beyond New Market by the end of his march of the twentieth because Jackson as well would reach that point by the evening of the twentieth.[23]

Jackson was arranging the fine points of his descent upon Strasburg, making sure his brigades did not waste time blocking each other at the New Market crossroads. To complete the attack Stonewall desired that Banks should know nothing of his approach while he gained detailed information on Banks's positions. The first requirement was supplied by Ashby, who had reoccupied the lines he had held in April along Stony Creek; from there he prevented southward penetration by Federal cavalry (although he was not, as is often asserted, vigorously demonstrating so as to draw Federal attention to the area; see Appendix A). The second need required a scouting mission, another job for Hotchkiss. Early on the nineteenth Jackson paired the mapmaker with the Army's engineer, Lieutenant Boswell, and sent them to reconnoiter. The two men rode to Ashby's camp outside New Market and then forward on the twentieth to pinpoint Federal pickets seven miles beyond Ashby's Stony Creek lines near the village of Maurertown. The pair split and prowled the Yankee front for the next two days; Boswell secured an infantry escort from a company of Mississippians that Ewell had stationed in the area and went as far as Three Topped Mountain overlooking Strasburg. Hotchkiss sketched several roads west of the Pike that might offer an undetected path around Banks's lines.[24]

Tuesday, May 20, saw the Confederate net closing. Southern raiders were dispatched to block roads in Hampshire and Hardy counties leading from Franklin to Strasburg or Winchester; Frémont must not be given easy passage to rescue Banks.[25] The brigades under Jackson gained the Valley Pike. The weather was fair, and on their first decent road in weeks these rebels raced northward. The way was marked by the aftermath of Federal occupation; everywhere were dead horses and their stench, and for miles fences had disappeared. "[The Yankees] have almost ruined the country about here," grumbled one rebel.[26]

Ewell had his wing moving across Columbia Bridge and up Massanutten Mountain with the sun. Trimble's Brigade reached New Market by evening, with Elzey a short distance back camped on the eastern slopes of the Massanutten.[27] During the day Ewell received assurance from his aide, Campbell Brown, that Branch's Brigade was starting its march across the Blue Ridge; Ewell forwarded the report to Jackson with a reminder that he had given no new orders to Branch. Jackson fired back: "Let the troops come on. I wish they were at New Market."[28]

By evening Jackson's lead regiments camped within sight of New Market,[29] and Southern concentration was almost complete when, about sundown, Taylor's Louisiana Brigade swung into view from the southeast after a march of more than twenty miles around Massanutten Mountain. His road slanted onto the Valley Pike ahead of Jackson's troops, so everyone had a chance to watch Taylor pass in review.

Taylor later recalled the moment through a romantic haze, writing of his regiments stepping jauntily, polished bayonets catching rays of the setting sun, every man neat in fresh gray uniform. The reality was likely less exquisite: the brigade had been marching for four of the past six days, had endured heavy rain the first two days, and had covered more than fifty miles over some of the poorer roads in the Shenandoah. The Louisianans must have been as dusty as everyone else, yet they made an impression. Some of Jackson's men were struck just by the regularity of their dress, "uniforms" being something of a rarity in the Valley; others wrote almost sheepishly of seeing Major Wheat's Tigers, whose reputation preceded them.[30] Certainly the strength and discipline of the command were evident: "They were a splendid looking set of fellows," admired one staff officer.[31] Taylor parked his regiments, then reported to Jackson, whom he found sitting on a fence rail. Old Jack received, quizzed, and dismissed him with four sentences, no doubt prompting Taylor to wonder, as had many others, about this strange, taciturn man.[32]

1. Major General Thomas J. "Stonewall" Jackson, commander of the Valley Army. *Courtesy of the Library of Congress*

2. Brigadier General Turner Ashby. This picture was taken shortly after Ashby's death. In accordance with the customs of the time, the body was cleaned and dressed in a fresh uniform. *Courtesy of the Chicago Historical Society*

3. Jackson and his staff. A wartime composite featuring rare photographs of some principal Valley Army staff members; missing are Major John Harman, the Army's indefatigable quartermaster, and Colonel Stapleton Crutchfield, chief of artillery. *Courtesy of the Library of Congress*

4. Major General Richard S. Ewell, second in command of the Valley Army during the decisive months of May and June 1862. He later admitted that he never saw a courier from Stonewall approach without anticipating orders to attack the North Pole. *Courtesy of the Library of Congress*

5. Brigadier General William W. Loring, second in command of the Valley Army during its disastrous march against Romney. He was the first of many officers with whom Jackson clashed during the Valley Campaign. *Courtesy of the Library of Congress*

6. The Shenandoah Valley from Maryland Heights, a wartime sketch by Alfred R. Waud. *Courtesy of the Library of Congress*

7. "Following Stonewall," a wartime sketch by Confederate artist William L. Sheppard depicting the march on Romney. *Courtesy of the Museum of the Confederacy*

8. "Adventure of Ashby at Winchester," a highly romanticized depiction of Ashby's exit from Winchester on March 12, 1862. The scene is typical of the myths that grew up around Ashby. *From* Wearing the Gray *by John Esten Cooke, New York, 1868*

9. Captain R. P. Chew, commander of Ashby's mounted battery. *U.S. Signal Corps Photo No. 111-BA-1251, Brady Collection, National Archives. Courtesy of the National Archives*

10. Typical terrain over which the Valley Campaign was fought. This picture, taken in the 1880s, shows the area around Strasburg as it would have appeared to Jackson's troops. The northern end of the Massanutten Mountain rises in the background. *Courtesy of the Massachusetts Commandery Military Order of the Loyal Legion and the U.S. Army Military History Institute*

11. Recruiting at Woodstock when the war was still a romantic adventure. *Courtesy of the Virginia State Library*

Classmates at West Point, Johnston and Lee found themselves issuing conflicting orders to the Valley Army in May 1862.

12. General Robert E. Lee. *Courtesy of the Library of Congress*

13. General Joseph E. Johnston. *Courtesy of the Library of Congress*

14. The Battle of Kernstown. This contemporary engraving by Alfred R. Waud evidently depicts the final moments of the battle, as Waud carefully included fleeing rebels and the setting sun. *From April 12, 1862, issue of* Harper's Weekly, *reproduced courtesy of the Virginia State Library*

15. Ashby's charge at Middletown. *Courtesy of the Virginia State Library*

16. Federal scouts approaching Strasburg, June 1, 1862. In this wartime sketch by Union artist Edwin Forbes, the last Confederate trains can be seen *(center, left)* pulling through Strasburg to escape the Union pincer operation set in motion by President Lincoln seven days earlier. *Courtesy of the Virginia State Library*

The brigade was the basic combat unit of the Valley Army, and on successive fields these brigadiers held center stage of the Valley Campaign.

17. Brigadier General Edward Johnson. *Courtesy of the Library of Congress*

18. Brigadier General Isaac R. Trimble. *Courtesy of the Library of Congress*

19. Brigadier General Charles S. Winder. *Courtesy of the Library of Congress*

20. Brigadier General Richard B. Garnett. *Courtesy of the Library of Congress*

No single group of soldiers left as significant a body of postwar recollections as did those who fought with the Valley Army. Here are only a few of the Army's many authors.

21. Gunner George Neese, a member of Chew's Battery and prolific diarist. *Courtesy of Lee L. Wallace, Jr., and Ben Ritter*

22. Brigadier General Richard Taylor. *Courtesy of the Library of Congress*

23. Captain William Poague. *U.S. Signal Corps Photo No. 111-BA-1253, Brady Collection, National Archives. Courtesy of the National Archives*

24. Colonel Bradley T. Johnson. *Courtesy of the Library of Congress*

25. Ashby's dying fight. This sketch by Confederate artist William L. Sheppard portrays the charge of the 1st Maryland Infantry during the brief but savage action at close quarters near Harrisonburg on June 6, 1862. *Courtesy of the Library of Congress*

26. The Valley Army's June retreat. This sketch depicts Confederate troops destroying the bridge at Mount Jackson, June 3, 1862. *From July 5, 1862, issue of* Frank Leslie's Illustrated Newspaper, *reproduced courtesy of the Virginia State Library*

27. The Valley Pike just north of Middletown. This picture, taken in the 1880s, shows the section of the Valley Pike along which Federal forces were trapped on May 24, 1862. Note how the stone walls on either side would funnel troops and wagon trains into an extended, indefensible column. *Courtesy of the Massachusetts Commandery Military Order of the Loyal Legion and the U.S. Army Military History Institute*

28. Captain Campbell Brown, aide and future son-in-law to General Richard S. Ewell. *Courtesy of the Tennessee State Library and Archives (Nashville, Tennessee)*

29. Captain S. J. C. Moore, Co. I, 2d Virginia Infantry, whose constant efforts to train his men culminated in a heroic stand that literally saved the Valley Army. *Courtesy of Ben Ritter*

30. The 199, a huge Baltimore & Ohio engine that Jackson's engineers struggled mightily to save. Their efforts were rewarded and the engine survived for a long life of service, as shown in this photograph taken many years after hostilities ceased. *Courtesy of the Baltimore and Ohio Railroad Museum*

With Taylor camped at the head of Jackson's troops, the Louisiana Brigade was very close to Trimble's command at New Market. Ewell therefore could easily reunite his division in the morning and move it the eight miles required to place it beyond Mount Jackson by next evening, all that Stonewall had asked of him. That would put Ewell's fresh troops in the lead, an excellent vanguard by the measure of Taylor's men. Jackson's veterans could follow and close up, and after they passed New Market Branch's command (which ought to be even then descending the Blue Ridge to Columbia Bridge) should finish its march over the Massanutten and form the rear.

Eight days earlier, Jackson had been probing Frémont's lines near Franklin; only three days earlier, the Confederates in central Virginia were dispersed from the fringes of the Alleghenies to Gordonsville; now they were poised to launch a major offensive. By the next evening, Wednesday the twenty-first, twenty thousand Southern infantry could bivouac along the Pike. With luck Hotchkiss would have returned by then with his observations of Banks's position, and the Valley Army could speed northward to destroy him somewhere outside Strasburg. The batteries of Ewell and Branch would add weight to the attack by increasing the Valley Army's artillery to more than fifty pieces. The cavalry attached to Ewell would stiffen Ashby's command and the total mounted force would equal a strong brigade. Only Johnston at Richmond and Beauregard in Mississippi wielded greater strength in the face of the enemy. Stonewall in fact now commanded the third largest army of the Confederacy.

Old Jack climbed off the fence from which he had watched Taylor's parade and rode to Headquarters; there one aide saw him smiling.[33] Perhaps he was enjoying a forethought of victory and perhaps as well relief at the lack of additional orders. There had been time enough for his message of the seventeenth from Mount Solon to reach Johnston and bring priority response if Johnston so chose, but there had been no word. Jackson had written that unless he heard from Johnston to the contrary he would continue his march until within striking distance of Banks. He was free to interpret silence as tacit authority for retaining Ewell. Stonewall had refused to abandon his goal of defeating Banks, and now he was nearly ready to do it. There was reason for satisfaction at Headquarters, but Jackson's smile was to vanish as he looked up and saw Richard Ewell coming his way.

II

Three times Ewell had ridden up to Army Headquarters: twice at Swift Run Gap before Jackson went to confront Frémont, and recently at Mount Solon. The visit of the twentieth, like that of the eighteenth, was unexpected, and it brought news just as bad. While Jackson west of the Massanutten could see a major offense taking shape that day, Ewell on the east side of the mountain was first to receive news that might end it.

Dawn of the twentieth found General Branch moving his North Carolina Brigade up the western slopes of the Blue Ridge according to plan; "the glorious sunrise saw the whole Brigade urging its way up the western ascent," wrote one Tarheel.[34] Before the march had proceeded barely three miles, however, Branch was overtaken by a courier bearing peremptory orders from General Johnston in Richmond to return there. Branch at once about-faced to Madison Court House, where he penned a note to Ewell advising him of this change.[35] Ewell received this message that afternoon and understood the word he earlier had passed to Jackson that Branch was near the Luray Valley was false. Ewell could hardly have looked forward to correcting the news for Jackson, but soon there was worse.

On the heels of Branch's courier came from Johnston a new order. It was dated May 17 and so was written before Jackson's request from Mount Solon for definite instructions had arrived on his desk. This order was born of Johnston's preference for massing strength by giving up territory and fighting only when there was nowhere else to retreat: "My general idea," Johnston explained, "is to gather [at Richmond] all troops who do not keep away from McClellan greatly superior forces." Johnston was particularly concerned with the idea of attacking entrenchments. "If Banks is fortifying near Strasburg the attack would be too hazardous. In such an event we must leave him in his works." Johnston's only permission for action in central Virginia was to write that if opportunity presented itself Ewell and Jackson might unite to attack Shields on his march to Fredericksburg; Johnston added that Branch's command, like Ewell's, also had been ordered east.[36] Thus by midafternoon of the twentieth Ewell had orders to move toward Richmond, and there was nothing to do but go and apprise Stonewall. Ewell's face was a mask of ill humor as he trotted up to Army Headquarters.

"General Ewell, I'm glad to see you. Get off!" said Jackson.

"You will not be so glad, when I tell you what brought me," replied Ewell.

"What—are the Yankees after you?"

"Worse than that. I am ordered to join General Johnston," Ewell groused as he dismounted.[37]

Jackson ushered Ewell into an adjacent grove out of earshot of his aides, but rumors flew as staffers began to buzz about what this visit meant. Sandie Pendleton was watching as the generals conferred and wrote home at that very moment: "Genl. Ewell and Genl. Jackson are now in close conclave and what the result may be I do not know. I surmise that Ewell is ordered to take his force which joined us today over the [Blue] Ridge tomorrow."[38]

No one overheard the conversation, but Henry Douglas could see that Jackson spoke very little.[39] Indeed there would seem to have been little to say. The latest knowledge about the Richmond front that can be attributed with any certainty to Jackson or Ewell would have been contained in Lee's letter of May 16 advising of the Battle at Drewry's Bluff and the suspension of Mahone's redeployment to the Valley. Johnston's peremptory instructions to Branch to head for Richmond (issued on the seventeenth) were consistent with Lee's actions and implied that some emergency had arisen at the capital. Alexander Boteler had written Jackson on the sixteenth from Richmond and noted there was much confusion at government offices as files were packed for transfer out of the city; he added that Johnston had "contracted" his lines, evidently against a movement by McClellan, who perhaps would act in concert with Burnside's forces from North Carolina.[40] Whether Jackson had this letter in hand by the twentieth is unknown, but if so it would only heighten concern about the state of things at the capital. Stonewall could not appreciate and manifestly did not even know the overall situation as viewed from Richmond; he could not know how an order that appeared wrong to him might be part of a larger plan. Indeed it was not a subordinate's right to such knowledge—that was the premise of his own unyielding silence.

It was a dramatic moment in the Shenandoah. With Branch and now Ewell called away there was little chance for a battle in the Valley. Jackson roiled at the idea of losing this opportunity, but it was his duty to obey. Stonewall groped within himself for the will to watch Ewell depart, but it was not there. Within himself Jackson clutched ambition, not obedience. Jackson had written to Johnston on the seventeenth, Ewell to Lee on the same day; the order Ewell had just showed him was written before either message could have been read in Richmond. Perhaps new instructions were already en route. Perhaps General Lee could do something to save the attack. Lee had nurtured the Shenandoah offensive; Lee was the last hope, and to him Jackson wrote:

Camp Near New Market, Va.
May 20, 1862

General R. L. Lee:

I am of the opinion that an attempt should be made to defeat Banks, but under instructions just received from General Johnston, I do not feel at liberty to make an attack. Please answer by telegraph at once.

T. J. Jackson
Major General[41]

Having taken one step toward insubordination, Jackson went all the way. He wrote across the bottom of Johnston's order, "Suspend the execution of the order for returning to the east until I receive an answer to my telegram," signed it, and handed it to Ewell.[42] There is no record that he sent word to Johnston of this telegram to Lee.

Had General Loring halted his Army of the Northwest during the march against Romney and surreptitiously petitioned Johnston that some other move be adopted, his conduct would not have been more insubordinate than Jackson's. Jackson had just directly countermanded the express orders of a superior officer, a graver offense than those for which Jackson had demanded Loring's court-martial. If Johnston had developed a plan to relieve Richmond dependent in part on Ewell's arrival, or if that force were needed for a desperate final defense against heavy odds, Jackson might have ruined everything. It would profit the Confederacy nothing to crush Banks if it cost Richmond in the bargain, and this was the risk Jackson had assumed. Ewell rode back to his headquarters, surely amazed at what had just happened. Jackson later that night sought out the Louisiana Brigade and spent some hours by the campfire of its commander. General Taylor recalled that he said little.[43]

Jackson's telegram to Lee was the origin of one of the minor mysteries of the war; there was no response from Lee, and yet Ewell remained in the Valley. Who authorized that, and with what authority? The questions have prompted several different conjectures.[44] In fact, there was a response, although not from Lee, who nonetheless probably played a role in handling the telegram. Another look at old and new sources offers a reasonably finite account of the course of Jackson's message from the time it left New Market.

Major Harman maintained a string of couriers from Jackson's Headquarters to Staunton; through that post telegrams were flashed to Richmond.[45] Harman demanded twelve miles an hour from his riders, a good average pace for Jackson's telegram of May 20 given the fact that night was coming on as the courier left the New Market area and he would have to cross the North River by ford since its bridges were destroyed. The telegram could hardly have been sent from Staunton before midnight, which was confirmed by William Allan. Allan quotes Jackson's telegram (original now lost) in full in his study of the campaign and gives the dateline as including the phrase "via Staunton, May 21."[46] Assuming a best-case scenario, all telegraph operators in central Virginia were awake at their posts and the message worked its way to Richmond before dawn of the twenty-first; then a presumably alert young man rode from the telegraph office to Lee's house (as opposed to his office) and roused him.

Wherever Lee received Jackson's appeal, he would have realized instantly that Jackson had placed him in an awkward position. Jackson would not have intended that, and probably he telegraphed under an assumption that Lee and Johnston each had some idea what the other was doing, but nothing suggests Lee knew what Johnston had ordered in the Valley. Lee therefore had only a request from Jackson to "answer" on something having to do with "instructions" from Johnston; the message did not even specify what help Jackson wanted. If Johnston's instructions were orders, as Jackson indicated by writing he no longer felt able to attack Banks because of them, then there was nothing about which Lee could answer him. Jackson should follow orders, as he knew perfectly well. If the instructions were not orders, it would have been impossible for Lee, not having seen them, to comment, and if Jackson was covertly suggesting Lee ought to intervene to get more freedom of action for him, then Old Jack had mistaken what was possible. Lee simply was not a man to interfere with Johnston's plans.

The conclusion is inescapable that Lee endorsed Jackson's message to Johnston for answer. He handled Ewell's telegram of the seventeenth that way,[47] and to do otherwise would have produced howls from Johnston about meddling in his command. No such protests are known. Johnston's army was now close to Richmond, so a courier spurring to his headquarters did not have far to go. If the same horseman rode from Lee's house to Johnston he faced the daunting prospect of awakening his second four-star general that morning, but such was the path of this message, because it was Johnston, not Lee, who responded. The reply was a telegram that rested for decades unnoticed in the papers of Major Dabney. It read:

By Telegraph. Via Staunton
Richmond May 21—1862

Maj. Genl. Jackson

If you and Genl. Ewell united can beat Banks do it. I cannot judge at this distance. My previous instructions warned you against attacking fortifications. If it is not feasible to attack let Genl. Ewell march towards Hanover C.H. reporting from time to time on his way. Only general instructions can be given at this distance.

J. E. Johnston[48]

This dispatch, an obvious reply to Jackson's call for an "answer" concerning Johnston's latest instructions, now had to make its way back to the Valley. A rider carried it to Richmond, whence it was telegraphed to Staunton. Although his recollections included many errors of fact, John Imboden (an officer based in Staunton) years later described a message so nearly identical with Johnston's as to guarantee that it in fact reached that point. Imboden's claim that the response was within an hour of sending Jackson's plea is unbelievable, but his statement that he forwarded the reply at once to Jackson is credible.[49] What cannot be determined is the time the answer cleared Staunton, but before end of day Johnston's telegram should have been in Jackson's hands, as were other instructions from Johnston.

It will be recalled that when Ewell halted all movements under his control on May 17 while he rode to Mount Solon, he also ordered Campbell Brown to Gordonsville with a telegram seeking guidance from Lee. That communication reached Lee the next day, but he had declined to respond, sending it instead to Johnston. Johnston replied with alacrity. He wrote at 2 P.M. on the eighteenth: "The whole question is whether or not General Jackson and yourself are too late to attack Banks. If so the march eastward should be made."[50] Johnston thought about the matter further and wrote Ewell again that day; he instructed him to send both letters on to Jackson. This second letter allowed great discretion to both of his commanders in the Shenandoah: "The object you have to accomplish is the prevention of the juncture of Genl. Banks' troops with those of Genl. McDowell. I cannot provide for modifications of the case, but having full confidence in the judgment and courage of both the division commanders, rely upon them to conform to circumstances, without fear for the result."[51]

Unaware of how urgently these two letters were needed in the Valley, Johnston did not expedite transmittal. They obviously had not reached Ewell by the twentieth, but given the two to three days it normally took messages to travel from Richmond to the Valley it is probable Ewell had them before noon of the twenty-first, which triggered a frantic ride for one of his couriers, Lieutenant Frank Myers. Myers commanded a detail of riders working for Ewell and recalled shortly after the war being summoned by Old Bald Head on the twenty-first. Ewell handed Myers a bundle of dispatches and told him to take the best horse he had and get them to Jackson: "[Go] to New Market and take the turnpike road to Harrisonburg; be quick now, I want to see you again today," piped Ewell in his high squeaky voice. Myers dashed.[52]

Johnston at last had supplied what had been absent in the Shenandoah, discretion (within some wide limits) from the superior officer directly commanding the theater of operations for Jackson and Ewell to conform to an evolving situation in pursuit of a designated goal. The question was whether any of these messages reached Jackson in time to influence his next move.

As he stirred on the morning of May 21, Jackson had no idea that couriers with vital instructions were approaching from opposite directions—one from the Staunton telegraph office while Lieutenant Myers came across the Massanutten from Ewell—and Confederate movements along the Pike lacked vigor. Wherever the rebels went that day it would be through New Market, and it seems that Jackson sought nothing more than to be closed up there when or if some word came from Lee. Winder put the Stonewall Brigade in motion at 6 A.M. but came upon the advance brigade—now Taylor's—halted and was forced to wait behind it a long time; Winder eventually grew impatient and trotted past the Louisianans into New Market to buy some personal items. As he did he would have been able to see regiments from Trimble's Brigade at morning drill outside of town.[53] A pivotal moment was at hand, but there was time for a shopping trip in the Shenandoah!

On his return, Winder found the Valley Army in frenetic motion. It is impossible to know whether Jackson finally had a message from Johnston subsequent to that of May 17 or had independently concluded that no matter what Richmond decided his plan for attacking Banks near Strasburg was untenable, yet in either case the drive on Strasburg was dead. If he had Johnston's telegram of the twenty-first, Jackson could read again the blunt warning against assaulting strong positions; if he had only Johnston's messages of the eighteenth forwarded from Ewell he still had to read the grant of discretion contained therein in light of Johnston's letter of May 17. The message of the seventeenth was caution enough for a man who had been in a military environment all his adult life, and especially for one who had just countermanded the orders of a four-star general, that a battle against fortifications was not desired by high command and therefore not an option. This conclusion could of course have been reached by Jackson in the absence of any word from Johnston subsequent to the seventeenth.

Based on activity that began about noon, it is logical to believe that Jackson by then either had what he construed to be written permission to retain Ewell (either the telegram from Staunton or the dispatches carried by Myers), or he had determined in the absence of new instructions that he could no longer justify Ewell's halt. Under either assumption his sole option was to cross Massanutten Gap into the Luray Valley. If Jackson had Johnston's permission to defeat Banks, the best place to avoid fortifications was east of the Massanutten. Alternatively, if Jackson felt compelled by an absence of orders to dispatch Ewell over the Blue Ridge, Stonewall's remaining chance for decisive action was to strike with Ewell somewhere beyond the Shenandoah. In both instances the village of Luray became the fulcrum of continued effort. Exactly where the Valley Army would go from Luray probably had not been decided by Jackson when he swerved in that direction, but as the day progressed he surely learned the decision would be his alone. Johnston's telegram was probably received, and Lieutenant Myers located him as well. Fooled by the general's sunburned coat and cap, Myers rode up and asked Stonewall where he could find General Jackson. "I am General Jackson, where are you from sir?" came the blunt reply. The shocked young man managed to deliver Ewell's dispatch pouch (containing Johnston's letters of the eighteenth) and escape without further embarrassment.[54]

Returning via New Market, Myers might have seen that Trimble's Brigade abruptly ended its drills and was on the road for Luray via Massanutten Gap by noon; Winder returned from his shopping trip to find the Stonewall Brigade hurrying in that direction as well.[55] Nearing Ewell headquarters, Myers could have observed more evidence of a sudden change of direction. Ewell initially must have assumed that Johnston's letters of the eighteenth—he had not seen Johnston's telegram of the twenty-first—meant that Strasburg would remain the target. Ewell accordingly had Elzey resume his march westward for New Market.[56] There was much confusion before this was corrected and the entire Valley Army headed eastward for Luray. One soldier in the 13th Virginia recalled of the events of that day, "We were faced to New Market where we stood waiting for orders. When they came we were again faced about and started in the opposite direction and at full speed until at the foot of the [Massanutten] mountain on the east side we came to forks of the road, one pike leading to Luray and other to Madison Court House. Jackson seemed determined to take both of these roads, went a short distance on Luray route, then faced us about and started back to New Market and the next thing we knew was off in the direction of Richmond via Madison Court House. We kept on to the river where we crossed and here again orders were changed and we started in the direction of Luray."[57]

Only Trimble and Elzey reached the vicinity of Luray village by nightfall, crossing the South Fork of the Shenandoah River by the White House Bridge (another of the bridges Hotchkiss had failed to burn with Ashby's drunken cavalrymen a month before). The remaining brigades slowed on the climb up and then down the Massanutten, and by dark the Army was scattered along more than a dozen miles with its rear brigade still just outside New Market.[58] It was a much different bivouac than had brought a smile to Old Jack twenty-four hours before.

III

Jackson on the evening of the twenty-first crossed White House Bridge and established Headquarters at a little church nearby.[59] It was sunset as he passed the 1st Maryland, which cheered eagerly at its first sight of Stonewall. Then the 16th Mississippi took up the cry, demanding Jackson show himself to receive its hurrahs.[60] The troops naturally had no idea of the convolutions into which their high command had twisted itself—although as usual they guessed much and about this time a joke began to pass through ranks that Jackson wished Richmond would send "fewer orders and more men"[61]—so those cheers simply expressed respect for a man who actually had been fighting while other Confederate armies were in retreat.

What next? Jackson met with Ewell to find the answer.[62] Without Branch's Brigade the Valley Army numbered on paper approximately 17,500, including 1,000 or so cavalry, although straggling, illness, and desertion were decreasing that number. With Chew's Battery there were forty-eight cannons.[63] It was a force greater than that of Banks, who was thought in late April to have about 21,000 men. The early reports of Shields's departing force counted 6,000, and more recent estimates suggested Shields had taken 10,000, with Banks's remaining strength at probably the same number.[64] Jackson must have believed he outnumbered Banks. The best plan now available was an advance down the Luray Valley against whatever Union force held the village of Front Royal. Front Royal lay twelve miles east of Union fortifications at Strasburg, and once in control of it and several river bridges nearby the Army might outflank Banks and drive him toward the Potomac. If Richmond changed orders again and it became necessary to move east, Front Royal lay opposite Manassas Gap, an easy passage across the Blue Ridge. Jackson once had pondered a move in this direction if Banks's entire army crossed the Blue Ridge. Front Royal was the obvious target, but Jackson's information on this region was out of date.[65] Ewell had had scouts patrolling the Luray Valley, and he shared whatever information they had provided. Campbell Brown later credited Ewell with arguing for a strike at Front Royal, and with whoever's insight it was resolved to force the issue there.[66]

The melding of two heretofore independent commands for offensive action naturally presented challenges. Colonel Crutchfield, artillery chief, would have no time to learn the composition of Ewell's batteries,[67] while the 1st Maryland had to be detached from Elzey's Brigade to form the nucleus of a new organization called the Maryland Line. The Confederate government had decreed that all units from that state should be consolidated in a force commanded by a newly arrived brigadier general from that state, George H. Steuart. Jackson had issued the necessary orders a few days earlier,[68] but initially the Maryland line comprised only the 1st Maryland and Brockenbrough's Baltimore Battery. Elzey's command was reduced to a mere regiment by the transfer of the 1st Maryland, and therefore the brigades of the Army of the Northwest were placed under him.[69]

This meeting of new commands and commanders would have happened, obviously, if the Army had been en route for Strasburg, but it now was superimposed upon a drive in a new direction. Jackson had planned a surprise attack over the smooth Valley Pike against Banks's freshly reconnoitered positions outside Strasburg. After much confusion, he would march instead with reduced numbers over by a miserable road against an enemy of uncertain strength without time to scout them. Hotchkiss remained south of Strasburg, and Ashby's cavalry was back in the Shenandoah around New Market, so the Confederates started toward Front Royal with little idea of what awaited there. At some point Ashby did task one of his lieutenants to scout Union positions at Front Royal, but it is impossible to know when the mission started. The work fell to Lieutenant Walker Buck of Company E, who had grown up in Front Royal and still had many family members there.[70]

To meet the danger of the unknown, Jackson concentrated every man. On the twenty-second Ashby gathered his riders and shifted his force into the Luray Valley, leaving only four companies south of Strasburg to attract Banks's attention there, while another company rode into the Alleghenies to provide extra observation of Frémont's movements.[71] The only other rebel force of any consequence remaining west of the Massanutten was the detachment of two cavalry companies (one led by Harry Gilmor) still observing Frémont near his last-known position at Franklin.[72] Someone even remembered to leave word for Hotchkiss to rejoin Headquarters.

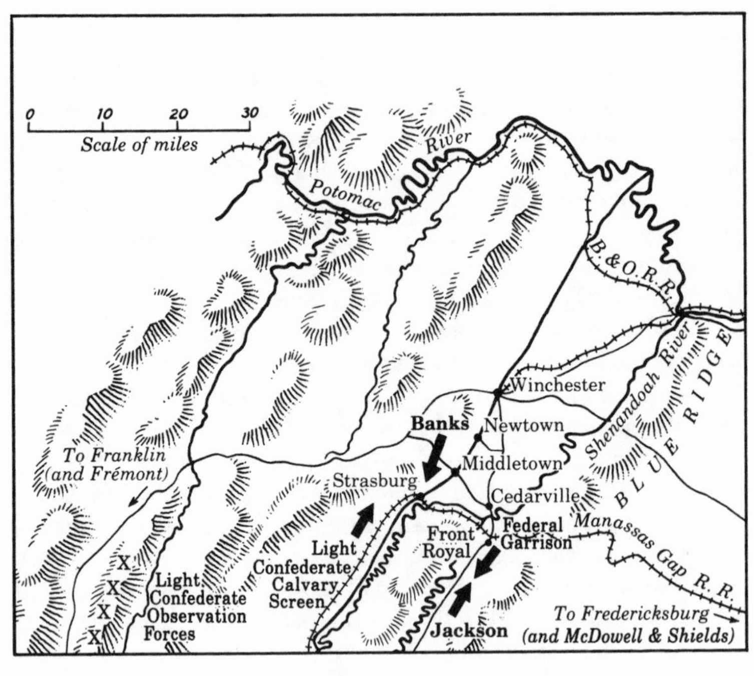

8. Situation in Lower Shenandoah, May 22, 1862

The infantry marched on May 22 under a blistering sun by a narrow strip of land between the Blue Ridge and the Shenandoah's South Fork River. The road was very rough, little more than miles of dry dirt, and the tramping of thousands of feet raised a pall of dust over the column—at least until a hard afternoon shower stirred the dust to slippery mud.[73] Lanty Blackford of the Rockbridge Artillery saw that his comrades "are about as nearly broken down as men well can be to get along at all." He calculated that this battery had marched twenty of the last twenty-three days and was "likely to go on so for a month to come for aught I see to the contrary."[74] The terrible marching conditions scattered the Army over almost fifteen miles from head to tail. The Rockbridge Artillery, at the rear, barely passed Luray by day's end; Trimble's Brigade, the van, camped within ten miles of Front Royal.

Those who had been marching and fighting since before the Battle of McDowell began to betray the despair of exhaustion: "Almost tired to death," Jim Hall scribbled in his diary.[75] The 10th Virginia had been with the Valley Army barely a month, but its Colonel Warren saw what his men had suffered and groused to his wife, "Jackson is killing up all my men. I have only half of them this morning fit for duty."[76] Warren's brigade commander, General Taliaferro, who had rejoined the Army in April, was already ill and had to be furloughed for recovery; Colonel Fulkerson again was in charge of that unit.[77]

In the Stonewall Brigade the 2d Virginia was temporarily under the command of Lieutenant Colonel Lawson Botts. That day Botts warned Winder that his command was near the end of its mettle: "The men are much fatigued by the constant marches they have recently made and need rest; . . . were it possible to issue rations at once, it would be impossible for the men, with the limited supply of cooking utensils, to cook them and obtain any rest tonight. This loss of rest, followed by a forced march tomorrow, would exhaust them as to hazard the hard earned reputation of the regiment."[78] Botts was not a fainthearted man; an 1844 graduate of V.M.I., he was a distinguished lawyer who following the 1859 Harpers Ferry raid appeared as counsel for John Brown, arguably the most reviled man in Southern history. Botts closed his letter to Winder with a promise that he would start next morning as ordered, but his warning spoke volumes about the condition of the Valley Army.

Among those enduring the stress of the campaign in Bott's 2d Virginia was Captain Sam Moore. Notwithstanding his wound at Kernstown, Moore had remained with his company as it slogged several hundred miles that spring. Now Moore was sensing a reward, for he knew the Army was pointed toward Front Royal. Only twelve miles beyond there lay Berryville, home. How he expected to deliver it is unclear, but Moore wrote to his wife, "I am today on the march in the direction of Front Royal, which is nearer home than I have been for some time."[79] Home!

Indeed, many themes of the Valley Campaign rose toward a climax on May 22. Old Jack continued to mold his infantry. He published a new rule that before battle two men should be detailed from each company to succor the wounded; only those men were authorized to leave ranks, and they were to have red bands tied around their hats. Roll would be called immediately after every engagement to enforce this rule.[80] Jackson was determined to tighten discipline, and his youths continued to resist. Joe Kaufman of the 10th Virginia saw his house from the ranks and dropped out to spend a refreshing afternoon at home.[81] These motifs and others—troubles with Ashby's cavalry, problems from the Confederacy's reorganization, compartmentalization of Union high command, Shields's redeployment to Fredericksburg, Lee's warnings of the danger from that point, and Jackson's ceaseless considerations on the question "What next?"—had primed the Shenandoah for the events to follow the march of May 22.

The Confederate bivouac that night was uneasy. During the afternoon the men had been ordered to clean their weapons,[82] and after dark came orders to cook rations and rise early. In the morning only ambulances and ammunition wagons would move with the regiments; wagons with food were to move at the rear of the Army; other vehicles would not move at all.[83] "This caps the climax, and we are really disconsolate," moaned Lanty Blackford.[84] There would be battle the next day. The rebels talked gravely of the prospect, ate their meager rations, and took fitful rest. Under a clear, moonless sky, silence enfolded the Valley Army.

IV

A scant twenty miles from the Valley Army's cheerless bivouacs in the Luray Valley were Banks's camps at Strasburg. Unlike the rebels, the Union soldiers were well contented and amply fed. They had heard rumors that rebels might be approaching, but they took little heed.[85] More interesting was the current gossip about Banks, who was now transporting himself in a carriage. Northern troops strolled the brightly lit streets of Strasburg, where they could buy oysters, lobsters, and the finest cheeses and meats. A traveling minstrel show was in town, and laughter roared from a canvas theater.[86]

Banks did not join that laughter, for his command was fragmented and much reduced from the twenty-two thousand men it had boasted after Kernstown. Shields had taken a full division of ten thousand men to Fredericksburg. Banks was also obligated to provide small detachments along the Manassas Gap Railroad from Strasburg to Manassas. The largest such detachment was roughly one thousand men of the 1st (Union) Maryland Infantry at Front Royal. Banks's effective strength around Strasburg was less than seven thousand: forty-five hundred infantry organized in two brigades, eighteen hundred cavalry, and sixteen guns.[87] Though his forces were entrenching rapidly, Banks worried that fortifications could not protect him from a determined assault. His sadly out-of-date intelligence located Jackson eight miles west of Harrisonburg and Ewell at Swift Run Gap, but he more accurately estimated these divisions to number sixteen thousand and believed he was their target.[88] On May 22 he begged reinforcements from Secretary Stanton, warning of "the persistent adherence of Jackson to the defense of the Valley and his well-known purpose to expel the Government troops from this country if in his power. This may be assumed as certain. There is probably no more fixed and determined purpose in the whole circle of the enemy's plans."[89] Had Banks been privy to the insubordination Jackson had just risked to keep the Shenandoah offense alive, he could not have written more shrewdly; Banks's only mistake was that he could not envision the Valley Army's vanguard already less than ten miles from his outpost at Front Royal.

Stanton made no known reply to Banks's forecast, for he was occupied with other fronts that May 22. A telegram had reached Washington from General McDowell at Fredericksburg that day, and with seven words it sentenced the Confederacy to an early end: "Major General Shields' command has arrived here."[90] The descent on Richmond could commence. Everything was prepared: wagons were heaped with five days' rations; beef cattle on the hoof were distributed to the brigades; four new bridges spanned the Rappahannock.[91] McDowell reported to

McClellan that day: "I have received the orders of the President to move with the army under my command and cooperate with yours in the reduction of Richmond."[92]

On May 22, 1862, McClellan's reassembled Peninsula Campaign stood on the edge of success. There was even to be a triumphal parade to mark the coming victory. President Lincoln and several of his cabinet members were journeying to Fredericksburg to issue McDowell final instructions.[93] Following the conference, they would be treated to a grand review of McDowell's army—four divisions totaling forty thousand men and more than one hundred guns—before it marched south for the "reduction of Richmond."

In Richmond, President Jefferson Davis and his cabinet shared no such bright prospects. General Johnston continued to draw near the city, having lost much valuable ammunition and artillery on his retreat from Yorktown. McClellan closed steadily after him. The treasury secretary kept steam up in a special train holding the South's gold reserves; the Secretary of War had discreetly begun to pack his records for "removal."[94] President Davis had bundled his family off to North Carolina and almost despaired that Johnston could reverse the situation. Johnston persisted in urging that all Southern forces be massed with his own army, yet it remained unknown if he would actually fight. Johnston had warned Lee on May 10: "If the President will direct the concentration of all the troops of North Carolina and Eastern Virginia, we may be able to hold Middle Virginia at least."[95] On May 14, with McClellan twenty-five miles away, the Cabinet debated where Johnston's army should rally if Richmond fell.

A prickly tension was growing throughout Richmond, whose badly frightened people began to feel the government was losing control. "The enemy are at the gates. Who will lead and act, act, act?" demanded the *Daily Dispatch*.[96] A correspondent for the Memphis *Daily Appeal* recorded scenes of "groups of excited men at every corner; dense crowds before bulletin boards of the newspaper offices; long lines of army wagons rattling over the clamorous pavements; . . . couriers, covered with dust of the road, on broken down horses in feeble gallop towards the War Department."[97]

Portents of disaster multiplied: the government took control of telegraph lines south and west of Richmond; foreigners literally besieged the passport office.[98] Every shop in town, even bookstores, was selling packing cases and trunks.[99] The Richmond & Danville Railroad dismantled its repair shops for shipment south; planks were being laid across the trestles spanning the James River to speed any withdrawal by Johnston's army.[100]

On May 20 Davis promised publicly that the capital would be defended to the end; that same day McClellan crossed the Chickahominy River at a point only twelve miles from Richmond. Then McClellan began to extend his right wing northward as if to link with the approach of a column from Fredericksburg. On May 22 McClellan took the village of Cold Harbor—eight miles from Richmond.[101] The day was McClellan's second wedding anniversary, and he started a letter to his wife in which he expressed the hope that, among other things, he would be able to control his army if it entered the enemy capital after a victorious assault. He would do his best to prevent outrage and pillage but feared he might soon see the sack of Richmond. "I am here on the eve of one of the great historic battles of the world," he confided.[102]

Communications between President Davis and General Johnston were not so open; in truth, they had become almost nonexistent. On May 22, while Lincoln was preparing to visit McDowell's troops at Fredericksburg, Davis could tolerate the uncertainty over Johnston's plans no longer and spurred through Richmond's suburbs to discover the whereabouts of the South's principal army. Davis found it in some places just in front of earthworks that had been dug early in the war within three miles of Richmond. At the front the president was under Federal shell fire. Johnston could not be found. Local field commanders apparently had no instructions or even an idea of what enemy force lay just beyond their positions. Everything was confused; Davis feared an alert Union commander "might easily have advanced on the Turnpike toward if not to Richmond."[103] Inside and out of the Confederate capital on May 22, 1862, no one thought of Jackson's frazzled army spread in the Shenandoah along the miserable track from Luray to Front Royal.

12

THREE DAYS OF RUNNING BATTLE

All sorts of a mixed up fight ensued.

—Henry Douglas

The village of Front Royal, a few hundred people in the spring of 1862, was the Luray Valley's northern exit. It existed because trails from two Blue Ridge gaps met there on the banks of Happy Creek, creating a natural stop for pioneers traversing the mountains in the 1700s. Originally called Helltown—early settlers could be rowdy—it was perhaps finally named when a frustrated Revolutionary War commander drilled his ragged militia by aligning them on a tree in the village square with the shout, "Front the royal oak!" George Washington passed close by on his many journeys to Winchester, though apparently he did not tarry in the area. The Manassas Gap Railroad threw a spur to the village in the 1850s but established its larger facilities elsewhere. Historically the village was a place people went through and not to, and on May 23 the Valley Army as well was to storm it on its way elsewhere.

A mile and a half north of Front Royal the forks of the Shenandoah River formed a right angle—the North Fork River flowing from the northwest, the South Fork (beside which the Valley Army was marching) from the southwest. Near the confluence the Manassas Gap Railroad viaduct spanned the South Fork. Another bridge suitable for wagons spanned the South Fork a short walk upstream (southward) from the viaduct. The main highway crossed that bridge and split into two roads. One roughly paralleled the Manassas Gap tracks westward to Strasburg. The other route continued across the peninsula between the two streams, passed the North Fork by another footbridge, and ran thence to Winchester. With both rivers deep and swift from recent rains,[1] Jackson needed those bridges.

Confederate intelligence placed Banks's main force at Strasburg, and given the numerical advantage Jackson could reasonably assume he would hold attacking Front Royal, he might have charged straight for the bridges with the Army's vanguard, Trimble's Brigade. But Jackson did not actually know how strong or weak he would find the enemy around Front Royal,[2] and other factors demanded caution as well. Any native of the region could have warned him that the road from Luray ran under river bluffs before reaching the village. A rebel who passed this way recalled one place where the highway coursed "along the base of a precipice which seemed almost perpendicular to the height of 250 feet."[3] Federals posted there might check the Confederate march sufficiently to allow destruction of the vital bridges. Moreover, the Valley Army was so spread out that most units were not within supporting distance of the vanguard. The column was so extended that Jackson had not even been able to find time to ride forward the prior evening to give personal orders for the twenty-third to Ewell, who was near Trimble's Brigade.[4]

The general therefore crafted a simple but effective descent upon Front Royal.[5] First, he would cut off the enemy garrison. Ashby would cross the South Fork of the Shenandoah at McCoy's Ford, a few miles south of Front Royal, and sever rail and telegraph links between Strasburg and Front Royal. As backup, Jackson ordered Colonel Flournoy to follow Ashby with his 6th Virginia Cavalry and all of Munford's 2d Virginia not east of the Blue Ridge to strike the railroad closer to Front Royal; Flournoy could also serve as a blocking force to prevent a Federal escape to Strasburg.[6]

Second, Jackson would kill the garrison. Confederate infantry, excepting Trimble, would march at dawn. Jackson ordered Ewell not to let Trimble proceed until the brigade behind him, Taylor's, caught up.[7] Jackson had learned something from the Army's piecemeal arrival at the Battle of McDowell, and he obviously hoped to have his infantry concentrated when he met the enemy. By quizzing soldiers recruited in the area he also learned of a sheltered approach. Four and a half miles outside Front Royal, at Asbury Chapel, a rugged path branched from the Luray road and ran up the heavily wooded slopes of the Blue Ridge to intersect Gooney Manor Road; that road traveled into Front Royal directly from the south. Jackson chose to make that detour, thereby skirting the Luray road defile where his attack might be stalled; additionally, a charge from the south, instead of from along the river, would lessen Union opportunity to escape over the Blue Ridge. The Federal garrison would be overwhelmed by an unexpected blow before it had time to destroy the bridges. These details Jackson probably reviewed as he rode to accompany the Army's vanguard; perhaps along the way he passed Ashby's cavalry splashing across the South Fork River.

Moving westward from the river and then around the base of Massanutten Mountain, Ashby's troopers approached Buckton Station, midway between Strasburg and Front Royal. Here behind a stout brick depot, the Manassas Gap tracks crossed Passage Creek by a small trestle. It was a likely point to cut Federal communications. Ashby sent pickets farther to the west to watch for enemy activity from Strasburg and then personally reconnoitered the station. Federal guidons warned that he faced two companies of Indiana and Wisconsin infantrymen, farm boys who would not shatter like Yankee cavalry. Tents for perhaps 150 Federals stood in rows near the depot, which was sandbagged and manned like a redoubt.[8] The trestle was fortified on both ends.

Ashby quickly rejoined his troopers, formed a rough line, and charged. The Yankees were surprised but rallied inside the depot to turn back the first rush. Ashby shouted for a second dash. Vaulting fences and ditches, the rebels roared in like Indians. The bluecoats had driven loopholes through the depot wall and kept up a steady fire on the Confederates. Captain Sheetz was killed; Captain Fletcher went down. Captain Winfield's horse was shot from under him. Winfield rolled free, gathered a squad, and hacked into the Union fort. After five minutes of room-by-room fighting he emerged with a Federal banner around his arm, signaling that the redoubt had fallen.

Federal survivors pulled into their revetments at the western end of the bridge. Ashby slashed telegraph wires and massed his men to go again. "Forward boys," he thundered, "we'll get every mother's son of them."

Yelping rebels swarmed into a leaden hail. They recoiled and charged again, and more troopers fell. Ashby drew off, but not without a characteristic show of nerve. He halted to ponder still another charge, and the Federals began to bang away at him. Ashby ignored them until a bullet tore the ear off his black charger. Such was his horsemanship that a few words quieted the animal, and to a private who urged his retreat, he merely replied, "That was only a stray ball, but you'd better see to yourself."[9] The paladin had not destroyed his foe today, but he would never fear them. He may, however, have underestimated his enemy. Ashby attacked with only five companies; one defender estimated his strength at about four hundred men.[10] Chew's Battery, which might have done good service against the brick depot, was absent. The horse artillery had started the day in Luray and apparently was never summoned forward to join the offense.[11] As Ashby rejected another attack and rode toward Front Royal, it was not in fact clear where much of his command was or what it was doing.

At about the same early afternoon hour that Ashby scouted Buckton, rebel infantry neared Asbury Chapel, the junction from which Jackson would launch his attack. The general was at the front now but apparently did not hurry the march. The day was extremely warm, reason enough not to press the troops until the last minute, yet the Luray road was already littered with scores of men who had fallen from ranks.[12] Trimble's Brigade had covered only six miles since leaving camp, a slow pace unless Jackson was trying to close up his tired regiments and conserve their strength. Trimble eased his brigade along the river past Asbury Chapel to cover the side detour.[13] Soon he had Federal prisoners; from them, or possibly from one of Ashby's scouts, Jackson discovered that the Northern defenders included the Union's 1st Maryland Infantry, which prompted him to recall his own Maryland Line.[14] Not averse to throwing brother against brother, Jackson dispatched a courier to bring the Confederate Marylanders to spearhead his drive for the bridges.

Jackson did not know it, but he had just ordered a regiment in mutiny to the forefront of the Valley Army! The previous evening, the festering dispute within the Maryland regiment as to whether its enlistments were for one year or the duration of the war had exploded. Many soldiers insisted they had intended to sign on for only twelve months, that their time had expired and any papers stating otherwise were trickery; the officers refused to listen, and discipline collapsed. Scores of men refused to serve any longer and were disarmed and placed under guard. The entire regiment fielded barely 350 men, and a large percent of those were under arrest. "The next morning, the 23rd," Colonel Johnson remembered, "the march was begun, the First Maryland in the worst possible condition—one half under arrest for mutiny, the rest disgusted with the service, and the colonel disgusted with them."[15]

This condition had been kept secret from Jackson, whose instructions to come forward were peremptory: "Colonel Johnson will move the First Maryland to the front and attack the enemy at Front Royal. The army will halt until you pass."[16] The regiment was stopped at a rest break a half dozen miles south of the goal when Stonewall's order arrived, and Colonel Johnson realized he had to try something dramatic. The 1860s were an age of fiery rhetoric; commanders often delivered an oration before battle. A prewar lawyer, Johnson had faced his share of juries and so gathered his men for a harangue. Johnson read the order and vowed to return it with an endorsement that the regiment refused to face the foe. In rapid fashion he touted the themes of state pride, individual dishonor, the ignominy of refusing to face the enemy, and the wrath of parents, sisters, and sweethearts. "You will wander over the face of the earth," Johnson thundered, "with the brand of 'coward,' 'traitor,' indelibly imprinted upon your foreheads, and in the end sink into a dishonored grave, unwept for, uncared for, leaving behind as a heritage to your posterity the scorn and contempt of every honest man and virtuous woman in the land."[17] Some of the bombast, likely the part about sweethearts, worked. Those under arrest called for their arms and were released to get them; before long Johnson was on his way with a combat-ready regiment. Parts of the Army did halt to make way as they double-quicked toward the Yankees.[18]

At Asbury Chapel the Marylanders took Jackson's detour; the narrow, gullied path already was crowded with Taylor's Brigade. The march slowed along the rough track, which twisted generally east at a steep incline. Within a short time the Marylanders climbed four hundred feet and must have wondered whether, after all else, they would scale the Blue Ridge as well. The afternoon was now very hot, and trees closely packed along the way blocked the air so that shade was more stifling than refreshing. Frazzled men reached Gooney Manor Road and turned northward, and then finally, about 2 P.M., the Marylanders emerged from the last stand of timber overlooking Front Royal. A handful of surprised Union pickets were dispersed in a brief firefight.

The Southerners could see down from the high ground to the courthouse square about a half-mile away. Near the square were newly built military hospitals, from which sniper fire was already coming toward them.[19] There also was much commotion visible in the streets of the village. A mile beyond was a flinty ridge of perhaps 150 feet, Richardson's Hill. The main enemy camp was there, with a two-gun battery planted on the summit. Just beyond the camp, near the confluence of the Shenandoah's forks, stood the bridges. Jackson with his staff was with the van, assessing how to seize the spans. Ewell and his aides arrived, then General Steuart of the Maryland Line, then Colonel Johnson, until the collection of officers began to look like a cavalry column. Everyone waited for Jackson to order the attack, but he was silent.

With timing so perfect it appeared providential, Jackson got information he needed to order the charge. Lieutenant Henry Douglas was at Jackson's side—where he would spend most of the next two days—when he spotted a young woman running frantically and waving her bonnet without regard to shots peppering the fields. Jackson sent him to investigate, and within minutes Douglas faced a winded eighteen-year-old girl he had known before the war, Belle Boyd. As loyal to the South as any man, Boyd would later gain notoriety as a Southern spy. She was raised in Martinsburg, where on July 4, 1861, she shot a Federal soldier who came to tear down the Confederate flag flying over the hotel her father managed. This was an unheard of act for a woman of the day, as evidenced by an absence of severe punishment despite the soldier's death. May 1862 found her living with her uncle in Front Royal. Good looks made her welcome in Federal camps, where she flirted with the occupants while counting them. When Confederates were sighted south of town, she immediately looked for a man to carry her information to them, and when none would go she started herself. Making a circuit to keep as much cover as possible between herself and Yankee sharpshooters, she was running for the first mounted men she saw and had the luck to head for Jackson.

"I knew it must be Stonewall, when I heard the first gun," she panted to Douglas. "Go back quick and tell him that the Yankee force is very small—one regiment of Maryland infantry, several pieces of artillery and several companies of cavalry. Tell him I know, for I went through the camps and got it out of an officer. Tell him to charge right down and he will catch them all."[20]

Douglas passed the news to Jackson. It was the sort of intelligence that helped lead the Army into Kernstown, but this time the citizen's words were remarkably accurate. There were in fact only about one thousand Federals present, drawn mainly from the 1st (Union) Maryland. At last Stonewall was sure of his foe: a mere regiment stood between him and the bridges! The Valley Army had almost thirty regiments, but these were spread over miles. Taylor's Brigade had not yet cleared

Gooney Manor Road; only the first of his units, Wheat's Tigers, was in sight, but Jackson attacked with the troops at hand.[21]

Though the Confederates had irresistible numbers within a five-mile radius, they began the battle with only the 350 men of the 1st Maryland. As those rebels came on they learned the identity of their opponents, and they hit howling like demons. A sharp, quick fight roiled through the village. Civilians dodged into the middle of it, cheering, bringing food and water, and pointing out hidden Yankees. Major Wheat brought up his Tigers and joined the street fighting. Campbell Brown of Ewell's staff never forgot watching Wheat surge into action: "[Wheat] was riding full gallop, yelling at the top of his voice—his big sergeant-major running at top speed just after him, calling to the men to come on—& they strung out according to their speed or 'stomach for the fight,' following after—all running—all yelling—all looking like fight."[22]

Rebels cleared the town, then advanced into wheat fields north of it. The Marylanders and Tigers were fewer than five hundred men,[23] and fully deployed they were only a line of skirmishers. Union skirmishers opened fire from behind stone walls crisscrossing the fields, and Union artillery on Richardson's Hill began to pound the rebels. The charge sputtered. Johnson's small force needed support, but support was not at hand. Colonel Crutchfield, chief of artillery, could not get much speed from the jaded horses in Ewell's two batteries, and when these guns did arrive Crutchfield realized that most were small pieces that could not reach the enemy. Longer-range rifled cannons were required to hit Richardson's Hill; Crutchfield found one in Captain Courtney's Battery and planted it on a rise west of the courthouse to shell the Federal artillery. He added two guns from Brockenbrough's Battery, only to see one disabled by accident. Overall the Confederate artillery accomplished little that afternoon.[24]

One hour, then more, slipped away as the Valley Army coiled. Trimble advanced his brigade along the Luray road to the sound of the guns; his 16th Mississippi was posted to support Crutchfield's artillery.[25] Colonel Johnson worked some of his Marylanders along Happy Creek to flank the Union position from the east.[26] Taylor got his brigade up and Jackson directed him to deploy three regiments behind Johnson and send one under forest cover along the South Fork River to outflank Yankee artillery from the west.[27] The flanking party would also cut off the enemy from the vital spans. The fight had lasted for two hours before Jackson was ready to get his bridges.

In the end, Southern infantry was saved an attack by the cavalry, which began to collect on hills across the South Fork River, waiting like vultures. This proved to be Colonel Flournoy's command. Pursuant to Jackson's orders, he had torn up track and telegraph west of Front Royal that morning; by 2 P.M. the mission was accomplished and Flournoy followed the tracks to Front Royal. He arrived on the peninsula between the forks of the Shenandoah and thus endangered the only Federal escape route.[28] Flournoy's appearance signaled to the Union commander, Colonel John Kenly, that it was time to evacuate. Shortly after 4 P.M., Kenly ordered his battery to move out, then started his infantry toward the wagon bridge over the South Fork and new positions from which to delay the rebel onslaught.[29]

Jackson watched the enemy retiring unmolested when long-range guns could have broken them. "Oh, what an opportunity for artillery!" moaned the former gunner, who was unhappy to find that the needed guns were somewhere on the road from Luray. Jackson sent orders to bring up every long-range rifled cannon in the Army, then pushed ahead with the Marylanders and Taylor's command.[30] Along the way the rebels tore through the Union camps; here some of the Tigers stopped to loot.[31] There were more spoils as the Confederates captured large depots of war stocks and two railroad trains packed with Army supplies.[32] Still the enemy was unbroken and might yet deny the true prizes Jackson sought. Before the rebels reached the South Fork wagon bridge, the Yanks were on the far bank of the North Fork deploying on a superb piece of real estate called Guard Hill. There the Federal battery unlimbered to decimate rebels charging across the South Fork highway bridge. And already smoke was rising from the North Fork bridge.

Sharp-eyed Dick Taylor met the crises. He saw that the Federal cannons could not sweep the railroad bridge; his men might get over it on the cross ties. Jackson approved, and the 8th Louisiana sprinted down the tracks. Dismounting, Colonel Henry Kelly led the way across the span under heavy musket fire; some men were shot or lost their balance and plunged into dark waters below. Most gained the opposite shore and dashed for the burning North Fork bridge. The structure was in flames, but Colonel Kelly's battle blood was up. "Come on, boys! We will yet have them!" he shouted. Floundering under fire from Federals seemingly directly overhead, a handful of rebels swam to the opposite shore and returned fire while others dodged Union bullets to douse the flames.[33] Taylor waved the rest of his brigade to their support in a pell-mell surge for the burning span. "It was rather a near thing," Taylor remembered. "My horse and clothing were scorched, and many men burned their hands severely while throwing brands into the river."[34] A large section of flooring collapsed, but the rebels stomped out the fire, and by bearing to the right in single file they reached the far bank, only to see the enemy withdrawing, still in good order, toward Winchester.

Jackson had what he needed, but he was not content. Colonel Flournoy was leading his regiment over the charred bridge one horse at a time; the general waited until he had four companies across and ordered him to pursue. Flournoy thundered off at once, with Jackson keeping pace. Three miles north of the river, near a hamlet called Cedarville, Kenly was overtaken. Still hundreds strong, Kenly deployed his two guns on the road with infantry on either side behind houses and stone fences.

Colonel Flournoy had no more than 250 riders, but each of those men was to relish a moment of romantic glory, was to experience what he had supposed every cavalry action to be. While one squadron massed on the road, others formed in fields on either side, then—charge! They came on over clean green fields, bugles blaring, sabers and pistols flashing. A point-blank fusillade dropped the front row of the company on the road. Twenty-one horses were killed, and two thirds of the thirty-six men in ranks were killed or wounded, but the remaining rebels waded in, hacking and shooting. The fight was hand to hand. Captain Baxter died leading his company. Lieutenant George Means was thrown to the ground when his mount was bayoneted; Federals swarmed to beat him with rifle butts when his sergeant rushed up to save him. Quickly the tide turned.

The Yanks scattered. Gunners fled for Winchester with one cannon; the other was deserted. The infantry collected in an orchard surrounded with a rail-and-post fence, but the Southerners hit them again as two more companies of cavalry appeared. Kenly went down badly wounded, men began to sneak away, and white flags waved. In the twilight the enemy dissolved.[35] A short distance away Jackson sat aglow. Never, he exclaimed, had he seen such a gallant charge, high praise from the reticent Stonewall.[36]

To the cavalry went the spoils. The riders merrily rounded up hundreds of prisoners and herded them southward. Two privates shadowed the last Union cannon and found it abandoned within sight of Northern outposts four miles from Winchester. Stealthily borrowing two plow horses from a neighboring field, they eased the gun back to Front Royal and earned Ewell's special mention.[37] Other riders had also done well. Captains G. W. Myers and Edward MacDonald were stationed west of Massanutten Mountain with a small contingent of Ashby's cavalry and orders to divert Banks. In a perfectly timed feint they occupied a hill outside Strasburg and entrenched at dusk. Darkness prevented Banks from estimating how weak they were but left him the whole night to worry about them.[38]

Southern casualties for the day were fewer than one hundred killed and wounded; Federal losses exceeded seven hundred, mostly prisoners.[39] The Union captives were turned over to the first infantry Flournoy met coming from the North River bridge, the Confederate 1st Maryland. There was thus a reunion of sorts, with tales of brothers, sons, and fathers on opposite sides greeting each other.[40] There was probably more postwar romance than reality in these stories, but certainly some acquaintances were renewed as the Southerners escorted their prisoners to Front Royal. The rules of war were observed by the one band of Marylanders guarding the other, although, Colonel Johnson remembered, "The conversations which generally passed between them were not of a polite or complimentary character."[41] The Federals would be kept there for several days before Jackson concluded what to do with them.[42]

Prisoners and immense stores were not necessarily what Jackson could anticipate during the battle. Front Royal was not a pretty victory, and but for Flournoy's exploit the results might have been less satisfactory. Having hastened the 1st Maryland into enemy view, Jackson had to commit it without backup; for a long time the few rebels actually fighting were outnumbered and outgunned. The march via Gooney Manor Road reflected sound planning, but this benefit was partially lost by not managing the final approach so that Taylor's entire brigade was positioned to support the 1st Maryland's charge. Time inevitably lost along the detour and generally inefficient artillery work handed the foe an opportunity to destroy the bridges (had they merely done it) and to escape. At Front Royal the Valley Army fought bravely and with such overall superiority that it eventually had to take the place, but it was also lucky that it secured everything desired.

Still, Old Jack had his bridges, and by morning any damage to them could be repaired. The Valley Army had smashed through Union defenses into the lower Shenandoah, had flanked Banks's entrenchments at Strasburg, cutting him off from central Virginia and opening the road to Winchester. The next target was Banks's army itself.

II

Long after dark Jackson rode weary and alone to the bivouac of the Louisiana Brigade, which was a little south of Cedarville.[43] Sitting down by General Taylor's campfire almost without a word, Jackson stared at the flames. Much time passed and Taylor deduced that the mute Jackson was at his prayers.[44] Doubtless so, yet even prayer must have often yielded to the problem of defeating Banks's main force.

Jackson analyzed this operation within the framework of a triangle. The base of the figure was the road between Front Royal and Strasburg. The Valley Pike ran northeast from Strasburg eighteen miles to the apex at Winchester. A road from Front Royal northwest to Winchester closed the triangle. Banks could be defeated somewhere within or near this triangle, depending upon which of four courses he elected. First, if Banks misread the situation (that is, construed the Army's attack as merely a raid with limited objectives), he might remain at Strasburg while detaching a small force to reclaim Front Royal. Second, he might retreat westward into the Alleghenies to join Frémont; there was no way to know if the rebel raiders earlier detailed to block mountain roads west of Strasburg had succeeded. Third, Banks could retreat to Winchester; this would protect his capacious warehouses there and keep him between the Confederates and the Potomac. Fourth, he might try to outthink Jackson. Banks might assume the rebels would swoop directly from Front Royal to Winchester. Such a move would open the way for Banks's escape via Front Royal and Manassas Gap; he could bide his time until the Southerners were miles down the road to Winchester, then slip across their rear. He would find good delaying positions in the Gap, and Union rail transport could rush reinforcements from Fredericksburg or Washington.

Discounting Shields, the casualties inflicted today, and scattered detachments, Banks probably had fewer than ten thousand men at Strasburg. Jackson outnumbered him substantially, but Old Jack could cor-

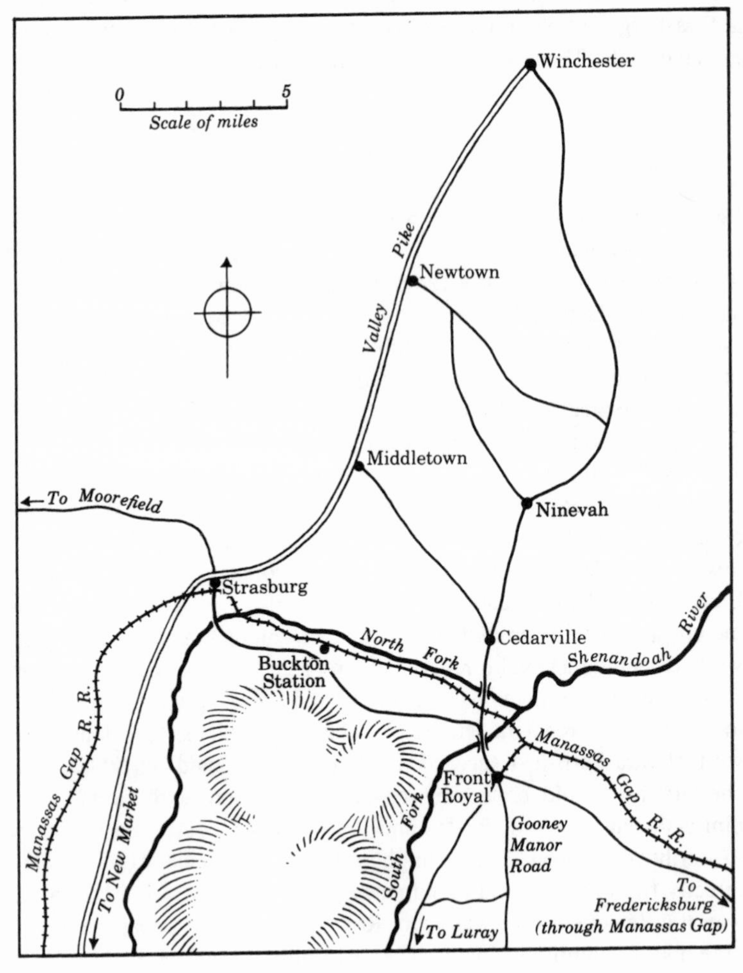

9. JACKSON'S OPERATIONAL TRIANGLE, MAY 24, 1862

rectly suppose that Union troops were well rested, while the Valley Army was drained. Confederate straggling was likely to grow despite every order Stonewall issued against it. His brigades in fact were dwindling from hunger and fatigue, and there was no guarantee numerical superiority would last, particularly if the enemy could not be brought to ground quickly.

From the constraints of geography, enemy options, and relative strength, Jackson searched for a plan. Two possibilities emerged. First, the Valley Army could seek Banks by crossing the base of the triangle to Strasburg. This would ready the Army to blunt a thrust on Front Royal or to pursue if Banks fled into the Alleghenies. Should Banks retire directly to Winchester, however, the Confederates probably could not catch him before he occupied good defensive terrain on high ground south and west of the city. Second, the Army might advance directly from Front Royal to Winchester and surely could outpace Banks there unless he abandoned his trains. Should the enemy bolt eastward from Strasburg, however, the rebels would have to countermarch from Winchester and might not be able to overtake the Federals before they escaped over Manassas Gap. Since the paramount objective of the Valley Army was to prevent the union of Banks's and McDowell's forces, this second course was no better than the first.[45]

In the end, Jackson again opted for a careful offense. He would advance on the Front Royal–Winchester side of the triangle keeping his infantry brigades together, at least until Banks's location was ascertained. The foot column was to be preceded by a cavalry cloud. Jackson thought of General Steuart, underutilized as head of the one-regiment Maryland Line (which Colonel Johnson manifestly could handle) and detached both of Ewell's mounted regiments to him. Jackson may have recalled Steuart as a cadet two years behind him at West Point, where he graduated thirty-seventh in the class of 1848. Steuart had extensive cavalry experience in the prewar Union army; that qualified him for what Jackson had in mind, which was to take Flournoy's and Munford's regiments on a sweep along the triangle almost to the apex, then cut across and intersect the Valley Pike at Newtown, only eight miles south of Winchester. If Banks was there Steuart could delay him; if not, he could so advise.[46] Ashby's troopers would conduct an even wider reconnaissance: one company rode east to observe the Shenandoah River ford leading to Ashby's Gap in the Blue Ridge; an unknown number of companies went from Front Royal to watch Banks in Strasburg. Some riders went eastward from Front Royal to attack the small Union garrison on the railroad at Linden; they would prevent any surprise from that direction.[47] With these movements Confederate operations on May 24 began.*

General Trimble started the infantry advance down the Front Royal–Winchester road at 6 A.M.; the 1st Maryland was with him.[48] Elzey's and Taylor's brigades marched behind Trimble. Jackson's old brigades departed from Front Royal and spent their early daylight hours filing over both forks of the Shenandoah. The Stonewall Brigade did not move until 8 A.M.,[49] at least one of Campbell's regiments had not marched by 9 A.M.,[50] and Fulkerson (commanding Taliaferro's Brigade) began the day four miles south of Front Royal, so it is unlikely he crossed the streams until after 9 A.M.[51]

At that hour, Banks had grasped his peril and was preparing to take to the Valley Pike or, as he explained later, "to enter the lists with the enemy in a race for the possession of Winchester."[52] Portions of his wagon train were in retreat by 4:30 A.M. Still dreading an attack from a possibly strong rebel column above Strasburg, he deployed his cavalry to parry that thrust. The infantry was readied with what Banks claimed to be "incredible celerity," yet they were not heading for Winchester until after 9 A.M.[53]

Jackson, meanwhile, accompanied the vanguard of his column to a point six or seven miles north of Front Royal, so that Federals and Confederates were traveling on opposite sides of Jackson's triangle. Trimble was closer to the apex and could have entered Winchester before the Yanks if the benefit of an early start had not been neutralized by want of information. Jackson perhaps expected that the cavalry would have discovered Banks's direction of march by now, but since the enemy did not leave Strasburg until midmorning, Jackson could have had no positive news. If any word came from scouts observing Strasburg, it was merely that Banks was preparing a move. Move where? Jackson did not know, and with every forward step his concern increased that Banks

* See Appendix B for a fuller discussion of what is known and what can be deduced of Jackson's plans and marches on May 24.

would get to Front Royal behind him. The village was still crowded with Union prisoners; moreover, Southern trains would pour into Front Royal today, and Major Harman was going to be replacing worn-out rebel equipment with better Yankee gear,[54] offering Banks the chance to do to Jackson's trains what Stonewall hoped to do to his. Stonewall could have left a brigade or two to defend the village, but that squandered the advantage of numbers at the battle he hoped to fight. Sometime after 8 A.M. Stonewall decided to go no farther until he had more information; he told Trimble to rest his men three miles north of Cedarville (near the hamlet of Ninevah), dismounted at a farmhouse, and asked for breakfast.[55]

Southern brigades came to a halt as they closed on Trimble, and this halt consumed the forenoon. Elzey (with Allegheny Johnson's command) and Taylor stopped; Jackson's late-moving units brought the rear of the Army to the vicinity of Cedarville by 11 A.M., then they too broke ranks. Thousands of men sprawled along the roadside swatting flies. Ewell joined Jackson near the head of the column, and the two generals discussed what to do.

About 11 A.M., a sweating courier interrupted this talk. The boy carried intelligence from General Steuart. Steuart had reached Newtown to find the Pike crowded with Union trains. His attack created a panic. Wrote one cavalryman of the fight: "The whole regiment charged with tremendous yell. The enemy took fright, threw off their knapsacks and guns and run [*sic*] for life. I rode up to a stonewall fence. There were seven blue coats hid behind the fence. I presented my pistol to them and ordered them over the fence; to my great releaf [*sic*] they soon hopped over. I marched them back to headquarters. . . . We took on that charge about 225 men and a great many waggons [*sic*] and horses.[56] Encumbered with prisoners and booty, and probably facing increasing pressure from Yankee formations coming along the Pike from the south, Steuart pulled eastward and sent a courier with word of his discovery, asking for cavalry and infantry reinforcement.[57]

Steuart's report was the first definite intelligence Stonewall had received, and it was hopeful news. It indicated that Banks was running for Winchester and might be spread along the Pike, and Jackson decided to risk splitting the Army. He ordered Ewell to stand fast around Ninevah with Trimble and Elzey while he backtracked to Cedarville, from whence a trail ran west seven miles to intersect the Pike at the village of Middletown. Taylor's Brigade was sitting around Cedarville and could diverge to the west immediately; the brigades still south of Cedarville could follow him without loss of time. For a final check the general sent Hotchkiss, who had rejoined the Army late the prior day, out the trail with a handful of cavalry. Within minutes Hotchkiss drew fire and asked for help, whereupon Jackson had Taylor reinforce him with three companies of Louisiana men. Less than two miles from Cedarville Hotchkiss uncovered a strong Union picket and got into a hot firefight.

That settled the matter. Jackson had all the hints he needed that Banks was running for Winchester. He wrote to Ewell to give Steuart such cavalry support as he could—although he still did not want Ewell to advance infantry—then bugled his men to their feet and started for Middletown. It was approximately noon. Ashby galloped forward with cavalry and Chew's Battery and ejected the Federal pickets.[58] The Yanks retired grudgingly; Chew recalled years later that the Southerners encountered strong resistance the entire way,[59] and Jackson fed in reinforcements. Still smarting from the want of long-range artillery at Front Royal, he ordered the Rockbridge Artillery's two rifled pieces to the van under Captain Poague's personal direction. Wheat's Tigers escorted the guns and capered along, hoping for another fight and more plunder.[60] The remainder of Taylor's Brigade, followed by the Stonewall Brigade and then Campbell's and Fulkerson's commands and most of the Army's artillery, joined the column. All of these men were exhausted and hungry. Their road grew rough and muddy; the terrain was hilly and densely forested; a light rain commenced, and two hours vanished despite cries for haste from Jackson and his staff.

Halfway to Middletown, Union riders dashed onto the road and entangled Ashby in a slow joust for time.[61] Behind him, the Confederates marched and stopped, marched and stopped, and another hour vanished. The drizzle ceased. A short distance from the Pike Ashby directed Major Funsten a mile northward with most of the cavalry; he would cut the Pike there while Ashby opened an attack with artillery outside the village.[62]

It was approximately 3:30 P.M. when the rebel guns, somewhat ahead of Taylor's Brigade, burst onto high ground overlooking Middletown. Federal wagon trains, ambulances, and cavalry were jammed on the macadam pike. There was not a Union cannon or infantryman in sight. Stone walls on either side of the road corseted the enemy into a thin line that stretched out of sight both to the north and south, an artillerist's delight. Without waiting for support, Chew and Poague wheeled their pieces into range, and a lopsided fight ensued. The first Southern salvo crushed some Union wagons and clogged the road, rendering Union cavalry a defenseless target. "At a half mile range," recalled George Neese, "we opened on the flying mixture with all of our guns, and as our shells plowed gap and gap through the serried column it caused consternation confounded, and vastly increased the speed of the mixed fugitive mass."[63]

The carnage spilled onto neighboring fields as more Northern squadrons blindly spurred forward in vain effort to hew their way to Winchester. Colonel Crutchfield was directing fire of the guns and saw a large force of cavalry charging along the Pike; Crutchfield threw the cannons to within eighty yards of the road and delivered a volley of canister. When the dust settled the dazed survivors, perhaps a hundred men, surrendered en masse.[64] Henry Douglas was watching by Jackson's side. He had never seen slaughter on this scale: "It was a dreadful sight. Killed and wounded men and horses in a struggling heap." It seemed murder and Douglas quietly muttered as much. "Let them alone," Stonewall replied implacably.[65] Soon, Jackson would report, the road was "literally obstructed with the mingled and confused mass of struggling and dying horses and riders."[66]

One band of Federal survivors threatened to escape. Ashby fixed on them and reached for his saber. Douglas was close enough to shout, "Colonel, surely you're not—" but Ashby was off. Alone he dashed into the retreating squadron and returned with a dozen captives.[67] Wheat's Tigers appeared, rifles blazing, and ended all organized resistance. Several hundred prisoners were collected, then looting began. General Taylor cantered up to see his Tigers "looting right merrily, diving in and out of the wagons with the activity of rabbits in a warren." (When the Tigers spotted their stern general this pillaging ceased, and they snapped to attention, looking, recalled Taylor, "as solemn and virtuous as deacons at a funeral.")[68] North of Middletown Funsten struck as well, stalling the Union wagons and driving the mounted escort off to the west. Riderless but fully equipped Union mounts and wagon horses were everywhere, and it did not take Asbhy's boys long to collect them; sometimes leading four or five animals, Southern riders disappeared with their trophies.[69]

Jackson was too busy to reprimand as he searched for clues to the whereabouts of Banks's main column. The absence of Union infantry and artillery hinted that he had intercepted only the Federal rear guard, and he decided to move on Winchester. At 4 P.M. he dispatched an order to Ewell to head for that city with everything he had and report his progress hourly.[70] Had the general followed his instinct, Banks might have been destroyed that day, but within a few minutes Union artillery joined the melee as shells fell around Middletown from the south, and Jackson spied what looked like large blue formations deploying from that direction. Perhaps Banks had not slipped past after all. Jackson started Taylor's Brigade southward to confront the enemy. Shortly it appeared that Banks was caught around Cedar Creek, a mile and a half from Middletown, and there a decisive battle loomed. At 4:30 Jackson dispatched another message to Ewell canceling the Winchester advance and telling him instead to stand in place with Trimble but move Elzey's command to Middletown.[71] Ashby, with a task force of cavalry, Chew's Battery, Poague's rifled guns and a few companies of the 7th Louisiana, pursued the enemy who had escaped along the Pike;[72] the bulk of the Army lunged southward.

Outside Middletown Taylor's Brigade was in range of Federal cannons, which concentrated against it. One shell exploded directly beneath Taylor's horse. He and an aide were showered with dirt and the edges of their saddle blankets were blown away, but neither men nor mounts were nicked.[73] Jackson placed fresh batteries to return the fire and a spirited duel ensued; the Yanks appeared to be posted beyond the bridge over Cedar Creek in strength, and Taylor moved his regiments toward them.[74] There was splendid turnabout here: two months ago to the day, almost to the hour, the survivors of Kernstown on low ground beyond Cedar Creek under Union fire from the high ground north of it. Now Confederates flushed with victory held the high ground. The result was as before: those south of the stream fled (to head for the Potomac via back roads), burning the bridge. As the Federals ran to the west it became obvious that this force was not Banks's main body and was not worth pursuit. Obviously Banks's main body had passed Middletown before 3 P.M. Jackson left a regiment to cover the rear and ordered his infantry to countermarch.

It was now 5:45 P.M.; almost two hours had been lost around Middletown, so haste was imperative to overtake Banks. Jackson scribbled another note to Ewell, telling him to march on Winchester.[75] The shift caught Winder with three regiments of the Stonewall Brigade heading south to support Taylor; those units about-faced, and Winder raced to turn the 27th and 33d Virginia from the Cedarville trail directly northward onto the Pike.[76] In November 1861 and again in March 1862 these regiments had followed the Pike from Strasburg to Winchester, and spirits rose when they started there again. To Winchester!

III

As Jackson started for Winchester, Ewell was already heading there on the Front Royal road. Old Bald Head had chafed at inaction since Jackson left him around Ninevah, particularly as he listened to the swell of artillery from the west. General Steuart joined him with prisoners taken at Newtown, and Ewell grew frantic to join the hunt. During the afternoon he dispatched a note to Jackson proposing to take his infantry by Steuart's route to Newtown and attack whatever he found there.[77] He received no quick response to this note, and the hours ticked by without any orders. "Without instructions my situation became embarrassing," Ewell recalled after the war. Finally Ewell concluded Banks was getting away, and he must advance on his own initiative. Once Ewell started, around 5 P.M., conflicting orders from Headquarters did not slow him. Wisely avoiding a westward drive to the Pike, where his men might be unable to tell friend from foe in the twilight, Ewell pushed directly toward Winchester with Trimble's Brigade, the 1st Maryland, two batteries, and the cavalry under Steuart. He reached a point about two miles southeast of the city by dark, drove in enemy pickets, and hunkered down for the night.[78]

Ewell's road to Winchester had been clear; on the Pike, the Southerners met the wreckage of Banks's command. Abandoned wagons littered the way for miles, some with teams still hitched. Other vehicles were smashed or overturned, with contents scattered. "I wish," wrote Lanty Blackford to his mother, "I could give you an adequate idea of the immense variety of their contents and of the evidences they afforded of the almost luxurious manner of living among the Yankee soldiery. Lemons, oranges, dates, hermetically sealed fruits and vegetables, candies, jellies, pickles, tea, coffee, sugars, etc."[79] Henry Douglas saw sutlers' stores, officers' luggage, knapsacks, Bibles, cards, photographs, songbooks, and cooking utensils, "a general wreck of military matter."[80]

Ashby's cavalry and artillery detachment followed the enemy toward Winchester through this wreckage. Some of Funsten's raiding detail had followed after the enemy they drove west from the Pike, so Ashby had no more than two hundred horsemen,[81] the two rifled guns of Poague and Chew's Battery; he promptly outpaced the small infantry support from Taylor's Brigade, and his strength declined steadily as his riders reined up to inspect the spoils. By the time Ashby neared Newtown, four miles from Middletown, only fifty men remained to cover the cannons. The artillerists halted, and Colonel Crutchfield, supervising Poague's guns, rode back for help. He urged a few dozen men of the 7th Louisiana forward, but Taylor's marchers could limp onward no faster. Only Ashby's ransacking cavalrymen, who were all around, could do any good. Crutchfield appealed to pride; he swore; he threatened. It was in vain: "Unable to force or persuade them to abandon this disgraceful employment and return to their duty, I returned to Newtown, and after consulting Colonel Ashby we concluded it would be imprudent to push the pursuit further."[82] The alert Union rear guard commander felt the pursuit slacken and probed southward to buy some time. Union artillery caught Chew's gunners feeding their horses in Newtown and forced them to retreat to a hill outside of town, then blue skirmishers joined the fight and drove them back farther.[83]

Southern infantry were coming to their aid, but not as fast as needed. Civilians now were lining the road, waving and encouraging the infantry, which only slowed them. "Everything in Middletown turned out to greet us: men, women, girls, children, dogs, cats and chickens, and nobody corrected the frequently repeated mistakes when some pretty girl would take some young man for her brother," wrote Private Bob Barton of the Rockbridge Artillery.[84] "Our march from Middletown to Newtown is a continual triumph," Sergent Kearns of the 27th Virginia wrote in his diary. "The ladies cheer and we bawl ourselves hoarse."[85] And the boys had to pick over the Union wagons, in which they found items to answer every need. The Rockbridge Artillery satisfied its collective sweet tooth: "Most of our men got plenty of simple sweet things to eat—a most greatful [*sic*] acquisition—and at one place where we halted, some of the fellows hoisted a whole barrel of ginger-cakes into our ambulance," wrote Lanty Blackford.[86] Winder's aide, McHenry

Howard, found a fine red sash that dressed up his uniform; he wore it for most of the war.[87] Even Jackson once was seen poking through an overturned wagon looking for something to eat; he found a tough, dirty cracker and made a meal.[88] Stragglers were lost every mile to exhaustion and plundering, and only with the most strenuous efforts did officers keep the infantry ranks partially full. It was near dusk before Jackson and the infantry approached the fight outside Newtown to find Union artillery bombarding the remnant of Ashby's pursuit.

Captain Poague was answering with his two long-range pieces, but the enemy fire was so strong that Jackson did not want to tempt it. He now had Ewell's note suggesting that he head for Newtown via the route followed earlier by Steuart; that could bring Ewell in on the Union flank. Jackson wrote back to Ewell to come on as he suggested,[89] then had Winder place the Stonewall Brigade under cover. Ewell never appeared, and the enemy held on until night, then withdrew.

Pursuit was not to be easy. The Army, summarized Henry Douglas, "had been marching almost daily for weeks, had been up nearly all the night before, had been living for some time on much excitement and very small rations; it was exhausted, broken down and apparently unfit for battle."[90] It would be difficult to coordinate with Ewell, who was somewhere east of the Valley Pike with his status unclear. Federals who escaped capture that afternoon were moving in unknown numbers toward the Potomac west of the Pike and might pose a danger to Jackson's flank from that direction. Federals on the Pike had just demonstrated they were still capable of vicious resistance. But there was high ground around Winchester that Jackson wanted. Jackson recalled the powerful cannon fire from Pritchard's Hill at Kernstown; there was good defensive terrain even closer to the city, and the rebels ought to be on it before daylight. There are few things more dangerous than a night skirmish, but that was not reason to relinquish the drive, and Jackson motioned to continue. Chew's Battery was too spent to obey, so Poague's guns and Ashby's handful took the van. Just behind came Jackson and his staff, then Winder's Brigade with Colonel John Neff's 33d Virginia in front.

It was now dark, but the Pike was lit for the next mile by burning wagons. The enemy had won at least two hours around Newtown, time to regroup and burn what they could not move. Jackson blamed the delay on Ashby's want of discipline, which had allowed his command to melt away. Had pressure been maintained, Jackson thought, Banks would not have reached Winchester with a wagon train and perhaps without an army.[91] Anger steeled the general's resolve to cover the last eight miles to the city.

"Moving at a snail's pace and halting," wrote gunner Bob Barton, "and then moving again and halting again, falling asleep at the halts and being suddenly wakened up when motion was resumed, we fairly staggered on, worn almost to exhaustion by the weariness of such a march."[92] Gunner Ed Moore left a similar narrative, commenting that of everything he endured during four years of war, this night was the worst.[93]

A volley roared from the dark. Ambush. "Charge them, charge them," Jackson ordered Ashby's cavalry. The tense riders drew another volley and stampeded. "Did you see anybody struck, sir?" Jackson demanded of Major Dabney. "Did you see anybody struck? Surely they need not have run, at least until they were hurt!"[94] A few riders reappeared, Colonel Neff threw out two companies of skirmishers, and the drive continued.[95] Seven miles to Winchester.

At Barton's Mill about 1 A.M. the Federals hit again. They seemed to be all around, in front, to the east and to the west of the Pike. Southern cavalry scattered; Poague's gunners dove under their caissons to avoid being trampled. Men of the 33d were run down, and the regiment was left in such disarray it could not be rallied.[96] Winder sent the 2d Virginia to the right to turn the Union flank, but it wandered into a marsh and could not proceed. Something in a burning wagon began to explode, someone thought it was artillery shells and yelled "Look out!" and rebels scampered into a field. The next regiments in line took them for Yankees and opened fire.[97] Finally Colonel Grigsby brought the 27th Virginia forward under heavy fire from the invisible enemy to clear the way.[98] Five miles to Winchester.

Jackson knew that the 5th Virginia was raised in Winchester and ordered Winder to put two companies from it in the lead. Captain George Kurtz of Company K had spent his life in the area and found himself inching forward astride the Pike; Winder and Jackson followed a short distance behind on foot. It was a night Kurtz never forgot: "Every time we fired upon the Pickets, I reported to Gen'l. Jackson. . . . His only reply to my reports was, 'Captain, move cautiously. I am confident you can drive every picket.'. . . We had much trouble with the enemy in front of us. When we reached Kernstown, I rallied men from both Companies and cleared the road by shooting a volley down the Pike through Kernstown."[99] Three miles to Winchester.

Stalking along the paths of youth, Kurtz drove on and on through the miserable dark. Near a tollgate he collided with Federal cavalry; a volley sent them running. One mile to Winchester. What was left of the deathly tired Army wove after him like drunks. Men swore they slept as they marched. John Apperson observed that many of his friends in the 4th Virginia fell down on the road asleep, reducing the regiment's strength by three quarters.[100] Between 2 and 3 A.M., Colonel Fulkerson stumbled out of the blackness with an urgent request of Jackson. His men were finished; many had collapsed and more were lost with every stop. The Army must rest, Fulkerson pleaded, or it would be nothing more than a skirmish line by dawn. Jackson reminded Fulkerson of the hills just ahead outside Winchester; after what Fulkerson had endured from Pritchard's Hill at Kernstown he ought to grasp the danger of that terrain. Getting to those hills tonight would spare lives in the morning. It was all true, but it no longer mattered. Jackson knew Fulkerson was right and gave orders for two hours' rest.[101]

The Army slumped down; men dropped wherever they stood. A blurry-eyed Henry Douglas noticed Jackson and Ashby, two silent sentinels, pacing at the front. Other than Kurtz's skirmishers, there was no one else between the Valley Army and Banks. This alone Douglas recalled. He touched the ground, and sleep was instantly upon him.[102]

IV

If while he stood sentinel Jackson remembered it was now Sunday, he would have prayed; certainly he shaped his battle. He intended to attack in strength; the exhausted Army might not have more than one hard blow left. The night turned cold, and when morning neared a fog lifted from the waters of a little creek, Abraham's, that wandered west to east between him and Banks; mist would complicate the battle.

Stonewall thought also of Ewell, from whom he had had no word since his offer to cross to the Pike at Newtown. Ewell did not march for Newtown, and there was no hint of his whereabouts. Ewell naturally did not allow campfires when close to the enemy, and thus there would have been nothing visible to Jackson to mark his location. Two of Old Jack's three messages on the twenty-fourth told Ewell not to advance, and the general apparently suspected that Ewell had not moved since noon or had gone only a short distance. When Jackson decided to get orders to Ewell, he chose one of his best staff officers, Colonel Crutchfield, and advised he look for Ewell four or five miles south of Winchester on the Front Royal road. Crutchfield in fact rode back to Newtown and east to Ninevah before he started north on the Front Royal road.[103] The precise orders he carried are unknown, but they could not have been far different than the simple message "Attack at dawn" one rebel remembered seeing on a note that accompanied a map of Winchester delivered to Ewell that morning from Jackson.[104]

If Jackson thought Ewell was miles south of Winchester, then he had to worry that the road from there east to Berryville remained open for Banks. The Federals might retire along it and then turn north to Harpers Ferry; alternatively, the enemy might continue their flight from Winchester to Martinsburg and the Potomac. Jackson had had enough of not knowing which road Banks would take, and he may have discussed this quandary with Ashby when they were alone during the early morning halt. Indeed, the best surmise about Ashby's mission for the day was that he was told in some fashion to cover the Berryville highway.[105] Ashby evidently thought he could choose where and how to cover it. Jackson for his part thought he made clear that he wanted Ashby in a certain place when the battle ended.[106] Whatever was said, around 5 A.M. Ashby began to gather his troopers, and Jackson began to rouse his infantry.

Ewell at this hour was only a mile or two away, but he could not have realized how close he was to Jackson. His last message from Stonewall—probably one of the two orders not to advance—was received about 9 P.M.[107] By roughly that hour he had halted outside Winchester and stationed his 1st Maryland left of the Front Royal–Winchester road to protect his flank and, he hoped, link up with Jackson.[108] Colonel W. W. Kirkland's 21st North Carolina of Trimble's Brigade was astride the highway to the right of the Old Line Staters. Fires were not permitted, and the rebels spent a cheerless few hours before Ewell had them probing northward at 5:40 A.M.[109] Jackson's position did not become known during the night, and with an equally inadequate idea of

Union dispositions and with the field shrouded by fog, Ewell was trying just to discover who was where. Inability of Jackson and Ewell to communicate during the previous evening's lurching advance in fact now committed the two major generals to fighting separate battles.

Ewell's Marylanders advanced slowly in open order for many minutes without contact, then a stone wall emerged through the half light. Colonel Johnson's men dashed over it into a large orchard. Sensing he had gone too far without striking Federals, Johnson feared he had penetrated the Union line. He drew his command in a tight knot and listened. The voices they heard had a distinctly Northern accent. Within a few minutes more the rebels could make out their location: a mile east and south of Winchester the Front Royal road crossed Abraham's Creek and joined a highway (Millwood Pike) leading east to the Shenandoah River. North of the intersection and creek lay Union troops shielding Winchester east of the Valley Pike. The 1st Maryland was in the middle of that line! Union shells began to scream overhead—then a thunderous volley somewhere off to the right rear, then another, then the sound of musketry to the west. Fog suddenly grew denser. Completely cut off and unsure of what was happening, Johnson kept his men quiet and waited.[110]

Trimble, meanwhile, had ordered the 21st North Carolina to advance along the Front Royal road into Winchester. A gap opened between the 21st and Trimble's other regiments, which broke ranks to allow Courtney's Battery to get forward to answer the Federal guns.[111] Mounted on a fine bay mare, Kirkland pressed onward. Foolishly for a professional soldier (Kirkland had entered West Point in 1852 but dropped out three years later to accept a commission in the U.S. Marine Corps) he failed to throw out skirmishers and lost track of units behind him. The 21st was in a column four men across as it waded the creek and began to pass stone fences and houses in Winchester's suburbs. "We were soon in a lane, and stone fences on either side," wrote one of Kirkland's privates. "We come [*sic*] to quite a short raise and ascent in the road and just at the top of the road . . . the Yankees who were concealed behind the left hand stone fence raised up and fired into us. . . . We were taken completely by surprise and fell back pell mell to the foot of the raise."[112]

One volley, then another, savaged the North Carolinians. Kirkland's richly caparisoned horse ran across the fields riderless and frantic;

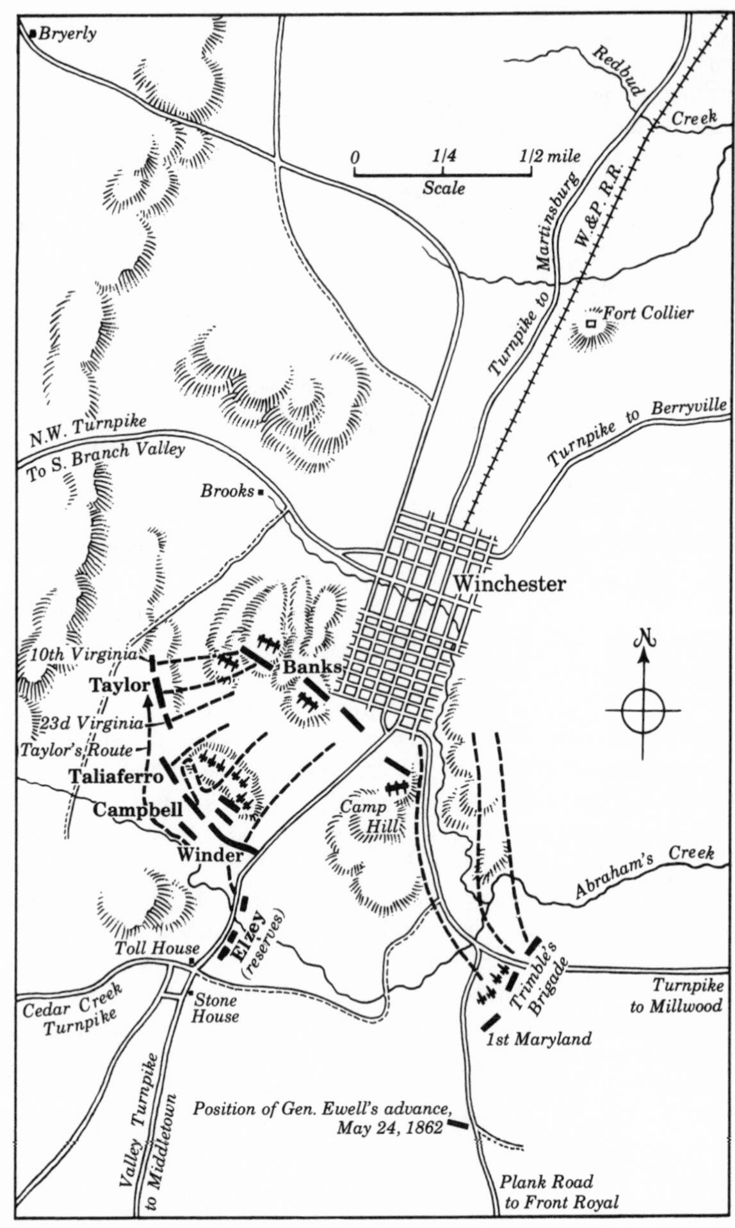

10. BATTLE OF WINCHESTER, MAY 25, 1862

Kirkland and his lieutenant colonel were down, along with a quarter of the rank and file.[113] Tarheel survivors rallied to return fire while Trimble swung the 21st Georgia to flank the Union ambush. The Georgians laid down a covering fire, which drove off the enemy while the 21st North Carolina retired.[114] This was the firestorm heard by the 1st Maryland; unknown to them, the regiment was only two hundred yards away from the Federals who cut down the North Carolinians.

Courtney's gunners unlimbered and pumped shells at a strong Union battery near the Pike, then turned their attention to infantry formations in that area. Brockenbrough's Battery came up. Trimble now had his Alabama and Mississippi regiments present, and he found Ewell to report about a ravine he had spotted. It led off to the northeast, a perfect avenue to get around the enemy left wing. Ewell was considering it when the battlefield suddenly and literally disappeared. A thick bank of fog rolled between him and the Yanks, making it impossible to see or shoot anything. Although Trimble preferred to plunge ahead in the mist, Ewell waited. During the enforced delay of the next thirty minutes, cannon fire swelled west of the Valley Pike; clearly Jackson was engaged there.

It was past 8 A.M. when the rising sun burned the fog off Ewell's sector. Confederate artillery opened a fierce cannonade on everything they could see to the left and front. Ewell told Trimble to begin his movement around the eastern end of the Union line. About this time Crutchfield dashed up. He delivered Jackson's orders for Ewell to attack and rode to check the divisional artillery; to his horror he found some of Courtney's guns laying down a heavy fire on Jackson's infantry west of the Pike.[115] Other rebels began to look that way as well, for the sound of battle there reached a crescendo. With daylight now flooding the field Ewell's men found themselves stopping to watch Confederates west of the Pike deciding the battle. "Moving as if on parade, with alert bearing, rhythmic steps, eyes on the foe," wrote one transfixed Georgian, "they swept smoothly on over ledge and fence."[116] It was Stonewall launching one of the great infantry charges of the war.

Depending on their place in the column when it halted, the brigades on the Valley Pike had gotten one to two hours' sleep before Jackson moved again. The hour was a little before sunrise, about the time Ewell advanced. The morning mist was less dense ahead of Jackson, but he proceeded cautiously, feeling for the last high ground outside Winchester. Soon it could be spotted ahead and west of the Pike. One hill was four hundred yards south of the others and commanded the road. "You must occupy that hill," was Jackson's laconic order to Winder.[117] Winder deployed and overran rows of tents a regiment or two of Union cavalry had just abandoned, but he met no resistance on his way to the target.[118]

Winder's troops clambered to the summit. The noise, if not the sight of Ewell's fight, was detectable east of the Valley Pike, but Banks's real strength was straight ahead. The Union line studded a ridge running northwest from the Pike roughly half a mile before curving forward so that its right flank enfiladed (from the left) the newly taken ground. It was the ridge Jackson had wanted last evening. Manning the elevation were several thousand men and a dozen guns, which began to plaster the rebel hill with accuracy. Colonel Allen pulled his 2d Virginia back from the crest. In those ranks was Captain Sam Moore's Company I, as usual posted where the action was hot, and today Moore's command was to have an exercise in endurance. Though on the reverse slope, Moore's men were under fire for more than an hour without opportunity to reply. At least two shells exploded directly overhead, killing and wounding several.[119] The other regiments of the Stonewall Brigade ducked under what cover there was.

Jackson threw in artillery to challenge Federal batteries from the rise held by Winder. Poague's two rifled guns, which had chased the enemy from Middletown, were closest to the front and first to the crest. The enemy saluted them with a devastating barrage from the hills west of Winchester. Northern sharpshooters took post behind stone walls below those Federal guns and inflicted heavy damage: when the rest of the Rockbridge Artillery joined Poague minutes later, casualties were already piled around the battery's two rifled pieces.[120] Poague waved the fresh guns to the left of the hilltop to answer this fire, but, heading through a gate, the first gun carriage caught a stout oak post between wheel and cannon. The horses reared and fell, jamming the obstacle fast, while the other guns stalled behind it under a murderous fire.

Private Alex Whitt stood in the middle of this hell. Whitt was not by nature a heroic man; there was nothing of Ashby about him, yet something heroic seized him at this particular moment. Veins taut, Whitt jerked an ax from his caisson and darted to the wreck. He dropped to his knees and whacked at the oak post, grunting with each stroke—"as if playing an accompaniment to the music of his axe," thought Private Bob Barton. Every Union gun seemed to train on Whitt. Barton, who was young enough to forget his own peril while he relished the scene, found himself standing in the open to watch as "eager faces watched the axe-man to see what would happen when the post should fall. Presently the last lick was struck and the post fell and the straining, struggling horses sprang forward with the gun, while the cool headed [Poague] called out above the din, 'Corporal Whitt from this hour.'"[121]

There were other Alex Whitts in the Valley Army this day. Carpenter's Battery, then Cutshaw's (formerly Waters's) entered the melee. They aligned on Poague's right under a cross fire from Northern artillery to the front and left. Cutshaw was killed and all his officers were either killed or wounded. Carpenter lent the survivors a lieutenant and ordered a mass fire on a Union battery to the north. After much punishment the Federal guns retired.[122]

The four crews Poague ordered to the left found the position untenable and rejoined him near the Rockbridge Artillery's rifled pieces.[123] Here Private Lanty Blackford watched the driver of his No. 5 gun stagger off with his arm in shreds. Then Private Washington Steuart's face was smashed by a minié ball. Bob Barton heard a scream and saw John Gregory carried away. He spun and saw friends drag Bob McKim from the field. A wheel of Barton's gun was hit, showering him with splinters. Undaunted, he ran for a new wheel.[124] Not far distant a second gun of the Rockbridge Artillery lay crippled and useless.[125]

Behind this horror, Jackson was arraying his infantry. He escorted forward the brigade under Colonel Campbell, and Winder used it to extend his line westward and support the batteries.[126] Campbell happened upon some Union entrenchments near the artillery and got his men into them; the brigade's field officers stayed on their horses and offered Federal snipers easy targets. Campbell went down, so Colonel John Patton of the 21st Virginia took charge of the brigade (on foot). The commander of the 48th Virginia was wounded, and Patton sent a major from the 21st to direct it. The only field officer with the 42d Virginia was hit; Patton had no other officers and left the senior captain in charge.[127] Colonel Fulkerson brought up his three regiments, and Winder packed them on the far left. Jackson's courier rode to hurry Taylor's Brigade, and the general sent orders as well for Elzey to deploy on the Pike as a general reserve.[128]

Stonewall was attaining the early concentration of force that had eluded him at Kernstown, McDowell, and Front Royal. Moreover, the two Southern wings, though fighting independently, were supporting each other. With only one of the Army's six full brigades, Ewell was keeping busy all Banks's regiments on the right. Jackson therefore had five brigades available to handle Banks's remainder, and not long past 7 A.M. he was ready to unleash superior numbers. Winder reported that the enemy was reinforcing its right and suggested a flank attack; Jackson nodded. "I shall send you up Taylor," Jackson said and went to give the orders.[129]

Jackson discovered the head of Taylor's Brigade coming and waited, impassive, as Taylor galloped up. Returning a salute, Jackson pointed out the ridge where the Federal guns stood and gave Taylor orders impossible to confuse: "You must carry it."[130] Taylor followed the sweep of Jackson's arm toward his objective. Abraham's Creek ran northwesterly from the Pike just behind Winder toward the opponent's right wing and afforded some shelter during an approach to it. A march of a mile up that stream should bring his men to the foot of the hill that was the Union right flank; from there the ascent would not be steep. Only two fences would slow the climb. The real test lay beyond the fences, for there the slope was completely exposed to Federal infantry and artillery.

The Louisiana Brigade sloshed up the bed of Abraham's Creek, passing under a vast walnut tree. The Federals began to drop shells in the area, using the tree as a marker. As shells burst over it small limbs rained on the Pelican Staters, and one rebel recalled branches of fresh green leaves stuck on a number of bayonets. Jackson chanced this fire to trot alongside the brigade. Richard Taylor was with him, ecstatic that after two days his command was becoming the Army's workhorse. He was about to take his men into a combat as a single unit for the first time, and it would be to carry the decisive point in plain view of both armies—and especially under the eyes of the tight-lipped Jackson. Federal artillery fire intensified, and some Louisianans ducked.

"What the hell are you dodging for?" Taylor rasped. "If there is any more of it, you will be halted under this fire for an hour."

The troops looked as if they had swallowed ramrods, but Jackson stared reproachfully. There was no excuse for such language, especially on a Sunday. He put his hand on Taylor's shoulder: "I am afraid you are a wicked fellow," he said, then went toward Winder's lines.[131]

Taylor was too excited to smile about his strange commander. He reached the base of the Federal hill and adjusted the dress and cover of his lines. His path had inserted his men into the middle of Fulkerson's regiments. On the left flank Taylor overlapped a small wooded rise where Fulkerson's 10th and 37th Virginia were posted, while Taylor's right touched the 23d Virginia close to the Confederate cannons. Fulkerson's men alertly aligned on both ends.[132] Other units were forming in anticipation of the climax, but the glory of the moment belonged to Louisiana. Still mounted, Taylor took his place in front. His lone saber flashed. Five pelican-bedecked battle flags began to flap. "Attention, forward march."

Fifteen hundred Louisianans stepped off on the left foot; the 10th and 37th Virginia moved in echelon. A forest of burnished steel paraded against the Union right. Taylor twisted occasionally to check the alignment. It did not falter, though shells chopped and chewed his ranks. Men stepped up to close the gashes. They skirted trees and re-formed, vaulted fences and re-formed, preserving a remarkable elbow-to-elbow formation and absorbing the gaze of hundreds. Private John Worsham of the 21st Virginia crawled from his place to get a better view: "That charge of Taylor's was the grandest I saw during the war; . . . every man was in his proper place. There was all the pomp and circumstance of war about it that was always lacking in our charges."[133]

"Steadily and in unbroken column they advance through a storm of rifle balls and cannon shot," wrote Watkins Kearns in his diary.[134] "I have rarely seen a more beautiful charge. This full brigade, with a line of glistening bayonets bright in that morning sun, its formation straight and compact, its tread quick and easy as it pushed on through the clover and up the hill, was a sight to delight a veteran," recollected Henry Douglas.[135] Jackson as well offered commendation with this description: "Steadily, and in fine order, mounting the hill, and there fronting the enemy where he stood in greatest strength, the whole line magnificently swept . . . across the field."[136]

Halfway to the crest Union cavalry menaced. The flank companies of the 8th Louisiana fanned out to meet them; one volley crushed the threat.[137] Directly ahead the rebels could see Union gunners madly limbering their pieces. Taylor rose in his stirrups and bellowed so that John Worsham heard him across the field: "Forward, double quick, charge!"[138]

The Louisianans surged over the top as the Union line crumbled. This was the charge that riveted the attention of everyone within sight, even among Ewell's troops on the opposite wing, and it at once signaled for Yanks retreat and for rebels a general advance. A breeze tore away the last tatters of the morning fog that had cloaked the Marylanders, and they too saw Taylor's steel-tipped line "sweeping over the crest of the ridge towards the enemy's batteries with the swiftness and regularity that a wave advances to the shore." Colonel Johnson watched the enemy break and whooped, "Get after them!"[139] As Ewell heard cheers west of the Pike, Trimble found the position he wanted on the Union left and charged.[140] Winder unleashed his regiments as Taylor gathered speed.[141] Even silent, wooden-faced Old Jack sensed the climax and waved his cap around his head like a child shouting: "Let's holler. Order forward the whole line, the battle's won."[142]

The brigades of Trimble from the east, Winder and Campbell from the south, and Taylor and Fulkerson from the west careened toward Winchester in pursuit. There would soon be heated argument over which Confederate units first entered town, but all agreed that the wildest scenes of the day awaited in Winchester. Smoke was rising from Union warehouses; citizens helped rebels extinguish the flames. Civilians were everywhere, laughing, shrieking, crying. They fairly dragged some men aside and smothered them with affection. Recalled John Worsham: "On passing through Winchester, the citizens met us with cheers and were perfectly wild with delight. . . . The bullets were flying through the streets, but it made no difference to those people; it seemed that joy had overcome fear. Such a scene I never witnessed."[143]

Captain Jim Edmondson elbowed through town at the head of his company and wrote, "I never saw such a demonstration as was made by the citizens—the ladies especially as we passed through—every window was crowded and every door was filled with them and all enthusiastically hurrahing for our generals and soldiers. I have never seen such an exhibition before."[144]

Federals were barricading some intersections in a bid for time. Some deployed around the courthouse square, but they scattered as the 5th Virginia's Winchester boys sprinted down side streets and charged the square. Citizens vied with soldiers to mop up other pockets of resistance. They sniped with handguns hidden since March; those without weapons threw kitchen knives and pots and even tubs of boiling water down on their oppressors. Southern batteries somehow lashed through the overjoyed crowds and opened whenever the civilians could be driven out of the way.[145] Banks's army spilled out of Winchester in confusion.

The Federals sped northward along the Valley Pike for the Potomac. It was over this ground, two and a half months earlier, that Jackson had proposed to rout Banks by a surprise dawn attack.[146] Now he had done more than that, and the victory needed only to be crowned with a grand sweep of cavalry. This was the moment for Ashby to storm after the enemy like a firedrake. Ashby! Jackson suddenly realized he had not seen him since before daybreak. The Union mob was the perfect target for Ashby, and none of his riders were at hand. Nor was Steuart in sight. "Never was there such a chance for cavalry," moaned Stonewall. "Oh, that my cavalry was in place."[147] Searching the fields for Ashby, Jackson instead spotted Taylor nearing at the head of his infantry. "Where is the cavalry?" asked Taylor. Stonewall's glower warned Taylor not to repeat the question.[148]

Jackson spurred on, angrily seeking to improvise a pursuit. He kept the infantry on the road for four or five more miles.[149] He tried to advance guns from the ground Poague had held, but those units were too worn out to do much good. "The physical man was so weakened it was impossible to go farther," declared one of Carpenter's gunners.[150] The general personally ordered the two long-range pieces of the Rockbridge Artillery to the van once again, but the horses' pathetic condition canceled that effort.[151] Jackson called for volunteer gunners with fresher animals to unhitch lead horses of their caissons and pursue like cavalry; he found men ready for the desperate sally but abandoned this idea as the enemy gained distance.[152]

Jackson had gotten all that his infantry and gunners had to offer. "We lay down and panted like dogs tired out in the chase," wrote one of Ewell's Alabamians.[153] Winder summed the day in his diary by noting that victory had exhausted everyone: "Very tired. Wagons did not come up until night. . . . Nothing to eat for 48 hours."[154] Men who had marched from Mount Solon a week before had come almost one hundred miles through weather hot or wet, over roads bad and good, and crossed high mountains and rivers with no bridges. In three days of running battle there was hardly a pause or a meal. They could do no more, nor should they have to. This was the time for cavalry. Where was Ashby? Where was Steuart?

Three miles north of town, with still no cavalry in sight, Jackson ordered Sandie Pendleton to find the mounted regiments Steuart commanded and bring them into action. Pendleton located Steuart's troopers two and a half miles east of Winchester, where they had spent the morning. The men were resting along the wayside as their mounts grazed in a clover field.

Urgently Pendleton repeated Jackson's order to move as rapidly as possible to the Valley Pike and "carry on the pursuit of the enemy with vigor."[155] Though time was precious Steuart refused. He explained that after his raid on Newtown he believed he had reverted to the direct control of Ewell, and in by-the-book military fashion Steuart stated he must have orders from his immediate superior to move. Pendleton rode to find Ewell, who was without knowledge of Steuart's attitude and whose anger about it evoked his blackest oaths. The cavalry then started in short time.[156]

Once he gained the Valley Pike Steuart pursued aggressively and collected many Union stragglers. Ashby joined him about twelve miles north of Winchester with a body of troopers. He later justified his absence with the claim that he had circled Ewell's line during the battle to cut off an enemy detachment. William Allan believed that Ashby had tried to interrupt Federal flight by assuming a blocking stance on the road from Winchester to Berryville.[157] Ashby evidently made a much wider circuit than Jackson had understood he planned, or perhaps had been diverted chasing some Yankees, but obviously Ashby was not where Jackson wanted him at the close of the action.

The rebel cavalry now presented a reasonable force astride the Pike, but they were too late to complete the rout. Banks's troops were no longer in panic. The Southerners tailed them to Martinsburg, applying sufficient pressure so that depots there were not burned and more booty fell into Confederate hands, but the true prize escaped.[158] Banks crossed the Potomac by sunset with his army heavily damaged but intact.

In Winchester, worn-down Confederates from private to general forgot about Banks. One cavalryman, detailed to herd in prisoners, finished his duty and simply dropped. "We laid [*sic*] down on the side of the street and slept till morning, fed our horses, laid down in the hot sun, slept soundly several hours among all the confusion and noise of the city," wrote the boy.[159] One major general did the same. Old Jack took a room in the principal hotel and climbed to his quarters, then utter weariness hit him. Still booted and spurred, Jackson fell face down on his bed and was instantly asleep.[160]

13

THREE DAYS OF RUNNING BATTLE: THE AFTERMATH

A certain plan I had much at heart had been adopted and was on the eve of execution when I received orders changing it.

—Irvin McDowell

Old Jack must have slept the balance of the Sabbath; his preliminary report of operations from Front Royal to Winchester was not written until May 26. It was a brief account without casualties or prisoner totals but did claim "brilliant success" in beating the enemy at several places and also reported large stores of captured supplies. This message he prepared for Adjutant General Cooper.[1] To ensure that his superiors understood so much as was then known on the scene, Jackson sent word of his victory to Richmond via one of his staff; perhaps believing there would be little work for an engineer in the coming days, Jackson selected Lieutenant Boswell. Boswell whipped his mount to Staunton, where he telegraphed a first report to Richmond. The telegram worked its way eastward until received by General Johnston on the morning of May 27. Johnston replied by a special courier with new instructions for Jackson: "If you can threaten Baltimore and Washington, do so. It may produce an important diversion. . . . Your movements depend, of course, upon the enemy's strength remaining in your neighborhood. Upon that depends the practicability of your advancing to the Potomac and even crossing it."[2]

Boswell arrived in person at Johnston's headquarters on the twenty-seventh, probably in the evening, to find Confederate hopes for the safety of Richmond at their nadir. Since May 22, when President Davis thought Federal troops might have walked into the city, affairs had gone badly at the Southern capital. On May 24 McClellan took Mechanicsville—five miles from Richmond—while Union observation balloons floated into view above the city. Johnston scrambled to gather all available Southern units; the Confederates near Fredericksburg under Brigadier General Joseph R. Anderson were summoned to Richmond, but it seemed as though they might not reach the city in time. Early on May 27 McClellan hurled a reinforced division against the brigade of General Branch at Hanover Junction, fifteen miles north of Richmond. Branch, it will be recalled, had been summoned back to the Richmond front from his march to join the Valley Army just three days before it hit Front Royal. Branch had hardly entered Hanover when McClellan hit him, and his outnumbered North Carolinians were driven south with heavy losses. On the heels of this disaster came couriers to Johnston from General Anderson advising that McDowell was following in strength his retirement from Fredericksburg. McDowell's advance guard was already less than twenty-five miles from Hanover and a juncture with McClellan.[3]

It was against this backdrop that Boswell appeared at Johnston's door with details of success in the Valley. Johnston heard him out and then, at 9:15 P.M., wrote the last message he was to write to Stonewall. After restating the essence of his morning letter and advising Jackson there were no Union forces beyond the Potomac to stop him if he ventured across it, Johnston stated:

> You cannot, in your present position, employ such an army as yours upon any enterprise not bearing directly upon the state of things here—either by preventing the reinforcements to McClellan's army, or by drawing troops from it by divisions. These objects might be accomplished by the demonstrations proposed above [that is, crossing the Potomac], or by a movement upon McDowell, although I fear that by the time this reaches you it will be too late for either.

To prevent reinforcements to McClellan or to draw troops from him—that had been the mission of the Valley Army for weeks, and Johnston had just given that goal its clearest expression. But was it too late? Johnston feared as much, but concluded his letter with a plea for action—now:

> The most important service you can render the country is the preventing the further strengthening of McClellan's army. If you find it too late for that, strike the most important body of the enemy you can reach.

Johnston signed his name and then added a postscript to advise Jackson of McDowell's descent upon Richmond: "It is probable," he closed.

This dispatch Johnston handed to Boswell, telling him to spare nothing getting it to Jackson with secrecy and haste. Boswell spurred to the nearest telegraph office, whence in the early hours of the twenty-eighth the message flashed to Staunton with instructions that it be sent through to Jackson immediately. Boswell even asked that Major A. W. Harman (commanding at Staunton) send word when his courier departed for Winchester.[4] Johnston badly needed Jackson to deliver one more blow before it was too late.

With the clearer light of day on the twenty-eighth, Johnston's fears that there was no longer time for Jackson to strike so as to aid Richmond seemed justified. Intelligence confirmed McDowell's southward advance; "There can be no doubt" of McDowell's approach, Johnston wrote to Lee.[5] In Richmond, the population verged on chaos. The morning papers carried an appeal from Mayor Joseph Mayo declaring, "The hour of battle and decision is upon us," and urging citizens to meet him at city hall. Hundreds came and heard Mayo discuss what once had been unthinkable: if Confederate authority collapsed, the city might be exposed to riots and pillage. Mayo's solution was the immediate formation of a home guard to protect citizens and their property, an idea greeted with applause. As if to underscore Richmond's plight, trains started to disgorge casualties from Branch's drubbing at Hanover the previous day. Carloads of dead and wounded and tales of "terrific slaughter" from demoralized troops only increased the prevailing dread.[6]

Johnston now was arranging a last-chance battle. On his map of the Peninsula was a ragged plus sign depicting McClellan's position. The vertical arm of that cross was McClellan's front, which ran generally north-south. The horizontal line was labeled Chickahominy River, which flowed eastward past Richmond on the north before curling southward to the James. McClellan was compelled to straddle the Chickahominy so that his right (northern) wing could link up with McDowell. Johnston had been weighing an assault on this exposed flank for several days, but news of McDowell's march prodded him to action. He now had to throw part of his army north of the Chickahominy and crush McClellan's right wing before McDowell swelled the Union host to 150,000 men.

It was after 1 P.M. on May 28 before Johnston finished sketchy orders for a dawn attack. The seventeen hours that remained were not sufficient to arrange it adequately, and many people betrayed pessimism that anything could be done to redeem Richmond. The city council began enrolling the home guard proposed that morning. The army provost marshal made ready to burn enormous stockpiles of tobacco leaf. Under cover of dark, the secretary of war carted his archives to the railway station.[7] A violent thunderstorm broke over Richmond.

Confederate division commanders gathered at Johnston's headquarters outside Richmond during that storm for a briefing by Major General Gustavus W. Smith, who would lead the attack on May 29. It had showered heavily during the past month, and the Chickahominy was swollen beyond its banks, Smith began. Worse, Federal outposts held the Chickahominy bridges that the rebels must use, so that the main attack could not even be launched until those structures were captured. That task was assigned to the only Confederate unit north of the Chickahominy, Major General A. P. Hill's Division, and it was not an ideal choice. Hill's command had been formed the day before and included one brigade, Branch's, which had been weakened by its drubbing at Hanover Junction; yet there was no time to get other troops into position to take the bridges. Assuming the spans were won, other divisions must funnel over them and across quagmires to assault enemy lines bristling with heavy artillery. There was no chance to achieve surprise.

Several officers interrupted Smith to argue against this slugging match. The obvious alternative was to outflank McClellan by circling to the north around his right, but there was no time for maneuver. Smith was of the opinion that a head-on assault could not be avoided and he later wrote, "It would be a bloody business, called for, however, by the necessity for prompt action if we expected to beat McClellan before he was joined by McDowell."[8]

Smith summarized: Hill's untested, two-day-old division must capture several Chickahominy bridges so that the main columns could cross that treacherous river to attack a carefully entrenched foe. And there were but forty-eight hours in which to win a decisive victory. The Confederates would be fighting east of the Fredericksburg-Richmond pike, and if success was not achieved within two days McDowell could slash into their rear. And, while Smith thrust at the Union right, Johnston had to retain some divisions south of the Chickahominy to keep McClellan from storming Richmond. Fourteen years later Johnston said of the prospect for communication between his separated wings: "I supposed that the bridges and fords of the little river would furnish means of sufficient communication between the two parts of the Confederate army."[9] Here lay the ultimate admission of tactical despair. About to gamble for his capital, Johnston could only "suppose" the halves of his army would fight in concert.

Yet, if Johnston dared, this last-chance battle might be avoided. A courier had brought him word before the conference that McDowell had about-faced and was returning to the Rappahannock. The Southern cavalry shadowing McDowell did not know why, but they seemed certain about his new direction of march.[10] The question was what credit to give the report. Johnston's opinion of cavalry was notoriously low, though this intelligence came from a young brigadier general named J. E. B. Stuart, and Johnston though well indeed of "Jeb." But had Jeb actually seen the withdrawal? Could he vouch that McDowell had given up a winning hand? If Johnston held off his attack on the authority of this report and it proved false . . . what then?

Johnston's thoughts returned to the reality of a room crowded with long-faced generals, one of whom, Major General James Longstreet, argued vigorously for immediate action.[11] Johnston hesitated, listened for a moment to the storm swirling outside, then announced his most fateful decision of the war. He canceled the attack on McClellan's right.

May 29 dawned quietly, without rain, and morning reports confirmed McDowell's retreat. Richmond listened in vain for cannon fire, then slowly began to understand it would not need a home guard to preserve order. Confederate authority would not collapse here. President Davis skimmed his office work and galloped out to the expected battle; as usual, Johnston had not shared his altered plans with the chief executive. Davis found whole divisions parked along the roadside in confusion: "I found Smith's division halted, and the men dispersed in the woods. Looking for some one from whom I could get information, I finally saw General Hood, and asked him the meaning of what I saw. He told me he did not know anything more than that they had been halted."[12] Recall orders had not reached some units until the early hours of May 29, even as they were stumbling into attack positions.[13]

Robert E. Lee rode directly to Johnston's headquarters that morning,[14] and only then did Lee learn of McDowell's about-face on May 28. Perhaps only then was he handed Jackson's dispatch from Winchester announcing "brilliant success." The Valley Army (of which Lee apparently had heard nothing since May 21 when he relayed to Johnston Jackson's telegram from New Market)[15] had carved its way to Winchester, and now McDowell had ended his descent on Richmond. Probably Lee linked McDowell's countermarch with "brilliant success" in the Shenandoah. Perhaps Johnston wondered whether Jackson had anticipated his second message on May 27 and already attacked "the most important body of the enemy you can reach." At seemingly the last hour of the last day, the Valley Army had saved Richmond.

In Washington, the sense of impending victory, so strong on May 22, had lessened since 11 P.M. of May 23, when first word of the fight at Front Royal arrived. In this report Banks estimated rebel strength at five thousand.[16] By midnight he relayed hearsay estimates of rebel strength as twenty thousand.[17] He soon reported that Ewell held Front Royal with six thousand to ten thousand men and Jackson was south of Strasburg with his command.[18] Banks's warnings were magnified by Brigadier General John Geary, who patrolled the Manassas Gap Railroad east of the Blue Ridge. Geary howled that Jackson was passing north of him and moving eastward in the general direction of Centreville with an army of twenty thousand; Geary reported additional thousands south of the railroad near Warrenton.[19] Luck favored the South with Geary's dispatch, for the Federals had just lost contact with General Anderson's Confederate force,[20] which was retreating from Fredericksburg to Richmond. Now here were thousands of rebels supposedly swarming into the Warrenton area northwest of Fredericksburg. Had Anderson joined Jackson for a general offensive? Lincoln and Secretary of War Stanton did not know.

For the first time in his presidency Lincoln was truly the commander in chief. The Valley Army had struck in a region where three of Lincoln's independent departments—those of Frémont, Banks, and McDowell—abutted, and any Northern reaction there must affect McClellan as well. None of the generals involved could act decisively in the overall situation, since each commanded only his own department. Lincoln stepped into this breach.

The commander in chief discerned two contrary opinions. He could forget all else and concentrate McDowell around Washington to ensure its safety. Yet this did not seem justified on the evening of May 24. Secretary Stanton sent four regiments to Banks from Washington and Baltimore on the twenty-fourth,[21] and there was every reason to suppose Banks would survive. Nor did a passive stance satisfy Lincoln, who, like Jackson, had been studying his map of Virginia. If Jackson was hurtling down the Valley or even east from the Blue Ridge, there could hardly be significant Confederate strength in the rebel rear around, say, Harrisonburg. With that thought Lincoln clutched a plan. At the same hour Jackson was piercing Banks's rear guard outside Middletown, at 4 P.M., May 24, Lincoln ordered Frémont to relinquish his Knoxville project and move from Franklin toward Harrisonburg: "The exposed condition of General Banks makes his immediate relief a point of paramount importance. You are therefore directed by the President to move against Jackson at Harrisonburg and operate against the enemy in such way as to relieve Banks."[22]

Within the hour Lincoln also instructed McDowell to forgo his movement on Richmond (scheduled to begin on May 26) and lead two of his four divisions, a total of twenty thousand men, to the Shenandoah. McDowell's objective was to capture the Valley Army, orders that McDowell called a "crushing blow."[23] At that moment, 5 P.M., May 24, the Valley Army won its Valley Campaign.

Because Lincoln soon did fear that the Valley Army might endanger Washington and because he unloaded that anxiety on McClellan, the traditional view of his crucial May 24 orders has been that they were motivated by this fear. There is no hard evidence to support this view. As of 5 P.M. Lincoln knew only that Jackson might be advancing east from the Blue Ridge[24] or down the Valley toward Winchester,[25] and Banks wired at 8 P.M. that the entire alarm was a mistake and that he would reoccupy Strasburg immediately.[26] Lincoln took no action on May 24 to bolster Washington's garrison; instead, troops were sent from Washington to the Valley. His orders to Frémont and McDowell show concern for Banks, not for Washington. Even Secretary Stanton, who imagined a rebel drive against the capital likely and who knew the city's garrison was not strong, routed Union troop trains directly from Baltimore to

Banks all day.[27] McDowell went to the Shenandoah to bag the Valley Army, an offensive rather than a defensive strike.[28] Perhaps the president wished to give sluggish McClellan a demonstration of what decisive action could accomplish, but whatever his motivation, he gave no hint that dread of the Valley Army controlled him when he issued his May 24 orders and changed the course of the war.

Only as reports of a collapse at Winchester were added to other bad news on May 25 did Lincoln and Stanton begin to worry about the Valley Army approaching Washington. Banks sought to minimize the extent of his rout, but he also relayed intelligence that the rebels, with reinforcements expected, would invade Maryland via Harpers Ferry and Williamsport.[29] Minor pro-Southern rioting flared in Baltimore.[30] The whereabouts of General Anderson's force from Fredericksburg remained undetermined. General Geary not only reiterated that Jackson was moving eastward from the lower Valley but also relayed a rumor that as many as ten thousand Southern cavalry were pressing northward from Warrenton.[31]

Coupled with the disappearance of Anderson's command from Fredericksburg, Geary's dispatches were especially grim. Stanton supposed the enemy capable of anything and read these dispatches as proof that Anderson had eluded McDowell. He pestered the latter for assurances that Anderson was not heading toward the Valley.[32] McDowell's well-reasoned response could not alleviate the secretary's fears, which were aggravated by escalating alarms from Geary. On May 26 Geary again wired that Jackson was pouring east over the Blue Ridge to surround him.[33] "In consideration of the hopeless circumstances surrounding us," Geary wrote, he fled with his entire force to Manassas.[34] Stanton spread the panic: Bristoe Station, forty miles east of the Blue Ridge, was abandoned on his orders.[35] At the van of McDowell's column moving to the Valley, Shields neared Manassas Junction on May 26 ready to fight his way through it.[36] Absurd as hindsight makes it, there was a genuine anxiety on the part of some high Union officials on May 25 and 26 that the rebels were nearing Manassas in force.

Two or three hundred half-armed Southern cavalry were responsible for this farce. Ewell, it will be recalled, had sent Colonel Munford with a detachment of his 2d Virginia Cavalry east of the Blue Ridge to track Shields in mid-May. Munford had ended his vigil when Shields passed Warrenton. By this time Munford's companies were swollen with unarmed recruits, and he was sent to secure arms in Richmond. Many of his riders returned to the Valley, but some had remained to observe Geary's command.[37] It was this motley handful that Geary multiplied into the rebel hordes that haunted Stanton. The only other known Confederate force east of the Blue Ridge during this period was one cavalry company,[38] and it merely burned Manassas Gap bridges deserted by Geary.[39] These cavalrymen did as much as anyone in the Valley Army to throw a scare into the Federal government.

Southern riders, however, were only the first of Stanton's worries. The secretary also was dogged by the knowledge that Washington's garrison was weak. When McDowell was held at Manassas after Kernstown the capital was entirely secure, and Stanton did little thereafter to tone up the flaccid garrison McClellan had provided. So little was done that when, on April 19, Stanton gave surprise orders requiring the garrison to assume the city was under attack and actually deploy to resist, it took four hours to assemble forty-one hundred men at several Potomac bridges, and many of them lacked ammunition.[40] He confided to Banks on May 9, "The probabilities at present point to a possible [rebel] attempt upon Washington. . . . Washington is the only object now worth a desperate throw."[41] Yet there is no record of Stanton prowling Washington's defenses to ensure their adequacy. Of course, a secretary of war normally does not attend to such matters, but since he and Lincoln had virtually become the Union high command in Virginia, the task devolved on him. Stanton had ignored the job, while at the same time allowing McDowell to dip into Washington's garrison before his descent on Richmond. Four regiments from the capital were on the Rappahannock by early May.[42] On May 11 four of the best regiments remaining in the city were siphoned to Catlett's Station as replacements for a brigade that strengthened McDowell.[43] Another regiment left Washington for Fredericksburg as late as May 22.[44]

It was one of the war's unnoted ironies that Stanton, so indignant over McClellan's chicanery in March, also let Washington be stripped of defenders, yet Union records amply document that the city was no better defended after Winchester than after Kernstown, and Stanton cannot evade culpability. He had personally supervised the deployment of McDowell's forces. McDowell noted some of the major shifts in the Washington garrison in dispatches to Stanton.[45] McDowell submitted frequent reports tallying the strength of his army and its subordinate command, Brigadier General James Wadsworth's Military District of Washington.[46] These reports openly charted a steady drain on the forces around Washington. The report of Saturday, May 24, which Stanton must have combed eagerly, was especially revealing of Washington's defenses. Wadsworth's effective aggregate strength was given as 18,779 men, and 3,300 of them were forty miles away at Catlett's Station; Wadsworth even doubted those 3,300 were still under his command. Stanton flashed special orders returning those men to Wadsworth,[47] but telegrams did not move them any closer, and there were other skeletons lurking among the neat rows of numbers. With a lawyer's passion for detail, Stanton noted that one of the regiments supposedly at Washington had marched for Fredericksburg on May 22; of the fewer than 15,000 "effectives" in the city, 2,000 were unequipped;[48] there was a total of only 300 cavalry fit for service.[49] Even the news, if Stanton heard it, that there were units available but not tallied in McDowell's report soured: those units proved to be several squadrons of cavalry so disorganized that even McClellan, who never felt he had enough men, had ejected them from the Peninsula.[50] Had Stanton been willing to empty Washington's military stockades and hospitals, he might have placed a man every ten feet around the capital on May 25.

Stanton did not stop to classify the fears that were battering him to the fringe of hysteria. Whereas the day before he had weakened Washington to bolster Banks, the afternoon of May 25 saw him drag one of McDowell's brigades back to Manassas and another into Washington.[51] Stanton wired the governors of thirteen states that Jackson was advancing full force on Washington and begged them to rush their militia to its rescue.[52] He seized operating control of every railroad in the North to speed the rescuers[53] and thereby immeasurably fueled his own crisis mentality.

After the war, zealous admirers of Jackson would claim the entire Union shared Stanton's fears for Washington; they would write of a panic-stricken North pouring men into the capital,[54] but this was not true. What panic there may have been was confined to a handful of public officials and journalists. Some governors did issue alarmed mobilization orders in response to Stanton's plea for militia. Ohio's Governor David Todd relayed the "astounding intelligence that the seat of our beloved Government is threatened with invasion."[55] Governor John Andrew of Massachusetts announced that a "wily and barbarous horde" was menacing Washington as he ordered his militia to assemble on Boston Common.[56] The Boston *Daily Advertiser* thereafter reported a "ferment" in Boston,[57] probably attributable more to the assembling militia than fears for Washington. The New York *Herald* headlined that five hundred thousand men responded to the governors' calls,[58] a report often cited by Jackson's admirers, though it was totally inaccurate.

The North was not stampeded by the Valley Army's drive. The stock market recorded no unusual activity from May 24 to 30. The New York *Times* immediately advised that stuffing Washington with militia would only produce undue excitement on the home front and assured its readers on May 27 that the Valley Army was already retreating.[59] One looks in vain for any large-scale evidence that the Union feared for Washington's safety during May 1862. One finds, rather, complacent comments such as that in a Philadelphia *Inquirer* editorial: "Strategic combinations, well made, have doubtless been in a slight degree disconcerted by the hurried retreat of General Banks. . . . But it is very improbable that any permanent damage has been done."[60]

Nor is there any evidence of panic in the streets of Washington itself. The *Sunday Morning Chronicle* of May 25 reported simply that Banks had retired safely to Winchester, where he had been heavily reinforced. The *Chronicle*'s front-page story concerned Benjamin Franklin's ledger kept while postmaster general.[61] The *National Intelligencer* denounced rumors of a Southern advance on the city as absurd and devoted its principal attention on May 27 to analysis of United States' relations with Mexico.[62]

One reporter, who had witnessed the frenzy in Washington following the defeat at Manassas a year ago, compared that with the current mood of the capital: "The alarm of the night of [May] 25th by no means was as general as it was [after Manassas]. We are all surprised, vexed; some of us are a little glad, though, that the enemy is doing something besides everlastingly running away. We don't apprehend any great catastrophe."[63]

But Abraham Lincoln did apprehend a catastrophe, at least during the afternoon and evening of May 25. Rumor stacked on rumor in the White House, and the president recalled glumly that this was the agony he had dreaded since McClellan first broached his Peninsula maneuver. McClellan had assured him it would never happen, but he also had promised to leave fifty-five thousand men around Washington. Fear and frustration marked every word as Lincoln wrote McClellan that day: "Jackson's movement is a general and concerted one, such as could not be if he was acting upon the purpose of a very desperate defense of Richmond. I think the time is near when you must either attack Richmond or give up the job and come to the defense of Washington."[64] Later, perhaps after a briefing by Stanton, the president wrote McClellan again to tell him the city was "stripped bare," adding, "If McDowell's force was now beyond our reach, we should be utterly helpless. Apprehensions of something like this, and no unwillingness to sustain you, has always been my reason for withholding McDowell's force from you."[65]

That last sentence has been cited as the strongest support for the traditional view that Lincoln diverted McDowell from Richmond for fear of the Valley Army.[66] As we have seen, however, this diversion had already taken place for offensive purposes when Lincoln penned those words. But while Lincoln's concern had not been the cause of McDowell's new orders, it did make them irrevocable. By May 25 Lincoln's worry was such that he was deaf when McDowell argued that he should go to Richmond as planned. More than anyone else, McDowell perceived the gravity of the error Lincoln was making. He lectured the president: "By a glance at the map it will be seen that the line of retreat of the enemy's forces up the valley is shorter than mine to go against him. It will take a week or ten days for the force to get to the valley by the route which will give it food and forage, and by that time the enemy will have retired. I shall gain nothing for you there, and shall lose much for you here [at Fredericksburg]. It throws us all back, and from Richmond north we shall have all our large masses paralyzed, and shall have to repeat what we have just accomplished."[67] He complained to General Wadsworth: "If the enemy can succeed so readily in disconcerting all our plans by alarming us first at one point, then at another, he will paralyze a large force with a very small one."[68]

McDowell had read the minds of Lee and Jackson, but Lincoln did not appreciate his vision. The president's orders stood. General Shields departed Fredericksburg for the Valley on May 25, and Major General E. O. C. Ord's Division followed the next day. At Stanton's direction, most of Ord's men moved first by water to Alexandria, then to the Valley, in order to afford Washington additional temporary security.[69] The Union counterattack was on.

To counteract the melodrama that has confused the Valley Campaign, it must be stressed here that Washington had not been an actual or feinted target for Jackson and that fear of Jackson did not dictate Lincoln's crucial redeployments of McDowell either in April or May. The rebels had wintered in 1861–62 within a few miles of Washington, had watched its fortifications grow, and could not have believed Jackson's small force capable of bothering it. The Lee-Jackson correspondence of this period does not contain the word "Washington," and there is only one possible allusion to it, Lee's letter of May 16 in which he suggested Jackson threaten the "Potomac line" after a successful move against Banks.

In fact no Confederate source reveals designs to create panic in Washington during the spring of 1862. It defies the facts to assert that Jackson intended to frighten Washington with his 3,600 soldiers on March 23, when his latest intelligence had McClellan's 150,000 men still near the Union capital. (Recall that McClellan's embarkation had begun only a few days before Kernstown and that Jackson was not apprised of developments on the Peninsula until the second week of April.) Jackson's dispatches show that he intended only to prevent Banks from leaving the Valley to worsen the odds against Johnston; Old Jack said nothing about Washington prior to or after Kernstown. It again defies the facts to assert that Lee and Jackson intended to stop McClellan on the Peninsula with a stampede at Washington when neither Confederate mentioned the city during the month-long correspondence preceding the Battle of Winchester. It is more realistic to read what they wrote and to acknowledge that they planned for a Southern offensive to strip the Union flank at Fredericksburg and prevent McDowell from crossing the Rappahannock.

Comparably, Union sources make clear that the specter of the Valley Army rampaging into Washington did not keep McDowell from McClellan. Lincoln's basic unease about his capital prompted him to require that McClellan's Peninsula effort have as a foundation a large garrison at Manassas. This general worry indirectly sponsored McDowell's detachment from the Peninsula drive after Banks was unable to reach Manassas (because of Kernstown) and it was discovered that McClellan had not provided a sufficient garrison there. But it must be remembered that after Kernstown Lincoln was attempting to establish the conditions under which McClellan had agreed to operate; it is not likely he retained McDowell on April 3 out of alarm about Jackson when that day the Valley Army was at Rude's Hill confronted by greatly superior forces. Lincoln's redirecting of McDowell to the Valley in May was an offensive move ordered prior to evidence of concern the Valley Army might approach Washington. The disturbance Lincoln suffered for the capital's safety following May 24 was a Confederate bonus that served to make McDowell's orders for the Shenandoah irrevocable.

There was, finally, an ironic footnote in the chronicle of the Union's response to the Valley Army's drive; this concerns the reprieve of May 28, which appeared so miraculous to Confederate high command. As Shields's and Ord's troops left Fredericksburg, McDowell sent his remaining forces south from the Rappahannock to conceal his departure to the Shenandoah.[70] It was this sham—and McDowell's march south was never more than that—that scared Johnston to the brink of a last-chance battle. Had McDowell actually been en route for Richmond—indeed, had his sham merely continued a little longer—Johnston would have thrown his army at McClellan on May 29. But as it was, the nightmarish jolt McDowell gave Johnston was all the help McClellan was to receive from his forty thousand men. McDowell soon called another of his divisions to the Valley, and the second front against Richmond dissolved.

II

"[Jackson] will paralyze a large force with a very small one"—that was McDowell's warning as his divisions lumbered off on a mission he knew to be a blunder, and it was high praise and fitting reward for the Valley Army. McDowell's redeployment climaxed an example of the operational level of war fighting so successful that the disruption of McClellan's 1862 master plan can be termed classic. The operational level of warfare introduces to the study of campaigns a new category in which to assess generalship; the "operational" category exists between stretegy and tactics. Strategy in this matrix embodies the overall war aims of the nation as they are pursued in a major geographic theater of conflict. Tactics remains the deployment and engagement of troops in the presence of the foe. Between strategy and tactics is operational art, a concept neither wholly offensive nor defensive in nature but one closely related to the spirit of maneuver (with which it is sometimes equated). The size of forces available does not determine whether a particular effort is operational (although operational art is typically expressed by a force equivalent to an army corps or larger). Rather, the province of the operational level of warfare is the combination of battles—and battle avoidance—with terrain and marches to achieve results in support of strategic ends without necessarily achieving those ends. The operational level does not shun combat, but it emphasizes celerity of movement to prevent costly engagements in favor of striking inadequately protected high-value assets. Enemy rear areas are frequently targeted. The nature of the operational task demands that the local commander have the greatest possible independence. The campaign conducted by the South in the Shenandoah in 1862 is a textbook example of the operational level of war.

The relevant theater of conflict was the state of Virginia from its Atlantic coast to the Alleghenies, to which should be added parts of eastern North Carolina. Confederate strategy there was formulated in reaction to the Union invasion begun on several fronts. The strategy sprang from a political/military assessment that the national capital, Richmond, and significant rail, population, industrial, and agricultural resources within the theater must be shielded through a combination of offensive and defensive means. The abandonment of large portions of Virginia by deep withdrawal into the Confederate interior was unacceptable to the supreme strategy generating authority represented by Jefferson Davis (in his role as chief executive and commander in chief) and his cabinet. This policy was reasonable. Defeats inflicted on the South during the first months of 1862 were such as to imperil the continued existence of the nation if capped by loss of the capital and the Confederacy's most populous and richest state.

In accord with the strategy of protecting the capital and surrounding territory through offensive/defensive means, the South confronted McClellan on the Peninsula with its principal army. Confederate commanders sought opportunity to draw McClellan away from his overwhelming naval support and then engage him on a favorable basis, as Johnston was doing when the intelligence reached him of McDowell's supposed approach on May 27 (and as Johnston and then Lee would continue to do until Lee unleashed the Seven Days battles at the end of June). As an integral element of preparation for the Richmond contest, the South sought to achieve favorable odds. Lee worked diligently to increase Johnston's numbers with troops from as far away as Georgia, and both Lee and Johnston urged an operational maneuver by Jackson. The goal of this operation was in support of the theater strategy (save Richmond by offensive/defensive means) by preventing significant Union forces in central Virginia from intervening at Richmond.

The letters of Lee and Johnston to Jackson are a summary of wise operational warfare planning. Areas of enemy weakness were sought: Lee wrote on April 25, "I have hoped in the present divided condition of the enemy's forces that a successful blow may be dealt them by a rapid combination of our troops before they [the enemy] can be strengthened themselves either in their positions or by re-enforcements." Federal rear echelon but high value targets were selected: Lee urged on May 16 that wherever Jackson hit Banks he should drive him "back toward the Potomac, and create the impression, as far as practicable, that you design threatening that line." Johnston even urged crossing the boundary river. Speed and maneuver were stressed over costly battles: Johnston warned Jackson against attacking fortifications, while Lee noted that the offensive must be fought with "efficient and light" troops. Despite conflicting communications that for a time hampered Jackson's exercise of judgment, Richmond eventually gave Stonewall freedom to execute his mission: Johnston wrote on May 18 that he could not provide for modifications of the mission, "but having full confidence in the judgement and courage of both the division commanders, rely upon them to conform to circumstances, without fear for the result." And it was made clear to Jackson that he should wield his force to benefit the capital's defense: Johnston wrote on May 27, "You cannot employ such an army as yours upon any enterprise not bearing directly upon the state of things here."

And that is precisely what Jackson had done in the Shenandoah. Stonewall had taken a swift force around enemy strongpoints to attack in a sensitive area of weakness far from the Union's front lines. He did so (finally) with freedom to react to Federal measures as they were discovered, and he had acted for the benefit of the main army more than one hundred miles away at Richmond. The Valley Army's success is a valuable demonstration of what can be attained at the operational level of war fighting.[71]

Examined from either the operational or the strategic level, the Valley Campaign from Kernstown to Winchester also offers several trenchant examples of well-known principles of war wisely followed in large-scale operations and as well object lessons highlighting the consequences of disregarding these maxims.

First, the Valley Campaign demonstrates that an offensive does not leap full grown from the mind of its planner. It begins, rather, with a series of suggestions, of alternatives typified by the Lee-Jackson correspondence. It matures in an atmosphere of vaguely understood enemy intentions, strength, and location, and it must always expect the unexpected. At the end of April Frémont's advance had driven Edward Johnson back on Staunton, Banks had a powerful column at Harrisonburg, and a dual threat to Richmond was worsening from Fredericksburg and the Peninsula. Stonewall had no overall solution to this imbroglio as he departed Swift Run Gap on April 30; it cannot be asserted definitely that he expected more than to oppose Frémont by a march from Swift Run Gap directly to Staunton. Problems arising from foul weather and the cavalry's inability to screen Jackson's march (probably due to Ashby's illness, exactly the sort of unanticipated event that typically occurs when a general attempts decisive action) forced Stonewall to abandon his original idea and detour via Brown's Gap to Staunton. There Jackson had reports that Milroy and Banks both were retiring, not what he initially anticipated. After the victory at McDowell Jackson plunged toward Franklin alert to any opportunity he might find to attack Banks from the west, but he could accomplish nothing in the face of Frémont's strong positions. Jackson thereupon retraced his steps to the Shenandoah determined to try something else. From May 12 to May 17, he clung to the mistaken notion that no part of Banks's column would leave the Valley, and what intelligence he received did not refine the picture. Ewell correctly sent word that portions of Banks's force were moving east, while Ashby erroneously reported they were moving west.[72] Such contradictory reports are the rule in war, and Jackson's demand was properly for more information.

As late as the evening of May 20, Jackson wanted to hit Banks around Strasburg, a markedly different operation than the one actually commenced the next day. At New Market and Luray Jackson rethought his offensive and ultimately attacked in a sector about which he had limited knowledge. The halt just north of Cedarville clearly reveals that Jackson was unsure how to corner Banks as late as 11 A.M. of May 24.

At no time was the Valley Campaign ever a fixed itinerary in Jackson's mind.[73] Flexibility is vital in war.

A crucial principle of war—concentration of maximum force at the point of decision—is vividly illustrated in both its negative and positive applications through this campaign. The principle itself, like all axioms of war, is readily comprehensible. Clausewitz expressed it thusly: "to concentrate our power as much as possible against that section where the chief blows are to be delivered and to incur disadvantages elsewhere, so that our chances of success may increase at the decisive point. This will compensate for all other disadvantages."[74]

Starting in obedience to this principle, the Union spring offensive ended in tragic violation of it. McClellan set out to capture the enemy capital by an end run with his entire army; for all his faults as a commander, he urged concentration of the Army of the Potomac. Unfortunately for McClellan, the Battle of Kernstown made it impossible for him to keep his army together and simultaneously guard Washington in the manner Lincoln desired. McClellan chose instead to inflate Washington's garrison with nonexistent or worthless troops. Discovery of that duplicity led directly to the severing of both Banks and McDowell from McClellan's control. The detachment of McDowell from the Army of the Potomac was especially unfortunate. His thirty thousand men at Fredericksburg were too powerful merely to guard the approaches of Washington yet too distant from McClellan or Banks to actively support either.

After Kernstown, Lincoln increasingly became supreme commander of the Union armies across Virginia, a role in which he ignored the need for concentration with the dispatch of Blenker's Division (ten thousand men) from McClellan to Frémont for operations against Knoxville. This was a gross blunder. Frémont had nineteen thousand men without Blenker,[75] an adequate force to defend his Mountain Department. McClellan was launching a possibly climactic endeavor to take the enemy capital, and every available Union soldier belonged with him. The conquest of Richmond would have outweighed anything Frémont might have won in the Alleghenies. Frémont should have been kept on the defensive with only sufficient strength to prevent Confederates opposite him from reinforcing Richmond. A Southern attack in the Alleghenies might even have been encouraged, for rebels pushing west there could not be at Richmond. Instead, Frémont advanced without concentrating his forces and thereby provided Jackson a superb opening: Milroy was dangerously far from the bulk of Frémont's command when the Valley Army started after him.

By ordering McDowell to Richmond in May, Lincoln attempted to concentrate his armies. It would have been best for McDowell to go by sea, since an overland march risked his destruction before reaching McClellan. Lincoln, however, would not uncover Washington, but he did brace McDowell with an additional ten thousand men. Unfortunately, Lincoln drew these reinforcements from the sensitive Valley. Banks was left with fewer than ten thousand men to garrison a large area and a long rail line, and his inadequate force was as a result thinly spread. (It should also be noted that, during May, Lincoln was ready to give up Frémont's advance on Knoxville and direct him toward Richmond by way of Salem, Virginia.[76] This course was preferable to the original mission for Frémont, but it still kept Frémont isolated and out of range for cooperation with other Federal armies.)

Shields's transfer was approved after Banks claimed Jackson had fled the Valley, but the Battle of McDowell signaled that Jackson had not. Immediately after Jackson left his front, Frémont reported that the rebels were returning to the Valley.[77] Even before this, Banks, reversing earlier claims, wired that Jackson and Ewell were both in the upper Valley,[78] and similar warnings came from at least one other source.[79] Washington seems simply to have ignored these signals in favor of reports more compatible with its notion of where the Valley Army should be. As he moved eastward, Shields assured the War Department that rebels in the Valley were not there to fight but to delay his own division and then retreat to Richmond via Charlottesville.[80] Washington adopted Shields's view, and late May found Union armies badly positioned: Frémont had too many men where they were not needed; Banks had too few where they were; Shields was on his way to Fredericksburg from whence, with McDowell, he faced a potentially dangerous march of one isolated army toward Richmond. Finally, responding to the Valley Army's offense, Lincoln further scattered his forces. Some of McDowell's brigades moved toward Washington; some of his divisions went to the Shenandoah; and the remainder feinted an advance on Richmond.

While Washington squandered its strength, the South sought ever greater concentration of resources. Lee's letter to Jackson of April 25 catches so clearly the essence of the principle of concentration of force that it deserves repetition. Lee wrote, "I have hoped in the present divided condition of the enemy's forces that a successful blow may be dealt them by a rapid combination of our troops before they [the enemy] can be strengthened themselves either in their position or by reenforcements."[81] A worthy companion to Lee's letter came from Jackson, who had explained his need for Loring's command and the subsequent march on Romney by writing Johnston on Christmas Eve 1861, "Our true policy is to attack the enemy in his present position before he receives additional re-enforcements, and especially never to permit a junction of their forces at or near Martinsburg."[82]

It is with such vision that campaigns are won. Jackson's goal after leaving Swift Run Gap was to unite with Edward Johnson; during the same march he gathered up the small V.M.I. Corps of Cadets. There were only two hundred cadets, but Jackson did not overlook a reinforcement of two hundred any more than he did one of two thousand. After dealing with Frémont, Stonewall's next step was to join Ewell. Their offensive through Front Royal was delivered by virtually the entire Valley Army; only a handful of cavalry were deployed south of Strasburg. The way to Staunton was thus temporarily opened for Frémont, a risk Jackson took to guarantee preponderance of numbers on the battlefield.

While seeking to unite his forces, Jackson tried always to preclude the enemy from doing the same. This desire possessed Jackson from the day he assumed command in the Valley and saw he must contend with two enemy fronts. The quest to keep those fronts apart led him to Bath and to McDowell. The persistence with which he pursued this matter was evidenced after the Battle of McDowell on May 8 when he had Hotchkiss block passes between Franklin and the Harrisonburg–New Market area. It was Jackson's desire never to leave enemy columns an easy road by which to unite.

The massing of Southern forces in the Valley, though ultimately successful, was not easily attained, which points to another lesson of the campaign: in war it is usually difficult to continue toward a chosen objective, even as vital an objective as concentration. Above all else General Lee desired to combine Southern detachments in central Virginia and the Valley for a major diversion to stop McDowell, certainly the Confederacy's best course. But even Lee lost sight of this goal when, on May 8, he prodded Ewell to attack Banks if he ventured to

Fredericksburg. Such a blow would have been struck without Jackson's and Johnson's commands, and it is questionable whether anything like the results of the descent on Winchester could have come from such a battle.

Johnston, too, wished Jackson and Ewell to unite against Banks. Yet, under the pressure of McClellan's approach and Shields's departure from the Valley, Johnston temporarily relinquished hope of a Valley attack. In his letter of May 17 he stated that Jackson and Ewell might unite to attack Shields, but then Ewell must reinforce Richmond while Jackson watched Banks, orders that would have dispersed the Confederates at the very moment they had an opening to crush Banks. Fortunately, Johnston was wise enough to grant freedom of action to the Valley Army after he saw Ewell's letter to Lee of May 17 and Jackson's telegram from New Market.

Jackson's response to Johnston's orders of May 17 was another example of the strain involved in holding to the objective. Johnston's instructions to send Ewell east were clear and peremptory. Jackson, however, prevented Ewell's compliance with that order while he appealed to Lee with a telegram that was not precisely clear as to what help he wanted; everything else aside, the act was certainly a renunciation of the exacting obedience by which Stonewall had always lived. His hands must have trembled as he wrote Lee, but Jackson was ready to exhaust every possibility before he abandoned a course he thought to be correct. For the military historian, failure to maintain focus on the true objective is among the easiest mistakes to detect. For the soldier it is among the most difficult blunders to avoid.

Constant planning, force concentration, and maintenance of the objective—these were fundamental elements of the operational art as demonstrated in the Shenandoah. And there is nothing particularly difficult to understand about these elements; they are simply the result of earnest effort. The Valley Campaign was a brilliant operational achievement, but brilliance sprang from much hard work. Ever rechecking his information, Jackson at length found a sensitive point, which he struck aggressively with his whole strength. That done, he had fulfilled his mission as a commander, and even had McDowell not been diverted from Richmond, Stonewall could have done no more. "Duty is ours," Jackson once declared; "consequences are God's."

III

The consequences of the Army's May offensive seemed to its victors the equal of Manassas—in fact the greatest Confederate triumph to date.[83] Banks had been stampeded from the Valley with more than three thousand casualties, the majority captured. More than one thousand were taken in hospitals at Strasburg and Winchester, so the roundup was not as great as might appear. Nevertheless, the Union force encountered from Front Royal to Winchester totaled approximately nine thousand men (counting the 1st Maryland and hospitalized prisoners), and since Union losses roughly matched casualties at Manassas, where a much larger force was defeated, the ratio of damage inflicted in the Valley exceeded the 1861 battle. Confederate loss during the three-day scramble was barely four hundred killed and wounded, mostly among a handful of units, such as the 21st North Carolina and Taylor's Louisianans. Many units had hardly any killed or wounded, although all regiments were reduced by straggling. In absolute and percentage terms Southern blood was shed at a much smaller rate than at Manassas. No Southern victory to date had inflicted comparable losses at such relatively light cost.[84]

Triumph was the sweeter in that it was charged to the accounts of Banks and Frémont. These men were not unknowns to the South, like McDowell when he advanced on Manassas. Rather, they were villains Southerners had disliked from before the war. Banks was a national figure during the bitter run up to the war, an ardent opponent of states' rights. Frémont was the 1856 Republican presidential candidate whose platform was anathema to the South. They stood second and third behind only McClellan in seniority among Union generals (Banks outranked Ulysses Grant until 1864!). By beating Banks and Frémont the Valley Army defeated prime examples of the kind of men most Southerners believed they were fighting.

It was therefore with extra glee that the spoils of victory were tallied. At Front Royal, Strasburg, Winchester, and Martinsburg military goods and eatables beyond anything yet won by a Southern army were taken, stores in such abundance that the rebels dubbed Banks their "Commissary." More than nine thousand small arms, two cannons, droves of horses, cattle, sheep, countless wagons, tons of ammunition, food, and other stores were seized. Especially important were medical supplies already in short supply across the South. Those goods filled one of the largest warehouses in Winchester: "a larger amount of medical stores than in the whole Southern Confederacy," marveled Sandie Pendleton.[85] Those stores were hurried to Charlottesville for reshipment.[86] Never was the largesse with which America sends its armies to war better displayed than in the abundance seized from "Commissary" Banks. It was with some justification that Colonel Warren of the 10th Virginia boasted to his wife, "We have today won the greatest and most decisive victory of the war."[87]

Beyond spoils, the victory reflected improved tactical performance of the Army's leadership. Ewell alertly marched to Winchester, the obvious target by the afternoon of May 24, despite conflicting orders. The next morning he tied up Union forces east of the Valley Pike while preparing to flank them; Banks had only two infantry brigades at Winchester, and one of them faced Ewell. Ewell occupied it fully, allowing Jackson to hurl almost five brigades against Banks's one other brigade. Had Jackson been able to get detailed orders to Ewell he could not have asked better assistance than that rendered. On his front, Jackson seized the important terrain for his artillery to soften the enemy while he massed infantry, swiftly exploiting the opportunity Ewell gave him to array overpowering numbers. Unlike at Kernstown, Jackson's orders at Winchester were clear, and he ensured that the final attack would come where he wanted it by riding with Taylor's Brigade on its approach march. There was no chance that confusion such as snarled the advance at Kernstown would be duplicated at Winchester.

Two other features of Jackson's leadership had emerged in the interval from Kernstown to Winchester. First, Stonewall displayed a penchant for the flank. He sought to "get around" the Union right at Kernstown, and he was exploring a wide turning movement when Milroy attacked at McDowell. He detoured as far as possible around Union positions at Front Royal, and at Winchester Taylor's charge rolled up the Federal right wing. If the enemy barred the road ahead, Jackson did not wait long to flank them. Anyone studying his career at the time would not have been surprised by the course of the Battle of Chancellorsville.

Another result of Chancellorsville, Jackson's wounding by his own skirmishers as he rode back in the dark from a scout of enemy lines, was equally predictable from the Valley Campaign. To an extent unimaginable (and inappropriate) today, Jackson as army commander led from the front. He was on the firing line with the Rockbridge Artillery at Kernstown; he and Johnson drew Union picket fire as they reconnoitered before McDowell. He was among the first over the burning bridge outside Front Royal, and he followed on foot after Captain Kurtz's Winchester boys as they skirmished down the Pike on May 24. He was near Colonel Campbell when he was wounded on the twenty-fifth. Richard Taylor recalled almost chasing him away from the Louisiana Brigade before its final charge.[88] Civil War generals oftentimes were at the front; only there could they make necessary adjustments immediately, as when Belle Boyd confirmed the weakness of the Union force at Front Royal. Yet Jackson manifested no regard whatsoever for bullets, and the wonder is that he lived long enough to be wounded at Chancellorsville.

Improved tactical handling, a quest for the flank, and leadership from the front helped give the Valley Army the advantageous position it held at dawn on May 24. At that point Taylor's large brigade was around Cedarville, and Trimble's was within easy supporting distance. Had both units started at first light for Middletown they could have reached the Valley Pike in time to cut off Banks and hold him for the balance of the Army. When the Union general obligingly tarried in Strasburg until midmorning, he even handicapped himself in the "race for the possession of Winchester." And intersecting the Valley Pike early was merely one of several opportunities to eliminate Banks. On paper Banks ought not to have left the Shenandoah with an intact army after Jackson secured the Front Royal bridges. Exactly why Banks escaped is a question worth closer examination.

That the rebels started from good ground on May 24 did not automatically translate into an operational advantage when the overall war picture is considered. The Valley Army was the third largest of the Confederacy and the only one not then facing greatly superior numbers; it represented an immense military investment. Other fronts, such as at Richmond and along the North Carolina coast, were weaker than desirable so that Jackson could have the force he wielded, but stresses on those fronts were draining units earmarked for the Valley, first Mahone's Brigade and then Branch's. Given its manpower constraints and McClellan's proximity to Richmond, the Confederacy could not hope to duplicate its concentration of force around Front Royal, particularly not in a zone offering such sensitive targets as the Potomac and the B & O Railroad.

Obviously the South needed Stonewall to return its investment in the Shenandoah with a victory there; paradoxically, the pressing need for victory fettered Jackson, because to win he had first to ensure that Banks would not escape. The Army's offense could come to naught if Banks slipped through Front Royal, and things would have been worse had Banks in the process crippled Jackson by wrecking his trains around Front Royal. It was for this reason that Jackson could not simply steamroll with his superior numbers toward the point where he was most likely to encounter the Federals; on May 24 Stonewall could not risk hitting air. Unsure of Banks's whereabouts, Jackson halted north of Cedarville while the enemy was being located. Old Jack thereby improved his ultimate chance to run Banks to the ground, even though in so doing he sacrificed the early chance to intercept Banks if the latter was fleeing along the most probable escape route, the Pike. The hours spent around Cedarville, if unfortunate from a purely local point of view, demonstrated a fine understanding of exactly why Jackson was attacking in the Valley, and not heading to Richmond. The failure to reach Middletown until midafternoon reflected no lapse of leadership, as some have thought,[89] but rather the fact that Jackson analyzed the situation very skillfully as he sat by Taylor's campfire the previous evening.

Jackson's second and perhaps best opening to destroy Banks developed as Ashby broke the Union column around Middletown. At that time, 4 P.M., Stonewall's impulse was to pursue northward, and had he done so it is questionable whether Banks would have escaped. Taylor's and Winder's tough brigades pushing after the Union flight at 4 P.M. with ample artillery—and Ewell moving shortly thereafter in the direction of Winchester (Jackson's order of 5:45 P.M. to that effect presumably would have been given earlier as well)—would have made a grimly effective sweep. Unfortunately, the principal Union force suddenly seemed to form above Middletown, and of course Jackson turned to confront it. The rear Union elements that wandered up and fooled Jackson, apparently without trying, into thinking they were the main blue column saved Banks. The two hours expended in correcting that tactical misapprehension handed Banks another reprieve, and for this there is no fault, for such confusion and miscues inevitably accompany battle; call it bad luck for Jackson.

Asbhy's pursuit north from Middletown began at the same hour the infantry might have commenced the chase, and Ashby's initial pace was unaffected by whether infantry was behind him. It is tempting to focus on cavalry looting as a cause for Banks's escape that afternoon, and Jackson did as much in his report. Carefully examined, however, the looting cannot be a wholly sufficient explanation. Had Ashby had half his companies available (five hundred men would be a generous total) and had none of them looted, the cavalry might have captured more wagons, but at some point Ashby was going to collide with the Union rear guard, and there he was going to stop unless supported by infantry. The Union retreat was covered by several infantry regiments and artillery sections adroitly managed by Colonel George Gordon (a classmate of Jackson's at West Point; it is another of the war's fascinating coincidences that Jackson, who worked so hard in the Valley to derail the campaign of his classmate McClellan, had his own efforts there thwarted in part by yet another member of the class of 1846). Cavalry did not generally challenge cohesive infantry and artillery, and Flournoy's heroic charge notwithstanding, the result of Ashby pressing beyond the Federal wagons with even a large mounted force would have been a pause for infantry aid whenever he ran up against Gordon's defenses. Had Confederate infantry marched northward at 4 P.M. instead of at 6 P.M., presumably foot support would have been available to Ashby outside Newtown at 6 P.M. instead of sunset, with an attendant increase in the chance for decisive action. Since the infantry was not there for two hours, Ashby was unlikely to have inflicted significantly greater damage than he did even had he led model troopers.

As the Union army was swept through Winchester it was again in jeopardy: Banks admitted his forces passed through town in "considerable confusion."[90] The failure to strike a crippling blow at this point lies squarely with the cavalry. General Steuart's inaction at the head of two excellent regiments was particularly harmful and can be explained, though not justified, only by a blurred chain of command.

Steuart's reports on his Newtown raid went to Jackson, but in response Jackson had Major Dabney write to Ewell directing him to "instruct General Steuart to use his own discretion as to advancing."[91] Ewell presumably relayed these instructions, which evidently gave Steuart the idea he was under Ewell's direction. Steuart was, after all, leading cavalry attached to Ewell's Division. According to aide Campbell Brown, Ewell believed Jackson would retain control over all cavalry;[92] other than to tell Steuart to move in tandem with him on the afternoon of the twenty-fourth, Ewell did not report giving Steuart any orders.[93] Yet since Ewell was forced to act independently on the twenty-fourth, it is unclear how he thought Steuart could be guided by Jackson, especially in the fog early on the twenty-fifth. Steuart apparently believed he was under Ewell's direct command, for which there was some reason, so it was technically correct for him to await orders from the latter to chase down Banks. Yet technicalities are a hindrance during the fluid situation that accompanies pursuit, and it is easy to understand why no one took time to clarify the chain of command. Generals such as Jackson and Ewell doubtless never imagined anyone would need orders to fulfill so basic a cavalry function as pouncing upon a beaten foe. Only a few weeks later, Jackson was to express a view that there was but one true rule for cavalry: "to follow as long as the enemy retreats."[94] Steuart ought not to have needed orders such as those he received from Pendleton, and the simple truth is that he lacked the spirit to lead large mounted units.

If Steuart lacked a killer instinct, the same could not be said of Ashby. Moreover, Jackson personally told him where he was to be at the close of the battle. He was not there, which raises interesting questions: where was he, with what force, and what was lost by his failure to be where Jackson wanted him?

Ashby's early biographer and regimental chaplain, James Avirett, argued that he had moved westward on the morning of May 25, perhaps to deal with Federal reinforcements or forces cut off at Middletown and moving parallel to the Pike since the previous afternoon, but three of Jackson's staff concurred that Ashby circled east of Winchester during the battle.[95] Dabney implied that this was an independent enterprise of some sort, while Allan and Hotchkiss can be read as indicating the ride at least began according to instructions. Jackson merely stated in his report that Ashby explained he went east of the Pike "for the purpose of cutting off a portion of" Federals; Jackson did not hint whether this movement could have evolved beyond orders. The general did state that the move left Ashby "not where I desired him at the close of the engagement"[96] but did not otherwise elaborate what he desired of Ashby.

It is reasonable to believe that Jackson had concerns over the area southeast of Winchester because he did not know until the fight opened how advanced Ewell was in that sector; it is certainly fair to accept that Jackson might have thought Ashby would find something worthwhile to do thereabouts. The best assumption is that the cavalryman moved east of Winchester believing he was in accord with instructions. Since it is inconceivable that Ashby was near the field when there were Federals to be ridden down and did not do so, a further assumption seems justified that he rode too far out, which would have been easy in the dense fog. He must have been farther east than two and a half miles from Winchester, since that is where Pendleton located Steuart, and there is no hint the cavalry leaders were in contact. Probably Ashby was too distant to know when the battle ended.

Whether Ashby could have enhanced Confederate success had he been on the field depends on what force he had, and this is impossible to know. In fact, it is impossible to reconstruct the whereabouts of Ashby's command between May 23 and 25. Avirett claimed Ashby had only a few companies with him during this time because most riders were spread around the Shenandoah on missions assigned by Jackson: ten companies picketing the Alleghenies to observe Frémont, four companies deployed south of Strasburg, one company deployed east of Front Royal, two companies guarding prisoners, at least one company sent to scout Strasburg from the east, and some men detailed to act as couriers for Headquarters.[97]

Avirett is correct to an extent, although the complete fragmentation he described is untenable. Only three companies, not ten, can be documented as deployed to observe Frémont.[98] This assessment was corroborated by Trooper Bill Wilson, who noted in his diary for May 22: "That portion of Ashby's cavalry which has been camped for the last three or four weeks at Mt. Crawford, Lacey Springs and this place [New Market] together with ten companies just returned from accompanying Jackson on his expedition to McDowell received marching orders."[99] The flow of this diary establishes that the cavalry crossed Massanutten Mountain with the infantry.

It is true that one or two companies were detached from Ashby's control to act as scouts and couriers for Headquarters. Four companies were deployed above Strasburg. Gilmor's unit and at least two other cavalry companies were watching Frémont in the Alleghenies, and another company can be documented on reconnaissance northeast of Front Royal on May 24.[100] The raid on Linden, just east of the Valley, perhaps was carried out by Ashby's command, although that is not certain. Some companies seem to have ridden from Front Royal west to observe Strasburg. Yet even assuming everything Avirett recalled except ten companies detailed to the Alleghenies, there is no accounting for almost half of Ashby's command. Some missing units may have been assigned to take charge of property seized in Strasburg, though the one source to comment on the cavalry there, Captain MacDonald, reported that he left the town under Captain Myers and pressed after Banks on the twenty-fourth with his command. MacDonald makes no mention of a sizable mounted contingent remaining with Myers.[101] It is simply impossible to number the companies that began May 24 with Ashby.

Since the units with Ashby on May 24 cannot be determined, it is impossible to know the number of men lost from duty because of looting. The looting was sufficient to reduce Ashby's force to fifty men outside Newtown, according to the sole observer to give specifics, Colonel Crutchfield. Some looters may have rejoined Ashby during the night, and some other units may have come in, yet there is nothing to indicate that the cadre with Ashby at Newtown had been materially enlarged by the morning of the twenty-fifth. It was against this background that the question of whether Ashby might have completed Banks's destruction must be answered. Had his been a disciplined force, and had it been concentrated, Ashby might have had five hundred or six hundred men ready to intervene at the close of battle, and that might well have meant disaster for Banks—if the cavalry had not been elsewhere. The few riders Ashby mustered seem inadequate to have interdicted Banks even if they had been present to ride down his fleeing troops; because they were not present, their location rather than their number becomes the salient factor in Banks's escape from Winchester.

Jackson's need to move deliberately and then confusion at Middletown helped Banks escape on the twenty-fourth. Poorly trained riders under an aggressive cavalryman in the wrong position and better-trained companies under an unaggressive commander in a better position combined to squander a third opportunity the following day. And so for reasons both preventable and unavoidable, the Union army in the Valley escaped to fight on other fields; call it good luck for Banks.

If Ashby's command is not solely at fault for the escape of Banks, blame was nonetheless disproportionate to its numbers. It accomplished the least of any branch of the Army while others—Flournoy's riders or Taylor's infantrymen in particular—were winning glory. Ashby's cavalry failed to break the Manassas Gap Railroad at Buckton Station, it achieved less than it could have north of Middletown, and it contributed nothing but rounding up stragglers on the twenty-fifth. The answer to the question of whether Ashby could operate effectively with the Army came along Jackson's operational triangle between May 23 and 25, and the answer was that Ashby's command was not prepared to carry out the basic functions of a modern cavalry force.

Jackson had moved early to improve discipline in Ashby's command, but this merely triggered the latter's resignation. Jackson might have tried to do something after Winchester, but fortune smiled on Ashby. On May 23, the day the cavalry began to unravel in the Valley, Richmond confirmed Ashby's elevation to brigadier general. Much lobbying for the promotion had come from Jackson's friend Congressman A. R. Boteler, also a friend of Ashby's. The chieftain received his star on May 27. According to Avirett, Ashby "smiled, took the paper, and was soon on his way back to camp."[102]

IV

Consequences, lessons, evaluations: these were not the concern of the young Confederates who triumphed in the Shenandoah. Victory was a more personal thing for them. It meant a visit home or the bliss of a real bed. As the Army gave up the pursuit of Banks on the twenty-fifth, Jackson camped it several miles from Winchester and issued his usual directive prohibiting unauthorized soldiers in the city,[103] an order that received as little attention as it had during the winter. Private Johnny Williams of the Rockbridge Artillery invited Ed Moore to spend a night at his house, which they found crowded with privates and officers alike.[104] Randy McKim of the 1st Maryland savored three days around Winchester reveling in civilized life and "the enjoyment of the ladies' society in particular."[105]

And there was food—courtesy of the Union. Before Stonewall could secure the prodigious quantities of captured stores, his men had picked through them, liberating oranges, lemons, figs, dates, oysters, lobsters, sardines, pickles, coffee, sugar, cheese, hams, and meats. "You have no idea of the extent of the booty," Ted Barclay of the Headquarters Guard wrote his sister.[106]

Because he was usually where the action was hottest, Captain Sam

Moore of the 2d Virginia was in the middle of this feeding frenzy. He was detached from his regiment and made assistant commandant of Winchester with particular responsibilities for captured sutlers' stores. For once he relaxed a little, he wrote, "and unfortunately I sampled too many of them, such as cakes, pickles, sauer krout [*sic*] and many other things." Actually, Moore ate himself sick and spent the last days of May in bed. Happily, while laid up he had liberty to arrange a reunion with his wife and family; it was short, for he soon had to send them away as refugees and return to his unit, but the brief visit was a fine reward for months of earnest soldiering.[107]

Beyond food there was drink—crates of the finest brandies and wines. Two Marylanders captured a dozen bottles of champagne and resolved to place them beyond risk of recapture, so they quaffed every one. The next day they marched, causing one man to admit in later years, "I have not forgotten the terrors of that day's march, particularly in the early hours until some friends gave me a bottle of Rhine wine. It healed my sorrows . . . and enabled me to make the march with comparative comfort. Many years have since rolled by; many varied experiences have I undergone, but never since have I attempted to put away six bottles of champagne in one sitting."[108]

The boys slept, bathed, ate, and drank. They riddled Federal breastplates (which were advertised to protect against all harm) at target-practice sessions.[109] They began to replace their meager wardrobes from a warehouse of Federal uniforms, until it almost seemed that Banks's army had returned. New regulations boomed from Headquarters in response. All men found wearing Union garb, Jackson directed, should be arrested until they could be identified as Confederates. Since the men obviously had too much time on their hands, daily drills were resumed.[110]

No chorus of squawks greeted these orders, for the troops had come to understand the ceaseless activity of their stern commander. On May 26 Jackson praised their victory in a general order and added, "The explanation of the severe exertions to which the Commanding General called the army, which were endured by them with such cheerful confidence, is now given, in the victory of yesterday."[111] Years later John Worsham recalled that order and what the troops learned from it about their general: "He had led us for three weeks as hard as men could march. In an order issued to his troops the next day he thanked us for our conduct, and referred us to the result of the campaign as justification for our marching so hard. Every man was satisfied with his apology; to accomplish so much with so little loss, we would march six months!"[112]

Old Jack had won by trading sweat for blood; this his men understood. "Our loss was small," concluded John Casler about the fight from Front Royal to Winchester, "it being a kind of a one sided fight all the time. General Jackson 'got the drop' on them in the start, and kept it."[113]

Part IV

14

IN THE LOWER VALLEY

We resumed our march north—50 minutes each hour, rest, then 50 minutes again.

—Franklin Riley

The Valley Army's initial operations following recapture of Winchester were an extension of the mission that had led it there. Although the Army's task was accomplished on May 24 when Lincoln derailed McDowell's push on Richmond, Jackson of course did not know it then. His immediate planning after May 25 would have been guided by Lee's letter of May 16 in which Lee wrote that if a strike against Banks went well Jackson should "drive him back toward the Potomac and create the impression, as far as practicable, that you design threatening that line."[1] The Valley Army had come to rest following the Battle of Winchester in positions that facilitated Lee's purpose. The cavalry ended its pursuit of Banks around Martinsburg, and work details promptly began removing supplies taken in the large warehouses there and tearing up B & O tracks. Colonel Munford returned from east of the Blue Ridge with the balance of his 2d Virginia Cavalry, now fully armed. He was dispatched with Brockenbrough's Baltimore Battery to join the advanced forces at Martinsburg and skirmished to within a mile of the Potomac. His raid drew fire from Union guns on the far side of the boundary river.[2] On the evening of May 27 Jackson ordered the Stonewall Brigade, minus the 2d Virginia Infantry, which had been detached to guard captured property in Winchester, to head the following morning in the direction of Charles Town for a show of strength against any Federal units there.[3]

If the Army was to operate in the lower Valley, its flanks had to be secured, since at Winchester the rebels were seventy-five miles beyond

Frémont's last known location at Franklin and far north of Shields's route to Fredericksburg. On May 27 Colonel Conner and his 12th Georgia with a section of Captain Rice's Battery were ordered to garrison Front Royal.[4] Jackson thought of the cavalry still watching Frémont and dispatched a reminder for Harry Gilmor to stay close to the Pathfinder. He also urged Major Harman's brother Asher, commanding at Staunton, not to keep many stores there and as well to organize even sick soldiers against mounted raids.[5]

There was much to be done in the lower Shenandoah. All Federal prisoners were assembled at Winchester. The 21st Virginia under direction of its second in command was assigned to guard the approximately twenty-three hundred "blue birds" able to march; sick and wounded Federals were paroled.[6] Since the tons of material seized from Banks surpassed available transport, Jackson gave Major Harman most of what few wagons the infantry brigades retained and detailed them to Front Royal to haul captured supplies. Typically, Jackson kept only ammunition wagons and ambulances with the Army.[7] Still unable to move all Union stores, Harman asked for more help, and Jackson used his authority to impress teams and wagons across the upper Shenandoah for government service. William Allan noted that the order directed officers in the southern Valley to gather "everything that can be made available to haul stores, and send them here forthwith, immediately, if not sooner."[8] There was an excellent response, and two columns of civilian wagons began moving down the Valley, one toward Winchester, the other toward Front Royal.

The Army also needed to reorganize. Brigadier General Taliaferro returned from sick leave and resumed command of the 3d Brigade of Jackson's original force. Colonel John Patton of the 21st Virginia, the last full colonel left in the 2d Brigade, would lead that unit in place of the wounded Colonel Campbell. Jackson reviewed the state of discipline in the ranks and raced to punish all breaches. On the twenty-seventh he published orders for each brigade to detail officers for court-martial duty; all offenders were to be charged at once. Jackson was unwilling to be long occupied with the administration of military justice and planned trials for the next day. Commanders were especially to report acts of pillaging; despite the fine overall performance of Taylor's command, Jackson recalled the looting around Middletown and singled out the Louisianans in an order directing Ewell to provide a list of men guilty of that particular violation.[9]

Some Louisianans, especially Major Wheat's Tigers, escaped Stonewall's version of due process on May 28 when the general received Johnston's telegram of May 27, which Lieutenant Boswell had expedited from Richmond. Jackson would have been galvanized by Johnston's call for action to counteract McDowell's push on the capital: "The most important service you can render the country is the preventing the further strengthening of McClellan's army," Johnston had written. If as Johnston feared Jackson was too late to cross the Potomac or even slash into McDowell's rear, then the telegram contained an even more urgent directive: "Strike the most important body of the enemy you can reach."

Johnston's telegram required an immediate effort in the Valley. The obvious target was Harpers Ferry, twenty-five miles northeast of Winchester. If the Union had not already reacted to the Army's offensive, it would be impossible to ignore once Confederate artillery opened on Harpers Ferry, a post as far north as Baltimore and barely fifty miles from Washington. Winder's Brigade had marched at 5 A.M. for Charles Town, which lay on the road to Harpers Ferry, to make the demonstration Jackson wanted, so the operation was already under way. Orders exploded for Ewell to assemble his division and follow Winder.[10]

As if to reinforce the decision, word soon came that Winder had discovered Federals in Charles Town. Winder had only four regiments and was without cavalry, but he pressed onward. He collected fifteen straggling cavalrymen and luckily met Captain Chew of Ashby's artillery, who volunteered to command them. Chew found the enemy's pickets, and in a quick firefight Winder drove back in confusion a force of fifteen hundred Yanks. Winder chased them to within sight of Bolivar Heights, a ridgeline on which Federals stood in battle array barring the southern approaches to Harpers Ferry.[11] Here lay the nearest important body of Federals the Valley Army could quickly reach, and throughout the rest of the day Jackson, who remained in Winchester, redeployed his army in that direction.

Shortly after midnight, Headquarters received a rumor that the thrust to the Potomac faced a massive Federal counteroffensive. In the early hours of the twenty-ninth an elderly civilian entered Winchester with news from beyond the Blue Ridge. Sandie Pendleton interviewed him and heard the gentleman describe how General McDowell's Union corps was marching from Fredericksburg for the Shenandoah. Shields was already within a day's march of Front Royal. The informant stated he had seen Shields's Division on the road and had galloped for twelve hours to bring warning. Pendleton was inclined to credit this report but decided to wait until morning to notify Jackson. When Jackson saw the gentleman he was not sure of the story.[12] He did not accept this report as more than a rumor, he told Major Harman, but he urged him nonetheless to accelerate removal of captured goods from Front Royal.[13]

Given the usual tardiness of Union movements, Jackson was justified in doubting that the enemy, who could not have discovered the extent and direction of his attack before late on May 24, would have a relief column within a day's march of Front Royal so soon. Nonetheless, rumors persisted. At 6 A.M. on May 29 Colonel Conner, commanding at Front Royal, forwarded to his brigade commander (Elzey) the product of his interrogation of a Federal prisoner. The Yank had been taken less than twenty miles west of Front Royal near Rectortown and claimed to be part of a brigade-size force there. He stated that Shields had hustled out of Fredericksburg on the twenty-fifth with fourteen thousand men and was moving on Front Royal. Conner was worried and asked if he should burn all stores at the first approach of the enemy and rejoin Elzey.[14] It is unknown when this word came to Jackson, but Johnston's peril at Richmond required the Valley Army to make a bold demonstration somewhere despite reports such as those of Conner's. Indeed, Jackson on the twenty-ninth elected to collect the Army outside Harpers Ferry. Ashby rode in the direction of the Ferry, as did the force at Martinsburg.[15] The last infantry brigades around Winchester, those of Taliaferro and Patton, marched to the northeast, and even the 2d Virginia was relieved from guard duties and hurried up to Winder.[16] The Army was massed south of Harpers Ferry by dark.

Headquarters that night was established at Charles Town in the home of Major Hawks. Having worked tirelessly to feed the troops for months, Hawks now played host to the Army's high command at his own dinner table.[17] Winder and Ewell could report that during the day they had skirmished energetically with the Yanks along Bolivar Heights; they had been busy enough that the enemy ought to feel anxious. Winder even had effected a partial encirclement of the Federals when he discovered that Loudoun Heights, on the Shenandoah River's east bank, was deserted. The enemy perhaps believed they need not man that high ground since they had cleared the river of all boats, but Colonel Allen got most of his 2d Virginia across the stream by the simple expedient of having his men hold the tail of a horse while a cavalryman swam it over.[18] The Army was at a fever pitch of excitement as rumors swirled that Confederate sympathizers in Maryland had risen. Supposedly there were riots in Baltimore, and some rebels wondered whether an assault on the Ferry or an outright invasion of Maryland was more likely.[19]

During the night, however, prospects for continued offense dimmed. From Harry Gilmor in the Alleghenies came word that Frémont had stirred. Gilmor had circled Frémont's camps persistently, and when Frémont pulled out of Franklin, Gilmor followed. Gilmor initially thought Frémont intended to head north to the Potomac and succor Banks. But at the mountain village of Moorefield Frémont took the road to Wardensville; from there a highway paralleled for a number of miles Little North Mountain, then curled around its tip to run southeast a few miles into Strasburg. Gilmor sent this news by his most trusty courier, who reached Headquarters during the night of the twenty-ninth.[20] The general did not cancel a vigorous probe of Bolivar Heights after reading this dispatch, but he must have begun to consider that his time in the lower Valley could be short.

As it turned out, Gilmor's information on Frémont, and as well the rumors about Shields, were essentially accurate. The counteroffensive Lincoln had launched to capture the Valley Army was gathering speed, and the Army's redeployment toward Harpers Ferry in response to Johnston's call aided the Union plan by taking the Confederates away from their lines of communication. Johnston's instructions were appropriate given his straits in Richmond, and Jackson's move to Harpers Ferry was his best response, but the result was that the Valley Army was at risk of being trapped.

Lincoln's operational level offensive had been designed on the afternoon of May 24 when the president knew little more than that rebels were dogging Banks northward. The president ordered Frémont to the southwestern Shenandoah as an anvil against which McDowell's divisions could hammer. Frémont specifically was ordered to prevent Confederate flight from the lower Valley by capturing Harrisonburg. McDowell would then pound the blocked Valley Army wherever it was cornered. Unfortunately for Lincoln, Frémont disregarded his instructions to enter the Valley near Harrisonburg; instead, he was tramping through the Alleghenies via Moorefield and Wardensville to enter the Valley at Strasburg. (One of Frémont's reasons for this course was obstruction of the passes between Franklin and the Harrisonburg–New Market area by Hotchkiss after the Battle of McDowell.) Frémont's decision eliminated much flexibility from Lincoln's maneuver. His march to Strasburg would bring him into the Valley at approximately the same time as and at a point opposite from Shields's entrance (Front Royal), thus converting Lincoln's net into a pincer movement. Timing is crucial and difficult in a pincer movement, but with Jackson sitting outside Harpers Ferry, the pincers represented by Frémont and Shields had a magnificent opportunity to snag the Valley Army.

Banks, meanwhile, also was showing signs of recovery. He had one regiment of cavalry across the Potomac by May 30; it advanced cautiously toward Martinsburg.[21] Union General Geary was probing the Blue Ridge twenty miles east of Winchester with a regiment. The remaining unit of McDowell's marching column, Ord's Division, was a day's march behind Shields. Banks, Geary, and Ord thus did not pose immediate danger to the Valley Army, but as Jackson would quickly discover, they were close enough to set off alarms of Federals approaching from all directions.

To summarize: late May found Federal pincers aiming for the Valley Army's rear. Frémont was bearing down on Strasburg from the west; McDowell's two divisions, with Shields in the van, were targeting Front Royal from the east. Banks along the Potomac and the Harpers Ferry garrison blocked the northern rim of the Shenandoah. A ring of fifty thousand soldiers was being forged around the Valley Army.*

May 30 dawned brightly, but soon rain clouds began stacking up over Harpers Ferry. Southern artillery opened on Federal positions along Bolivar Heights. Federal big guns boomed in response, and for a time the artillery fire grew lively. Using dips and breaks in the ground, several companies from the 1st Maryland sneaked through an unguarded stretch of Union lines to the top of Bolivar Heights. They helped themselves to camp items strewn about in the usual abundance before being

* For an account of this extraordinary phase of the Valley Campaign from the Northern viewpoint, see Appendix C.

driven off.[22] As Jackson watched the skirmishing, Generals Winder and Elzey joined him. Winder mentioned that the enemy apparently had been heavily reinforced; Elzey, a man renowned for his courage, remarked that some long-range Union guns were planted across the Potomac. "General Elzey, are you afraid of heavy guns?" snapped Jackson, whose attention then was diverted by a messenger.[23] Elzey flushed, though he said nothing. Stonewall had been too tactless to realize he had just humiliated one general in the presence of another.

Fatigue and worry sharpened Jackson's want of tact that day, for he had received several grim dispatches in addition to Gilmor's report on Frémont. From various sources came confirmation that Shields was closing on Front Royal and (erroneous) report of a second column under McDowell crossing the Shenandoah River as if to enter Berryville. Other intelligence claimed Banks was reinforced and able to recross the Potomac below Martinsburg.[24] Jackson must have guessed that all these reports could not be valid, but there was no way to separate the true, the false, and the maybe. A significant reaction was under way, and news of Union armies converging on the Valley gave assurance that Richmond's need for a diversion had been met. Johnston hoped Jackson might draw forces from McClellan "by divisions"; that had been done. The problem now was to avoid or defeat those divisions. In the absence of definitive information on the Union offensive, Jackson's best option was to regroup at Winchester, if not even farther south.

Shortly past noon Jackson ordered the Army to march for Winchester, save Winder's Brigade, which continued to skirmish along Bolivar Heights to screen the withdrawal. Most troops followed the rail line back to Stephenson's Depot; Taylor's Brigade marched directly from Charles Town to Berryville to blunt any Union advance from the lower fords of the Shenandoah River.[25] The orders given, Jackson curled up under a large tree for a nap.

When Jackson awoke, Alexander R. Boteler, the Valley's representative in the Confederate Congress, was sketching him on a pad. Jackson had promised during the spring to alert Boteler if he pushed down the Valley again (perhaps to give the latter a chance to visit his home in Shepardstown), and Jackson kept his pledge by advising Boteler of his drive from Harrisonburg on May 19. Boteler headed for the Valley quickly, arriving after the Battle of Winchester to find that his son had been wounded there. The boy's wounds were not critical, so Boteler came on to join Jackson's staff as a special aide with the honorary rank of colonel. Boteler had an artistic side and would later gain fame for drawings of Confederate leaders. The sketch that now occupied him did not survive (it rendered Stonewall somewhat in the mold of a crusader, with arms folded over the chest and feet crossed) but Old Jack got a look. The general glanced over the drawing, then mused as if very far away, "My hardest tasks at West Point were the drawing lessons, and I never could do anything in that line to satisfy myself, or indeed, anybody else."

Suddenly Jackson returned to the present, pulled himself into an upright position, and talked business: "I want you to go to Richmond for me," he said to Boteler. "I must have reinforcements. You can explain to them what the situation is here. Get as many men as can be spared, and I'd like you, if you please, to go as soon as you can."

Boteler requested details of the situation, and Jackson shared as much as he knew. Shields and Frémont were probably planning to link up around Strasburg, he said. Banks's resurrected army and the Harpers Ferry garrison would likely come south as the Confederates withdrew toward Winchester. Stonewall was confident he could puncture this circle and was equally confident of regaining the initiative if reinforced. Perhaps thinking of Johnston's telegram that he must employ his army on projects bearing directly upon the state of things at the capital, he outlined a great new drive to lift the siege of Richmond: "If my command can be gotten up to 40,000 men, a movement may be made beyond the Potomac which will soon raise the siege of Richmond and transfer this campaign from the banks of the Potomac to those of the Susquehanna."

Boteler realized that the Susquehanna flowed through central Pennslyvania; this was a major drive indeed! And Jackson wanted the idea conveyed to Richmond at once. He instructed Boteler to proceed to the train depot at Charles Town. The rebels had managed to restore service on the railroad between Harpers Ferry and Winchester, and Boteler would find a train in Charles Town. Jackson told him to take it to Winchester, thence go by road to Staunton and rail to Richmond and urge the help he needed. Boteler left at once while the general joined the column receding from Bolivar Heights.[26]

The road was full of marching soldiers, all curious as to their destination. What of the invasion of Maryland? What about the rumors of

Federals approaching? What next? One young lieutenant of Ashby's command wandered up and, accustomed to the cavalry's informality, decided to quiz Jackson. Riding past several of the staff, including Hotchkiss, the cavalryman asked Stonewall, "General, are the troops going back?"

"Don't you see them going?" grunted Jackson.

"Are they all going?" he persisted.

Jackson had had enough conversation. He turned to one of his staff and snapped, "Arrest that man as a spy." Happily, Ashby trotted along soon and got his trooper off by explaining, as Hotchkiss recorded it, that the boy "had not much sense."[27]

Arriving in Charles Town, Jackson saw Boteler's train still at the station and elected to take the cars back to Winchester. Joined by Sandie Pendleton and perhaps others of the staff, Jackson took a seat in the coach and dozed off again. Someone laid aside a dispatch pouch holding Johnston's telegram of May 27 and other sensitive documents. The engine hissed out beneath a hard rain, but Jackson slept on. Boteler was less comfortable and watched the horizon anxiously during the slow journey south. After some miles Boteler spotted a lone Confederate horseman whipping his mount toward the train as if pursued by half the Yankee army. Boteler nudged Jackson, who ordered a halt. The rider, a messenger from Winchester, closed and handed up a dispatch that must have numbered among the most disheartening Jackson ever received: Shields held Front Royal! Wooden faced, Jackson tore up the message and motioned to continue. Soon they reached Winchester, and in their hurry to deal with this latest crisis the general and his staff bolted off the train, leaving behind the dispatch pouch with Johnston's message.[28] Clearly Jackson had troubles on his mind.

II

Since midafternoon on the thirtieth hints of a disaster near Front Royal had been reaching Winchester. First came runaway wagons and stray rebels talking of a Federal avalanche. Later Colonel Conner arrived, stammering that his regiment had been overrun by enormous numbers and that he had ordered his men to disperse to save themselves; Conner

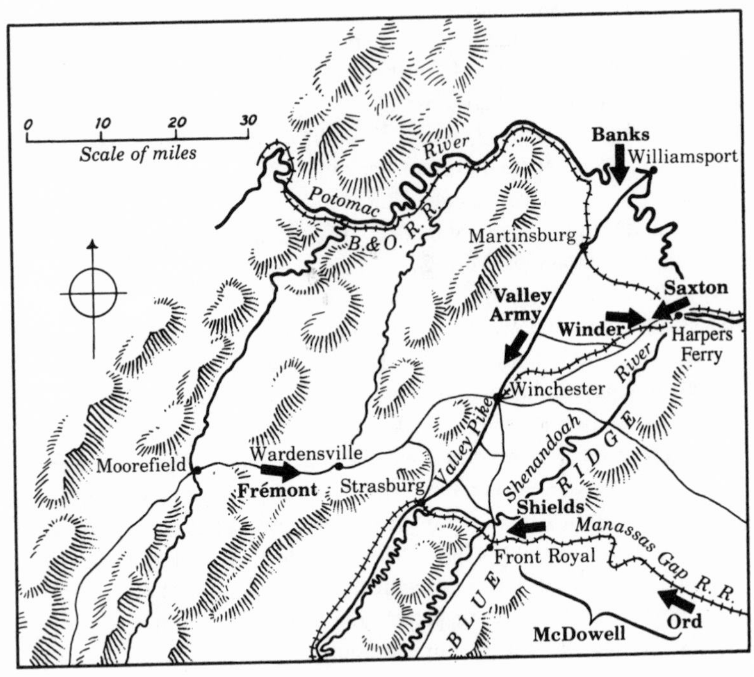

11. Situation in the Lower Valley, May 31, 1862

claimed the Federals were pursuing toward Winchester.[29] Conner wrote a hasty report to Ewell, and it was this note, or the essence of it, that halted Jackson's train on its return from Charles Town.[30]

During the next hours a fuller picture of events at Front Royal became available, and it was indeed dire. On the twenty-ninth rumors had begun to circulate around the village that Shields was coming,[31] but Colonel Conner apparently formulated no response. The next day Conner belatedly ordered an evacuation as Federals were nearing the village. The wagons from Jackson's brigades were started back to Winchester, and word went to the convoy of civilian wagons approaching Front Royal from the south to reverse direction. One of Major Harman's assistants stayed to torch a still bulging depot, but many captured wagons, some loaded, were abandoned.[32] Rebel infantry took off on the road for Winchester as Federal cavalry secured the bridges and stormed after them. In a melee two miles north of Front Royal the section of guns from Rice's Battery stood alone blasting Union cavalry, which charged within eighty yards. Rice had to destroy one of the chests on a caisson to escape, and in the confusion a cannon from Brockenbrough's Battery was lost.[33] The main Union weight fell on the 12th Georgia, part of which was cut off, and here Conner lost his head. He told his men to flee and ran himself; the next in command was equally shaken. Major Willie Hawkins ordered his men to lay down their arms and surrender, but a sixty-year-old captain refused to obey, rallied the troops, and continued the withdrawal. "We had to run some distance to save ourselves and retreat to Winchester; a good many of the boys tired down and scattered through the woods, where they were picked up by the enemy's cavalry," wrote one Georgian.[34] Thus occupied, the enemy did not head for Winchester on the evening of May 30.

The action was almost a mirror image of the encounter at Front Royal six days earlier. An infantry regiment and two guns were routed by superior numbers and overtaken around Cedarville. One hundred fifty Georgians had been made prisoner by swarming cavalry, which came on "shooting and cutting."[35] As before, much property was lost, and the vital bridges over both Shenandoah forks were surrendered intact. The difference was that this time there had been no courageous delaying fight, no effort comparable to the stand of the Union 1st Maryland. Perhaps the 12th Georgia had not recovered from its punishment at McDowell, but that was not an excuse in the Valley Army. At Headquarters that evening Old Jack erupted when he met Conner. "Colonel," he barked, "how many men did you have killed?"

"None."

"How many wounded?"

"None, sir."

"Do you call that much of a fight?" snapped Jackson as he placed Conner under arrest.[36]

By the time Conner was disposed of and the fragments of his regiment collected, it was dusk. The majority of the Valley Army was finishing its march from Harpers Ferry and camping around Stephenson's Depot. The only combat-effective force in Winchester was Chew's Battery, now reduced to two pieces after an accident disabled its best gun during the drive against Banks. That unit was hustled to the outskirts of Winchester and deployed where the road from Front Royal entered town; happily no Federals challenged it.[37] Jackson doubtless spread his maps and restudied the triangle formed by Front Royal, Winchester, and Strasburg. This time the enemy would have to decide which way to go on the morrow. They might come northward toward Winchester, perhaps uniting with Federals crossing the fords of the lower Shenandoah River; alternatively, they might dash toward Strasburg and a junction with Frémont. The course for the Valley Army was self-evident: with Shields in Front Royal the single road on which the Southerners could evacuate with prisoners and captured property was the Valley Pike. Shields and Frémont both threatened that road at Strasburg, so a march there must be swift. Federal prisoners were herded south at an early hour, followed by trains and infantry.

At 3 A.M. on May 31 Jackson roused Hotchkiss with his latest intelligence summary. Federals were closing on every side, he said: Frémont was in the vicinity of Wardensville if not already east of it; that put him perilously near Strasburg. Shields was in Front Royal, Banks was to the north, McDowell to the east.[38] The Army probably would have to confront at least one Union column that day. The general implied that the fight might be around Winchester because he spoke of trying to keep the city open for Winder. Jackson wanted Hotchkiss to return to Harpers Ferry with this news and start Winder's Brigade to rejoin the Army. This assignment could have been handled by any courier, and the general revealed the gravity of their plight when he explained why he gave Hotchkiss the mission. Stonewall was uncertain he could hold Winchester until Winder got there; in such event Hotchkiss must guide Winder back to the Army—through the Alleghenies if necessary. It was more than possible that the Stonewall Brigade was going to need an expert mapmaker.

There were crucial orders for Ashby as well. Jackson instructed him to picket all the roads from Front Royal toward Winchester and the Pike. The general designated the crossroads from Ninevah to Newtown and Cedarville to Middletown for special surveillance; he had not forgotten his use of those byways a week earlier.[39] Ashby as always interpreted his orders aggressively. With Chew's Battery and perhaps five hundred riders, Ashby rode up the Winchester–Front Royal road until within sight of Guard Hill, the position from which Yankees had attempted to impede Confederate pursuit on May 23. Once again Federal guns were posted there. Rebel artillery opened and kept up a noisy skirmish until the enemy took cover in a ravine. Ashby could only observe a regiment of Federals, but prisoners were collected who confirmed that Shields held the village in force. Ashby's presence handcuffed the Yanks at Front Royal and left them afraid to move from it. After several hours of what may have been his most valuable service of the war, Ashby retired to the Pike.[40]

Along that highway the bedraggled, overloaded rebels must have heard the sound of Ashby's guns and quickened their trek for Strasburg. First came the trains, a jumble of captured U.S. Army wagons, civilian carriages, and Conestogas. Many wagons from the upper Valley were part of traffic jam Major Harman estimated to be eight miles in length. Hotchkiss claimed the trains stretched "in double lines, 8 miles long when well closed up."[41] Eight miles would have swallowed hundreds of vehicles, so it is no wonder they were tallied by the mile.

Federal prisoners, on the other hand, were accounted for to a man. There were twenty-three hundred of them, and they crowded Harman's caravan. "We have no place to put them, and they are in the way. I wish now they had been paroled," groused the quartermaster.[42] The Yanks guessed that liberation was near, and they grew rowdy. One of the surrounded rebel guards of the 21st Virginia, John Worsham, almost felt himself a captive: "One of the Yankee prisoners marched at my side, talking about what he was going to do with me when they were retaken, and how he would take care of my gun."[43]

Next came the infantry brigades, first Taliaferro's and Patton's commands and then Ewell's Division. Those in ranks were showing the effect of this forced march; perhaps they outnumbered the stragglers, but it would have been impossible to know. Colonel Thomas Garnett of the 48th Virginia estimated half his men were left behind just on the march from Charles Town to Winchester.[44] Hundreds of stragglers were strewn in the rear of Ewell's command. Many found aid from Flournoy's and Munford's cavalrymen. Recalled Munford: "Hundreds of our best infantry fell by the wayside, but the riders would help them, often taking them up behind them on their horses, or carrying their rifles or allowing them to hold on and be supported by the stirrups as they limped forward."[45]

Noon of May 31 found the Army spread along the Pike for miles. A few squadrons of Federal cavalry could have revenged the slaughter at Middletown, and rumors of such a trap racked the column. But there was no ambush, only the distant mutter of Ashby's fight outside Front Royal, which ended that afternoon as the rebels reached Cedar Creek. Units from Taliaferro's Brigade went farther ahead to camp within a mile of Strasburg.[46]

To the north, Winder's Brigade kept on the road. Hotchkiss had reached Charles Town early with Jackson's instructions to retire; he found the Stonewall Brigade preparing to skirmish again while the 2d Virginia remained on the east bank of the Shenandoah River. Also present was the 1st Maryland, which somehow had not received orders to withdraw.[47] Winder assumed command of the Old Line Staters and brought the 2d Virginia over the river from Loudoun Heights. As before, each infantryman paddled across clinging to the tail of a horse. Several hours were lost before the column began a marathon that was to be one of the great marches of the war. Hour after hour the troops sprinted without pausing to eat; for the 2d Virginia it was the second day without rations. Early on there was an alarm: Yanks were on the Valley Pike north of Winchester and would cut off the trains. The rumor was false, like most that stirred ranks that day. The pace was maintained under a hot sun to Winchester, which was devoid of organized Confederates when Winder reached it. One woman wrote in her diary: "Jackson's old Brigade—the 'Stonewall'—did not pass until long after dark, so we waited for it. . . . We were standing in the door giving the soldiers bread as they passed." Another lady described how the soldiers, from private to

General Winder himself, crowded her table for anything she had to feed them.[48]

Winder soon led his men over the battlefield of Winchester and along the same road they had traveled on the miserable night of May 24. A cold rain began to fall. Toward midnight, as the rebels dragged past charred Union wagons outside Newtown, Winder realized they could not reach Strasburg that night. The exhausted shell of his brigade was outnumbered by its stragglers. Pointing his men into an orchard, he let them sleep. Every soldier left in ranks had slogged thirty miles, those in the 2d Virginia more than thirty-five, in approximately sixteen hours.[49] Wrote Lanty Blackford of that camp: "It was cold and rainy and we put up no tents or shelters of any kind, so the night was almost as miserable as it well could be. Beds spread on the ground with mud 3 or 4 inches deep below and rain above are not the most comfortable."[50] One of the Marylanders echoed that thought: "Never was I so tired in my life as I lied [*sic*] down that night in a dark rain to rest my weary limbs and blistered feet."[51]

Not many hours after Winder let his troops sleep, Hotchkiss rode up to Headquarters at the Hupp estate just north of Strasburg to report Winder's progress.[52] With the Stonewall Brigade outside Newtown Jackson knew it was nearer to Strasburg than Shields, who from Front Royal was twelve miles away over a hilly country road. Winder was at most ten miles away via the Valley Pike. He ought to avoid entrapment if Frémont could be held at bay. Jackson had only a small outpost on the Wardensville road, and Frémont hit it early on the morning of June 1.[53] Frémont thus was closer to Strasburg, and Jackson spent the first daylight hours of June 1 blocking this threat. While the trains continued up the Pike, Ewell took his division to the northwest along the Wardensville road with orders to delay Frémont without becoming heavily engaged.[54] Jackson remained near the Pike to supervise and hurry the trains.

Ewell's vanguard footed four miles of gently ascending terrain until its way was intersected by a small vale two or three miles long; the road from Wardensville curled around Little North Mountain, on the vale's far side, and ran across the low ground and up to the point where Confederates stood. Federal pickets were already moving forward, so Ewell acted at once to secure the high ground with Elzey's and Taylor's brigades, held Trimble's men in reserve and unleashed two batteries. Union artillery replied.[55] The cannon fire grew vigorous and worrisome enough that Jackson dispatched other units to this front. Taliaferro's Brigade and then at least part of Patton's arrived, so at one point most Southern infantry was deployed northwest of Strasburg.[56]

The cannonade lasted for several hours, exactly the sort of time wasting the Valley Army needed to slip away, but it tormented Ewell, who was mystified by enemy passivity when attack was the obvious course. General Taylor overheard him fretting about Jackson's instructions not to bring on a general engagement and volunteered that his brigade might slip around the Union left, near the Wardensville highway, and learn something of enemy intentions. "Do so; that may stir them up, and I am sick of this fiddling about," Ewell replied.

Taylor put his troops in motion, and swiftly they struck the Pathfinder's flank. The probe gathered speed as the enemy seemed to disappear. "It was nothing but a 'walk over,'" scoffed Taylor. "Sheep would have made as much resistance as we met. Men decamped without firing, or threw down their arms and surrendered, and it was so easy that I began to think of traps. At length we got under fire from our own skirmishers, and suffered some casualties, the only ones received in the movement."[57] Taylor called a halt to his drive and resumed the defensive, capping Ewell's successful bluff. Frémont thought he confronted fifteen thousand men with eight thousand more coming up, and he did not press.[58] During the day Jackson visited the area and judged that Frémont was neutralized; Stonewall began shifting units from Ewell's fight back to high ground overlooking the road from Front Royal to Strasburg.

The road from Front Royal to Strasburg had been silent all morning. Soon after dawn, Jackson sent Lieutenant Boswell, just returned from carrying to Richmond word of the victory at Winchester, on a scout to the east. Boswell was barely two miles toward Front Royal when he encountered Federal cavalry. He hastened back to Headquarters but found only Ashby there to receive his report; Ashby immediately flung out a portion of his command to block the highway.[59] Chew's Battery joined them. There the Southerners made a great display of fight for the benefit of Federal cavalry approaching without, significantly, blue infantry support. Eventually Ashby's riders were joined by Trimble's Brigade from Ewell's front, but the Federals did not test them.[60]

Winder's column, meanwhile, renewed its march at 5:30 A.M.[61] Because Frémont's road followed the base of Little North Mountain to a point several miles north of Strasburg before it curled back, his clash with Ewell took place almost directly west of Middletown, and Ewell's fight sounded ominously close to Winder's dead-tired marchers.[62] Rumors of disaster were everywhere, especially among the innumerable stragglers. One of them, Watkins Kearns, described his worries as he tried to overtake his unit: "Report of the advance of the enemy up the pike in our rear, off to the left at North Mountain and to the right by way of Front Royal. We are all told to hurry forward or the enemy will cut us off at Newtown—then at Middletown—then this side of Strasburg."[63] The worst rumors hit above Middletown: there the word was certain that Shields was athwart the road waiting for them.[64]

Winder's aide, McHenry Howard, was slightly in advance of the column as Middletown came in sight. At the juncture of the Cedarville cutoff, the same road Jackson had surged along on the afternoon of May 24, Howard spotted a small group of horsemen. Federals? Howard pressed a little farther, and as he did one of the riders in the group came northward slowly. In a moment Howard recognized—Ashby.

"Is that General Winder coming up?" called the cavalryman.

Howard whooped yes, and Ashby relaxed. Winder trotted up, and the chieftain pumped his hand; he had not forgotten Winder's friendship during his standoff with Jackson at Swift Run Gap. "General," Ashby smiled, "I never was so relieved in my life. I thought that you would be cut off and had made up my mind to join you and advise you to make your escape over the mountains to Gordonsville."[65]

Ashby's smile assured Winder this would not be necessary. The road ahead was open for the last of the Valley Army, which Colonel Johnson of the 1st Maryland described as "a column of limping stragglers, two miles long."[66] The Stonewall Brigade pushed over Cedar Creek and then halted for an hour while laggers rejoined; Colonel Johnson estimated that at least a thousand men caught up during the halt, but hundreds more were behind them.[67] Ashby dispatched riders to warn them to head southwestward through the Alleghenies until they could return to the Army.[68] Then Ashby burned the bridge over Cedar Creek, and by noon Winder had his magnificent troops in Strasburg.

With Trimble in position to blunt any drive from Front Royal, and with Ewell holding Frémont, Jackson could give Winder's troops a little rest while the trains lurched on. By midafternoon, however, rest time was over; under a breaking thunderstorm, Jackson withdrew up the Pike. Behind him, Federals appeared from Front Royal, while Frémont's van moved in from the west. They took Strasburg and several hundred prisoners, and several hundred more Confederates were destined to pick their way through the Alleghenies before rejoining the Army, but no organized Southern infantry, artillery, or trains were captured. The Federal pincers from east and west slammed shut twelve hours too late.

Like Banks a week earlier, the Valley Army's evasion of destruction was, on paper, improbable as of noon on May 30, but two days of hard marching and skirmishing had whisked the Army through a ring of fifty thousand foe. Many Confederates departing Strasburg assumed Old Jack raced to the Potomac anticipating the Union counterthrust and that their deliverance was a brilliantly calculated maneuver.[69] Their faith in their general and in themselves soared. In reality Jackson had done no more than target an obvious point for the demonstrations Johnston urged in his telegram of May 27. The peril at Richmond necessitated risk taking in the Valley, and as demanded by the overall situation Jackson prolonged the most serious threat he could make (at Harpers Ferry) until it became certain the enemy was responding. He then took his only escape route with the greatest possible speed. Brilliance had sprung once again from hard work.

And it was the hard work of soldiers on the march more than any other factor that permitted escape. While the Stonewall Brigade won just praise for its superb effort backtracking from Harpers Ferry, every man in the Army had been on the road almost continually since the twenty-eighth. With start times ranging from early on the twenty-eighth to the morning of the twenty-ninth, all units had trudged twenty or more miles to Harpers Ferry, then back to Winchester, then eighteen miles to Strasburg and three or four miles out to stop Frémont. In the approximately one hundred hours between dawn of May 28 and noon of June 1, most units had covered between sixty and seventy miles, during which time they won major skirmishes at opposite ends of the lower Valley.

"We have come to be veterans—have no tents, carry our knapsacks and blankets, never ride on caissons . . . and, in case of necessity, can live on half rations and not think it anything remarkable," boasted one rebel.[70] Another agreed, "I can stand almost anything; lay down at night on the ground without a tent with my clothes perfectly wet in a single blanket and sleep as sound as if on a feather bed."[71] A veteran army was emerging, men who knew they could prevail and were determined to do so. No longer did they talk of going home until the war was won: "I mean to keep at it as long as there is any necessity for it, if it should be the rest of my life," wrote Private Dick Waldrop, who, with his entire company, had refused to reenlist last February.[72] One of the Georgians put it more simply; he would stay with his unit "as long as I can raise one foot before the other."[73]

Trotting up and down the Shenandoah, the hard core of the Valley Army was becoming Jackson's "Foot Cavalry." The men were adopting that curious sobriquet, bragging they could break down cavalry on a long march. The endless drills and training, to say nothing of weeks of practice on the road, had toughened them beyond their appreciation. One Confederate depicted how the constant marching "so hardened our muscles that when fatigue came there was no soreness or stiffness of the muscles, but just a general exhaustion."[74] Such were the words of veterans. And it was well the soldier's life had been mastered, for things were about to become much harder than these men had yet known.

15

UP THE VALLEY

This trip has broken me down completely and at one time.

—JAMES EDMONDSON

The passage through Strasburg opened an ordeal greater than anything the Valley Army had yet withstood. The blizzards of January, defeat at Kernstown, the march through mud and mountains from Swift Run Gap to McDowell, not even the punishing drive to defeat Banks were worse than what now awaited. Ahead lay brutal weather, endless day and night slogging, confusion, ambush, numbing fatigue, and hunger. The Army confronted one of the most taxing operations in warfare, a fighting retreat encumbered with prisoners and an enormous train. And this withdrawal was doubly difficult since it was before not one Union column but two. "I am inclined to think we are going to be hard up," Major Harman predicted.[1]

In fact, as Jackson pondered his next move on June 1, he had to question whether escape had been too easy. Frémont had sparred feebly with Ewell for a day; Shields had held Front Royal since noon on May 30 but had not neared Strasburg in force. This almost disinterested effort could mean a Union trap was to be sprung from another direction, probably from beyond Massanutten Mountain. That tangled barrier screened the Army's advance northward to Front Royal; it would cover a Federal lunge southward from that point as well. Even while Confederates breathed freer around Strasburg, Shields might be stealing into the Luray Valley to bag them.[2] If Shields crossed the Shenandoah's South Fork at Luray and vaulted Massanutten Gap to New Market, the Army would be bottled between him and Frémont. Once again, the Valley Army faced a threat from two directions, north along the Pike (Frémont) and to the east (Shields).

Around 2 P.M. on the first Jackson sent Captain Sam Coyner, commanding D Company of Ashby's regiment, to scout Page County and if necessary torch the White House and Columbia bridges. Coyner started promptly for Mount Jackson, where he was overtaken by new and peremptory orders to burn the bridges. Coyner's force was already frazzled, with many horses broken down, but he pushed on to New Market and thence eastward to Massanutten Mountain. Halfway up Coyner was overwhelmed by a stupendous thunderstorm, a downpour so violent he literally had to stop on the road and wait for the worst to clear before proceeding; his only guide was lightning. "About halfway down the mountain," he recollected, "the storm was repeated. The rain fell in torrents and the thunder rolled, and oh, the darkness, it was so thick I could almost clutch it in my grasp." Somehow Coyner got his men to the South Fork, found dry materials, and had all spans around Luray in flames by sunup.[3]

West of the Massanutten Jackson wanted more distance from Frémont, and so after dark on June 1 he gave Taylor orders to place his brigade near the Pike south of Strasburg and hold—Jackson did not say how long—while the Army lurched southward. The only support was Steuart's cavalry force, the 2d and 6th Virginia, and there was word that Ashby still had one company out somewhere in the area. These cavalry were every bit as worn down as the infantry. Men and horses had had little to eat for three days; some men were sleeping on their mounts. Taylor placed his troops and tried vainly to rest as rain fell swiftly; the 2d Virginia lay north of the Louisianans with most riders asleep; ahead of them and closest to the enemy was the 6th Virginia.

It was a night so intensely dark men could hardly see the Pike, but the Federals found it and came clattering out of the black rain toward rebel pickets. When challenged they shouted they were "Ashby's cavalry" and were allowed to approach; they were almost inside Southern ranks when they charged and scattered the Confederates. The 6th bolted, overrunning many of the sleeping 2d, and the whole thrashing mass poured down on two companies of Louisianans on the Pike. "There was a little pistol shooting and sabre-hacking," wrote Taylor, "and for some minutes things were rather mixed."[4] Hard fighting finally ended the affair, and Taylor judged it was time to pull out. Throughout a night of crackling thunder and stinging rain, he held the snapping Union cavalry at bay.

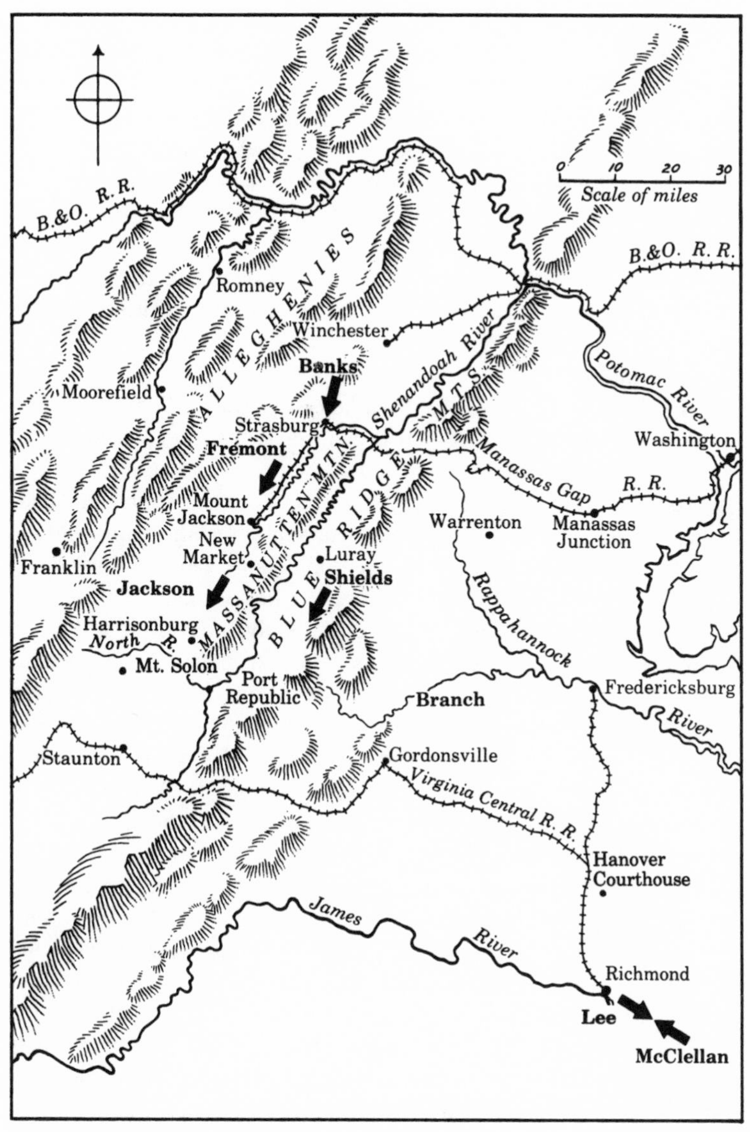

12. General Situation, June 1 to 6, 1862

Meanwhile the main column was on a horrendous journey. It required unremitting effort to get even a little more mileage from the drained troops. Henry Douglas remembered that night many years later: "Of course a thousand different obstacles impeded the movement of the train and consequently of the troops. One brigade divided another, and generals and colonels were wandering through the mass in search of their commands." Jackson stumbled into one officer whose brigade had broken into two or three parts.

"Colonel, why do you not get your brigade together, keep it together and move on?" Jackson rasped, as if it were a drill field maneuver.

"It's impossible, general: I can't do it."

"Don't say it's impossible," barked Stonewall. "Turn your command over to the next officer. If he can't do it, I'll find someone who can, if I have to take him from the ranks."[5]

The column stopped and started, stopped and started, and at times soldiers needed to lock arms to steady each other lest they slide into the muck that covered the road. Mud had been churned into the consistency of batter; beneath the mud the road was a relief of rocks and potholes, and the many barefoot marchers suffered greatly.[6] "The road was shoemouth deep in mud," remembered one Alabamian. "My feet were blistered all over, on top as well as on the bottom. I never was so tired and sleepy."[7] The prisoners moved like a glacier and could only be driven beyond Tom's Brook, five miles from Strasburg. By dawn the van had dragged barely beyond that point to within sight of Woodstock, but there was no halt. Hotchkiss could have reminded Jackson that his scout of the Strasburg area during May had revealed roads west of the Pike suitable for marching, and certainly Jackson had to anticipate that Frémont's cavalry might advance along those byways to get ahead of him. Jackson still had no report on Conyer's bridge-burning party in the Luray Valley. Colonel Crutchfield rode to check on Conyer's work, and the retreat continued.[8]

Colonel Patton's command, now reduced to only two and a half regiments after detachment of the 21st Virginia for guard duties, was the best force Jackson had available to stiffen the cavalry rear guard. Taylor started his Louisianans southward while Ashby and Steuart, on opposite sides of the Pike and somewhat north of Patton, each planted a battery and selected a position for their respective forces. The 2d and 6th

Virginia Cavalry were placed west of the road in support of Caskie's Battery; Ashby's troopers went east behind Brockenbrough's Baltimore Light Artillery. For some hours the enemy did not challenge, and the main column inched forward to gain a little more distance. When Union cannon fire eventually did swell, the rebels made ready to retire.

As orders came to start the withdrawal, Munford assumed the batteries would retire by echelon, one staying to cover the other as it rumbled back, then the first stopping to cover the second, with cavalry close by to discourage an enemy dash. Munford led his riders to the east side of the Pike and south a few hundred yards toward the stationary battery, but he never made it, as a disordered mass of riders and guns came flooding along the Pike. What had happened was not entirely clear. Munford would rail that Steuart bungled the maneuver, evidently by attempting a general retreat instead of withdrawal in echelon. It is also likely that at the moment the rebels retired in whatever order Northern squadrons charged, and the result was a fiasco.

Companies from both the 6th Virginia and Ashby's regiment bolted. Federals thundered after them, almost surrounding two guns from the Baltimore Battery, whose quick-thinking officers simply refused to be captured and lashed through the whirling fight. Rebel cavalry and guns slammed into Munford's 2d Virginia, which fled into Patton's infantry. Mounted men stormed through the 48th Virginia, knocking its colonel off his horse, injuring several soldiers, and so disordering the regiment that it could not be rallied for a time. The 42d Virginia mistook the gray riders for Yankees and opened fire, wounding several, while Federals waded in, taking prisoners.[9] The Confederate cavalry scampered on, threatening to overrun the next unit in the column, the Stonewall Brigade, so that Colonel Allen had to deploy his 2d Virginia Infantry. Lanty Blackford of the Rockbridge Artillery saw the boiling mass pouring his way: "In a few moments the road and fields on either side were filled with C.S. Cavalry flying pell-mell in the wildest confusion and with all the indications of panic, some horses without riders, and some riders without horses, all rushing on indiscriminately. I . . . felt more apprehension just then of being run over by our own terrified cavalrymen than of being cut down by the enemy's."[10] The entire Confederate rear was endangered.

Ashby saved the day. Jumping to the ground, he called for infantry stragglers to join him. Something of the look, the voice, the spirit of the man renewed these laggers, and quickly he formed them in a copse near the Pike. At virtually the last instant he bellowed to fire, and a point-blank volley erupted in the enemy's face. It was an extraordinary display of the dynamic combat leadership that Ashby exuded; it was what one of Jackson's staff had in mind when he marveled that Ashby "seemed to possess a magnetic influence over his men. They would follow wherever he would lead, and he was always foremost. . . . As a scout, and as a ranger, and in battle as a leader, he was a genius."[11] Few men could have changed stragglers, mostly strangers to each other, wet, weary, hungry, and without officers, into a steady rear guard to blunt a cavalry onslaught, and Stonewall himself praised the stand as "one of those acts of personal heroism and prompt resource which strikingly marked [Ashby's] character."[12] The Federals were staggered, and Colonel Garnett brought enough of his 48th Virginia to the fight to finish driving them away.[13]

It had been a close call. Behind Ashby the rebel cavalry was still fleeing; Colonel Johnson had to stretch his 1st Maryland Infantry, now little more than two hundred men, across the street in Woodstock with fixed bayonets to arrest the flight.[14] Patton's command was so shaken that Winder's Brigade, fatigued though it was, had to take the rear. Just north of Woodstock Winder formed a line of battle, faced the enemy down, and began a slow retreat, pulling his regiments back in echelon, maintaining a bristling front but avoiding any more firefights.[15]

Munford, meanwhile, sorted out his command and, fuming about General Steuart's handling of the retreat, began talking to Colonel Flournoy. Soon both men were mad, and perhaps with Ashby's heroics in mind, they rode to Ewell and so derided Steuart's management that Ewell appealed to Jackson to have their regiments transferred to Ashby. For colonels to savage their commander so openly was not unheard of in the Confederacy, but it betokened the Army's peril that Stonewall listened. In this kind of close-in, desperate fighting, Ashby was the best man, disciplinarian or not. Steuart, who had not proven adept with the mounted arm, was returned to his Maryland Line in Ewell's Division, to which were added Scott's Brigade from Edward Johnson's old force.[16]

Ashby now stood at the summit of his career. Jackson heard Ewell's comments and moved promptly, if without recorded enthusiasm, to realign the cavalry. Before end of day Ashby alone commanded the entire Valley Army cavalry, three regiments with paper strength equaling a full brigade.[17] Only Jeb Stuart at Richmond headed a larger cavalry corps in Virginia; among Virginia cavalrymen only Stuart also was a brigadier general. And, in fact, of the two men Ashby was the better known, known well enough to have gained special attention from the North. Frémont's unusually spirited cavalry was commanded by Brigadier General George Bayard, one of whose regiments was led by a veteran English soldier of fortune, Colonel Sir Percy Wyndham. Wyndham had crowed he would bag Ashby the first time he came within sight of him. Wyndham led part of the action that day, and so had failed to bag Ashby at the first encounter, yet it was the sort of attention Jeb could not then command—at this point of the war he had not seen half Ashby's combat. Ashby was the most famous cavalryman in Virginia that June, and now he was master of all Valley horse.

While Ashby collected his riders during the afternoon another shower opened, which meant the simple effort to move grew more exhausting. Federal prisoners from occasional hills along the Pike could see blue cavalry hammering the rear guard, and they became rowdy. Some had to be pounded to the ground to be kept under control. Part of the 6th Virginia Cavalry was detailed to help guard them, "as mean looking set of men as I ever saw," thought one of the riders.[18] The trains inched along, prodded by the staff and often by Old Jack himself. That great wagon throng was becoming as much a danger as a trove, for it clogged the way and had to be thrust onward for anyone else to move. Instructions were given that all vehicles should stay to the right and keep moving, without pause even to water horses, but progress was in slow motion. Part of the problem lay at a bottleneck over the North Fork of the Shenandoah between Mount Jackson and New Market; there all wagons had to squeeze across the bridge single file, and only the van of the trains reached New Market toward dark.[19]

By then rain fell in torrents. There was little rest for the troops that night as they took whatever shelter they could find. The lucky ones built makeshift protection of scantlings picked from the rail bed outside Mount Jackson.[20] The ranks were severely thinned: "I never saw a Brigade so completely broken down and unfitted for service as our Brigade," wrote the 27th Virginia's Captain Jim Edmondson of his Stonewall Brigade. "I am satisfied that the Brigade has lost at least 1,000 men broken down, left on the way and captured." Edmondson was pained to admit that his own company had lost at least one hundred men from these causes, and his entire regiment (which numbered 418 men one month ago) had shriveled to 150.[21] The entire Army suffered comparably.

Tuesday, June 3, dawned overcast but without rain. Ashby with riders and Chew's Battery skirmished from every hillock and bend in the road. Sometimes supported by infantry, sometimes just unlimbering his guns, Ashby blunted the Union pursuit hour after hour, forcing them to stop only to slip away when the Federals were deployed.[22] He was buying time for the great bottleneck at the North Fork, and slowly it eased as infantry and trains cleared the bridge and stopped on familiar ground atop Rude's Hill. Here Jackson arrayed part of the Army in line of battle while efforts were completed to destroy the bridge. This was the structure Ashby's riders had failed to burn in April, and its destruction now was arranged with much care. The roofing was stuffed with dry, split wood. Scattered through piles of kindling were two dozen artillery shells and several kegs of gunpowder. A party from Ashby's command under Captain Edward MacDonald was stationed with orders to throw in torches at the last moment.

Ashby and Chew crossed, and the rebel flow decreased to a trickle of stragglers. Captain MacDonald trotted through the bridge to hurry the last of them and saw Federals thundering his way. His men did not wait, immediately setting their fires. Flames jumped, and amid a hail of Yankee bullets MacDonald clattered over the blazing span. He made the far side just before the structure collapsed into the river; then his problem was to lead his men across the bare terrain of Meem's Bottom under Union fire from the far bank. His luck held, and his men escaped without casualties to cheers of the Southerners watching the action from the high ground at Rude's.[23]

Headquarters was pitched that evening in a field outside of New Market. By this time Jackson knew of Captain Coyner's success burning the South Fork bridges; he confided to Ewell that this relieved him greatly,[24] because this neutralized for a time Shields's threat from the east. However, Jackson that day ordered Ashby to have Captain Coyner prowl the region opposite Luray for Yanks and as well send riders to Conrad's Store to burn the South Fork span there.[25] Jackson was thinking very far ahead now, and by destroying all the bridges in the middle Valley he hoped to ensure that Frémont and Shields stayed apart while gaining a little respite for his troops.

Respite was not to be. New downpours—"tremendous rains" according to Hotchkiss[26]—deluged the Army that night. The field in which the Headquarters tent stood became a creek; water gushed from hills on either side, collected into a stream, and deluged the tent, floating the general's hat and boots. Douglas recalled peeking inside the tent the next morning to see some of Jackson's personal items, and even furniture, bobbing like little boats.[27] Ewell pitched his headquarters too close to the river and awoke during the night to find rising waters had turned his campsite into an island; without coat or hat he had to swim his mount over to higher ground.[28] The entire Army was drenched and no one was rested; wrote Lanty Blackford, "Cooking was out of the question, so hunger was added to our other discomforts. We lay disconsolately under our shanties with puddles of water here and there beneath us, about as miserable as outward surroundings could make us."[29] Frémont's engineers somehow threw a pontoon bridge across the North Fork, and his cavalry began to cross on the fourth. They did not get far, however, before the river swelled and snapped the Union pontoon.[30]

Jackson suppressed any impulse to lunge at the enemy isolated on his side of the stream and gave orders to get two days' cooked rations into haversacks; his men needed food more than battle.[31] Soon, however, a new threat emerged. Reports came that Frémont was trying a flanking movement from the west by sliding along the North Fork where it curled southward on the far side of a ridge west of New Market. Jackson had to shift the Army two miles south of New Market to high ground overlooking a possible crossing site. The troops deployed in the ceaseless rain to blunt the flanking thrust; Frémont did not appear.[32] After a miserable vigil Old Jack gave word to stand down, but he could not give his men a long rest. If Frémont could bridge the North Fork, Shields to the east as well might find a way around the destruction of the bridge at Conrad's Store. Nothing could be taken for granted. At 10 P.M. Jackson summoned Hotchkiss and told him to get to the southern tip of Massanutten Mountain the next morning and report on Shields's activity in the Luray Valley.[33] Orders were issued to resume the retreat at 1 A.M.

"Aroused and started at the appointed hour, marched down to the turnpike and stopped in mud and water till day, waiting till the Army and trains pass by," wrote a Mississippian.[34] It had been a week since the Army left Harpers Ferry. The distinction between day and night, sleep and marching was blurring, but the Army slogged on through the predawn hours of June 5. "How far south are we going?" scribbled one infantryman in his field diary.[35]

II

Jackson as well was mulling the question of destination, but in a double sense; he had to be concerned not only with the direction of march but also with the Army's future goal. Doubtless he was looking for some result from the mission to secure reinforcements on which he had dispatched Colonel Boteler from Harpers Ferry. Depending on what aid Richmond might supply, Jackson could develop several offensive schemes. There had been time enough by June 5 for a response, and Old Jack must have been getting anxious to know the result of Boteler's trip.

Boteler had departed Winchester during the still-dark morning hours of May 31 and hastened to Staunton, whence he took a train for Richmond. He arrived in Charlottesville by June 1 and discovered the rail line had been broken by Federal raiders and that reaching the capital required a detour south and east through Lynchburg. Alarmed by the loss of time, he telegraphed to the new Confederate secretary of war, G. W. Randolph, the status of affairs at Winchester and urged reinforcements "immediately if possible."[36] Boteler traveled on to Richmond as expeditiously as the overworked Confederate rail system would permit, which was fortunate, for the circumstances that greeted him there were such as to allow the government to forget the Valley unless someone was present to lobby for it.

On May 31 Johnston had launched a massive assault on McClellan. In a battle of many blunders, the largest battle in Virginia to date, Johnston rammed portions of the Union line back a mile, then lost the ground to fresh Federal divisions. Among the thousands of casualties was Johnston himself, blown off his horse with severe wounds to the chest and thigh. For a time it was not clear he would survive; at a minimum he was incapacitated for months.

That would be sad news when learned in the Shenandoah, for Johnston's place in the history of the Valley Campaign was an honorable one. Johnston had backed Jackson during the Romney winter, and he had risked President Davis's ire by permitting Jackson to retain the Virginia regiments and batteries of Loring's command. Johnston allowed

Ewell's shift to the Valley, and though he had almost recalled Ewell, he corrected his error. He finally came to see the mission of Jackson and Ewell as preventing a juncture of Banks and McDowell, essentially what Lee had urged as early as May 1 when he advised Jackson that his movements might relieve pressure at Fredericksburg. Johnston's only fault was that he had not grasped the wider scheme as early as Lee did.

Robert E. Lee now commanded in Johnston's stead. This officially made Lee what he had been informally for weeks, Jackson's supervisor, so a man with much interest in the Valley now headed Southern forces in Virginia. Nonetheless, in the unsettled immediate aftermath of Johnston's battle Lee thought it impossible to reinforce Jackson. Secretary of War Randolph was more hopeful. Checking troop transfer rosters, he noted that a sizable brigade of Georgians under Brigadier General A. R. Lawton had begun redeployment to Virginia some days ago. The Confederate rail system had them spread across several states, so they had not yet been incorporated into Lee's army. Randolph confirmed that with Lee and, on June 7, ordered the command to move toward the Shenandoah via Mechum's River Station.[37]

Boteler took his assignment of reminding the government about Jackson's plight to the highest levels. He saw President Davis and portrayed the situation in the Valley; evidently he left the impression that Jackson might have to fight his way through Front Royal,[38] and that attracted attention. Lee on June 4 telegraphed to Major Harman's base in Staunton for the commandant there to collect every man who could move, raise civilians, and march down the Valley toward Jackson, spreading rumors to magnify the numbers coming. It was a desperate ploy but all Lee could think of at first.[39] Davis also wrote to Jackson on the fourth, advising that it did not seem practicable to send reinforcements, but adding congratulations for a brilliant campaign. "The army under your command encourages us to hope for all which men can achieve," wrote the Confederacy's president.[40]

Whether Boteler met personally with Lee is unclear, but undeniably Lee heard in detail of Jackson's plans to march for the Susquehanna. Lee reflected much about reinforcing Stonewall and overcame his initial reluctance. He wrote to Davis on the fifth that if it were "possible to reinforce Jackson strongly, it would change the character of the war. This can only be done by the troops in Georgia, South Carolina and North Carolina. Jackson could in that event cross Maryland into Pennsylvania. It would call all the enemy from our Southern coast and liberate those states. If these states will give up their troops I think it can be done."[41] Lee was recommending the Atlantic coast be stripped to give Jackson numbers within a few thousand of the second biggest army of the Confederacy so that he could invade the Union, strong testimony to the confidence Stonewall now inspired. Something good might yet come of Boteler's efforts, but reinforcements were still far away and could do nothing for the Confederates trudging the Valley Pike. Any word Jackson received from Richmond during the first week of June told him only that he would have to survive on his own resources for a while longer.

That fact made critical a decision about the Army's destination as it evacuated New Market. Jackson had faced this challenge previously, in mid-April, when he withdrew from Rude's Hill before Banks's advance. Then Jackson had sent his excess trains to Staunton, burned the North River bridges after them, and retired to Conrad's Store. The first part of that option would have been attractive in June; getting excess baggage safely across the North River and into Staunton would have unburdened the Army for a counterattack. Unfortunately, none of the North River bridges near the Pike had been rebuilt, nor was it likely that a temporary expedient could be contrived after a week of wild rains. Indeed, that experiment had already failed. On the fourth, while the Army was facing Frémont's rumored flanking movement west of New Market, Jackson dispatched Lieutenant Boswell to the North River at Mount Crawford. There he met the ingenious Captain Mason, probably summoned by Major Harman, but both concurred that a bridge was hopeless. The river was extremely rapid and higher than it had been in twenty years; the engineers had been fortunate to fashion two boats from loose lumber and ferry the sick out of harm's way.[42] The North River washed across the Valley only eight miles south of Harrisonburg, which meant the rebels were literally running out of room to maneuver as they marched from New Market to Harrisonburg on June 5. Almost two months earlier, the Southerners turned east at Harrisonburg for Conrad's Store. This choice was no longer available since the bridge there had been destroyed and Shields in any event might already be in that vicinity. There was thus only one other way to go. Running southeast from Harrisonburg was a trail to the village of Port Republic; there a bridge spanned the North River. A road led southwestward back to Staunton from Port Republic; moreover, from there it was not many miles to the Blue Ridge via the route the Army followed across Brown's Gap to

Mechum's River Station in May. That route could be vital if instructions came, as was always a possibility, to move for Richmond. Port Republic was the best, indeed the only, answer to the question of how far south the Army would go.

To protect his march to Port Republic, Jackson summoned Colonel John Imboden to bring a mixed command of artillery and cavalry he had been recruiting around Staunton up to Mount Crawford to guard the south bank of the river. Though the stream had been pronounced uncrossable, the general made sure Frémont would not somehow slip over it and take him from behind. Of that threat he need not have worried, for the Pathfinder was delayed getting over the river below New Market and hung back out of striking distance on the fifth. Union prisoners were driven beyond Port Republic by dusk, while the van of Major Harman's trains came close to the North River bridge there. The infantry cleared Harrisonburg in the afternoon and headed for Port Republic. Jackson moved his old brigades first, and Ewell's command took the rear. Toward evening Hotchkiss came down from his observation post and rode through Harrisonburg, finding it deserted except for cavalry. A mile or so out the Port Republic road he found Headquarters and reported that he had watched Shields's column encamp that afternoon at 4 P.M. within two miles of Conrad's Store.[43]

In May it had taken the Valley Army two days to go from Conrad's Store to Port Republic; one day's good effort tomorrow ought to bring the rebels to the village, so Shields should be too late to outpace the Army there. But there was no guarantee the Army was safe. As torn up as the Valley Pike had been, it was infinitely better than the road now to be followed; in fact, some men thought this route as bad as the track from Swift Run Gap to Port Republic in May. The path shook many in the Stonewall Brigade loose from ranks when they hit it: "The road in miserable condition and the troops all break down. The army marches within a mile of Port Republic but the men are mostly on the road," Sergeant Kearns of the 27th Virginia wrote in his diary.[44] Units dissolved, with men drifting away to march in the rear, or in the fields, and only catching up to their regiments the next morning.

The trains, meanwhile, floundered on the miserable Port Republic road. "Such a road! How our wagons are to get over it I scarcely know," penned one Confederate who walked it.[45] The condition of the draft animals was pathetic. That night Major Harman pleaded with his brother

Asher to get him twenty fresh horses or some guns might be abandoned.[46] In the Rockbridge Artillery Lanty Blackford wrote that "our horses were so completely broken down we could not get up to our wagons and had to stop and bivouack [*sic*] in a field 5 miles [outside Harrisonburg]." Of the condition of the gunners he added, "We had nothing to eat of course and had to go in the morning supperless and breakfastless. I was weak from hunger and really suffered from exhaustion."[47]

The same was true everywhere in the Army; even the strongest men approached a point where the crushing need for sleep conquered all else.* Major Harman virtually collapsed on the evening of June 5: "Nature could stand it no longer; I had to knock under last night," he admitted to his brother.[48] One weary scavenger had the luck to find a hot meal but fell unconscious before he could eat it; Captain John Winfield of the cavalry was so weak his troopers had to lift him into his saddle.[49]

In the nine days since the Army marched to Harpers Ferry from Winchester virtually every man had plodded close to 120 miles, most of the way in savage weather. The long march had demanded the courage of a battle, and it was far more costly. The Army lost four hundred men fighting its way from Front Royal to Winchester; more prisoners than that were lost during the retreat, and thousands of stragglers dropped from ranks.[50] They spread out like a gray mist, behind and around trains stopped by the mud. Jackson gave orders for the wagons to move at 5 A.M. on the sixth with fifty men from each brigade to assist them, then canceled the order as if unsure the men, if found, could nudge the wagons.[51] During the morning of June 6 the trains would remain dangerously mired.[52] Hotchkiss reestablished his observation point atop the Massanutten and there spent anxious hours waiting to see if he could spot a new Federal advance either from Shields out of the Luray Valley or from the aggressive cavalry of Frémont.[53] The Army required time to finish its escape.

III

No one appreciated better on June 6 the importance of the rear guard than Turner Ashby, who in a sense had become the rear guard. A proud

---

* Jackson was among the exhausted. A full account of his state of mind as the retreat closed, and its effects on subsequent operations, is presented in Appendix D.

man, he must have heard bitterly those who spoke derisively of his cavalry. One night he unburdened himself to Colonel Munford, complaining that his men had been on the move since they were first recruited, that there was no time, equipment, or officers to make better soldiers of them. Munford understood his dilemma and recalled later, "Provided with just such arms as they could pick up, with no organization, it was simply impossible for him to do anything with them but to lead them."[54]

And lead Ashby did, spurring his men by example to feats sufficient, just barely, to keep at bay an implacable pursuit. Everything he did now added to his mystique. On the night of June 2, after his incredible stand by the Pike, he had come to Headquarters, and there Jackson's staff surrounded him. Sandie Pendleton urged him to expose himself less, advising he could not beat death for long if he continued as he had been doing. Ashby was unconvinced, explaining that he did not fear being in close combat. There the enemy might take careful aim, but shots fired directly at him by Northern marksmen did not concern him since the enemy invariably missed their mark.[55] For Ashby it was a simple statement of credo; the impact upon men less insensible to danger can be imagined. His legend grew.

Ashby rose early on June 3, checked his pickets, supervised Captain MacDonald's preparations for demolishing the North Fork bridge, and was with Chew's Battery as it retired toward that point. On the fourth he covered high ground below New Market while the Army shifted above it to thwart Frémont's supposed advance from the west, then defended that position after Jackson vacated it. During the fifth he withdrew slowly to end the day in a meadow a little north of Harrisonburg near an old sawmill.[56] A number of officers gathered at his tent that night and fell to discussing the boast of Sir Percy Wyndham to capture Ashby, which doubtless produced mirth among those present.

Wyndham was an English soldier of fortune and something of a dandy, a man who sported a huge mustache, slouch hat, and plume. Only twenty-eight years of age, he had seen service with the British, Austrian, and Italian armies, and even the French navy. (He later would command the army of the King of Burma, in which country he died when a balloon he had fashioned plunged into the Royal Lake.) Some of these facts the Confederates could have learned from Major Wheat, of Taylor's Brigade, for Wheat had fought with Wyndham under Garibaldi in Italy. The mercenary had tendered his service to the Union and been rewarded with a colonel's commission and a supposedly picked cavalry unit, the 1st New Jersey. Ashby as usual said little about all of this, though he did make clear that he did not wish Wyndham to gain any reputation at his expense, and before the evening ended he outlined his intentions. Wyndham was given to bold charges, and several of them had done the rebels harm. Ashby announced that if Wyndham attempted one of those dashes the next day he would do the same; Ashby would meet charge with countercharge to capture Wyndham.[57]

June 6 dawned without rain or much chance Ashby would encounter Wyndham. The Yankees held well back. Ashby retired through Harrisonburg and along the Port Republic road for about a mile until he reached high ground, Chestnut Ridge, where the rear guard could stand. Chew planted his two serviceable pieces here. Ewell unlimbered several batteries as well; his division was deployed to protect the guns, and Ashby was authorized to call upon it for infantry support. Hotchkiss reported some Federals approaching from Frémont's direction, but no sign of Shields. Hours passed quietly, and the weather turned fine. The trains were by now a good distance toward Port Republic; Jackson was there already. Ewell started his artillery for Port Republic and moved his infantry after it. Chew's Battery also started in that direction. Ashby pulled back with the 6th Virginia Cavalry on the road and his old regiment, now led by Major Funsten, south of it. Union cavalry seemed to keep its distance; only occasionally would a Federal rider fire a harmless shot at long range toward the rear guard. A little past midafternoon, Ashby ordered a halt to rest and feed the mounts.[58]

As he had done in the past, Colonel Wyndham somehow picked this moment, with the rebels dismounted and their horses grazing, to charge. The rebels scrambled to form. Funsten believed the retreat would continue and aligned his troops toward Port Republic, but Ashby would have no withdrawal. He dashed by, ordering Funsten to attack. "Follow me," he blared. Never taught to maneuver, Ashby's men were thrown into confusion trying to about-face, but they knew what to do once around. Vaulting a high fence, the rebels made a disorganized, wild rush at the enemy.

These Yanks had never faced an Ashby charge, and its fury startled, then splintered them. A headless mass of Federal horsemen boiled back to the outskirts of Harrisonburg. A few Yanks attempted to rally and were trampled: the Union banner was scooped up from the mud, as was Sir Percy. As the last pockets of resistance collapsed, the rebels counted more than sixty-four prisoners; there were also thirty-six Federals killed and wounded against only one Confederate casualty. Reminding the English braggart of his pledge to snare Ashby, crowing rebels led Wyndham away, the maddest prisoner anyone ever saw. One Southerner recalled about the mercenary, "He would have stopped right there in the road and engaged in fisticuffs if he could have found a partner."[59]

Toward nightfall Federal cavalry reappeared, this time with infantry. Ashby had anticipated this and sent to Ewell's retiring division for aid. The hindmost of Ewell's brigades was Steuart's, who received Ashby's call but, as in Winchester, refused to move without orders from Ewell. Ashby's appeal to Ewell brought help and Ewell himself, as the latter personally led Steuart's command to Ashby. Approximately two miles from Harrisonburg Ewell overtook Ashby with the 58th Virginia in the van of his infantry column.[60]

Quickly Ashby offered a plan. The enemy might advance down the road, and Ashby wanted to encourage them to do it. He would dangle Munford's 2d Virginia Cavalry there and draw them on. Munford would have a surprise for the Yanks, because Chew would deploy behind his riders, sheltered from enemy sight but ready to blast away when needed. In the meantime, let Southern infantry enter a dense forest of oaks to the right of the road and storm out on the Yankee flank. They would need to spring their trap at once, because it was already twilight.[61]

Ewell agreed. Steuart's Brigade was not fully up when he directed the 58th Virginia and 1st Maryland into the timberline. The 44th Virginia sprinted after them but did not overtake the main column for a time; the 52d was still further back. Munford's riders took their places as bait while Ewell and Ashby joined the foot column. The two generals rode together, the chieftain explaining the nature of the ground to Old Bald Head. Riding at the head of his regiment, Colonel Johnson was too far back to hear what was said, but even in the gathering twilight he could see how the prospect of battle thrilled the cavalryman. "Look at Ashby," Johnson remarked to his adjutant. "See how happy he is!"[62]

Soon the rebels deployed in the woods, the 58th Virginia to the right and the 1st Maryland on the left. Ashby came back to the Old Line Staters, grabbed two companies, and took them forward as skirmishers. Stealthily, listening for the sounds of battle from Munford's cavalry on the road, the rebels advanced.

Before long there was a cascade of musket fire! But it was to the front, not from the road, and in a moment another volley tore the 58th.

The Pennsylvania Bucktails, a crack battalion of Federal sharpshooters who wore their namesake bucktails on their headgear, had beaten the rebels into the forest to set their own trap. The rebels were almost on top of a well-sheltered fence protecting the Federals when they took the first volley, which shattered the 58th. The Virginians bolted, then stopped and returned a wild fire, some of it hitting the Marylanders. As those rebels came forward Colonel Johnson's horse was shot from under him. The drive threatened to collapse, but then the heroes went to work. Ewell rode along the lines, ordering the Marylanders to fix bayonets. General Steuart brought the 44th Virginia to their support. Ashby was everywhere, weaving his sleek mount between the tangled hardwoods, shouting, steadying, leading. He was in front of the 58th when his horse crumpled. He rolled free, bounced up, and ran at the enemy. The 58th followed.[63]

The Confederate attack gathered strength. Steuart led the 1st Maryland and 44th Virginia in on the Union right flank under a galling fire. Twice the Maryland color bearer was hit, but each time the flag was caught before it touched the ground, and the rebels kept coming. From the road Munford spotted Federal cavalry trotting to the Bucktails and opened Chew's Battery, then charged to scatter the blue riders. Rebel infantry came roaring in on all sides of the Bucktails and hurled them out of the woods into a clearing, where many were shot down.[64] As dark fell the sharp, bloody fight ceased, with heavy casualties on both sides. The Federals lost perhaps 50 men, almost half of those engaged. The 58th Virginia suffered worst, losing 53 killed, wounded, and missing; the 1st Maryland lost 17 of 150 engaged, so that in one brief episode the Southern regiments sacrificed greater than 10 percent of their strength.[65] Ewell was especially proud of the 1st Maryland, writing of its "dashing charge." In recognition he ordered one of the bucktail ornaments to be attached to their regimental flag as a trophy.[66]

As the hot fight was ending the rebels looked for Ashby to be on the enemy's tail, but he was not. Now they remembered his horse taking a wound. They returned to the spot and found Ashby close by, lying with his face toward the Union line. He was dead. No certain account exists of his last moments; no last words can be reliably quoted. He was shot through the chest, the bullet passing through the right arm and exiting the body under the left breast; he apparently died instantly.[67]

Troopers escorted the body from the field in disbelief. Ashby was the first general of heroic stature to die in Virginia, and his youngsters had never imagined that heroes met such a fate. Activity ceased as men learned the news. "There is a gloom throughout the whole camp," wrote Trooper Bill Wilson, "an awful stillness that can be almost heard."[68] The corpse was carried to Port Republic. Wrapped with a Confederate flag, it remained the night. Cavalrymen came to mourn, honoring Ashby in death as they had followed him in life, singly or in little bands. Many sobbing openly, they thought their sad thoughts and rode off as they saw fit.[69]

The news spread like a stain. Jackson was interrogating Wyndham when word reached him. He dismissed the Englishman at once, went to his room, and locked the door. The staff heard him pacing a long, long time. "A loss irreparable," recorded Hotchkiss that night.[70] "A great loss to our cause," thought General Winder.[71] Sandie Pendleton confided to his mother, "It is a staggering blow to us."[72] In Richmond Lee knew of it the next day and wrote to the secretary of war, "I grieve at the death of General Ashby."[73]

On June 7, beneath azure skies, Ashby's body was carried across the Blue Ridge for burial in Charlottesville. The cortege was attended by an honor guard of survivors from the company Ashby had led to war as a captain fourteen months earlier. Captured Federals and their guards, many with uncovered heads, lined the way in respectful silence.[74] At some point the body was dressed in a fresh uniform and propped up for a photograph. The picture is of a rough-hewn man, much thinned by hard service, and probably by his May illness, but at peace. After the war Ashby's remains were taken to Winchester for reburial. On October 15, 1866, they were laid to rest in the Stonewall Cemetery of that city.

Ashby's final day mirrored his life as a soldier. In his last cavalry fight his men could not maneuver, but they fought savagely under his eye and bested a vengeful foe. Yet it is also true that attention to drill and picketing might have prevented Wyndham's column from getting within range without warning. Moreover, ignoring the chain of command brought Ashby to the spot where he met death. As commander of the Army's cavalry he had no business leading infantry skirmishers in a woodland firefight. Both the division and brigade commanders of the infantry engaged were present to direct those troops, as of course were the regimental commanders. Ashby's proper place was on the road with his riders.

It is also true that Ashby's twilight battle achieved little to justify the rough handling of the 58th Virginia and 1st Maryland. That morning the trains had been at risk, but the Federals had not attacked, and if they had the artillery barrier on Chestnut Ridge should have stopped them. By midafternoon, when Ashby turned toward Port Republic, the trains were safely approaching that point, and Ewell's infantry still was between the wagons and any Federal incursion. If Ashby could provide Ewell adequate warning of any Federal lunge, there was no chance that Frémont's cavalry would overtake the trains. It may be that Ashby wanted to drive the enemy off lest they attempt another night ambush, but with dark at hand Ashby had little chance to exploit any success he might gain. The Federal cavalry was already stunned from the fight with Wyndham, and without evidence of a really determined Union drive under way, there was no reason for this final battle. The better decision would have been to avoid it.

Ashby had never thought of avoiding battle, and therein lay his essence. Jackson knew that. When the time came to report this phase of the campaign, Stonewall offered an extraordinary tribute to Ashby: "As a partisan officer I never knew his superior; his daring was proverbial; his powers of endurance almost incredible; his tone of character heroic; and his sagacity almost intuitive in divining the purposes and movements of the enemy."[75] Such praise was unheard of from Jackson, and Ashby had won it by always being willing to fight. He had fought many valuable fights, including at Kernstown, in distracting Shields outside Front Royal on May 31, and during the retreat.

Such successes only made more glaring Ashby's failures. As the campaign progressed Jackson grew distrustful of his mounted arm. Rarely since April had Stonewall given Ashby an important mission without detailing one of his staff to surpervise. Hotchkiss was tasked to burn the bridges on the Shenandoah's South Fork in April. Hotchkiss, not Ashby's scouts, reconnoitered Milroy's position before the Army started for the Alleghenies. When Jackson wanted the Allegheny passes between Franklin and the Harrisonburg area blocked, he again assigned Hotchkiss to lead the work. As he was racing to overtake Banks, Jackson had Ashby merely hold his position in front of Banks and collect information on enemy strength. Ashby was entrusted with an independent mission in the Buckton Station attack on May 23, though Jackson guarded against failure there by committing a much larger force under Flournoy to the same work of cutting communications some miles nearer Front Royal. The next day Jackson flung a mounted column to Newtown. He had not sent Ashby, whose riders knew every byway in the Valley, but Steuart, whose men were strangers to the region. Colonel Crutchfield had checked the work of Ashby's bridge-burning parties during the retreat from Harpers Ferry. Even the prime achievements that can be claimed for Ashby—that Jackson was usually well informed of Union movements, while the enemy remained ignorant of his—resulted as much from Stonewall's own deceptive ways and from the poor quality of Northern cavalry as from Ashby's efforts.

Ashby was not exclusively at fault for the weaknesses that sometimes made his squadrons worthless. Stonewall had made incessant demands on him for information and security; since the beginning of the campaign, Ashby's troopers had been kept on patrol and the picket line, work that kept them off the drill field. The vast expanse of the Shenandoah could be patrolled only by numerous small parties, and this too prevented close supervision by Ashby. Many of those who disgraced him had just enlisted during March and April, immediately before the Valley Army's explosive May drive, and Ashby had had little opportunity to fashion soldiers of them. Further, each Southern cavalryman was required to furnish his own horse. No central reserve of remounts existed (as it did in the Union army), and when a horse was lost there was nothing for the owner to do but leave to find another. Much of the Valley cavalry's rampant absenteeism arose in this way.[76]

It was also true, as Ashby's defenders pointed out, that Jackson's control over his infantry was sometimes tenuous. Infantrymen were as willing as Ashby's troopers to loot or slip home. Jackson never made professionals of his infantry. But—and here lay the essential difference—starting with volunteers who thought much like Ashby's, Jackson drilled those boys until most would stay in ranks at critical times if physically able. On May 24 Jackson brought a much larger percentage of infantry to Winchester than did Ashby of cavalry, and the infantry were as exhausted as the cavalry. Any doubt about whose methods made the better soldier, Jackson's or Ashby's, was resolved along the Valley Pike between Middletown and Winchester.

There were many competent men in Ashby's cavalry, but he never mobilized their abilities; he never made a real attempt to organize his command. A few hours per month could have been spared for drill. Smaller, more compact regiments could have been formed to provide additional officers. Ashby never grasped the importance of such things. He admitted as much when, during his standoff with Jackson at Swift Run Gap, he protested to Hotchkiss "that Jackson was treating him very badly in desiring to divide his command into two regiments and requiring him to drill them. He seemed to think that although he had so many companies he could easily manage them all himself and that it was unnecessary to have them drilled."[77] The lost opportunities of May 24 and 25 did not alter Ashby's view. On the day of his promotion to general he asserted that though his discipline was ragged, it did not worry him. His men followed when he led, and that alone was important.[78]

Ashby relied upon sheer courage to answer every challenge. He always fought with incredible boldness, staking his life each time on a conviction that the valor aroused in his men through his own fearlessness was ample substitute for discipline—and at the same time revealing that he, like his men, had succumbed to generations of Southern thinking that glorified cavalry action as glittering adventure. General Taylor sensed this delusion and complained, "Graceful, young cavaliers, with flowing locks, leaping cannons to saber countless foes makes a captivating picture . . . but ''tis not war.' Valor is necessary now as ever in war, but disciplined, subordinated valor, admitting the courage and energies of all be welded and directed to a common end."[79]

Such a union of energies never existed in Ashby's command, where every trooper was a general. One who rode with Ashby's regiment remembered, "It was more like a tribal band held together by the authority of a single chief. Increase of numbers rather diminished than increased its efficiency as a whole and made it more unmanageable."[80] Ironically, it was this very tribal band mentality that denied Ashby's troopers their dream of a glittering adventure. Flournoy's well-schooled companies at Cedarville on May 23, not Ashby's carefree squadrons, made the one truly romantic cavalry charge of the campaign. Ashby's riders were offered their chance for a grand charge two days later, but the band was not together to overtake Banks as he fled north from Winchester.

Still, Ashby's courage was magnificent; his bravery as a battle captain must be weighed against his failures as an administrator, and which was greater becomes a matter of opinion. Any summary of his career must stress that he was out of step with his times and therefore never able to achieve his full potential in them. "Riding his black stallion," remembered Henry Douglas, "he looked like a knight of the olden time,"[81] and so he was. Ashby was a splendid paladin, and, as such, he was also an anachronism, a knight-errant at the dawn of modern, total war.

16

TRAP

When we were not expecting the enemy,
the first thing we knew they were firing into our camp.

—Joe Kaufman

Saturday, June 7, dawned dry and fair, the kindest weather since the rebels had left Harpers Ferry, and it seemed to portend a respite for the Valley Army. Jackson the prior day had found his first opportunity in some time to report to Richmond. Unaware of who commanded there, Jackson addressed his letter of June 6 to General Johnston. He advised that his army was so placed that it could attack Shields if he found a way across the South Fork of the Shenandoah and tried to join Frémont. Jackson evidently thought Shields unlikely to attempt such a march and that he might leave the Shenandoah instead, for he asked Johnston, "If Shields crosses the Blue Ridge shall my entire command, or any part of it, move correspondingly?" Jackson concluded he could not do more now than rest his troops and devote time to drill.[1]

And so June 7 was a quiet day by Valley Army standards. Southern guards concentrated their prisoners beyond chance of recapture along the Virginia Central near Waynesboro; from there the Federals were moved to Lynchburg.[2] Jackson joined Ewell's Division during the morning and maneuvered to lure Frémont into battle, but the latter declined.[3] After noon, Stonewall left Ewell to watch Frémont and rode past the thinned ranks of his old division as it limped toward the village of Port Republic. There, approximately four miles from Ewell's lines, Jackson established Headquarters; the general took rooms in the home of a locally famous physician, Dr. George Kemper, pitching tents for some of the staff in an orchard a few hundred feet across the green fields of Kemper's estate (known as Madison Hall). Close by was Captain Joseph Carrington's Charlottesville Light Artillery, which had joined the army after the Battle of Winchester. It was so recently formed, and the press of events so rapid during the past weeks, that Carrington's Battery had not been properly outfitted. It was not yet formally attached to a brigade and apparently had wandered along with the ordnance and baggage trains during the retreat.

The Port, as local residents called the village, was a small inland harbor. It lay on a peninsula created by two streams—the North River, which flowed from the northwest, and the South River, which flowed from the southwest; these streams merged into the South Fork of the Shenandoah, which rolled on to Front Royal. (It was this stream, bank-high from recent rains and its bridges destroyed by Ashby's troopers, that separated Shields and Frémont.) Valley residents brought bulk goods to Port Republic for barge shipment downriver to Harpers Ferry. Mills, a foundry, and a tannery were built along the South River; the path behind them eventually became known as Water Street. Parallel to Water was the Port's other street, Main, which ran north-south. At its southern end Main Street took a right angle turn and ran westward across the front of Dr. Kemper's property; at Kemper's far corner the road turned another 90 degrees toward Staunton. If reinforcements were to reach Jackson, their easiest march from Staunton would be via this road into Port Republic.

At the other end of Main Street was the travelers' bridge carrying the highway from Harrisonburg over the North River. It was a nondescript structure, wooden roofed and sided, no different than many built in the Shenandoah before the war. Its importance simply was that it still stood, one of the few functional spans left in the Valley. Beyond the bridge, on the west bank of the South Fork, was a line of bluffs that dominated all ground on the east bank. Exit from the Port to the east was by a ford, known as the lower ford, that crossed the South River a few dozen yards from the bridge. Beyond the ford the road divided: one branch ran roughly northward across several miles of wheat fields, then through heavy forest to Conrad's Store and Swift Run Gap; the other branch led southeastward over the Blue Ridge at Brown's Gap. The Valley Army had utilized these two roads on its march to join Allegheny Johnson in May. Shields was positioned at Conrad's Store to follow Jackson's previous route south, but if he did so it would be over the same horrendous road, and he would have to approach the Port east of the South Fork across fields that could be pounded by Confederate artillery on the west bank bluffs. Finally, near the south limits of the Port was another ford known as the upper ford.

To keep Shields from Frémont and to secure his own communications both to Brown's Gap and Staunton, Jackson had to control the bluffs, the North River bridge, and the South River fords. The best way to do that was to crown the bluffs above the bridge with artillery reinforced by infantry and throw strong cavalry patrols well forward of the South River, but that was not ordered. Instead, Southern deployment around Port Republic was haphazard. The trains rumbled through the long wooden bridge, south along Main Street, turned across the front of Madison Hall, and then turned again to head out the Staunton road; the vehicle park was established less than a mile above Madison Hall. That meant both Major Harman's wagons and Headquarters were not shielded by the main force and were connected with it solely by the North River bridge. No batteries were planted on the bluffs to protect that vital structure. The Rockbridge Artillery, for example, came to rest at least a half-mile west of the bluffs.[4] The infantry camp was even farther away.[5]

After dark Jackson received intelligence that Shields was advancing in the direction of Port Republic, but this report evidently did not convince Old Jack the thrust was serious. He dispatched only a small cavalry patrol from Ashby command, under Captain Emanuel Sipe, to investigate. A few hours later, Captain G. W. Myers, who had helped decoy Banks outside Strasburg on the evening of May 23, was directed to move in support of Sipe; the only other cavalry on guard in the village was a company of Munford's 2d Virginia under Captain J. J. Chipley. The three main regiments of cavalry, now under overall command of Colonel Munford, were arrayed as follows: Ashby's old regiment and Colonel Flournoy's troopers were above Port Republic along the Staunton road; they could protect against a long-range raid that might strike from the south. Munford's 2d Virginia was deployed at the base of Massanutten Mountain (principally along the road from Conrad's Store to Harrisonburg) and could provide warning if Shields somehow advanced into the Confederate right rear from Conrad's Store.[6] Although the main cavalry formations protected against less likely threats, they could be little help against a thrust straight at the North River bridge. Parts of only two foot companies from the 2d Virginia Infantry were stationed around town, one by the bridge and another at the lower ford.[7] Probably fewer than two hundred men, including Carrington's Battery, which had never fired a shot in anger, were within sight of the crucial span.

It was as if the Army was too tired to keep up its guard. Sandie Pendleton wrote home on June 7, "Our whole force is nearly broken down and needs rest. I am sadly in need of it myself and the men worse than the officers. Gen. Jackson is completely broken down."[8] As the rebels found campsites they dropped without concern for anything but that their march seemed at an end: "At last we are come to a halt!" rejoiced Lieutenant James Dinwiddie of Carrington's Battery in a letter that day.[9] The units of Jackson's old command stopped along the Harrisonburg road and spent their time, wrote a very tired Lanty Blackford, "quietly in camp, reading, writing, sleeping etc., as only Jackson's army can, enjoying the luxury and sweetness of rest."[10]

Rest seemed in store on June 8 as well. The morning dawned so quietly as to seem unnatural. Headquarters slept late; it was after 8 A.M. as most of the staff finished breakfast and collected on Dr. Kemper's porch to enjoy the tranquil day at a leisurely pace. Hotchkiss, like many others, was exhausted from his labors during the retreat. He was suffering a violent headache, and Jackson had excused him from duty; the mapmaker was reclining in his tent. Dr. McGuire was at a small church on Main Street. There the wounded from Ashby's final fight were being tended to, and McGuire had ridden down to supervise getting them into ambulances for removal to safer points.[11] It was a Sunday, the first the Army might keep holy since Jackson's meeting with Ewell at Mount Solon. The soldiers had not failed to notice that of late the incredibly devout Stonewall always had them in battle or on the road on Sundays, but today no military emergency threatened.[12] Jackson told Major Dabney, also feeling ill after the retreat, that he would not fight that day if the Yanks would leave him alone, and the cleric was in his tent trying to outline a sermon for the Stonewall Brigade. In the peace of the morning he had exchanged his uniform for his parson's garb.[13]

The general and some staffers were walking in Dr. Kemper's meadows, watching the horses graze in the lush grass, when a courier arrived from Captain Sipe. He reported finding a few Yanks around the bridge early that morning and chasing them northward along the east bank of the Shenandoah's South Fork, only to run into a regiment of Union cavalry. Sipe wrote from a point several miles north of the Port, but his message was otherwise unclear as to the exact strength or current loca-

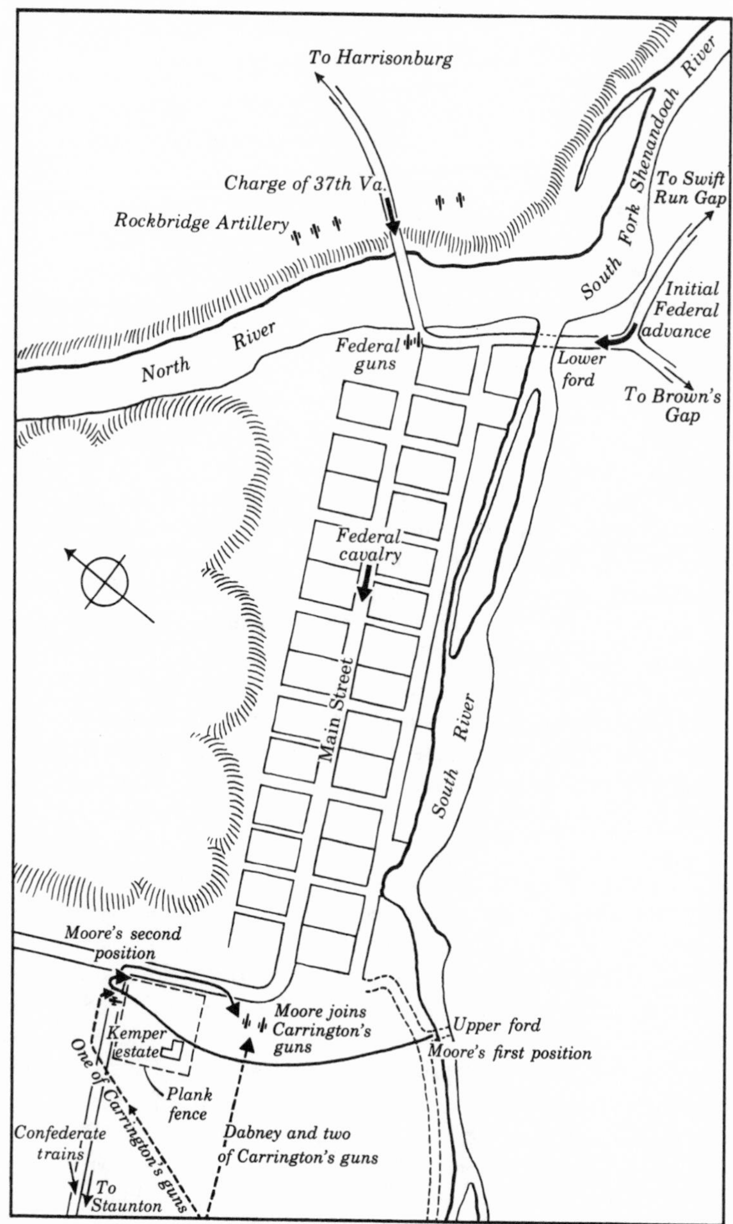

13. Skirmish in Port Republic, June 8, 1862

The above is reproduced from a tracing of an original in the Hotchkiss Papers, Library of Congress. The original (prepared under the direction of Jedediah Hotchkiss in 1896) reconstructed wartime Port Republic with infinite care; unfortunately, the original is no longer reproducible. Troop locations and movements are approximate and have been added by the author.

tion of the enemy. Jackson decided to check on Captain Sipe himself; in the meantime he relayed Sipe's news to Ewell with orders not to take aggressive action until he heard what Jackson had learned of the situation by his personal inspection.[14] A few of the staff went to saddle their horses, but there was no hurry.

Southern camps stretching along the road to Harrisonburg were equally calm, save at headquarters of the Stonewall Brigade, where General Winder had a morale problem. Unhappy about the effects of the campaign on his men, Winder found himself "grossly disgusted with Jackson." He rose later than usual, then penned a note to Jackson requesting to leave his army.[15] Winder's aide, McHenry Howard, knew nothing of this and was taking inventory of his clothing; he had it spread out on the ground and knelt surrounded by it, no doubt letting damp garments dry while he looked for holes.[16] Not far away, General Taliaferro had ordered a general inspection in his brigade. He wanted to give officers an opportunity to check arms and take an accurate roll call, and the troops were forming ranks; Taliaferro himself was getting into clean clothes.[17] In the Rockbridge Artillery the horses were loose and grazing, the cannons unlimbered, while many men had gone to fish or swim. Lanty Blackford had in hand a rubber blanket he had captured at Winchester. After the ceaseless rains of the past week he had come to regard it as among his most valuable possessions, one requiring a name on it. He found a shady spot and began marking.

Blackford had just completed his *B* when, around 9 A.M., he heard a shell explode from the direction of Port Republic. As veterans do, Blackford weighed the situation and concluded that some Confederate battery must be firing off damp or defective rounds. He resumed marking but heard a second, then a third shell.[18] McHenry Howard heard the cannon fire and began stuffing clothes back into his carpetbag. Someone asked what he was doing. "Well," Howard replied, "it's Sunday and you hear that shot."[19] General Taliaferro heard it too and shoved his arms through his shirt quicker "than man ever put on shirt before."[20] Captain Poague assumed the worst and ordered his battery to fall in; Blackford threw aside his rain gear and joined his comrades chasing down the battery horses.[21] And within a few minutes Confederates along the Harrisonburg road saw a sight they could never forget: Stonewall Jackson thundering their way yelling to no one in particular to get moving.[22] Something was wrong!

II

That something was very wrong had become obvious to Jackson no more than twenty minutes before. Following receipt of Captain Sipe's warning of Yanks in the area, Jackson had lingered in Dr. Kemper's yard, still enjoying the splendid morning. But moments later another rider came dashing toward Madison Hall. The boy was a private of Myers's cavalry company, Henry Kerfoot, with horrific news: Federal riders were charging the South River's lower ford! The enemy had swept away the Confederate cavalry there and was perhaps already at the river. A glance could verify it; Confederate riders were careening about Port Republic in panic. Even the infantry guard near the bridge was retiring to the north side of the stream. "Go back and fight them" was Jackson's stern instruction to the lone Kerfoot.[23]

A shell exploded near the North River bridge, a blast that rocked Southerners along the Harrisonburg road. More rounds came shrieking in, battering the steeple of the church Dr. McGuire used as a hospital and showering the rebels with wood chips. The drivers tensed to flee, and only with much profanity did McGuire keep them at their posts even while rebel cavalry stampeded past. "Disgraceful disorder" and "shameful" were Jackson's words describing the pandemonium that afflicted the mounted units guarding Port Republic that morning; the cavalry vanished, leaving the Valley Army's rear unprotected.[24]

Dr. McGuire frantically loaded his ambulances, while at the Kemper estate officers and orderlies threw tack on jittery animals. Hotchkiss heard the noise and forgot his headache; he helped pack the headquarters vehicles then started south with them, going past wagons scrambling to flee. Henry Douglas happened to have his mount saddled and offered it to Jackson, but Stonewall declined, and anxious seconds followed before Old Jack's servant brought his horse, then the Valley Army's command spurred for the bridge. Jackson led the way, racing down Main Street and past Dr. McGuire, who was still swearing at his drivers to get the wounded loaded. "Doctor," shouted Stonewall, "don't you think you can manage these men without swearing?" McGuire promised to try, and the general, Boswell, Sandie Pendleton, and others clattered across the span even as Federals splashed up from the lower ford to Main Street. "I was last to get over," remembered Henry Douglas, "and I passed in front [of Union cavalry] as they rode up out of the water and [I] made my rush for the bridge. I could see into their faces plainly and they greeted me with sundry pistol shots."[25]

Yanks swarmed up behind Douglas to capture the Army's artillery chief, Colonel Crutchfield, and his assistant, Lieutenant Edward Willis. They had missed Jackson by seconds, but soon enough more than a hundred Union cavalrymen thronged the northern end of Main Street. Before long two Federal guns arrived and Federal scouts discovered the transport column beyond Madison Hall; the Southern wagons were ridiculously conspicuous in newly issued white canvas tops.[26]

The profanity, noise, and confusion at both ends of the North River bridge must have been as thick as the dust thrown up by galloping hooves. The war had not yet come to this part of the Valley, and terrified civilians were streaming from their homes for the woods.[27] Stray shots were falling, Union troopers were bringing in rebel prisoners,[28] and Yanks were unlimbering two guns at their end of the bridge. In the confusion Dr. McGuire could not tell who held Main Street; he started his ambulances southward then wandered into Federals at the bridge and was taken prisoner.

Someone appeared on the bluffs across the river and shouted at the Yank gunners. It may have been Stonewall, or one of any number of other officers, trying to sort friend from foe or give commands to bewildered troops. Historical romance has credited Old Jack with attempting to trick the Federals into bringing their gun across the bridge. Supposedly he was impersonating a Union officer and was yelling for the Federals to bring their cannon to him. Reliable observers dismiss any such incident. It is impossible to know today what happened, but the tale highlights the extraordinary turmoil of the moment.[29]

Federal scouts galloped up to report to their commander, Colonel Samuel Carroll, that Confederate trains were beyond the Kemper home. The Union leader turned to prisoner Crutchfield and demanded to know if the wagons were there. "You must find that out for yourself," snarled the artillerist, who knew the report was true and gloomily contemplated the fate of those vehicles while the Federal commander motioned a strong detail to check. Not knowing what else to do with Dr. McGuire, his Federal guard told him to join the ride. One of the Union cannons swung around to bolster the probe. Probably no more than two miles away, a Northern infantry column was coming rapidly up the road from Conrad's Store to support the cavalry. The Valley Army faced disaster as Carroll's troopers formed to advance up Main Street toward Madison Hall.[30]

The Kemper estate, which at that moment was virtually deserted, was about to become the fulcrum of the action, and perhaps drawn by that fact a rebel who seemed always to be at flash points appeared. Scrambling into Kemper's yard came Captain Sam Moore of the 2d Virginia. Moore had been assigned to picket the upper ford of the South River the previous afternoon and had marched with a small detail via the North River bridge to his post. Always serious about duty, Moore had not slept like many others but had instead sent a private to a high point to survey the terrain around him, and thus he learned the location of the army's trains and as well Carrington's Battery. When bullets and shells began to splatter Port Republic, Moore assembled his detail for combat, only to find that two recently drafted men had just disappeared. Private Kerfoot (who had served for a year in Moore's company before transferring to the cavalry) came trotting back, muttering Jackson's instructions to "Go back and fight them." Moore had only two officers and twenty muskets, but in the greatest decision of his life he decided to "fight them." He formed his soldiers and sprinted to the Kemper home, sending Trooper Kerfoot to Carrington's Battery for help.

No one remained at Madison Hall to give him orders when Moore arrived, so he studied the ground by himself. On a knoll surrounded by a panel fence, Dr. Kemper's house and yard were like a little fort at the southwestern edge of Port Republic. Main Street, at the head of which Federal cavalry was plainly visible, ran 800 yards from the North River bridge to Kemper's acreage, turned 90 degrees to the west, and rose gently for 150 yards to intersect the Staunton road. The board fence surrounded Kemper's house in such a way that it paralleled the highway for the last yards before it met the Staunton road, then paralleled the road toward Staunton for some distance. To attack the wagons, the Yankees had to either turn right at the head of Main Street and advance uphill toward the Staunton road with their flank crowded against the fence, or dash across Kemper's open fields. If the enemy kept to the road the grade would slow them a little and the fence might afford Confederates protection against the Federals deploying to charge. If the enemy took to the fields, Moore would be on their flank.

Moore's best position therefore was along the western boundary of Kemper's property, and there he elected to stand. "My object," he recalled years later, "was to defend the trains, and this seemed to be the best position for that purpose."[31] He spread his men behind the fence, speaking bluntly of what they must do. The preservation of the Army depends on us, he said; there is no one else. They must hold or die. Moore then gave orders any combat veteran would recognize: he told his men to stay low, and when the Federals came, each man should pick a target but hold fire until ordered.

Moore's men crouched and waited, but not for long. A large body of blue cavalry came down Main Street at a walk. They turned the right angle at the head of Main Street. Be ready, Moore said quietly. The Yanks came on, unaware of their reception. Then, at close range, Moore bellowed, "Fire!"

The volley startled the Federal riders, who were unable to deploy to the side because of the fence. Saddles were emptied, then another volley ripped into blue ranks. In the middle of the Union swarm was Dr. McGuire, whose guard was hit and fell to the ground. McGuire thought Moore's fire sounded like it came from a thousand muskets, and in the confusion he bolted down an alley to escape. The Yankees staggered, and Moore's men charged toward them, firing as they came. The Federals recoiled down Main Street.[32]

A few minutes had been gained, but the enemy was regrouping. Moore hustled his troops back to their fence and awaited the next onslaught. No rebels had been hit. So far so good, then came even better news. As the infantry reloaded they were joined by four men and a twelve-pound howitzer from Carrington's Battery. Carrington's guns had initially been ordered to flee; then gunners with the last piece ready to move had seen Moore's stand, and some men shouted to join it. Others were less enthusiastic, and when an officer ordered the piece to make for Moore's fence, one burly Irishman jumped from the wheel horse and disappeared. A black barber with the battery courageously abandoned his noncombatant role, vaulted onto the wheel horse, and whipped the gun toward the fence. There the four new men worked like demons: they dropped the tail of the piece, swung it around behind the fence, and loaded. Federal cavalry was returning, this time in battle formation.

The gunner was a sixteen-year-old private, L. W. Cox, who saw what looked like eighty Federal riders. He yelled for a double charge of canister. Another man shouted that there was no canister in the limber chest, so Cox called for whatever there was. Sam Shreve ran forward with a bag of powder and a round shell, Julius Goodin stuffed them into the mouth of the cannon, and Cox rammed it home. Federal cavalry now was at the charge and only half pistol range away. There was no time to elevate the piece. Cox jumped around and yanked his lanyard. The rebel gun barked. The shot blew down the fence and sent splinters flying like pinwheels. The shell was wide and not a Federal was scratched, but they reined up, then scampered back into Main Street.[33]

Major Dabney next roared into the skirmish. He had not left the Kemper estate at the first alarm; focused on his sermon, he was unaware of what was happening until a servant started uprooting the ground pins of his tent. By the time Dabney wiggled out of his vestments and back into uniform Jackson and the rest of the staff were gone. Dabney gave brief encouragement to Moore's detail, then rode south to Captain Carrington. The artillerist had been approached by Trooper Kerfoot to join the fight, but in the confusion he did not know who the rider was or exactly what was happening; Carrington probably had already begun withdrawing when Dabney found him. Encouraged by the clergyman and learning more of the situation, Carrington changed his orders. Two guns were still in sight, and officers spurred to reverse direction. Lieutenant Dinwiddie had to draw his pistol to turn back the gunners with one piece, but soon they were advancing, following Dabney across Kemper's fields to the head of Main Street. Moore led his infantry forward to support the two guns.[34]

A determined force was collecting at the south end of Port Republic. Captain Sipe had managed to corral some of his company and brought them back to the guns.[35] Moore began plotting with Sipe to advance down the side alleys and pick off Federals. While Carrington's two guns unlimbered the Yanks advanced again, but with Dabney shouting directions the rebels opened with canister. The two pieces swept the street and kept the Yanks pinned down. From his corner Gunner Cox's piece lobbed shells at the enemy.[36]

While Moore made his heroic stand, Jackson was pounding down the road to Harrisonburg looking for help. Gone now was the composure that allowed him to await his own horse being saddled or to correct Dr. McGuire's language. He did not know what force Shields was hurling at him, only that his army was about to be trapped on the same side of a swollen river with the numerically superior forces of Frémont and cut off from its reserve ammunition and food. For all Jackson knew, at that very moment the Yanks were tossing firebrands into the bridge. Captain Poague recalled, "I never saw Jackson as much stirred up at any other time";[37] Lanty Blackford reported that Jackson showed "more signs of excitement that I ever saw him manifest before."[38]

"Have the guns hitched up, have the guns hitched up!" he yelled, then directed Poague to make for the bridge. Poague's independent decision to assemble when he first heard the Union cannon fire now paid off; his guns were quickly ready and started to the Port. Captain Carpenter, who also had rallied his men at the first sound of the Federal raid, followed with his battery. Jackson next dashed to Winder's tent. If Winder's letter requesting transfer had been either sent or received, nothing was said of it. From Winder Jackson received immediate response to an order to get a regiment moving. Within five minutes the 2d Virginia was pressing to the sound of the guns.[39] More quickly ready was Taliaferro's Brigade, to which Jackson dispatched Sandie Pendleton.[40] Those troops were just forming ranks for inspection and moved immediately, with Wooding's Battery; Taliaferro led the way in his fresh shirt. Jackson also dispatched a staff officer in "hot haste" for Taylor to bring his brigade.[41]

Returning to the North River, Stonewall overtook the lead gun of Poague's Battery and guided it to a position directly above the bridge. As the rebels swung their gun around, the general spotted blue-clad men serving a piece at the far end of the span. He ordered the cannon near him to sweep them away, but a chorus of voices protested that those men were Confederates. Poague stated he had visited Carrington earlier and thought his men wore blue uniforms.

In what may have been the basis for the impersonation myth, Jackson rose in his stirrups and called the errant gunners to the safe side of the stream: "Bring that gun up here," some of the rebels thought they heard him shout. The blue-clad men ignored him.

"Bring that gun up here, I say," Jackson repeated. The gunners screwed their piece to its highest elevation and blasted the ground from under his feet. "Let 'em have it," raged Old Jack, who turned back to hurry on the infantry.[42]

Closest to the front was Colonel Fulkerson and his 37th Virginia. "Charge right through, Colonel!" Jackson yelled as the 37th topped the bluffs. In the heat of the moment Jackson was waving his cap around his head, just as he had done at Winchester.

Two Union guns were in action on Main Street, Poague's cannons were firing from the bluffs, and Carrington's were blazing from Kemper's property as Fulkerson started down the ridgeline. He had no time to deploy. His panting Virginians were strung out and advanced in a long, ragged column. The rear was just coming over the crest as the front ranks stormed onto the bridge. A Northern gun fired at point-blank range. The shot was high and wide, damaging the sides of the bridge but leaving its understructure untouched. In a trice the Confederates held the Union gun and were shooting down Federals as they bolted for the lower ford. Amid the whirling dust and smoke the rear companies of the 37th could not tell friend from foe and took aim at the men on the gun, now Confederates.[43] The second Union gun was taken. Colonel Crutchfield escaped in the melee.

The Southerners had no time to rejoice before new alarms pealed out. The Federal infantry column, at least a regiment and looking to some to show the strength of four,[44] was observed pressing for the ford. But now Poague's, Carpenter's, and Wooding's batteries studded the bluffs. The blue foot soldiers had no cannons and were just out of musket shot, so the rebels could drop shells among them without risk. The Yankee infantry were fifteen minutes too late, and both retiring cavalry and advancing foot received a savage fire from the high ground. Wrote Bob Barton of the Rockbridge Artillery, "We had it all our own way and we did tremendous execution. So fast was our firing that we had to cool our guns by pouring water down them from our canteens. Gen. Jackson sat like a Statue immediately by the gun I was assisting to work and he seemed quite to enjoy the firing."[45]

The Union troops collapsed under this barrage. As Federals retired via the road to Conrad's Store, rebel guns shifted correspondingly along the bluffs. For more than a mile they kept up the fire, one battery leapfrogging another so that a constant barrage hit the Yanks. Only when the Federals literally disappeared around a bend in the South Fork did the artillery pursuit halt.[46] Federal casualties totaled at least forty killed and wounded among infantry and artillery, with sizable losses among the cavalry contingent. The Confederate loss was three men from the 37th; amazingly, neither Moore nor Carrington had a man scratched.[47]

The victorious Confederates reestablished control in Port Republic. They found Moore's detail coming south along Main Street to announce their lines had held. Messengers rode to bring back the fleeing trains. Major Harman realized that the cavalry that earlier had scampered away would head to Staunton with tales of disaster. He notified his brother Asher that the situation was restored, although he urged him to get supplies out of Staunton as fast as he could without creating panic. Harman added that "the gallantry of Capt. Moor's [*sic*] company from Clarke who was on picket duty save [*sic*] the whole thing."[48] Taliaferro moved all his regiments into the village to guard key fords. Winder deployed the Stonewall Brigade to protect the artillery on the bluffs; units of Patton's Brigade were assigned there as well.[49]

As calm returned Major Harman's assistant, William Allan, also penned a letter to Asher Harman, and in it he pleaded, "Don't allow any infernal reports of this affair to get to Richmond."[50] That news of the near debacle ought not to reach higher authorities was not a surprising attitude for Headquarters, because in this instance it had not performed well. The power Jackson mustered around the North River bridge after he almost lost it (and which he maintained there for some time while Ewell was fighting against odds at the Battle at Cross Keys) underscored the importance of that span as well as the arrangements he should have made before the enemy was handed a chance to burn it.

The Federal raid had not been in overwhelming force, nor even one with a precise goal. Carroll thought himself under orders to save the bridge and had driven forward from Conrad's Store in the van of Shields's command with just two guns and 150 cavalrymen; his only other close support was one infantry regiment. It was not Union numbers, therefore, but the point at which they struck that set the stage for ruin. Had the Union commander been focused on burning the bridge a calamity would have befallen the Valley Army. Days later, even a private could not think of that span aflame without shuddering: "I was fully aware how much, indeed how entirely, upon the preservation of this bridge depended the safety of our wagon train and the integrity, if not the existence of our army," wrote Lanty Blackford.[51]

With the bridge denied, the rebels had no means to get over the North River for at least several days. Frémont could have pounded them at his leisure. If nothing else, lack of food and fodder would have soon left the Army impotent. Almost as devastating would have been just the destruction of the trains, upon which depended Jackson's ability to make any move for the relief of Richmond. Years later Sam Moore would bluntly state the consequences from loss of the trains alone: "An army without ammunition cannot fight, and without food cannot exist."[52]

Hotchkiss had spotted elements of Shields's command in the vicinity of Conrad's Store as early as June 5, and evidence that the victor of Kernstown had to be thought enterprising was contained in Jackson's letter to Johnston of June 6, in which Stonewall related efforts to guard against Shields's crossing the South Fork to join Frémont. There was ample warning that Federals were prowling the vicinity before dawn of the eighth, yet Jackson initially investigated with a small party under Sipe despite the fact that the bridge was protected by only a handful of infantry. All of these were sufficient reasons to defend the area with solid infantry and artillery units from the outset by at least dawn.

That the Army's trains and sole escape route were caught defenseless is surprising considering the attention Jackson had lavished heretofore on the Valley's rivers. Crutchfield had monitored the work of Ashby's bridge-burning parties to ensure that Frémont and Shields stayed apart, and Imboden had been summoned to Mount Crawford with the last disposable troops in the Shenandoah to defend the North River even though the redoubtable Captain Mason could not cross there. Southern cavalry guarded against approach from west of the South Fork (unlikely, given destruction of the bridge at Conrad's Store) or a raid against the trains from above, yet the most obvious Federal target had been seized by the enemy virtually without opposition. Such a lapse is the sort of thing that happens to an army when its officers and men have reached the limits of endurance. The inattention to detail, unusual for Jackson, probably reflected his own exhaustion after the retreat.

The Confederates had assumed they were out of trouble and relaxed; with the exception of a handful of heroes like Moore's men, they had not been preparing for the worst, but they got it. Drawing on a figure of speech in his letter to Asher Harman, William Allan literally summarized the whole episode when he admitted, "Shields' army this morning made a dash on Port Republic and almost caught us napping."[53]

17

TWO DAYS OF STAND-UP BATTLE

The balls whistle by our heads as fast and thick as ever I saw hail fall in Georgia.

—T. M. HIGHTOWER

No sooner had the Union lunge at the North River bridge been foiled than the grumble of cannon fire swelled from the west. It was Frémont coming in on Ewell. Were the pincers Jackson had evaded since May 31 about to snap shut?

The prior afternoon, when Jackson had assigned Ewell to hold Frémont while he trudged on to Port Republic, Old Bald Head and his subordinates had surveyed the terrain, and General Elzey found an excellent position on a low ridgeline four miles northwest of the Port.[1] The elevation was a natural fortification; on its northern side, toward Frémont, was a creek that served as a moat. The ridge paralleled that creek for more than a mile with heavy stands of oak on either end. Through the middle ran the Harrisonburg road, and on either side of the highway the ground could be swept by guns on the high ground. The location was two miles southeast of a village called Cross Keys, which took its name from the insignia of hospitality (crossed keys) on a wall of its tavern. Ewell bivouacked his division near the ridge on the seventh; the 15th Alabama was left outside Cross Keys as skirmishers, while Munford's cavalry patrolled the right of Ewell's line and the South Fork of the Shenandoah.

On the eighth Ewell learned that Jackson planned no march that day, so he assumed a defensive posture.[2] He massed his divisional artillery where the road from Harrisonburg bisected the high ground. In what would be the center of his line Ewell stationed five batteries, those of Captains Courtney, Raines, Lusk, Brockenbrough, and Rice. Almost twenty guns dominated the fields to the north; Ewell stationed the 21st North Carolina to protect them.[3] Left of the guns General Steuart posted his brigade, consisting of the 1st Maryland and Colonel Scott's regiments from Allegheny Johnson's command. To the right went Trimble's Brigade; Trimble spotted ground more to his liking a few hundred yards ahead and got Ewell's permission to occupy it. This was a wooded hill roughly parallel to the main battleline with its right protected by a ravine, its left close enough to rebel guns to be covered by them, and with completely open terrain beyond. Trimble arrayed his 21st Georgia and 16th Mississippi at this point. Taylor's Brigade took a position in the center behind the guns.

These dispositions were made in a deliberate, almost leisurely fashion because Frémont did not press until long after dawn.[4] Elzey's Brigade was farthest back from the ridge, safe enough that it could think of worship services, and the chaplain of the 25th Virginia even commenced preaching in a field to his flock. The cleric had just reached "thirdly" when orders came to move.[5] Cannon fire was heard from the Port Republic, and Taylor's Brigade had been summoned there; Ewell brought Elzey's unit to the front to replace Taylor. He confronted Frémont with only three brigades, fewer than five thousand men, but he remained confident as, about 10 A.M., battle commenced.

Although Frémont had in excess of ten thousand men, his stroke was hesitant. Nor was this attack coordinated with Colonel Carroll's raid at Port Republic; Frémont was ignorant of Jackson's need to mass troops against that threat. The Pathfinder lurched toward battle with the mistaken notion that he was opposed by the majority of the Valley Army and outnumbered by it. He reasoned his best plan was to turn the Confederate right flank, which would permit him to link up with Shields while driving the Southerners away from their escape route, and he gave orders accordingly to a brigade composed of German immigrants with no combat experience. Unfortunately for them, those orders put the attackers on a collision course with Isaac Trimble.[6]

The combative sexagenarian had been spoiling for a fight for weeks. The quiet spring on the Rappahannock and at Swift Run Gap had not been to his liking, nor had Trimble been contented even with the action he had seen in the Valley. He felt Ewell had been less than sufficiently aggressive at Winchester, where Trimble had pressed him to strike the Union flank regardless of the thick fog.[7] Trimble was a man perpetually ready to fight, and it must have been with eagerness that he awaited the battle. His Alabama skirmishers put up a noisy fight, withdrawing grudgingly to form on the right wing of the brigade's line. After them came Federal artillery, which deployed generally opposite Ewell's guns and opened a thunderous duel.[8] It was this firing that reached Confederate ears after the raid at Port Republic, and the artillery duel consumed several hours.

It was noon before a mass of blue infantry emerged out of the timber 150 yards north of Trimble's position and separated from it by a field of buckwheat. Trimble was ready. He had taken care to conceal his men along a brushy fence slightly below the crest of his elevation. He dismounted all officers, save himself; as Union infantry came on he patrolled his lines, telling the troops to stay low and hold their fire. The Federals advanced in parade formation, banners flapping, much like Taylor's Brigade at Winchester, except that at Winchester Taylor knew what he faced. The Federals were coming on without skirmishers and were ignorant of Trimble's ambush. A few rounds flashed from overeager Alabamians, but Trimble squelched it and the Federals kept coming. Recalled one rebel who awaited the attack: "These were almost breathless moments; not a word, not a whisper by the men, only a word of caution was whispered by the officers. See them advancing; keep cool, Alabamians; take good aim, and do not fire too high."[9]

At fifty paces Trimble shouted, "Fire!" He subsequently wrote that a murderous volley dropped "the deluded victims of Northern fanaticism and misrule by scores." Trimble's prose, if florid, was accurate, and two more volleys cleared the field. When the smoke of a thousand muskets drifted away the Yanks had run, leaving behind several hundred killed and wounded and many too stunned to flee.[10]

Trimble waited fifteen minutes for the enemy to return. When they did not he took the battle to a Union battery that had opened half a mile to his front. The 13th and 25th Virginia arrived from Elzey's Brigade with Ewell's instructions to support the right, and soon Trimble had five regiments advancing. The attack gained momentum for an hour or more, during which time the rebels pushed forward three times, occasionally exposed to flanking fire and sometimes delivering it, until they had taken fully a mile. The 16th Mississippi's Colonel Posey was wounded in the fighting.[11] The Northern battery pulled back to avoid capture, but many Federals were less lucky. Confederates picked up dispirited Yanks everywhere; one Georgian brought in ten prisoners captured at one time.[12]

By now Trimble's blood was boiling, and from his newly gained ground he felt able to sweep around Frémont's whole line if given some help. He sent to Ewell for reinforcements, and when they were refused, repeated the request.[13]

Ewell replied that Trimble must stop. Wisely he did not permit Trimble to entice him into a bigger fight on the right, for he was not positive that there lay the enemy's main effort. Ewell remained in the center, from which he could survey the entire field, and there he received word that Frémont seemed to be throwing a column around his left wing. The artillery duel raged on and was hitting troops even well behind the Southern guns. To some the cannonade seemed the fiercest yet.[14] General Elzey was knocked off his horse and out of action as he steadied the center. About the time Trimble was gathering speed Federals began to grapple with the Confederate left wing, and Ewell directed Elzey's 12th Georgia and 31st Virginia to General Steuart.[15]

The Union action on the Confederate left was more a series of firefights than a coordinated attack, although given the weakness of most Southern units there the battle was strenuous enough to the men enduring it. Major Joseph Chenoweth of the 31st Virginia recorded in his field diary as he lay under Union artillery fire, "This is decidedly the warmest battle with which I have ever had anything to do. The artillery fire is superb. . . . We are in reserve, but the shells fly around us thick and fast."[16] Steuart deployed Colonel Johnson's 1st Maryland near Brockenbrough's Baltimore Battery, and the Marylanders repulsed two attacks before the Yanks settled down behind a fence three hundred yards off and subjected them to a hot fire. At length Johnson drove them off, then dispersed what seemed to be another Northern regiment. After hours of combat his ammunition was exhausted and he had taken almost 30 casualties, serious losses since his unit numbered only 175 men on entering the battle. The even smaller 44th Virginia, numbering at most 130 men, was equally steady in blunting two Union regiments.[17] General Steuart took a severe shoulder wound; he was the second general officer disabled that day.

By midafternoon help was coming to Ewell. Colonel Crutchfield, none the worse for having spent part of his morning as a prisoner of war, came to direct Southern batteries. He found ammunition running low and slowed the rate of fire accordingly.[18] Jackson sent first Taylor's Brigade, which Ewell placed in reserve, then Patton's, which Ewell used to extend and bolster his left flank. This support was welcome, for Frémont deployed the brigades of Milroy and Schenck against Ewell's left during the afternoon. Those were the troops who had stressed the Valley Army at McDowell, and the pressure was mounting as Patton's Brigade arrived.[19] Patton directed Colonel Garnett's 48th Virginia to support an exposed battery, and Garnett recalled parrying one infantry drive before deploying near the guns in case of another assault. Union artillery never ceased to bombard the area: "I can give you some idea of the danger here when I tell you," he wrote his father, "that altho' my men were lying down the explosion of a single shell killed 4 and mangled terribly 8."[20]

Though Frémont had started his main effort against the Confederate right, he eventually assembled more and better troops opposite Ewell's left. Ewell felt this pressure and, toward 4 P.M., released his last reserves, Taylor's Brigade. In doing so he divided the Louisiana regiments, two going to the left while Taylor joined Trimble with two regiments and Wheat's Tigers. As if in response to Ewell's determination, Union fire began to slacken. Frémont had by now learned of Shields's stab at Port Republic and calculated the latter would be in strength around there the next day. The Pathfinder decided to break off the engagement with the idea of resuming the next morning in conjunction with Shields.[21]

Ewell could hear the enemy fire faltering, but recalling Jackson's instructions not to become entangled, he held back for a time, then ordered a careful advance of both wings. By dark the Southerners claimed the ground from which Frémont had attacked.[22]

Like the fight at McDowell (and fought by many of the same troops on both sides) the Battle of Cross Keys was essentially a rambling skirmish. Frémont had not gone in with a killer instinct. He had begun with roughly a two-to-one superiority, though that margin was narrowed as Confederate brigades returned from the Port. Had the Pathfinder focused his strength against one wing (as Jackson did at Winchester), Ewell's defenses might have cracked, especially while Taylor's Brigade was redeployed to the North River bridge. Frémont cannot be criticized for failing to exploit Carroll's raid at Port Republic (since he had no way to know of it beforehand), but blame is his for not forcing a decision either by hammering home the attack against the Southern right or responding to Milroy and Schenck when they appeared to make progress on the Confederate left. Frémont did neither, settling for disjointed assaults that cost 557 killed or wounded and another 127 captured[23] while accomplishing nothing but the waste of an opportunity to defeat a foe cornered by a swollen river.

Cross Keys was a valuable victory for the South, and one that had to be won. The Valley Army had no room to maneuver on June 8; in the four miles from the ridge held by Ewell back to Port Republic there was no strong defensive ground.[24] Had Ewell been forced off his ridge, Frémont's aggressive cavalry and strong artillery might have reached Jackson's camps and the North River bridge, leaving the Valley Army in a hopeless position. The Southern troops around Port Republic understood that fact of geography and listened anxiously to the wax and wane of Ewell's battle.[25] Furthermore, Ewell had to hold without becoming so ensnared with Frémont that Jackson would be impeded in freeing the Army from the narrow band of real estate it controlled. Ewell did precisely that in his skillful stand against heavy odds. His losses were half those of Frémont, fewer than three hundred.[26]

Only General Trimble was dissatisfied with these results. He believed the Confederates had stopped short of routing Frémont and pestered Ewell to resume the assault, even to make a night attack. Ewell refused but gave Trimble permission to see Stonewall. The old general galloped to Headquarters that night, where Jackson heard him briefly, then told him, "Consult General Ewell and be guided by him." Trimble tried again, and Ewell shook his head a second time. "You have done well enough for one day," he said.[27]

For Jackson to grant a subordinate such discretion was his supreme, if unspoken, compliment, and Ewell had earned it. During the past month he had led his division well. He had loyally supported Jackson's offensive as Stonewall was fighting at McDowell, convincing Lee that his command ought to remain where Jackson wanted it while he dealt with Frémont in the Alleghenies; later, Ewell joined Jackson in risking Johnston's ire by delaying compliance with orders to track Shields. When on May 24 the order of march left Ewell on the Front Royal–Winchester road while Jackson shifted west, Ewell watched until his picture clarified, then acted independently and wisely. He pushed on to reach Winchester that night and open the battle the next day. Unsure of Jackson's location or Union strength opposite him, he refused to be drawn by Trimble's enthusiasm into a hasty attack at Winchester.

Ewell shrewdly bluffed Frémont outside Strasburg on June 1, and at

Cross Keys he effectively wielded his division in combat for the first time. Again he displayed excellent judgment in resisting Trimble's urge to press forward on the right. Confederate casualties were almost evenly divided between left and right wings, which emphasizes the danger Ewell faced on his left. Such threat made it unreasonable to strip that wing or commit reserves to Trimble's scheme, even though nothing would have given Ewell more joy than to lead the attack. But he had kept his perspective, remembering that this day it was imperative to stop Frémont, not to destroy him. Old Bald Head had begun the campaign questioning what "President Davis made me a major general for"; his record now supplied the answer.

II

Confident Ewell could check Frémont, Jackson limited his time on that front during June 8. He visited Ewell briefly around noon,[28] then returned to the Port, from which he kept in touch with Ewell by courier.[29] For several hours Jackson was with Winder's Brigade on the bluffs commanding the South Fork of the Shenandoah; there he mostly stood staring at the ground.[30] He must have been planning, or praying, or both.

The general expected Shields to resume the attack; that was the logical course with Frémont battling Ewell. But Shields did nothing that afternoon, compelling Jackson to decide what to do next; plainly he could not remain sandwiched between two Union armies. Shields was closer to the North River Bridge than Frémont. Jackson had observed Shields's column during the artillery pursuit that morning and thought it "a considerable body of infantry,"[31] and there was no way to measure whether additional Union forces had reached the vicinity during the day. Nonetheless, Jackson believed Shields's local force was less than Frémont's. If Shields could be overcome he would have to flee via the miserable road from Port Republic to Conrad's Store, whereas if Jackson thrashed Frémont's larger and more distant army the Pathfinder had the Valley Pike on which to escape, and Shields would still remain to endanger the North River bridge. In a worst-case scenario, if Jackson struck Frémont and lost he would have farther to withdraw (and the additional impediment of the North and South rivers to cross) than if a fight with Shields went against him.[32] As the sound of Ewell's battle ended, Jackson resolved to hit Shields the next morning.

One requirement for this attack was that Jackson hold the west bank bluffs along the Shenandoah's South Fork, because if Frémont planted guns there he might decimate infantry attacking to the east, as Southern artillery had just done. Thus the entire Army could not be hurled against Shields; some troops had to protect the high ground, and a vigorous commander must retard Frémont while Shields was mastered. Two brigades were a minimum for the west bank force, leaving Jackson at most five road-weary brigades to challenge Shields's unknown strength.

Avoiding any fight by withdrawing into Brown's Gap during the night probably suggested itself to everyone in the Valley Army except Jackson; in truth another contest offered the Confederates more peril than promise. All Confederates had seen action that day and would need most of the night to return to camp, find something to eat, and resupply. Ewell's men would be drained by their battle. On the other hand, there was time before dawn to funnel through Port Republic and burn the North River bridge, thus isolating Frémont for more valuable days. Dawn could see the Army out of enemy reach in the Blue Ridge, and a powerful rear guard could dispute Shields if he followed. Southern cavalry could lay in ambush for any Union strike from Port Republic to Staunton. From Brown's Gap Stonewall would block any Union raid eastward against the Virginia Central Railroad, which would also provide him ready communications with Richmond. Withdrawal to Brown's Gap was an attractive option, especially since Jackson planned to send the wagon train there anyway while he hit Shields.

Given the risk and complexity of offensive action around Port Republic, and the safety of Brown's Gap, it can be asked why Jackson weighed who to fight rather than how to retire, but the record is silent. The general never specified any goal to be won the next day; in his official report he stated only, "As no movement was made by General Shields to renew the action that day [June 8], I determined to take the initiative and attack him the following morning."[33] Perhaps Jackson calculated that if Shields was forced to retire Frémont would do so as well; one victory might win a second without bloodshed. Or, Old Jack may have recalled Johnston's telegram of May 27. "The most important service you can render the country is the preventing the further strengthening of McClellan's army. . . . Strike the most important body of the enemy you can reach," were among Johnston's instructions.[34] June 9 would be the first occasion in days for Jackson to deliver a hard blow. It is also possible Jackson thought reinforcements were detraining at Mechum's River Station and might reach him quickly, opening the way for a general counteroffensive to exploit a victory over Shields.[35]

Since there were possible gains from the battle, the decision to attack cannot simply be termed rash. Nonetheless, it reflected risk taking to a degree not heretofore seen. Timing was crucial, because nothing must delay the defeat of Shields. The rebels left to occupy Frémont would be heavily outnumbered. If they could not hold as long as necessary, and especially if Frémont took the high ground west of the river, the attack against Shields could become a Confederate disaster. The Army was going to fight inside a potential trap, and if anything went wrong the trap might close on it. Dr. McGuire, Crutchfield, Boswell, and others on the staff exchanged looks when they learned of the attack; Jackson was "crazy again," muttered Sandie Pendleton. "We were getting used to this kind of aberration, but this did seem rather an extra piece of temerity," Henry Douglas recalled afterward. "But the General seemed to like traps and, at any rate, was not yet satisfied with the risks he had run and the blows he had inflicted."[36]

The battle had to be arranged with haste, for it needed to start at early dawn, before Frémont became active. The work of organizing it kept Old Jack and his soldiers from sleep most of the night and fatigued all who would challenge Shields.* The most pressing need was passage at the South River. Federal cavalry had proven that morning that teams and wheeled vehicles could cross there, but it was unrealistic to think infantry could do likewise, and even if possible it would take too much time. Jackson called upon Captain Mason and his African Pioneers for another bridge-building feat, and construction began after dark. Like the expedient of vehicles standing side by side at Bridgewater, a span of wagons was contrived by Mason. But instead of vehicles side to side, Mason this night stripped wagons to their running gear, dragged them into the river one after the other, and lashed the tongue of each under the rear axle of the one ahead. Planks were laid from one to the next, and in the moonlight it seemed two men could cross abreast.[37]

---

* Jackson's own fatigue may have played a role in his decision to seek battle by rendering him too tired to evaluate his circumstances objectively. See Appendix D.

Past Mason's toiling laborers Colonel Munford took his 2d Virginia Cavalry. While some troopers picketed the road toward Conrad's Store and Shields's forces, Munford reconnoitered toward Brown's Gap to ensure the way there was clear for the trains.[38] Before the wagons could head in that direction, however, they had much to do. Long lines filed west to resupply Ewell's troops, then returned to the Port to ford the South River and rumble east. In the dark they oftentimes could not find their soldiers, who were also in motion. Colonel Johnson recalled missing his wagons, which left his Marylanders without food for the second day, while many batteries were unable to replenish limber chests.[39] Winder marched his brigade (minus the 33d Virginia, which remained on the bluffs above the North River bridge) a mile or two south of Madison Hall and bivouacked.[40] Taliaferro spent the night with his men in Port Republic, then marched to the high ground above the bridge.[41]

Jackson's plan can be discerned from these movements. As soon as possible the trains would seek the safety of Brown's Gap. Taliaferro's Brigade would hold the Port Republic bluffs; Trimble's Brigade, bolstered by the 42d Virginia and the Irish Battalion under Colonel Patton, was to remain in place to blind the Pathfinder. Patton's other regiment, the 48th Virginia, would march early through Port Republic; Ewell would lead the brigades of Taylor, Elzey (now commanded by Colonel Walker of the 13th Virginia), and Steuart (once again under Colonel Scott) on the same march. The Stonewall Brigade, already near the Port, would march first and be across the South River before other units reached Captain Mason's bridge. Jackson envisioned an orderly flow of troops out the road to Conrad's Store. Wherever Shields was found he would be routed immediately. As usual when Jackson thought of battle, he wanted all his forces to converge; he recalled Colonel Imboden's mixed detachment of artillery and cavalry guarding the North River at Mount Crawford. Imboden had some howitzers that might be useful for digging Shields out of a hiding place in the Blue Ridge, and Jackson ordered him to the Port.[42]

A movement this extensive required many orders, and officers hurried to Headquarters all night for instructions. Ewell was first, coming before midnight.[43] Next was Trimble, still urging a night attack against Frémont; Jackson felt Ewell understood the overall design sufficiently that he could trust him to direct Trimble, and the latter was sent back for

Ewell's guidance.[44] Jackson scribbled a brief note for a courier to take to Staunton to be telegraphed to Lee, then Taliaferro arrived. Jackson gave him necessary orders; while doing so Jackson found the brigadier so exhausted that he offered him his own bed for a short nap.[45] By 2 A.M. Colonel Patton was at the door.

Patton would operate under direction of Trimble, but Jackson wanted to make explicit what was expected: "I wish you to throw out all your men, if necessary as skirmishers, and to make a great show, so as to cause the enemy to think the whole army are behind you," explained Jackson. "Hold your position as well as you can; then fall back when obligated; take a new position; and hold it in the same way; and I will be back to join you in the morning." Patton ventured to ask how long he must hold, and Jackson replied: "By the blessing of Providence, I hope to be back by ten o'clock."[46]

These instructions were vintage Jackson: they outlined what must be done but gave little understanding of the overall picture, and other commanders were receiving similarly unenlightening directions. It caused confusion at the time, and it today impairs understanding exactly what Jackson hoped to accomplish on June 9. Patton believed Jackson was telling him that he wished to crush Shields and get enough of the Army back by 10 A.M. so that a second battle could be waged against Frémont; writing shortly after the war, Dabney adopted that idea, the first of several to do so.[47] Jackson actually never revealed that this was his purpose, and Patton's recollection, which is the strongest evidence that can be claimed for Jackson's intention about a dual battle, really says nothing about it. Patton was merely told Jackson would be back by 10 A.M., not that Jackson would bring an army to fight Frémont. It would not be unusual for a commander leaving a subordinate to delay greatly superior numbers to promise to return to share the peril as soon as possible, and Jackson's comment probably was merely assurance that Patton would not be forsaken.

To argue otherwise is to imply that Stonewall believed he could move all his batteries and five infantry brigades over both the North and South rivers, fight a battle, and then shift back over the same two rivers in at most eight hours. River crossings, even via bridges, are notoriously protracted affairs, and it is unreasonable to attribute to Jackson a belief that he could manage four of them in so short a time, especially since he would want to pursue vigorously if Shields was routed; pursuit would take many Confederates out of position to encounter Frémont. The foregoing conclusion also seems probable since Jackson left no artillery behind for another bout with Frémont or even to join in the attack on Shields from the west bank heights. Guns positioned atop those bluffs would have greatly leveraged Stonewall's attack on Shields, and it seems unlikely that Jackson would have forgone this advantage if he harbored any serious plans for more than one victory on June 9.[48]

Whatever Jackson wanted to accomplish, he was running out of time to do it. Colonel Imboden reported during the early morning hours and was given his assignment; he was told to keep his guns ready to pound Shields if he took defensive positions in Blue Ridge hollows that would otherwise be difficult to assail. Preparations were completed to burn the North River bridge if necessary; several loads of kindling were piled inside it and men were stationed with orders to have flame ready. Around 4 A.M. Jackson dispatched Boswell across the Blue Ridge to Mechum's River Station in case reinforcements were detraining there from Richmond.[49] About that time Captain Garbar, Harman's assistant, hurried in to report Captain Mason had finished his bridge, and a courier spurred with orders for General Winder to be in Port Republic within an hour.[50]

The instructions to Winder required immediate movement but did not specify the goal. Evidently neither Winder nor any other infantry commander knew a battle was imminent. For example, Colonel Garnett of the 48th Virginia got word simply to report to Jackson in Port Republic. He marched at an early hour from the lines near Cross Keys, but when he neared the Port, Jackson had departed for the front, leaving Garnett to wander about looking for a mission.[51] The Confederates knew nothing as they shuffled off, nothing except that they were stumbling into Port Republic as the sun topped the Blue Ridge.

III

General Winder was awakened at 3:45 A.M. by a courier with Jackson's orders to march; he had his brigade winding around Madison Hall before 5 A.M. The way was congested by wagons waiting to pass the South River; from the far bank a line of the white-canvased vehicles lurched toward Brown's Gap. Winder spotted Jackson, who told him to cross

Mason's bridge and follow the road to Conrad's Store. Winder summoned Colonel Neff's 33d Virginia from its camp beyond the North River, then headed for the wagon bridge, to which adjustments were yet being made.[52]

The structure was unstable from the first. The problem was that one of the middle wagons settled, creating a step down, or that the planks were not well secured and bounced under the tread of marching boots. Either explanation (both are possible and may have coexisted) reflects the haste with which Mason had toiled. Several men were tossed into the water, and the soldiers instinctively funneled into a single file that threaded its way slowly. More than an hour was lost just getting the Stonewall Brigade beyond the stream.[53]

The time lost jeopardized the scheme to pummel Shields before Frémont intervened. Before a shot was fired, the worst possible thing had happened: the Valley Army was off schedule. There is no hint that Old Jack thought now of withdrawing into Brown's Gap, and that in fact was no longer an option. Had he wanted to, Jackson could not simply cover the trains and batteries moving through the Port; any defensive line he could establish now would be dangerously close to the river crossings. Confederate artillery had been pulled off the west bank bluffs and was snarled in the growing bottleneck at the Port. When the sun mounted a little higher, any officer in Shields's command with a spyglass would see that Southern artillery no longer dominated from across the river; armed with such knowledge Shields might advance so as to bombard Port Republic. Jackson had to locate Shields and drive him back at once. Old Jack had taken the risk to fight within a potential trap; if he did not fight quickly, the trap could close on him.

Quickly then Jackson led Winder's regiments down the east bank of the South Fork. Poague's and Carpenter's Batteries joined the push. In the van was the 2d Virginia; in front of it were two companies of skirmishers, D and I, so that Captain Sam Moore was taking his men into combat yet again. Entitled to no special treatment for having saved the trains the day before, Moore proceeded a few hundred yards and encountered proof of the effect on Shields's raiders of rebel cannon fire from the bluffs. Recalled McHenry Howard, who also passed that way, "We came to several dead bodies by the roadside, one with the head missing, a few inches of the spinal column projecting above the shoulders, testifying to the effect of our fire yesterday."[54] It was extra incentive if anyone required it to dispose of Shields before Frémont's artillery gained the high ground.

Federal pickets were rousted a mile and a half out. Moore waved his skirmishers forward while Jackson surveyed the ground. Stonewall was looking generally north and east: ahead of him, between the South Fork on the left and the forested slopes of the Blue Ridge on the right, was slightly less than a mile of level, dew-covered wheat fields. A spur jutted out from the Blue Ridge and commanded this plain; atop the spur was a coaling, a flat area where charcoal was produced. Cannon shells were searching for the gray column from this post. Running northwesterly from the coaling to the river, directly ahead of the rebels and several hundred yards off, lay a worm fence that in places rose on a small elevation. The main Union infantry line was behind it, and there also were additional Federal cannons. Jackson apparently had no idea of exact enemy strength, though some rebels thought the colors of five regiments could be counted along the worm fence.[55]

It was now approximately 7 A.M., and Jackson had to work swiftly if he was to support Colonel Patton by 10 A.M. As was his practice when Federals barred the way, he sought the flank. He started the 2d and 4th Virginia and Carpenter's Battery through the matted foothills of the Blue Ridge to circle the coaling and attack from its flank. Poague was ordered to answer Federal artillery with his long-range pieces from a point near the road, while Winder deployed the 5th and 27th Virginia in support.[56] A weak and hasty Southern attack commenced.

Union artillerists gauged the range to Poague's guns and Northern fire swelled powerfully: six, eight, then perhaps ten guns thundered. Confederates ducked the first salvo and looked back for help—and saw that the road from the Port was deserted. A short ride to Port Republic would have accounted for the absent brigades. The main strength of the Army was tangled around the bridges. Not even the Stonewall Brigade was totally through this jumble. Colonel Neff's 33d Virginia was stalled there, and his report of the battle contains a lucid account of havoc in the Southern rear. Approaching Port Republic from beyond the North River, Neff asked one of Winder's aides where the brigade was. The aide, Neff wrote, "replied he was not sure whether it was on the Brown's Gap road or whether it would go down the river. . . . I pushed on, but before I got to the [North River] bridge I found the way blocked by wagons, ambulances, artillery, and infantry; it was with great difficulty and considerable loss of time that I at last got my regiment across the main bridge, and encountered almost every obstacle in crossing the temporary one across the [South River]. I was without any definite knowledge as to the whereabouts of the brigade, but took it for granted it was somewhere on the battle-field."[57]

Choas erupted behind Neff as he marched off to find his brigade. The temporary bridge had broken down, making it possible for men to trickle over only a few at a time. Major Dabney was in charge here, but he lacked the means to repair the bridge and could not persuade the troops to attempt fording the stream. Artillery, cavalry, and wagon trains plowed through the jammed infantry seeking their crossing point,[58] and the peninsula was swamped by what Dabney termed "almost inextricable confusion."[59] Whatever battle orders Jackson had left with Dabney were lost in this turmoil. General Taylor, obviously without instructions, squeezed over both rivers after Winder, then parked his brigade a few hundred yards downstream and allowed his men to eat breakfast.[60]

A mile north of Taylor, Jackson looked to the Stonewall Brigade's flanking column for relief from Northern artillery on the coaling. He was disappointed. Carpenter's Battery abandoned the attempt to flank the Union cannons and joined Poague in the wheat fields. The 2d and 4th Virginia, no more than five hundred men,[61] went on hacking their way through dense mountain laurel. The Virginians crept within a hundred yards of the coaling and counted six guns. Three regiments of Union infantry supported them. Too heavily outnumbered to charge and knowing Garnett's fate for retiring, Colonel Allen of the 2d Virginia filtered some marksmen ahead to pick off enemy gunners, but two wild shots from overanxious rebels spoiled his tactic. Federal gunners swung around, firing grapeshot, and riddled the Southerners, who fell back.[62]

The Stonewall Brigade was neutralized. While the officers of Allen's flanking column sought to steady their men on the mountainsides, the 5th and 27th were being shelled furiously in the lowlands. The 33d still had not found the front. Colonel Neff was lost, utterly ignorant of enemy location and forced to rely on rumors to find the battle:

> I came up to an ambulance which the driver told me belonged to the Second Virginia Infantry, and from him I learned that the Second Regiment had gone up the same road upon which I was then moving. I continued to march in that direction, expecting to meet General Winder or some of his aides. [In fact Neff, was head-

> ing into the laurel thickets in the direction of the coaling.] . . . I had gone, as I supposed, half a mile farther, when I met several members of the Fourth Virginia, who told me the regiments were falling back, and their regiment was ordered back to support Carpenter's battery. I was now in the woods; there was sharp firing in front of me; I was totally ignorant of our position or that of the enemy, and scarcely knew what to do. I accordingly halted the regiment and rode forward to ascertain, if possible, something of the conditions of affairs.[63]

The condition of affairs was grim. Jackson was stalled under the Union bombardment, a fire all the more galling because there were many Southern guns available but without ammunition. Colonel Crutchfield scoured the rear for rifled pieces to match the Union guns and found battery after battery without shells, a consequence of rapid shifting of the trains during the night. It required time to refill limber chests, and until that was done Confederate batteries sat while infantry below the coaling was hammered. Some of Carpenter's pieces had to be withdrawn after firing their last rounds, and Crutchfield could only replace them piecemeal.[64]

About this time, Taylor's Louisianans double-quicked toward the firing. Taylor had not waited for orders when he heard the fight explode; instantly forming his men from their breakfasts, Taylor started them northward along the highway from Port Republic and cantered ahead to find Jackson. Stonewall was not far from the hottest part of the action. Looking about, Taylor grasped the Army's peril: "Ewell was hurrying his men over the bridge, but it looked as if we should be doubled up on him ere he could cross and develop much strength."

"Delightful excitement," said Jackson.

The Louisianan replied he was happy the general was enjoying himself but commented that pleasure might turn to indigestion if Northern artillery at the coaling was not silenced.[65] Jackson agreed and elected to reinforce his flanking operation. He motioned Hotchkiss to his side and shouted over the roar, "Take General Taylor around and take those batteries!" Taylor was to move with his entire brigade, save the 7th Louisiana, which Jackson wanted to brace Winder's line.[66]

As Taylor and Hotchkiss headed into the rising sun to launch the envelopment, Colonel Harry Hays brought his 7th Louisiana into the wheat fields. Hays was directed by Winder into the center of the line, with the 5th Virginia to his left and the 27th to his right. The enemy

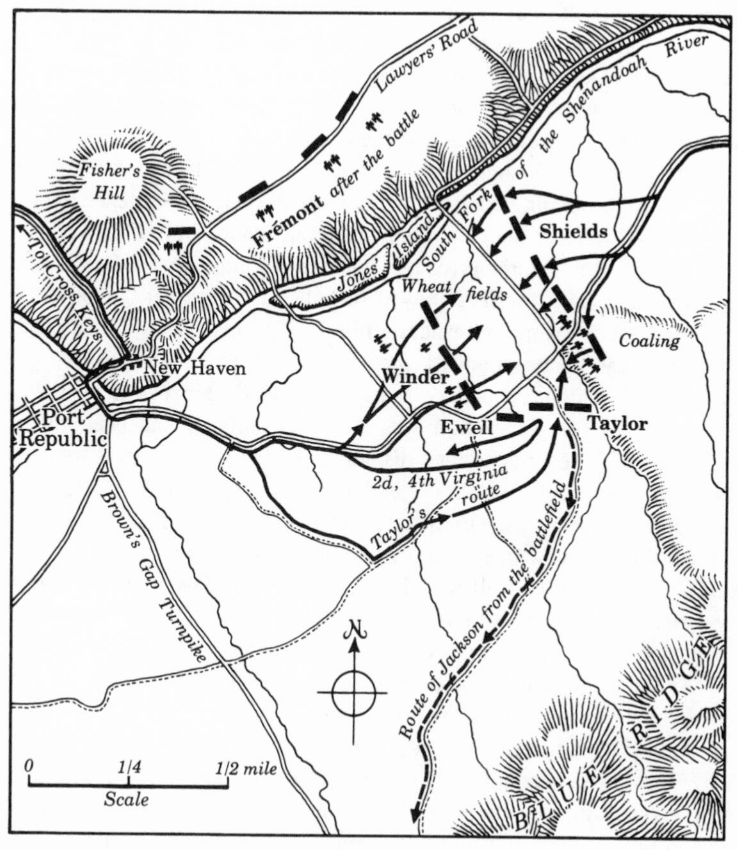

14. Battle of Port Republic, June 9, 1862
Redrawing of a map prepared under the direction of Jedediah Hotchkiss for William Allan's *History of the Campaign of General T. J. (Stonewall) Jackson in the Shenandoah Valley.*

was arrayed against them in heavy force, larger numbers than the Valley Army now engaged. Winder knew he was "greatly outnumbered." He must have understood that the Army faced a worse defeat than at Kernstown, especially if doubled back on Ewell's brigades packed together at Port Republic, and in response to the precarious situation Winder made a courageous tactical decision—he attacked. Ordering Poague's and Carpenter's guns to move, he led his three regiments, probably not more than one thousand infantry, across the bottomland.[67]

The ground was soggy, and it was hard going to get through the mud and rich, ripening wheat.[68] Winder's men dodged to a fence within two hundred yards of the Union line and crouched to return fire. Yankees hidden along the riverbank caught the 5th Virginia in the flank. The 27th was torn by a "perfect shower of ball," and Colonel Grigsby had his horse shot from underneath him.[69] Colonel Hays of the 7th Louisiana was badly wounded, then his lieutenant colonel was killed; the regiment fought on under its major. Winder's horse was hit once, then again. Before the action was ended the animal had been thrice wounded and Winder continued dismounted; "the musketry was tremendous," he thought.[70] The rebels endured an unequal contest for thirty long minutes, then disheartened Confederates began to slip away as ammunition grew scarce. More minutes passed. Winder pleaded for reinforcements. Stonewall found some of Ewell's Division coming to the front; among them was the 31st Virginia from Walker's (formerly Elzey's) Brigade, and Walker was told to hurry the 31st to Winder.

At about the same time, perhaps 8:30 A.M. or a little later, Jackson realized Shields's resistance was more obstinate than he had anticipated and that he would need all Confederate strength to prevail. The Valley Army must be concentrated. A messenger was dispatched to Trimble to bring his holding force to the battle at once. Jackson dispatched another rider in quick succession with the same message to ensure its receipt. Similar orders went to General Taliaferro.[71] These orders meant Jackson was abandoning the west bank bluffs. Taliaferro's men would leave them now, and when Trimble's rear guard cleared the North River there would be nothing to prevent Frémont's artillery from taking that high ground and firing on the lowland where Winder was being punished. Such was possible within two hours.

At the front, it appeared the battle might be lost regardless of Frémont. Colonel Hoffman led his 31st Virginia to report to Winder, but Winder saw it was too late to bolster the line. Instead he reserved the 31st in anticipation of what was to come.[72] Winder's volleys weakened as man after man shot away his last cartridge. Courage gave way to strength, and the rebel front broke. Virginians and Louisianans scampered back across the wheat fields; a few companies rallied, only to wash away as Yanks flowed over them. Winder spotted Lieutenant Davis of Poague's Battery fleeing with his piece and ordered him to make a stand. Davis tried, but his gunners began to drop. Federals were only a hundred yards away when the gun was loaded. Davis fell pulling the lanyard, even as the battery horses were killed. "We could almost tell the colors of the eyes of the enemy before we were ordered to cease firing and fall back leaving the gun to its fate," wrote one of the party: "Lt. Davis lay wounded on the ground, other of the men of the gun were killed or wounded; the whole field just there was thick with dead and wounded, and under other circumstances the screams of pain would have been more than I could stand. The enemys [*sic*] infantry was firing its shot into us and the bullets whistled in a weird way as they cut through the wheat or sounded with a dull thud as they hit some retreating Confederate."[73] The last gunners fled and the cannon was lost.[74]

Winder deployed the 31st Virginia to give his men a chance to rally behind it. The Federals charged to within a short distance and thinned its ranks terribly; soon it broke. One of Jackson's staff found the 31st almost panic stricken and retreating in disorder; he set to work to rally them, though his efforts, like those of officers across the plain, were only partially successful.[75] It seemed that the Union drive might bring Federal lines to a point at which their artillery would be within range of the jumble at the South River. About this time Chew's Battery entered the melee, and its George Neese remembered, "The musketry right in front of us raged fearfully. . . . The shells from the battery on the coaling were ripping the ground open all around us, the air was full of screaming fragments of exploding shells, and I thought I was a goner.[76]

Ewell salvaged the day. Like Jackson, he had sprinted forward with the first organized force he found beyond the wagon bridge, Scott's Brigade. Jackson apparently grabbed one of Scott's regiments, the 52d Virginia, and sent it to Winder, but it was brushed aside by the Federal advance.[77] Ewell meanwhile had neared the fight with Scott's other regiments, the 44th and 58th Virginia; unable to locate Jackson, Ewell decided to support Taylor with the new troops. Their route of march led to the right of the Confederate line and onto the slopes of the Blue Ridge. Greatly reduced by the retreat from Harpers Ferry and the Battle of Cross Keys, these regiments were barely more than a corporal's guard; the 44th Virginia numbered no more than 130 men.[78] Ewell rode with the command as it entered the forests, but he had not gone far when his attention was drawn to the tumult in the wheat fields. From his elevation he saw Winder's line fracture and blue regiments (he thought they looked like at least two brigades) charging after them, until the Union flank was almost at right angles to Scott's little regiments. Now it was Ewell's turn for a brash move, and without hesitation he threw Scott's men on the Union flank.

"The two regiments, bravely led by Colonel Scott, rushed with a shout upon the enemy, taking him in flank," wrote Ewell.[79] The sally was too weak to break the Federals, but it diverted them. Blue regiments shifted their direction from south to east and herded Scott's little force against the Blue Ridge with heavy loss. The repulse was severe; the 44th Virginia suffered fifty men killed and wounded, so that its casualties were virtually 40 percent of those engaged.[80] Scott's troops were forced away from the Federal flank, and the enemy re-formed for a final drive upon Winder.

During the time Scott's troops had earned him Winder made some progress rallying his troops, but he was not ready to stop another drive. Since beginning the fight with only two regiments, Winder had received piecemeal three additional regiments from three different brigades. All those troops had been mauled by Union artillery and infantry fire. Winder's lines were shattered and about to be swept aside. They needed help.

Help for Winder seemed at hand as three regiments under Colonel Walker filled the Port Republic road while Walker, who once had challenged Jackson to a duel at V.M.I., rode forward for orders. Despite Winder's predicament, however, the coaling remained the key to victory, and probably thinking of the inevitable approach of Frémont's army, Jackson continued to thrust against that point. He ordered Walker to follow Taylor's path to the Federal guns. Walker requested a guide. Jackson had none. The colonel took a long look at the Federal battery, tried to grasp a landmark or two, and headed into the laurel thickets.[81]

As if prompted by Jackson's resolve, General Taylor was, by about this time or perhaps a little earlier, smashing away some underbrush to get a better view. His men had been groping through a maze of low-branched laurel for more than an hour. The Louisiana Brigade had reached a point on the flank of Union guns at the coaling but were separated from it by a ravine; the Yanks apparently were unaware of them. Perhaps Taylor might have found better ground by completing his circuit of the Yankee position, but the fading sound of Winder's battle demanded immediate succor. Taylor pointed his regiments toward the Union guns and the rebels surged instinctively. Breaking into little groups, unable to see or hear their officers, Pelican State men rolled out of the woods, down, then up the ravine and onto the coaling before the Federals could open fire. Six Union guns were taken.

It had been too easy! Federal infantry supporting the guns counterattacked savagely and caught the Confederates before they could form to resist. Fearing to lose the guns, rebels began to shoot the battery horses; Major Wheat pulled out his bowie knife and slit the throats of animals close to him. "It was a sickening sight," said one rebel who saw Wheat later. "Major Wheat was as bloody as a butcher."[82] One man estimated that eighty or ninety horses died in less than an acre.[83] Despite tenacious individual fighting, the rebels were battered back to their original positions. There they rallied and blasted Union gunners who tried to drag away the cannons. Only one was removed.

Taylor brought his brigade raging out of the forest again. It was nothing like the charge at Winchester. Undergrowth made it impossible to form ranks. Rebels tripped on roots and vines; the leaf-caked ground slipped away under their feet, and they stormed up like a savage mob. Federal guns opened with canister at point-blank range. The battle swirled over dozens of dead battery horses as Southerners lunged in with bayonets. Men grappled hand to hand. Writhing wounded piled hub high around the guns, but the rebels were thrown back across the gorge.[84]

All order was gone, but the rebels fought on in small groups, sweeping the Union guns with a deadly fire. Northern artillery from other sections of the field hit the Louisianans in turn, and the Federal advance against Winder stopped as the regiments that had almost destroyed him swerved toward the coaling. There was no sign of help for Taylor, who could see the Northern regiments in the wheat fields shifting to attack him: "With colors advanced," he recalled, "like a solid wall [the enemy] marched straight upon us. There seemed nothing left but to set our backs to the mountain and die hard."[85]

This thought had barely cleared Taylor's mind when a ragged line of infantry burst from a fringe of trees to his left. It was Ewell, flinging profanities and waving on the survivors of the 44th and 58th Virginia. Ewell had pulled these men together after the repulse of their flank attack and marched with them to the coaling. Doubtless the heavy foliage kept anyone from detecting how few they were. They were the first support to reach Taylor, and their fire helped stagger the enemy. Ewell marveled at these Virginians, who had taken everything a battle could give: "It would be difficult to find another instance of volunteer troops after a severe check rallying and again attacking the enemy," he wrote in praise of their day's work.[86] Ewell as always was in the thick of the fighting, and a shell exploded under his horse, killing it.[87]

Old Bald Head would not have realized it, but his arrival signaled a turn of the tide. When the enemy shifted toward the coaling Winder was able to regroup his regiments, and help reached him. Colonel Garnett came up with the 48th Virginia, followed by Taliaferro with his entire brigade. These four fresh regiments stiffened Winder's lines.[88] At about the same time the 33d Virginia was racing to the front; Colonel Neff had gotten a messenger to Winder, learned the situation, and was actually passing some regiments in his hurry to join the fray.[89] The rest of the Stonewall Brigade, Colonel Allen's flanking party of the 2d and 4th Virginia, was coming up to align on Taylor, and, better still, Colonel Walker was bringing his three regiments to the coaling after a long and frustrating climb.[90]

Prior to the climax of the action, the enemy had never met more than a few Southern regiments at one time, and Confederate attacks by even those small bodies had been delivered separately. As the hour passed 10 A.M. Taylor was collecting ten regiments in the vicinity of the coaling, while Winder had that many in the flatland. Southern batteries, their limbers at last full, were adding their weight, while Union artillery fire was halved as Taylor dueled over the guns in front of him. The Union lines began to buckle under this long-delayed concentration of perhaps eight thousand men.

Seeing the enemy pause, rebels everywhere attacked. Winder got all forces within his reach moving northward. The Louisianans swarmed out of the woods once again to claim the now deserted Union guns. Ewell ran up to one, gave an instant lesson in gunnery to a handful of infantrymen, and began to drop shells amongst the Federals on the plain. Eyes ablaze with the fire of combat, Jackson rode onto the coaling; he pumped Taylor's hand and promised the captured guns to him.[91] The enemy staggered.

Yet the Federals did not break. They preserved formation even as Taliaferro's Brigade and Winder's regiments pressured them off the field. Keeping generally just out of Confederate range, the Yanks retired along the road to Conrad's Store; Southerners, understandably weary after the last two days, were not able to pursue with rapidity. Rebel infantry pounded out four or five miles, and Munford's cavalry pushed a few miles farther; the spoils included approximately 450 prisoners, eight hundred muskets, one more cannon, and some wagons.[92] Ever laconic, Jackson dispatched a one-sentence telegram to Richmond advising, "Through God's blessing the enemy near Port Republic was this day routed with the loss of Six (6) pieces of his artillery."[93] Jackson's prose notwithstanding, the enemy retreat indicated nothing consistent with a rout.

The battlefield indicated everything consistent with a savage fight, the hardest of the campaign. Total Southern casualties were 816 killed and wounded; Union losses (including prisoners) were estimated from 800 to 1,000.[94] "The ground," wrote one of Jackson's staff, "in many places [was] covered with the dead and wounded."[95] The site of Taylor's clash was a snapshot from hell: dead horses were strewn among charcoal pits; one animal stood upright, but dead, supported by a fallen tree.[96] At one captured gun was a young Northern soldier shot through the heart; his left arm was over the muzzle and in his right hand was the shell he died trying to load. Behind the dead man, recorded a rebel who inspected the gruesome scene, "was the gunner, his body lying over the sight, one eye open, shot in his tracks, and near him one [man] with a broken rammer in his hand, the other part having snapped off in the piece as he was ramming the charge home."[97] Long after the war Richard Taylor recalled, "I have never seen so many dead and wounded in the same limited space.[98]

With the pursuit launched and aid to the wounded of both armies under way, Jackson received good news from the rear: Trimble had completed his mission to block and then escape Frémont. Trimble had begun his day on the same ground outside Cross Keys from which he had fought on June 8. He had with him his four regiments and Colonal Patton's

42d Virginia and Irish Battalion; his task force could not have exceeded two thousand men. Trimble could hear the battle four or five miles to his east,[99] as presumably did Frémont, but the latter advanced timidly. It was after 9 A.M. before the Federals had unlimbered a battery opposite Confederate lines. Without guns himself, Trimble had to withdraw along the Port Republic road, a movement that accelerated as he received Jackson's two couriers, dispatched about 8:30 A.M., to hasten to the battlefield. Trimble sprinted for that point immediately with Union cavalry in pursuit.[100]

One Alabamian thought infantry had never covered so many miles so quickly. As Trimble's panting column reached the heights overlooking the North River bridge, his Deep South men could see Jackson's battle on the far side of the South Fork.[101] The way through the village was open: other rebels had cleared the Port, and the last of the trains was beyond the South River lashing for Brown's Gap. While Trimble prodded his marchers through the covered bridge, one cavalryman, Lieutenant Thomas Waller of Munford's 2d Virginia, tarried to observe the onrushing Union riders. Too late he turned to give warning that the enemy was at hand; he found the bridge afire. The river was swift and swollen, filled with floating trees, but Waller took his chances, plunged his mount in, and drowned trying to escape.[102]

The long wooden bridge, meanwhile, had become an inferno, and just as Frémont's riders crested the bluffs it collapsed. The Yanks raced down to the river and fired on the last of Trimble's infantrymen darting across the wagon bridge while Captain Mason's Pioneers worked to dismantle it. Captain Garbar, Harman's assistant, was with them. Draft animals were needed to drag wagons out of the stream, but the big animals made perfect targets for Union marksmen, who were killing them rapidly. One courageous black worker stayed at his task until all was ready, then mounted the saddle horse of his team only to have it shot dead. The man calmly removed the harness, leaped on the wheel horse and drove off, "as brave an act as we witnessed during the war," wrote Garbar. Sandie Pendleton came to check on things, saw nineteen dead animals, and responded to Garbar's pleas for orders with a shout: "Run like the devil, you fools!"[103]

The last members of the Valley Army dashed from the South River and out of range of Yankee rifles. Within an hour Frémont's artillery was on the high ground positioned to devastate the bottomland where

Winder's regiments had fought, but the only rebels there now were ambulance orderlies and doctors attending the wounded of both armies. In a display of incredible stupidity, Union gunners opened fire on rebel ambulances, with the result that Jackson pulled them off the field as soon as all Southern casualties were removed.[104] To the Confederates returning from the pursuit of Shields that afternoon Frémont's guns posed no threat. Jackson found a path along the foot of the Blue Ridge out of Union cannon range, so Frémont's bombardment did nothing but condemn Union soldiers to needless suffering.

Southerners slogging back to Brown's Gap, where Jackson had ordered them to join the trains that night, felt the numbing fatigue that comes with the end of battle. Most soldiers had nothing to eat; many dropped from exhaustion and slept by the roadside.[105] Those who made it to the trains near the summit found the ground so steep they had to pile rocks into little retaining walls to keep from rolling away.[106] The rebels made their bulwarks, the last act of a long soldier's day, and fell asleep beneath a cold rain.

IV

The Valley Army slept the night of June 9 in the same positions it could have occupied twelve hours earlier without the intervening costly battle, raising the question of what was achieved that morning. The answer is not certain. Shields and Frémont remained apart, but the flooding of rivers in the upper Shenandoah was such that separation was assured for a few days more even if Jackson had simply withdrawn into Brown's Gap (provided of course that the North River bridge was destroyed). With Shields now in retreat to Conrad's Store there was no chance for Frémont to unite with him near Port Republic and hammer the Valley Army by sheer weight of numbers; however, nothing prevented the enemy from attempting the same thing by trying to bridge the South Fork at Conrad's Store and then moving to an attack.

Had Jackson been privy to the counsels of the Union high command he might have concluded the battle was justified, once again, to keep Union forces entangled in the Shenandoah. President Lincoln had by early June decided that his Valley counteroffensive had achieved what could be expected, and the chief executive wanted to reassemble

McDowell's force for a march on Richmond. Probably at the same hour that the battle was raging below Port Republic, orders flowed from Washington for both Frémont and Shields to cease the pursuit of Jackson; specific directions were given to Shields to collect his division at Luray and prepare to redeploy to Fredericksburg.[107] Jackson did not know Union plans, but he could assume that something of the sort was a possibility and that any fight would retard Shields from crossing the Blue Ridge. In fact, the action contributed to that result, although Shields's ability to redeploy was additionally compromised by tardy movements of other Federal units in the Valley, supply difficulties, and exposure to miserable weather and rigorous marching that had been just as strenuous for his troops as for the Confederates. His command was unable to leave the Valley for more than a week after receipt of Lincoln's directive, and it cannot be estimated how many days were added to the holdup by the drubbing at Port Republic.[108] When Shields fell back toward Conrad's Store, Frémont began a corresponding movement along the Valley Pike that took him as far as Mount Jackson and thus liberated additional Shenandoah territory.

Against the uncertainty of what could be and was achieved, Jackson fought an extremely hazardous battle, one that put at risk the South's largest maneuver element in Virginia. As was true when he chased down Banks on May 24, Jackson on June 9 was fighting at the operational level of war, which meant he needed to recall the strategic goal sought by the Confederacy, namely, securing Richmond. The Valley Army represented the decisive reinforcement for any campaign to save the capital, and preservation of the army either to succor Richmond or continue to occupy Federal masses in the Shenandoah was Jackson's operational goal in support of overall rebel strategy. That point seems to have been ignored. One of the critical elements of the operational art is an ability to know when to refuse combat, and in initiating battle under the constraints that he faced at Port Republic Stonewall's judgment on this point is open to doubt.

Had Frémont opened his attack against Trimble at 6 A.M. instead of three hours later, had the South River crossing been more difficult than it was, or had Taylor's Brigade been retarded another few minutes on its trek for the coaling, the Valley Army might have been defeated in detail. The same is particularly true if Shields's forces had been present in greater numbers. There is nothing to indicate that Jackson had any reliable estimate of Northern strength on June 9, and in fact he was lucky that he collided with only two Union infantry brigades and supporting artillery. Shields had not even been on the field. Several days earlier he had thrust forward two brigades under Brigadier General Erastus Tyler to strike the Port Republic bridge, and it was this force—eight infantry regiments, three batteries, and a small cavalry contingent, a task force of about thirty-five hundred men—that had almost vanquished the Valley Army. Richard Taylor would later admit, in an masterpiece of understatement: "Had Shields himself, with his whole command, been on the field, we should have had tough work indeed."[109]

Little about the battle's tactical handling was impressive. Not until the end of the contest did the numerically superior Confederate infantry utilize its strength; only then as well, with Federal guns at the coaling silenced, did Southern artillery contribute powerfully.

The piecemeal nature of Confederate infantry assaults was the worst feature of the battle: the first two hours consisted of isolated firefights in which the rebels were outnumbered. Colonel Allen's original flanking detail against the coaling contained only two reduced regiments, fewer than five hundred men, an inadequate force to storm a large battery with solid infantry support. Winder charged the Union line with only three regiments, and Colonel Scott's counterattack on the Federals pursuing Winder was delivered by two tiny units. Campbell Brown summarized the problem accurately in a letter written one week after the battle: "each regiment and each brigade was hurried into the fight as it came up, without being allowed time to form or to collect a large body & make a strong simultaneous attack. The consequence was that when our [Ewell's] division came up, three or four brigades having been successively sent up against a force of Yankees just strong enough to whip them, our whole force previously engaged was in full retreat from the field having suffered heavily. The whole battle hung on a thread."[110]

The impossibility of easily crossing the South River, which became apparent too late for the battle to be canceled but too early to permit a buildup of Southern forces before being thrown into the attack, was the immediate cause of Jackson's difficulties at Port Republic. Henry Douglas wrote in postwar years that Jackson had gone into battle "impetuously and was disappointed,"[111] and he was correct to an extent. However, the ultimate impetuosity was less the hurried march to get Winder into a fight before other units were available to support him—

that was almost required to keep the enemy well away from Port Republic once it was clear there was major congestion behind the Army—than Jackson's insistence on fighting at all.

Once committed to action, Jackson showed again his unyielding determination to destroy the enemy. Realizing victory hinged on the coaling, he moved against it with the first troops to reach the field and held to his goal throughout the morning. After Allen's party marched for the Federal guns, Taylor's, Scott's, and Walker's brigades followed, even though this risked opening the way to Port Republic. Without such determination there could have been no victory on June 9. Nonetheless, Jackson's tendency to get into battle piecemeal and his inability to handle subordinates skillfully remained weaknesses among otherwise sound leadership traits.

The men in ranks had fewer concerns about Jackson's leadership: to them he had become the Confederate Mars. The men realized they now formed the most successful army of the South, and they believed Jackson would lead them to perpetual victories. A young private caught the spirit when he wrote a few days later: "If all of our Generals was [*sic*] like Jackson this war would not last long."[112] Thinking beyond the privations of the campaign, one Marylander spoke for the Army when he described the past weeks under Jackson: "The campaign in the Valley was the most exciting in this war. . . . Now it is all over. I look back with pride—and for all the world I would not have missed it."[113]

18

WHAT NEXT?

We are being heavily reinforced
and I suppose will soon be on
the march again after the enemy.

—JEDEDIAH HOTCHKISS

By June 12 both Frémont and Shields were retreating into the northern Shenandoah, and Jackson had left Brown's Gap to return to the Valley. Munford occupied Harrisonburg with his cavalry, capturing several hundred wounded abandoned by Frémont.[1] Jackson moved the infantry through Port Republic and several miles to the southwest along the Staunton Road. Near the lip of a beautiful grotto called Weyer's Cave he pitched his camps and ordered a general cleanup.[2] The boys soaked away a chalky compound of sweat and mud, and the strain of the past weeks eased. They basked beneath a warm Valley sun and fished or played cards or prowled the nearby cavern, "the most beautiful hole in the ground I ever was in," thought George Neese.[3]

Two days of this unaccustomed repose fortified even the weariest Confederate for further adventure. Captain Campbell Brown obtained a short furlough to Staunton with his friend John Jones. They met some comrades from the Louisiana Brigade at the hotel and decided to toast their victories; a few hours later one of the Louisiana men was dead drunk on a lobby bench, while Jones was tottering toward his room in a "perfectly limp state." (Like many boys writing home from war, and surely to prevent word of such mischief reaching Ewell via the woman of the general's dreams, Brown omitted the drinking episode when he penned a letter to his mother, instead recounting only that he had purchased soap in Staunton, a town he innocently depicted as "a thousand times more intensely dull than the most vivid imagination could conceive.")[4]

Never willing to permit time for such frolics, Jackson resumed daily infantry drills.[5] He instructed his staff to help Munford organize Ashby's cavalry.[6] In an order that highlighted Jackson's zealous devotion to duty, religious as well as military, the general both announced new courts-martial and invited his soldiers to join him at divine worship.[7] Major Dabney administered the sacrament before Taliaferro's Brigade, and Old Jack was there, standing unobtrusively at the rear.[8]

News from beyond the Shenandoah also occupied Jackson's attention. Alexander Boteler, whom Jackson had dispatched to Richmond from Harpers Ferry, returned after Port Republic with much to tell.[9] He had seen something of the rejoicing excited by the Valley Army's triumphs, rejoicing typified by the diary of one Richmonder, who wrote, "[Jackson] has swept [the Federals] out of the valley, scattering their hosts like quails before the fowler. They fly in every direction; and the powers at Washington are trembling for the safety of their own capital. Glorious Jackson!"[10] The Richmond *Whig* outdid itself: "Glorious Old Stonewall is fast becoming the HERO OF THE WAR," it trumpeted.[11] Upon learning of Cross Keys and Port Republic, the *Whig* proclaimed, "[Jackson] is a game cock and he does wheel with a vengeance. He 'cuts and comes again,' and reminds us of that queer and terrible Australian implement which deals death and destruction by the unexpected and unward-off-able process of the circumbendibus. Let Jackson be called the Great Gyrator or the Confederate Boomerang."[12]

News of the Valley Campaign spread beyond Richmond. The Macon, Georgia, *Daily Telegraph* hurrahed for the Valley Army: "The men have little baggage, and [Jackson] moves, as nearly as he can, without encumbrance. He keeps so constantly in motion that he has no need of hospitals. In these habits, and in a will as determined as that of Julius Caesar, are read the secret of his great success. His men adore him . . . because he constantly leads them to victory, and because they see he is a great soldier."[13] The news spread through the rural regions of the South, and from far-off Walthourville, Georgia, a country parson rejoiced, "We have cause of gratitude to God for the manifest indications of his returning favor. Great has been His blessing upon his servant General Stonewall Jackson. That pious man and able commander has executed one of the most brilliant passages at arms during the war."[14]

An army nurse at Mobile, Alabama, wrote in her diary, "A star has arisen: his name ('Stonewall') the haughty foe has found, to his cost, has been given prophetically, as he has proved a wall of granite to them. For four weeks he has kept at bay more than one of the boasted armies."[15]

A South parched for victory eagerly drank in news of the Valley Army. Some of these reports were fantastic—the Army was reported to the north of the Potomac[16] or even outside Washington[17]—and the reports were believed. After a springtime of little hope, news of triumphs in the Valley revived confidence across the South, and many of the misconceptions that attached themselves to the campaign doubtless sprang from this sudden outpouring of much-needed relief. The Confederacy had discovered its talisman, and the headline "Stonewall is behind them" would comfort a nation for the next year.

This was the commendation Jackson had written about to his wife after Manassas, but he had no time to relish it as his troops relaxed around Weyer's Cave.[18] Instead Jackson discussed with Boteler events at Richmond. In addition to Boteler's news from that front, Jackson received a response from General Lee to his letter of June 6 to Johnston; Lee's reply, dated June 8, explained his concept of the Valley Army's next mission: "I desire you to report the probable intentions of the enemy and what steps you can take to thwart them. Should there be nothing requiring your attention in the Valley so as to prevent your leaving it for a few days, & you can make arrangements to deceive the enemy & impress him with the idea of your presence, please let me know, that you may unite at the decisive moment with the army near Richmond. Make your arrangements accordingly, but should an opportunity occur for striking the enemy a successful blow do not let it escape you."[19]

Jackson answered Lee's letter on the day received, June 13, first sharing his latest intelligence. Shields was about ten miles south of Luray; Frémont had retired as far as Mount Jackson. Stonewall's current plans were to rest his men, who were "greatly fatigued." As to the idea of another blow in the Shenandoah, Jackson did not think any offensive that might go as far as Winchester was prudent unless he was strong enough to hold that town. Because Lee indicated a summons to Richmond was likely, Jackson added that troops en route to the Valley could be halted without endangering his ability to move eastward.[20]

These last must have been difficult words for Jackson; he had never before stopped reinforcements for the Valley. Even now the fruits of Boteler's Richmond trip were entering the Shenandoah; the lead elements of Lawton's Brigade marched to the vicinity of Port Republic on June 10, followed at intervals over the next days by several thousand more sturdy Georgia infantry.[21] With aid at hand and the enemy in retreat, Stonewall found it hard to forgo thoughts of an offensive beyond the Potomac. This was the scheme he had thought of outside Harpers Ferry two weeks earlier—indeed, he had been thinking of it when he commanded only the Stonewall Brigade in the autumn of 1861. Now he imagined anew a foray into the Northern heartland. On the evening of June 13 Jackson directed Boteler back to the capital to make formal application that the Valley Army be increased to forty thousand men so that it could cross the Potomac. He felt certain this thrust would compel the Union to switch large forces from Richmond in response. McClellan's entire army might be redeployed, because Jackson had in mind a drive so relentless it would transfer the war into Pennsylvania. Jackson even outlined his invasion route: he would cross the Blue Ridge and skirt secretly along its eastern slopes until he reached a convenient gap somewhere opposite Winchester, then storm back over the mountains into the lower Shenandoah. With any Federal commands found there disposed of, the general would drive down the Valley Pike through Martinsburg to ford the Potomac at Williamsport—no doubt after again interrupting the B & O and taking another crack at Dam No. 5. From Williamsport the way into Pennyslvania was open.

Fired by this vision, Boteler rode for Staunton and took the train to Richmond; he carried with him Jackson's letter of the thirteenth.[22] It was after office hours the next day when Boteler gained his destination, but he went to the residence of the secretary of war, who recommended he see President Davis. Boteler hurried on to the Confederate White House, and when the president referred him on to General Lee's headquarters, he spurred there. Dismounting after dark, Boteler found Lee in the last hours of an anxious vigil.

Boteler could not have realized the extent of Lee's concerns just then. To secure intelligence on McClellan's dispositions, Lee a few days earlier had dispatched Jeb Stuart with twelve hundred cavalrymen to scout the rear of the Army of the Potomac, a mission Stuart transformed into a ride around McClellan's entire command. The dazzling raid would turn Stuart into Virginia's foremost cavalryman, but for longer than anticipated he had not been heard from and there was suspense about his fate. Lee likely knew nothing of Stuart's whereabouts when he received Boteler. Worse, word had come during the day of heavy reinforcements joining McClellan from Fredericksburg or perhaps North Carolina.[23]

Lee was courteous and attentive as Boteler presented Jackson's letter and set out Stonewall's proposal, but clearly he had other ideas. "Colonel," he said after hearing the plan, "don't you think General Jackson had better come down here first and help me to drive these troublesome people away from before Richmond?"

Boteler answered in the negative, citing worry about the effect of Tidewater weather on the Valley troops, but Lee pressed until he had Boteler's true view, which doubtless echoed that of his chief. "Jackson had been doing so well with an independent command that it seems a pity not to let him have his own way," said Boteler.

"I see," Lee replied, "that you appreciate General Jackson as highly as I myself do, and it is because of my appreciation of him that I wish to have him here."

Lee quizzed Boteler at length on the condition of the Valley Army and its recent victories, but he revealed nothing of his decision. Nonetheless, this conversation helped Lee finalize a strategy he had been considering during the past week of conflicting news from the Shenandoah.[24]

On June 5 Lee had shown enthusiasm for building the Valley Army to invasion strength, but efforts to find the troops stalled.[25] By the seventh, with news of Ashby's death and no certainty about Jackson's fate, Lee seemed concerned primarily with helping the Valley Army survive. That day he urged Secretary of War Randolph to hurry Lawton's Brigade to the Shenandoah: "We must aid a gallant man if we perish," he wrote.[26] Next day Lee received Jackson's letter of June 6 reporting the evident security of the Valley Army and Stonewall's belief that he could do little more than rest and drill. This news turned Lee's thoughts again to a battle at Richmond, which implied that reinforcements might be lost on Jackson.[27] On the morning of the ninth came a brief, vague telegram announcing the June 8 repulse of Frémont and Shields at Port Republic;[28] that suggested that Jackson remained in contact with the

Federals. Lee assumed that if more details confirmed this initial impression Jackson soon would resume the offensive; he therefore again urged Secretary Randolph to expedite Lawton's move to Jackson.

On June 10 another telegram was received in Richmond verifying triumph in the Shenandoah—indeed, the second victory there in as many days: "Through God's blessing," advised Jackson, "the enemy near Port Republic was this day routed with the loss of Six (6) pieces of his artillery."[29] Jackson gave no other details, but the term "rout" seemed confirmed by the large artillery capture and implied that the Valley Army was secure. This freed Lee to focus on the relief of Richmond, and his plan was centered upon the Valley Army marching to the capital and falling on McClellan's right rear north of the Chickahominy River. As groundwork for this envelopment, Lee wished Jackson to undertake a limited offensive in the Shenandoah and destroy—"wipe out" was his term—the enemy so that he could shift to Richmond without impediment, and Lee offered the means to ensure Jackson's success in these preliminaries. On June 10 he proposed to Davis that two strong brigades be moved from his own army to the Valley. Those units, with Lawton's Georgians, would give Jackson enough hitting power to defeat any close threat. Lee allotted a week or ten days for the operation, about as much time as he might hope McClellan would dawdle, so haste was vital. He cautioned the president that the operation ought to commence that night.[30]

In his memoirs Davis remembered a visit to Lee's headquarters to discuss the redeployment but erroneously gave the date as June 2.[31] More likely Davis responded to Lee's communication on June 10 with a personal visit and authorized the undertaking after studying it. In postwar conversations with Colonel William Allan, Lee stated that after he made his proposal Davis "came out to see him and talked the whole matter over, and after considering another day, granted finally his permission."[32] In any event, by June 11 a demidivision of eight regiments (Brigadier General John B. Hood's Texas Brigade and a command of Deep South units under Colonel Evander Law) commanded by General W. H. C. Whiting had transportation orders for the Shenandoah.[33] With Lawton's Brigade, Jackson had been assigned fourteen new regiments, about eight thousand infantry. Lee's instructions to Jackson, written on the eleventh, were clear: Stonewall was to crush Union opposition at hand and then come to Richmond. Absolute discretion was afforded Jackson in implementing these orders. Subject only to the goal of defeating McClellan outside Richmond, Old Jack was unfettered as to how and where he dealt with his front.[34]

Lee's next actions signaled how far he had moved from any idea of a Pennsylvania invasion: he made arrangements for the soldiers departing Richmond to be as obvious as possible. Lee actually wished spies to observe the entraining troops, which he hoped would convince the Union that Jackson was readying a new drive.[35] The rebels evacuated their camps in daylight. Lee sent staff officers to the depots to drop hints that Jackson was only awaiting these regiments to surge down the Valley.[36] So that the stratagem would not be too obvious, Lee sought to restrain the Richmond newspapers from any mention of the transfer.[37] Had Lee still considered a northward offensive by Jackson, this counterintelligence would have been unlikely.

The same day Whiting began his shift to the Valley, Lee sent orders to Stuart to begin his exploration of McClellan's rear. Stuart departed early on the morning of the twelfth, riding northward from Richmond as though to turn west for the Shenandoah, so that everything was done to create the impression that Jackson was being reinforced for a new drive. Then Stuart headed east and disappeared. For three long days there was no news of him. It was against this background that Boteler arrived with Stonewall's plan to invade the Union. Lee could not tell from Jackson's letter if he had received his own letter of June 11, so Lee did not know to which reinforcements Jackson referred when he mentioned stopping them. Boteler did not know what letters Jackson had and could shed no light.

Perhaps Lee was unscrambling this point when, at last, a courier reported Stuart's cavalry was returned after completely circling McClellan with the loss of only one man. Surely by the next day, the fifteenth, all thought of Jackson's plan ended when Stuart himself rode up to headquarters with the intelligence Lee required. McClellan's deep flank and rear were exposed, offering a superb chance to break his lines of communications and isolate him from his base of operations. The possibility loomed of destroying the Union's premier army, but the opportunity had to be grasped immediately, for rumors persisted of new thousands coming to McClellan. Probably that day Lee endorsed Jackson's letter of June 13 as follows: "I think the sooner Jackson can move this way, the better. The first object now is to defeat McClellan. The enemy in the Valley seem at a pause. We may strike them here before they are ready there to move up the Valley. They will naturally be cautious & we must be secret & quick." Jackson's letter then was delivered to Davis, who seconded Lee: "Views concurred in," he wrote.[38] The Valley Army would go to the Chickahominy, not the Susquehanna.

Whether Lee missed an opportunity to win the war by not adopting Jackson's course is, naturally, unknowable, though he has been criticized for not affording Stonewall the opportunity to reach the Susquehanna. The criticism is understandable given the badly coordinated Southern offensive during the Seven Days battles and the horrendous casualties of that struggle. The idea, although it is largely a hindsight view, is that almost anything would have been better than those staggering losses, which did not annihilate McClellan. It is fair to recall, however, that with the Valley Army on the Peninsula the South effected its greatest concentration of force, and the actions fought there came temptingly close to destroying McClellan. Moreover, those battles were fought against a commander whose measure the Southern high command believed it had. The Southerners correctly believed McClellan would crack under pressure, a factor that ought to have weighed in selecting the target of their offensive.[39]

Nor was success inherent in Jackson's proposal. The Valley Army in April had opened an extended operational maneuver wherein it overcame major geographical obstacles (the Alleghenies), united with new forces (Ewell), and conquered difficult terrain (Massanutten Mountain and the Luray Valley) before attacking a numerically inferior enemy with total surprise. In these outstanding accomplishments the Valley Army was driven to its limit and left too exhausted to pursue Banks after Winchester; despite being much outnumbered, Banks, a very mediocre opponent, managed to escape beyond the Potomac.

Jackson's June design committed his army to an even bolder drive. Once again it would have to cross mountains, the Blue Ridge, unite with thousands of new troops, and traverse rough country along the base of the Blue Ridge. Ewell had traveled roads in that region and found them to vary from good to nearly impassable,[40] exactly what the Valley Army had faced during May. And this time Jackson's attack in the lower Valley would be delivered back over the Blue Ridge and against forces that rivaled Confederate numbers.* Major Harman had struggled to provide transportation for at most sixteen thousand infantry in May and June; how he was to support more than twice that number over longer distances was a question Jackson never addressed.

Equally unexplored was how and where 20,000 more men were to join the Valley Army. It is generally estimated that Jackson brought to Richmond 18,500 infantry, including Lawton's and Whiting's commands. Only light cavalry forces were left in the Shenandoah, so there is no reason to calculate that Stonewall could muster other strength from his own district for the invasion. Thus to meet Jackson's manpower needs the South had not only to free up another 20,000 men but also to get them to him, presumably somewhere east of the Blue Ridge.

The requirements for such transportation within the time reasonably to be anticipated before McClellan hit Richmond—Lee was worried about waiting ten days—were beyond the South. The rail net in Virginia worked overtime getting Lawton and Whiting to the Shenandoah, a trip in some ways as toilsome as a road march for the soldiers. Packed troops endured days of slow shuttling beneath rain or hot sun, and some units arriving at Lynchburg had to be given rest periods to recover.[41] Disease following the exposure was common. The average transit between Richmond and the Valley was three to four days, with several changes of trains, and approximately ten days of sustained effort were needed to put Lawton and Whiting in the Valley.[42] Redeployment to a point east of the Blue Ridge necessitated fewer miles, and therefore less time, but it could not start before the cars had delivered Lawton's and Whiting's troops, meaning the bulk of the reinforcements would not depart Richmond before mid-June. There would then be double the number of rebels to move (and even this assumes, optimistically, that the troops would all come from Richmond; if they came from the Deep South, even more time would be needed and there would be increased pressure on limited rail resources). Tracks might be rejected in favor of a march toward the Blue Ridge, but that entailed a wearying journey just to get into position to launch the operation. Jackson likely could not have assembled a strike force east of the Blue Ridge prior to the last

---

* The assumption here is that the commands of Frémont, Shields, Ord, Banks, and Saxton at Harpers Ferry would in some way be combined against Jackson's march to the Potomac, a scenario for which Jackson had to plan. He could not assume that the enemy would again be encountered piecemeal or, for that matter, that they would not be expecting his return.

week of June, and by that time even McClellan had steeled himself to action. On June 25 he opened the first of three partial attacks designed to seize advantageous terrain for his final assault on Richmond.

Thousands of troops streaming from Richmond to central Virginia would not have gone unnoted by the spies Lee knew to be everywhere; indeed, he believed Confederate plans were immediately carried to the Federals. It thus must be accepted that the Union would learn of Jackson's extra strength and heighten its vigilance. Indeed, Jackson or his staff had inadvertently warned the Union he was coming. Johnston's telegram of May 27, wherein he discussed crossing the Potomac to draw divisions from McClellan for the benefit of Richmond, had been lost at Winchester when Jackson scrambled off his train there to deal with the reoccupation of Front Royal. Though the rebels later tried to burn the rail yard, the passenger car was partially saved, and Jackson's dispatch pouch was found. Johnston's message worked its way north and appeared on the front page of the New York *Herald* on June 16. A Confederate invasion a few days later might well have been regarded by the Federals as nothing but a feint such as Johnston desired; if McClellan took that view and at the same time opened a major assault on Richmond, things could have gone very badly indeed for the Confederacy.

Units merging with the Valley Army for invasion from distant seaport garrisons, or even from Lee's army, had not known the intense activity of Old Jack's veterans. New troops subjected to Stonewall's relentless marches would report enormous losses from straggling and disease. There was, additionally, no guarantee that Federals in the lower Valley would be swept aside. Troops now under Frémont were deadly opponents at McDowell, Banks's men fought well along the Valley Pike and at Winchester against impossible odds, and Shields's troops proved their mettle at Kernstown and Port Republic. Even a victorious battle against a partially concentrated Union force that included fighters such as these would bring high Southern casualties.

Nor would Jackson's way be clear if he did beat some Federals in the lower Valley. Assuming not all Union formations there were crushed in the first lunge, the rebels might be plagued by Yankees remaining behind in the area of operations, just as Frémont's column moved from Franklin to menace Jackson after the Battle of Winchester. Jackson took no account of a Northern garrison holding out in Harpers Ferry, which slowed Lee's incursion into Maryland in September 1862.

Moreover, a problem that drained Southern ranks during the Antietam campaign awaited Jackson in a way he could not have foreseen. The reluctance of Southerners to wage an aggressive war thinned Lee's ranks when he entered Maryland, and there is no reason to grant Old Jack immunity from the same discontent among troops peeled from Deep South states to invade Pennsylvania even earlier in the conflict. (Only one reaction to such quibbling by the troops was imaginable from Jackson—execute the shirkers; that was not likely to send morale soaring among the invading host.)

It will never be known what Jackson might have derived from his invasion. Such discussion is hypothetical since twenty thousand more troops could not be located for him. What can be assumed is that Stonewall would never have gotten forty thousand men in fighting condition across the Blue Ridge into the lower Valley, and that whatever reduced power he had subsequent to clashes there would have been as exhausted as the Valley Army following Winchester. To then ford the Potomac and start into the North would have been a wildly desperate gamble.

Of course, such a gamble might have altered the character of the war, as Lee wrote, but changing its character would not inevitably bring an end. To maneuver McClellan's entire army off the Peninsula was to beat neither it nor the massive naval force that sustained it, and for this reason Lee's resolve to settle accounts on the Peninsula seems wise. McClellan was vulnerable in a way that permitted his annihilation, and annihilation of the Army of the Potomac was the surest path to Southern independence. Jackson's plan postponed that trial; Lee's compelled it on terms as favorable as he might ever expect and before McClellan could turn the campaign for Richmond into the one contest wherein he was unbeatable, an artillery match.

McClellan in fact was assembling outside Richmond an incredible siege train, and when it was in position he could open a barrage like nothing ever seen on the North American continent. On June 15, at virtually the same time Lee was deciding Jackson's next mission, McClellan was writing, "I shall make the first battle [against Richmond] mainly an artillery contest—I think I can bring some 200 guns to bear & sweep everything before us."[43] As if he had read McClellan's mind, Lee measured the throw weight of McClellan's huge guns against the hope of what Jackson might do beyond the Potomac: "Unless McClellan can be driven out of his intrenchments," Lee wrote to Jackson on June 16, "he will move by positions under cover of his heavy guns within shelling distance of Richmond. I know of no surer way of thwarting him than that proposed"—meaning Jackson must come east.

Action followed analysis. Lee's letter to Jackson of June 16 continued, "The present, therefore, seems to be favorable for a junction of your army and this. If you agree with me, the sooner you can make arrangements to do so the better."[44] Lee's considerate wording notwithstanding, it was not for Old Jack to disagree. Lee's letter was an order and was so understood by Jackson when received the next evening. Within a short time of being handed Lee's message, Jackson had orders flowing to the Army to move. Soon the troops were forming up and heading for the Blue Ridge.[45] The Valley Campaign of 1862 was over.

II

What may be said in summary of the campaign just concluded? Unquestionably it was a tribute to the legs of the Foot Cavalry. Those who marched with Jackson from Swift Run Gap on April 30 and survived to fight at Port Republic had, in the intervening forty days of mostly adverse weather, traveled approximately 400 miles over much difficult terrain: mountains, burning forests, swollen rivers, and terrible roads. The 10 miles a day average compares favorably with other operations in which maneuver played a greater role than fighting. Sherman left Atlanta on November 15, 1864, and was outside Savannah on December 13, having come approximately 240 miles—8.5 miles average for each of his twenty-eight days—against enfeebled opposition. Grant struck out from the east bank of the Mississippi on May 1, 1863, raced to Jackson, Mississippi, and back to Vicksburg, approximately 125 miles, by May 18; the several midsize battles he fought slowed him to an average of 7 miles per day. It would take veterans of the Foot Cavalry to beat their own marching time: from Lynchburg on June 17, 1864, Early would travel nearly 360 miles to approach Washington and return to the Valley in a month.

Swift marching spared the Valley Army large battle casualties. Confederate losses at the principal engagements of Kernstown, Mc-

Dowell, Front Royal, Winchester, Cross Keys, and Port Republic tallied approximately 2,750 killed, wounded, and captured; total Union losses were double, just in excess of 5,400. Additions to the butcher's bill from smaller actions such as the retaking of Front Royal, skirmishes around Strasburg on June 1, and Ashby's final fight might raise the sum for each side by a few hundred but would not alter a ratio of two to one in favor of the South. Basically the same ratio pertained to the exchange of artillery, the South losing four guns (two at Kernstown, one when Shields took Front Royal, one at the Battle of Port Republic) while capturing ten (two at Front Royal on May 23, two at Port Republic on June 8, and six the next day). Thousands of small arms and much valuable property had been seized during the final half of the campaign. It is difficult to value this property because unknown but large quantities of it were lost or destroyed during Front Royal's reoccupation on May 30,[46] but it can be asserted that the Confederacy supplied itself liberally from Union warehouses during May.

These familiar statistics might be argued as confirmation for a view that maneuver was the preferred way to conduct the Southern war of independence. The case has been made that the Confederacy beat itself in bloody stand-up combats that foolishly sacrificed its manpower. The idea is that the South should have avoided massive engagements, particularly of an offensive nature, in favor of "deception, surprise and distraction."[47] But this campaign offers no such general prescription, for the level of effort required of the Valley Army drained it as surely as a major battle.

The combination of strenuous marching and many small engagements badly strained the Army's leadership. In Jackson's original force, no brigade fought at Port Republic under the commander it had only two and a half months earlier at Kernstown. Garnett was arrested and replaced with Winder, and by early June Winder was "grossly disgusted with Jackson" and requesting to be transferred from his command.[48] The 2d Brigade had seen one temporary commander after another since Jackson's dispute with Colonel Gilham in January: Colonel Burks (originally commander only of the 42d Virginia) had given way due to a severe hernia suffered at Kernstown to Colonel Campbell of the 48th Virginia, who, wounded at Winchester, was replaced by Colonel Patton of the 21st Virginia. The day after Port Republic Patton was too ill to continue and handed the brigade over to the acting commander of the

48th Virginia, Lieutenant Colonel Thomas Garnett, who four days later gave way to sickness that had dogged him for weeks.[49] The 42d Virginia had no more officers to contribute to brigade command; it had operated under a major from the time of April reorganization until the Battle of Winchester, where that officer was wounded, leaving the senior captain in charge. Only then did the lieutenant colonel elected in April appear. Lieutenant Colonel Cunningham, second in command of the 21st Virginia, handled the brigade when his regiment completed prisoner escort duty and rejoined it on the march to Richmond, but the shortage of officers was so acute it became necessary to promote the second in command of the 33d Virginia, John R. Jones, to head this brigade.[50] In the brigade led by Colonel Fulkerson at Kernstown, Taliaferro had returned to his post only to succumb to a May illness, although he was active during a few weeks in June before again relinquishing command to Fulkerson.[51]

Of the twelve regiments that made up the Valley Army as of March 1, only the 2d and 4th Virginia went into battle under the same colonel at Kernstown and Port Republic, and it should be recalled that Colonel Ronald of the 4th was injured early in the March battle and the regiment fought on Sandy Ridge under its major.[52] Some regiments changed commanders by ballot, and in others the difference was due to a senior colonel supervising a brigade, but there was a steady hemorrhage of regimental leadership during the campaign.

This trend was apparent in other segments of the Army. Edward Johnson fell at McDowell, and of his two brigade commanders one, Colonel Conner, was placed under arrest after panic at Front Royal. Only Colonel Scott finished the campaign, and he soon would leave the service. Of the six officers commanding Johnson's regiments at McDowell, only Scott of the 44th and James Hoffman of the 31st Virginia were still with their units one month later at Port Republic.[53] Ewell's officers, who served the shortest time in the Valley, suffered two brigadier generals wounded, Elzey and Steuart, and as well Colonels Kirkland of the 21st North Carolina, Posey of the 16th Mississippi, and Hays of the 7th Louisiana wounded. The strain experienced by Taylor during May and June must have triggered a recurrence of a rheumatoid arthritis that soon incapacitated him for an extended period.[54]

In sum, four of the Army's six brigades changed command during the campaign, some more than once; a comparable rate for the Army of

Northern Virginia during the Seven Days (where nine of thirty-eight infantry brigade actually changed leaders) would have entailed turnover in twenty-five brigades! Of eleven general officers active between March and June, Ashby was dead, Johnson and Steuart were badly wounded, and Elzey was slightly wounded. Garnett was under arrest. Taylor and Taliaferro were physically unfit to command in the Army's next offensive. Winder was at the point of resigning due at least in part to the rigors of soldiering under Stonewall; only two days after Port Republic he was confiding in his diary, "Oh, how tired I am of this constant moving. Really worn out."[55] And Jackson himself was so broken down as to make questionable his handling of the Army during its operations around Port Republic as well as during its subsequent battles on the Peninsula.

Losses in the ranks from illness, breakdown, straggling, and desertion were significant. Such hemorrhage is reflected in much correspondence home. "I only wish I was with you to tell you of all we have gone through in the past month, not only in the fighting but in the marching line," wrote one of Taylor's Louisianans to his wife. "You cannot think . . . how much we have suffered. One meal a day and that only bread and meat; from five to six hours sleep and two thirds of the time it rained every night. When it did not it was very cold and our sleep did us little good. Were it not for the oil cloths that we captured from the enemy I do not know what we would have done as a good many times our wagons did not catch us in time to get our blankets."[56] The combined effects of fatigue, hunger, and bad weather increased straggling even as it aggravated illness: "Some," wrote one rebel, "a good many indeed, have given way under the exposure of our late marches and have severe attacks of fever & pneumonia."[57]

Gaps in Confederate documentation make it impossible to quote nonbattle casualties during the Valley Campaign, but fairly good statistics from the commands of Winder and Taylor offer a valid approximation. On May 3 Jackson listed the Stonewall Brigade's strength at 3,681.[58] Unfortunately, he did not specify whether this number counted only those present for duty or all men carried on the roles, which would include deserters, missing, and sick. Assuming the latter, and assuming that absence could produce a 25 percent reduction from its overall strength even during a period of recruitment and reorganization, such as April, the Stonewall Brigade fielded approximately 2,800 officers and men when it marched out of Swift Run Gap for Staunton. These Virginians saw strenuous marching during the next weeks but little combat prior to Port Republic. They were not engaged at McDowell or Front Royal and took only 67 casualties around Winchester, yet Winder reported of the Battle of Winchester, "The entire strength of the brigade on going into action was 1,529, rank and file."[59] It was only 1,313 on going into action at Port Republic.[60] Obviously, something on the order of 1,250 men were absent because of nonprojectile injuries, roughly confirming the June 3 estimate of Captain Edmondson that the brigade had lost 1,000 men broken down and captured. The artillerist Captain Carpenter had much the same to write to his father on June 16: "We have had three days rest in the last two months—the balance of the time either on a forced march or fighting—one or the other. A few more marches and fights will ruin [Jackson's] Old Brigade unless he allows them to recruit now, but the enemy appears to be determined to press us hard in our unorganized condition."[61] When Jackson resumed daily drills after Port Republic, the 27th Virginia's Company G had an experience that must have been repeated often throughout the Army: the company's ranks were so reduced it was unable to muster even a full squad on the drill field![62]

Similar losses can be documented from the Morning Report of Taylor's Brigade for June 11, 1862.[63] This tally suggests about thirty-two hundred Louisianans were present for duty in early May and that at least six hundred were shaken loose from ranks by the rigor of their efforts.[64]

The Stonewall Brigade and Taylor's command were each molded by a ruthless disciplinarian who would rise to the rank of lieutenant general while winning many victories; these units were as proficient in the school of the soldier as Confederate infantry brigades were going to be. The two commands were the Valley Army's largest (approximately six thousand effectives between them) and reflect the varying experiences of the campaign, from hard marching with somewhat limited action to repeated attacks. Despite occasionally savage fighting, battle casualties for both brigades were a relatively small source of loss compared with other reasons. Taking the brigades together, nonbattle losses drained 25 to 30 percent of available manpower.

Not all Confederate units offer the same level of detail, though this trend is generally apparent. For example, the 2d Brigade of Jackson's original force was estimated at 2,516 on May 3. Again it is unknown if this was paper strength or officers and men actually present for duty, but assuming the former and allowing a 25 percent reduction for normal "wastage," that unit should have had 1,900 men ready for service during May. The brigade took only 9 killed and wounded at McDowell and hardly more at Winchester. Only 13 casualties were suffered at Cross Keys.[65] The 21st Virginia of that command was absent at Cross Keys assigned to prisoner escort duties; on May 3 the 21st was estimated to have 600 men, and assuming not a single one of them was afflicted with nonbattle injuries, there should have been 1,300 officers and men in the brigade on the morning of June 9 when Jackson assigned it to bluff Frémont. Instead, Patton recalled, "My brigade at that time numbered only about 800 effective men . . . the rest having been a good deal thinned out by the hardships of the campaign."[66] Trimble's Brigade in early May had 2,382 officers and men actually present for duty. It took only 97 casualties at Winchester and 138 at Cross Keys and did not fight at Port Republic. Those 235 killed and wounded should have left roughly 2,100 men in ranks by mid-June, whereas only 1,172 were present.[67]

The records are not clear with regard to noncombat losses in Taliaferro's Brigade.[68] The trend in question appears in Elzey's Brigade, although its exact loss is difficult to tally because of its mingling of Edward Johnston's regiments with the 13th Virginia.[69] But it is possible in a gross way to estimate the campaign's punishment across the entire Army. In early May, Jackson could wield approximately 16,000 infantry and artillery in his own, Johnson's, and Ewell's commands. During the next forty days he suffered almost exactly 2,000 battle casualties, after which he received about 8,500 replacements in 14 regiments under Whiting and Lawton. Those replacements gave him, by general agreement, 18,500 men when he headed for the Peninsula, so that after Port Republic the original Army was reduced to at most 10,000.[70] That in turn means 4,000 soldiers drifted away from ranks during the Campaign. (Eighty percent of that number is satisfied by the four brigades studied above; remaining units could easily fill the balance.) It is thus both a reasonable and a conservative estimate that one quarter of the infantry and artillery were lost from nonbattle causes throughout the campaign. Maneuver losses on a scale of one in four were double combat losses (one in eight from McDowell to Port Republic) and pushed total Southern casualties toward 40 percent, a figure that would likely have been touched were it possible to include figures on Ashby's cavalry. Such a percent was greater, and sometimes very much greater, than that of any major battle in Virginia.

Following his death, Jackson had no stronger partisan than Major Dabney, who praised Stonewall for decades. But three days after Port Republic, racked with fatigue and illness and seeing the same among the men around him, Dabney shared a very different opinion with his wife. After describing how the Valley Army was too exhausted to pursue Shields effectively following Port Republic, Dabney confided, "Jackson's great fault is that he marches and works his men with such disregard of their physical endurance. His victories are as fatal to his own armies as to his enemies. The [latter] he kills, the [former] he works nearly to death. With all the rigidity of his character, I think him a poor disciplinarian. He is in too much of a hurry to attend to the physical needs of his soldiers."[71] Admittedly Dabney's was not a great military mind, but Charles Winder was a sound observer, and his opinion of the stress of the campaign, expressed in a private diary on June 5 after watching his spent men trudge along the Valley Pike, echoed that of Dabney: "Jackson is insane on these rapid marches."[72] Winder and Dabney certainly did not know the larger framework that constrained Jackson. They did not understand that Jackson had been warned by Johnston against attacking fortifications (initiating his long march to attack Banks via Front Royal instead of Strasburg) and then urged on May 27 to strike the most important enemy concentration he could reach (virtually demanding the advance to Harpers Ferry and the exhausting escape from Lincoln's counteroffensive). The comments of Winder and Dabney might have been muted by such knowledge, but their thoughts do highlight the price that victory by maneuver extracted.

That a long marching campaign can deplete an army is not a discovery; it has occurred often enough. As with all statistics, it is necessary to question what nonbattle losses from the Valley Campaign truly mean. It could be argued that they mean little and are acceptable since some of those dropping from exhaustion or illness would be expected to return to ranks. But many wounded in large battles returned to their units as well. The same was often true of those captured; whether taken on the march or in battle, captives were equally subject to exchange. Again, it might be contended that the Valley Army's nonbattle losses represent a unique circumstance reflecting Southern draft laws and the large number of unmotivated men swept by them into ranks in early 1862. The argument would assert that Jackson's nonbattle losses would not be replicated in a maneuver campaign waged by a hard core of veterans, but that point is weakened by studies demonstrating that desertion from Southern armies remained at roughly constant levels until the war's last, dark days; during all this time the South was, of course, utilizing the draft.[73]

Certainly statistics do not "prove" that battle was a better choice for Southern commanders than maneuver. The Valley Campaign does, however, provide a valuable perspective on the issue of whether they were unreasonably eager to fight large battles. It is well to be reminded by Jackson's complete losses of what Confederate officers would have understood full well: relying on deception, surprise, and distraction to avoid a main force engagement might be more costly than the battle. A rebel army was a very dangerous place to be whether on the march or on the battlefield.

In truth a Confederate army offered innumerable opportunities for death or debility no matter what it was doing, and that applies fully to the question of maneuver versus battle. Boots, wagons and teams, food and medicines—all the things necessary to keep an army functioning on the road and out of battle—were in short supply after 1862; those factors made the maneuver more risky. Moreover, as enemy numbers increased a Southern maneuver column inevitably confronted higher risks. The pincers avoided by the Valley Army in late May and the razor-thin margin of safety on the morning of June 8 illustrate how the dangers of a maneuver campaign could equal those of battle; in both instances Jackson was closer to destruction than at large battles, such as Second Manassas or Antietam.

To be sure, the campaign proved that an operational maneuver to hit the enemy in sensitive areas could be a winning Southern plan. It was an option to be employed where appropriate. That choice had to be accompanied, however, by an appreciation that it might produce losses that rivaled a stand-up fight. Put another way, there was no certainty that surprise or distraction was the best means to gain Southern independence. Perhaps Lee had concluded so when he kept hammering McClellan on the Peninsula in the face of ghastly losses.

It is also interesting to examine the relative contributions of Lee, Johnston, and Jackson to the campaign, particularly in light of Johnston's newly appreciated dispatches to Jackson. Unquestionably Lee provided the operational framework. Prior to Lee contacting Jackson in mid-April, Stonewall seems to have had no wider vision than the orders from Johnston to unite with Ewell and give battle to Banks on the Blue Ridge, and Jackson was proceeding in that general fashion.[74] After Lee opened their correspondence, Jackson (on April 29) thought of following up a victory over Banks by moving across the Blue Ridge to Warrenton, Fredericksburg, or some similar point.[75] As late as May 17, in his letter to Johnston from Mount Solon, Jackson stated he would exploit the defeat of Banks by threatening Frémont's rear.[76] Such a maneuver would have taken the Valley Army into the Alleghenies and away from the most productive area of exploitation, which was north toward the Potomac. Jackson was thinking like a district commander—precisely what he was—and given his isolation and lack of intelligence on other fronts, it may have been unreasonable to expect more of him.

The wider view came from Lee, who from his first letter to Jackson tied operations in the Shenandoah to the concept of retarding Federal movements from Fredericksburg. He also was the first to mention enhancing a victory over Banks by driving toward the Potomac. This was a classic example of what is now termed "operational" art, and Lee's embrace of it is at odds with the current notion of an incurable desire on his part to fight large battles. Johnston came to share Lee's vision; when on May 18 he wrote that Jackson's mission was to prevent the juncture of Banks's troops with McDowell's, he was giving much the same instruction as Lee when he urged Jackson to crush Banks so as to relieve pressure at Fredericksburg. And Johnston was, if anything, more aggressive than Lee in urging Jackson to reach the Potomac.

If Lee and Johnston eventually presented a common operational concept, the direct impact of their instructions on Jackson was much different. It cannot be asserted that Lee guided Stonewall on any specific move, whereas Johnston's hand can be seen at several points. His letter to Jackson of March 19 was meant to prod Jackson closer to Banks; it must have been a factor in Stonewall's decision to fight at Kernstown. Johnston's cautions against attacking fortifications were involved in redirecting Jackson's May offense from Strasburg to Front Royal, while the telegram of May 27 must have been a prime motivation in Jackson's scramble to Harpers Ferry. And, of course, Johnston's telegram of

May 21 permitted the campaign to continue against Banks in the Valley as opposed to requiring a strike against Shields elsewhere.

Jackson, in summary, received during April and May an excellent correspondence course in military operations from Lee and Johnston, who provided the general goals of the campaign. In implementing their thoughts Jackson in turn achieved something of great difficulty. In four of six encounters with an overall numerically superior foe, the Valley Army held the advantage of numbers on the battlefield. There were 30,000 Federals within the area of operations on May 8, but only 2,200 fought at McDowell against 4,700 Confederates out of 17,000 around the upper Valley. On May 23, 70,000 Union troops (including McDowell, Shields, Frémont, Banks, and smaller details along the B & O and Manassas Gap railroads) might have been concentrated against Jackson; instead, Jackson fought 1,100 Federals at Front Royal and 7,000 at Winchester with his entire force, overwhelming odds even if the Army was exhausted by the maneuver to launch the attack. Frémont did muster odds against Ewell at Cross Keys, but it is well to note that those odds would have been worse had Jackson's forethought in burning bridges along the South Fork not left Shields cut off from Frémont. Lastly, at Port Republic the Valley Army eventually marshaled perhaps 8,000 men (of roughly 11,000 available) against 3,500 Federals, though there were approximately 20,000 enemy troops within the region.

These victories were sometimes won despite tactical missteps; indeed, the primary criticism of Jackson's leadership in the campaign must be his tactical handling of the Army, particularly at the start of battles. Always leading from the front, Jackson had a tendency to hurl the Army into battle piecemeal, as occurred at Kernstown, McDowell, Front Royal, and Port Republic. However, the manpower advantage he enjoyed still made victory likely. Matching one's strength against enemy fragments is the right way to fight when the time comes; it is the best insurance against the uncertainty that accompanies battle, and it was Jackson's principal contribution to the Southern effort.

Finally, the campaign illustrates in a salient way the value of fighting—or not fighting—at the right time. By electing to withdraw from Franklin rather than battle Frémont there, and by his orders to Ewell to avoid entanglement with Frémont outside Strasburg on June 1 and again at Cross Keys, Jackson demonstrated that he realized when not to bring on battle. Nothing gained on those days could have improved materially the overall strategic situation for the South, whereas restraint made possible other more productive efforts. With the arguable exception of Port Republic, Jackson likewise chose the right moment for the battles he started. Though Stonewall was misinformed about enemy intentions prior to Kernstown, he knew a major redeployment from the Valley was under way. An opponent in the midst of a troop shift signals vulnerability, and Jackson was well rewarded at Kernstown for reading those signals. That battle locked Banks in the Shenandoah for many weeks. Comparably, the drive to McDowell was well timed, occurring as soon as Ewell's force was positioned to replace the troops Jackson took out of Swift Run Gap and before Frémont had pressed close enough to Staunton to guarantee its fall. Finally, as quickly as Jackson realized Shields's march for Fredericksburg, which suggested a Union drive from that point but a weakened Yankee presence in the Valley, Stonewall swarmed over Banks. Had the Valley Army delayed only three days, its thrust would have come too late to divert McDowell's march against Richmond.

It is in the events surrounding McDowell's diversion that the Valley Campaign's ultimate significance rests. By May 23 the life of the Confederacy had trickled down to a handful of days. Only the Valley Army was available to retrieve the situation, and it is possible to project events with unusual confidence if the Army had not punched through Front Royal that day. First, McDowell would have lumbered south from Fredericksburg. Orders for this push had been given by Lincoln, and abundant men and materiel were available to execute those orders. Second, because the South mistook McDowell's feint for a march on Richmond, we know what the Southern response would have been if McDowell's feint had been a real march: Johnston's desperate battle of May 29 against McClellan's right flank. Only the melodramatic reversal of McDowell's onslaught prevented Johnston's attack: Generals Johnston, Smith, Longstreet, and others left ample evidence of Confederate determination to strike if McDowell approached closer. Given the chaotic Southern preparations and the formidable Federal positions to be assaulted, a result similar to the stalemate following the battle of May 31 would have been likely. Further, this would have been a stalemate without Lee rising to command the Army of Northern Virginia and complicated by forty thousand fresh Northern soldiers. Without the Valley Army's intrusion, this "if" scenario leads irresistibly to an outcome in which McClellan claws his way into Richmond in June, probably landing the mortal blow he set out to deliver. Whatever opportunity the South possessed to win its independence during the battles it was to wage on the Peninsula, and thereafter, sprang in large measure from the Valley Campaign.

The campaign, in conclusion, should be seen as a shrewd example of how and where to concentrate resources and accept losses. Confederate resources were used in the right way and at the right time in the Shenandoah. Lee and Johnston provided the right goal, Jackson concentrated force and sought the enemy tirelessly, and the soldiers endured and fought with courage. And so the Confederacy bought time in the spring of 1862, time in which McClellan was stalled, and time in which the South massed for a deadly counterattack on the Peninsula.

EPILOGUE

On June 18 the Valley Army crossed the Blue Ridge, bound for Richmond. Only Munford's cavalrymen held the Shenandoah, and they were swarming after Frémont as if every rebel within fifty miles were with them. The infantry, including General Whiting's eight thousand men just off the trains from Richmond, were bewildered by their new march, for Jackson shrouded the goal with impenetrable silence. He deserted his own staff in his quest for secrecy.[1] The aides attached themselves to Ewell, who had orders only to move toward Charlottesville.[2] The troops guessed eagerly at their destination—at least, until a covey of stills was discovered along the way and hundreds of canteens were brimming with applejack.[3]

The mood in Mr. Lincoln's Washington, meanwhile, was anything but tranquil. During early June, Lincoln had lost interest in the Valley and concentrated again on the stalled drive for Richmond. He shipped McDowell's last units at Fredericksburg to McClellan by sea. He transferred General Burnside's large command from the North Carolina coast to the Peninsula. The president extended Frémont's Mountain Department to the Massanutten, extended Banks's command to a line twenty miles east of the Blue Ridge, and ordered the two men to cooperate. Frémont would plug the Valley at Mount Jackson, while Banks held the line at Front Royal. These two Federal fronts, so long encased within unrealistic, arbitrary departmental boundaries, were at last unified to guard the Potomac, liberating McDowell, with Shields, to resume his overland march on Richmond from Fredericksburg.[4] Frémont questioned this design, but Lincoln's response indicated he had learned something: "I think Jackson's game—his assigned work—now is to magnify the accounts of his numbers and reports of his movements, and thus by constant alarms keep three or four times as many of our troops away from Richmond as his own force amounts to. Thus he helps his friends at Richmond three or four times as much as if he were there. Our game is not to allow this."[5]

This came on June 15. Had Lincoln "not allowed this" three weeks earlier, when McDowell had offered him essentially the same reason for not redeploying to the Valley, Richmond might already have fallen. By June 15 many factors combined to sap Lincoln's resolve. Frémont and Banks were terrified of the Valley Army. On June 19, with the rebels seventy miles away, Banks fretted that they were upon him.[6] Both generals were inexcusably slow reaching their assigned positions, which delayed Shields's and McDowell's return to Fredericksburg.[7] Rumors persisted of a new Valley Army offensive: the Army was reported moving on Richmond, Charlottesville, Fredericksburg, Luray, Front Royal, and into the Alleghenies.[8]

So it went. Lincoln's generals fretted, demanded more troops, and accomplished nothing. The president grew weary of it and sought a better solution, but he also forgot his recent insight and abandoned his intention to push McDowell on to Richmond and a linkup with McClellan. On June 26 Lincoln consolidated Frémont's, Banks's, and McDowell's detachments under command of Major General John Pope. Pope was to do three things: "attack and overcome the rebel forces under Jackson and Ewell, threaten the enemy in the direction of Charlottesville, and render the most effective aid to relieve General McClellan and capture Richmond."[9]

Largely because of a Valley Army phobia, McDowell's march on Richmond was scrapped anew, and the South won the Valley Campaign a second time. A Federal army was created in central Virginia, where it could not aid McClellan as it might have at Richmond. Pope's army deployed where it was needed least, eighty miles northwest of the Confederate capital, while McClellan was left dangling. McClellan anticipated McDowell would join him and waited with his right wing extended northward toward Fredericksburg until June 26. That flank was exposed, and as word of Pope's new army reached McClellan, Jackson's divisions, not McDowell's, were descending on McClellan's isolated wing.

The Valley Army swept over McClellan's right, but during a week of unparalleled carnage the South bungled its opportunity to annihilate the Army of the Potomac. Jackson, who strove as mightily as any man to isolate McClellan, did as much as any to permit his escape. Old Jack promised that his column would begin the battle before it was humanly possible, and the rebels never recovered the time lost waiting for Stonewall. As in the Valley, the general was plagued by fatigue at a decisive hour.* Jackson once fell asleep before Federal positions he should have stormed. When he awoke, he sat on a stump gaping at the ground. Officers requested orders. He had none.[10] He called for dinner but could hardly eat because of fatigue.[11] The Army of the Potomac, hurled back from Richmond, its grasp on the city broken, survived to fight again.

In the broadest sense, the Valley Campaign and the Peninsula Campaign were phases of one immense conflict that raged across Virginia in the spring of 1862, and there was a sequel. The Valley Campaign halted McClellan and created Pope's army; while Pope was organizing, the rebels drove McClellan away from Richmond. Now the Valley Army was free to turn against Pope. Its new theater of operations was within sight of the Blue Ridge but eastward from it, in the rolling countryside north of Charlottesville. At the furious Battle of Cedar Mountain on August 9 the Army bested Pope's vanguard under Banks. Three weeks later the Army tore into Pope's rear via Thoroughfare Gap, the same route by which some of those rebels had journeyed to the Valley so long ago in November 1861. At the ensuing Second Battle of Manassas on August 29–30 Pope was crushed completely enough to satisfy even Jackson.

With the climax of this summer's fighting the generals who had contended in the Valley Campaign began to disappear from Virginia. Refusing service under Pope, Frémont was relieved of his command on June 28, 1862, and spent the remainder of the war "awaiting orders." He later caught the public eye when convicted for complicity in a railroad swindle. Banks was shunted off to Louisiana. In 1864 he mismanaged a drive up the Red River against an old antagonist, Richard Taylor, and was routed as badly as in the Valley Campaign. He was relieved of command and suffered congressional censure, but he redeemed himself after being elected to the House of Representatives. There Banks enjoyed far greater success than he had known as a warrior. Shields left the army in March 1863 and pursued a political career in Missouri. Damned because

---

* See Appendix D.

of blunders he was ordered to make and by McClellan's undying enmity, McDowell was court-martialed during the winter of 1862. He was exonerated, but he was never trusted against the rebels again. He finished the war commanding Union forces on the Pacific coast.

Valley Army officers disappeared from Virginia more swiftly than the Federals. Richard Taylor departed to rally Confederate strength in western Louisiana. He never saw his splendid brigade thereafter, but he did have the pleasure of thrashing Banks once again. During Reconstruction he energetically advocated fair treatment of the South to his personal friends Presidents Johnson and Grant. The Battle of Cedar Mountain saw the death of Winder, perhaps the Army's best brigade commander. Generals Trimble and Taliaferro were both wounded at Second Manassas. Feisty old Trimble mended in time to lose a leg and be made prisoner at Gettysburg. After the war he resumed his work as a railroad executive headquartered in Baltimore. Taliaferro later commanded Confederate defenses at Charleston, South Carolina, and passed the balance of his years on his Virginia estate.

Ewell was also among the wounded at Second Manassas, and his was the hardest fate of all Valley Army officers. He was an unmatched division commander when he fell. When he recovered, after Jackson's death, leadership of Stonewall's troops went to him. Without time to master duties three times greater than those he had known, Ewell marched northward to Gettysburg; the dragoon who once had worried lest anyone beat him into battle showed his former dash as he overran a Union garrison outside Winchester. His operations in the lower Valley were flawless, to the point that Douglas Southall Freeman would write that it seemed a second Jackson had come. Yet on the first day of Gettysburg Ewell balked at a crisis of the battle. His failure to attack Cemetery Hill on the evening of July 1—which all present grumbled Jackson would have carried—ignited a controversy that has not ended to this day. During the next months the effects of amputation and the strain of high command mounted until Lee eased him into less arduous garrison duty. By then he had at least the consolation of having married Campbell Brown's mother, the Widow Brown. In his curious way Ewell sometimes would introduce her as "my wife, Mrs. Brown."[12] He met death quietly in 1872 as a gentleman farmer and, in this he had taken up Jackson's mantle, as a devout Christian.

The summer of 1862 was significant in yet another respect, for it witnessed the last battles of the Valley Army. Jackson continued as the head of the Valley District until December, and he sometimes prefixed his orders "Headquarters, Valley District." Nevertheless, the Army became an integral element of Lee's command, and only local infantry and cavalry formations defended the Shenandoah after the Army left in June. Veterans of the Valley Campaign became Lee's II Corps. As though to consecrate the merger, Jackson donned an elegant uniform one autumn day and apprised his staff: "Young gentlemen, this is no longer the headquarters of the Army of the Valley, but of the Second Corps of the Army of Northern Virginia."[13]

Six months later Jackson was dead. Reconnoitering in advance of Confederate lines at Chancellorsville on May 2, 1863, he was mistaken for Union cavalry and brought down by his own soldiers, the worst "friendly fire" episode of American history. His death, on May 10, a year to the day after he marched from McDowell to exploit his first victory, closed a legendary time of the war; those months saw Southern victories on the Peninsula and at Cedar Mountain and Second Manassas, capture of eleven thousand Federals at Harpers Ferry, a magnificent defense at Sharpsburg, and more victories at Fredericksburg and Chancellorsville. With the exception of the Peninsula fighting, much of this success came from the efforts of Jackson and his troops. After the Valley Campaign Stonewall wielded a degree of moral ascendancy over his enemies that no American, of any era, has ever equaled,[14] and his death at Chancellorsville, more than Pickett's Charge two months later, was the war's great turning point.

The staff Old Jack had assembled so carefully began to dissolve as he fell. Henry Douglas noted that before Jackson's death the staff never lost a man, but "after the protection of his presence and his prayers had been withdrawn, death played havoc with them."[15] Captain Boswell, Jackson's engineer, died with his chief in the hail of Confederate fire at Chancellorsville. Sandie Pendleton remained with the staff and served Ewell at Gettysburg, then rose to be chief of staff for Early in the 1864 Valley Campaign; he was not yet twenty-four when mortally wounded in that contest. He had become, in the opinion of his friend Douglas, "the most brilliant staff officer in the Army of Northern Virginia and the most popular with officers and men."[16] At his death his widow carried his unborn child. Douglas, wounded and captured at Gettysburg, was exchanged, fought in the 1864 Valley Campaign, and surrendered at

Appomattox. A respected member of the Maryland bar in the postwar years, he lived until 1903. His long life allowed him to collect many biographies and studies of Jackson, including those by Dabney, Mrs. Jackson, and the British Colonel G. F. R. Henderson, so that as he grew older Douglas had the rare privilege of reading about events that he had witnessed described as classic military history. His fascination with those events is reflected by marginal jottings in his books. The volumes still exist, with marginalia offering insightful—and doubtless spontaneous—commentary on many who rode with Stonewall.

Major Dabney left the staff because of ill health following the Peninsula battles; in 1866 he was among the first to publish a life of Jackson, and he thereafter enjoyed a distinguished teaching career in theology at the University of Texas. Dr. McGuire became medical director for Lee and later joined the Virginia Medical College faculty. In peace as in war he proved an innovative healer, and his term as president of the American Medical Association was a credit to his profession. John Harman continued at his duties throughout the war, then returned to his home in Staunton and became a Republican and postmaster of the area; he died in 1874. The invaluable Hotchkiss served Lee, Ewell, and Early, then returned to Staunton to repair his ruined fortunes. Among his first work was a contract with a group of men including John Harman to teach private students. Over the next decades he was active in many fields, particularly in promoting Virginia's industrial development. He also undertook meticulous historical research, especially concerning Jackson's operations. His studies brought him into contact with Colonel Henderson, and in 1894 Hotchkiss escorted the visiting Englishman on a tour of some Valley battlefields. His efforts were acknowledged by Henderson to be of prime importance in his great biography of Jackson.

Fought often by local forces, including the companies that had been Ashby's command, the war in the Shenandoah raged on after 1862 in battles and skirmishes that sometimes replayed segments of Jackson's Valley Campaign. April 1863 saw Confederate Brigadier General William E. Jones lead a cavalry force beyond Romney and destroy B & O bridges and track, thereby undertaking one of Jackson's favorite enterprises. Many of the troopers had ridden with Ashby. Perhaps because of those early days, the Valley cavalry never accommodated the idea of discipline, and Confederate infantry commanders never could work well with it. Bradley Johnson, who took over a brigade of Valley riders in 1864, would describe them as "half armed and badly disciplined mountaineers from Southwest Virginia, who would fight like veterans when they pleased, but had no idea of permitting their own sweet wills to be controlled by any orders, no matter from whom emanating."[17]

As a new corps commander on his way to Gettysburg in June 1863, Ewell led Jackson's old units, including Taylor's Louisianans and the Stonewall Brigade, through Front Royal and once again out the road to Winchester they had followed on May 24, 1862. Driving to within a few miles of Winchester, Ewell, assisted by Allegheny Johnson's skillful handling of his division, captured a large contingent of Federals commanded by Johnson's former foe, Milroy.

In January 1864 Southern cavalry repeated the Romney winter in a massive foraging raid into the South Branch Valley, an operation that again became an arctic ordeal. In May 1864 Federals came surging down the Valley Pike from Strasburg, and as Jackson had done, the Southern commander opposing them, John C. Breckinridge, called out the V.M.I. Corps of Cadets, which included some of the same boys who had marched to succor the Valley Army before McDowell. The Corps force marched the ninety miles from Lexington to New Market and was thrown into the center of a bloody battle. Within sight of the crossroads where Stonewall had wished Richmond would send "more men and fewer orders," the cadets delivered a decisive charge to thrash the Yanks; doing so, they suffered 20 percent killed and wounded.

A month after the Battle of New Market Federals drove down the Valley yet again, burning the Virginia Military Institute only to be stopped by the return of Confederate forces commanded by General Jubal Early. Among his thinned regiments were veterans of the 1862 campaign. Early began his Valley Campaign by chasing the Federals back into the Alleghenies, then turned north for the lower Valley. His way led first through Lexington, site of Jackson's burial, and the veterans of Old Jack's original division paraded past the grave. Henry Douglas was there and recalled, "Not a man spoke, not a sound was uttered. Only the tramp, tramp of passing feet told that his surviving veterans were passing in review. . . . Alas, how few of them were left."[18]

Handling those veterans as if inspired by Jackson, Early raced up the Valley Pike, vaulted the Potomac, and stormed to the gates of

Washington. But there, again, exhaustion and nonbattle losses thwarted the rebels. At a moment of vast opportunity, Early's ranks were too drained by the maneuver for attack. Major William Pfohl, a North Carolinian with Early outside Washington who also had marched with Jackson against Banks, wrote home, "When we reached Washington the number of men in our Brigade up for immediate duty did not exceed 250 out of 1600 and this was a fair proportion throughout the whole army."[19] Early was too weak to take Washington and had to content himself with achieving an objective Jackson would have recognized, drawing off forces from Grant's army, then locked in combat with Lee on the Peninsula.

Early withdrew into the lower Shenandoah, then turned around and, on July 24, cornered a Union force at Kernstown. Once again the rebels double-timed around the Union flank by a dash to Sandy Ridge. John Worsham, who had fought there in March 1862, ran for that same ridge in 1864. "Soon after we began to advance," he remembered, "we came in sight of the hill [Pritchard's] that was occupied by a battery which fired at our regiment in March, 1862, when we crossed this same field."[20] This time Kernstown was a Southern victory, completing the sweep Jackson once tried.

In August 1864 Major General Philip Sheridan came with orders from Ulysses Grant to end trouble in the Valley. As he had been willing to do in 1862, Lee bled other fronts to reinforce the Shenandoah; Lee's instructions to Early—"Maneuver so . . . as to keep the enemy in check until you can strike him with all of your strength"[21]—might have been penned during 1862 when the Valley Army bivouacked at Swift Run Gap wondering, What next? But there were no more miracles from the Valley. On September 19 was fought the third battle at Winchester; this time the armies collided north and east of the city, on the ground across which Southerners had chased Banks on May 25, 1862. The outnumbered Confederates were defeated in detail, suffering the fate of every smaller force that tried to defend this place. A month later, Early attempted what Jackson had urged upon his only council of war, a dawn surprise attack. The outnumbered and half-starved Confederates stampeded Sheridan's Army northward from the banks of Cedar Creek only to meet an unstoppable counterattack. The rebels were driven back through Middletown, some retiring along the same route where Federal cavalry had been slaughtered on May 24, 1862.

With Early now too weak to offer more than token resistance,

Sheridan rode on to devastate the Valley. He captured or destroyed 71 flour mills, 1,200 barns, 435,000 bushels of wheat, 75,000 bushels of corn, 25,000 cattle and sheep, and 4,000 horses and mules.[22] The Valley was lost, and as Jackson had augured, Virginia was also lost. Within weeks of Sheridan's onslaught Lee's men were reduced to impossible rations. Within months, Lee surrendered at Appomattox.

Of the seventeen thousand men who were the Valley Army, few were still in the field at Appomattox. Units like Taylor's Louisiana Brigade and the Stonewall Brigade had shriveled to a handful by then. The Liberty Hall Volunteers had suffered a staggering 125 percent casualties. Hundreds of the Army's finest, men like Joe Kaufman, Bull Paxton, and soldier of fortune Chatham Wheat, had died in battle. Others, like Jim Edmondson, were crippled from wounds and waited out the struggle in painful frustration. The irrepressible Harry Gilmor rose to the rank of major during the war and commanded a cavalry battalion; after many adventures, he was taken prisoner toward the end.

Many of the survivors went on to lives of great public service. Gilmor became police commissioner of Baltimore in the 1870s. Trooper Bill Wilson obtained a law degree and enjoyed a distinguished career in law and education. He served as postmaster general in the second Cleveland administration and was president of Washington and Lee College, thus assuming the position once held by Robert E. Lee. Lanty Blackford was principal of Episcopal High School, a distinguished academy outside Washington, for almost forty years.

Other veterans of the campaign led lives of quiet service during which they helped to rebuild the Valley. Ted Barclay returned to Lexington where he was for a time coeditor of the local newspaper and manager of a manufacturing concern. John Casler began a contracting business around Winchester; William Poague opened a law office in Lexington. George Neese returned to his home at New Market and worked hard to support himself as a painter.

Whatever their careers, these men never ceased to recall their war. There were Confederate Veterans camps for discussing old battles and friends, and sometimes the recollections found their way into print. John Worsham, William Poague, and John Casler, among many others, published memoirs of their wartime service. George Neese revised and expanded his diary into one of the great personal accounts of the war: *Three Years in the Confederate Horse Artillery.*

And there were reunions. In 1890, for example, there was a gathering of Ashby's command, including Chew's Battery, and George Neese was there, joining twenty-nine of his friends to fire an eleven-gun salute with two cannons borrowed from the Staunton Artillery.[23] In 1898, as war with Spain loomed, the Winchester Confederate Veterans camp resolved to offer its services to President McKinley. Neese heard of it and felt compelled to write (at age fifty-eight) to his former commander Colonel Chew: "I think that there is a little bunch of Buncombe wrapped up somewhere in that resolution, but be that as it may, if the time ever comes that you will consider it your duty to take the field once more, call on me and I will go with you."[24]

In 1891 there was a reunion of Stonewall Brigade survivors for dedication of an impressive statue of Jackson on his grave in Lexington. The townspeople planned to give the gray-haired veterans the best accommodations after a long day of ceremonies, but the old Confederates could not be found when night fell. Following a frantic search of homes, hotels, and dining rooms the veterans were located huddled in blankets around Jackson's grave. The old soldiers refused shelter, and one man explained: "We've slept around him many a night on the battlefield, and we want to bivouc once more with Old Jack."[25]

Both in war and peace Captain Sam Moore kept turning up where the action was hottest. He was wounded in the summer fighting of 1862 but retook the field as assistant adjutant general of the old Burks/Campbell/Patton brigade of the original Valley Army; he saw action at Fredericksburg and Chancellorsville. He was wounded again during the 1864 Wilderness fighting but mended and served on Early's staff; he was at his post for the Battles of Winchester and Cedar Creek. He was still on duty in March 1865 when the final agony exploded in the Shenandoah, near Waynesville. The Yankees came on in overwhelming numbers, and the last fragment of Valley defenders was swept away. After the war Moore was an honored member of the bar and then judge of the county court of Clarke County. To the end he was committed to his duty, and until late in the century, when he began corresponding with Hotchkiss about the June 8 skirmish in Port Republic, he published nothing of that extraordinary event, lest, he wrote, "I should seem to be seeking notoriety for doing that which it was only my duty to do."[26]

In December 1908, as Moore lay on his deathbed, his son Scollay, a clergyman, was with him. Sam Moore had often shared his war recollections with his son, and as a child Scollay had watched Union troops passing his Berryville home en route to the Battle of Kernstown. But now there was no talk of the war; the eighty-two-year-old man was unconscious. There came a ring of the doorbell, and the son learned that an old comrade of his father's had come. Scollay Moore advised that the patient was unable to speak or even understand. "It will not be much comfort to you and none to him to have you see him," warned the younger Moore.

"I was one of the twenty-three men with him at Port Republic," the visitor replied.

No more needed to be said. "If any one of those twenty-three men wishes to see him now I think he has the right to do so," said the son.[27]

Sam Moore's fight at Port Republic was the kind of heroism that inspires forever, and in it Moore typified many soldiers of Jackson's Valley Campaign. There were many splendid feats in the Shenandoah in 1862, countless displays of sacrifice and endurance. The bonds created by those acts, and the pride with which they were passed from one generation to the next, are the enduring legacy of those who fought with Stonewall in the Valley.

APPENDIX A

STRASBURG OR FRONT ROYAL: CONFEDERATE ATTACK PLANS, MAY 17–21, 1862

The Valley Army's May drive against Banks via Massanutten Gap and Front Royal was one of the most successful operations of the Civil War, and that Jackson led the march would seemingly ensure that the maneuver executed a carefully crafted plan. That premise underpins much written about the Valley Campaign. The traditional view of the operation (including the first edition of this work) has implied or directly accepted the notion that the flanking movement unfolded as originally conceived—in other words, that Jackson "got the drop on Banks" by accomplishing an operational design dating from at least the conference with Ewell at Mount Solon on May 18.[1] Repetition of this view has elevated it to dogma and made difficult an examination of the question of whether Jackson in fact planned the offensive from the outset as it eventually occurred. Like many unasked questions, however, once broached this inquiry led to interesting answers and prompted this author to reject what he once assumed and offer the account found in chapter 11.

The established view that Jackson defeated Banks as he always intended is buttressed by three ideas common to Valley Campaign literature: that Jackson's written orders to Ewell to unite with him at New Market (hardly consistent with a march east of Massanutten Mountain to attack Front Royal) were understood by Jackson and Ewell to mean something different; that Ewell conformed to the unstated master plan by moving the bulk of his division only from Conrad's Store to Luray, where on May 21 he was joined by Jackson from New Market; and, finally, that Ashby demonstrated fiercely in front of Banks for several days before May 21 to blind him to Jackson's eastward shift.

Although Jackson's orders for Ewell to join him at New Market appear—when looked at without assumptions about Jackson's intentions—to be straightforward and inconsistent with an attack on Front Royal, even so great a scholar as Freeman could not avoid the idea that they reflected some sort of code worked out at Mount Solon to send only Taylor's Brigade westward around the Massanutten. Freeman therefore presented Jackson as intending always to attack Front Royal; Chambers implied at least that by suggesting Taylor's march to New Market was to convince Banks (should he learn of it) that Ewell's force was joining Jackson west of the Massanutten and thus blind Banks to the attack on Front Royal.[2]

The idea that Ewell's Division (minus Taylor) marched directly down Luray Valley to await Jackson along the banks of the South Fork of the Shenandoah River is strong evidence for the proposition that Jackson aimed all along at Front Royal; moreover, this appears to be confirmed by participants' accounts. For example, Hotchkiss wrote after the war that the majority of Ewell's Division "marched down the eastern, or Page valley, to opposite New Market," and there awaited Jackson.[3] Allan wrote much the same, stating that as a result of the Mount Solon meeting it was agreed Taylor's Brigade would join Jackson at New Market while the "remainder of his [Ewell's] force followed the course of the south fork of the Shenandoah to Luray. . . . Jackson, on the 21st, turned off at New Market to the right, on the way to Luray. He crossed the Massanutton [*sic*] mountains, and the south fork of the Shenandoah at White-House bridge. Here he met Gen. Ewell with the other brigades of his division, which had marched down the Luray Valley and encamped at the eastern entrance of the New Market gap of the Massanuttons [*sic*]."[4] Apparently neither Allan nor Hotchkiss was with Jackson prior to May 22, so they were not writing on personal knowledge. However, two staff officers who were by Jackson's side, Dabney and Douglas, both expressed the same idea,[5] so it is not surprising that by the time Colonel Henderson came to describe the campaign he would write, "On the 20th Jackson arrived at New Market, thirty miles from Mount Solon. Ewell had meanwhile marched to Luray, and the two wings were now on either side of the Massanuttons [*sic*]. On his way to New Market Jackson had been joined by the Louisiana Brigade of

Ewell's Division. This detachment seems to have been made with the view of inducing Banks to believe, should information filter through Ashby's pickets, that the whole Confederate force was advancing direct on Strasburg."[6] Henderson goes on to describe Jackson moving to Luray the next day without mention of Ewell moving westward to New Market.

As indicated by Henderson, Ashby's supposed contribution to the masked approach to Front Royal was to decoy Banks while Jackson's column moved down the Valley Pike to turn east at New Market. In the first full-length study of the campaign, William Allan praised Ashby for just that work, and others continued to award credit there.[7]

If Jackson's written orders to Ewell to take his division to New Market really meant something else (either that Ewell should launch only Taylor's Brigade as a decoy or that he should otherwise retain the bulk of his command in the Luray Valley), if Ewell remained in the Luray Valley, and if Ashby misled Banks by active operations before the march across Massanutten Mountain began on May 21, then the assumption that Stonewall intended his turning march all along would be inescapable. In fact, and as narrated in the text, there is an absence of factual support for any of these themes. Moreover, compelling contemporary documents dispute the venerable view that Jackson always plotted to destroy Banks as he did and suggest a different initial plan. While it perhaps seems improbable for there to be new insight into Jackson's plans so long after the war, such is the case. Because Stonewall's plans remain a source of fascination for many, and to explain the divergence from the standard view of the campaign, facts supporting the new interpretation are offered in detail.

Confederate Orders

In his report of the campaign, Jackson cloaked the time of his decision to attack Front Royal. He merely reported, "We moved from Harrisonburg down the Valley turnpike to New Market, in the vicinity of which a junction was effected with Ewell's division, which had marched from Elk Run Valley. Leaving the Valley turnpike at New Market we moved via Luray toward Front Royal, with the hope of being able to capture or disperse the garrison at the latter place."[8] Fortunately, Jackson's contemporary orders to Ewell reveal his thinking. Indeed, the most persuasive evidence of Jackson's persistent intention to attack Strasburg instead of Front Royal comes from his written instructions.

Every day between May 17 and 20 Jackson expressed in writing his desire for Confederate forces to be encamped between New Market and Mount Jackson by the evening of May 21. The first message was written at 5 A.M. on the seventeenth[9] and asked Ewell to encamp beyond, or north of, New Market by May 21. This was prior to the Mount Solon conference, which was initiated by Ewell's unexpected appearance at Jackson's tent flap. Stonewall could hardly have anticipated an opportunity to explain to Ewell that this order meant anything other than exactly what it stated when he wrote it. In this communication Jackson gave detailed instructions that Branch's command should also move for New Market via Fisher's Gap. He even asked Ewell to scout the possibility of moving his division from Luray to the Valley Pike at Edinburg, which would have involved a trek across some very primitive Massanutten pathways but that would have brought him to the Pike seven miles closer to Strasburg than at Mount Jackson.

Jackson asked Ewell to camp between New Market and Mount Jackson in the letter he handed to Ewell at Mount Solon on the morning of the eighteenth,[10] and he even asked Ewell to be beyond Mount Jackson in a letter of the nineteenth.[11] Finally, as late as 4 P.M. of the twentieth Jackson replied to Ewell's note on the progress of Branch's column that he wished it was in New Market.[12]

That Ewell understood Jackson's orders to be taken at face value is reflected by the instructions he gave to General Branch, to whom he served as liaison for Jackson. Immediately upon returning from the meeting at Mount Solon, Ewell had an aide relay the following to Branch: "I am instructed by Gen'l. Ewell to say that in consequence of conflicting orders he paid a visit to Gen'l. Jackson the result of which is an order to proceed with this Division to New Market, arriving at that place on the 21st (Wednesday). You are requested to move to the same point with your brigade arriving there if possible about the same time."[13]

To ensure there was no confusion, the next morning Ewell wrote again to Branch, explaining to him Campbell Brown's mission to Gordonsville with a telegram for Lee. Ewell made it clear that if Brown communicated orders from Richmond in response to that telegram Branch must be governed by them, then went on to state that in the absence of new orders Branch should continue his march in the direction of New Market. Ewell closed by writing, "Gen'l. Jackson's orders, if not changed by those received by Lt. Brown, require this Division to be between Mount Jackson and New Market on Wednesday night, the 21st."[14]

No one valued secrecy more than did Stonewall, but it is unreasonable to believe that these continued references to a full concentration beyond New Market were a code for anything else. Jackson did not at any other time in the war send repeated orders for movement to a specific point that was not actually intended to be reached. Indeed, such a practice embodied an unacceptable risk of confusing those receiving the "decoy" orders, Branch and Ewell, who had never before operated with Stonewall. Jackson's orders must be taken at face value.

Ewell's Movements

The movements of Ewell's force prior to the actual descent upon Front Royal have been obscure. The reference to the New Market juncture with "Ewell's Division" (not just with Taylor's Brigade) in Jackson's report (quoted above) seems clear enough, although conceivably that reference might describe only the dramatic arrival of Taylor's command. In any event, the newly found diaries and other sources drawn upon in chapter 10 make clear that Old Bald Head did not go down the Luray Valley from Conrad's Store as part of an operation against Front Royal. It is certain he moved on May 15 to Columbia Bridge with the idea of forcing a fight there or wherever he could find Shields. Two days later he was moving his division eastward out of the Shenandoah in response to Johnston's orders. If at Mount Solon it was determined that the Confederates would attack Front Royal, Ewell was in position: he had only to return to Columbia Bridge and march the short distance to Luray. To say that Ewell's movement from Conrad's Store to the vicinity of Luray was part of a planned approach to Front Royal flies in the face of well-settled facts.

Moreover, by his march of the twentieth, Ewell demonstrated he understood that Jackson's orders to concentrate at New Market were literal. It was certainly for this reason that he had his division near New Market by the twentieth and in position to move beyond Mount Jackson the next day. The newly considered material noted in chapter 11 confirms the presence of the majority of Ewell's command near New Market (not in the Luray Valley) on the twentieth.[15] To those sources should be added the diary of Private Joseph Snider of the 31st Virginia, who would have been near the head of Jackson's column as it marched through New Market on May 21. Snider recorded, "We marched through New Market and turned to the right following Gen. Ewell's Division which countermarched back across the Mountain."[16] Another diary from Trimble's Brigade, that of Private Franklin Riley of the 16th Mississippi, also speaks unequivocally of a juncture around New Market on May 20.[17]

That Ewell was both ordered to move his division beyond Mount Jackson and completed most of that march by the twentieth must reflect Jackson's intentions; nor can the march be explained away as an elaborate ruse. To start the march against Front Royal from anywhere north of Mount Jackson would place Ewell in a foolish posture. It would force Ewell to retrace his route over the bridge near Rude's Hill, traverse once again the Massanutten his men had just climbed, and get over the White House bridge. By adding two river crossings, a mountain climb, and many toilsome miles to Ewell's way before he could get back to Luray and even begin to advance toward Front Royal, Jackson would delay a Southern attack by at least a full day. (The same would apply to Branch's Brigade moving to New Market.) In view of that delay it is unlikely Jackson would have plotted to bring Ewell to Mount Jackson to deceive any Federal spies about a Front Royal attack; the time wasted returning Ewell to his starting point near Luray, to say nothing of the extra fatigue, would have been excessive. Time was of the essence in May. The pressure from Richmond to strike quickly was great, and Jackson was not a man to waste an hour.

Jackson's Staff

Two principal staff officers provide powerful circumstantial evidence that Jackson intended to strike Banks at Strasburg. Hotchkiss was dispatched early on May 19, along with Lieutenant Boswell, to reconnoiter Banks's positions around Strasburg and spent several days doing so.[18] No comparable scout is documented around Front Royal, which must explain why Jackson approached the village with limited intelligence on Federal dispositions. Jackson relied heavily on Hotchkiss throughout the campaign. It is unthinkable that the general deprived himself of his invaluable assistant by a scouting mission that had no real purpose while planning at the same time to attack Front Royal without detailed advance investigation. Such a move would merely handicap Jackson in an attack he had long been urged to make, and upon the success of which perhaps depended the fate of Richmond, if not the Confederacy.

A written note from Major Harman is also of importance on this issue. Harman was working on the assumption that the Army would need food for a march along the Valley Pike to Strasburg. On May 20 he wrote his brother of the need for corn for the transport animals. This was all important if the Army's artillery and trains were to keep pace. That day Harman advised that all possible grain "will have to come at least to Mount Jackson."[19] With time running out, there was no point in detouring Harman's trains through Mount Jackson if the target was actually Front Royal. As was true with placing Ewell near Mount Jackson, such a detour would only needlessly exhaust the trains, clog roads, and waste time.

Ashby's Movements

In his campaign report, Jackson summarized Ashby's activities during the approach to Banks thus: "To conceal my movements as far as possible from the enemy, Brigadier-General Ashby, who had remained in front of Banks during the march against Milroy, was directed to continue to hold that position until the following day, when he was to join the main body."[20] This passage comes immediately after a sentence describing the infantry leaving the Valley Pike at New Market for Luray (on May 21), so the entire section seems to define Ashby's mission as essentially defensive (as opposed to an active decoy operation) and as not commencing until May 21. If in fact Jackson did plan before the twenty-first to slip over the Massanutten, then it would have been logical for Ashby to draw Banks's attention to the Valley Pike before that date. Nowhere, however, does Jackson imply Ashby was to decoy Banks by aggressive action before May 21.

That the cavalry's role was passive before the twenty-first is suggested by a newly discovered order from Jackson to Ashby. Major Dabney wrote to Ashby on the seventeenth from Mount Solon (which was reached only toward the end of the day): "Jackson directs me to say that he desires you will continue to hold your position before Gen. Banks, and send all the information you can collect concerning his movements, & Gen. Shields', and their numbers."[21] This mission was completely passive, and while the intelligence Ashby might gain would be helpful, Jackson's failure in this order to even suggest that his cavalry chief make an effort to attract Union attention to his front is inconsistent with the general considering a march toward Front Royal.

Just as the actual movements of Ewell's infantry prior to the evening of May 20 establish that Jackson's orders for Ewell to place himself north of New Market were meant to be read literally—and thus argue against an early plan for attack on Front Royal—so Ashby's known operations before evening of May 20 confirm that Jackson's instructions for him provided a specific mission inconsistent with an attack on Front Royal. The records in fact are silent about any significant Confederate cavalry demonstrations from May 17 to May 20. This is to be expected if Jackson intended to move on Strasburg; given such a goal he would not have wanted Ashby to attract Union attention to the Valley Pike at all.

George Neese recorded no activity for Chew's Battery, which spent the days in question camped near New Market.[22] One young rider recalled light skirmishing below Woodstock on May 18, but his company returned to camp at New Market the next day and began drilling twice a day.[23] Trooper Bill Wilson participated in a seven-man scout below Woodstock on the seventeenth and then returned to New Market on the eighteenth and had time to attend church. The following day he was on picket: "Everything is quiet and I have been amusing myself by perusal of Yankee papers."[24]

During these days Hotchkiss was prowling the area below Mount Jackson on his mission to reconnoiter Banks's lines. It is hard to imagine that he could have done his job in the midst of a constant firefight, and in fact Hotchkiss recorded no combat on the nineteenth or twentieth. Indeed, Hotchkiss may have best described the role of Ashby's cavalry in a handwritten summary of the Valley Campaign. The document seems to be an amplification of his diary and states for May 20: "Ashby held closely the line of Stony Creek [which Hotchkiss had identified in April as a good defensive position]. . . . I went by myself and reconnoitred on the Middle and Back roads, finding the enemy quiet, tho' he drives in our pickets almost daily."[25]

In the absence of any reliable source to confirm heavy skirmishing before May 21 (in truth there is no reference to active deceptions on the twenty-first or twenty-second) it seems probable that Ashby was doing just what Hotchkiss describes: holding the Stony Creek line against Federal probing and doing nothing to attract Federal attention to that point or otherwise alert them to any possibility of an impending march toward Strasburg.

Jackson's Correspondence of May 17

Jackson's letter to Johnston of May 17 from Mount Solon explained that his intention "was to try and defeat Banks, and then, by threatening Frémont's rear, prevent him from advancing up the South Branch."[26] Although that would seem to imply an attack near Strasburg, it is not incompatible with an attack via Front Royal. But Jackson's other letters of the same date, read with the message to Johnston, strongly dispute that Jackson then had in mind a march via Front Royal. It was on that day he first notified Ewell to move his division to the vicinity of New Market and instructed Ashby just to hold his position and gather information on Banks's numbers. Those three messages come as close as the secretive Jackson will allow us to knowing his plans, and those plans point toward Strasburg.

Nor was Strasburg an unattractive target; there was in fact something to be said for it as a point of attack, while the drive through Front Royal posed difficulties fully as large as attacking fortifications. There was no reason for Jackson to assume that the Federals at Front Royal would not also be fortifying, and in any event neither side in this war had yet experienced the awful price to be paid for assaulting well-fortified infantry. If Banks could be pried out of his works at Strasburg his flight along the Valley Pike could be hounded immediately, solving the problem of finding the enemy army, which slowed Southern operations from Front Royal on the twenty-fourth (see Appendix B). And Hotchkiss's scout of back roads around Strasburg suggests that Jackson probably included some wide-turning maneuver as part of an attack on Strasburg.

On the other hand, and as chapter 12 describes, an attack on Front Royal against even inferior numbers was not a walkover. Just getting into and out of the village could not be taken for granted. The approach to Front Royal along the South Fork River road, which Jackson fortunately was able to sidestep at the last minute, offered an excellent blocking position from which a small Union force might have delayed a much larger attacker. Bridges across both Shenandoah forks had to be captured to permit a drive anywhere in the lower Shenandoah. Without those bridges crucial time would be lost with repairs or fording; it might even allow Banks time to shift forces to oppose the crossing, one thing Jackson really needed to avoid. Stonewall could well have concluded before he was forced to adopt it that a drive via Front Royal was not the preferred approach to Banks.

Ewell's Headquarters

One final source of support exists for the reconstruction offered herein and it springs, logically enough, from Ewell's Headquarters. In a narrative apparently written after the war, and little known until recently, Campbell Brown bluntly stated what has been laboriously reconstructed herein: "On the 20th Jackson returned to the Valley, & the 'Valley Campaign' began. Gen. Jackson came to Harrisonburg, and his original intention was that Ewell should join him at New Market & both move to attack Banks at Strasburg. But in his absence Ewell had carefully scouted toward Front Royal . . . & become certain that only a small force held it. This he told Jackson who immediately concluded to move on Front Royal."[27] Brown was probably not in the Valley on May 20th—a letter written by him to his mother is dated "Gordonsville, May 21st"[28]—so he likely related subsequent information given him by Ewell.

There is support for Brown's version in an undated fragment of a history of the Valley Campaign penned by Ewell. Parts of this rough document have been lost, but the middle section, dealing with operations near Winchester, has survived. Ewell wrote of the period around May 20: "some of my command was on the march for Gordonsville when I received conflicting orders from Genl. Jackson & halting those troops already in motion rode all night to Mt Solon & was directed to retake my position on [above this he adds the word 'near'] Luray and be ready to follow the enemy."[29] The uncertainty whether Jackson wanted him "on" or "near" Luray establishes that this document was not Ewell's final word; it was obviously the first draft of an uncompleted effort. The quoted passage could be read as indicating that Ewell always was to move on Front Royal, since that would be, in a general sense, "following" Shields, who had marched that way. Equally plausible is an interpretation that Ewell recollected Jackson wanted him near Luray, that is, at New Market, and that from there they were to follow Banks, who had moved to Strasburg when Shields went to Front Royal. This is the view accepted herein.

Conclusion

Taken together, there is ample evidence both direct and circumstantial that Jackson intended until at least the evening of May 20 to strike Banks near Strasburg, while there is virtually nothing to prove that he had decided upon Front Royal as a target before that time. A spate of communications from higher command, including Johnston's warning against attacking fortifications, apparently forced Jackson to rethink this offensive, which doubtless explains why he started off toward Front Royal with so little knowledge of what awaited there. Warriors from the Caesers to the Gulf War would recognize this experience; great soldiers have responded by doing as Jackson did, scrambling to find a new way to complete their missions. While it would have been a master stroke had Jackson always intended the offensive as it ultimately was delivered, it speaks equally well of him that he reacted to the evolving situation and drove home a successful attack after he was forced to alter his plans on short notice.

APPENDIX B

JACKSON'S PLANS AND MARCHES, MAY 24, 1862

Jackson's intentions and actual movements on May 24, 1862, have been a persistent source of confusion, and the major recountings of this day have compounded the uncertainty. The account offered in chapter 12 disputes all previous accounts and therefore requires detailed explanation.

Previous Accounts

Jackson's report of the Valley Campaign was prepared during the winter of 1862–63, and it reflected the long lapse between the events and their chronicling. The preliminary draft was written for Jackson by Colonel Charles J. Faulkner, who was not with the general during the campaign, and recollections conflicted among those Faulkner interviewed even at this comparatively early date.[1] Jackson edited out many of Faulkner's clarifying explanations, lest the enemy "learn [our] mode of doing."[2] The report, therefore, was not intended to be a completely reliable history, but it can be read as if Jackson planned, during the night of May 23–24, to proceed directly from Front Royal to Middletown the following morning. The reported stated:

> I determined with the main body of the army, to strike the turnpike near Middletown, a village 5 miles north of Strasburg and 13 miles south of Winchester.
>
> Accordingly, the following morning General Ashby advanced from Cedarville toward Middletown, supported by skirmishers from Taylor's brigade.[3]

Dabney in 1866, William Allan in 1880, and Colonel G. F. R. Henderson in 1898 each accepted the report on its face and asserted that Jackson moved directly from Front Royal to Middletown. By doing so, these authors were compelled to provide excuses for the fact that the Army did not reach the village until afternoon, though the distance from Front Royal was only ten miles. Henderson, for example, stressed rough terrain and enemy delaying tactics as reasons for the Army's supposed slowness.[4] But such factors, while certainly to be considered, fail to justify a pace of barely a mile and a half per hour.

In an incisive appendix to his 1942 *Lee's Lieutenants,* D. S. Freeman probed this matter and challenged the view that Jackson initially planned to advance toward the Valley Pike at Middletown. In essence, Freeman's argument was as follows: The initial Confederate march of May 24 led north from Front Royal, past the road from Cedarville to Middletown, and on to Ninevah; this is known from Hotchkiss's reliable diary and from Ewell's report. Such a march was pointless and a serious waste of time if Stonewall intended to strike Banks at Middletown. What was more likely, according to Freeman, was that Jackson contemplated a move to Winchester along the Front Royal road, but, as he neared Ninevah still without word of Banks's location, he grew fearful the enemy would dash for Front Royal. This fear was such that, without additional information, Jackson halted and soon countermarched to Middletown.[5] (The present account suggests Jackson began the day without a definite plan but with a preference to follow the Front Royal road to Winchester—perhaps only a difference in degree from Freeman—and that Jackson began his Middletown thrust *after* locating Banks—a major difference from Freeman.[6])

Freeman's analysis was an important step away from the idea that Jackson lunged directly at Middletown on the twenty-fourth. It also helped to explain why the Army took so long to reach the Valley Pike. But Freeman relied almost exclusively upon Hotchkiss's diary for his account, and this perhaps led him to overlook other evidence that, if analyzed in conjunction with the Hotchkiss diary, would have brought the operations of May 24 into even sharper focus. This evidence concerns the Valley Army's midmorning halt between Ninevah and Cedarville. When the duration of this halt is understood, a detailed timetable of the day's events becomes possible.

The Halt North of Cedarville

This halt is well documented. In his report (dated June 4, 1862) Ewell wrote that the head of his column was stopped by Jackson eight miles north of Front Royal; this placed it around Ninevah.[7] Colonel Ronald of the 4th Virginia wrote (June 4, 1862): "Arriving at the Forks of the road [Cedarville] the brigade was halted for several hours."[8] Colonel Neff of the 33d Virginia implied a lengthy halt, writing (June 4, 1862): "Moved from bivouac at 8 A.M. and marched with the brigade on the Winchester road about three miles, where we halted. About 12 n. we again moved, taking the Middletown road."[9] Hotchkiss noted in his diary that he accompanied the van of the Army to Ninevah, then returned with Jackson to Cedarville, "going by the troops which were halted." Hotchkiss then recorded that Jackson sent him to reconnoiter the Cedarville-Middletown road.[10] A letter dated May 26, 1862, from Hotchkiss to his wife has also survived, and by relating it to the diary it is possible to time the beginning of Hotchkiss's reconnaissance at after 11 A.M. In the letter Hotchkiss wrote that "shortly after 11 A.M." he was sent on the reconnaissance, found the enemy, and alerted Jackson, who thereupon started the Army westward.[11] The time occupied by these events could hardly have been under an hour. Thus the Hotchkiss material also demonstrates that the Army started toward Middletown about noon and after a halt.

John Apperson, a careful diarist with the Stonewall Brigade, recorded on May 24 that the brigade was detained three miles from Front Royal for three or four hours.[12] "W.W.H.," an otherwise unidentified soldier whose generally accurate narrative of the campaign was written on May 25 and published in the Lynchburg *Republican* of May 31, described a halt lasting several hours before moving on Middletown.[13] Jim Hall of the 31st Virginia, Elzey's Brigade, noted in his diary, "Marched a mile or two along the road and halted to await orders. . . . About 2 o'clock we started at a brisk pace for Middletown."[14] (Hall's estimate of the hour at which Elzey marched west was too early, but a lengthy halt is clear from his diary.)

General Trimble, who led Ewell's Division to Ninevah, left additional documentation of the midmorning halt. In a postwar letter to author William Allan, Trimble noted that his advance was halted, on Jackson's orders, at 8 A.M.[15] With Trimble breaking ranks at 8 A.M., units marching behind him, some of which only departed Front Royal at that hour, would have been catching up and halting at 10 A.M., just as many rebels affirm.

To recapitulate: seven individuals ranging in rank from brigadier general to private (six of them writing either on or shortly after May 24) agree that a halt of one to four hours, depending upon the writer's position in the column, occurred north of Cedarville. These reports accepted, it is reasonable to accept further that the halt was made in order to ascertain Banks's whereabouts; Jackson hardly would have been sitting still had he known where Banks was fleeing. Finally, allowing for the hours lost at Cedarville makes possible the following timetable of the events of May 24:

6 A.M.	Ewell moved north from Front Royal on the Road to Winchester (Ewell's report).
8 A.M.	Ewell's van, Trimble's Brigade, reached a point eight miles from Front Royal and halted (Ewell's report; Trimble's letter). The brigades of Jackson's command began to follow Ewell's rear brigades out of Front Royal (Winder's, Campbell's, and Fulkerson's reports).
9 A.M.	Ewell's rear brigades began to halt behind Trimble (Hall's diary). Winder's Brigade neared Cedarville; Campbell's and Taliaferro's brigades were behind it (positions computed by allowing a conservative march rate of two miles per hour over the known distances).
9–10 A.M.	Banks began to evacuate Strasburg for Winchester (Banks's report).
10 A.M.	Jackson, still lacking word of Banks's movements, ordered the brigades of his division to halt as they reached Cedarville (Ronald's and Neff's reports; Apperson's diary).
10–12 A.M.	The Army closed up, until the rear was at Cedarville and the entire force was halted (Hotchkiss's diary).
10–11 A.M.	Steuart intercepted the Valley Pike around Newtown, swept south, threw enemy trains into a panic, and sent word of this to Jackson. (Captain Samuel Zulich, 29th Pennsylvania, who was stationed at Middletown that morning, reported, "At 11 A.M. an excitement was

	created among the teamsters by an advance of enemy cavalry from Newtown."[16] For the effect of Steuart's raid to have spread the four miles from Newtown to Middletown by 11 A.M., Steuart obviously had to arrive at the former point sometime before 11 A.M.; 10 A.M. was the earliest reasonable time of Steuart's arrival.)
11–11:30 A.M.	Jackson received work of Steuart's attack and sent Hotchkiss toward Middletown to search for enemy pickets (Hotchkiss's letter).
11:30 A.M.–12:30 P.M.	Hotchkiss found enemy pickets one and a half miles west of Cedarville and informed Jackson, who started the Army westward (Hotchkiss's letter; Neff's report). Federal vedettes on the Cedarville-Middletown road began skirmishing with advancing rebels. (In his report Colonel C. S. Douty, 1st Marine Cavalry, wrote, "At about 12 o'clock . . . the most advanced vedettes came in and reported the enemy's cavalry and infantry advancing. . . . After a delay of half an hour the enemy opened on us with artillery, throwing shell into my column. I drew off my force and proceeded slowly to Middletown.")[17]
12:00 or 12:30 P.M.–3:00 or 3:30 P.M.	The Valley Army marched to Middletown.
3:30–4:00 P.M.	The Confederates attacked at Middletown (Jackson's message to Ewell in *OR,* vol. 51, pt. 2, p. 562).

Considering the countermarch of some units to Cedarville, rain, a poor road, enemy delaying tactics—which caused frequent halts—and exhaustion in the ranks, the Valley Army's march of six or seven miles from Cedarville to Middletown in roughly three hours was a respectable feat, and, given the timetable offered above, there is no reason to fault the Army for slowness in reaching Middletown.

Contrary Evidence

Two Union officers reported that the main Confederate attack at Middletown occurred between noon and 2 P.M. An attack at this time would refute the timetable offered here; however, there are serious inconsistencies in both of these officers' reports.

Colonel G. H. Gordon, who commanded one of Banks's brigades on the trek from Strasburg, stated that soon after passing Newtown, at approximately 2 P.M., he heard artillery rumbling behind him and learned that the Union column had been pierced at Middletown. Gordon immediately countermarched to aid the rear guard.[18] To have been even one mile beyond Newtown at 2 P.M. Gordon, who evacuated Strasburg at 10 A.M.,[19] would have had to cover ten miles in four hours. This was possible on the Valley Pike, but it was unlikely Gordon maintained such a pace, since his brigade trailed an immense train of wagons. Gordon also halted for reconnaissance around Middletown, which cost more time. Further, Gordon certainly was more than only one mile behind Newtown when he heard the Middletown news. One of Gordon's regimental commanders, Colonel George Andrews, reported that he was within five miles of Winchester when Gordon ordered him to countermarch.[20] Gordon's Brigade probably traveled as a unit, so Andrews's report located it thirteen miles north of Strasburg, or four miles north of Newtown, when it about-faced. In an 1863 monograph Gordon corroborated Andrews's statement,[21] and it can confidently be asserted that the brigade was roughly thirteen miles north of Strasburg when news of trouble at Middletown was received. If that news was received at 2 P.M., Gordon had hurtled thirteen miles in four hours, an almost impossible feat given the conditions under which the Federals were retreating. (One Union regiment, the 29th Pennsylvania, required eight hours to cover thirteen miles from Middletown to Winchester on May 24.)[22] It thus is doubtful that Gordon had reached the point where he learned of the Middletown attack by 2 P.M., although he could have reached it about 4 P.M.

Gordon's report is suspect in another way, for it leaves several hours unaccounted for. Assume Gordon did learn of the Middletown struggle at 2 P.M. and took two hours to reoccupy Newtown,[23] arriving about 4 P.M. Upon arrival Gordon reported sighting rebel artillery south of town and attacking at once. A skirmish of one "hour or more" followed. But at the conclusion of this combat, Gordon gave the time as 8 P.M.[24] His report thus contains a major gap, a gap eliminated with the assumption that Gordon received word of the Middletown trouble at 4 P.M., if not later.

In a personal letter dated May 29, 1862, Lieutenant C. F. Morse of Gordon's Brigade supported the contention that the brigade was ordered back toward Newtown after 4 P.M. Morse wrote that the time from the first shots of the brigade's skirmish at Newtown until a point "just as it began to get dark"[25] was about two hours. Assume Morse's regiment countermarched at 2 P.M., took even two hours to complete the march to Newtown, and fought there for two more hours. This covers the day until only 6 P.M., hardly twilight time in late May. The problem, however, is resolved by beginning Morse's countermarch at 4 P.M.

Gordon was not at Middletown when the main Confederate attack surged over it. Major William P. Collins, 1st Vermont Cavalry, was there and set the time of this attack as between noon and 1 P.M.[26] In fact, there was a skirmish near Middletown during the late morning or early afternoon; on this fact most Federal sources concur. Three lines of evidence, however, refute Collins's assertion that this attack was delivered by the main Southern column.

First, if the main Confederate attack came during the early afternoon, we would be compelled to believe the tussle at Middletown lasted two or three hours, until 4 P.M., when Jackson informed Ewell that the enemy had begun to retreat northward. Given Federal panic and superior Confederate numbers, a contest of more than thirty minutes is inconceivable. Nor is it logical to think Jackson shattered the enemy column in the early afternoon and waited until 4 P.M. to inform Ewell that the enemy was retreating northward in his direction.

Second, the report of Colonel Douty, Collins's commanding officer, contradicts Collins. Collins reported that he spent the day with or near Douty's command. Douty, in his official statement, positioned his command at least four miles *east* of Middletown between noon and 1 P.M. and wrote that he fell back slowly from this position as the rebels advanced.[27] To have been with Douty at noon, Collins could not have been around Middletown.

Third, the weight of Federal evidence denies a determined attack on the Pike at noon. No other Union officer suggested that the raid that did occur then was serious. None reported Confederate artillery present at this time, and all agreed the rebels were brushed aside easily. Finally, no report credited this early foray with the great destruction and panic known to have accompanied the main attack.[28]

In summary, sources that accelerate to 2 P.M., or earlier, the hour of the principal fight at Middletown must be ruled in error, and the brief fight that did occur then must be attributed to some portion of Steuart's cavalry as it swept south from Newtown. To do otherwise ignores a larger body of evidence, from both armies, which sets the attack between 3 and 4 P.M. To ignore such evidence merely returns the operation of May 24 to a state of confusion.

Lenoir Chambers, in his excellent biography of Jackson, suggested that Freeman's appendix study of Confederate movements on May 24, persuasive at it was, failed to explain (1) why Jackson did not mention the crucial events of the day's early hours in his official report; (2) why Jackson, who wished to "deal effectively" with Banks, "changed his mind" (Chambers's words) after reaching Front Royal and decided to march for Winchester instead of Strasburg; and (3) how he would have dared to march toward Winchester on the morning of May 24 knowing that it exposed his flank and rear to Banks at Strasburg.[29]

The present account is subject to the same questions and cannot offer definitive answers. Such answers, resting with a man long dead, probably will never be known. Of the first question, it can only be repeated that Jackson's report was drafted for him by an aide who did not witness the campaign. Further, this report was purposely edited to conceal reasons for major maneuvers. The implication of the second question (that by marching on Winchester instead of Strasburg Jackson had somehow abandoned his intention to deal effectively with Banks) may be argued: nothing indicates Jackson thought that moving directly on Winchester from Front Royal would not deal effectively with Banks, and thus nothing establishes that he changed his mind. Vast stores had accumulated at Winchester, and Banks was known to be cautious. It was reasonable for Jackson to believe that by descending on Winchester directly he could flush Banks into the open and deal effectively with him. Concerning Chambers's third question, it should be noted that no matter what he did, Jackson could hardly avoid offering Banks his flank on May 24. If the Valley Army had closed on Strasburg by a route north of the Shenandoah's North Fork while Banks was retreating toward Winchester, the Confederates would have been inviting Banks to about-face and strike their right. Jackson could have countered this threat by moving on Strasburg south of the North Fork, via the main Front Royal–Strasburg road, but this route would have required him to cross that stream near Strasburg, seriously hampering the Army if Banks were found there. By the same token, an advance from Cedarville to Middletown potentially opened the Southern left flank to a stab from Strasburg or, if Banks had passed Middletown, opened the right flank to a stab from the north. It can be argued that Banks probably would not have interrupted his retreat from Strasburg to attack the rebels, but this was equally true in the case of Confederates moving directly on Winchester from Front Royal. Finally, it should be recalled that Jackson knew Banks was well entrenched at Strasburg, and Jackson may have calculated that any risk he took of exposing his flank to Banks was preferable to attacking those fortifications.

Steuart's Raid and Jackson's Start for Middletown

A final disagreement with Freeman arises over his view that Jackson started to Middletown without positive knowledge of Banks's location because of a growing fear that Banks would dash from Strasburg to Front Royal. According to Freeman, by hurrying to Middletown Jackson achieved the best position to deal with this possibility, as well as with the possibility that Banks would flee to Winchester.[30] This was a strange contention. Had he ventured to Middletown "blind" and discovered there that Banks had made a dash for Front Royal, Jackson would have confronted three unfavorable courses. First, he could have trekked back to Cedarville, united with the brigades under Ewell, moved south to Front Royal, and possibly not have been able to cross the North Fork because Banks already had occupied the area and burned the highway bridge (a possibility Freeman admitted). Second, Jackson could have marched sixteen miles via Strasburg to Front Royal with less than half his army. Third, he could have waited for Ewell to reinforce him at Middletown and then marched via Strasburg after losing much time. The two last choices avoided the necessity of crossing the North Fork near Front Royal. Nevertheless, the South Fork remained to be crossed at Front Royal, as it would in the first alterative (upon which Freeman made no comment). If Banks destroyed the bridges over this stream, and it was logical to assume he would, Jackson would have had to cross by fords. Valley streams were high from recent heavy rains, and fording them would have consumed many hours. Additionally, the Federals could have taken superb positions from which to retard the rebels once they entered Manassas Gap. Jackson doubtless considered these contingencies. Given the importance of preventing Banks's escape to the east (and the danger such an escape posed to Confederate wagon trains packed around Front Royal on May 24), it was unlikely that Jackson burdened himself with the unfavorable options he might have faced by starting to Middletown without word of Banks's direction of march.

With the present timetable, it seems probable that the information Stonewall needed so desperately reached him about 11 A.M. Assume that General Steuart, in execution of the mission Jackson gave him to cut the Pike at Newtown, moved from Front Royal at 6 A.M. Steuart would have needed to move only approximately three miles per hour to sight Newtown at 10 A.M., not a strenuous pace for cavalry on an important reconnaissance. Steuart's courier, dispatched about 10 A.M., could have reached Jackson by 11 A.M. and no later than noon, early enough to prompt, and certainly to confirm, Hotchkiss's discovery that enemy pickets lay west of Cedarville. Jackson's report cited a dispatch from Steuart that indicated Banks was preparing to evacuate Strasburg.[31] As only this dispatch was recalled many months after the event, its information was doubtless significant.

Hotchkiss bolstered the view that Steuart's news was the decisive factor of the start to Middletown when he wrote, in a postwar journal: "after the position of the enemy had been ascertained by an advance of cavalry on the Newtown road . . . General Jackson sent Col. Ashby with some artillery and cavalry to aid the small force [presumably Hotchkiss's initial scouting party] that went toward Middletown."[32] Jackson very much desired the intelligence this passage asserted he had received. Jackson took risks, but not the kind of risk inherent in throwing less than half his army toward Middletown without a strong indication Banks would be found there.

APPENDIX C

Three Days of Running Battle: The Union Response

This study has stressed, by design, the Southern viewpoint, a more compelling story than that of the fumbling campaign mounted by the Valley Army's opponents. For this very reason, the Army's deliverance through Strasburg on June 1 has a leaden, unsatisfying ring. Viewed from rebel ranks, Federal divisions remained strangely passive during the critical period from May 30 to June 1. This inactivity cannot be fully explained by anything the rebels did. Jackson pushed his marchers hard; Ashby executed a brilliant diversion on May 31; Ewell handled Frémont well on June 1. Yet these efforts could not retrieve the fact that, at noon on May 30, the Valley Army was demonstrating before Harpers Ferry, while Shields was mopping up Front Royal and Frémont was barely thirty miles west of the Valley Pike at Strasburg. Umpires judging such a situation during peacetime maneuvers would have declared the Army eliminated—yet it escaped. How? The answer requires investigation into the details of Union movements not attempted by those who have studied the Valley Campaign from the Northern viewpoint.[1]

Lincoln's Plan: May 24–27

In its most important respect, Lincoln's decision to hurl McDowell into the Valley was a colossal blunder. Even total success there would have been purchased at the prohibitive price of delaying a final battle at Richmond, of stranding McClellan in an awkward position on the Peninsula, and of granting Johnston much-needed time to concentrate additional strength against the Army of the Potomac. Johnston did, in fact, use the time allowed him by McDowell's diversion to effect such a concentration. He massed the bulk of his army against McClellan's southern wing and hit it very hard on May 31.

But in other respects Lincoln evidenced much ability with his plan to trap the Valley Army. Viewed at the operational level of war, Lincoln's design was reasonable. Federal columns targeted the undefended Confederate rear. Frémont was to plug the principal Confederate escape route by occupying the Harrisonburg area. McDowell was to reach the Valley by a march along the Manassas Gap Railroad or in "advance" (presumably Lincoln meant south) of it.[2] What became a pincer movement began as something much simpler. Frémont was to harass the deep Southern rear; McDowell was to deliver the knockout blow as opportunity offered.

Nor was Lincoln's plan based upon Jackson's tarrying in the lower Valley. Lincoln could read a map and see that if Jackson retired from Winchester on May 25 or 26, neither Frémont nor McDowell could be there to follow him, but this made little difference. Frémont was closer to Harrisonburg than Jackson. Had the rebels begun a withdrawal into the upper Valley on May 26, Frémont still should have been able to beat them there and fight a delaying action until McDowell arrived. Further, the plan had the advantage that every day Jackson lingered around Winchester brought McDowell closer, swelled Banks's forces on the Potomac, and gave Frémont additional opportunity to do serious damage in Jackson's rear. Every day Jackson remained in the lower Valley made Lincoln's plan a better one. By dawn of May 31, had others not meddled with it, this plan would have borne excellent results: compact Northern forces would have held Front Royal, while Frémont would have stood solidly athwart the Valley Pike.

Unfortunately, Frémont meddled with the plan, deciding on his own initiative to ignore Lincoln's directive to operate against Jackson at Harrisonburg and to proceed instead through the Alleghenies to Strasburg. This decision was based on four factors: (1) Jackson had blocked the passes between Franklin and Harrisonburg, except one that necessitated a long detour; (2) occupation of Harrisonburg would open an escape corridor through the Alleghenies along the road from Moorefield to McDowell; (3) Frémont's communications were vulnerable if Jackson entered that corridor; and (4) only by moving through the Alleghenies could he secure adequate rations for his army.[3] These reasons provide a controversy in themselves. Beyond the question of whether Frémont was correct to enter the Valley via Strasburg, his decision had one sure result: it eliminated the flexibility Lincoln originally provided.

Frémont, however, was not the only culprit. Apparently writing without Lincoln's knowledge, Secretary of War Stanton advised Frémont on May 25 that he was to fall "upon the enemy at whatever place you can find him with all speed."[4] Without a genuine Union chain of command, Frémont could accept Stanton's message as clarification of the president's order, clarification that allowed him discretion to select his road into the Valley. Frémont read it that way and trudged northward as one arm of a pincer no one at Washington knew was under way.

Next, Stanton shackled what would become the pincer's other arm. On May 25 he required two of the three brigades of Ord's Division, which McDowell had scheduled to march for the Valley on May 26, to forgo the direct road through Manassas and to come first to Alexandria by steamer.[5] His idea was to give Washington extra protection by funneling Shenandoah-bound troops through its environs, but the result was to interfere seriously with Lincoln's plan. (Ultimately, the lack of a single commander directing all Union efforts did more than anything else to defeat those efforts.) Stanton had compelled improvisation of a land-sea-rail movement, and the Union lacked logistical talent to carry that off without notice. An unexpected night march from Fredericksburg to the docks at Aquia broke up some of Ord's regiments, which wandered onto the wharves in groups of three or four.[6] The Union Navy was caught unprepared. The steamers it had available could not reach Aquia's shallow wharves, so precious hours were lost lightering the soldiers aboard.[7] Debarked at Alexandria, Ord's brigades faced a lurching trip over clogged railroads to Manassas. The recently captured Confederate rails also were overwhelmed by the freshet of blue-clad soldiers; McDowell experienced something of the problem when he journeyed from Alexandria to Manassas and lost valuable time while bleary-eyed dispatchers tried to clear the track for him.[8] Worse, the navy scrambled Ord's supply and baggage wagons, which left him completely dependent on the jammed railroads.[9] As late as May 28 Ord was assembling his regiments at Manassas.[10]

In contrast, by moving directly from Fredericksburg through Manassas, Shields cleared the latter point and was probing westward along the Manassas Gap Railroad by May 28. His advance was west of Thoroughfare Gap that afternoon, and he had three brigades in supporting range of it.[11] Had Ord, whose men initially were fresher than Shields's, not been detoured through Alexandria, he could have stayed up with Shields. As it was, his division lagged many hours behind Shields. Those hours, lost to pacify Stanton, were among the most costly ever sacrificed by the Union and completed the disruption of Lincoln's plan by deranging McDowell's orderly redeployment to the Shenandoah.

A New Plan: May 28–29

With Frémont moving on Strasburg there was need for someone to coordinate his operations with those of McDowell, a need not immediately recognized. Before May 29 Frémont and McDowell were each given one sentence on the other's progress. On May 27 Frémont was informed, "General McDowell has a strong force concentrated at Manassas to pursue the enemy and cut off his retreat, if he can be overtaken."[12] Lincoln casually wrote to McDowell on May 28, "By the way, I suppose you know Frémont has got up to Moorefield, instead of going to Harrisonburg."[13] Each commander was briefed only that the other was on the march, hardly adequate orchestration for a pincer movement involving forty thousand men.

These minimal communications are explainable in part by the fact that Lincoln and Stanton knew little of Frémont's whereabouts. Lincoln did not learn until May 27 that Frémont was en route to Strasburg.[14] At 1 P.M. the next day the president instructed him to stop at Moorefield and await orders.[15] It happened that Frémont was ten miles east of Moorefield when this order was received, and, stung by an implied presidential rebuke for bypassing Harrisonburg, he responded literally. He promised to turn around and march back to Moorefield the next morning.[16] The president then was too disgusted to reply. Stanton relayed Lincoln's instructions: Jackson was somewhere between Winchester and Martinsburg; Frémont was to move against him without delay.[17] Positive though these orders were, they contained no hint of concerted action with McDowell.

Stanton's message of May 28 required Frémont to acknowledge. Not uncharacteristically, Frémont's acknowledgment—"The President's order will be obeyed as promptly as possible"[18]—masked his inaction the next day. His army remained in camp on May 29. To be sure, it needed a rest. Frémont's medical director had made a written plea for one day's halt. Stragglers numbered in the thousands; morale was abysmal; artillery and wagon teams were starving.[19] Nevertheless, Frémont knew the enemy was before him, and he had been enjoined by Stanton as early as May 25: "You must not stop for supplies, but seize what you need and push rapidly forward."[20] Had Frémont pushed forward even slowly on the twenty-ninth, had he covered only six or seven miles, he probably could have slipped athwart the Valley Pike ahead of Jackson. As with the circuit Stanton arranged for Ord, Frémont's halt on May 29 squandered irretrievable hours.

That halt bordered on insubordination after the receipt of new, urgent, and peremptory orders from Lincoln. About noon of May 29 the president grasped the obvious. Shields was moving in the direction of Front Royal, and Frémont supposedly was nearing Strasburg, while Jackson was loitering outside Harpers Ferry. Lincoln suddenly realized that he might close both halves of the Shenandoah under the best possible circumstances, no enemy forces between the tips of his armies. The president moved to accelerate the pincer movement he had discovered. He wrote to Frémont: "General McDowell's advance, if not checked by the enemy, should, and probably will, be at Front Royal at 12 (noon) to-morrow. His force, when up, will be about 20,000. Please have your force at Strasburg, or, if the route you are moving on does not lead to that point, as near Strasburg as the enemy may be by the same time."[21]

As Lincoln indicated, Shields was making excellent progress despite problems similar to Frémont's. His men were tired, forage was scarce, and the Manassas Gap Railroad was blocked,[22] but Shields kept coming with supreme confidence. He half seriously advised McDowell to keep Ord at Manassas, claiming his own division could thrash all the rebels in the Valley.[23] At dawn of May 29 Shields's advance brigades were at Rectortown, twenty miles from Front Royal.[24] During the day a supply train jumped the track in Thoroughfare Gap, and Shields feared he would lose twenty-four hours as a result. But shown a telegram from the president urging speed, Shields promised to march through the night with only what supplies his men could carry.[25]

So Shields kept driving, and the gap between him and Ord kept getting wider. Ord was still in the vicinity of Manassas by sunrise of May 29.[26] To complicate matters, McDowell had received intelligence on May 28 that the rebels who had confronted him at Fredericksburg had slipped westward to join Jackson.[27] This rumor never quite died during the Valley Army's operations in the lower Shenandoah, and now McDowell, who had doubted it a few days earlier, feared it might hold some truth. On the twenty-eighth and twenty-ninth he started Bayard's cavalry brigade and Brigadier General Rufus King's infantry division from Fredericksburg to the Valley.[28] These units were, of course, farther behind Shields than Ord, so that McDowell's column was strung out badly. The position of Bayard's Brigade, which only reached Catlett's Station on May 29, was especially bad: Shields was grumbling that very day about his want of cavalry.[29]

Nevertheless, McDowell's forces were approaching the Valley, and Lincoln sent McDowell his pincer plan during the afternoon of May 29: "General Frémont's force should, and probably will, be at or near Strasburg by 12 (noon) to-morrow. Try to have your force or the advance of it at Front Royal as soon."[30] Lincoln dispatched identical information to Banks and Saxton and told them to pursue if Jackson withdrew from the Potomac.[31]

These dispatches were Lincoln's outstanding contribution to the pincer maneuver. He had coordinated his forces to the extent that four separate detachments had orders to strike specific targets in the lower Valley. More important, Frémont and McDowell knew (1) approximately where the other was supposed to be; (2) the point toward which the other was moving; and (3) the other's estimated time of arrival. This information was distorted by Frémont's failure to march on May 29, but this was a small matter compared with Jackson's troubles. Throughout May 29 he hammered at Harpers Ferry, farther than Frémont or Shields from his escape route. Stanton gave this news to both Frémont and McDowell at 11:30 P.M. on May 29,[32] supplementing the information of each with the exact enemy location. Despite meddling, despite a disorganized command structure, despite futile delay, Lincoln had thousands of men converging from superior positions. The situation was becoming, in the commander in chief's oft-quoted phrase, "a question of legs."[33]

Failure: May 30–June 1

May 30

The day began unbelievably well. Shields's advance capped a strenuous night march by storming Front Royal at 11 A.M., one hour ahead of schedule. Thunderstruck rebels abandoned the highway bridges over the

North and South forks and left them intact, throwing the roads to Strasburg and to Winchester open to the enemy. Shields's rear brigades arrived at Front Royal before midnight.

Shields now estimated Jackson's strength at approximately twenty thousand and pondered a rumor of powerful Confederate reinforcements from Richmond approaching Front Royal. Forgetting the boast that his division could clear the Valley unaided, Shields telegraphed McDowell to hurry Ord's and King's divisions to him. He added, "Frémont has not yet reached Strasburg, and I fear that he will not reach it in time."[34]

Frémont, in fact, had already awarded himself extra time. During the afternoon of May 30 Lincoln received a letter from Frémont dated the twenty-ninth. Frémont attempted to put a good face on his halt of that day with a promise that he would reach Strasburg at 5 P.M. of the thirty-first.[35] This was the worst possible news, and Lincoln pleaded, "You must be up to time you promised, if possible."[36]

Shields read such words and staggered on; Frémont seemed indifferent. His efforts on May 30 are a mystery. It is known that he camped ten miles east of Moorefield on the twenty-ninth. He later reported that only on the thirty-first did he pass "the mountain between Lost River and Cedar Creek,"[37] a point roughly twenty miles east of Moorefield, indicating that he lumbered a mere ten miles on the thirtieth. Frémont offered excuses for this mediocre performance, which he fancied novel to his army: rain, mud, and fatigue.[38]

Lincoln, growing worried, noted Frémont's delay to McDowell and authorized him to act accordingly.[39] Unfortunately, the precious discretion the president gave had already been curtailed by the secretary of war. Ord's Division was exhausted by Stanton's worthless detour through Alexandria. McDowell came to herd Ord forward and found chaos. He wrote Stanton, "This place [Rectortown] is filled with stragglers and broken-down men from every brigade." Ord's Division was, as McDowell described it, "in much confusion," and its van was only five miles west of Rectortown at noon of May 30. Its rear brigade was still east of Rectortown. Ord had collapsed under the pressure and surrendered command to Brigadier General James Ricketts. Bayard's cavalry also was out of range; it did not reach Rectortown until after dark.[40]

Nevertheless, on balance, the day's events did not augur ill for the Union. Shields had done everything planned and wanted more work. Frémont and Ord had managed less, yet had achieved better positions than

Jackson, whose army stretched from Harpers Ferry to Newtown encumbered by eight miles of wagons and twenty-three hundred prisoners. One final heroic effort might bring the kill.

May 31

Frémont was incapable of a final spurt. He plodded along, his army grossly strung out, for another fifteen or so miles on May 31. The effort he reported to Washington, however, was excellent. He announced that his cavalry had the enemy in sight and added, "The army is pushing forward, and I intend to carry out operations proposed."[41] Reading those words, Lincoln could not have guessed that Frémont had halted for the day several miles out of Strasburg without a skirmish.

Shields, on the other hand, was eager for action. He had entered the Shenandoah looking for a fight. As early as May 29 he was considering what to do after he captured Front Royal. Shields had envisioned his command moving from Front Royal to Strasburg, while Ord's forces swept from Front Royal to Winchester. Shields saw no way for Jackson to escape such a net.[42] But Ord was not up—Shields's reasonable plan for Ord's deployment illustrates how costly Stanton's detour had been—and other factors conspired to deny Shields the action he craved. Shields left a meager record of his activities during this day, which therefore must be reconstructed according to what Shields can be assumed to have known, the orders he received, and the situation that developed around him.

Shields knew several things on May 31, though the sum was less than the parts. First, he knew Ord and Bayard were nowhere in sight. Second, he knew Frémont was supposed to occupy Strasburg but doubted he would do it. Third, his intelligence from the previous day placed Jackson at Winchester, and Shields had to assume Jackson had moved somewhere since then. Shields did not know where. Lastly, there was the nagging concern that a large enemy column from Richmond or Fredericksburg was approaching Front Royal.[43] When he marshaled these facts, Shields found he knew little of friend or foe.

Shields's bleak prospect was darkened further by orders arriving from McDowell. McDowell stated, among other things, that Frémont had promised to reach Strasburg by 5 P.M. and that Shields must "Get your division well in hand to go forward to his support."[44] This order was ambiguous. Should Shields go forward before 5 P.M., so as to reach

Strasburg in concert with Frémont, or was he to go later, after Frémont had arrived? Shields evidently made the latter interpretation, perhaps believing the overall chance of trapping Jackson was better if he stayed at Front Royal. If he occupied Strasburg with his entire division, he would have to abandon Front Royal, opening it for Jackson. If he moved with a fraction of his division, he risked either that fraction or the fragment left at Front Royal running afoul of superior enemy forces. Certainly it was better to barricade one escape road (Front Royal) than to open it in an effort to block the other (Strasburg) when Frémont was only a few hours away from the latter and enemy reinforcements were believed to be approaching Front Royal.

Shields's decision to remain at Front Royal promptly appeared wise. Ashby came knocking on the Winchester road, and Shields advanced four regiments to meet him. A brisk skirmish ensued. Though Ashby was driven off, Shields, having only a token contingent of cavalry, was unable to pursue effectively and discover what force the rebels possessed.[45] Thus ensnarled, he was compelled to remain at Front Royal. One of his brigades was engaged all afternoon with a force of uncertain size; to send other units west toward Strasburg without Ord near was to scatter McDowell's column in Jackson's immediate presence. Ashby slipped away at dark, having performed the invaluable service of wasting Shields's afternoon.

So ended May 31, a day of lost opportunity. It also proved to be the last day Lincoln might have trapped Jackson in the lower Valley. Still, the advantage held by Lincoln's columns was such that much might have been salvaged on June 1. Rebel wagon trains were within range of determined cavalry and artillery; the Stonewall Brigade was isolated and exhausted. If it was too late to encircle the Valley Army, the Federals could inflict a grievous wound—if only they would act.

June 1

This day was a sad monument to the lack of an overall Federal commander at the front. Frémont complained, "We hear nothing of McDowell";[46] McDowell echoed, "General Frémont's forces have not yet made their appearance";[47] Banks fretted, "Have heard nothing of Frémont."[48] McDowell comprehended so little of Banks's movements that at one point he believed Banks, who actually was at Martinsburg, was battling Jackson around Middletown.[49] Though the president had coached Banks along in pursuit of Jackson for several days, McDowell was denied news of Banks's progress until the early hours of June 1.[50] Then, however, it was too late for anyone to coordinate the Federal thrust.

Ewell jumped Frémont's van before dawn, and kept it five miles from Strasburg. It was 10 A.M. before Frémont's main strength reached the front and began to skirmish with Ewell. Frémont then told Washington that there would probably be a battle that afternoon. Later, he reported that the morning skirmish had ended with Ewell's retreat after only two hours, yet it was 6 P.M. before Frémont advanced again.[51] That he should cling to the retiring Ewell with every man capable of holding a rifle apparently escaped Frémont's consideration. At any rate, he failed to account for the unfilled hours cited in his own report.

Frémont did serve one useful function by squatting west of Strasburg. Ewell had to pull off the Valley Pike to get at him, which exposed his rear to Shields—and this was an opportunity for which Shields was at last free. The problems that had trussed him the day before were unraveling. The van of Ord's Division entered Front Royal on the morning of June 1. These troops were in poor condition but were reviving with the prospect of action. Bayard's cavalry also was present. McDowell had come in on May 31 and huddled long with Shields planning for this day. They decided to implement the dragnet originally envisioned by Shields, with his division sweeping to Strasburg and Ord's infantry and Bayard's cavalry marching on to Winchester.[52]

Shields actually began this sweep. His division marched. His ten thousand doughty Midwesterners, men who had seen the Valley Army's back, were unleashed. And yet, with everything at last arranged, Shields never crossed the South Fork of the Shenandoah. Why? The answer was a mistake that altered many events of this war: somehow, Shields wandered onto the wrong road.

The blunder apparently happened this way: as the march commenced, two officers dispatched by Shields to scout Jackson's movements galloped up with a false report that the Valley Army had cleared Strasburg. This report was accepted, and it was hastily decided to hurl Bayard upon the rebels before they moved too far south of Strasburg. The cavalry therefore was redeployed from the Winchester to the Strasburg road.[53] The shift entailed considerable confusion, and in starting out again, Shields wandered off the Strasburg and onto the Winchester road.

When Shields's Division had initially left the Valley for Fredericksburg in mid-May, it had marched via Front Royal; it had spent the previous two days picketing the area; Shields was an alert commander who knew where he went. Though it hardly seems credible that such soldiers took the wrong road, the evidence is supplied by men who were there. George L. Wood, an intelligent member of the 7th Ohio, recorded, "Shields, with his entire division, was ordered out on the road to Strasburg, for the purpose of intercepting the retreat of the enemy. But instead of taking the road which he was ordered to take, he crossed over the north branch of the Shenandoah River on the road to Winchester."[54] Private William Kepler of the 4th Ohio agreed: "Our division must again rush forward, this time to intercept the enemy by way of the Strasburg road. For some reason, Shields, having taken the wrong road, was permitted to continue up the Luray Valley."[55] Major James Huntington of Shields's 1st Ohio Artillery also concurred: "It was late in the afternoon before Shields got ready to move, and then, owing to some blunder never clearly explained, he took the road to Winchester."[56] McDowell reported the error in testimony before the infamous Committee on the Conduct of the War: "I then went to see where Gen. Shields was, and found him over on the road towards Winchester. He had sent his troops on that road, instead of on the one I had ordered him to send them on."[57]

Whatever the cause of this mistake, it is certain that Shields started out on the wrong road, and by the time he could have been set right, it was too late. Bayard advanced to Strasburg unsupported and could do nothing against "heavy masses of [rebel] infantry, artillery and cavalry all plainly discernible, drawn up on commanding positions around [Strasburg]—a force so largely exceeding my own that an attack was utterly out of the question. The enemy threw a couple of shells at us, and just before dark I withdrew my forces."[58]

Conclusion

The Valley Army escaped from the lower Shenandoah for many reasons. Some were the product of its own effort. Swelling with notions of their invincibility as they cleared Strasburg, the rebels would have resented the suggestion that deliverance was also the result of Federal misjudgments and bad luck. Nevertheless, five discernible Union blunders helped to open the gates for the Valley Army.

First, Frémont altered Lincoln's flexible plan into a pincer operation with little margin for delay. He then proceeded to make an unpardonably slow march. His delay on May 29 proved especially damaging and made it almost certain that he would be halted just far enough from Strasburg to be little more than a nuisance.

Second, and most telling, the Federal operation was never synchronized. This was the inevitable concomitant of Lincoln's compartmentalized command structure, a system totally unsuited for the operational level of warfare it was to direct. Three of Lincoln's independent commanders, Frémont, Banks, and McDowell, were involved, and none of them could do no more than suggest deployment of the others. Only Lincoln and Stanton, who were too far away during the critical hours, could coordinate this drive, and they failed, as illustrated by the absurd oversight that left McDowell without word of Banks's location until June 1. The entire operation should have been delegated to one general officer rather than kept in the hands of two civilians who were necessarily distracted during the crucial period of May 31–June 1 by the great battle before Richmond.

Another failure of coordination was Stanton's decision to route two thirds of Ord's Division through Alexandria. In this instance the secretary was even out of touch with the president. Lincoln was trying to shuttle twenty thousand men from Fredericksburg to the Valley with all speed; Stanton wanted additional protection for Washington. These objectives were incompatible. Required to do two things at once, Ord accomplished neither fully and was rendered a negative factor until June 1. Stanton's detour was the third blunder.

The fourth mistake was the oversight that kept Bayard's cavalry from reaching the Shenandoah before June 1. The necessity to have Bayard at the van of Shields's march should have been manifest. Even a cursory knowledge of the Valley Army should have warned McDowell that he would require mounted reconnaissance to find the elusive rebels when he entered the Valley. McDowell's inexcusably late marching order for Bayard was the former's principal miscalculation of the drive.

Finally, on one of the few occasions of his military career, Shields followed the wrong road on June 1.

And yet, until Shields took that wrong turn, the Union might have smashed at least part of the Valley Army. The North had no monopoly on mistakes or bad luck in the Shenandoah. If Frémont lost precious time by pausing on May 29, Jackson did the same by ignoring signals of Shields's approach on May 28. If Shields was unlucky in taking the wrong road, Jackson was unfortunate in garrisoning Front Royal with a colonel who lost his nerve, the town, and its vital bridges to an enemy attack that had been rumored for a day. If Shields was harassed by reports of rebel reinforcements entering the Shenandoah, Jackson's scouts made mighty columns of Banks's and Geary's regimental-sized reconnaissances. Where the Federals were slowed by want of supplies, Jackson was handicapped by miles of captured booty and several thousand prisoners. The Union had its opportunities to destroy the Valley Army; it simply missed them.

APPENDIX D

Jackson's State of Mind at the Close of the Campaign

In his *R. E. Lee,* Douglas Southall Freeman chronicles Jackson's strenuous activities during the period preceding and including his strange failures on the Peninsula (June 22–30). Freeman examined Jackson's activities both during the daylight and nighttime hours of this crucial eight-day period and wrote:

> In summary, during the eight days from noon, June 22, to noon, June 30, Jackson rode approximately 100 miles with no rest intervening except while in conference at Lee's headquarters; he lost all of four nights' sleep or else had no sleep after midnight; he was probably up at dawn on the four mornings following a night of sleep; two of these four nights were spent on or close to fields where battles had been fought the preceding day; finally, on six of the eight days, he was either making his hurried ride to Richmond or else was on the march with his troops, under the most exacting conditions.[1]

This activity, which Freeman believed denied Jackson sleep upon which he was very dependent, was, in Freeman's opinion, a significant cause of Jackson's poor performance on the Peninsula. Later, in *Lee's Lieutenants,* Freeman modified this opinion only somewhat,[2] and more recent authors have tended to emphasize even more strongly than Freeman the debilitating effect of Jackson's want of sleep.[3]

The final days of the Valley Campaign saw Jackson endure a similar period of concentrated effort allowing little sleep. This was the ten-day retreat beginning with the Valley Army's withdrawal from Harpers Ferry and ending with the Battle of Port Republic. During these days and nights of alternating severe summer heat and hard rain, the Valley Army retreated approximately one hundred miles, fighting numerous skirmishes against a numerically superior foe while encumbered with enormous trains. It is the author's contention that the rigors of this retreat impaired Jackson almost as greatly, if not just as greatly, in the fighting around Port Republic as the strain of the march to Richmond impaired him on the Peninsula. This impairment is evident in the careless dispositions of the Army on the morning of June 8, in the haphazard construction of the bridge over the South River (the one structure on which everything Jackson wished to accomplish depended) and in the generally disjointed fighting at the Battle of Port Republic itself. In support of these contentions Jackson's daily activities from noon, May 30, to noon, June 9, are rostered below:

Day of May 30:	Napping and riding train from Charles Town to Winchester.
Night of May 30–31:	Conferring late with Boteler; conferring with Hotchkiss at 3 A.M.
Day of May 31:	Marching to Strasburg.
Night of May 31–June 1:	Talking and praying for "some time"[4] at Taylor's campfire.
Day of June 1:	Observing day-long skirmish against Frémont's army.
Night of June 1–2:	Marching from Strasburg to Woodstock in a heavy rain and hail storm; arriving at Woodstock "late";[5] eating about midnight and marching again soon thereafter.
Day of June 2:	Marching and observing skirmishing of the Army's rear guard; heavy rainstorm in the afternoon.
Night of June 2–3:	Riding six or more miles through a heavy rainstorm in response to a false alarm attributable to Ashby's cavalry; rising "very early."[6]
Day of June 3:	Marching to Rude's Hill under a heavy rainstorm; "having lost much sleep,"[7] Jackson retires early.
Night of June 3–4:	Sleeping in the mud beneath a torrential downpour; rising after a "very unpleasant night,"[8] Jackson appears "wet and wearied."[9]

Day of June 4:	Studying Valley geography and being interviewed by a Union war correspondent.[10]
Night of June 4–5:	Marching during early hours of the night; conferring with Hotchkiss as late as 10 P.M.[11]
Day of June 5:	Marching beyond Harrisonburg beneath light to moderate rainstorms.
Night of June 5–6:	Conferring with Hotchkiss "quite late."[12]
Day of June 6:	Marching along "very, very muddy"[13] roads to Port Republic.
Night of June 6–7:	Interviewing Sir Percy Wyndham until "late";[14] meditating about Ashby for "some time"[15] thereafter.
Day of June 7:	Maneuvering throughout the day to tempt Frémont into an attack near Cross Keys.
Night of June 7–8:	No record; probably sleeping; rising by least 7 A.M.
Day of June 8:	Skirmishing in and around Port Republic.
Night of June 8–9:	Planning battle beyond 2 A.M. (including conference with Colonel John Imboden);[16] up in time to send order to Winder before 3:45 A.M. to move his brigade to Port Republic.
Day of June 9:	Battle of Port Republic.

Descriptions of the terrible physical punishment suffered by the Valley Army during its retreat from Harpers Ferry to Port Republic are legion. Strong men such as John Harman admitted to "knocking under" from fatigue,[17] and they carried fewer burdens than Jackson. It is little wonder, then, that as the Army stumbled toward Port Republic its general was hardly as alert as he had been earlier in the campaign. Lieutenant McHenry Howard spent several hours near Jackson on June 8 and recalled that most of the time the general stood gazing at the ground with his cap pulled tightly over his eyes—a description strikingly similar to some of those of Jackson on the Peninsula.[18] Sandie Pendleton's June 7 description of Jackson can well serve as a conclusion regarding his physical and mental condition at the campaign's close: "General Jackson is completely broken down."[19]

APPENDIX E

VALLEY ARMY TABLES OF ORGANIZATION, JANUARY TO JUNE 1862[1]

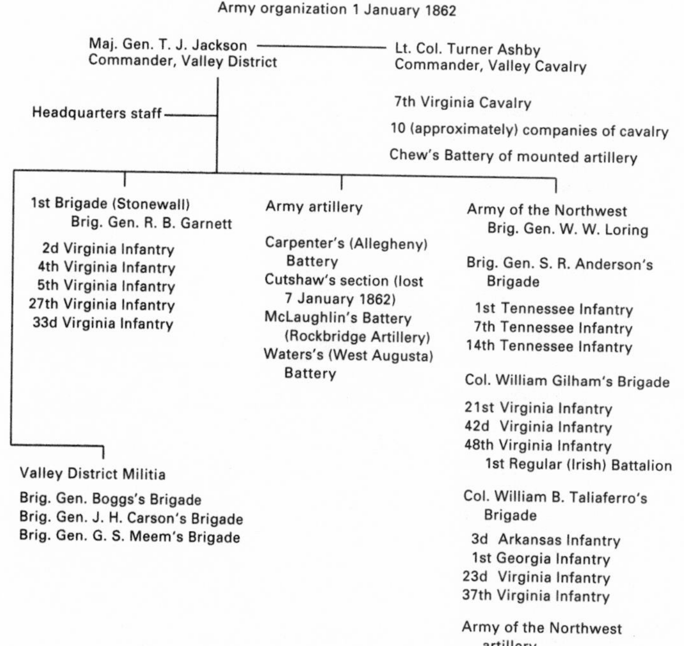

Army organization at Kernstown, 23 March 1862

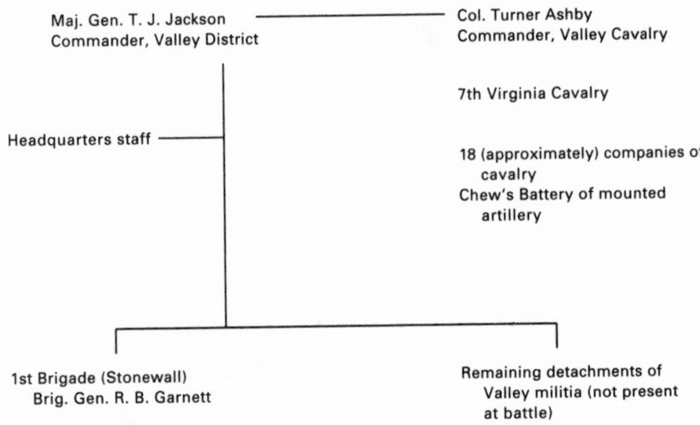

2d Virginia Infantry
4th Virginia Infantry
5th Virginia Infantry
27th Virginia Infantry
33d Virginia Infantry
Carpenter's (Allegheny) Battery
McLaughlin's Battery
(Rockbridge Artillery)

2d Brigade
Col. Jesse Burks

21st Virginia Infantry
42d Virginia Infantry
48th Virginia Infantry
1st Regular (Irish) Battalion
Marye's (Hampden) Battery
Waters's (West Augusta) Battery

3d Brigade
Col. S. V. Fulkerson

23d Virginia Infantry
37th Virginia Infantry
Shumaker's (Danville) Battery

Army organization at McDowell, 8 May 1862

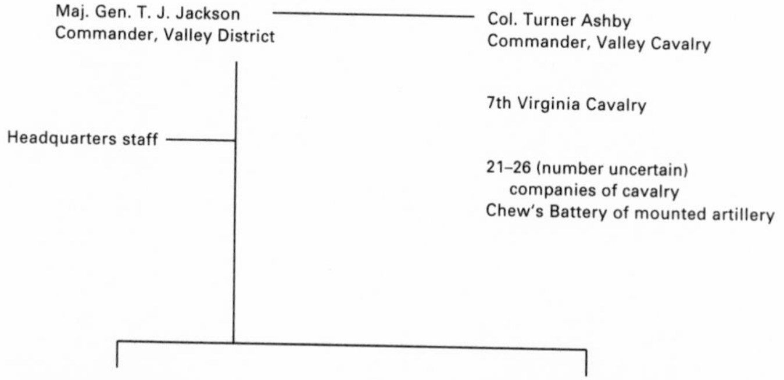

1st Brigade (Stonewall)
Brig. Gen. Charles S. Winder

2d Virginia Infantry
4th Virginia Infantry
5th Virginia Infantry
27th Virginia Infantry
33d Virginia Infantry
Carpenter's (Allegheny) Battery
(Rockbridge Artillery)

2d Brigade
Col. John A. Campbell

21st Virginia Infantry
42d Virginia Infantry
48th Virginia Infantry
1st Regular (Irish) Battalion
Caskie's (Hampden) Battery
Cutshaw's (West Augusta) Battery

3d Brigade
Brig. Gen. William B. Taliaferro

10th Virginia Infantry
23d Virginia Infantry
37th Virginia Infantry
Wooding's (Danville) Battery

Army of the Northwest
Brig. Gen. Edward Johnson

1st Brigade
Col. Z. T. Conner

12th Georgia Infantry
25th Virginia Infantry
31st Virginia Infantry

2d Brigade
Col. W. C. Scott

44th Virginia Infantry
52d Virginia Infantry
58th Virginia Infantry

Army of the Northwest artillery

Lusk's (2d Rockbridge) Battery
Raine's (Lynchburg "Lee") Battery
Rice's (8th Star) Battery

Army organization from action at Front Royal, 23 May 1862, to end of the Campaign

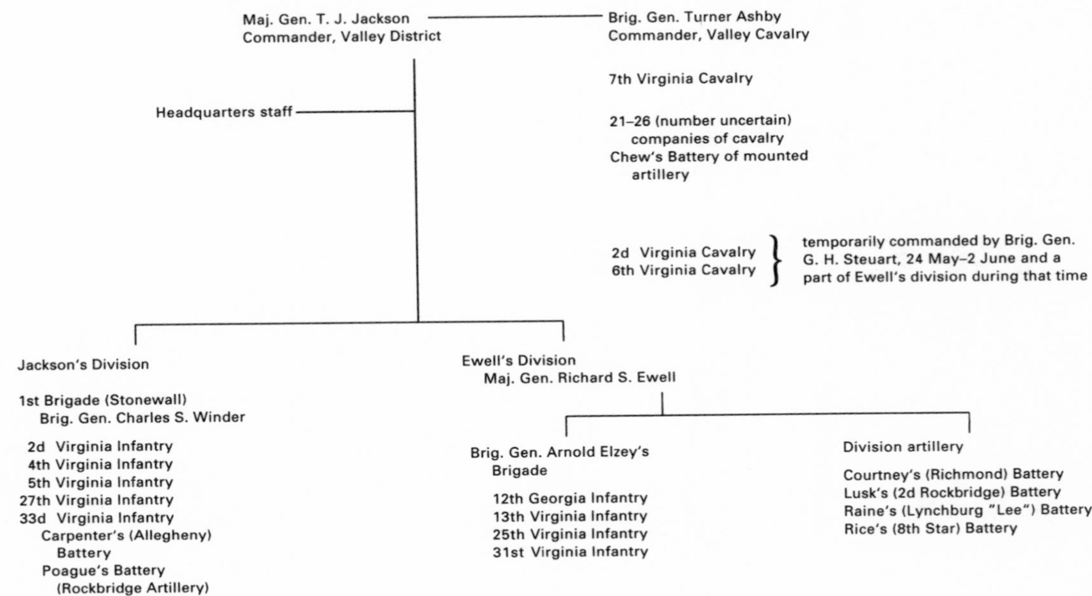

2d Brigade
Col. John M. Patton (as of 25 May)

21st Virginia Infantry
42d Virginia Infantry
48th Virginia Infantry
1st Regular (Irish) Battalion
Caskie's (Hampden) Battery
Cutshaw's (West Augusta) Battery

3d Brigade
Brig. Gen. William B. Taliaferro

10th Virginia Infantry
23d Virginia Infantry
37th Virginia Infantry
Wooding's (Danville) Battery

Carrington's (Charlottesville) Battery
(present as of 7 June)

Col. W. C. Scott's Brigade
(after 2 June commanded by Brig. Gen. G. H. Steuart)

44th Virginia Infantry
52d Virginia Infantry
58th Virginia Infantry

Brig. Gen. Richard Taylor's Brigade

6th Louisiana Infantry
7th Louisiana Infantry
8th Louisiana Infantry
9th Louisiana Infantry
Maj. R. C. Wheat's Battalion
(Louisiana Tigers)

Brig. Gen. Isaac Trimble's Brigade

15th Alabama Infantry
21st Georgia Infantry
16th Mississippi Infantry
21st North Carolina Infantry

Maryland Line
Brig. Gen. George H. Steuart
(Steuart temporarily assigned to command of 2d and 6th Virginia Cavalry, 24 May–2 June, then to command of Scott's Brigade; Maryland Line acted as a part of Steuart's Brigade after 6 June)

1st Maryland Infantry
Brockenbrough's Battery
(Baltimore Light Artillery)

NOTES

INTRODUCTION

1. Robert Leonhard, *The Art of Maneuver* (Novato, Calif.: Presidio Press, 1991), pp. 8–9.
2. Ibid., pp. 7–13; Christopher Bellamy, *The Evolution of Modern Land Warfare: Theory and Practice* (London: Routledge, 1990), pp. 60–61; Edward N. Luttwak, *Strategy* (Cambridge: The Belknap Press, 1987), pp. 90–112; John Romjue, "From Active Defense to AirLand Battle: The Development of Army Doctrine 1973–1982." TRADOC Historical Monograph Series, June 1987.
3. Joseph T. Glatthaar, *Partners in Command* (New York: The Free Press, 1994); Jay Luvaas, "Lee and the Operational Art: The Right Place, the Right Time," *Parameters* (Autumn 1992), pp. 2–18.

PROLOGUE

1. James K. Edmondson to his wife, 11 November 1861, Edmondson Letters, Rockbridge Historical Society, Lexington, Virginia
2. S. J. C. Moore to his wife, 11 November 1861, Moore Papers, Southern Historical Collection, Chapel Hill, North Carolina.
3. Henry Kyd Douglas, *I Rode with Stonewall* (Chapel Hill: University of North Carolina Press, 1940), p. 54.
4. Samuel R. Watkins, *Company Aytch* (Nashville: Cumberland Presbyterian Publishing House, 1882; reprint ed., Jackson, Tenn.: McCowart-Mercer Press, 1952), p. 52.
5. John N. Opie, *A Rebel Cavalryman with Lee, Stuart and Jackson* (Chicago: W. B. Conkey Co., 1899), pp. 48–50.
6. Henry K. Douglas to "Miss Tippie," 16 November 1861, Douglas Letters, Duke University Library, Durham, North Carolina.
7. Opie, *Rebel Cavalryman,* p. 50.
8. John O. Casler, *Four Years in the Stonewall Brigade* (Girard, Kans.:

Appeal Publishing Co., 1906; reprint ed., Marietta, Ga.: Continental Book Co., 1951), p. 60.

9. George Baylor, *Bull Run to Bull Run* (Richmond: B. F. Johnson Publishing Co., 1900), pp. 29–30.

CHAPTER 1

1. J. Lewis Peyton, *History of Augusta County* (Staunton, Va.: Yost and Son, 1882), pp. 5–6.
2. Samuel Kercheval, *A History of the Valley of Virginia,* 4th ed. (Strasburg, Va.: Shenandoah Publishing House, 1925), pp. 36–37.
3. John W. Wayland, *The German Element of the Shenandoah Valley of Virginia* (Charlottesville, Va.: Michie Co., 1907), pp. 11–14.
4. Ibid., p. 9.
5. Ann Maury, ed., *Memoirs of a Huguenot Family* (New York: G. P. Putnam's Sons, 1901), pp. 288–89.
6. Hermann Schuricht, *History of the German Element in Virginia* (Baltimore: Theo. Kroh & Sons, 1898), pp. 86–88.
7. Wayland, *German Element of the Shenandoah,* pp. 24–26.
8. Kercheval, *History of the Valley,* p. 178.
9. Ibid., p. 80.
10. John C. Fitzpatrick, ed., *The Writings of George Washington,* 39 vols. (Washington, D.C.; Government Printing Office, 1931–44), vol. 1, p. 144.
11. Ibid., pp. 203–6.
12. Louis K. Koontz, *The Virginia Frontier: 1754–1763* (Baltimore: Johns Hopkins University Press, 1925), p. 99.
13. Fitzpatrick, ed., *Writings of Washington,* vol. 1, p. 494.
14. Ibid., vol. 2, p. 153.
15. Stanislaus Hamilton, ed., *Letters to Washington and Accompanying Papers,* 5 vols. (Boston: Houghton Mifflin and Co., 1898–1902), pp. 398–400.
16. Schuricht, *German Element in Virginia,* p. 109.
17. Charles Campbell, *History of the Colony and Ancient Dominion of Virginia* (Philadelphia: J. B. Lippincott, 1860), p. 585.
18. Ibid., pp. 585–86.
19. Wayland, *German Element of the Shenandoah,* pp. 143–44.
20. Quoted in Harry M. Strickler, *A Short History of Page County* (Richmond: Dietz Press, 1952), p. 86.
21. Kercheval, *History of the Valley,* p. 147.
22. Frederic Morton, *The Story of Winchester* (Strasburg, Va.: Shenandoah Publishing House, 1925), p. 136.
23. Ibid., p. 53.

24. T. K. Cartmell, *Shenandoah Valley Pioneers* (Winchester, Va.: Eddy Press, 1909), p. 162; Morton, *Winchester,* p. 124.
25. Cartmell, *Valley Pioneers,* p. 149.
26. Ibid., p. 143.
27. Morton, *Winchester,* pp. 123–25.
28. Ibid., pp. 233; Cartmell, *Valley Pioneers,* p. 158.
29. Freeman H. Hart, *The Valley of Virginia in the American Revolution* (Chapel Hill: University of North Carolina Press, 1942), p. 99.
30. Thomas A. Ashby, *Life of Turner Ashby* (New York: Neale Publishing Co., 1914), p. 75.
31. U.S. War Department, *War of the Rebellion: A Compilation of the Official Records of the Union and Confederate Armies,* 128 vols. and index (Washington, D.C.: Government Printing Office, 1880–1901), ser. IV, vol. 1, p. 385. (Cited hereafter as *OR.* Unless otherwise specified, all references are to series I.)
32. Ibid., p. 382.
33. Virginia Militia Laws (Richmond, Va., 1855), p. 24.
34. See Jean Gottman, *Virginia at Mid-Century* (New York: Henry Holt and Co., 1955), pp. 99–104.
35. John W. Wayland, *History of Rockingham County* (Dayton, Va.: Ruebush-Elkins Co., 1912), pp. 376–77; John W. Wayland, *History of Shenandoah County* (Strasburg, Va.: Shenandoah Publishing House, 1927), pp. 207, 291.
36. Wayland, *Rockingham County,* pp. 418, 423.
37. Cartmell, *Valley Pioneers,* p. 54; Wayland, *Shenandoah County,* pp. 262–66.
38. "Thirty-Sixth Annual Report of the Baltimore and Ohio Railroad Company, 1862," Baltimore, Maryland, 1864.
39. Wayland, *Shenandoah County,* p. 293.
40. "Twenty-Sixth Annual Report of the Virginia Central Railroad Company," Richmond, Virginia, 1861, p. 17.
41. Peyton, *Augusta County,* pp. 227–29.
42. Winchester *Virginian,* 21 November 1860.
43. Thomas Jefferson, *Notes on the State of Virginia,* ed. by William Peden (Chapel Hill: University of North Carolina Press for the Institute of Early American History and Culture, 1955), p. 24.
44. Samuel V. Leech, *The Raid of John Brown at Harper's Ferry* (Washington, D.C.: De Soto Press, 1909), p. 5.
45. Ibid., pp. 7–8; "Report of Colonel Robert E. Lee, Report of the Select Committee of the Senate appointed to inquire into the Late Invasion and Seizure of the Public Property at Harper's Ferry" (Senate Com. Report No. 279, 1st Sess., 36th Congress, Washington, D.C., 1866), pp. 40–43.
46. Leech, *Raid of John Brown,* p. 13.
47. Mary Anna Jackson, *Life and Letters of General Thomas J. Jackson* (New York: Harper & Brothers, 1892), pp. 130–32.

CHAPTER 2

1. Robert U. Johnson and C. C. Buel, eds., *Battles and Leaders of the Civil War,* 4 vols. (New York: Century, 1887–88; reprint ed., New York: Thomas Yoseloff, 1956), vol. 1, pp. 115–17. (Cited hereafter as *B & L.*)
2. Casler, *Four Years,* p. 19.
3. Opie, *Rebel Cavalryman,* p. 19.
4. James B. Avirett, *The Memoirs of General Turner Ashby and His Compeers* (Baltimore: Selby and Dulany, 1867), p. 62.
5. J. K. Edmondson to his wife, 3 and 17 May 1861, Edmondson Letters.
6. George W. Booth, *Personal Reminiscences of a Maryland Soldier in the War Between the States* (Baltimore: Fleet, McGinley and Co., 1898), p. 10.
7. *B & L,* vol. 1, p. 118.
8. John Esten Cooke, *Stonewall Jackson and the Old Stonewall Brigade,* ed. by Richard Harwell (Charlottesville: University of Virginia Press, 1954), p. 10.
9. Baylor, *Bull Run,* p. 14.
10. Henry D. Monier, *Military Annals of Louisiana* (New Orleans, 1875), p. 89.
11. *B & L,* vol. 1, p. 121.
12. Thomas J. Jackson Order Book, 1861, 12 April–30 May 1861, Hotchkiss Papers, Library of Congress, Washington, D.C.
13. *B & L,* vol. 1, p. 118.
14. *OR,* vol. 2, pp. 832–33.
15. Ibid., pp. 809–10.
16. *B & L,* vol. 1, p. 122.
17. Ibid., pp. 121–22.
18. Ibid., p. 123.
19. Hunter McGuire, "General Thomas J. Jackson," *Southern Historical Society Papers* XIX, p. 302. (Cited hereafter as *S.H.S.P.*)
20. *OR,* vol. 2, p. 183.
21. Jackson, *Life of Jackson,* p. 168.
22. Edward Hungerford, *The Story of the Baltimore and Ohio Railroad,* 2 vols. (New York: G. P. Putnam's Sons, 1928), vol. 2, p. 28; "Annual Report of the Baltimore and Ohio Railroad, 1861," p. 7.
23. Cornelia McDonald, *A Diary with Reminiscences of the War and Refugee Life in the Shenandoah Valley* (Nashville: Cullom and Ghertner Co., 1934), p. 77.
24. Origins of the name "Stonewall" are traced in Douglas Southall Freeman, *Lee's Lieutenants,* 3 vols. (New York: Charles Scribner's Sons, 1942–44), vol. 1, Appendix V.
25. See chapter 3, notes 21–23 and accompanying text, infra.

26. Roy Bird Cook, *The Family and Early Life of General Thomas J. Jackson,* 3rd ed. (Charles Town, W.Va., 1948), pp. 160–62.
27. Jackson, *Life of Jackson,* pp. 179–80.
28. Casler, *Four Years,* p. 47.
29. Ibid., pp. 41, 51.
30. Henderson, *Stonewall Jackson and the American Civil War,* p. 133.
31. Marcus B. Toney, *The Privations of a Private* (privately printed, Nashville, 1905), p. 20.
32. John H. Worsham, *One of Jackson's Foot Cavalry* (New York: Neale Publishing Co., 1912), p. 43.
33. James E. Hall, *The Diary of a Confederate Soldier,* ed. by Ruth Woods Dayton (Philippi, W.Va., 1961), 25 and 27 November 1861.
34. *OR,* vol. 5, pp. 942–43.
35. Ibid., pp. 889, 943.
36. Ibid., p. 936.
37. Ibid., p. 937.
38. Ibid., pp. 378–80.
39. Ibid., pp. 239–48, 898–99, 920; Avirett, *Ashby,* p. 127.
40. *OR,* vol. 5, p. 899.
41. Ibid., p. 919.
42. Ibid., p. 890.
43. Douglas, *I Rode with Stonewall,* p. 28.
44. A. S. Pendleton to his mother, 21 March 1862, William G. Bean, ed., "The Valley Campaign of 1862 as Revealed in Letters of Sandie Pendleton," *Virginia Magazine of History and Biography,* vol. 78, no. 3, July 1970, p. 340. (Cited hereafter as Bean, ed., "Pendleton Letters.")
45. *OR,* vol. 5, p. 913.
46. Ibid., p. 909; vol. 51, pt. 2, p. 361. Concerning other candidates for the command, see Linda Lasswell Crist and Mary Seaton Dix, eds., *The Papers of Jefferson Davis,* vol. 7, 1861 (Baton Rouge: Louisiana State University Press, 1991), p. 365.
47. *OR,* vol. 5, p. 913.
48. Jackson, *Life of Jackson,* pp. 183–84; *OR,* vol. 2, p. 863.
49. Campbell Brown to his mother, 31 May 1862. Polk, Ewell, Brown Papers, Southern Historical Collection, University of North Carolina, Chapel Hill, North Carolina.
50. Wells Hawks to Robert L. Dabney, 17 January 1866, War Letters 1861–1865 Collection, New York Historical Society, New York, New York. The brief delay in Jackson's departure from Centreville is noted in *OR,* vol. 51, pt. 2, p. 364.
51. *OR*, vol. 5, pp. 936–37.
52. Ibid., p. 937.
53. Ibid., p. 938.
54. Ibid., p. 939.

55. Ibid., p. 940.
56. Casler, *Four Years,* p. 49.
57. John H. Graybill, *Diary of a Soldier of the Stonewall Brigade* (privately printed, Woodstock, Va., n.d.), 10 November 1861.

CHAPTER 3

1. McDonald, *Diary,* p. 37.
2. John G. Paxton, ed., *Elisha F. Paxton: Memoir and Memorials* (privately printed, New York, 1907), p. 38.; J. H. Langhorne to his father, 21 November 1862, Langhorne Letters, Virginia Historical Society, Richmond; H. K. Douglas to "Miss Tippie," 16 November 1861, Douglas Letters, MS Diary of John S. Apperson, Rockbridge Historical Society, Lexington, Virginia, 23 and 30 November 1861.
3. S. J. C. Moore to his wife, 22 November 1861, Moore Papers.
4. S. J. C. Moore to his wife, 30 November 1861, Moore Papers.
5. L. M. Blackford to his mother, 12 November 1861, Blackford Family Papers, University of Virginia, Charlottesville, Virginia.
6. H. K. Douglas to "Miss Tippie," 16 November 1861, Douglas Letters.
7. Opie, *Rebel Cavalryman,* p. 56.
8. Baylor, *Bull Run,* p. 31.
9. Judith W. McGuire, *Diary of a Southern Refugee* (Richmond: E. J. Hale and Son, 1867), p. 72.
10. Recollections of John N. Lyle (unpublished typescript entitled "Stonewall Jackson's Campguard"), Rockbridge Historical Society, Lexington, Virginia, p. 300.
11. L. Minor Blackford, ed., *Mine Eyes Have Seen the Glory* (Cambridge, Mass.: Harvard University Press, 1954), p. 181.
12. Abraham S. Miller to his wife, 24 February 1862; letters in possession of Dr. James A. Miller, Winchester, Vïrginia.
13. Opie, *Rebel Cavalryman,* p. 57.
14. Lyle Recollections, p. 313.
15. Opie, *Rebel Cavalryman,* pp. 57–58.
16. Gen. D. H. Hill, "Address," *S.H.S.P.* XIII, p. 261.
17. Opie, *Rebel Cavalryman,* p. 15.
18. Randolph H. McKim, *A Soldier's Recollection* (New York: Longmans, Green and Co., 1910), p. 99.
19. William Couper, *One Hundred Years at V.M.I.,* 4 vols. (Richmond: Garrett and Massie, 1939), vol. 3, p. 178.
20. Couper, *V.M.I.,* vol. 1., p. 313.
21. Richard Taylor, *Destruction and Reconstruction* (New York: D. Appleton and Co., 1879; reprint ed., New York: Longmans, Green and Company, 1955).
22. *B & L,* vol. 2, p. 297.

23. Taylor, *Destruction and Reconstruction,* p. 37.
24. Jackson Letter Book, 1862, 31 July 1861, Hotchkiss Papers, Library of Congress, Washington, D.C.
25. Jackson Letter Book, 1862, 11 February 1862, Hotchkiss Papers.
26. Couper, *V.M.I.,* vol. 4, p. 76.
27. Elizabeth P. Allan, *The Life and Letters of Margaret Junkin Preston* (Boston: Houghton Mifflin and Co., 1903), p. 72.
28. Taylor, *Destruction and Reconstruction,* pp. 89–91.
29. *OR,* vol. 12, pt. 3, pp. 841–42.
30. John Esten Cooke, *Wearing of the Gray* (New York, 1867; reprint ed., Bloomington: Indiana University Press, 1959), p. 45.
31. Jackson Letter Book, 1862, 25 February 1862, Hotchkiss Papers.
32. Allan, *Valley Campaign,* p. 16.
33. Apperson Diary, 26 November 1861.
34. Carlton McCarthy, *Detailed Minutiae of Soldier Life in the Army of Northern Virginia* (privately printed, Richmond, 1882; reprinted in *Soldier Life of the Union and Confederate Armies,* ed. by Philip Van Doren Stern. Bloomington: Indiana University Press, 1961), p. 305.
35. *OR,* vol. 5, pp. 942, 965.
36. Jackson to Alexander R. Boteler, 6 May 1862, Boteler Papers, Duke University, Durham, North Carolina; Allan, *Preston,* p. 125; J. H. Langhorne to "Aunt Nannie," 12 December 1861, Langhorne Letters, Virginia Historical Society, Richmond, Virginia. There is no known evidence of favoritism in the selection of Garnett to command the Stonewall Brigade.
37. *OR,* vol. 5, p. 977.
38. Ibid., p. 976.
39. Ibid., pp. 390, 976.
40. Jackson, *Life of Jackson,* p. 160.
41. William T. Poague, *Gunner with Stonewall* (Jackson, Tenn.: McCowart-Mercer Press, 1957), p. 12.
42. Jennings C. Wise, *The Long Arm of Lee,* 2 vols. (Lynchburg, Va.: J. P. Bell Co., Inc., 1915), vol. 1, pp. 163–64.
43. William N. McDonald, *A History of the Laurel Brigade* (Baltimore: Sun Job Printing, 1907), pp. 22–24.
44. *OR,* vol. 2, p. 881.
45. *B & L,* vol. 1, p. 124.
46. *OR,* vol. 2, pp. 861–62.
47. Ibid., p. 868.
48. Ibid., pp. 832–33.
49. Ibid., p. 954.
50. Avirett, *Ashby,* p. 190.
51. William C. Kean to "Susan," 11 April 1862, Kean Letters, University of Virginia, Charlottesville, Virginia.
52. L. M. Blackford to his mother, 10 December 1861, and to his father, 17 June 1862, Blackford Papers.

53. Avirett, *Ashby,* p. 173.
54. Thomas Clarence, *General Turner Ashby* (Winchester, Va.: Eddy Press Corp., 1907), p. 193; *OR,* vol. 5, p. 919.
55. Harry Gilmor, *Four Years in the Saddle* (New York: Harper and Brothers, 1866), p. 15.
56. Margaretta Barton Colt, *Defend the Valley* (New York: Orion Books, 1994), p. 156.
57. Laura Virginia Hale, *Four Valiant Years in the Lower Shenandoah Valley* (Front Royal, Va.: Hathaway Publishing, 1986), pp. 236–37.
58. Baylor, *Bull Run,* p. 37.
59. Ibid., p. 48.
60. *OR,* vol. 5, p. 892; vol. 12, pt. 3, p. 880; vol. 51, pt. 2, p. 336; Ashby to Benjamin, 7 November 1861, Ashby Letters, Chicago Historical Society, Chicago, Illinois.
61. *OR,* vol. 5, p. 974.
62. Ibid., p. 969.
63. Jackson, *Life of Jackson,* p. 209.
64. Alexander M. Garbar, *Sketch of the Life and Services of Major John A Harman* (privately printed, Staunton, Va., 1876), pp. 7–19, 39.
65. "Sketch of the Life and Career of Hunter Holmes McGuire," *S.H.S.P.* XXVIII, p. 273; Garbar, *Sketch of Harman,* p. 13; Clement Evans, gen. ed., *Confederate Military History,* vol. 3, *Virginia,* by Jedediah Hotchkiss (Atlanta: Confederate Publishing Co., 1899; reprint ed., Dayton, Ohio: Morningside Bookshop, 1975), p. 1019. (Cited hereafter as *C.M.H.*)
66. Lyle Recollections, pp. 313, 315.
67. Elizabeth P. Allan, *Life and Letters of Margaret Junkin Preston* (Boston: Houghton Mifflin and Co., 1903) p. 121. As to other activities, see generally J. N. Lash, *Destroyer of the Iron Horse* (Kent, Ohio: The Kent State University Press, 1990), p. 22.
68. *OR,* vol. 5, p. 965.
69. Ibid., p. 966. By late December, Johnston was more supportive of the drive. Ibid., p. 1007.
70. Ibid., p. 968.
71. Ibid., p. 983.
72. Ibid., pp. 988–89.
73. Edwin C. Bearss, "War Comes to the Chesapeake and Ohio Canal," *West Virginia History,* vol. 28, no. 4, October 1966, p. 167. This article provides a comprehensive discussion of operations against the canal.
74. J. H. Langhorne to his father, 15 December 1861, Langhorne Letters.
75. Theodore "Ted" Barclay to his sister, 23 December 1861, Barclay Letters, Rockbridge Historical Society, Lexington, Virginia.
76. Apperson Diary, 16 December 1861.
77. W. Morton Brown to Dr. Lee Holt, 17 January 1862. Bowman-Howard-Domingos Collection, Washington Library, Macon, Georgia.
78. *OR,* vol. 5, p. 395.

79. Apperson Diary, 17 December 1861.
80. Theodore Barclay to his sister, 23 December 1861, Barclay Letters; J. H. Langhorne to his mother, 23 December 1861, Langhorne Letters.
81. Apperson Diary, 18 December 1862.
82. Typescript diary of William T. Kinzer, 19 December 1861, West Virginia Collection, West Virginia University, Morgantown, West Virginia.
83. Poague, *Gunner with Stonewall,* pp. 13–14.
84. J. H. Langhorne to his mother, 23 December 1861, Langhorne Letters.
85. *OR,* vol. 5, p. 390; Jackson Order Book, 1861, 24 December 1861, Hotchkiss Papers.
86. S. J. C. Moore to his wife, 21 December 1861, Moore Papers.
87. Douglas, *I Rode with Stonewall,* p. 19.
88. S. J. C. Moore to his wife, 27 December 1861, Moore Papers.
89. J. H. Langhorne to his mother, 31 December 1861, Langhorne Letters.
90. Jackson to Ashby, 27 December 1861, Dabney Papers, Virginia State Library, Richmond, Virginia.
91. *OR,* vol. 5, pp. 1003–4.
92. Ibid., p. 1004.
93. Lavender R. Ray to his father, 7 December 1861, Ray Letters, Georgia Department of Archives and History, Atlanta, Georgia.
94. Jackson Order Book, 1861, 26 December 1861, Hotchkiss Papers.
95. L. R. Ray to his father, 7 December 1861, Ray Letters.
96. J. H. Chamberlayne, *Ham Chamberlayne—Virginian,* ed. C. G. Chamberlayne (Richmond: Dietz Printing Co., 1932), p. 55.
97. R. W. Waldrop to his father, 26 December 1861, Waldrop Letters, Southern Historical Collection, University of North Carolina, Chapel Hill, North Carolina.
98. L. R. Ray to his sister, 13 December 1861, Ray Letters.
99. Toney, *Privations,* pp. 25–26.
100. Allan, *Life of Preston,* pp. 126–27.
101. Jackson Order Book, 1861, 26 December 1861, Hotchkiss Papers.
102. J. H. Langhorne to his mother, 31 December 1861, Langhorne Letters.
103. A. S. Miller to his wife, 1 January 1862, Miller Letters.
104. Apperson Diary, 31 December 1861.
105. J. H. Langhorne to his mother, 31 December 1861, Langhorne Letters.
106. John H. Graybill, *Diary of a Soldier of the Stonewall Brigade* (privately printed, Woodstock, Va., n.d.), 31 December 1861.

CHAPTER 4

1. Toney, *Privations,* p. 27; Baylor, *Bull Run,* p. 31; unpublished manuscript recollections of William Allan, Allan Papers, Southern Historical Collection, University of North Carolina, Chapel Hill, North Carolina., p. 96.

2. Garbar, *Sketch of Harman,* p. 14.
3. Ibid.; Apperson Diary, 1 January 1862.
4. Casler, *Four Years,* p. 73.
5. Unpublished manuscript journal of Clement D. Fishburne, Fishburne Journal, University of Virginia, Charlottesville, Virginia, p. 23.
6. Douglas, *I Rode with Stonewall,* p. 20.
7. Apperson Diary, 3 January 1862; William S. White, *Sketches of the Life of Captain Hugh A. White* (Columbia, S.C.: Columbia Steam Press, 1864), p. 71.
8. L. R. Ray to his brother, 12 January 1862, Ray Letters.
9. A. K. Kelley to his mother, 19 January 1862, Kelley-Williamson Papers, Duke University, Durham, North Carolina; R. W. Waldrop to his father, 12 January 1862, Waldrop Letters.
10. MS Journal of Jedediah Hotchkiss, Hotchkiss Papers, p. 2.
11. Ibid.
12. L. R. Ray to his brother, 12 January 1862, Ray Letters.
13. Henderson, *Stonewall Jackson,* p. 144.
14. A. S. Miller to his wife, 6 January 1862, Miller Letters.
15. William Gilham to Jedediah Hotchkiss, 25 November 1866, Hotchkiss Papers; George A. Porterfield, "A Narrative of the Service of Colonel George A. Porterfield in Northwestern Virginia in 1861–1862," *S.H.S.P.* XVI, p. 90.
16. Porterfield, p. 90.
17. *OR,* vol. 5, p. 1066. Loring later denied the comment. Ibid., p. 1070.
18. Typescript of diary of Samuel J. Mullins, in possession of R. P. Gravely, Martinsville, Virginia, 3 January 1862.
19. A. S. Miller to his wife, 6 January 1862, Miller Letters.
20. William Gilham to Jedediah Hotchkiss, 25 November 1866, Hotchkiss Papers.
21. See *OR,* vol. 5, p. 1070 for Loring's side of this incident; Jackson's version is on pp. 390, 1066.
22. Ibid., p. 391.
23. Ibid.; William Gilham to Jedediah Hotchkiss, 25 November 1866, Hotchkiss Papers.
24. MS Journal of J. Hotchkiss, Hotchkiss Papers, p. 3.
25. H. K. Douglas to his mother, 12 January 1862, Douglas Letters.
26. Frank Moore, ed., *The Rebellion Record,* 12 vols. (New York, 1862–71), vol. 4, p. 16.
27. Winchester *Daily Republican,* 18 January 1862.
28. Gilmor, *Four Years in the Saddle,* p. 28.
29. MS Journal of J. Hotchkiss, Hotchkiss Papers, p. 3; Allan, *Valley Campaign,* p. 22.
30. Watkins, *Co. Aytch,* p. 56.
31. MS Diary of George Neese, 6 January 1862, Virginia State Library, Richmond, Virginia. (This source, the original from which Neese's printed volume *Three Years in the Confederate Horse Artillery* was

largely drawn, occasionally contains material omitted in the later work. It will be referred to as MS Diary when utilized instead of the printed work.)

32. MS Journal of J. Hotchkiss, Hotchkiss Papers, p. 3.
33. Toney, *Privations,* p. 31; C. A. Fonerden, *A Brief History of the Military Career of Carpenter's Battery* (New Market, Va.: Henkel & Co., 1911), pp. 17–18.
34. *OR,* vol. 5, p. 392.
35. MS Memoirs of Edward H. MacDonald, MacDonald Memoirs, Southern Historical Collection, University of North Carolina, Chapel Hill, North Carolina, p. 34.
36. H. K. Douglas to his mother, 12 January 1862, Douglas Letters.
37. Lyle Recollections, p. 327.
38. H. K. Douglas to his mother, 12 January 1862, Douglas Letters; Douglas, *I Road with Stonewall,* p. 23; Worsham, *Foot Cavalry,* p. 59.
39. Moore, *Rebellion Record,* vol. 4, p. 17.
40. Casler, *Four Years,* p. 63.
41. Fishburne Journal, p. 33.
42. Fonerden, *Carpenter's Battery,* pp. 17–18.
43. Lyle Recollections, p. 328; H. J. Langhorne to his mother, 12 January 1862, Langhorne Letters.
44. Watkins, *Co. Aytch,* p. 57.
45. MS Journal of J. Hotchkiss, Hotchkiss Papers, p. 4.
46. Fishburne Journal, pp. 31–32; Worsham, *Foot Cavalry,* p. 63.
47. Paxton, *Elisha Paxton,* p. 43.
48. *OR,* vol. 5, p. 392.
49. Ibid., p. 1018.
50. Ibid., p. 1026.
51. Ibid.
52. Ibid.; here Jackson reviewed the disposition of his forces, including the fact that twenty-three hundred men were spread over the lower Shenandoah in small detachments. Such a deployment clearly suggests a defensive posture.
53. Apperson Diary, 10 January 1862.
54. Moore, *Rebellion Record,* vol. 4, p. 16.
55. *OR,* vol. 51, pt. 1, p. 461.
56. Diary of Julia Chase, typescript in Handley Library, Winchester, Virginia, 12 January 1862.
57. William Gilham to J. Hotchkiss, 25 November 1866, Hotchkiss Papers, supports the view that Jackson had abandoned the attempt to take Romney prior to learning the enemy had evacuated it.
58. H. K. Douglas to his mother, 12 January 1862, Douglas Letters; Fishburne Journal, p. 33.
59. MS Journal of J. Hotchkiss, Hotchkiss Papers, p. 4.
60. *OR,* vol. 5, p. 636.
61. Ibid., pp. 631, 678.

62. Ibid., p. 404.
63. Ibid., pp. 676, 697.
64. Ibid., p. 696.
65. William Gilham to J. Hotchkiss, 23 November 1866, Hotchkiss Papers.
66. MS Journal of J. Hotchkiss, Hotchkiss Papers, p. 5; Jackson Order Book, 1862, 12 January 1862, Hotchkiss Papers.
67. Allan Recollections, p. 102.
68. Fishburne Journal, p. 35.
69. Allan Recollections, p. 102.
70. R. W. Waldrop to his father, 19 January 1862, Waldrop Letters.
71. Ibid.
72. J. H. Langhorne to his father, 19 January 1862, Langhorne Letters.
73. Worsham, *Foot Cavalry,* p. 60.
74. J. H. Langhorne to his father, 19 January 1862, Langhorne Letters.
75. Watkins, *Co. Aytch,* p. 57; Fishburne Journal, p. 37.
76. *OR,* vol. 5, p. 1036.
77. Ibid., p. 1035.
78. Ibid., p. 1039; Apperson Diary, 17 January 1862.
79. *OR,* vol. 5, p. 1034.
80. Apperson Diary, 21 January 1862.
81. J. H. Langhorne to his father, 19 January 1862, Langhorne Letters.
82. William F. Harrison to his wife, 23 January 1862, Harrison Letters, Duke University, Durham, North Carolina.
83. *OR,* vol. 5, p. 1039.
84. Ibid. p. 1034.
85. Ibid.
86. Ibid., pp. 1043–44.
87. S. M. Barton, Loring's chief engineer, evaluated the possibility of defending the Romney area much less favorably. *OR,* vol. 5, pp. 1055–56. Other views are found in *OR,* vol. 5, pp. 201–4, 378–79.
88. Ted Barclay to his sister, 22 and 25 January 1862, Barclay Letters.
89. Apperson Diary, 15 January 1862.
90. Poague, *Gunner,* p. 17.
91. R. W. Waldrop to his father, 28 January 1862, Waldrop Letters.
92. Baylor, *Bull Run,* p. 33.
93. Fishburne Journal, p. 37.
94. Apperson Diary, 25 January 1862.
95. Paxton, *Elisha Paxton,* p. 47.
96. Although the Union had planned no pincer movement toward Martinsburg prior to January 1, 1862, plans had been made for a strike from the Alleghenies to Winchester. Allan, *Valley Campaign,* pp. 19–20.
97. *OR,* vol. 51, pt. 1, pp. 461–62.
98. W. H. Harrison to his wife, 31 January 1862, Harrison Letters.
99. Dabney, *Jackson,* pp. 274–75.
100. *OR,* vol. 5, pp. 1046–48.

101. Ibid., pp. 1040–41.
102. Ibid. p. 1042.
103. William H. Taliaferro to "Conrad," 11 July 1877, Taliaferro Papers, College of William and Mary, Williamsburg, Virginia. Davis never verified this interview.
104. *OR,* vol. 5, p. 1040.
105. Ibid., p. 1050.
106. Ibid., p. 1044.
107. Ibid., p. 1049.
108. Ibid., p. 1051.
109. Ibid., pp. 1071, 1050.
110. Ibid., p. 1059.
111. Ibid., p. 1050.
112. Ibid., p. 1053.
113. Ibid., p. 1044.
114. Ibid., p. 1053.
115. Ibid., p. 1056.
116. Ibid., p. 1063.
117. Ibid., pp. 1059–60, 1062, 1071–72.
118. MS Diary of Thomas Bragg, 30 January 1862, Bragg Papers, Southern Historical Collection, University of North Carolina, Chapel Hill, North Carolina.
119. Ibid., pp. 1053, 1064; Douglas, *I Rode with Stonewall,* p. 26.
120. J. H. Harman to his brother, 6 February 1862, Hotchkiss Papers.
121. R. W. Waldrop to his father, 7 and 14 February 1862, Waldrop Letters.
122. T. J. Jackson Papers (a), Typescript, "Charge and Specifications Preferred by Maj. Gen. T. J. Jackson P.A.C.S. against Col. William Gilham 21st Regt. Va., Vols." Southern Historical Collection, University of North Carolina, Chapel Hill, North Carolina.
123. *OR,* vol. 5, pp. 1065–66.
124. Ibid., vol. 1, pt. 2, p. 469.
125. Ibid., p. 468.
126. A. S. Miller to his wife, 22 December 1862, Miller Letters.
127. In his answers to Jackson's court-martial specifications, Loring blamed this delay entirely upon Jackson. *OR,* vol. 5, p. 1070.
128. Poague, *Gunner,* p. 18.
129. Jonathan Green to "Miss Sallie," 1 February 1862, Green Letters, Duke University, Durham, North Carolina.
130. George K. Harlow to his family, 8 and 17 February 1862, Harlow Letters, Virginia Historical Society, Richmond, Virginia.
131. H. K. Douglas to his mother, 12 January 1862, Douglas Letters.
132. J. H. Langhorne to his mother, 12 January 1862, Langhorne Letters.
133. G. K. Harlow to his family, 23 January 1862, Harlow Letters.
134. John Garibaldi to his wife, 25 January 1862, Garibaldi Letters, Virginia Military Institute, Lexington, Virginia.
135. A. S. Miller to his wife, 24 February 1862, Miller Letters.

136. *OR,* ser. IV, vol. 1, pp. 1011, 1114–15.
137. Ibid., vol. 5, p. 1016.
138. Graybill, *Diary,* 28 February and 17 March 1862.
139. Paxton, *Elisha Paxton,* p. 44.
140. S. J. C. Moore to his wife, 12 January 1862, Moore Papers.
141. L. M. Blackford to his mother, 16 January 1862, Blackford Papers.
142. Joseph M. Kern to "Sue," 4 February 1862, Kern Letters, Southern Historical Society Collection, Chapel Hill, North Carolina.
143. Ted Barclay to his sister, 10 February and 3 March 1862, Barclay Letters.
144. Baylor, *Bull Run,* p. 34.
145. *OR,* vol. 12, pt. 3, p. 880.
146. Turner Ashby to J. P. Benjamin, 17 March 1862, Ashby Letters.
147. McDonald, *Laurel Brigade,* p. 21.
148. R. W. Waldrop to his father, 14 February 1862, Waldrop Letters.
149. Robert W. Hooke to his family, 9 March 1862, Hooke Letters, Duke University, Durham, North Carolina.
150. *OR,* vol. 5, p. 1086.
151. Apperson Diary, 19 February 1862.

CHAPTER 5

1. Dunbar Rowland, ed., *Jefferson Davis: Constitutionalist* (Jackson, Miss.: Mississippi Department of Archives and History, 1923), pp. 198–203.
2. *OR,* vol. 3, pp. 525–26; vol. 51, pt. 2, p. 497.
3. *OR,* vol. 5, p. 1074.
4. Ibid., p. 1081.
5. Testimony of General Irwin McDowell before the Committee on the Conduct of the War, Senate Documents, 37th Congress, 1863, vol. 2, p. 139.
6. *OR,* vol. 5, pp. 41, 56, 57; *B & L,* vol. 2, p. 163.
7. *OR,* vol. 5, pp. 50, 56; vol. 12, pt. 1, p. 223.
8. Ibid., vol. 5, pp. 55–56; vol. 12, pt. 1, pp. 228–29.
9. Ibid., vol. 12, pt. 1, p. 224.
10. Ibid., vol. 5, pp. 19–22.
11. Ibid., vol. 11, pt. 3, p. 15.
12. Ibid., vol. 51, pt. 1, p. 523
13. The essence of these orders can be found in *OR,* vol. 5, p. 1087, and Joseph E. Johnston, *Narrative of Military Operations* (New York: D. Appleton and Co., 1874; reprint ed., Bloomington: Indiana University Press, 1959), p. 106.
14. Crist and Dix, *Papers of Davis,* vol. 8, p. 68. The strength figures are reported in *OR,* vol. 5, p. 1086 and Allan, *Valley Campaign,* p. 39.

15. Robert K. Krick, *Lee's Colonels* (Dayton, Ohio: Morningside Bookshop, 1979), p. 66.
16. Charles C. Walker, *Memorial, Virginia Military Institute* (Philadelphia: J. B. Lippincott, 1875) pp. 210–216.
17. Jackson to Turner Ashby, 14 March 1862, Jackson Papers (b), Virginia Historical Society, Richmond, Virginia.
18. *OR*, vol. 5, p. 735.
19. J. H. Langhorne to his father, 8 March 1862, Langhorne Letters.
20. Chase Diary, 9 March 1862.
21. Colt, *Defend the Valley*, p. 115.
22. R. W. Waldrop to his mother, 21 February 1862, Waldrop Letters.
23. White, *Hugh White*, pp. 73–74.
24. S. J. C. Moore to his wife, 10 March 1862, Moore Papers.
25. T. J. Jackson to General D. H. Hill, 25 February 1862, Jackson Papers (c), Virginia Military Institute, Lexington, Virginia.
26. White, *Hugh White*, p. 75.
27. *OR*, vol. 5, p. 1095.
28. Douglas, *I Rode with Stonewall*, p. 27.
29. J. K. Edmondson to his wife, 8 March 1862, Edmondson Letters.
30. J. H. Langhorne to his father, 8 March 1862, Langhorne Letters.
31. Apperson Diary, 9 March 1862.
32. MS Diary of Harry R. Morrison, Rockbridge Historical Society, Lexington, Virginia, 8–10 March 1862.
33. John Harman to his brother, 7–10 March 1862, Hotchkiss Papers.
34. J. Se Cheverell, *Journal History of the 29th Ohio* (Privately printed, Cleveland, 1883), pp. 36–37.
35. Morrison Diary, 11 March 1862; MS Diary of Randolph Tucker, 12 March 1862, Museum of the Confederacy, Richmond, Virginia.
36. Ibid.; Paxton, *Elisha Paxton*, p. 51.
37. Morrison Diary, 11 March 1862.
38. Edinburg (Virginia) *Sentinel*, "Stray Recollections of a Private of Co. C, 7th Virginia Cavalry," 28 June 1900.
39. Morrison Diary, 11 March 1862. Other observers indicated Federals were feared from the direction of Bath. See Colt, *Defend the Valley*, p. 116.
40. Johnston, *Narrative*, p. 106.
41. Morrison Diary, 11 March 1862.
42. A. S. Pendleton to his mother, 13 March 1862, Bean, ed., "Pendleton Letters," p. 336.
43. *OR*, vol. 5, p. 740.
44. MS Diary of William P. Parker, Washington and Lee University, Lexington, Virginia, 1 February 1862; Jedediah Hotchkiss typescript "Journal of Jed. Hotchkiss, Campaigns of 1861, 1862," Hotchkiss Papers.
45. John Harman to his brother, 10 March 1862, Hotchkiss Papers.
46. 3 *C.M.H., Virginia*, p. 216. Hotchkiss, author of this volume, was not

with Jackson on March 11, but he worked closely for an extended time with many of those present at the council. He is the only source to specify where Jackson intended to attack.

47. *OR,* vol. 12, pt. 3, p. 837.
48. Jackson, *Life of Jackson,* pp. 240–43, 500–501.
49. Jackson possessed unusually reliable information on this point. See *B & L,* vol. 2, p. 302 for the recollection of General Nathan Kimball, who wrote that the bulk of Shields's Division remained around Martinsburg on the night of the eleventh while his brigade made a night march toward Winchester.
50. Kinzer Diary, 11 March 1862; Tucker Diary, 12 March 1862.
51. John Harman to his brother, 10 March 1862, Hotchkiss Papers.
52. Jackson, *Life of Jackson,* p. 243.
53. A. S. Pendleton to his mother, 13 March 1862, Bean, ed., "Pendleton Letters," p. 336.
54. Morrison Diary, 12 March 1862.
55. A. S. Pendleton to his mother, 13 March 1862, Bean, ed., "Pendleton Letters, p. 337; Edinburg (Virginia) *Sentinel,* "Stray Recollections of a Private of Co. C, 7th Virginia Cavalry," 28 June 1900.
56. Henderson, *Stonewall Jackson,* pp. 174–75.
57. Alpheus S. Williams, *From the Cannon's Mouth* (Detroit: Wayne State University Press and Detroit Historical Society, 1959), p. 63.
58. Jackson, *Life of Jackson,* p. 242.

CHAPTER 6

1. Cooke, *Jackson,* pp. 106–7. A more realistic account of this episode is found in Dabney, *Jackson,* p. 311.
2. MS Neese Diary, 12 March 1862.
3. Gilmor, *Four Years,* pp. 30–31.
4. Henderson, *Stonewall Jackson,* p. 170.
5. MS Diary of S. J. C. Moore, 16 March 1862, Moore Papers.
6. *OR,* vol. 51, pt. 2, p. 534.
7. A. S. Pendleton to his mother, 16 March 1862, Bean, ed., "Pendleton Letters," p. 339.
8. *OR,* vol. 51, pt. 2, p. 495.
9. Ibid., vol. 5, p. 1097.
10. J. S. Waddell, *Annals of Augusta County* (Richmond: William Ellis Jones, 1886), p. 44.
11. Jedediah Hotchkiss, *Make Me a Map of the Valley: The Civil War Journal of Stonewall Jackson's Topographer,* ed. by Archie P. McDonald (Dallas: Southern Methodist University Press, 1973), 18–26 March 1862. (Cited hereafter as Hotchkiss, *Diary,* in distinction to other versions of his diary, which exist in an original state and will be noted as such when utilized for information not appearing in the edited volume.)

12. *OR,* vol. 5, p. 1088.
13. Ibid., p. 1092.
14. Johnston to Jackson, 19 March 1862, T. J. Jackson Papers (b). In his postwar recollections, Johnston confirmed that his order was meant to convey to Jackson that he needed to draw nearer to Banks. Johnston, *Narrative,* p. 107.
15. *OR,* vol. 12, pt. l, pp. 380, 386.
16. Kinzer Diary, 21 March 1862.
17. MS Diary of Watkins Kearns, Virginia Historical Society, Richmond, Virginia, 22 March 1862.
18. L. M. Blackford to his mother, 27 March 1862, Blackford Papers.
19. MS Neese Diary, 22 March 1862.
20. Charles T. O'Ferrall, *Forty Years of Active Service* (New York: Neale Publishing Co., 1904), p. 26
21. *OR,* vol. 12, pt. 1, p. 385.
22. Testimony of T. J. Jackson at Court-Martial of General R. B. Garnett, 6 August 1862, Garnett Court-Martial Papers, Museum of the Confederacy, Richmond, Virginia.
23. *OR,* vol. 12, pt. l, p. 389.
24. S. J. C. Moore to his wife, 16 and 24 December 1861, Moore Letters.
25. *OR,* vol. 12, pt. 1, p. 386; MS Neese Diary, 23 March 1862.
26. *OR,* vol. 12, pt.1, p. 389–90.
27. Ibid., p. 385.
28. Ibid., p. 389.
29. Ibid., p. 381.
30. A. S. Pendleton to his mother, 28 March 1862, Bean, ed., "Pendleton Letters," p. 342 speaks rather routinely of "Our spy, who was in Winchester."
31. Ashby's report merely states that he "learned" of the arrival of Jackson's column and "received" Jackson's order to prepare to advance after he fell back from his skirmish of the morning. Ibid., p. 385.
32. Testimony of T. J. Jackson, 6 August 1862, Garnett Court-Martial Papers.
33. *OR,* vol. 12, pt. 1, pp. 381, 387.
34. Ibid.; T. J. Jackson testimony, 6 August 1862, Garnett Court-Martial Papers.
35. *OR,* vol. 12, pt. l, pp. 408, 387.
36. Ibid., p. 399.
37. Baylor, *Bull Run,* p. 36.
38. *OR,* vol. 12, pt. l, p. 383.
39. Ibid., p. 390.
40. Ibid., p. 385.
41. Ibid., p. 381.
42. Ibid., p. 408.
43. Fonderen, *Carpenter's Battery,* p. 20.
44. *OR,* vol. 12, pt. l, p. 399.
45. Ibid., p. 408.

46. Ibid.
47. Ibid., p. 386.
48. Testimony of T. J. Jackson, 6 August 1862, Garnett Court-Martial Papers.
49. Testimony of A. S. Pendleton, 6 August 1862, Garnett Court-Martial Papers; the order to Garnett is implied in Garnett's report of the battle and stated directly in his written defense of his conduct at the battle sent to General Samuel Cooper on June 20, 1862. Both are found in the Garnett Court-Martial Papers and are quoted extensively herein.
50. Testimony of T. J. Jackson, 6 August 1862, Garnett Court-Martial Papers.
51. *OR,* vol. 12, pt. 1, p. 381.
52. Report of General R. B. Garnett of Battle of Kernstown, 30 March 1862, Garnett Court-Martial Papers.
53. Testimony of T. J. Jackson, 6 August 1862, Garnett Court-Martial Papers.
54. Report of General R. B. Garnett, 30 March 1862, Garnett Court-Martial Papers; OR, vol. 12, pt. 1, p. 391.
55. Pile, George. Memoir of Co. A, 37th Virginia, Manuscript Section, Tennessee State Library and Archives, Nashville, Tennessee.
56. *OR,* vol. 12, pt. 1, p. 408.
57. Report of General R. B. Garnett of 30 March 1862, Garnett Court-Martial Papers.
58. R. B. Garnett to Samuel Cooper, 20 June 1862, Garnett Court-Martial Papers.
59. *OR,* vol. 12, pt. 1, pp. 390, 394.
60. Ibid., p. 394.
61. Ibid., p. 388.
62. R. B. Garnett to Samuel Cooper, 20 June 1862, Garnett Court-Martial Papers.
63. Report of R. B. Garnett, 30 March 1862, Garnett Court-Martial Papers.
64. MS Diary of Frank B. Jones, 23 March 1862, Handley Library, Winchester, Virginia.
65. *OR,* vol. 12, pt. l, p. 388.
66. Ibid., p. 390.
67. Ibid., p. 393; Henry S. Shanklin to his father, 31 March 1862, Shanklin Papers, Virginia State Library, Richmond, Virginia.
68. *OR,* vol. 12, pt. 1, p. 396.
69. Edward Moore, *The Story of a Cannoneer under Stonewall* (New York: Neale Publishing Co., 1907), pp. 24–26, 30; Clement Fishburne, "Historical Sketch of the Rockbridge Artillery," *S.H.S.P.* XXIII, p. 130.
70. Lanty Blackford to his mother, 27 March 1862, Blackford Papers.
71. Moore, *Cannoneer,* pp. 30–31.
72. Testimony of A. S. Pendleton, 6 August 1862, Garnett Court-Martial Papers.

73. Fishburne Journal, p. 41.
74. Ibid.; Moore, *Cannoneer,* p. 31.
75. *OR,* vol. 12, pt. 1, p. 396.
76. Ibid., p. 405.
77. Ibid., p. 400.
78. Henry S. Shanklin to his father, 31 March 1862, Shanklin Papers.
79. Testimony of A. S. Pendleton, 6 August 1862, Garnett Court-Martial Papers.
80. Jones Diary, 23 March 1862.
81. Report of R. B. Garnett, 30 March 1862, Garnett Court-Martial Papers. In his battle report, Fulkerson merely stated that at this juncture he reported his position to Jackson; he wrote nothing about awaiting orders. However, he preceded this statement with a comment that as he reached the ridge the enemy placed infantry support near the guns on Pritchard's Hill "seemingly for the purpose of resisting a charge." *OR,* vol. 12, pt. 1, p. 396. It is dangerous to read too much into this clause, but it may hint that Fulkerson interpreted his mission as a charge; if he felt a charge impossible, it was not unreasonable for him to await new orders, and in the absence of other evidence Garnett's attribution of the statement to Fulkerson is accepted.
82. Report of R. B. Garnett, 30 March 1862, Garnett Court-Martial Papers.
83. John Echols to R. B. Garnett, 30 July 1862, Garnett Court-Martial Papers.
84. Statement of Elliott Johnston, volunteer aide to Garnett, 25 July 1862, Garnett Court-Martial Papers.
85. Report of R. B. Garnett, 30 March 1862, Garnett Court-Martial Papers.
86. Pile, Memoir of Co. A; *OR,* vol. 12, pt. 1, p. 409.
87. Morrison Diary, 23 March 1862.
88. *OR,* vol. 12, pt. 1, p. 388.
89. S. J. C. Moore to his wife, 26 and 28 March 1862, Moore Papers.
90. *OR,* vol. 12, pt. 1, p. 388.
91. R. B. Garnett to Samuel Cooper, 20 June 1862, Garnett Court-Martial Papers.
92. A. S. Pendleton to his father, 29 March 1862, Bean, ed., "Pendleton Letters," p. 342.
93. *OR,* vol. 12, pt. 1, p. 388.
94. Cooke, *Jackson,* p. 114.
95. Baylor, *Bull Run,* p. 37.
96. Casler, *Four Years,* p. 69.
97. Worsham, *Foot Cavalry,* p. 68.
98. Jackson, *Life of Jackson,* p. 248.
99. R. B. Garnett to Samuel Cooper, 20 June 1862, Garnett Court-Martial Papers.
100. *OR,* vol. 12, pt. 1, p. 386.
101. Ibid., p. 397.
102. Fishburne Journal, p. 43.

103. Sworn statement of W. H. Harman to unidentified correspondent, 20 June 1862, Garnett Court-Martial Papers.
104. *OR,* vol. 12, pt. 1, p. 409.
105. Testimony of T. J. Jackson, 6 August 1862, Garnett Court-Martial Papers.
106. Henderson, *Stonewall Jackson,* p. 186.
107. Worsham, *Foot Cavalry,* p. 68.
108. Lyle Recollections, p. 398.
109. *OR,* vol. 12, pt. 1, p. 387.
110. Ibid., p. 398.
111. Ibid., p. 397.
112. Summerfield Smith to his brother, 31 March 1862, Edmund B. Smith Papers, University of Virginia, Charlottesville, Virginia.
113. Fishburne Journal, p. 45.
114. R. B. Garnett to Samuel Cooper, 20 June 1862, Garnett Court-Martial Papers.
115. Sworn statement of W. H. Harman to unidentified correspondent, 20 June 1862, Garnett Court-Martial Papers.
116. Ibid.; *OR,* vol. 12, pt. 1, p. 392.
117. Ibid., pp. 392, 404.
118. Richard L. Armstrong, *7th Virginia Cavalry* (Lynchburg, Va.: H. E. Howard Inc., 1992), p. 24; *OR,* vol. 12, pt. 1, p. 385.
119. McDonald, *Laurel Brigade,* p. 45.
120. Neese, George M., *Three Years in the Confederate Horse Artillery* (New York: Neale Publishing Co., 1911) p. 36.
121. A. S. Pendleton to his father, 29 March 1862, Bean, ed., "Pendleton Letters," p. 342.
122. G. K. Harlow to his family, 26 March 1862, Harlow Letters.
123. J. K. Edmondson to his wife, 25 March 1862, Edmondson Letters.
124. *OR,* vol. 12, pt. 1, p. 383.
125. Paxton, *Elisha Paxton,* p. 54.
126. Henderson, *Stonewall Jackson,* pp. 188–89.
127. *OR,* vol. 12, pt. 1, p. 379. Jackson maintained this opinion for some time. Jackson, *Life of Jackson,* p. 248.
128. *OR,* vol. 5, p. 750.
129. Ibid., vol. 12, pt. 1, pp. 346–47.
130. Ibid., pp. 335–36.
131. Ibid., p. 341.
132. Ibid., pt. 3, p. 16.
133. Ibid., pt. 1, pp. 234–35.
134. Ibid., pp. 226–27.
135. Ibid., pp. 224–25.
136. Ibid., pp. 112–15, 228–29.
137. Ibid., pp. 228–29.
138. Ibid., pp. 230–31.
139. Ibid., pt. 3, p. 43.

140. Ibid., vol. 9, p. 605.
141. Ibid., vol. 12, pt. 1, p. 5.
142. Turner Ashby to J. P. Benjamin, 17 March 1862, Ashby Letters.
143. *OR,* vol. 12, pt. l, p. 386.
144. Ibid., p. 382.
145. Ibid. pp. 384, 408.
146. A. S. Pendleton to his mother, 3 April 1862, Bean, ed., "Pendleton Letters," p. 344.
147. R. B. Garnett to R. M. Hunter, April 1862, Garnett Court-Martial Papers.
148. R. B. Garnett to Samuel Cooper, 20 June 1862, Garnett Court-Martial Papers.
149. Sworn statement of W. H. Harman to unidentified correspondent, 20 June 1862, Garnett Court-Martial Papers.
150. Henderson, *Stonewall Jackson,* p. 193; Poague, *Gunner,* p. 20.
151. Jackson Letter Book, 1862, 29 April 1862, Hotchkiss Papers.
152. Jones Diary, 2 April 1862.
153. Douglas, *I Rode with Stonewall,* p. 37; Colt, *Defend the Valley,* p. 130.
154. R. B. Garnett to Samuel Cooper, 20 June 1862, Garnett Court-Martial Papers.
155. Douglas, *I Rode with Stonewall,* p. 38.
156. Jackson, *Life of Jackson,* pp. 246–47.

CHAPTER 7

1. J. Hotchkiss to his wife, 25 March 1862, Hotchkiss Papers, reported passing on the preceding day ambulances bearing all degree of wounded away from the front, indicating where transportation was located.
2. Jones Diary, 24 March 1862; MS Neese Diary, 24 March 1862; Worsham, *Foot Cavalry,* p. 70.
3. MS Neese Diary, 24 March 1862; Moore, *Cannoneer,* p. 35.
4. Lanty Blackford to his mother, 3 April 1862, Blackford Papers; Moore, *Cannoneer,* p. 35; Jones Diary, 24 March 1862.
5. Kearns Diary, 24 March 1862.
6. Jones Diary, 24 March 1862.
7. Moore, *Cannoneer,* p. 35
8. Lanty Blackford to his mother, 3 April 1862, Blackford Papers.
9. Turner Ashby to J. P. Benjamin, 17 March 1862, Ashby Letters; *OR,* vol. 12, pt. 1, p. 386.
10. *OR,* vol. 12, pt. 3, p. 844.
11. Ibid., pt. l, p. 383.
12. Ibid., p. 384. As to the aborted effort to succor the Valley Army, see ibid., vol. 11, pt. 2, p. 401.
13. Ibid., pt. 3, p. 838.

14. Ibid., p. 841.
15. Neese, *Horse Artillery,* pp. 37–38; *OR,* vol. 12, pt. 3, p. 420.
16. Hotchkiss, *Diary,* 31 March 1862.
17. Hungerford, *Baltimore and Ohio Railroad,* vol. 2, pp. 7–14.
18. A. S. Pendleton to his sister, 12 April 1862, Bean, ed., "Pendleton Letters," p. 347.
19. Jackson Letter Book, 14 April 1862, Hotchkiss Papers.
20. Ibid., 4 April 1862; Krick, *Lee's Colonels,* p. 71.
21. A. S. Pendleton to Ashby, 1 April 1862, Ashby Papers, Virginia Historical Society, Richmond, Virginia.
22. MS Diary of Charles S. Winder, 1 April 1862, Maryland Historical Society, Baltimore, Maryland.
23. Jones Diary, 2 April 1862.
24. Casler, *Four Years,* p. 73.
25. McHenry Howard, *Recollections of a Maryland Staff Officer under Johnston, Jackson and Lee* (Baltimore: Williams and Wilkins Co., 1914), p. 83.
26. Poague, *Gunner,* pp. 19, 21.
27. S. J. C. Moore to his wife, 28 March 1862, Moore Letters.
28. Paxton, *Elisha Paxton,* p. 53.
29. Graybill, *Diary,* 28 April 1862.
30. Neese, *Horse Artillery,* pp. 41, 43; Moore, *Cannoneer,* p. 37.
31. Worsham, *Foot Cavalry,* p. 71.
32. Avirett, *Ashby,* p. 170.
33. *OR,* vol. 12, pt. 3, p. 843.
34. Ibid., pp. 843–44.
35. Ibid., vol. 11, pt. 2, p. 419.
36. These instructions must be inferred from letters written by Jackson in *OR,* vol. 12, pt. 3, pp. 845, 848, 863. As to rebel estimates of food resources in the Shenandoah, see ibid., vol. 11, pt. 3, p. 573.
37. Ibid., vol. 12, pt. 3, p. 848.
38. Ibid., pp. 845, 850.
39. Ibid., pt. 1, p. 426.
40. Avirett, *Ashby,* p. 401–2.
41. *OR,* vol. 12, pt. 3, p. 426.
42. John W. Wayland, *Virginia Valley Records* (Strasburg, Va.: Shenandoah Publishing House, 1930), pp. 280–82; Hotchkiss noted that Ashby personally torched the span, *Diary,* 17 April 1862, which was confirmed by other observers; Colt, *Defend the Valley,* p. 133.
43. Avirett, *Ashby,* p. 174.
44. Neese, *Horse Artillery,* p. 46; Wayland, *Virginia Valley Records,* pp. 278–80.
45. Kearns Diary, 17 April 1862.
46. Douglas, *I Rode with Stonewall,* p. 41
47. *OR,* vol. 12, pt. 3, p. 855.
48. John Harman to his brother, 18 April 1862, Hotchkiss Papers.

49. Jedediah Hotchkiss, MS "Memoranda—Valley Campaign of 1862," 18 April 1862, Hotchkiss Papers, Manuscript Department, New York Historical Society, New York, New York, provides details on movement of the trains. TS Diary of Jasper Hawse, Handley Library, Winchester, Virginia, p. 10, records the killing of Ashby's trooper.
50. Moore, *Cannoneer,* pp. 41–42.
51. *OR,* vol. 12, pt. 3, p. 848.
52. Jedediah Hotchkiss to his wife, 19 April 1862, Hotchkiss Papers; Hotchkiss, *Diary,* 19 April 1862.
53. W. H. Taylor to Jackson, 16 April 1862, Dabney Papers.
54. Avirett, *Ashby,* p. 176.
55. Hotchkiss, *Diary,* 24 April 1862.
56. Ibid.
57. Clarence, *General Ashby,* p. 209.
58. John Harman to his brother, 25 April 1862, Hotchkiss Papers.
59. Hotchkiss, *Diary,* 24 April 1862.
60. Clarence, *General Ashby,* p. 204.
61. Dabney, *Jackson,* p. 397.
62. Winder Diary, 25 April 1862; Howard, *Staff Officer,* p. 90; Hotchkiss, *Diary,* 25 April 1862.
63. John Harman to his brother, 26 April 1862, Hotchkiss Papers.
64. *OR,* vol. 51, pt. 2, p. 543.
65. Ibid., ser. IV, vol. 1, pp. 1045 ff.
66. Ted Barclay to his sister, 15 April 1862, Barclay Letters.
67. White, *Hugh White,* p. 87.
68. Robert E. Lee, Jr., *Recollections and Letters of General Robert E. Lee* (New York: Doubleday, Page, & Co., 1924), p. 70.
69. Lanty Blackford to his mother, 24 April 1862, Blackford Papers.
70. Poague, *Gunner,* p. 21; 3 *C.M.H.,* pp. 1119–20.
71. Baylor, *Bull Run,* p. 37.
72. Gilmor, *Four Years,* p. 32.
73. Jackson reported that Ashby had given him a total of twenty-one companies, *OR,* vol. 12, pt. 3, p. 880; Avirett, *Ashby,* p. 169 and Clarence, *General Ashby,* p. 72 reported 26 companies; McDonald, *Laurel Brigade,* p. 49 reported twenty companies. The most accurate estimate is twenty-four and is contained in a newly discovered letter from one of Ashby's captains dated May 5, 1862. In it James Marshall reports to the then ill Ashby that his commanders had tentatively agreed upon a division of the cavalry into two regiments of ten companies each with four remaining units to form a battalion; names for the commander of each company in the larger units are given. There are twenty-four officers listed. Ashby is not known to have acted upon this idea. James E. Marshall to Ashby, 5 May 1862, Ashby Papers.
74. S. J. C. Moore to his wife, 27 April 1862, Moore Papers.
75. Neese, *Horse Artillery,* p. 54.
76. S. J. C. Moore to his wife, 26 March 1862, Moore Papers. On the

improving state of Army morale in general, see also White, *Hugh White,* p. 81 and Paxton, *Elisha Paxton,* p. 55.

77. Jennings C. Wise, *The Military History of the Virginia Military Institute from 1839–1875* (Lynchburg, Va.: J. P. Bell, 1915), p. 188.
78. Casler, *Four Years,* p. 72.
79. *OR,* vol. 12, pt. 3, p. 879.
80. Hotchkiss, *Diary,* 14 April 1862.
81. Douglas, *I Rode with Stonewall,* p. 56.
82. Robert L. Dabney, "Stonewall Jackson," *S.H.S.P.* XI, p. 129.
83. Thomas C. Johnson, *The Life and Letters of Robert Lewis Dabney* (Richmond: Whittet and Shepperson, 1903), p. 244.
84. Douglas marginalia in Henderson's *Stonewall Jackson and the American Civil War* in custody of Antietam National Battlefield Park.
85. MS Journal of Sandie Pendleton, 23 April 1862, Pendleton Papers, Duke University, Durham, North Carolina.
86. Douglas, *I Rode with Stonewall,* p. 27.
87. John Harman to A. W. Harman, 17 April 1862, Hotchkiss Papers.
88. Shepard G. Pryor to his wife, 21 April 1862, Pryor Letters, Georgia Department of Archives and History, Atlanta, Georgia.
89. Howard, *Staff Officer,* p. 86.
90. Hotchkiss, *Diary,* 20 April 1862.
91. *OR,* vol. 12, pt. 3, pp. 458, 859–60.
92. Ibid., vol. 5, p. 1099. Douglas Southall Freeman, *R. E. Lee,* 4 vols. (New York: Charles Scribner's Sons, 1934), vol. 2, p. 31 offers the best analysis of Lee's status with the Confederate high command in the spring of 1862.
93. Ibid., vol. 12, pt. 3, p. 855.
94. Ibid., p. 852
95. See *OR,* vol. 12, pt. 3, pp. 878, 884, 885, and 887 for Lee's repeated references to this mission.
96. Ibid., pp. 859–60.
97. Ibid., pp. 862–63.
98. Ibid., pp. 863–64.
99. Ibid., p. 861
100. Ibid., pp. 865–66.
101. Ibid., pp. 868–69
102. Hotchkiss, *Diary,* 24 April 1862.
103. *OR,* vol. 12, pt. 3, p. 875.
104. Ibid., pt. 1, p. 466.
105. Ibid.
106. Ibid., pp. 446–47.
107. Ibid., pt. 3, p. 118.
108. Ibid., p. 122.
109. Ibid., p. 872.
110. S. G. Pryor to his wife, 21 April 1862, Pryor Letters.

111. Jackson used the phrase in a May 3 letter to Superintendent Smith of the Virginia Military Institute quoted in Couper, *One Hundred Years,* vol. 2, p. 151.
112. Jackson specified to Lee that his preferred route was to Staunton via Port Republic. *OR,* vol. 12, pt. 3, p. 872, which is assumed here to mean a direct march as opposed to the course ultimately taken. See also Couper, vol. 2, p. 151, in which is quoted a letter from Jackson to Superintendent Smith regretting that the roads had prevented "my reaching Staunton, as I hoped by marching across the country by Port Republic."
113. *OR,* vol. 12, pt. 3, p. 872; Hotchkiss, *Diary,* 26 April 1862.
114. *OR,* vol. 12, pt. 3, pp. 876, 878.
115. Ibid., pp. 871, 876. The evidence for ascribing to Jackson an estimate of approximately ten days to deal with Frémont is persuasive even if circumstantial. Ashby's biographer, Avirett, cites a letter from Ewell to Ashby dated May 11 in which Ewell, the best source of knowledge on Jackson's projections, complained that "Gen. Jackson has stayed much longer than I anticipated." Avirett, *Ashby,* p. 402. Four days earlier Ewell wrote to L. O'Brian Branch that he anticipated not being able to leave Swift Run Gap for "several days." *OR,* vol. 12, pt. 3, p. 882. Ewell's conduct after May 10 is consistent with the view that he thought by then Jackson would have been seeking other targets than Frémont's vanguard. Finally, on April 30, when Jackson summoned the V.M.I. Corps to Staunton, he assured Superintendent Smith that they would be absent from the Institute "for a few days." Couper, *One Hundred Years,* vol. 2, p. 146. A belief by Jackson that he could deal swiftly with Frémont is also indirect support for the proposition that he intended to march directly to Staunton via Port Republic, a march that with better weather should have been completed in two or three days. Such a direct move, as opposed to the longer and slower detour that occurred, would have permitted Jackson to thrust Frémont back and rejoin Ewell by approximately May 10.
116. Hotchkiss, *Diary,* 26–28 April 1862.
117. Ibid., 29 April 1862.

CHAPTER 8

1. MS Diary of Joseph Kaufman, Southern Historical Collection, University of North Carolina, Chapel Hill, North Carolina, 30 April 1862; Hotchkiss Diary, 30 April 1862.
2. Kaufman Diary, 1 May 1862.
3. E. T. H. Warren to his wife, 5 May 1862, Warren Papers, University of Virginia, Charlottesville, Virginia.

4. Thomas M. Wade, Jr., to Mrs. S. L. Hopkins, 6 May 1862, Wade Letters, Stonewall Jackson House, Lexington, Virginia.
5. Apperson Diary, 1 and 2 May 1862.
6. Lanty Blackford to his mother, 3 May 1862, Blackford Letters
7. Apperson Diary, 2 May 1862; Douglas, *I Rode with Stonewall,* pp. 47–48.
8. J. Hotchkiss to his wife, 3 May 1862, Hotchkiss Papers.
9. Hotchkiss, *Diary,* 1 May 1862.
10. Kaufman Diary, 2 May 1862.
11. TS Memoirs of William Allan, p. 41, Southern Historical Collection, University of North Carolina, Chapel Hill, North Carolina.
12. Hotchkiss, *Diary,* 30 April 1862, places Ashby with his troopers during the operations outside Harrisonburg. The exact nature of the illness is unknown, but it was known to Jackson by May 3; see Dabney to Ashby, 3 May 1862, War Letters 1861–65.
13. Diary of W. H. Arehart, 2 May 1862, printed in the Rockingham (Virginia) *Recorder,* vol. I, no. 2, December 1946.
14. Dr. Harvey Black to his wife, 3 May 1862, Black Family Papers, Virginia Polytechnic Institute, Blacksburg, Virginia. See also Apperson Diary, 2 May 1862.
15. *OR,* vol. 12, pt. 3, p. 126.
16. Dabney to Ashby, 3 May 1862, War Letters 1861–65.
17. Kearns Diary, 3 May 1862
18. *OR,* vol. 12, pt. 3, p. 879.
19. Kearns Diary, 4 May 1862; Apperson Diary, 4 May 1862.
20. Kaufman Diary, 4 May 1862, for example, reported only three trains in operation when the 10th Virginia reached the tracks; James Huffman, *Ups and Downs of a Confederate Soldier* (New York: William E. Rudge's Sons, 1940), p. 46 noted the crowded conditions inside the cars.
21. Journal of J. A. Waddell, 5 May 1862, Hotchkiss Papers.
22. Winder Diary, 5 May 1862, indicates that his brigade marched as far as Afton Station, easily ten miles beyond Mechum's and only fifteen miles from Staunton, and still waited most of the night for trains; the Stonewall Brigade did not reach Staunton until the early hours of the sixth. From Port Republic the brigade had marched more than twenty-five miles before it got a train ride, hardly the sort of journey Jackson would have taken to move his troops the short remaining distance into Staunton by rail or to decoy the enemy. See also Kaufman Diary, 5 May 1862, wherein it is noted that the 10th Virginia was not picked up at Afton until daybreak on the fifth, probably at the same time as the 21st Virginia, which did not reach Staunton until 11 A.M. on the fifth. TS "Memoirs of Asa Wyatt," Southern Historical Papers, University of North Carolina, Chapel Hill. Clearly the railroad had mobilized capacity for only a few regiments at a time and therefore required until May 6

to complete the transfer to Staunton—which further supports the contention that the march to Mechum's was hastily arranged. Six weeks later, when Jackson had at least some opportunity to plan a rail move, the same line mustered trains able to transport fifteen hundred to two thousand men at a time. See Carter Anderson, "Train Running for the Confederacy," *Locomotive Engineering,* July 1892.

23. Kearns Diary, 6 May 1862.
24. Hotchkiss, *Diary,* 4 May 1862.
25. A. S. Pendleton to his mother, 6 May 1862, Bean, ed., "Pendleton Letters," p. 355.
26. Couper, *One Hundred Years,* vol. 2, p. 150.
27. Hotchkiss, *Diary,* 4 May 1862.
28. *OR,* vol. 12, pt. 1, p. 487 provides the organizational details; Allan, *Valley Campaign,* p. 69 gives Johnson's strength as about three thousand, with which Hotchkiss, in 3 *C.M.H.,* p. 226, concurs. Richard L. Armstrong, *The Battle of McDowell* (Lynchburg, Va.: H. E. Howard Inc., 1990), pp. 43–44 gives Johnson slightly higher strength.
29. Krick, *Lee's Colonels,* pp. 87, 311.
30. Irby G. Scott to his father, 4 May 1862, Scott Papers, Duke University, Durham, North Carolina.
31. Order of T. J. Jackson, 4 May 1862, Ashby Papers.
32. Jackson to Johnson, 24 April 1862, Jackson Papers (d), Museum of the Confederacy, Richmond, Virginia.
33. T. J. Jackson to A. R. Boteler, 6 May 1862, Boteler Papers.
34. Howard, *Staff Officer,* p. 100; O'Ferrell, *Forty Years,* p. 32.
35. Hotchkiss, *Diary,* 5 May 1862.
36. *OR,* vol. 12, pt. 3, p. 881.
37. Ibid., pt. 1, p. 456; Gilmor, *Four Years,* p. 34.
38. Hotchkiss, *Diary,* 6 May 1862
39. *OR,* vol. 12, pt. 3, p. 881.
40. MS Diary of Joseph C. Snider, 6 May 1862, Snider Papers, West Virginia University Libraries, Morgantown, West Virginia.
41. *OR,* vol. 12, pt. 3, p. 882.
42. A. S. Pendleton to his mother, 10 May 1862, Bean, ed., "Pendleton Letters," p. 356.
43. Toney, *Privations,* p. 19.
44. Wise, *Military History of V.M.I.,* p. 206
45. R. W. Waldrop to his mother, 6 April 1862, Waldrop Letters; McCarthy, *Soldier Life,* p. 295.
46. Wise, *Military History of V.M.I.,* p. 206.
47. Moore, *Cannoneer,* p. 47.
48. *OR,* vol. 12, pt. 3, p. 884; Snider Diary, 7 May 1862.
49. Winder's Brigade, for example, only reached the top of North Mountain, some eight miles by road east of Johnson's skirmish site, by evening. Winder Diary, 7 May 1862.

50. Snider Diary, 8 May 1862. Johnson reported that he halted his troops on the slopes of Bull Pasture Mountain and advanced approximately two miles beyond to begin his examination of McDowell. *OR,* vol. 12, pt. 1, p. 483.
51. *OR,* vol. 12, pt. 3, p. 884.
52. Hotchkiss, *Diary,* 8 May 1862.
53. According to Johnson as reported in *OR,* vol. 12, pt. 1, p. 483.
54. Colonel Scott of the 44th Virginia understood that artillery was to be brought to the top of the hill to bombard the enemy in the morning. Ibid., p. 485. In an entry evidently made after the event, Hotchkiss stated he discovered a trail for the purpose of bringing guns to the crest on Jackson's orders. Hotchkiss, *Diary,* 8 May 1862. In a postwar work (3 *C.M.H.,* p. 229), however, Hotchkiss suggested that Jackson had decided to follow the envelopment strategy. Allan, *Valley Campaign,* p. 74, agrees. There was no explanation by Jackson of his intentions in his official report. Dabney implied that both courses were actively considered for some time (Dabney, *Jackson,* p. 344), but he does not appear to have been with Jackson that afternoon. *OR,* vol. 12, pt. 1, p. 473.
55. Worsham, *Foot Cavalry,* pp. 79–80.
56. *OR,* vol. 12, pt. 1, pp. 483, 485.
57. Dabney, *Jackson,* p. 345
58. *OR,* vol. 12, pt. 1, p. 471.
59. See Armstrong, *Battle of McDowell,* pp. 43–44, 52 for strength comparisons. Milroy had almost eighteen hundred infantry in his command, to which he added perhaps five hundred more men from one of Schenck's brigades, the 82nd Ohio. With the 31st Virginia initially out of the fight while holding the road and Southern artillery unable to participate at all, Johnson's five regiments probably did not exceed twenty-eight hundred men actively engaged for the first hour or so.
60. *OR,* vol. 12, pt. 1, p. 486.
61. Ibid., p. 483.
62. Howard, *Staff Officer,* p. 97.
63. Snider Diary, 13 May 1862.
64. Hotchkiss, *Diary,* 9 May 1862; see also John Harman to his brother, 11 May 1862, Hotchkiss Papers.
65. *OR,* vol. 12, pt. 1, pp. 481, 486.
66. Kaufman Diary, 8 and 9 May 1862.
67. Jackson to Boteler, 6 May 1862, Boteler Papers.
68. Hotchkiss, *Diary,* 8 May 1862.
69. Worsham, *Foot Cavalry,* p. 73.
70. Hotchkiss, *Diary,* 8 May 1862; *OR,* vol. 12, pt. 1, p. 483.
71. Winder Diary, 8 May 1862; Kearns Diary, 8 May 1862; Howard, *Staff Officer,* pp. 96–97.
72. Kearns Diary, 8 May 1862.
73. Apperson Diary, 8 May 1862.

74. Jones Diary, 13 May 1862.
75. Kearns Diary, 8 May 1862.
76. See, e.g., *OR,* vol. 12, pt. 1, p. 481.
77. Kearns Diary, 8 May 1862; Winder Diary, 8 May 1862.
78. Hotchkiss, *Diary,* 8 May 1862.
79. *OR,* vol. 12, pt. 1, p. 470 contains the report, directed to Adjutant General Cooper. Emphasis is often laid upon this dispatch as an example of Jackson's laconic style of communication. Of Jackson's secretive nature there can be no doubt, but in this instance Jackson may simply have assumed that his deputy in Staunton, Major Asher Harman (in whom he placed great trust), would collect and forward pertinent details of the battle to Richmond, as in fact he did by telegram on May 9 to Lee. Ibid., vol. 51, pt. 2, pp. 553–54. Details of Jackson writing his report are provided by Imboden, *B & L,* vol. 2, p. 287.
80. *OR,* vol. 12, pt. 1, p. 463.
81. Armstrong, *Battle of McDowell,* p. 100 offers the most detailed analysis of casualties and concludes they were slightly higher than those given by *OR,* vol. 12, pt. 1, pp. 462, 476.
82. Howard, *Staff Officer,* p. 98; Apperson Diary, 9 May 1862.
83. *OR,* vol. 12, pt. 1, p. 476; Kearns Diary, 9 May 1862.
84. *OR,* vol. 12, pt. 1, p. 483.
85. Jackson Letter Book, 10 February 1863, Hotchkiss Papers. On May 12, in a brief summary of the battle to Major Rhett, the assistant adjutant general in Richmond, Jackson stated that Johnson's "gallant conduct entitles him to great praise." Jackson Letter Book, Hotchkiss Papers.
86. Jackson to Boteler, 6 May 1862; Boteler Papers; Robert K. Krick, "The Army of Northern Virginia's Most Notorious Court Martial: Jackson vs. Garnett," *Blue and Gray Magazine,* vol. 3, no. 6 (July 1986), p. 29.
87. *OR,* vol. 12, pt. 1, p. 472.
88. Ibid., p. 484.
89. Ibid., pt. 3, p. 889.
90. Johnston to Jackson, 12 May 1862, Dabney Papers.
91. *OR,* vol. 12, pt. 3, p. 886.
92. Ibid., pt. 1, p. 472. Johnson, writing as early 17 May 1862, thought he had information that allowed him to estimate Federal losses between five hundred and one thousand. Ibid., p. 483.
93. Winder Diary, 9 May 1862; Snider Diary, 9 May 1862.
94. Lanty Blackford to his mother, 10 May 1862, Blackford Papers.
95. *OR,* vol. 12, pt. l, p. 720.

CHAPTER 9

1. *OR,* vol. 12, pt. 3, pp. 884, 887.
2. Ibid., pt. 1, p. 472. Allan, *Valley Campaign,* p. 80 and Dabney, *Jackson,* p. 352 claimed that this operation was assigned to local civilians.
3. J. Hotchkiss, undated, three-page MS "Account," Hotchkiss Papers; Hotchkiss, *Diary,* 10 May 1862.
4. James Marshall to Ashby, 5 May 1862, Ashby Papers. This interesting and newly discovered letter is a suggestion to Ashby by one of his senior officers on how the cavalry might be split into regiments and a battalion under the senior captains. It included a roster of all Ashby's companies but does not mention Sterrett's unit.
5. J. Hotchkiss, undated "Account," Hotchkiss Papers.
6. Apperson Diary, 11 May 1862.
7. Fishburne Journal, p. 55.
8. Allan Memoirs, handwritten continuation of typescript, unnumbered.
9. Dabney, *Jackson,* p. 352.
10. Howard, *Staff Officer,* pp. 101–2.
11. Ted Barclay to his sister, 16 May 1862, Barclay Letters.
12. Howard, *Staff Officer,* pp. 102–3; Kearns Diary, 11 May 1862.
13. *OR,* vol. 12, pt. 3, p. 887.
14. Kearns Diary, 12 May 1862; Snider Diary, 12 May 1862.
15. *OR,* vol. 12, pt. 3, p. 887.
16. Ibid., p. 888.
17. Ibid., pp. 883–84.
18. See, e.g., Ewell to Jackson, 4 P.M., 13 May 1862, Dabney Papers.
19. Philip Slaughter, *A Sketch of the Life of Randolph Fairfax* (Baltimore: Innen and Co., 1878), pp. 25–26; Lanty Blackford to his mother, 25 May 1862, Blackford Letters.
20. Gilmor, *Four Years,* p. 38.
21. *OR,* vol. 12, pt. 3, pp. 143, 180.
22. Ewell to Jackson, 2 A.M., 13 May 1862, Dabney Papers.
23. Ewell to Jackson, 4 P.M., 13 May 1862, Dabney Papers.
24. Hall, *Diary,* 14 May 1862.
25. Wise, *Military History of V.M.I.,* p. 209.
26. E. T. H. Warren to his wife, 16 May 1862, Warren Letters.
27. Lanty Blackford to his mother, 11 May 1862, Blackford Letters.
28. Hotchkiss, *Diary,* 14 April 1862; Garbar, *Sketch of Harman,* pp. 40–41.
29. *OR,* vol. 12, pt. 1, p. 472.
30. John Harman to his brother, 15 May 1862, Hotchkiss Papers.
31. John Harman to his brother, 18 May 1862, Hotchkiss Papers.
32. See McCarthy, *Soldier Life,* pp. 308–9.
33. Apperson Diary, 14 May 1862.
34. Charles L. Powell, Jr., to his sister, 26 May 1862, Powell Family

Papers, Swem Library, William and Mary University, Williamsburg, Virginia.

35. See William Gilham, *Manual of Instruction for the Volunteers and Militia of the United States* (Philadelphia: Charles Desilver, 1861), section 771.
36. Jackson Letter Book, 1862, 13 May 1862, Hotchkiss Papers.
37. Dabney, *Jackson,* p. 354; a copy of the order was kept in the archives of the 3d Brigade, Taliaferro's. Taliaferro Papers, War Records Group 109, chapter II, vol. 16, National Archives, Washington, D.C.
38. Kearns Diary, 15 May 1862.
39. This subject is treated in interesting detail and from the firsthand perspective of a marching soldier in Lanty Blackford to his mother, 29 May 1862; see also Shepard Pryor to his wife, 27 May 1862, Pryor Letters.
40. Hall, *Diary,* 15 May 1862.
41. Kaufman Diary, 15 May 1862.
42. Wise, *Military History of V.M.I.,* p. 203.
43. Jackson Letter Book, 1862, 16 May 1862, Hotchkiss Papers.
44. William L. Wilson, *A Borderland Confederate,* ed. by Festus P. Summers (Pittsburgh: University of Pittsburgh Press, 1962), 13 May 1862. (Cited hereafter as Wilson, Diary.)
45. Frank M. Myers, *The Comanches: A History of White's Battalion* (Baltimore: Kelley Piet and Co., 1871), p. 48.
46. Apperson Diary, 16 May 1862.
47. W. W. Scott, ed., "Diary of H. W. Wingfield," *Bulletin of the Virginia State Library* (July 1927), 16 May 1862.
48. Ted Barclay to his sister, 16 May 1862, Barclay Letters.
49. Kaufman Diary, 17 May 1862.
50. Winder Diary, 17 May 1862.
51. Jackson, *Life of Jackson,* pp. 257–58.

CHAPTER 10

1. William C. Oates, *The War Between the Union and the Confederacy: A History of the 15th Alabama Regiment* (New York: Neale Publishing Co., 1905), p. 93.
2. James C. Nisbet, *Four Years on the Firing Line,* ed. by Bill I. Wiley (Jackson, Tenn.: McCowart-Mercer Press, 1963), p. 33.
3. Oates, *The War,* p. 93.
4. R. H. Peck, *Reminiscences of a Confederate Soldier* (privately printed, Fincastle, Va., 1913), p. 13; J. William Jones, "Reminiscences of the Army of Northern Virginia," *S.H.S.P.* IX, p. 187. (Cited hereafter as Jones, "Reminiscences.")

5. Taylor, *Destruction and Reconstruction,* pp. 33–38; Peck, *Reminiscences,* p. 13; T. T. Munford, "Reminiscences of Jackson's Valley Campaign," *S.H.S.P.* VII, p. 523. (Cited hereafter as Munford, "Jackson's Valley Campaign.")
6. MS Memoirs of Campbell H. Brown, Manuscript Unit, Tennessee State Library and Archives, Nashville, Tennessee, p. 39; see *OR,* vol. 5, p. 1089 concerning Trimble's rail challenges during the withdrawal from Manassas.
7. Cooper, *One Hundred Years at V.M.I.,* vol. 3, p. 179.
8. Johnson, 2 *C.M.H.,* p. 69; McKim, *Soldier's Recollections,* p. 86
9. Taylor's recollections are found in *Destruction and Reconstruction,* pp. 48–49, 68, 87. Modern scholarship on these regiments is contained in the valuable T. Michael Parrish, *Richard Taylor, Soldier Prince of Dixie* (Chapel Hill, N.C.: University of North Carolina Press, 1992), pp. 129, 158 and Terry L. Jones, *Lee's Tigers* (Baton Rouge, La.: Louisiana State University Press, 1987), pp. 238–243.
10. Taylor, *Destruction and Reconstruction,* p. 17; Jones, *Lee's Tigers,* pp. 35, 249; New Orleans *Daily True Delta,* 15 August 1861; Brown Memoirs, p. 31.
11. Taylor, *Destruction and Reconstruction,* pp. 21–22; Parrish, *Richard Taylor,* pp. 140–141.
12. Taylor, *Destruction and Reconstruction,* pp. 35, 40.
13. Wise, *The Long Arm of Lee,* vol. 1, p. 170.
14. *OR,* vol. 12, pt. 3, pp. 850–51.
15. Ibid., p. 876; Hotchkiss, *Diary,* 30 April 1862.
16. Brown Memoirs, p. 33.
17. Dispatches for all days between May 3 and May 12 except May 9 and 11 are found in *OR,* vol. 12, pt. 3. Ewell's Letter Book contains an unpublished note from Jackson dated 9 May advising of the victory at McDowell and expressing his hope to be with Ewell in a few days. Brown Papers.
18. Jones, *S.H.S.P.* IX, pp. 364–65.
19. *OR,* vol. 12, pt. 3, pp. 880–81.
20. Ibid., p. 885.
21. Ibid., pp. 883, 885. This movement was later ended by the Union advance culminating in the Battle of Drewry's Bluff, and only two of Mahone's regiments reached Branch.
22. Ibid., pp. 881, 887.
23. See, e.g., ibid., pp. 883–84.
24. Ibid., p. 882.
25. Ibid., p. 881.
26. Ibid., p. 887.
27. Munford, "Jackson's Valley Campaign," *S.H.S.P.* VII, p. 526.
28. Ewell to Jackson, 2 A.M., 13 May 1862, Dabney Papers, specified that divisional cavalry was ready to go after Shields. The letter does not specify that Munford was the commander, but the letter so closely

coincides with Munford's recollections (*S.H.S.P.* VII, p. 526) that the inference seems justified that the operation Munford describes in his postwar recollection is the one Ewell related to Jackson.

29. *OR,* vol. 12, pt. 1, p. 502; Ewell to Jackson, 4 P.M., 13 May 1862, Dabney Papers, specifically complains of the lack of news.
30. Percy G. Hamlin, *The Making of a Soldier: Letters of General R. S. Ewell* (Richmond, Va., Whittet and Shepperson, 1935), p. 108.
31. *OR,* vol. 12, pt. 3, pp. 888–89.
32. Ibid., p. 890.
33. Ibid.
34. Ibid., p. 889.
35. TS Diary of James William Thomas, 15 May 1862, in possession of Mr. A. Thomas Wallace, Annapolis, Maryland, indicates that the head of the column was the 1st Maryland. Ewell to Jackson, typescript of 16 May 1862 letter, erroneously rendered as 18 May in Jackson Papers (a), indicates that the head of Ewell's column reached Columbia Bridge on the fifteenth. Overall the division made good speed. See "The Civil War Diary of James J. Kirkpatrick, 16th Mississippi Infantry, C.S.A," 15 May 1862. Thesis presented by Eugene Matthew Ott, Jr., Texas A & M University, 1984. (Cited hereafter as Kirkpatrick Diary.)
36. *OR,* vol. 11, pt. 3, pp. 499–500. In his memoirs, Johnston stated that he had left instructions for Ewell and Jackson to correspond to him but that the messages were evidently intercepted in Richmond, because he received no such letters until he drew nearer the capital. Johnston did not assign blame for this lapse. Johnston, *Narrative,* p. 129. For examples of the occasional reports on Valley conditions received by Johnston from Lee, see *OR,* vol. 11, pt. 2, pp. 459, 519.
37. Johnston to Jackson, 12 May 1862, Dabney Papers.
38. Crist and Dix, *Papers of Davis,* vol. 8, pp. 174, 203.
39. *OR,* vol. 12, pt. 3, p. 888. Ewell specified he had received Johnston's letter of the thirteenth the day before, that is, on the fifteenth, in Ewell to Jackson, 16 May 1862, Jackson Papers (a).
40. Ibid., p. 891.
41. Ewell to Branch, 16 May 1862 (letter apparently written in Swift Run Gap in the morning), L. O'Bryan Branch Papers (a), University of Virginia, Charlottesville, Virginia.
42. Ewell to Jackson, 16 May 1862, Jackson Papers (a).
43. *OR,* vol. 12, pt. 1, p. 498.
44. Munford, *S.H.S.P.* VII, p. 527.
45. *OR,* vol. 12, pt. 3, p. 894.
46. Ewell to Branch, 16 May 1862 (letter written at Columbia Bridge), Branch Papers (a).
47. *OR,* vol. 12, pt. 3, p. 895 contains Jackson's response to Ewell's note. Ewell's dispatch had not been found.
48. Jno. Lucas, Chief of Staff, Ewell's Division to Branch, 17 May 1862, Branch Papers (a).

49. Munford, *S.H.S.P.* VII, p. 523.
50. *OR,* vol. 12, pt. 3, p. 893.
51. McKim, *Soldier's Recollections,* p. 86.
52. Thomas Diary, 17 May 1862.
53. Austin C. Dobbins, *Grandfather's Journal: The Journal of Franklin L. Riely* (Dayton, Ohio: Morningside Bookshop, 1988), p. 79.
54. TS Diary of W. P. Harper, 17 May 1862, Tulane University Library, New Orleans, Louisiana; MS Diary of George P. Ring, 17 May 1862, Tulane University Library, New Orleans, Louisiana; TS Diary of Isaiah Fogleman, 17 May 1862, Fredericksburg Spotsylvania National Military Park, Fredericksburg, Virginia.
55. *OR,* vol. 12, pt. 3, p. 895.
56. Jno. Lucas to Branch, 18 May 1862, L. O'Bryan Branch Papers, North Carolina State Archives, Raleigh, North Carolina. (Cited hereafter as Branch Papers (b).)
57. Jno. Lucas to Branch, 19 May 1862, Branch Papers (b) records the fact that Brown was sent. In Brown Memoirs, p. 37, Brown recalled the trip to Gordonsville but recollected he carried a telegram to Johnston. The message went to Lee, who forwarded it to Johnston for decision; Johnston had it by 2 P.M. on the eighteenth. Johnston to Ewell, 18 May 1862, Jackson Papers (b).

CHAPTER 11

1. Moore, *Cannoneer,* p. 50.
2. Ibid.
3. Shephard G. Pryor to his wife, 18 May 1862, Pryor Letters.
4. John W. Wayland, *Stonewall Jackson's Way* (Staunton, Va.: The McClure Co., 1940), p. 102.
5. McGuire, *Diary,* p. 112.
6. Hotchkiss, *Diary,* 18 May 1862.
7. *OR,* vol. 12, pt. 3, p. 894.
8. Ibid., pp. 892–93.
9. Dabney, *Jackson,* p. 359.
10. *OR,* vol. 12, pt. 3, p. 897.
11. Hotchkiss, *Diary,* 18 May 1862.
12. Hotchkiss, MS "Memoranda—Valley Campaign of 1862," 18 April 1862.
13. Ibid., 18 May 1862; Garbar, *Sketch of Harman,* p. 19.
14. Moore, *Cannoneer,* p. 53; Worsham, *Foot Cavalry,* p. 80.
15. MS Record Book of William B. Taliaferro, 19 May 1862, Taliaferro Papers, National Archives, Washington, D.C.
16. *OR,* vol. 12, pt. 3, p. 202.
17. Jno. Lucas to Branch, 19 May 1862, Branch Papers (b).

18. Diary of George B. Johnston, 8 June 1862, Johnston Papers, North Carolina Department of Archives and History, Raleigh, North Carolina.
19. See, e.g., McKim, *Soldier's Recollections,* p. 88; Thomas Diary, 19 May 1862; TS Diary of Joseph M. Kern, 19 May 1862, Southern Historical Society Papers, University of North Carolina, Chapel Hill, North Carolina.
20. Harper Diary, 19 May 1862; Ring Diary, 19 May 1862.
21. Snider Diary, 19 May 1862; TS Diary of John Griffin, 19 May 1862, Emory University Library, Atlanta, Georgia.
22. See, e.g., Kearns Diary, 19 May 1862; Winder Diary, 19 May 1862.
23. *OR,* vol. 12, pt. 3, p. 898.
24. Hotchkiss, *Diary,* 19–22 May 1862.
25. Dan Oates, ed., *Hanging Rock Rebel: Lt. John Blue's War in West Virginia and the Shenandoah Valley* (Shippensburg, Pa.: Burd Street Press, 1994). Blue, a Confederate irregular, encountered a party of cavalrymen in Brock's Gap on May 23 on this mission. It is to be presumed the task was given by Jackson, but there is no official record of it, and in any event it does not appear to have been fulfilled, unlike Hotchkiss's pass-blocking mission.
26. Hall, *Diary,* 20 May 1862; see also Wilson, *Diary,* 18 May 1862; Apperson Diary, 20 May 1862.
27. The position of Trimble's Brigade is based upon the location of two regiments, the 16th Mississippi, Kirkpatrick Diary, 20 May 1862, and the 15th Alabama, Lieutenant Joseph M. Ellison to his wife, 26 May 1862 in Calvin J. Billman, ed., "Joseph M. Ellison: War Letters (1862)," *Collections of the Georgia Historical Quarterly,* vol. 48, 1964, p. 230. No sources pinpoint Trimble's other regiments, but there is no reason to believe his command was not together. The position of Elzey's command is confirmed for the 1st Maryland in Thomas Diary, 20 May 1862, and the 13th Virginia in Notes on Company K, Compiled Service Records for the 13th Virginia, National Archives, Washington, D.C. As to the position of the 13th see also Samuel D. Buck, *With the Old Confeds* (Baltimore: H. E. Houch & Co., 1925), p. 29.
28. *OR,* vol. 51, pt. 2, p. 560.
29. Snider Diary, 20 May 1862.
30. Worsham, *Foot Cavalry,* p. 81; Apperson Diary, 20 May 1862.
31. William Allan Memoirs, handwritten continuation of initial writing, unnumbered pages.
32. Taylor, *Destruction and Reconstruction,* p. 49.
33. Douglas, *I Rode with Stonewall,* p. 93.
34. Johnston Diary, 8 June 1862.
35. *OR,* vol. 12, pt. 3, p. 898.
36. Ibid., pp. 896–97.
37. Douglas, *I Rode with Stonewall,* p. 93. Freeman in *Lee's Lieutenants,* vol. 1, p. 362, footnote 2 disputed the accuracy of this exchange as

quoted by Douglas and assumed it referred to Ewell's arrival at Mount Solon on May 18. Were that the case the conversation would have made no sense and Freeman's doubts would have been justified. However, the words are perfectly consistent with the situation on the evening of the twentieth, and Ewell's visit was contemporaneously verified by Sandie Pendleton, infra. Therefore no good reason exists to doubt Douglas on this conversation.

38. A. S. Pendleton to his mother, 20 May 1862, Bean, ed., "Pendleton Letters," p. 360.
39. Douglas, *I Rode with Stonewall,* p. 93.
40. Boteler to Jackson, 16 May 1862, Dabney Papers.
41. *OR,* vol. 12, pt. 3, p. 898.
42. Ibid., p. 897. The wording of this endorsement is further evidence, if any is needed, of the actual meeting of Jackson and Ewell on the twentieth. If Ewell had not been present to see what Jackson wrote to Lee and by what means, he could not have known to what telegram the endorsement referred, without which there would be little reason for Jackson to expect Ewell to ignore Johnston's instructions.
43. Taylor, *Destruction and Reconstruction,* p. 50.
44. Freeman in *R. L. Lee,* vol. 2, p. 57, for example, speculated about a visit by Lee to Davis to secure permission to override Johnston's orders, conjectures followed and amplified by Jackson's most assiduous biographers. See Lenoir Chambers, *Stonewall Jackson* (New York: William Morrow & Co., 1959), vol. 1, p. 521. Unable to offer a more satisfactory solution, an earlier work by this author followed these speculations; see Robert G. Tanner, *Stonewall in the Valley* (Garden City, N.Y.: Doubleday & Company, Inc., 1976), p. 201.
45. Garbar, *Sketch of Harman,* p. 17; A. W. Harman, "The Valley after Kernstown," *S.H.S.P.* XIX, pp. 318–19.
46. Allan, *Valley Campaign,* p. 89. The reprint in *OR,* vol. 12, pt. 3, p. 898 omits this line of detail.
47. Johnston to Ewell, 18 May 1862, Jackson Papers (b) makes this clear. See note 50 and accompanying text.
48. Dabney Papers. The handwriting of the telegram might be read to indicate that it was dated the twenty-seventh, but that is unreasonable. Jackson's victory at Winchester was already known on the streets of Richmond by the twenty-seventh (see McGuire, *Diary,* p. 117), and it is impossible to believe Johnston was so far out of touch that he would only that day be authorizing the battle begun four days earlier.
49. *B & L,* vol. 2, p. 288.
50. Johnston to Ewell, 18 May 1862, 2 P.M., Jackson Papers (b) states that Johnston had received from Lee the telegram forwarded by Ewell's aide, and Campbell Brown is the only man known to have been sending messages to Richmond for Ewell at this time.
51. Johnston to Ewell, 18 May 1862, Jackson Papers (b). In his postwar recollection, Johnston confused these letters with the telegram,

writing that he authorized Jackson to attack—the telegram of the twenty-first—in response to Jackson's description of Banks's position—which was given in his letter from Mount Solon. See Johnston, *Narrative,* p. 129.

52. Myers, *The Comanches,* pp. 48–49. Myers does not specify the contents of the dispatches, but nothing else Ewell had to communicate to Jackson that day demanded frantic delivery.
53. Winder Diary, 21 May 1862; Kirkpatrick Diary, 21 May 1862.
54. Myers, *The Comanches,* p. 49. The details of Jackson's uniform were recorded later that day by Captain Kirkpatrick in his diary.
55. Kirkpatrick Diary, 21 May 1862; Winder Diary, 21 May 1862.
56. Myers, *The Comanches,* p. 49; Thomas Diary, 21 May 1862 confirms that the 1st Maryland initially marched a mile or two westward before reversing direction.
57. Buck, *With the Old Confeds,* p. 30.
58. Kirkpatrick Diary, 21 May 1862; Thomas Diary, 21 May 1862; the Stonewall Brigade was in the rear camped only partially up Massanutten Mountain. Winder Diary, 21 May 1862.
59. Hotchkiss, *Diary,* 21 May 1862.
60. Booth, *Maryland Soldier,* p. 31; W. W. Goldsborough, *The Maryland Line in the Confederate States Army* (Baltimore: Kelly Piet and Co., 1869), p. 45; Kirkpatrick Diary, 21 May 1862.
61. Bradley Johnson, "Memoir of the First Maryland Regiment," *S.H.S.P.* X, p. 52.
62. Myers, *The Comanches,* p. 49 is the only source for this meeting, and he places it the next morning. However, Jackson's presence near Luray on the evening of the twenty-first is undisputed, and it is difficult to imagine he would not have conferred with Ewell as quickly as possible after nightfall on the twenty-first. Ewell's lead brigade, Trimble's, marched at 6 A.M. on the twenty-second (Kirkpatrick Diary, 22 May 1862), indicating that the decision had been made before dawn to move in the direction of Front Royal. Had that decision been taken at the conference with Jackson in New Market on May 20, Ewell would not have started his division westward as he did when it initially moved on the twenty-first (see note 56, supra). Campbell Brown wrote of a discussion between Ewell and Jackson in which it was determined to attack Front Royal, but his recollection would set the discussion during Ewell's visit to Mount Solon, a point clearly too early in view of Jackson's subsequent orders for Ewell to move on New Market (Brown Memoirs, p. 37). In both his Memoirs and a fragment of writing entitled "From Fairfax C.H. to Richmond," in the Polk, Ewell, Brown Papers, Brown credited Ewell with scouting the Luray Valley and becoming aware soon after Front Royal was occupied by Union forces (May 16) that enemy strength there was limited. Ewell of course would have shared that information with Jackson, but it is assumed here that the information would not have been utilized on the day when Jackson

was flirting with insubordination and could not know what direction his campaign was about to take (May 20) but, rather, on the next evening.

63. Allan, *Valley Campaign,* p. 92.
64. *OR,* vol. 12, pt. 3, p. 870. The larger estimate of Shields's strength came to Ewell in a message from Captain Brown, who headed the company of Mississippi infantry Ewell had operating in the Shenandoah in mid-May. Brown to Ewell, 16 May 1862, Brown-Ewell Papers, Manuscript Unit, Tennessee State Library and Archives, Nashville, Tennessee.
65. *OR,* vol. 12, pt. 3, p. 895.
66. See note 62, supra.
67. *OR,* vol. 12, pt. 1, p. 725.
68. Ibid., pt. 3, p. 897.
69. Ibid., vol. 51, pt. 2, p. 563 establishes that Scott's Brigade from Johnson's old command had been assigned to Elzey by May 24; Allan, *Valley Campaign,* p. 110 listed Conner's old brigade as part of Elzey's command (although he showed Scott's Brigade as separate) at the Battle of Winchester on May 25. The few diaries available suggest the regiments of Conner's former command moved in the same direction as did Elzey during this time; see Hall, *Diary,* 24 May 1862. Brown Memoirs, pp. 40–41 noted that the two brigades from Johnson's old command basically were attached to Elzey, although he recalled it slightly differently in *S.H.S.P.* X, p. 256. Operationally, it appears that the Army of the Northwest became Elzey's Brigade about the time of the juncture with Ewell's Division, and it is considered so hereinafter, unless otherwise noted.
70. Buck's report of his mission is printed in the New York *Herald,* 16 June 1862. For independent confirmation that there was a Lieutenant Walter Buck in Ashby's Company E see McDonald, *Laurel Brigade,* p. 396. That confirmation serves to verify the authenticity of the documents quoted in the article. Unfortunately, the report is not dated, so it is not possible to say more than does the article, which is that the scout took place shortly before the battle on May 23. For the story of how Buck's dispatch, and others even more important, came to be printed in a New York daily, see chapter 13, note 4.
71. Avirett, *Ashby,* p. 198 and Baylor, *Bull Run,* p. 40 each reported four companies left opposite Strasburg; McDonald, *Laurel Brigade,* p. 59 gave the total as three. Hawse, Diary, 22 May 1862, recorded that his company was dispatched that day into the Alleghenies from New Market to watch Frémont.
72. Gilmor, *Four Years in the Saddle,* p. 39 reported that two days after Jackson withdrew from Franklin the company he headed was relieved by the company of a Captain Davis, and Gilmor was sent to watch Frémont west of Shenandoah Mountain.

73. Thomas Diary, 22 May 1862.
74. Lanty Blackford to his mother, 22 May 1862, Blackford Papers.
75. Hall, *Diary,* 22 May 1862.
76. E. T. H. Warren to his wife, 23 May 1862, Warren Papers.
77. *OR,* vol. 12, pt. 1, p. 772; Mary Anna Jackson, *Memoirs of Stonewall Jackson* (Louisville: Prentice Press, 1895), p. 513.
78. Lawson Botts to John F. O'Brien, 22 May 1862, Botts Papers, Virginia Military Institute, Lexington, Virginia.
79. S. J. C. Moore to his wife, 23 May 1862, Moore Papers.
80. *OR,* vol. 12, pt. 3, p. 898.
81. Kaufman Diary, 22 May 1862.
82. Hall, *Diary,* 22 May 1862.
83. *OR,* vol. 51, pt. 2, p. 561.
84. Lanty Blackford to his mother, 22 May 1862, Blackford Letters.
85. David Strother, *A Virginia Yankee in the Civil War: Diaries of David Strother,* ed. by Cecil Eby (Chapel Hill, N.C.: University of North Carolina Press, 1961), 22 May 1862.
86. George H. Gordon, *Brook Farm to Cedar Mountain* (Boston: Osgood and Co., 1863), pp. 191–92.
87. *OR,* vol. 12, pt. 1, p. 524.
88. Ibid., pp. 523–54.
89. Ibid., p. 524.
90. Ibid., pt. 3, p. 213.
91. Ibid., pt. 1, pp. 278, 281.
92. Ibid., pt. 3, p. 214.
93. Ibid., pt. 1, p. 282.
94. Ibid., vol. 11, pt. 3, p. 504.
95. Ibid., pp. 502–3, 506.
96. Richmond *Daily Dispatch,* 16 May 1862.
97. Memphis *Daily Appeal,* 22 May 1862.
98. Mobile *Daily Advertiser and Register,* 22 May 1862; Richmond *Daily Dispatch,* 19 May 1862.
99. E. A. Pollard, *Southern History of the War* (New York: Charles B. Richards, 1866), p. 382.
100. W. A. Christian, *Richmond* (Richmond: L. H. Jenkins, 1912), pp. 230–32.
101. J. B. Jones, *A Rebel War Clerk's Diary,* ed. by Earl Schneck Miers (New York: Sagamore Press, 1958), 20 and 23 May 1862.
102. Stephen W. Sears, ed., *Civil War Papers of George B. McClellan* (New York: Ticknor & Fields, 1989), pp. 273–74.
103. *OR,* vol. 11, pt. 3, p. 536. See William C. Davis, *Jefferson Davis* (New York: Harper Collins, 1991), pp. 421–23.

CHAPTER 12

1. Fogelman Diary, 23 May 1862.
2. Douglas, *I Rode with Stonewall,* p. 51. Dabney, *Jackson,* p. 364 also noted Jackson's lack of knowledge on enemy numbers in Front Royal, which may explain the slow pace of the assault upon it. Hotchkiss recalled in later years that Jackson's information about Front Royal came from Ashby's cavalrymen who lived thereabouts and as well some of Ewell's Mississippians. See Hotchkiss's "Comments on G. F. R. Henderson's Military Life of Stonewall Jackson," 1 May 1895, Hotchkiss Papers. The role of Ashby's cavalry is confirmed by a report to Ashby from Lieutenant Buck, Company E of Ashby's regiment; Buck, a native of Front Royal, scouted Federal positions there and reported his findings to Ashby, who must have sent them on to Jackson since the observations were among papers later captured at Winchester and printed in the New York *Herald,* 16 June 1862. (For the background of this article, see chapter 11, note 70 and chapter 13, note 4.) Buck reported the presence of the 1st (Union) Maryland and as well artillery and cavalry units but unfortunately did not date or time his message, and it is impossible to know when Jackson received it. That question is considered, with some speculation, in note 14, infra.
3. MS Neese Diary, 24 May 1862.
4. *OR,* vol. 51, pt. 2, p. 561.
5. Ewell noted that the plan was entire Jackson's. Ibid., p. 778.
6. Ibid., pp. 702, 733.
7. Ibid., vol. 51, pt. 2, p. 561.
8. Ibid., vol. 12, pt. 1, p. 560.
9. Avirett, *Ashby,* pp. 187–88; Wayland, *Valley Records,* p. 287.
10. Avirett, *Ashby,* p. 187; Edwin C. Bryant, *History of the Third Regiment of Wisconsin Veteran Volunteer Infantry* (Cleveland: A. H. Clark Co., 1891), p. 55.
11. MS Neese Diary, 22–23 May 1862.
12. Lanty Blackford to his mother, 28 May 1862, Blackford Letters; Apperson Diary, 23 May 1862.
13. There is some speculation here. Several sources from Trimble's Brigade are generally consistent with an advance along the river road into Front Royal. See Kirkpatrick Diary, 23 May 1862, which noted that his 16th Mississippi was, upon reaching Front Royal, "immediately thrown into line of battle on left of the pike"; and Nisbet, *Four Years,* p. 40, who stated that "Trimble's Brigade was leading the division [Ewell's] but just before entering the town we were halted fronting the pike." See also Dobbins, *Grandfather's Journal,* p. 79. No source rules out Trimble following the detour to the Gooney Manor road, but likewise none specifically mentions his unit making that wearying march. It would have been prudent for Jackson to push his lead unit

some distance beyond Asbury Chapel to cloak his turning maneuver, and the idea that Trimble so advanced also explains why his brigade, which had been in the vanguard of the Army for several days, did not lead the descent into Front Royal. Taylor's Brigade appears to have been behind Trimble in the order of march on the twenty-third, so that when Trimble moved beyond Asbury Chapel the head of the flanking column became Taylor. In this regard, it is interesting to note that Lucy Buck, a civilian diarist in Front Royal who recorded some valuable details of the action on the twenty-third, noted that some of the Confederates advanced along the Front Royal–Luray Turnpike. William P. Buck, ed., *Sad Earth, Sweet Heaven: The Diary of Lucy R. Buck* (Birmingham, Ala.: Buck Publishing Co., 1992), p. 78. It seems most probable that this was Trimble's Brigade.

14. L. W. Conerly, *A Historical Sketch of the Quitman Guards, Company E, Sixteenth Mississippi Regiment* (New Orleans: Isaac T. Hinton, 1866), p. 18 establishes the taking of Federal pickets but does not verify the unit. Jackson's order for the Confederate 1st Maryland Infantry to come forward from a position well back in the column is documented infra and was totally unexpected by the troops; the hasty summons is consistent with Jackson learning at the last minute of the presence of the Union 1st Maryland in Front Royal. Had he known earlier that the Federal Marylanders were present, it is impossible to explain why Jackson would have waited to bring forward his own Gamecocks. A brush with enemy pickets that revealed this information (such as is described by Conerly) is the best explanation why Jackson moved up his 1st Maryland so hastily in order for it to open the battle. It is also possible that Jackson received the information on the 1st Union Maryland via Ashby in the report from Lieutenant Buck as printed in the New York *Herald,* 16 June 1862. See note 2, supra.
15. 2 *C.M.H.,* p. 69. Goldsborough, *Maryland Line,* p. 46 agreed that nearly one half the regiment was in mutiny. Booth, *Maryland Soldier,* p. 31 thought roughly one third were mutineers.
16. 2 *C.M.H.,* p. 69.
17. Goldsborough, *Maryland Line,* p. 48; Jackson recalled generally the same tone in 2 *C.M.H.,* pp. 69–70.
18. J. E. H. Post to his mother, 17 June 1862, R. R. Bierne, ed., "Three War Letters," *Maryland Historical Magazine,* vol. 40, no. 4, December 1945, p. 291. Booth, *Maryland Soldier,* p. 32 also notes this interesting detail.
19. J. E. Post to his mother, 17 June 1862, Bierne, ed., "Three War Letters," p. 291.
20. Douglas, *I Rode with Stonewall,* pp. 51–52. The incident, which might be disregarded as a bit of romance, was separately verified by Campbell Brown, Memoirs, p. 38, in a version remarkably similar to that of Douglas. It was described by Boyd herself in *Belle Boyd in Camp and Prison* (New York: Blelock and Co., 1866), pp. 125–28. Taylor recalled

the episode somewhat differently, featuring himself as the recipient of her intelligence. Taylor, *Destruction and Reconstruction,* p. 52. There is no reason to doubt the essence of this episode as historical fact.

21. In marginal comments made in his copy of Henderson's *Stonewall Jackson,* p. 402 (in custody of Antietam National Battlefield Park), Douglas noted that Henderson had erroneously followed Taylor's account of the Boyd interview: "It was I who had the interview with Belle Boyd and gave the General her information. I am sure the General did not have the full information she gave, for immediately upon hearing it, he ordered an immediate attack and sent me with it." In an interesting handwritten memo entitled "Ewell's Division at Front Royal," Campbell Brown confirms that the attack continued much more forcefully after receipt of Boyd's information, all of which suggests her report on Union strength was significant. Ewell Papers, Swem Library, College of William and Mary, Williamsburg, Virginia.
22. Brown Memoirs, p. 38.
23. Booth, *Maryland Soldier,* pp. 31–32 and Post to his mother, 17 June 1862, Bierne, ed., "Three War Letters," p. 291 agree on these numbers. There are slightly higher or lower estimates from other sources, but five hundred men in combat seems reasonable given the known small size of these two commands.
24. *OR,* vol. 12, pt. 1, p. 725.
25. Kirkpatrick Diary, 23 May 1862.
26. 2 *C.M.H.,* p. 72.
27. *OR,* vol. 12, pt. 1, pp. 702, 800.
28. Ibid., p. 733.
29. Ibid., p. 557.
30. Dabney, *Jackson,* p. 366; *OR,* vol. 23, pt. 1, p. 788.
31. Goldsborough, *Maryland Line,* p. 51.
32. MS Diary of John Griffin, 23 May 1862; Apperson Diary, 23 May 1862; and Hotchkiss, *Diary,* 23 May 1862 all reported the capture of two entire trains.
33. Taylor, *Destruction and Reconstruction,* p. 56; Opelousas (Louisiana) *Courier,* 22 June 1862 letter of Robert A. Rowe, 6 September 1862; Oates, *The War,* p. 97.
34. Taylor, *Destruction and Reconstruction,* p. 56.
35. *OR,* vol. 12, pt. 1, p. 734; John C. Donohoe, "Fight at Front Royal," *S.H.S.P.* XXIV, p. 134; J. T. Mann to "Sarah," 27 May 1862, in possession of James Mann, Fredericksburg, Virginia.
36. Dabney, *Jackson,* p. 368.
37. *OR,* vol. 12, pt. 1, p. 779.
38. MacDonald Memoirs, p. 42; McDonald, *Laurel Brigade,* p. 59.
39. *OR,* vol. 12, pt. 1, p. 702.
40. Howard, *Staff Officer,* p. 106.
41. Bradley, T. Johnson, "Memoir of the First Maryland Regiment," *S.H.S.P.* X, p. 55.

42. Charles Camper, *Historical Record of the First Maryland Infantry* (Union) (Washington, D.C.: Gibson Brothers, 1871), pp. 47–48.
43. Ring Diary, 23 May 1862.
44. Taylor, *Destruction and Reconstruction.*, p. 58. 3 *C.M.H.*, p. 239 confirms that Jackson and his staff spent the night near Cedarville, thus putting the general in the vicinity of Taylor's command.
45. *OR,* vol. 12, pt. 1, p. 703.
46. Ibid., pp. 735, 754.
47. Avirett, *Ashby,* p. 193; the scout of Berry's Ford was conducted by Snipe's Company. Arehart Diary, 24 May 1862 in Rockingham *Recorder.* A strong probe to Linden is established by Federal sources. *OR,* vol. 12, pt. 1, p. 566. The units involved are unknown, but the assumption seems warranted that it was a detachment from Ashby's command. No other Confederate cavalry are known to have been operating in the area, and a move that would shield the Confederate right flank while Jackson probed for Banks would not have been coincidence.
48. *OR,* vol. 12, pt. 1, p. 779.
49. Ibid., pp. 735, 754.
50. Ibid., p. 764. Lanty Blackford of the Rockbridge Artillery reported that the main body of the Army did not leave Front Royal until about 9 A.M. Blackford to his mother, 7 June 1862, Blackford Letters.
51. *OR,* vol. 12, pt. 1, p. 772.
52. Ibid., p. 546.
53. Ibid., pp. 546–57.
54. Ibid., p. 722.
55. Allan, *Valley Campaign,* p. 128 (quoting a letter from Trimble); MS Hotchkiss Diary, 24 May 1862.
56. J. T. Mann to "Sarah," 27 May 1862, Mann Letters.
57. Jackson noted the significance of Steuart's report in *OR,* vol. 12, pt. 1, p. 703. A dispatch from Jackson to Ewell of May 24, not timed, states Jackson had received two letters from Steuart and now desired to reinforce Steuart with cavalry and infantry support. *OR,* vol. 51, pt. 2, p. 563. This is probably a morning response to a request for help from Steuart; Jackson had little time during the afternoon for directing Ewell how to aid Steuart.
58. Hotchkiss to his wife, 26 May 1862, Hotchkiss Papers and Hotchkiss, *Diary,* 24 May 1862 are generally consistent and supply the bulk of these details. Colonel Neff of the 33d Virginia noted that the column moved at about noon. *OR,* vol. 12, pt. 1, p. 754.
59. Address of Colonel R. P. Chew Delivered at the V.M.I. 19 June 1912 (Lexington, Va.: Rockbridge Co. News Press, 1912), p. 26.
60. Taylor, *Destruction and Reconstruction,* p. 58; *OR,* vol. 12, pt., 1, p. 760.
61. Dabney, *Jackson,* p. 371.
62. Avirett, *Ashby* (quoting an 1867 letter from Chew), p. 270 and

Douglas, *I Rode with Stonewall,* p. 54 both note that Funsten was sent to strike the Pike some distance north of Middletown, doubtless explaining why the fight at that village was primarily an artillery affair.

63. Neese, *Horse Artillery,* p. 56.
64. *OR,* vol. 12, pt. 1, p. 726.
65. Douglas marginalia in Henderson, *Stonewall Jackson,* p. 407 (in custody of Antietam National Battlefield Park).
66. *OR,* vol. 12, pt. 1, p. 703.
67. Douglas, *I Rode with Stonewall,* p. 54.
68. Taylor, *Destruction and Reconstruction,* p. 58.
69. Lanty Blackford to his mother, 7 June 1862, Blackford Letters. Kearns Diary, 24 May 1862, also noted cavalrymen returning from the Middletown skirmish with "any amount" of horses.
70. *OR,* vol. 51, pt. 2, p. 562.
71. Ibid., pt. 3, p. 899.
72. Ibid., pt. 1, pp. 703, 761.
73. Taylor, *Destruction and Reconstruction,* pp. 59–60.
74. *OR,* vol. 12, pt. 1, p. 704; Clyde L. Cummer, ed., *Yankee in Gray: The Civil War Memoirs of Henry E. Handerson, with a Selection of His Wartime Letters* (Cleveland: The Press of Western Reserve University, 1962), p. 42.
75. *OR,* vol. 12, pt, 3, p. 899.
76. Ibid., pt. 1, p. 735.
77. Ibid., pt. 3, p. 900.
78. Ibid., pt. 1, p. 799. Dobbins, *Grandfather's Journal,* p. 80, confirms that the sound of gunfire could be heard to the left of Ewell's position during the afternoon and that Ewell advanced around 5 P.M. Ewell recalled his "embarrassment" in an undated fragment of the history of the campaign found in the Polk, Ewell, Brown Papers.
79. Lanty Blackford to his mother, 7 June 1862, Blackford Papers.
80. Douglas, *I Rode with Stonewall,* p. 55.
81. Chew, Address Delivered at V.M.I., p. 27; see also Chew's letter in Avirett, *Ashby,* p. 270.
82. *OR,* vol. 12, pt. 1, p. 720; Poague reported the same looting by Ashby's men in *Gunner,* p. 23.
83. MS Diary of Neese, 24 May 1862.
84. Colt, *Defend the Valley,* p. 143.
85. Kearns Diary, 24 May 1862.
86. Lanty Blackford to his mother, 7 June 1862, Blackford Papers.
87. Howard, *Staff Officer,* p. 107.
88. Douglas, *I Rode with Stonewall,* p. 55.
89. *OR,* vol. 12, pt. 3, p. 900.
90. Douglas, *I Rode with Stonewall,* p. 56.
91. *OR,* vol. 12, pt. 1, p. 704.
92. Colt, *Defend the Valley,* p. 144.
93. Moore, *Cannoneer,* pp. 54–55.

94. Dabney, *Jackson,* p. 375.
95. *OR,* vol. 12, pt. 1, p. 735.
96. Poague, *Gunner,* p. 23; *OR,* vol. 12, pt. 1, p. 735.
97. Apperson Diary, 24 May 1862; *OR,* vol. 12, pt. 1, p. 743.
98. *OR,* vol. 12, pt. 1, p. 751.
99. George W. Kurtz, "Account of the Valley Campaign of 1862." *Winchester–Frederick County Historical Society Papers,* vol. 3, p. 47.
100. Apperson Diary, 24 May 1862; Hall, *Diary,* 24 May 1862; James H. Wood, *The War* (Cumberland, Md.: Eddy Press, 1910), p. 52.
101. Avirett, *Ashby,* pp. 196–97; Douglas, *I Rode with Stonewall,* p. 57.
102. Douglas, *I Rode with Stonewall,* pp. 56–57.
103. Brown, "Ewell's Division at Front Royal," William and Mary Library; *OR,* vol. 12, pt. 1, p. 725 confirms that Crutchfield was the bearer and gives the route he followed.
104. Myers, *The Comanches,* p. 52.
105. Hotchkiss, "Memoranda—The Valley Campaign of 1862," 25 May 1862 suggests that this was the assignment, writing, "Ashby had already gone to the enemy's left and covered the Berryville road."
106. *OR,* vol. 12, pt. 1, p. 706.
107. Brown, "Ewell's Division at Front Royal," William and Mary Library.
108. Johnson, *S.H.S.P.* X, pp. 98, 108; *C.M.H.,* vol. 2, p. 74.
109. *OR,* vol. 12, pt. 1, p. 779; Oates, *The War,* p. 97.
110. Booth, *Maryland Soldier,* p. 34; Goldsborough, *Maryland Line,* p. 55.
111. *OR,* vol. 12, pt. 1, p. 779; W. A. McClendon, *Recollections of War Times by an Old Veteran under Stonewall Jackson and General James Longstreet* (Montgomery: Paragon Press, 1909), p. 56.
112. MS Reminiscences of Eli S. Coble, North Carolina Department of Archives and History, Raleigh, North Carolina, pp. 32–33.
113. Oates, *The War,* p. 98; *OR,* vol. 12, pt. 1, pp. 779–80.
114. Nisbet, *Four Years,* p. 46; *OR,* vol. 12, pt. 1, p. 794.
115. *OR,* vol. 12, pt. 1, pp. 727, 794; Crutchfield's arrival shortly after the fog burned off is established by Brown. "Ewell's Division at Front Royal," William and Mary Library.
116. Nisbet, *Four Years,* p. 46.
117. *OR,* vol. 12, pt. 1, p. 736.
118. Lanty Blackford to his mother, 7 June 1862, Blackford Letters; *OR,* vol. 12, pt. 1, p. 749.
119. *OR,* vol. 12, pt. 1, p. 743; Thomas D. Gold, *History of Clarke County Virginia and Its Connection with the War Between the States* (privately printed, Berryville, Va., 1914), p. 174.
120. *OR,* vol. 12, pt. 1, p. 761.
121. Colt, *Defend the Valley,* pp. 146–47; Poague, *Gunner,* p. 24.
122. *OR,* vol. 12, pt. 1, pp. 736, 758.
123. Ibid., p. 751.
124. Lanty Blackford to his mother, 7 June 1862, Blackford Papers.
125. Moore, *Cannoneer,* p. 56.
126. *OR,* vol. 12, pt. 1, p. 736.

127. Ibid., pp. 764–65, 767.
128. Ibid., p. 705; Taylor, *Destruction and Reconstruction,* p. 61.
129. Howard, *Staff Officer,* p. 110; *OR,* vol. 12, pt. 1, p. 736.
130. Taylor, *Destruction and Reconstruction,* p. 61; Douglas, *I Rode with Stonewall,* p. 58 reported this interchange somewhat differently.
131. Taylor, *Destruction and Reconstruction,* p. 62; Colt, *Defend the Valley,* p. 149.
132. E. T. H. Warren to his wife, 25 May 1862, Warren Papers; *OR,* vol. 12, pt. 1, p. 772.
133. Worsham, *Foot Cavalry,* pp. 87–88; Worsham gave a few more details in *S.H.S.P.* XXXVIII, pp. 331–32.
134. Kearns Diary, 25 May 1862.
135. Douglas, *I Rode with Stonewall,* p. 59.
136. *OR,* vol. 12, pt. 1, p. 705.
137. Taylor, *Destruction and Reconstruction,* pp. 63–64; the repulse of the Union cavalry is confirmed in the Opelousas (Louisiana) *Courier,* 22 July 1862.
138. Worsham, *Foot Cavalry,* p. 87.
139. Johnson, *S.H.S.P.* X, p. 99.
140. *OR,* vol. 12, pt. 1, p. 704.
141. Ibid., p. 736.
142. Douglas, *I Rode with Stonewall,* p. 59.
143. Worsham, *Foot Cavalry,* p. 87.
144. J. K. Edmondson to his wife, 26 May 1862, Edmondson Letters.
145. *OR,* vol. 12, pt. 1, pp. 748–49.
146. See chapter 5.
147. Avirett, *Ashby,* p. 293.
148. Taylor, *Destruction and Reconstruction,* p. 64.
149. *OR,* vol. 12, pt. 1, pp. 737, 764.
150. Fonerden, *Carpenter's Battery,* p. 47.
151. *OR,* vol. 12, pt. 1, pp. 759, 762; Lanty Blackford to his mother, 7 June 1862, Blackford Papers.
152. *OR,* vol. 12, pt. 1, p. 772.
153. Oates, *The War,* p. 99.
154. Winder Diary, 25 May 1862.
155. *OR,* vol. 12, pt. 1, p. 706.
156. Ibid., pp. 709–10; Brown Memoirs, p. 43.
157. *OR,* vol. 12, pt. 1, p. 706; Allan, *Valley Campaign,* p. 115. Hotchkiss confirmed that idea in 3 *C.M.H.,* p. 243.
158. *OR,* vol. 12, pt. 1, pp. 706–7.
159. J. T. Mann to "Sarah," 17 May 1862, Mann Letters.
160. Dabney, *Jackson,* p. 384.

CHAPTER 13

1. *OR,* vol. 12, pt. 1, p. 706.
2. Johnston's message does not appear in the official records but is quoted in Douglas, *I Rode with Stonewall,* p. 65; later that day, Johnston wrote again, infra, and mentioned an earlier dispatch, which must have been the one Douglas saw. J. E. Johnston to Jackson, 27 May 1862, New York *Herald,* 16 June 1862.
3. Gustavus W. Smith, *Confederate War Papers* (New York: Atlantic Publishing and Engraving Co., 1884), pp. 146–47.
4. Johnston's telegram, and as well Boswell's covering instructions, were not part of the official record and in fact appear not to have been considered in Valley Campaign literature prior to this point. They appeared in the New York *Herald,* 16 June 1862. As discussed in chapter 11, note 70, the evidence for the accuracy of dispatches reported in the article is compelling. Johnston's letter to Jackson is significant, explaining as it does Jackson's move to Harpers Ferry at the end of May and his persistence in that enterprise despite warnings of a Union counteroffensive (see chapter 14). Nor is it difficult to know how these secret dispatches came to be printed on the front page of a New York City daily: the article makes clear that Jackson lost them. Johnston's dispatch, along with several others of a sensitive nature that would only have gone to Jackson, were found in a partially burned railroad car in Winchester. Jackson in fact returned to Harpers Ferry by rail on May 30 at a time of great pressure, and it seems clear that he or one of the staff left them behind when the train reached the station. See chapter 14, note 28.
5. *OR,* vol. 11, pt. 3, p. 555.
6. Richmond *Daily Dispatch,* 29 and 30 May 1862.
7. *B & L,* vol. 2, p. 223; *OR,* vol. 11, pt. 3, p. 557.
8. Gustavus W. Smith, *The Battle of Seven Pines* (New York: G. Crawford, 1891), p. 14.
9. Johnston, *Military Narrative,* p. 131.
10. Ibid., pp. 131–32; *B & L,* vol. 2, p. 224.
11. James Longstreet, *From Manassas to Appomattox* (Philadelphia: J. B. Lippincott Co., 1896; reprint ed., Bloomington: Indiana University Press, 1960), p. 86.
12. Jefferson Davis, *Rise and Fall of the Confederate Government* (New York: D. Appleton and Co., 1881), vol. 2, p. 121.
13. Longstreet, *Manassas to Appomattox,* p. 86.
14. Washington *Daily National Intelligencer,* 16 June 1862.
15. See chapter 11, notes 41–48.
16. *OR,* vol. 12, pt. 1, p. 525.
17. Ibid.
18. Ibid., p. 526.

19. Ibid., p. 626.
20. Ibid., pt. 3, pp. 233, 323; pt. 1, p. 626.
21. Ibid., pt. 1, p. 528.
22. Ibid., p. 643.
23. Ibid., pt. 3, pp. 219–20.
24. Ibid., pt. 1, p. 626.
25. Ibid., vol. 11, pt. 1, p. 20.
26. Ibid., vol. 12, pt. 1, p. 527.
27. Ibid., pt. 3, p. 222.
28. In his outstanding *Lincoln Finds a General,* 5 vols. (New York: MacMillan, 1949), vol. 1, p. 175, Kenneth P. Williams is one of the few historians to note this distinction.
29. *OR,* vol. 12, pt. 1, pp. 528–29.
30. Ibid., pt. 3, pp. 230–31.
31. Ibid., p. 241.
32. Ibid., pp. 232, 234.
33. Ibid., p. 242.
34. Ibid., p. 247.
35. Ibid.
36. Ibid., p. 248.
37. Ibid., pt. 1, pp. 729–30.
38. Avirett, *Ashby,* p. 198.
39. This work was evidently quite successful. See *OR,* vol. 12, pt. 3, p. 273.
40. *OR,* vol. 12, pt. 1, pp. 225–26.
41. Ibid., pt. 3, p. 150.
42. Ibid., pp. 109, 185.
43. Ibid., pp. 160, 185.
44. Abram P. Smith, *History of the 76th New York Infantry* (Syracuse: Smith & Miles, 1867), p. 55.
45. *OR,* vol. 12, pt. 3, pp. 109, 160, 185.
46. The fluctuating strength of the Washington garrison during the spring of 1862 will provide a fascinating study for the scholar attuned to detail. In outline, the following can be asserted (only infantry regiments, the backbone of the garrison, are considered here): In 1863 McClellan prepared a roster of Wadsworth's command as of April 1, 1862 (*OR,* vol. 5, pp. 22–23). This roster appears generally accurate, but it nevertheless was part of McClellan's effort to justify his command of the Army of the Potomac and cannot be accepted uncritically. At least one discrepancy is immediately evident. McClellan reported that the entire 26th Pennsylvania was assigned to Washington, yet in the same roster he listed that regiment as part of Hooker's Division (ibid., p. 17), which moved to the Peninsula with McClellan. Other sources indicate that only one company of this regiment was left in Washington (ibid., vol. 12, pt. 3, p. 313). Still, since there is little else available, we must begin with McClellan's totals. Subtracting

the 26th Pennsylvania from the twenty-one full infantry regiments claimed for Washington's garrisons leaves twenty regiments, a generous estimate of the infantry actually provided.

Of these twenty regiments, ten are known to have transferred to points some distance from Washington during April and May of 1862. The 95th New York was stationed ten miles north of Fredericksburg as of April 27 (ibid., pt. 3, p. 109). The 97th and 104th New York and 105th and 107th Pennsylvania moved to Catlett's Station on May 11 and passed from Wadsworth's control (ibid., pp. 160, 185, 241). The 26th and 94th New York and 88th Pennsylvania became part of Rickett's Brigade, which reached the Fredericksburg area on May 14 (ibid., pp. 144, 313). The 54th Pennsylvania was not in or near Washington on April 1 and thereafter became part of a special brigade guarding the B & O; it was in the Shenandoah when the Valley Army struck at Winchester (ibid., p. 211). The 76th New York moved to Fredericksburg on May 22 (Smith, *History of 76th N.Y.*, p. 55).

Of the remaining ten regiments, eight were in Washington in May, according to Wadsworth's end-of-the-month report. These were the 2d D.C.; 59th, 86th, and 101st New York; 10th New Jersey; and 91st and 99th Pennsylvania. One regiment, the 112th Pennsylvania, had been converted into a heavy artillery unit and was present as such. Of the remaining two units, the 91st New York redeployed to Florida (*OR*, vol. 12, p. 363), and the 12th West Virginia returned to its native state (ibid., vol. 12, p. 338); both transfers must have been completed before May 24, 1862, as neither unit is rostered in the weekly report of the Army of the Rappahannock for that date (see note 48, infra).

These detachments were only very partially made good. The Army of the Rappahannock's weekly report of 24 May rostered only two infantry regiments not with the Washington garrison in April—78th New York and 109th Pennsylvania (see note 48, infra). Thus two regiments had been made available to supply the place of ten taken from Wadsworth's command.

Because McClellan clearly lacked authority over this command after April 4, only Stanton and McDowell—and, ultimately, Lincoln—can be responsible for the steady drain on it. Stanton and McDowell clearly left Washington weakly garrisoned in May 1862, and this weakness made Lincoln's redeployment of McDowell irrevocable.

47. *OR*, vol. 12, pt. 3, p. 241.
48. "Morning Report of 24 May 1862," Record Group 94, Record of the Adjutant General's Office, Civil War Organization Returns, Army of the Rappahannock, National Archives, Washington, D.C.
49. *OR*, vol. 12, pt. 3, p. 267.
50. Newel Cheney, *History of the 9th Regiment of New York Cavalry* (privately printed, Jamestown, N.Y., 1901), pp. 44–45.
51. *OR*, vol. 12, pt. 3, p. 231.
52. Allan, *Valley Campaign*, footnotes pp. 121–22.

53. *OR,* ser. III, vol. 2, pp. 59–70.
54. See, e.g., Davis, *Rise and Fall of the Confederate Government,* vol. 2, pp. 107–9; Henderson, *Stonewall Jackson,* p. 263.
55. Allan, *Valley Campaign,* footnotes pp. 121–22.
56. Ibid.
57. Boston *Daily Advertiser,* 28 May 1862.
58. New York *Herald,* 26, 27, and 29 May 1862.
59. New York *Times,* 26 and 27 May 1862.
60. Philadelphia *Inquirer,* 27 May 1862. A similar account is found in the Harrisburg (Pa.) *Daily Telegraph,* 27 and 28 May 1862. Freeman collected a number of such accounts in *Lee's Lieutenants,* vol. 1, p. 410, note 94.
61. Washington *Sunday Morning Chronicle,* 25 May 1862.
62. Washington *Daily National Intelligencer,* 27 May 1862. Equally low-key coverage is found in the Washington *National Republican,* 26 May 1862. The Washington *Evening Star,* 26 May 1862, is the only major city paper to refer to any alarm, and, interestingly, it noted that this alarm was confined to excitable abolitionists.
63. New York *Times,* 27 May 1862.
64. Allan, *Valley Campaign,* p. 120.
65. Ibid., p. 121.
66. See chapter 15, notes 47–49, infra, and accompanying text for an analysis of this view.
67. *OR,* vol. 12, pt. 3, pp. 22–23.
68. Ibid., p. 221.
69. Ibid., pp. 230, 235.
70. Ibid., pp. 232–33.
71. See generally Walter P. Lang, Jr., J. Frank Hennessee, and William E. Bush, Jr., "Jackson's Valley Campaign and the Operational Level of War," *Parameters* (Winter 1985), pp. 48–58 for an interesting discussion of the campaign in this theoretical light.
72. *OR,* vol. 12, pt. 3, pp. 889, 893.
73. On this point, see especially Appendix A.
74. Carl von Clausewitz, *Principles of War,* trans. and ed. by Hans W. Gatzke (Harrisburg, Pa.: Stackpole Company, 1942), p. 46.
75. *OR,* vol. 12, pt. 1, p. 14.
76. Ibid., p. 10.
77. Ibid., pt. 3, pp. 146, 171, 184, 192.
78. Ibid., pp. 162, 180; pt. 1, p. 458.
79. Ibid., pt. 3, p. 202.
80. Ibid., p. 160.
81. Ibid., p. 865.
82. Ibid., vol. 5, p. 1004.
83. White, *Hugh White,* p. 85.
84. Allan, *Valley Campaign,* pp. 117–18 offers the best computation of losses.

85. A. S. Pendleton to his mother, 28 May 1862, Bean, ed., "Pendleton Letters," p. 361.
86. *OR*, vol. 12, pt. 1, p. 708.
87. E. T. H. Warren to his wife, 25 May 1862, Warren Papers.
88. Taylor, *Destruction and Reconstruction,* p. 63.
89. See, e.g., Freeman, *Lee's Lieutenants,* vol. 1, pp. 481, 484 and Chambers, *Stonewall Jackson,* vol. 1, p. 595.
90. *OR*, vol. 12, pt. 1, p. 528.
91. Ibid., vol. 51, pt. 2, p. 563.
92. Brown Memoirs, p. 43.
93. *OR*, vol. 12, pt. 1, p. 779.
94. Munford, *S.H.S.P.* VII, p. 533.
95. Avirett, *Ashby,* p. 199; see chapter 12, note 157 and Dabney, *Jackson,* p. 382 for the opinions of Allan, Hotchkiss, and Dabney.
96. *OR*, vol. 12, pt. 1, p. 707.
97. Avirett, *Ashby,* p. 198.
98. See chapter 11, notes 71 and 72.
99. Wilson, *Diary,* 22 May 1862.
100. See chapter 12, note 47.
101. MacDonald Memoirs, p. 43.
102. Avirett, *Ashby,* p. 206; A. R. Boteler, "Stonewall Jackson in the Campaign of 1862," *S.H.S.P.* XL, p. 171 took credit for getting Ashby the promotion.
103. *OR*, vol. 12, pt. 3, p. 900.
104. Moore, *Cannoneer,* p. 59.
105. McKim, *Soldier's Recollections,* p. 106.
106. Ted Barclay to his sister, 26 May 1862, Barclay Letters; see also McKim, *Soldier's Recollections,* p. 106.
107. S. J. C. Moore to Hotchkiss, 9 September 1896, Hotchkiss Papers.
108. Booth, *Maryland Soldier,* p. 37.
109. Ibid.
110. *OR*, vol. 12, pt. 1, p. 900.
111. Jackson Letter Book, 1862, 26 May 1862, Hotchkiss Papers.
112. Worsham, *Foot Cavalry,* p. 88.
113. Casler, *Four Years,* p. 78.

CHAPTER 14

1. *OR*, vol. 12, pt. 3, pp. 892–93.
2. Ibid., pt. 1, p. 730.
3. Winder Diary, 27 May 1862.
4. Griffin Diary, 27 May 1862; *OR*, vol. 12, pt. 1, p. 727 reports the presence of the artillery.
5. A. W. Harman, "The Valley after Kernstown," *S.H.S.P.* XIX, p. 320.

6. Worsham, *Fort Cavalry,* p. 89. The derisive term "blue birds" was used by R. Waldrop in a letter to his father, 12 June 1862, Waldrop Letters.
7. *OR,* vol. 12, pt. 1, p. 722; pt. 3, p. 903.
8. William Allan to A. W. Harman, 27 May 1862, Hotchkiss Papers.
9. MS record book of William B. Taliaferro, 27 May 1862, Taliaferro Papers, National Archives; *OR,* vol. 12, pt. 3, p. 902.
10. Kirkpatrick Diary, 28 May 1862, suggests Ewell's march to Harpers Ferry began hastily around midday, evidence for the proposition that Jackson received Johnston's telegram of May 27 at about the earliest possible moment (noon on May 28) and responded immediately. To the same effect see Kate Sperry, Diary, typescript in Handley Library, Winchester, Virginia, 28 May 1862; Sperry identifies Elzey's Brigade as heading away from Winchester in the afternoon.
11. *OR,* vol. 12, pt. 1, p. 738.
12. Douglas, *I Rode with Stonewall,* p. 63. This information came in after midnight on the twenty-seventh (presumably in the early hours of the twenty-eighth) and was given to Jackson after dawn according to Douglas, who goes on to state that the general and his staff then started from Harpers Ferry. Since Jackson clearly spent the day in Winchester on the twenty-eighth (see, e.g., John Harman to his brother, 28 May 1862, Hotchkiss Papers), Douglas's recollection is accepted but modified to reflect the later date given in the text.
13. John Harman to his brother, 29 May 1862, Hotchkiss Papers.
14. Z. T. Conner to Elzey, 29 May 1862, New York *Herald,* 16 June 1862.
15. *OR,* vol. 12, pt. 1, p. 730; Thomas Diary, 29 May 1862.
16. E. T. H. Warren to his wife, 29 May 1862, Warren Letters, and Huffman, *Ups and Downs,* p. 47 established that the 10th Virginia left Winchester on the twenty-ninth; the remainder of Taliaferro's Brigade is assumed to have moved with it, which is also assumed of Patton's Brigade. There is no record of Patton leaving Winchester before the twenty-ninth. All sources, however, agree that the entire army was concentrated around Harpers Ferry by the end of that day. Jackson established that the 2d Virginia was with Winder by at least the twenty-ninth. *OR,* vol. 12, pt. 1, p. 707.
17. A. S. Pendleton to his mother, 30 May 1862, Bean, ed., "Pendleton Letters," p. 361.
18. *OR,* vol. 12, pt. 1, p. 730; Lanty Blackford to his father, 13 June 1862, Blackford Papers.
19. See, e.g., Opelousas (Louisiana) *Courier,* 22 July 1862 and Kirkpatrick Diary, 29 May 1862. For rumors of the Baltimore riots, see J. S. S. Green to Thomas Flournoy, 29 May 1862, New York *Herald,* 16 June 1862.
20. Gilmor, *Four Years,* p. 40; Hotchkiss, "Memoranda—The Valley Campaign of 1862," 29 May 1862 noted that the information on Frémont arrived on the night of the twenty-ninth; he did not specify Gilmor as the source.
21. *OR,* vol. 12, pt. 1, p. 535.

22. Thomas Diary, 30 May 1862.
23. Howard, *Staff Officer,* p. 114.
24. Hotchkiss, *Diary,* 30 May 1862.
25. Harper Diary, 30 May 1862; Ring Diary, 30 May 1862.
26. Boteler, *S.H.S.P.* XL, pp. 164–65. Jackson's promise to advise Boteler when he started down the Valley (curiously unlike his normal secrecy) is found in T. J. Jackson to A. R. Boteler, 19 May 1862, Jackson Papers (c).
27. Hotchkiss, *Diary,* 30 May 1862.
28. Boteler, *S.H.S.P.* XL, pp. 165–66; the New York *Herald,* 16 June 1862, related the finding of Johnston's dispatch, and others, in a partially burned railroad car in Winchester, thus justifying the assumption made here that the documents were left behind by Jackson or one of his staff when they detrained.
29. Brown Memoirs, p. 44; William Allan to Asher Harman, 31 May 1862, Allan Letters, Huntington Library, San Marino, California.
30. *OR,* vol. 12, pt. 1, p. 793; Hotchkiss, *Diary,* 30 May 1862, claimed he sent the word to Jackson after receiving the first messenger from Conner.
31. Buck, *Diary,* 29 May 1862; Griffin Diary, 29 May 1862; Z. T. Conner to Elzey, 29 May 1862, New York *Herald,* 16 June 1862.
32. *OR,* vol. 12, pt. 1, p. 722.
33. Ibid., p. 727; probably the gun accidentally disabled during the action on May 23; ibid., p. 725.
34. Irby Scott to "Loved Ones at Home," 12 June 1862, Scott Papers.
35. Ibid.; Griffin Diary, 30 May 1862.
36. Hotchkiss, *Diary,* 30 May 1862. Charges, now lost, were sent to Richmond on July 12; Jackson's Letter Book, 1862, Hotchkiss Papers. Brown, *S.H.S.P.* X, p. 258 stated that the charges were for "misbehavior in the face of the enemy." No record of a trial exists, and Conner apparently was allowed to resign to avoid trial. Krick, *Lee's Colonels,* p. 87. For having ordered his men to lay down their arms and surrender, Major Hawkins was charged with cowardice. Brown, *S.H.S.P.* X, p. 258.
37. Neese, *Horse Artillery,* p. 62. The injury to the best gun of Chew's Battery, although not the exact cause, is noted in *OR,* vol. 12, pt. 1, p. 727.
38. Hotchkiss, *Diary,* 31 May 1862. It is not certain that Jackson specifically mentioned to Hotchkiss the whereabouts of Frémont at this time; Hotchkiss does not reference it in his diary. Nevertheless, it was known at Headquarters on the thirty-first that Frémont was east of Wardensville according to William Allan's letter of that date (see note 29). Also, essentially this information on Frémont was related by Colonel Boteler to Richmond when he was first in position to telegraph Jackson's plea for aid. The telegram was sent June 1, and Boteler states therein that he had left Jackson at Winchester "yesterday," certainly meaning in the early hours of May 31. The latest intelligence Boteler

could have included in the telegram would have been what was known at Headquarters early on the thirty-first, and that must be what Boteler reflected when he wired that "Frémont has 20,000 at Wardensville, Hardy, Co." Boteler to G. W. Randolph, 1 June 1862, Jackson Papers (e), Virginia State Library, Richmond, Virginia.

39. Jackson to Ashby, 31 May 1862, Ashby Papers.
40. Neese, *Horse Artillery,* p. 63; Wilson, Diary, 31 May 1862.
41. Hotchkiss, *Diary,* 1 June 1862; John Harman to his brother, 2 June 1862, Hotchkiss Papers.
42. John Harman to his brother, 31 May 1862, Hotchkiss Papers.
43. Worsham, *Foot Cavalry,* p. 94.
44. Thomas Garnett to his father, 2 July 1862, typescript at Fredericksburg-Spotsylvania National Military Park, Fredericksburg, Virginia.
45. Thomas Munford, MS "Recollections," Munford Papers, Duke University, Durham, North Carolina.
46. Strickler, *A Short History of Page County,* p. 180.
47. 2 *C.M.H.,* p. 75. Johnson blamed this on lack of a brigade structure, the Maryland Line at this point not being attached to any larger unit.
48. Sperry Diary, 31 May 1862 (quoted); see also Mrs. Hugh Lee Diary, typescript in Handley Library, Winchester, Virginia, 31 May 1862.
49. J. K. Edmondson to his wife, 3 June 1862, Edmondson Letters.
50. Lanty Blackford to his father, 13 June 1862, Blackford Papers.
51. J. E. H. Post to his mother, 17 June 1862, Beirne, ed., "Three War Letters," p. 293.
52. Hotchkiss, *Diary,* 1 June 1862.
53. *OR,* vol. 12, pt. 1, p. 708.
54. Ibid., pt. 3, p. 904; Taylor, *Destruction and Reconstruction,* p. 71.
55. Oates, *The War,* p. 100; Brown Memoirs, p. 45.
56. *OR,* vol. 12, pt. 1, p. 708. The presence of Taliaferro's command is established in Jackson, *Life of Jackson,* p. 513 and by E. T. H. Warren to his wife, 4 June 1862, Warren Letters. Patton's Brigade was short the 21st Virginia, guarding prisoners, but one of the two remaining regiments was northwest of Strasburg, so it is reasonable to believe the entire unit was there. Thomas Garnett to his father, 2 July 1862, Garnett Papers.
57. Taylor, *Destruction and Reconstruction,* p. 72.
58. *OR,* vol. 12, pt. 1, p. 649.
59. Ibid., p. 718.
60. Oates, *The War,* p. 100; Kirkpatrick Diary, 1 June 1862.
61. Winder Diary, 1 June 1862.
62. William Humphreys to his mother, 14 June 1862, letter in possession of Mr. David Updike, Staunton, Virginia.
63. Kearns Diary, 1 June 1862.
64. McKim, *Soldier's Recollections,* pp. 107–8; Booth, *Maryland Soldier,* p. 38.
65. Howard, *Staff Officer,* pp. 116–17.

66. Johnson, *S.H.S.P.* X, p. 102.
67. Ibid.
68. Casler, *Four Years,* pp. 80–81.
69. Howard, *Staff Officer,* p. 130; Goldsborough, *Maryland Line,* p. 62.
70. Slaughter, *Randolph Fairfax,* p. 26.
71. Irby Scott to "Loved Ones at Home," 12 June 1862, Scott Letters.
72. R. W. Waldrop to his mother, 27 May 1862, Waldrop Letters.
73. S. G. Pryor to his wife, 12 June 1862, Pryor Letters.
74. McKim, *Soldier's Recollections,* p. 107.

CHAPTER 15

1. John Harman to his brother, 1 June 1862, Hotchkiss Papers.
2. *OR,* vol. 12, pt. 1, p. 711. Jackson discussed this possibility with Taylor as early as the evening of May 31; Taylor, *Destruction and Reconstruction,* p. 67.
3. Hale, *Four Valiant Years,* p. 164.
4. Taylor, *Destruction and Reconstruction,* pp. 75–76; *OR,* vol. 12, pt. 1, pp. 730–31.
5. Douglas, *I Rode with Stonewall,* p. 71.
6. Dobbins, *Grandfather's Journal,* p. 82; McClendon, *Recollections,* p. 60.
7. Oates, *The War,* p. 101.
8. Hotchkiss, *Diary,* 1–2 June 1862.
9. Goldsborough, *Maryland Line,* p. 67; William H. Humphreys to his mother, 14 June 1862, confirmed that at one point two guns were feared lost, although Humphreys, a member of Carpenter's Battery, understood the cannons were from the Rockbridge Artillery. The role of the 48th Virginia in this melee is related by Thomas Garnett to his father, 2 July 1862, and in *OR,* vol. 12, pt. 1, p. 731.
10. Lanty Blackford to his father, 13 June 1862, Blackford Papers.
11. William L. Jackson to his wife, 8 June 1862, Jackson Letters, West Virginia and Regional History Collection, West Virginia University, Morgantown, West Virginia
12. *OR,* vol. 213, pt. 1, p. 711.
13. Thomas Garnett to his father, 2 July 1862.
14. Thomas Diary, 2 June 1862; J. E. H. Post to his mother, 17 June 1862, Beirne, ed., "Three War Letters," p. 293 confirmed that the Marylanders threatened to shoot some fleeing riders to stop the flight.
15. Howard, *Staff Officer,* p. 118.
16. *OR,* vol. 12, pt. 1, pp. 731, 788.
17. Ibid., pp. 712, 731.
18. J. T. Mann to "Sarah," 7 June 1862, Mann Papers; Worsham, *Foot Cavalry,* p. 90.

19. Hotchkiss, *Diary,* 2 June 1862.
20. Lanty Blackford to his father, 13 June 1862, Blackford Papers.
21. J. K. Edmondson to his wife, 3 June 1862, Edmondson Letters; *OR,* vol. 12, pt. 3, p. 879 gives the strength of the 27th in early May.
22. MS Neese Diary, 3 June 1862.
23. MacDonald Memoirs, p. 48.
24. Brown Memoirs, p. 46.
25. Pendleton to Ashby, 3 June 1862, Ashby Papers.
26. Hotchkiss to his wife, 3 June 1862, Hotchkiss Papers.
27. Douglas, *I Rode with Stonewall,* p. 75; Hotchkiss, *Diary,* 3 June, confirmed this episode.
28. Myers, *The Comanches,* p. 61.
29. Lanty Blackford to his father, 13 June 1862.
30. *OR,* vol. 12, pt. 1, p. 16.
31. Ibid., pt. 3, p. 905.
32. Hotchkiss, *Diary,* 4 June 1862.
33. Ibid., 4–5 June 1862.
34. Kirkpatrick Diary, 5 June 1862.
35. Dobbins, *Grandfather's Journal,* p. 82.
36. Boteler to Randolph telegram, 1 June 1862, Jackson Papers (d); Boteler described his journey generally in *S.H.S.P.* XL, pp. 166–69.
37. Lee, ibid., endorsed Boteler's June 1 telegram [Jackson Papers (d)] without recording a date but noting an inability to reinforce Jackson. The movement of Lawton's Brigade, including the secretary of war's order, is carefully related in Alton J. Murray, South Georgia Rebels (privately printed, St. Marys, Ga.: 1976), pp. 43–49 and indicates that the initial movement of only part of the brigade did not begin from Richmond until June 7 and was not completed until after June 10.
38. *OR,* vol. 12, pt. 3, pp. 905–6.
39. Ibid., p. 906.
40. Ibid., p. 905.
41. Clifford Dowdey and Louis H. Manarin, eds., *The Wartime Papers of Robert E. Lee* (New York: De Capo Press, 1987), p. 184. For the end result of the strategic considerations set in motion by these letters, see chapter 18, notes 30–38.
42. *OR,* vol. 12, pt. 1, pp. 718–19; John Harman to his brother, 4 June 1862, Hotchkiss Papers.
43. *B & L,* vol. 2, p. 292; Hotchkiss *Diary,* 5 June 1862; Worsham, *Foot Cavalry,* p. 94.
44. Kearns Diary, 5 June 1862.
45. Wilson, *Diary,* 6 June 1862.
46. John Harman to his brother, 5 June 1862.
47. Lanty Blackford to his father, 13 June 1862, Blackford Papers.
48. John Harman to his brother, 6 June 1862, Hotchkiss Papers.
49. Allan Recollections, p. 132; Wayland, Valley Records, p. 289.

50. Frémont claimed that by the time his pursuit reached Woodstock on June 2 he had collected more than five hundred prisoners. *OR,* vol. 12, pt. 1, p. 15. This probably is an approximation, but it seems realistic in view of Confederate straggling, and of course the number of prisoners certainly grew during the following days. Descriptions of straggling are legend and justify an estimate, although it is only that, of thousands of stragglers; see generally, McClendon, *Recollections,* pp. 60–63; Casler, *Four Years,* pp. 81–93; Cummer, ed., *Yankee in Gray,* p. 43. The effect of this straggling is considered at length in chapter 18, notes 57–70 and accompanying text.
51. *OR,* vol. 12, pt. 3, p. 906.
52. Wilson, *Diary,* 6 June 1862; Booth, *Personal Reminiscences,* p. 40.
53. Hotchkiss, *Diary,* 6 June 1862.
54. Munford, *S.H.S.P.* VII, p. 528.
55. Douglas, *I Rode with Stonewall,* p. 75.
56. These details are scattered through Avirett, *Ashby,* pp. 213–17 and MS Diary of Neese, 3–5 June 1862. With regard to the latter, Neese does not specify that Ashby was with Chew's Battery on June 5, but it is reasonable to infer since the battery during this time remained close to the enemy.
57. MacDonald, *Memoirs,* p. 50; the description of Wyndham is that of Taylor, *Destruction and Reconstruction,* p. 23.
58. MS Diary of Neese, 6 June 1862; Brown Memoirs, p. 46 noted the disposition of Ewell's Division. The infantry nearest the guns was apparently Trimble's Brigade. Dobbins, *Grandfather's Journal,* p. 83; Hotchkiss, *Diary,* 6 June 1862; Goldsborough, "How Ashby Was Killed," *S.H.S.P.* XXI, p. 225.
59. McClendon, *Recollections,* p. 40; *OR,* vol. 12, pt. 1, p. 732; MacDonald Memoirs, p. 51.
60. *OR,* vol. 12, pt. 1, p. 788; Avirett, *Ashby,* p. 273.
61. *OR,* vol. 12, pt. 1, p. 732.
62. Johnson, *S.H.S.P.* X, p. 104; *OR,* vol. 12, pt. 1, p. 788.
63. Johnson, *S.H.S.P.* X, pp. 104–5; Booth, *Maryland Soldier,* pp. 41–42; Goldsborough, *Maryland Line,* p. 70.
64. *OR,* vol. 12, pt. 1, pp. 732, 788.
65. Confederate losses are given in *OR,* vol. 12, pt. 1, pp. 788 and 817. Federal losses are cited in Allan, *Valley Campaign,* p. 143.
66. *OR,* vol. 12, pt. 1, p. 782.
67. Details of the last moments were related to Campbell Brown by Ewell, who had been near Ashby when struck but had not realized in the heat of battle who had fallen. Brown Memoirs, p. 47. William Jackson to his wife, 8 June 1862, Jackson Papers, recorded the trajectory.
68. Wilson, *Diary,* 6 June 1862.
69. O'Ferrall, *Active Service,* p. 38; Avirett, *Ashby,* p. 226; Brown Memoirs, p. 48.

70. Hotchkiss, *Diary,* 6 June 1862.
71. Winder Diary, 6 June 1862.
72. A. S. Pendleton to his mother, 7 June 1862, Bean, ed., "Pendleton Letters," p. 364.
73. *OR,* vol. 12, pt. 3, p. 907.
74. Wilson, *Diary,* 7 June 1862; Douglas, *I Rode with Stonewall,* p. 82; Avirett, *Ashby,* pp. 234–35.
75. *OR,* vol. 12, pt. 1, p. 712.
76. Ashby's very formidable problems are discussed in McDonald, *Laurel Brigade,* pp. 51–52; Ashby, *Life of Ashby,* pp. 185–86; and Clarence, *General Ashby,* p. 85.
77. Hotchkiss, *Diary,* 24 April 1862.
78. Douglas, *I Rode with Stonewall,* p. 75.
79. Taylor, *Destruction and Reconstruction,* p. 81.
80. McDonald, *Laurel Brigade,* p. 51.
81. Douglas, *I Rode with Stonewall,* p. 82.

CHAPTER 16

1. *OR,* vol. 12, pt. 3, pp. 906–7.
2. Worsham, *Foot Cavalry,* p. 96.
3. Hotchkiss, *Diary,* 7 June 1862.
4. Lanty Blackford to his father, 13 June 1862, Blackford Papers, placed the distance at roughly one half-mile. Moore, *Cannoneer,* p. 66, recalled the battery was a mile away from Port Republic.
5. *OR,* vol. 12, pt. 1, pp. 712–13.
6. Ibid., pp. 712, 732.
7. Cleon Moore, "Personal Narrative," *Confederate Veteran Magazine,* vol. 22, p. 511 established it was his company, K, near the bridge. As will appear, the company on the lower ford was Captain Moore's I Company.
8. A. S. Pendleton to his mother, 7 June 1862, Bean, ed., "Pendleton Letters," p. 364.
9. J. L. Dinwiddie to "Bettie," 7 June 1862, Dinwiddie Papers, University of Virginia, Charlottesville, Virginia.
10. Lanty Blackford to his father, 13 June 1862, Blackford Papers.
11. Hunter McGuire to Jedediah Hotchkiss, 23 May 1896, Hotchkiss Papers; Allan Recollections, p. 135–37; Hotchkiss, *Diary,* 8 June 1862.
12. See Howard, *Staff Officer,* p. 122, footnote 1.
13. Dabney, *S.H.S.P.* XI, p. 146.
14. *OR,* vol. 12, pt. 3, pp. 907–8; Douglas, *I Rode with Stonewall,* p. 85.
15. Winder Diary, 5–8 June 1862; it is not known whether the note was

delivered to Jackson before the events about to explode around Port Republic, or, in fact, if it was ever delivered.

16. Howard, *Staff Officer,* p. 122.
17. Jackson, *Life of Jackson,* pp. 515–16; *OR,* vol. 12, pt. 1, p. 773.
18. Lanty Blackford to his father, 13 June 1862, Blackford Papers.
19. Howard, *Staff Officer,* p. 122.
20. J. L. Dinwiddie to "Bettie," 12 June 1862, Dinwiddie Papers.
21. *OR,* vol. 12, pt. 1, p. 739.
22. See notes 37–38.
23. Samuel J. C. Moore, "Clarke County Men at Port Republic," unpublished typescript, p. 3, Moore Papers; Cleon Moore, *Confederate Veteran,* vol. 22, p. 511.
24. *OR,* vol. 12, pt. 1, p. 713; Hunter McGuire to Jedediah Hotchkiss, 23 May 1896, Hotchkiss Papers.
25. McGuire to Hotchkiss, 23 May 1896, Hotchkiss Papers; Douglas, *I Rode with Stonewall,* p. 85; *OR,* vol. 12, pt. 1, p. 719 specifies that Boswell was among those who raced over the span with Jackson.
26. Robert L. Dabney, "Memoranda for Colonel Henderson," unpublished typescript (probably 1896 but undated), Hotchkiss Papers; Allan Recollections, p. 137; Cleon Moore, "Stonewall Jackson at Port Republic," *Confederate Veteran,* vol. 22, p. 511.
27. J. L. Dinwiddie to "Bettie," 12 June 1862, Dinwiddie Papers.
28. Lanty Blackford to his mother, 13 June 1862, Blackford Papers, established that at least one rebel besides the known staff officers was taken.
29. This incident has been recounted many times but without conclusive result as to Jackson's role, if indeed he played one at all. The idea that he was attempting to decoy the Federal gun to the north side of the river was an early and very popular one. See Jackson, *Life of Jackson,* pp. 516–17. Dabney, on the other hand, disputed that anything of the kind happened. Johnson, *Life of Dabney,* p. 571. Another version, offered with the authority of those who would have been near Jackson, has him trying to determine whether the gun on the far side might be Confederate. See note 40, infra. The most recent examination of the episode is Darrel L. Collins, *The Battles of Cross Keys and Port Republic* (Lynchburg, Va.: H. E. Howard Inc., 1993), pp. 44–45.
30. Hunter McGuire to Jedediah Hotchkiss, 23 May 1896, Hotchkiss Papers; *S.H.S.P.* XI, pp. 147–48.
31. S. J. C. Moore to Jedediah Hotchkiss, 18 June 1896, Hotchkiss Papers.
32. Much correspondence exists on this episode, especially among Hotchkiss, Dabney, and Moore in the Hotchkiss and Moore Papers. The present narrative follows principally Moore, "Clarke County Men at Port Republic"; Hunter McGuire to Jedediah Hotchkiss, 23 May and 12 June 1896 (Moore Papers); and Moore to Hotchkiss, 3 and 18 June 1896 (Hotchkiss Papers). An undated four-page handwritten document

in the Moore Papers also seems trustworthy on Moore's comments to his men before their first volley.

33. L. W. Cox to Jedediah Hotchkiss, 17 August 1896, Hotchkiss Papers. A slightly expanded version of Cox's story is found in his typescript "Memoirs," Albemarle County Historical Society, Charlottesville, Virginia.
34. James Carrington to Hotchkiss, 17 June 1896, Hotchkiss Papers; Johnson, *Life of Dabney,* pp. 571–75.
35. Moore, "Clarke County Men at Port Republic," p. 4 notes that Sipe returned from the direction of Staunton. In all probability Sipe's men were part of the initial panic of Confederate cavalry, but the return to action saved them from disgrace. On June 17 Jackson published a general order specifically condemning the commands of Captain Myers and Chipley for "at the mere approach of the enemy [fleeing] from anticipated danger, regardless of the fate of the gallant army they so disgracefully deserted." Hotchkiss Papers. That Sipe's command was not included in Jackson's commendation of "cowardly conduct" suggests Sipe's unit redeemed itself in some fashion.
36. W. F. Davis, "Recollections of My Life," unpublished typescript in the possession of J. Harvey Bailey, Charlottesville, Virginia; James Carrington to Hotchkiss, 17 June 1896, Hotchkiss Papers.
37. Poague, *Gunner,* p. 26.
38. Lanty Blackford to his mother, 13 June 1862, Blackford Papers.
39. *OR,* vol. 12, pt. 1, pp. 739, 744–45; Poague, *Gunner,* p. 26.
40. Douglas, *I Rode with Stonewall,* p. 86.
41. *OR,* vol. 12, pt. 1, p. 801; Taylor, *Destruction and Reconstruction,* p. 74.
42. Moore, *Cannoneer,* pp. 68–69. Douglas, *I Rode with Stonewall,* pp. 85–86, tells the story in reverse. That is, he recorded that Jackson initially assumed the gun was Southern while being told by his staff around him that it was a Federal piece. An 1879 letter from Poague recalling the incident much as Moore does is quoted in Allan, *Valley Campaign,* p. 150, footnote 1.
43. Wood, *The War,* p. 59; Moore, *Cannoneer,* p. 70.
44. *OR,* vol. 12, pt. 1, p. 728. One of Carpenter's Battery, William Humphreys, thought the enemy column was "every man of 3 or 4 large regiments." Humphreys to his mother, 14 June 1862. In fact, there was only one Union regiment, the 7th Indiana, in the column.
45. Colt, *Defend the Valley,* p. 158.
46. *OR,* vol. 12, pt. 1, pp. 713, 728.
47. Federal losses given in *OR,* vol. 12, pt. 1, p. 699 do not include their mounted casualties. Taliaferro reported capturing "several" of the enemy and also gave Fulkerson's loss. Ibid., p. 773. Colonel Garnett reported the rebels took twenty-seven prisoners, including seventeen horses, which likely sets the outside limit of Federal cavalry losses. Thomas Garnett to his father, 2 June 1862, Fredericksburg-Spotsylvania National Military Park.

48. John Harman to his brother, 8 June 1862, Hotchkiss Papers.
49. *OR,* vol. 12, pt. 1, pp. 740, 768, 774.
50. William Allan to Asher Harman, 8 June 1862, Hotchkiss Papers.
51. Lanty Blackford to his mother, 13 June 1862, Blackford Papers. As to Carroll's mission, see Collins, *Cross Keys and Port Republic,* p. 33.
52. Moore, "Clarke County Men at Port Republic," p. 9, Moore Papers.
53. William Allan to Asher Harman, 8 June 1862, Hotchkiss Papers.

CHAPTER 17

1. *OR,* vol. 12, pt. 1, p. 781; Brown, Memoirs, p. 48.
2. Brown Memoirs, p. 48.
3. *OR,* vol. 12, pt. 1, pp. 713, 799.
4. Ibid., pp. 781, 795.
5. J. William Jones, "Reminiscences of the Army of Northern Virginia," *S.H.S.P.* IX, p. 280.
6. The entire battle is well covered by Peter Svenson, *Battlefield* (Boston: Faber and Faber, 1992); also thorough is Collins, *Cross Keys and Port Republic,* pp. 48–81.
7. *OR,* vol. 12, pt. 1, p. 794.
8. Ibid., p. 782.
9. McClendon, *Recollections,* p. 66; Oates, *The War,* p. 103.
10. *OR,* vol. 12, pt. 1, p. 796.
11. Nisbet, *Four Years,* p. 53.
12. *OR,* vol. 12, pt. 1, pp. 798–99; Allan, *Valley Campaign,* pp. 154–55.
13. *OR,* vol. 12, pt. 1, p. 798.
14. Kearns Diary, 8 June 1862.
15. *OR,* vol. 12, pt. 1, p. 781; Brown Memoirs, p. 57.
16. Walker, *V.M.I. Memorial,* p. 113 (Joseph Chenoweth Diary, 8 June 1862).
17. *OR,* vol. 12, pt. 1, pp. 789, 818.
18. Ibid., p. 728.
19. Ibid., p. 770.
20. Thomas Garnett to his father, 2 July 1862.
21. *OR,* vol. 12, pt. 1, pp. 21–22.
22. Ibid., p. 782.
23. Ibid., pp. 664–65.
24. Dabney, *Jackson,* pp. 420–21 attributes this opinion to Colonel Patton, who was required to defend the area the next day.
25. Moore, *Cannoneer,* p. 70.
26. *OR,* vol. 12, pt. 1, pp. 782–84.
27. Ibid., p. 798.
28. Dabney, *Jackson,* p. 418. Campbell Brown recalled seeing Jackson in the vicinity of a field hospital during the action, although he did not specify time or location of that aid station. Brown Memoirs, p. 52.

29. *OR,* vol. 12, pt. 1, p. 719.
30. Howard, *Staff Officer,* p. 124.
31. *OR,* vol. 12, pt. 1, pp. 713–14.
32. Jackson's reasoning was recorded secondhand, but carefully, by Hotchkiss almost a year later. Hotchkiss, *Diary,* 4 April 1863.
33. *OR,* vol. 12, pt. 1, p. 714.
34. Johnston to Jackson, 27 May 1862, New York *Herald,* 16 June 1862.
35. Boswell reported being sent by Jackson at 4 A.M. from Port Republic to Mechums for the purpose of "meeting reinforcements which were expected at that point." *OR,* vol. 12, pt. 1, p. 719. In reality, no such succor was at hand. Instead, Lawton's Georgians were moving past this point on the way to Staunton.
36. Douglas, *I Rode with Stonewall,* p. 89.
37. Garbar, *Life of Harman,* p. 20.
38. *OR,* vol. 12, pt. 1, p. 732.
39. Ibid., p. 728; *S.H.S.P.* X, p. 147.
40. *OR,* vol. 12, pt. 1, pp. 740, 757; Howard, *Staff Officer,* p. 127; Colt, *Defend the Valley,* p. 158.
41. *OR,* vol. 12, pt. 1, p. 774.
42. *B & L,* vol. 2, p. 293.
43. Patton, *S.H.S.P.* VII, p. 529.
44. *OR,* vol. 12, pt. 1, p. 798.
45. It can be stated with certainty only that Jackson wrote his telegram to Lee that night. See chapter 18, notes 28–30. The arrival of Taliaferro can be established more precisely from his recollections as contained in Jackson, *Life of Jackson,* p. 517.
46. Dabney, *Jackson,* pp. 420–21, quotes a statement recorded by Patton shortly after the war, infra.
47. Patton's assumption is described by him in an unpublished manuscript entitled "Reminiscences of Jackson," Roy Bird Cook Papers, University of West Virginia, Morgantown, West Virginia. For others following this assumption, see 3 *C.M.H.,* p. 260; Douglas, *I Rode with Stonewall,* p. 90; Howard, *Staff Officer,* p. 131; Allan, *Valley Campaign,* p. 157. In the first edition of this book, pp. 296–97, this author also accepted the idea and was critical of Jackson for attempting the dual battle.
48. *OR,* vol. 12, pt. 1, p. 708; General Trimble specifically noted that he had no artillery the next morning, and Colonel Crutchfield, p. 728 implied that all of Ewell's batteries were directed to the Port Republic front early.
49. Ibid., p. 719.
50. Winder stated he received the order at 3:45 A.M. Ibid., p. 740; Garbar, *Life of Harman,* p. 20.
51. *OR,* vol. 12, pt. 1, p. 768.
52. Ibid.; Winder Diary, 9 June 1862; Howard, *Staff Officer,* p. 126.
53. Dabney, *Jackson,* p. 420 offered the first explanation; Munford,

S.H.S.P. VII, p. 530, the second. There is general agreement that the defect, whatever it was, substantially slowed the crossing. Allan, *Valley Campaign,* p. 158

54. Howard, *Staff Officer,* p. 126; the assignment of Moore's company as skirmishers is reported in *OR,* vol. 12, pt. 1, p. 745. Gold, *History of Clarke County,* p. 176 notes that Company I bore its part in the Battle of Port Republic. Although he does not specify that Moore and the detail from the skirmish at Madison Hall were with the company, there is no reason to believe they were absent.
55. Howard, *Staff Officer,* p. 127.
56. *OR,* vol. 12, pt. 1, p. 740.
57. Ibid., p. 757.
58. Allan, "Recollections," p. 137.
59. Dabney, *S.H.S.P.* XI, pp. 151–52.
60. Taylor, *Destruction and Reconstruction,* p. 83; Henry B. Kelly, *Port Republic* (Philadelphia: J. B. Lippincott Co., 1886), pp. 15–16.
61. *OR,* vol. 12, pt. 1, pp. 745, 747.
62. Ibid., p. 745.
63. Ibid., p. 757.
64. Ibid., pp. 729, 760. One piece reported to the front minus gunners; p. 741.
65. Taylor, *Destruction and Reconstruction,* p. 84.
66. Hotchkiss, *Diary,* 9 June 1862; *OR,* vol. 12, pt. 1, p. 802. See Parrish, *Taylor,* pp. 208–9, footnote 43 for a discussion of postwar differences among Taylor, Colonel Kelley of the 8th Louisiana, and Hotchkiss on the question of exactly who led this march. The text has adopted the traditional view that Hotchkiss guided Taylor based upon a note made by Hotchkiss in his field diary that day: "I guided Taylor's La. Brigade around through the woods to the E. of Gen. Lewis and they charged and took a battery." MS Diary, 9 June, Hotchkiss Papers. Hotchkiss was credited by Boswell with having conducted the brigade at Jackson's order. *OR,* vol. 12, pt. 1, p. 719.
67. *OR,* vol. 12, pt. 1, p. 741.
68. Colt, *Defend the Valley,* p. 161.
69. *OR,* vol. 12, pt. 1, p. 753.
70. Winder Diary, 9 June 1862.
71. The time of Jackson's decision to abandon the west bank is approximate only. It is based upon Trimble's statement that he received Jackson's order at some point after 9 A.M. and while he was already pulling back toward Port Republic. *OR,* vol. 12, pt. 1, p. 798. It is unknown how far Trimble had retired (and thus how much closer he was to the Port) when he received the order. Whatever that distance, Jackson's courier had to ride a mile and a half from the battlefield, ford the South River, work his way through Port Republic and over the crowded North River bridge, and then ride out the Harrisonburg road to find Trimble. Thirty minutes would seem a bare minimum, so reverse calculation

would indicate that Jackson dispatched his courier sometime after 8:30 A.M. In his report, Jackson lumped the order to Trimble to come to the front with similar instructions given to Taliaferro (ibid., p. 715), upon which is based the assumption that they were given at the same time.

72. *OR,* pp. 741, 792.
73. Colt, *Defend the Valley,* p. 161.
74. *OR,* vol. 12, pt. 1, p. 763.
75. William Jackson to his wife, 10 June 1862, Jackson Letters.
76. Neese, *Horse Artillery,* p. 74.
77. *OR,* vol. 12, pt. 1, p. 790.
78. Ibid., p. 789.
79. Ibid., p. 786.
80. Ibid., p. 787.
81. Ibid., p. 792.
82. Buck, *With the Old Confeds,* p. 38.
83. Moore, *Cannoneer,* p. 75.
84. Taylor, *Destruction and Reconstruction,* pp. 84–85, and Henry B. Kelly, *Port Republic* (Philadelphia: J. B. Lippincott Co., 1896), pp. 18–22 are the best overall recollections of the battle. Taylor described three separate charges, but it is impossible to verify that number, and given the nature of the terrain and general confusion it is unlikely there were discrete attacks after the first one. Probably different regiments hit the coaling at different times, making it impossible to describe specific attack waves. In his official report, written 11 June 1862, Taylor described only one major followed eventually by one withdrawal before the battle was decided by arrival of reinforcements. *OR,* vol. 12, pt. 1, p. 800.
85. Taylor, *Destruction and Reconstruction,* p. 86.
86. *OR,* vol. 12, pt. 1, p. 786.
87. Wingfield, *Diary,* 14 June 1862.
88. *OR,* vol. 12, pt. 1, pp. 768, 774.
89. Ibid., p. 758.
90. Ibid., pp. 745, 792.
91. Taylor, *Destruction and Reconstruction,* p. 76; Nisbet, *Four Years,* p. 56.
92. *OR,* vol. 12, pt. 1, p. 715.
93. Jackson to Cooper, 9 June 1862, Jackson Papers (d).
94. Allan, *Valley Campaign,* p. 162.
95. William L. Jackson to his wife, 10 June 1862, Jackson Letters.
96. Moore, *Cannoneer,* p. 75.
97. Garbar, *Life of Harman,* p. 21.
98. Taylor, *Destruction and Reconstruction,* p. 76.
99. The commander of one of Trimble's units, the Irish Battalion, heard it clearly. *OR,* vol. 12, pt. 1, p. 771.
100. *OR,* vol. 12, pt. 1, p. 708. Dobbins, *Grandfather's Journal,* p. 84

noted that the march was made in "quick-step," a recollection supported by McClendon, *Recollections,* p. 67.

101. Oates, *The War,* p. 104.
102. *OR,* vol. 12, pt. 1, p. 732.
103. Garbar, *Sketch of Harman,* p. 20.
104. *OR,* vol. 12, pt. 1, p. 716; Douglas, *I Rode with Stonewall,* p. 90. At least one observer understood that Union artillery fired on a hospital in Port Republic. Percy G. Hamlin, *Old Bald Head* (Strasburg, Va.: Shenandoah Publishing House, 1940), p. 104.
105. *OR,* vol. 12, pt. 1, p. 751.
106. Buck, *With the Old Confeds,* p. 39; Dobbins, *Grandfather's Journal,* p. 84.
107. *OR,* vol. 12, pt. 1, p. 689.
108. The predicament of Shields's Division following Port Republic is well covered in Collins, *Cross Keys and Port Republic,* pp. 129–31.
109. Taylor, *Destruction and Reconstruction,* p. 76.
110. Brown to his mother, 17 June 1862, Polk, Ewell, Brown Papers.
111. Douglas, *I Rode with Stonewall,* p. 90.
112. Barnett H. Cody to Henrietta Burnett, 13 June 1862, E. C. Burnett, ed., "Letters of Barnett Hardeman Cody and Others, 1861–4," *Georgia Historical Quarterly,* vol. 23, no. 4, December 1939, p. 365.
113. William H. Murray to a friend, 28 June 1862, Maryland Historical Society, Baltimore, Maryland.

CHAPTER 18

1. *OR,* vol. 12, pt. 1, p. 716.
2. Hotchkiss, *Diary,* 12 June 1862.
3. Neese, *Horse Artillery,* p. 56.
4. Brown Memoirs, p. 56; Brown to his mother, 17 June 1862, Polk, Ewell, Brown Papers.
5. Kaufman Diary, 16 June 1862.
6. *OR,* vol. 12, pt. 3, p. 911.
7. Jackson Letter Book, 1862, 13 June 1862, Hotchkiss Papers.
8. Dabney, *Jackson,* p. 430.
9. Boteler, *S.H.S.P.* XL, p. 172 states that he returned just after Port Republic but does not specify the date.
10. Jones, *War Clerk's Diary,* 22 May 1862.
11. Richmond *Whig,* 27 May 1862.
12. Richmond *Whig,* 11 June 1862.
13. Macon *Daily Telegraph,* 3 June 1862. The same sort of praise could be found throughout the South. See Augusta (Ga.) *Daily Constitutionalist,* 8 June 1862, and Charlotte *Whig,* 17 June 1862.

14. Robert M. Myers, ed., *The Children of Pride* (New Haven, Ct.: Yale University Press, 1972), p. 908.
15. Kate Cummings, *The Journal of a Confederate Nurse,* ed. by Richard B. Harwell (Baton Rouge: Louisiana State University Press, 1959), pp. 53–54.
16. Atlanta *Intelligencer,* 3 June 1862; Americus (Ga.) *Sumter Republican,* 30 May 1862.
17. Jones, *War Clerk's Diary,* 22 May 1862.
18. For an excellent discussion of Jackson's reputation following the Valley Campaign, see Charles Royster, *The Destructive War* (New York: Alfred A. Knopf, 1991), pp. 68–70.
19. *OR,* vol. 12, pt. 3, p. 908.
20. Dowdey, *Wartime Papers of Lee,* p. 193.
21. Murray, *South Georgia Rebels,* p. 50.
22. Dowdey, *Wartime Papers of Lee,* p. 194.
23. Freeman, *R. E. Lee,* vol. 2, p. 98 describes in detail the worries of Lee's day.
24. Boteler, *S.H.S.P.* XL, pp. 172–74.
25. See generally Freeman, *R. E. Lee,* vol. 2, p. 93.
26. *OR,* vol. 12, pt. 3, p. 907.
27. Ibid.
28. Jackson to Lee, 9 June 1862, Jackson Papers (d), stated simply, "Yesterday God crowned our arms with success by repulsing the attacks of Frémont and Shields at Port Republic." That telegram, sent via Staunton, was received in Richmond on the morning of June 9. Dowdey, *Wartime Papers of Lee,* p. 188. Since it refers to the battle against Frémont as occurring "yesterday," it must have been written early on June 9, while Jackson was hurrying to prepare his attack on Shields.
29. Jackson to Cooper, 9 June 1862, Jackson Papers (d).
30. Dowdey, *Wartime Papers of Lee,* p. 188.
31. Davis, *Rise and Fall,* p. 131.
32. William Allan conversation with Lee, 17 December 1868, p. 16. Typescript in Allan Papers.
33. *OR,* vol. 11, pt. 3, p. 594
34. Ibid., vol. 12, pt. 3, p. 910.
35. William Allan conversation with Lee, 17 December 1868, p. 16. Allan Papers.
36. Charles Marshal, *An Aide-de-Camp to General Lee* (Boston: Little, Brown & Co., 1927), p. 84.
37. *OR,* vol. 11, pt. 3, p. 590.
38. Dowdey, *Wartime Papers of Lee,* p. 193.
39. See Stephen W. Sears, *To the Gates of Richmond* (New York: Ticknor & Fields, 1992), pp. 248, 300 for a discussion of points at which Northern disaster on the Peninsula became a real possibility despite Southern operational bungling. The Southern high command's assess-

ment of McClellan is reviewed on p. 47. A recent illustration of the criticism leveled at Lee for not supporting Jackson's invasion is found in Bevin Alexander, *Lost Victories: The Military Genius of Stonewall Jackson* (New York: Henry Holt and Company, 1992), pp. 80–91.

40. See *OR,* vol. 12, pt. 3, pp. 857, 860.
41. R. W. Waldrop to his father, 12 June 1862, Waldrop Letters.
42. Murray, *South Georgia Rebels,* pp. 44–48 and Harold B. Simpson, *Hood's Texas Brigade: Lee's Grenadier Guard* (Dallas: Alcor Publishing, 1983), p. 110 reflect the difficulties of the actual rail movement.
43. Stephen W. Sears, ed., *The Civil War Papers of George B. McClellan* (New York: Ticknor & Fields, 1989), p. 301. As early as the siege of Yorktown, McClellan had assembled firepower that dwarfed even that of the European powers at the siege of Sevastopol. See Sears, *To the Gates of Richmond,* pp. 57–58.
44. *OR,* vol. 12, pt. 3, p. 913.
45. Hotchkiss, *Diary,* 17 June 1862.
46. *OR,* vol. 12, pt. 1, p. 722.
47. The phrase is that of Alexander, *Lost Victories,* p. 80. See also Grady McWhiney and Perry D. Jamieson, *Attack and Die* (Tuscaloosa: University of Alabama Press, 1982), p. 7 and Alan T. Nolan, *Lee Considered: General Robert E. Lee and Civil War History* (Chapel Hill: University of North Carolina Press, 1991), pp. 77–79.
48. Winder Diary, 7 and 8 June 1862.
49. Thomas Garnett to his father, 2 July 1862, Fredericksburg-Spotsylvania National Military Park.
50. John D. Chapla, *42nd Virginia Infantry* (Lynchburg, Va.: H. E. Howard, Inc., 1983), pp. 12–15.
51. *OR,* vol. 11, pt. 2, p. 592.
52. For ease of analysis, the 10th Virginia is included in the original Valley Army even though it was not at Kernstown; but it follows the trend. The 10th's Colonel Gibbons fell during its first Shenandoah fight at McDowell. The 21st Virginia, which was not at Port Republic, is also included. It fought at Kernstown under Colonel Patton, but follows the trend because Patton had the brigade and the 21st was led on the prisoner escort mission by the next in command.
53. Colonel Hoffman, who was ill prior to McDowell, took the field during the engagement and remained even after being wounded. *OR,* vol. 12, pt. 1, p. 484. For purposes of this analysis his leadership of his unit at McDowell was limited, but he is grouped with Scott since he did participate in both battles.
54. Parrish, *Richard Taylor,* p. 225.
55. Winder Diary, 11 June 1862. Taylor, *Destruction and Reconstruction,* p. 79 recalled that Winder actually resigned two or three days later after being denied leave by Jackson, a flap that Taylor took credit for ending satisfactorily. The resignation is not otherwise documented and apparently went no further.

56. G. P. Ring to his wife, 14 June 1862, Ring Papers.
57. J. L. Dinwiddie to "Bettie," 18 June 1862, Dinwiddie Papers.
58. *OR,* vol. 12, pt. 3, p. 879.
59. Ibid., pp. 737–38.
60. Ibid., p. 742.
61. Carpenter's letter is quoted in Keith Bohannon, *The Giles, Allegheny and Jackson Artillery* (Lynchburg, Va.: H. E. Howard, 1990), p. 18. Edmondson's estimate is noted in chapter 15, note 21.
62. Kearns Diary, 16 and 17 June 1862.
63. Morning Report of the 8th Brigade, 11 June 1862, Henry E. Huntington Library, San Marino, California.
64. The calculations are as follows: The brigade aggregate on June 11 was 4,204 men. The report also states the aggregate for the last report (date unknown) was 4,252; the difference was attributed almost entirely to killed in action, and since the death tally almost equals deaths listed in Taylor's battle reports from Front Royal to Port Republic, it seems clear that the total roster before the Louisiana Brigade's strenuous efforts would have been 4,250 officers and men. Taking again a one-quarter reduction for normal absence, Taylor should have had 3,200 officers and men ready for action when he left Swift Run Gap, and, indeed, Taylor recalled that his brigade was in excess of 3,000 when it joined Jackson outside New Market. Taylor, *Destruction and Reconstruction,* p. 50. In an interesting postwar article, Jubal Early, infra, cited field returns also indicating that at the beginning of May Taylor's unit was slightly in excess of 3,000 men fit for duty. Taylor reported that his losses between Front Royal and Winchester (17 killed and 100 wounded and missing), at Cross Keys (2 killed and 15 wounded), and at Port Republic (33 killed and 255 wounded) totaled 52 killed and 370 wounded and missing. He should have had approximately 2,800 available after Port Republic, yet on June 11 his command fielded only 2,167 officers and men present, including 134 sick (presumably minor illnesses) and 166 on extra duty. The greater than 600 man difference between that figure and the presumed 2,800 would be attributed to nonbattle casualties after mid-May. This analysis is consistent with the report of Jubal Early, "Strength of Ewell's Division in the Campaign of 1862—Field Returns," *S.H.S.P.* VIII, p. 304. Early, writing in 1880, claimed to have received official papers on the strength of Ewell's Division from one of its staff officers. He quotes a Morning Report for the division for June 14, 1862, listing 1,899 officers and men present for duty in Taylor's Brigade. That number generally is consistent with the June 11 report, which, excluding sick and those on extra duty, would have 1,880 officers and men present. This accuracy gives comfort that Early's numbers are reliable with regard to other units as well. See note 67, infra, for numbers, including those suggested by Early, on Trimble's Brigade's nonbattle losses.
65. *OR,* vol. 12, pt. 1, pp. 476, 764–67, 784.

66. Patton, "Reminiscences of Jackson," Cook Papers. In *S.H.S.P.* I, p. 420 Early pointed out that this brigade was so reduced by the severity of its service in the Valley that it was kept back in the Peninsula fighting, and in fact it suffered negligible casualties there. See *OR,* vol. 11, pt. 2, p. 975.
67. Early, *S.H.S.P.* VIII, p. 302 gives the present-for-duty strength of Trimble's Brigade in early May and as of June 14. Trimble's battle losses are in *OR,* vol. 12, pt. 1, pp. 780, 784. It is significant to note that in describing his division at Cross Keys, including Trimble's Brigade, Ewell reported that he entered the battle with only three "small brigades." Ibid., p. 783.
68. *OR,* vol. 12, pt. 3, p. 879 estimated the brigade as of May 3 at 2,200 men. Assuming a 25 percent normal absent tally, the brigade ought to have had 1,650 officers and men ready. It took 101 casualties at McDowell (ibid., pt. 1, p. 482), but few thereafter. Unfortunately, its strength by campaign's end is not reported with precision. Collins, *Cross Keys and Port Republic,* p. 151 estimated the end strength at 1,200 men; Early, *S.H.S.P.* I, p. 420 noted that this brigade, like the 2d, was so reduced that it was kept back from heavy fighting in the Peninsula, which is confirmed by light losses there (*OR,* vol. 11, pt. 2, p. 975). Assuming Collins's numbers, nonbattle losses from this command would be consistent with the one quarter noncombat loss figure found in other data.
69. Jubal Early assumed command of the seven regiments of this brigade (the original force under Johnson plus the 13th Virginia, which campaigned with Elzey and was not engaged in any significant fighting before Cross Keys) on the Peninsula on July 1; he found its total strength was 1,052 officers and men present. There was only one colonel present, Walker of the 13th, and two lieutenant colonels (of the 25th and 52d Virginia). The other regiments were commanded by captains—again reflecting the strain of the campaign on the Valley Army's high command. Jubal Early, *Autobiographical Sketch and Narrative of the War Between the States* (Bloomington, IN: Indiana University Press, 1960), p. 78. Roughly 1,000 men were lost in the Valley Campaign battles of this unit, especially at McDowell, Cross Keys, and Port Republic, with significant additional losses to the 12th Georgia when Front Royal was recaptured. Some of the weakness Early found was doubtless due to the stressful march from the Valley to Richmond; the brigade was not heavily engaged on the Peninsula before Early took it over. With the 13th Virginia, Johnson's initial command must have counted in excess of 3,000 men present for duty as of early May; battle losses in the Shenandoah and even deductions for the march to Richmond seem insufficient to account for the small total Early found unless allowance is also made for sizable nonbattle losses during the Valley Campaign.
70. Recent scholarship supports this figure. Collins, *Cross Keys and Port*

Republic, p. 154 estimated the strength of the Valley Army before the dual battles and including 800 cavalry to have been 11,470. Without the mounted arm and approximately 1,000 casualties, this estimate is close to, though lower than, the 10,000 used here. Jubal Early, *S.H.S.P.* I, p. 420 was even less generous, claiming that the portion of Jackson's command that came to the Peninsula excluding Whiting and Lawton would not have exceeded 8,000.

71. Johnson, *Dabney,* p. 266.
72. Winder Diary, 5 June 1862.
73. See generally, James M. McPherson, *Ordeal by Fire* (New York: Alfred A. Knopf, 1982), p. 468.
74. *OR,* vol. 12, pt. 3, p. 863.
75. Ibid., p. 872.
76. Ibid., p. 894.

EPILOGUE

1. Douglas, *I Rode with Stonewall,* p. 97.
2. Jones, "Reminiscences," *S.H.S.P.* IX, p. 363.
3. J. B. Powley, *A Soldier's Letters to Charming Nellie* (New York: Neale Publishing Co., 1908), p. 46.
4. *OR,* vol. 12, pt. 3, p. 354; pt. 1, pp. 542–43.
5. Ibid., pt. 1, p. 661.
6. Ibid., pt. 3, p. 411.
7. McDowell would later assert that, had he been able to leave the Valley on the day he was ordered to depart (8 June 1862), he could have joined McClellan by 26 June 1862, the opening day of the Seven Days. Ibid., pt. 1, p. 288.
8. Ibid., pt. 3, pp. 382, 384, 392, 395, 407, 434.
9. Ibid., p. 435.
10. Ibid., vol. 11, pt. 2, p. 810.
11. Dabney, *Jackson,* p. 467.
12. Taylor, *Destruction and Reconstruction,* p. 78.
13. James P. Smith, "With Stonewall Jackson in the Army of Northern Virginia," *S.H.S.P.* XLIII, p. 24.
14. Royster, *Destructive War,* pp. 42–44 offers an excellent review of this aspect of Jackson's reputation.
15. Douglas, *I Rode with Stonewall,* p. 111.
16. Ibid., p. 313.
17. Bradley T. Johnson, "My Ride around Baltimore in 1864," *S.H.S.P.* XXX, pp. 216–17.
18. Douglas, *I Rode with Stonewall,* p. 292.
19. Hale, *Four Valiant Years,* p. 387. That the Confederate army suffered heavily by nonbattle losses on this campaign is confirmed in Douglas, *I Rode with Stonewall,* pp. 290–94.

20. Worsham, *Foot Cavalry,* p. 220.
21. *OR,* vol. 43, pt. 2, p. 880.
22. Ibid., pt. 1, p. 37.
23. Charles W. McVicar, "Chew's Battery," *S.H.S.P.* XVIII, pp. 285–86.
24. Neese to Chew, 28 March 1898, Robert Preston Chew Papers, Jefferson County Museum, Charles Town, West Virginia.
25. Elizabeth R. P. Allan, *A March Past* (Richmond, Va., 1938), pp. 153–54.
26. S. J. C. Moore, unpublished manuscript "Clarke County Men at Port Republic," p. 1, Moore Papers.
27. S. Scollay Moore, unpublished typescript "Recollections of My Father," p. 48, Moore Papers.

APPENDIX A

1. See, e.g., Freeman, *Lee's Lieutenants,* vol. 1, p. 363.
2. Ibid., and see also p. 366; Chambers, *Stonewall Jackson,* vol. 1, p. 517.
3. Hotchkiss, 3 *C.M.H.,* p. 236.
4. Allan, *Valley Campaign,* pp. 88, 91.
5. Dabney, *Jackson,* pp. 363–64; Douglas, *I Rode with Stonewall,* p. 51.
6. Henderson, *Stonewall Jackson,* p. 236.
7. Allan, *Valley Campaign,* p. 91; see also McDonald, *Laurel Brigade,* p. 57.
8. *OR,* vol. 12, pt. 1, p. 701.
9. Ibid., pt. 3, p. 895.
10. Ibid., p. 897.
11. Ibid., p. 898.
12. Ibid., vol. 51, pt. 2, p. 560.
13. Jno. Lucas to Branch, 18 May 1862, 11:10 P.M., Branch Papers (a).
14. Jno. Lucas to Branch, 19 May 1862, Branch Papers (a).
15. See chapter 11, note 27, and accompanying text.
16. Snider Diary, 21 May 1862.
17. Dobbins, ed., *Grandfather's Journal,* p. 79.
18. See chapter 11, note 24, and accompanying text.
19. John Harman to his brother, 20 May 1862, Hotchkiss Papers.
20. *OR,* vol. 12, pt. 1, p. 701.
21. Dabney to Ashby, 17 May 1862, Ashby Papers.
22. MS Neese Diary, 17–20 May 1862.
23. Arehart Diary, 18–21 May 1862.
24. Wilson, *Diary,* 17–19 May 1862.
25. Hotchkiss, "Memoranda—Valley Campaign of 1862," 20 May 1862. One of Ashby's riders recalled long after the war that following Banks's retreat to Strasburg "the cavalry moved back to Stony Creek and picketed along that stream." Edinburg (Virginia) *Sentinel,* "Stray

Recollections of a Private of Co. C, 7th Virginia Cavalry," July 12 1900.

26. *OR,* vol. 12, pt. 3, p. 894.
27. Campbell Brown, "From Fairfax Courthouse to Richmond," undated fragment of manuscript in Polk, Ewell, Brown Papers. Typescript in possession of Terry L. Jones, Monroe, Louisiana.
28. Brown to his mother, 21 May 1862, Polk, Ewell, Brown Papers.
29. Richard S. Ewell, undated account of the 1862 Valley Campaign in Polk, Ewell, Brown Papers. Typescript in possession of Donald Pfanz, Fredericksburg, Virginia.

APPENDIX B

1. Hotchkiss, *Diary,* 4 April 1862.
2. Ibid., 31 March 1863.
3. *OR,* vol. 12, pt. 1, p. 703.
4. Henderson, *Stonewall Jackson,* pp. 251–52.
5. Freeman, *Lee's Lieutenants,* vol. 1, pp. 735–39.
6. See notes 30–32 and accompanying text, infra, for a detailed discussion of this point.
7. *OR,* vol. 12, pt. 1, p. 779.
8. Ibid., p. 746.
9. Ibid., p. 754.
10. Hotchkiss, *Diary,* 24 May 1862.
11. J. Hotchkiss to his wife, 26 May 1862, Hotchkiss Papers.
12. Apperson Diary, 24 May 1862.
13. Lynchburg (Virginia) *Daily Republican,* 31 May 1862.
14. Hall, *Diary,* 24 May 1862.
15. Allan, *Valley Campaign,* p. 128.
16. *OR,* vol. 12, pt. 1, p. 623.
17. Ibid., p. 576.
18. Ibid., p. 614.
19. Ibid.
20. Ibid., p. 620.
21. Gordon, *Brook Farm to Cedar Mountain,* p. 215.
22. *OR,* vol. 12, pt. 1, p. 623.
23. Gordon, *Brook Farm to Cedar Mountain,* p. 215, indicated that it in fact took two hours to countermarch to Newtown.
24. *OR,* vol. 12, pt. 1, p. 615.
25. C. F. Morse, *Letters Written during the Civil War* (privately printed, 1898), pp. 58–60.
26. *OR,* vol. 12, pt. 1, p. 587.
27. Ibid., p. 576.
28. Ibid., pp. 567, 579, 605, 612. It should be noted further that the other

Federal sources fixing a time for the main Confederate attack place it at or after 3:30 P.M. Ibid., pp. 568, 586.

29. Chambers, *Stonewall Jackson,* vol. 1, pp. 530–31.
30. Freeman, *Lee's Lieutenants,* vol. 1, pp. 386, 737–38.
31. *OR,* vol. 12, pt. 1, p. 703.
32. MS Journal of J. Hotchkiss, Hotchkiss Papers, p. 19.

APPENDIX C

1. The most readable and best researched study of Lincoln's May counterthrust is found in Williams, *Lincoln Finds a General,* vol. 1, chapter 7.
2. *OR,* vol. 12, pt. 3, p. 219.
3. Ibid., pt. 1, p. 11.
4. Ibid., p. 644.
5. Ibid., pt. 3, p. 235.
6. Ibid., p. 244.
7. Ibid., pp. 244–45.
8. Ibid., p. 258.
9. Ibid., pt. 1, p. 283.
10. Ibid., pt. 3, p. 260.
11. Ibid., p. 266.
12. Ibid., pt. 1, p. 644.
13. Ibid., pt. 3, p. 267.
14. Ibid., pt. 1, p. 644.
15. Ibid., p. 645.
16. Ibid.
17. Ibid., p. 646.
18. Ibid., p. 647.
19. Ibid., p. 11.
20. Ibid., p. 644.
21. Ibid., p. 647.
22. Ibid., pt. 3, p. 259.
23. Ibid.
24. Ibid., p. 276.
25. Ibid., pp. 277, 278–79.
26. Ibid., p. 285.
27. Ibid., p. 269.
28. Ibid., pp. 265, 284.
29. Ibid., p. 282.
30. Ibid., p. 277.
31. Ibid., pt. 1, p. 533.
32. Ibid., pt. 3, p. 278.
33. Ibid., p. 267.
34. Ibid., pp. 293–94.

35. Ibid., pt. 1, p. 647.
36. Ibid., p. 648.
37. Ibid., p. 13.
38. Ibid.
39. Ibid., pt. 3, pp. 290–91.
40. Ibid., p. 291.
41. Ibid., pt. 1, p. 649.
42. Ibid., pt. 3, p. 281.
43. Ibid., pp. 293–94.
44. Ibid., p. 302.
45. Ibid., pt. 1, pp. 682–83.
46. Ibid., p. 649.
47. Ibid., pt. 3, p. 314.
48. Ibid., pt. 1, p. 538.
49. Ibid., pt. 3, p. 315.
50. Ibid., pp. 299–300.
51. Ibid., pt. 1, pp. 649–50.
52. Ibid., p. 283.
53. Ibid. This explanation is that of McDowell. Shields left no known explanation of his false start.
54. George L. Wood, *History of the 7th Ohio* (New York: J. Miller, 1865; reprint ed., Louisville, Ky.: Lost Cause Press, 1958), p. 114.
55. William Kepler, *History of the 4th Regiment of Ohio Volunteers* (privately printed, Cleveland, Ohio, 1886), p. 67.
56. Military Historical Society of Massachusetts, *Papers of the Military Historical Society of Massachusetts,* vol. 6, *The Shenandoah Campaigns of 1862 and 1864* (Boston, 1907), p. 19.
57. Allan, *Valley Campaign,* p. 135.
58. *OR,* vol. 12, pt. 1, p. 677.

APPENDIX D

1. Freeman, *R. E. Lee,* vol. 2, p. 580.
2. Freeman, *Lee's Lieutenants,* vol. 1, p. 659.
3. See, e.g., Clifford Dowdey, *The Seven Days* (Boston: Little, Brown and Co., 1964), pp. 196–205.
4. Taylor, *Destruction and Reconstruction,* p. 61.
5. Hotchkiss, *Diary,* 1 June 1862.
6. Douglas, *I Rode with Stonewall,* p. 74.
7. Ibid.
8. Hotchkiss, *Diary,* 4 June 1862.
9. Douglas, *I Rode with Stonewall,* p. 75.
10. Ibid.
11. Hotchkiss, *Diary,* 4 June 1862.

12. Ibid., 5 June 1862.
13. Ibid., 6 June 1862.
14. Ibid.
15. Ibid.
16. *B & L,* vol. 2, p. 293.
17. John Harman to his brother, 6 June 1862, Hotchkiss Papers.
18. Howard, *Staff Officer,* p. 124.
19. A. S. Pendleton to his mother, 7 June 1862, Bean, ed., "Pendleton Letters," p. 364.

APPENDIX E

1. Compiled from Allan, *Valley Campaign; B & L,* vol. 12, pp. 300–301; and *OR,* vol. 12, pt. 1.

BIBLIOGRAPHY

MANUSCRIPT MATERIAL

Allan Letters. Unpublished letter (31 May 1862) of William Allan, an officer in the Valley Army Quartermaster Department, to Asher Harman. Huntington Library, San Marino, California.

Allan Papers. Unpublished manuscript written by William Allan after the war. Southern Historical Collection, University of North Carolina, Chapel Hill, North Carolina.

Apperson Diary. Unpublished diary of John Apperson, a hospital orderly with the 4th Virginia Infantry, covering the years 1861 and 1862. Rockbridge Historical Society, Lexington, Virginia.

Arehart Diary. Printed copy of 1862 diary of W. H. Arehart, a member of Ashby's command. Found in Rockingham (Virginia) *Recorder,* vol. 1, nos. 2 and 3, December 1946 and December 1947.

Army of the Rappahannock, Morning Reports, April–May 1862. Record Group 94, Record of the Adjutant General's Office, Civil War Organizations Returns, National Archives, Washington, D.C.

Ashby Letters. A few unpublished wartime letters of Turner Ashby, written during 1862. Chicago Historical Society, Chicago, Illinois.

Ashby Papers. A collection of orders to and from Turner Ashby, written during 1862; important given the rarity of Ashby material. Virginia Historical Society, Richmond, Virginia.

Barclay Letters. Unpublished wartime letters of Theodore Barclay, a member of the 4th Virginia Infantry; scattered dates. Rockbridge Historical Society, Lexington, Virginia.

Black Papers. Unpublished wartime letters of Dr. Harvey Black of the 4th Viriginia Infantry; scattered dates. Virginia Polytechnic Institute and State University Libraries, Blacksburg, Virginia.

Blackford Papers. Typescript of largely unpublished wartime letters of L. M. Blackford (referred to herein by his popular name, "Lanty") of the Rockbridge Artillery, along with much other material on the Blackford family. University of Virginia, Charlottesville, Virginia.

Boteler Papers. Unpublished letters and papers of Alexander R. Boteler, who served briefly as a member of the Valley Army Staff during 1862. Duke University Manuscript Collection, Durham, North Carolina.

Botts Papers. Miscellaneous items of Lawson Botts of the 2d Virginia Infantry; scattered dates. Virginia Military Institute, Lexington, Virginia.

Bowman, Howard Domingos Collection. One wartime letter of interest by Private W. Morton Brown of the Rockbridge Artillery describes operations around Romney. Washington Library, Macon, Georgia.

Bragg Papers. Diary of Thomas Bragg concerning inner workings of the Confederate government. Southern Historical Collection, University of North Carolina, Chapel Hill, North Carolina.

Branch Papers (a). Wartime letters, official and private, of L. O'Bryan Branch. University of Virginia, Charlottesville, Virginia.

Branch Papers (b). Same as above, but of different dates. The two sets read together provide much useful informaton on the thinking of Jackson and Ewell and how they maneuvered Branch's column. North Carolina Department of Archives and History, Raleigh, North Carolina.

Brown Memoirs. Papers of Campbell Brown and Richard S. Ewell. Military reminiscences of Captain Campbell Brown, Chief of Staff, R. S. Ewell's Division. Manuscript Unit, Tennessee State Library and Archives, Nashville, Tennessee. (These papers were the gift of Campbell Brown of Franklin, Tennessee, grandson of Captain Campbell Brown.)

Chase Diary. Typescript of unpublished wartime diary of Miss Julia Chase, a resident of Winchester. Handley Library, Winchester, Virginia.

Chew papers. Scattered postwar correspondence to and from Chew. Jefferson County Museum, Charles Town, West Virginia.

Clewell Letters. Unpublished wartime letters of Augustus A. Clewell of the 21st North Carolina Infantry; scattered dates. North Carolina Department of Archives and History, Raleigh, North Carolina.

Coble Reminiscences. Unpublished postwar recollections of Eli S. Coble of the 21st North Carolina Infantry. North Carolina Department of Archives and History, Raleigh, North Carolina.

Cook Papers. A fairly extensive collection of material relating to Jackson collected by Roy Bird Cook. Of particular interest is a handwritten account of the fighting around Port Republic by Colonel John Patton entitled "Reminiscences of Jackson." West Virginia and Regional Libaries, University of West Virginia, Morgantown, West Virginia.

Cox Memoir. Typescript of unpublished postwar recollection of Leroy Wesley Cox of Carrington's Battery. Albemarle County Historical Society Library, Charlottesville, Virginia.

Dabney Papers. Extensive material collected by Jackson's principal assistant in the Valley Campaign, Robert L. Dabney, including some correspondence to Jackson not cited elsewhere. Virginia State Library, Richmond, Virginia.

Davis Memoir. Typescript of unpublished postwar manuscript of W. F. Davis of Carrington's Battery entitled "Recollections, 1839–1864." In possession of J. Harvey Bailey, Charlottesville, Virginia.

Dinwiddie Papers. Unpublished wartime letters of James L. Dinwiddie of Carrington's Battery; scattered dates. Dinwiddie Family Papers, University of Virginia, Charlottesville, Virginia.

Douglas Letters. Unpublished wartime letters of Henry Kyd Douglas, a member of the Valley Army Staff, written during 1861 and 1862. Duke University Manuscript Collection, Durham, North Carolina.

Edmondson Letters. Manuscript wartime letters of James K. Edmondson, a member of the 27th Virginia Infantry. Rockbridge Historical Society, Lexington, Virginia. A published collection has been brought out by Dr. Charles W. Turner under the title *My Dear Emma (War Letters of Col. James K. Edmondson, 1861–1865),* Verona, Virginia, 1975.

Ewell Order Book. A copy of the order book kept at Ewell's headquarters in 1862, with scattered other documents pertaining to Ewell's Division. Manuscript Department, New York Historical Society, New York, New York.

Ewell Papers. Miscellaneous writings relating to the war, many by Campbell Brown, Ewell's son-in-law. Swem Library, College of William and Mary, Williamsburg, Virginia.

Fishburne Journal. Unpublished manuscript journal of Clement D. Fishburne, a member of the Rockbridge Artillery, written after the war. (This journal formed the basis of Fishburne's "Historical Sketch of the Rockbridge Artillery," *Southern Historical Society Papers* XXIII.) University of Virginia Manuscript Collection, Charlottesville, Virginia.

Fogleman Diary. Typescript of unpublished diary of Isaiah Fogleman, of Taylor's Brigade. Park Headquarters, Fredericksburg-Spotsylvania National Military Park, Fredericksburg, Virginia.

Garibaldi Letters. Unpublished wartime letters of John Garibaldi, a member of the 4th Virginia Infantry, written for the most part in 1861 and 1863. Virginia Military Institute Manuscript Collection, Lexington, Virginia.

Garnett Court-Martial Papers. Typed transcript of testimony and various supporting documents collected for court-martial of Brigadier General Richard B. Garnett during August 1862. Museum of the Confederacy, Richmond, Virginia.

Garnett Letter. Typescript of unpublished letter (2 July 1862) of Thomas S. Garnett of the 48th Virginia Infantry Park Headquarters, Fredericksburg-Spotsylvania National Military Park, Fredericksburg, Virginia.

Green Letters. Unpublished wartime letters of Jonathan Green, a member of the 21st Virginia Infantry and later of the Rockbridge Artillery; scattered dates. Duke University Manuscript Collection, Durham, North Carolina.

Griffin Diary. Typescript of unpublished diary of John Levi Griffin, a member of the 12th Georgia Infantry, 1861–62. Emory University Library, Atlanta, Georgia.

Harlow Letters. Unpublished wartime letters of George K. Harlow, a member of the 23d Virginia Infantry; scattered dates. Virginia Historical Society, Richmond, Virginia.

Harper Diary. Typescript of unpublished diary of W. P. Harper, a member of the 7th Louisiana Infantry. Tulane University Library, New Orleans, Louisiana.

Harrison Letters. Unpublished wartime letters of William F. Harrison, a member of the 23d Virginia Infantry; scattered dates. Duke University Manuscript Collection, Durham, North Carolina.

Hawks Papers. A vast collection of receipts, rosters, and various documents relating to the work of Major W. J. Hawks, Valley Army Commissary Officer, throughout the war. Duke University Manuscript Collection, Durham, North Carolina.

Hawse Diary. Scattered entries of a wartime diary of Jasper Hawse, a private in Ashby's cavalry. Typescript in Handley Library, Winchester, Virginia.

Hightower Letters. Unpublished wartime letters of Thomas M. Hightower, a member of the 21st Georgia Infantry; scattered dates. Georgia Department of Archives and History, Atlanta, Georgia.

Hooke Letters. Wartime letters of Robert W. Hooke, a member of the 5th Virginia Infantry; scattered dates. Duke University Manuscript Collection, Durham, North Carolina.

Hotchkiss Papers. The essential source on the Valley Campaign. This vast collection contains the complete wartime letters of Jedediah Hotchkiss, a member of the Valley Army staff. Also included are Hotchkiss's diary, postwar unpublished journal, and various short recollections. The wartime letters of John Harman, Valley Army quartermaster, are contained herein, as are copies of T. J. Jackson's Order and Letter Books covering the entire war. Finally, these papers contain the fruits of Hotchkiss's postwar research, including dozens of letters to and from surviving participants of various battles. This postwar correspondence extends to 1896. Manuscript Division, Library of Congress, Washington, D.C. A postwar writing entitled "Memoranda—Valley Campaign of 1862" by Hotchkiss is found in the Manuscript Department, New York Historical Society, New York, New York. It presents a summary of the campaign in which Hotchkiss drew on a number of his writings.

Humphreys Letter. Unpublished wartime letter (14 June 1862) of William H. Humphreys of Carpenter's Battery. In possession of Mr. David Updike, Staunton, Virginia.

Jackson Letters. Typescript of unpublished wartime letters of William L. Jackson, for a time a member of General Jackson's staff; scattered dates. West Virginia and Regional History Collection, West Virginia University Libraries, Morgantown, West Virginia.

Jackson Papers (a). Wartime letters of T. J. Jackson; scattered dates. Southern Historical Collection, University of North Carolina, Chapel Hill, North Carolina.

Jackson Papers (b). Wartime letters of T. J. Jackson; scattered dates. Virginia Historical Society, Richmond, Virginia.

Jackson Papers (c). Wartime letters of T. J. Jackson; scattered dates. Virginia Military Institute Manuscript Collection, Lexington, Virginia.

Jackson Papers (d). Wartime correspondence of T. J. Jackson; scattered dates. Museum of the Confederacy, Richmond, Virginia.

Jackson Papers (e). Wartime correspondence of T. J. Jackson; scattered dates. Virginia State Library, Richmond, Virginia.

Johnston Diary. Unpublished 1862 diary of George B. Johnston, a member of Branch's Brigade during its march toward the Valley. Johnston Papers, North Carolina Department of Archives and History, Raleigh, North Carolina.

Jones Diary. Manuscript of the field diary of Frank Jones of the 2d Virginia Infantry, 1862. Handley Library, Winchester, Virginia. (This material is now available in Colt, *Defend the Valley.*)

Kaufman Diary. Typescript of unpublished diary of Joseph Kaufman, a member of the 10th Virginia Infantry, written during 1862. Southern Historical Collection, University of North Carolina, Chapel Hill, North Carolina.

Kean Letters. Unpublished wartime letters of William C. Kean of the Rockbridge Artillery; scattered dates. University of Virginia, Charlottesville, Virginia.

Kearns Diary. Typescript of unpublished diary of Watkins Kearns of the 27th Virginia Infantry, written in 1862. Virginia Historical Society, Richmond, Virginia.

Kelly Letters. Unpublished wartime letters of A. K. Kelly, a member of the 21st Virginia Infantry; scattered dates. Kelly-Williamson Papers, Duke University Manuscript Collection, Durham, North Carolina.

Kern Letters. Unpublished wartime letters of Joseph M. Kern of the 13th Virginia Infantry, scattered dates, with typescript "Memorandum History of Movements of Hampshire Guards, Co. K, 13th Virginia Infantry, C.S.A." Southern Historical Society Collection, Chapel Hill, North Carolina.

Kinzer Diary. Typescript of unpublished diary of William T. Kinzer, a member of the 4th Virginia Infantry, primarily covering 1862. West Virginia and Regional Collection, West Virginia University Libraries, Morgantown, West Virginia.

Kirkpatrick Diary. An unpublished diary edited and annotated in "The Civil War Diary of James J. Kirkpatrick, 16th Mississippi Infantry, C.S.A.," a thesis by Eugene Matthew Ott, Jr., Texas A&M University, 1984.

Langhorne Letters. Wartime letters of James Langhorne, a member of the 4th Virginia Infantry, primarily written during 1861 and 1862. Virginia Historical Society, Richmond, Virginia.

Lee Diary. Wartime diary of Mrs. Hugh Lee, a Winchester civilian. Typescript in Handley Library, Winchester, Virginia.

Lyle Recollections. Recollections (entitled "Stonewall Jackson's Campguard") of John N. Lyle, a member of the 4th Virginia Infantry, written during or shortly after the war. Typescript in Rockbridge Historical Society, Lexington, Virginia. A printed edition has been produced in limited numbers by Dr. Charles W. Turner under the title *A Reminiscence of Lieutenant John Newton Lyle of the Liberty Hall Volunteers.* Roanoke, Virginia, 1986.

MacDonald Memoirs. Unpublished manuscript of Edward H. MacDonald, a member of Ashby's cavalry, written in 1866. Southern Historical Collection, University of North Carolina, Chapel Hill, North Carolina.

Mann Letters. Unpublished wartime letters of J. T. Mann of the 6th Virginia Cavalry; scattered dates. In possession of James Mann, Fredericksburg, Virginia.

Miller Letters. Wartime letters of Abraham S. Miller, a Virginia Militia surgeon, written primarily during 1861 and 1862. In possession of Dr. James A. Miller, Winchester, Virginia.

Moore Papers. Wartime letters of Samuel J. C. Moore of the 2d Virginia Infantry, with postwar recollections and other material on Moore and his family. Southern Historical Collection, University of North Carolina, Chapel Hill, North Carolina.

Morrison Diary. Unpublished diary of Harry R. Morrison, a member of the 4th Virginia Infantry, covering the month of March 1862. Rockbridge Historical Society, Lexington, Virginia.

Mullins Diary. Typescript of unpublished diary of Samuel Mullins of the 42d Virginia Infantry. In possession of R. P. Gravely, Martinsville, Virginia.

Munford Papers. Unpublished reminiscences of Thomas Munford, commander of the 2d Virginia Cavalry, and subsequently of the entire Valley cavalry, written after the war, and numerous letters and papers. Duke University Manuscript Collection, Durham, North Carolina.

Murray Letters. Typescript of unpublished wartime letters of William H. Murray of the 1st Maryland Infantry; scattered dates. Maryland Historical Society, Baltimore, Maryland.

Nadenbousch Papers. Scattered wartime orders, letters, and so forth, of J. Q. A. Nadenbousch, a member of the 2d Virginia Infantry. Duke University Manuscript Collection, Durham, North Carolina.

Neese Diary. Manuscript of wartime diary of George Neese of Chew's Battery. This document was the basis for Neese's *Three Years in the Confederate Horse Artillery* but was heavily edited and in some instances added to for the published version. Where the contemporaneous writing is more authentic, it is utilized and identified as MS Diary of Neese. Virginia Historical Society, Richmond, Virginia.

Parker Diary. Wartime diary of surgeon William Parker, a member of the 7th Tennessee Infantry. Washington and Lee University, Lexington, Virginia.

Pendleton Papers. Family letters and papers of the William N. Pendleton family, including wartime letters of A. S. Pendleton, a member of the Valley Army Staff, written until his death in 1864. Duke University Manuscript Collection, Durham, North Carolina.

Penn Letters. Unpublished wartime letters of Thomas G. Penn, a member of the 48th Virginia; scattered dates. Duke University Manuscript Collection, Durham, North Carolina.

Pile Memoir. Unpublished printed recollection of George C. Pile of the 37th Virginia Infantry. Tennessee State Library and Archives, Nashville, Tennessee.

Polk, Ewell, Brown Papers. Scattered war and postwar material, some rare and of interest concerning Ewell and his aide Campbell Brown. Southern Historical Collection, University of North Carolina, Chapel Hill, North Carolina.

Powell Papers. Unpublished wartime letters of Charles L. Powell, who briefly accompanied the Rockbridge Artillery during the Valley Campaign; scattered dates. Powell Family Papers, Swem Library, William and Mary University, Williamsburg, Virginia.

Pryor Letters. Unpublished wartime letters of Shephard G. Pryor, a member of 12th Georgia Infantry, written 1861–63. Typescript in Georgia Department of Archives and History, Atlanta, Georgia.

Ray Letters. Typescript of unpublished wartime letters of Lavender R. Ray, a member of the 1st Georgia Infantry, 1861–65. Georgia Department of Archives and History, Atlanta, Georgia.

Richardson Letters. Unpublished wartime letters of Sidney J. Richardson, a member of the 21st Georgia Infantry; scattered dates. Georgia Department of Archives and History, Atlanta, Georgia.

Ring Papers. Unpublished wartime diary and letters of George P. Ring, a member of Taylor's Louisiana Brigade; scattered dates. Tulane University Library, New Orleans, Louisiana.

Scott Papers. Unpublished wartime letters of Irby Scott, a member of the 12th Georgia Infantry. Duke University Manuscript Collection, Durham, North Carolina.

Shaner Papers. Typescript of wartime letters of Joseph F. Shaner of the Rockbridge Artillery, scattered dates, with short diary transcript. University Library, Washington and Lee University, Lexington, Virginia.

Shanklin Letters. Scattered wartime letters of Henry Shanklin, a private with the 27th Virginia Infantry. Virginia State Library, Richmond, Virginia.

Smith, Edmond B., Papers. Scattered wartime letters of Summerfield Smith of the Rockbridge Artillery. University of Virginia, Charlottesville, Virginia.

Snider Diary. Unpublished wartime diary of Joseph Snider of the 31st Virginia Infantry, written in 1862. West Virginia and Regional History Collection, West Virginia University Libraries, Morgantown, West Virginia.

Sperry Diary. Wartime diary of Kate Sperry, a Winchester civilian. Rich in details. Handley Library, Winchester, Virginia.

Taliaferro Papers (a). Scattered wartime papers, letters, orders, and so forth, of William B. Taliaferro, commander of the 3d Brigade, Jackson's Division, Army of the Valley. National Archives, Washington, D.C.

Taliaferro Papers (b). A large collection of scattered papers, useful primarily on the expedition to Romney in January 1862. College of William and Mary Library, Williamsburg, Virginia.

Taylor's Brigade, Morning Report, 11 June 1862. Huntington Library, San Marino, California.

Thomas Diary. Typescript of unpublished wartime diary of James W. Thomas of the 1st Maryland Infantry. In possession of A. Thomas Wallace, Annapolis, Maryland.

Tucker Diary. Unpublished wartime diary of Randolph Tucker, a member of the 21st Virginia Infantry. Museum of the Confederacy, Richmond, Virginia.

Wade Letters. Wartime letters of Thomas M. Wade, a member of the Rockbridge Artillery; scattered dates. Stonewall Jackson House, Lexington, Virginia.

Waldrop Letters. Wartime letters of Richard W. Waldrop, a member of the 21st Virginia Infantry, written throughout the war. Southern Historical Collection, University of North Carolina, Chapel Hill, North Carolina.

War Letters 1861–1865 Collection. Miscellaneous letters of some interest, including correspondence of Wells Hawks to Robert L. Dabney. New York Historical Society, New York, New York.

Warren Letters. Unpublished wartime letters of E. T. H. Warren of the 10th Virginia Infantry; scattered dates. University of Virginia, Charlottesville, Virginia.

Winder Diary. Unpublished wartime diary of Charles Winder, commander of the Stonewall Brigade. Maryland Historical Society, Baltimore, Maryland.

Wright Recollections. Unpublished manuscript of Charles C. Wright, a V.M.I. cadet, written after the war. Virginia Historical Society, Richmond, Virginia.

Wyatt Memoir. Typescript of unpublished postwar recollection of Asa Wyatt, a member of the 21st Virginia Infantry. Southern Historical Society Collection, University of North Carolina, Chapel Hill, North Carolina.

PERSONAL REMINISCENCES AND UNIT HISTORIES

Avirett, James B. *The Memoirs of General Turner Ashby and His Compeers.* Baltimore: Selby and Dulany, 1867.

Baylor, George. *Bull Run to Bull Run.* Richmond: B. F. Johnson Publishing Co., 1900.

Booth, George W. *Personal Reminiscences of a Maryland Soldier in the War Between the States.* Baltimore: Fleet, McGinley and Co., 1898.

Bosang, J. N. *Memoirs of a Pulaski Veteran.* Privately printed. Pulaski, Virginia, 1912.

Bryant, Edwin C. *History of the Third Regiment of Wisconsin Veteran Volunteer Infantry.* Cleveland: A. H. Clark Co., 1891.

Buck, Samuel D. *With the Old Confeds.* Baltimore: H. E. Houch & Co., 1925.

Casler, John O. *Four Years in the Stonewall Brigade.* Girard, Kans.: Appeal Publishing Co., 1906; reprint ed., Marietta, Ga.: Continental Book Co., 1951.

Chamberlayne, John Hampden. *Ham Chamberlayne—Virginian,* Edited by C. G. Chamberlayne. Richmond: Dietz Printing Co., 1932.

Conerly, L. W. *A Historical Sketch of the Quitman Guards, Company E, Sixteenth Mississippi Regiment.* New Orleans: Isaac T. Hinton, 1866.

Cooke, John Esten. *Wearing of the Gray.* New York, 1878; reprint ed., Bloomington: Indiana University Press, 1959.

Cummer, Clyde L., ed. *Yankee in Gray: The Civil War Memoirs of Henry E. Handerson, with a Selection of His Wartime Letters.* Cleveland: Press of Western Reserve University, 1962.

Dobbins, Austin C. *Grandfather's Journal: The Journal of Franklin L. Riley.* Dayton, Ohio: Morningside Bookshop, 1988.

Douglas, Henry Kyd. *I Rode with Stonewall.* Chapel Hill: University of North Carolina Press, 1940.

Early, Jubal. *Autobiographical Sketch and Narrative of the War Between the States.* Bloomington: Indiana University Press, 1960.

Fonerden, C. A. *A Brief History of the Military Career of Carpenter's Battery.* New Market, Va.: Henkel & Co., 1911.

Gill, John. *Reminiscences of Four Years as a Private Soldier in the Confederate Army.* Baltimore: Sun Printing Office, 1904.

Gilmor, Harry. *Four Years in the Saddle.* New York: Harper & Brothers, 1866.

Goldsborough, W. W. *The Maryland Line in the Confederate States Army.* Baltimore: Kelly Piet & Co., 1869.

Graybill, John H. *Diary of a Soldier of the Stonewall Brigade.* Privately printed. Woodstock, Virginia, no date.

Hall, James E. *The Diary of a Confederate Soldier.* Edited by Ruth Woods Dayton. Privately printed. Philippi, West Virginia, 1961.

Hamlin, Percy G., ed. *The Making of a Soldier: Letters of General R. S. Ewell.* Richmond: Whittet and Shepperson, 1935.

Hotchkiss, Jedediah. *Make Me a Map of the Valley: The Civil War Journal of Stonewall Jackson's Topographer.* Edited by Archie P. McDonald. Dallas: Southern Methodist University Press, 1973.

Houghton, W. R. *Two Boys in the Civil War and After.* Montgomery, Ala.: Paragon Press, 1912.

Howard, McHenry. *Recollections of a Maryland Staff Officer under Johnston, Jackson and Lee.* Baltimore: Williams and Wilkins Co., 1914.

Huffman, James. *Ups and Downs of a Confederate Soldier.* New York: William E. Rudge's Sons, 1940.

Johnston, Joseph E. *Narrative of Military Operations.* New York: D. Appleton and Co., 1874; reprint ed., Bloomington: Indiana University Press, 1959.

Jones, J. B. *A Rebel War Clerk's Diary.* Edited by Earl Schneck Miers. New York: Sagamore Press, 1958.

Kelly, Henry B. *Port Republic.* Philadelphia: J. B. Lippincott Co., 1886.

Longstreet, James. *From Manassas to Appomattox.* Philadelphia: J. B. Lippincott Co., 1896; reprint ed., Bloomington: Indiana University Press, 1960.

McCarthy, Carlton. *Detailed Minutiae of Soldier Life in the Army of Northern Virginia.* Privately printed. Richmond, Virginia, 1882; reprinted in *Soldier Life of the Union and Confederate Armies,* ed. by Philip Van Doren Stern, Bloomington: Indiana University Press, 1961.

McClendon, W. A. *Recollections of War Times by an Old Veteran under Stonewall Jackson and General James Longstreet.* Montgomery: Paragon Press, 1909.

McDonald, Cornelia. *A Diary with the Reminiscences of the War and Refugee Life in the Shenandoah Valley.* Nashville: Cullom and Ghertner Co., 1934.

McDonald, William N. *A History of the Laurel Brigade.* Baltimore: Sun Job Printing Office, 1907.

McGuire, Judith W. *Diary of a Southern Refugee.* Richmond: E. J. Hale and Son, 1867.

McKim, Randolph H. *A Soldier's Recollections.* New York: Longmans, Green and Co., 1910.

Moore, Edward A. *The Story of a Cannoneer under Stonewall Jackson.* New York: Neale Publishing Co., 1907.

Myers, Frank M. *The Comanches: A History of White's Battalion.* Baltimore: Kelly Piet and Co., 1871.

Neese, George M. *Three Years in the Confederate Horse Artillery.* New York: Neale Publishing Co., 1911.

Nisbet, James C. *Four Years on the Firing Line.* Edited by Bill Irvin Wiley. Jackson, Tenn.: McCowart-Mercer Press, 1963.

Oates, Dan, ed. *Hanging Rock Rebel: Lt. John Blue's War in West Virginia and the Shenandoah Valley.* Shippensburg, Pa.: Burd Street Press, 1994.

Oates, William C. *The War Between the Union and the Confederacy: A History of the 15th Alabama Regiment.* New York: Neale Publishing Co., 1905.

O'Ferrall, Charles T. *Forty Years of Active Service.* New York: Neale Publishing Co., 1904.

Opie, John N. *A Rebel Cavalryman with Lee, Stuart and Jackson.* Chicago: W. B. Conkey Co., 1899.

Peck, R. H. *Reminiscences of a Confederate Soldier.* Privately printed. Fincastle, Virginia, 1913.

Poague, William T. *Gunner with Stonewall.* Jackson, Tenn.: McCowart-Mercer Press, 1957.

Powley, J. B. *A Soldier's Letters to Charming Nellie.* New York: Neale Publishing Co., 1908.

Smith, Gustavus W. *Confederate War Papers.* New York: Atlantic Publishing and Engraving Co., 1884.

———. *The Battle of Seven Pines.* New York: G. Crawford, 1891.

Taylor, Richard. *Destruction and Reconstruction.* New York: D. Appleton and Co., 1879; reprint ed., New York: Longmans, Green and Co., 1955.

Toney, Marcus B. *The Privations of a Private.* Privately printed. Nashville, 1905.

Watkins, Samuel R. *Company Aytch.* Nashville: Cumberland Presbyterian Publishing House, 1882; reprint ed., Jackson, Tenn.: McCowart-Mercer Press, 1952.

Wilson, William L. *A Borderland Confederate.* Edited by Festus P. Summers. Pittsburgh: University of Pittsburgh Press, 1962.

Wood, James H. *The War.* Cumberland, Md.: Eddy Press, 1910.

Worsham, John H. *One of Jackson's Foot Cavalry.* New York: Neale Publishing Co., 1912.

OTHER PRIMARY SOURCES

Allan, William. *History of the Campaign of General T. J. (Stonewall) Jackson in the Shenandoah Valley of Virginia.* Philadelphia: J. B. Lippincott, 1880; reprint ed., Dayton, Ohio: Morningside, 1974.

Ashby, Thomas A. *The Valley Campaigns.* New York: Neale Publishing Co., 1914.

Blackford, L. Minor, ed. *Mine Eyes Have Seen the Glory.* Cambridge, Mass.: Harvard University Press, 1954.

Buck, William P., ed. *Sad Earth, Sweet Heaven: The Diary of Lucy R. Buck.* Birmingham, Ala.: Buck Publishing Co., 1993.

Chew, Roger P. Address of Colonel Roger P. Chew Delivered at the V.M.I., June 19, 1912. Lexington, Va.: Rockbridge Co. News Press, 1912.

Colt, Margaretta B. *Defend the Valley.* New York: Orion Books, 1994.

Crist, Lynda Laswell, and Mary A. Dix, eds. *The Papers of Jefferson Davis, Vol. 7,* 1861. Baton Rouge: Louisiana State University Press, 1991.

———. *The Papers of Jefferson Davis, Volume 8,* 1862. Baton Rouge: Louisiana State University Press, 1995.

Davis, Jefferson. *Rise and Fall of the Confederate Government.* 2 vols. New York: D. Appleton and Co., 1881.

Dowdey, Clifford, and Louis H. Manarin, eds. *The Wartime Papers of Robert E. Lee.* New York: De Capo Press, 1987.

Evans, Clement A., gen. ed. *Confederate Military History.* 13 vols. Atlanta: Confederate Publishing Co., 1899; reprint ed., Dayton, Ohio: Morningside Bookshop, 1975.

Garbar, Alexander M. *Sketch of the Life and Services of Major John A. Harman.* Privately printed. Staunton, Virginia, 1876.

Gilham, William. *Manual of Instruction for the Volunteers and Militia of the United States.* Philadelphia: Charles Desilver, 1861.

Gold, Thomas D. *History of Clarke County Virginia and Its Connection with the War Between the States.* Privately printed. Berryville, Virginia, 1914.

Johnson, Robert U., and C. C. Buel, eds. *Battles and Leaders of the Civil War.* 4 vols. New York: Century, 1887–88; reprint ed., New York: Thomas Yoseloff, 1956.

Lee, Robert E., Jr. *Recollections and Letters of General Robert E. Lee*. New York: Doubleday, Page, & Co., 1924.

Marshal, Charles. *An Aide-de-Camp to General Lee*. Boston: Little, Brown & Co., 1927.

Paxton, John G., ed. *Elisha F. Paxton: Memoir and Memorials*. Privately printed. New York, 1907.

Pollard, E. A. *Southern History of the War*. New York: Charles B. Richards, 1866.

Sears, Stephen W., ed. *The Civil War Papers of George B. McClellan*. New York: Ticknor & Fields, 1989.

Slaughter, Philip. *A Sketch of the Life of Randolph Fairfax*. Baltimore: Innen and Co., 1878.

Southern Historical Society. *Southern Historical Society Papers*. 52 vols. Richmond, Virginia, 1876–1959.

U. S. War Department. *War of the Rebellion: A Compilation of the Official Records of the Union and Confederate Armies*. 128 vols. Washington, D.C.: Government Printing Office, 1880–1901.

Waddell, Joseph A. *Annals of Augusta*. Richmond: William E. Jones, 1886.

Walker, Charles. *Memorial, Virginia Military Institute*. Philadelphia: J. B. Lippincott, 1875.

White, William S. *Sketches of the Life of Captain Hugh A. White*. Columbia, S.C.: South Carolina Steam Press, 1864.

Williams, Alpheus S. *From the Cannon's Mouth*. Detroit: Wayne State University Press and Detroit Historical Society, 1959.

Wise, Jennings C. *The Long Arm of Lee*. 2 vols. Lynchburg, Va.: J. P. Bell Co., Inc., 1915.

———. *The Military History of the Virginia Military Institute from 1839–1875*. Lynchburg, Va.: J. P. Bell, 1915.

BIOGRAPHICAL WORKS

Allan, Elizabeth P. *The Life and Letters of Margaret Junkin Preston*. Boston: Houghton Mifflin and Co., 1903.

———. *A March Past*. Richmond: privately printed, 1938.

Arnold, Thomas J. *Early Life and Letters of General Thomas J. Jackson*. New York: Fleming H. Revell Co., 1916.

Ashby, Thomas A. *Life of Turner Ashby*. New York: Neale Publishing Co., 1914.

Bean, W. G. *Stonewall's Man: Sandie Pendleton*. Chapel Hill: University of North Carolina Press, 1959.

Boyd, Belle. *Belle Boyd in Camp and Prison*. New York: Blelock & Co., 1866.

Bushong, Millard K. *General Turner Ashby and Stonewall's Valley Campaign.* Berryville, Va.: Virginia Book Co., 1980.

Caldwell, Willie W. *Stonewall Jim.* Elliston, Va.: Northcross House, Publishers, 1990.

Casso, Evans J. *Francis T. Nicholls: A Biographical Tribute.* Privately printed. Thibodaux, Louisiana, 1988.

Chambers, Lenoir. *Stonewall Jackson.* 2 vols. New York: William Morrow and Co., 1959.

Clarence, Thomas. *General Turner Ashby.* Winchester, Va.: Eddy Press Corp., 1907.

Cook, Roy Bird. *The Family and Early Life of Stonewall Jackson,* 3rd ed. Privately printed. Charles Town, West Virginia, 1948.

Cooke, John Esten. *Stonewall Jackson.* New York: D. Appleton and Co., 1876.

Dabney, Robert L. *Life and Campaigns of Lieutenant General Thomas J. Jackson.* New York: Blelock and Co., 1866.

Davis, William C. *Jefferson Davis: The Man and His Hour.* New York: Harper Collins, 1991.

DuFour, Charles L. *Gentle Tiger.* Baton Rouge: Louisiana State University Press, 1957.

Farwell, Byron. *Stonewall.* New York: W. W. Norton, 1992.

Freeman, Douglas Southall. *R. E. Lee.* 4 vols. New York: Charles Scribner's Sons, 1934.

Hamlin, Percy G. *Old Bald Head.* Strasburg, Va.: Shenandoah Publishing House, 1940.

Henderson, G. F. R. *Stonewall Jackson and the American Civil War.* New York: Longmans, Green and Co., 1936.

Jackson, Mary Anna. *Life and Letters of General Thomas J. Jackson.* New York: Harper & Brothers, 1892.

———. *Memoirs of Stonewall Jackson.* Louisville: Prentice Press, 1895.

Johnson, Thomas C. *The Life and Letters of Robert Lewis Dabney.* Richmond: Whittet and Shepperson, 1903.

Martin, Samuel J. *The Road to Glory: Confederate General Richard S. Ewell.* Indianapolis: Guild Press of Indiana, 1991.

Miller, William J. *Mapping for Stonewall.* Washington, D.C.: Elliott and Clark, 1993.

Moore, Alison. *He Died Furious.* Privately printed. Baton Rouge, 1983.

Parrish, T. Michael. *Richard Taylor, Soldier Prince of Dixie.* Chapel Hill: The University of North Carolina Press, 1992.

Roper, Peter W. *Jedediah Hotchkiss: Rebel Mapmaker and Virginia Businessman.* Shippensburg, Pa.: White Mane Publishing Company, Inc., 1992.

Symonds, Craig L. *Joseph E. Johnston.* New York: W. W. Norton & Company, 1992.

Vandiver, Frank E. *Mighty Stonewall.* New York: McGraw-Hill Book Company, 1957.

Waugh, John C. *The Class of 1846*. New York: Warner Books, 1994.
Wessels, William L. *Born to Be a Soldier*. Fort Worth: Texas Christian University Press, 1971.

GENERAL SOURCES

Alexander, Beven. *Lost Victories: The Military Genius of Stonewall Jackson*. New York: Henry Holt and Company, 1992.
Armstrong, Richard L. *The Battle of McDowell*. Lynchburg, Va.: H. E. Howard, 1990.
———. *7th Virginia Cavalry*. Lynchburg, Va.: H. E. Howard, 1992.
Baltimore & Ohio Railroad Company. "Thirty-sixth Annual Report, 1862." Baltimore, Maryland, 1862.
Bean, W. G. *The Liberty Hall Volunteers*. Charlottesville: University of Virginia Press, 1964.
Beck, Brandon H., and Charles S. Grunder. *The First Battle of Winchester*. Lynchburg, Va.: H. E. Howard, 1992.
Bellamy, Christopher. *The Evolution of Modern Land Warfare: Theory and Practice*. London: Routledge, 1990.
Bill, Alfred Hoyt. *The Beleaguered City*. New York: Alfred A. Knopf, 1946.
Black, Robert C., III. *The Railroads of the Confederacy*. Chapel Hill: University of North Carolina Press, 1952.
Bohannon, Keith. *The Giles, Allegheny and Jackson Artillery*. Lynchburg, Va.: H. E. Howard, 1990.
Brice, Marshall. *The Stonewall Brigade Band*. Verona, Va.: McClure Printing Co., 1967.
Campbell, Charles. *History of the Colony and Ancient Dominion of Virginia*. Philadelphia: J. B. Lippincott, 1860.
Camper, Charles. *Historical Record of the First Maryland Infantry (Union)*. Washington, D.C.: Gibson Brothers, 1871.
Cartmell, T. K. *Shenandoah Valley Pioneers*. Winchester, Va.: Eddy Press Corp., 1909.
Chapla, John D. *42nd Virginia Infantry*. Lynchburg, Va.: H. E. Howard, Inc., 1983.
———. *48th Virginia Infantry*. Lynchburg, Va.: H. E. Howard, Inc., 1989.
Cheney, Newel. *History of the 9th Regiment of New York Cavalry*. Privately printed. Jamestown, New York, 1901.
Christian, W. A. *Richmond*. Richmond: L. H. Jenkins, 1912.
Clausewitz, Carl von. *Principles of War*. Translated and edited by Hans W. Gatzke. Harrisburg, Pa.: Stackpole Company, 1942.
Collins, Darrell L. *The Battles of Cross Keys and Port Republic*. Lynchburg, Va.: H. E. Howard, Inc., 1993.
Cooke, John Esten. *Stonewall Jackson and the Old Stonewall Brigade*. Edited by Richard Harwell. Charlottesville: University of Virginia Press, 1954.

Cooling, Benjamin Franklin, III. *Symbol, Sword and Shield: Defending Washington during the Civil War.* Shippensburg, Pa.: White Mane Publishing Company, Inc., 1991.

Couper, William. *One Hundred Years at V.M.I.* 4 vols. Richmond: Garrett and Massie, 1939.

Crute, Joseph H. *Units of the Confederate Army.* Powhaten, Va.: Derwent Books, 1987.

Cummings, Kate. *The Journal of a Confederate Nurse.* Edited by Richard B. Harwell. Baton Rouge: Louisiana State University Press, 1959.

Dowdey, Clifford. *The Seven Days.* Boston: Little, Brown and Co., 1964.

Driver, Robert J. *52nd Virginia Infantry.* Lynchburg, Va.: H. E. Howard, Inc., 1986.

———. *The 1st and 2nd Rockbridge Artillery.* Lynchburg, Va.: H. E. Howard, Inc., 1987.

Fitzpatrick, John C., ed. *The Writings of George Washington.* 39 vols. Washington, D.C.: Government Printing Office, 1931–44.

Freeman, Douglas Southall. *Lee's Dispatches to Jefferson Davis.* New York: G. P. Putnam's Sons, 1957.

———. *Lee's Lieutenants.* 3 vols. New York: Charles Scribners Sons, 1942–44.

Frye, Dennis E. *2nd Virginia Infantry.* Lynchburg, Va.: H. E. Howard, Inc., 1982.

Fuller, J. F. C. *Grant and Lee.* Bloomington: Indiana University Press, 1957.

Glatthaar, Joseph T. *Partners in Command: The Relationships Between Leaders in the Civil War.* New York: The Free Press, 1994.

Gordon, George H. *Brook Farm to Cedar Mountain.* Boston: Osgood and Co., 1863.

Gottman, Jean. *Virginia at Mid-Century.* New York: Henry Holt and Co., 1955.

Hale, Laura Virginia. *Four Valiant Years in the Lower Shenandoah Valley.* Front Royal, Va.: Hathaway Publishing, 1986.

Hamilton, Stanislaus, ed. *Letters to Washington and Accompanying Papers.* 5 vols. Boston: Houghton Mifflin and Co., 1898–1902.

Hart, Freeman H. *The Valley of Virginia in the American Revolution.* Chapel Hill: University of North Carolina Press, 1942.

Hungerford, Edward. *The Story of the Baltimore and Ohio Railroad.* 2 vols. New York: G. P. Putnam's Sons, 1928.

Jefferson, Thomas. *Notes on the State of Virginia.* Edited by William Peden. Chapel Hill: University of North Carolina Press for the Institute of Early American History and Culture, 1955.

Johnston, Angus J., II. *Virginia Railroads in the Civil War.* Chapel Hill: University of North Carolina Press, 1961.

Jones, Terry L. *Lee's Tigers: The Louisiana Infantry in the Army of Northern Virginia.* Baton Rouge: Louisiana State University Press, 1987.

Kellogg, Sanford C. *The Shenandoah Valley and Virginia, 1861–1865.* New York: Neale Publishing Co., 1903.

Kepler, William. *History of the 4th Regiment of Ohio Volunteers.* Privately printed. Cleveland, Ohio, 1886.

Kercheval, Samuel. *A History of the Valley of Virginia,* 4th ed. Strasburg, Va.: Shenandoah Publishing House, 1925.

Kleese, Richard B. *Shenandoah County in the Civil War.* Lynchburg, Va.: H. E. Howard, Inc., 1992.

Koontz, Louis K. *The Virginia Frontier: 1754–1763.* Baltimore: Johns Hopkins University Press, 1925.

Krick, Robert K. *Lee's Colonels.* Dayton, Ohio: Morningside Bookshop, 1979.

Lash, J. N. *Destroyer of the Iron Horse.* Kent, Ohio: The Kent State University Press, 1990.

Leech, Samuel V. *The Raid of John Brown at Harper's Ferry.* Washington, D.C.: DeSoto Press, 1909.

Leonhard, Robert. *The Art of Maneuver.* Novato, Calif.: Presidio Press, 1991.

Luttwok, Edward N. *Strategy.* Cambridge: The Belknap Press, 1987.

Luvass, Jay. *Military Legacy of the Civil War.* Chicago: University of Chicago Press, 1959.

Manarin, L. H., ed. *Richmond at War: The Minutes of the City Council, 1861–1865.* Chapel Hill: University of North Carolina Press, 1966.

Maury, Ann, ed. *Memoirs of a Huguenot Family.* New York: G. P. Putnam's Sons, 1901.

McPherson, James M. *Ordeal by Fire.* New York: Alfred P. Knopf, 1982.

McWhiney, Grady, and Perry D. Jamieson. *Attack and Die.* Tuscaloosa: University of Alabama Press, 1982.

Monier, Henry D. *Military Annals of Louisiana.* New Orleans, 1875.

Moore, Frank, ed. *The Rebellion Record.* 12 vols. New York, 1862–71.

Moore, Robert H., II. *The Charlottesville, Lee Lynchburg and Johnson's Bedford Artillery.* Lynchburg, Va.: H. E. Howard, Inc. 1990.

Morse, C. F. *Letters Written during the Civil War.* Privately printed. 1898.

Morton, Frederic. *The Story of Winchester in Virginia.* Strasburg, Va.: Shenandoah Publishing House, 1925.

Murphy, Terrence V. *10th Virginia Infantry.* Lynchburg, Va.: H. E. Howard, Inc., 1989.

Murray, Alton J. *South Georgia Rebels.* Privately printed. Saint Marys, Georgia, 1976.

Musick, Michael P. *6th Virginia Cavalry.* Lynchburg, Va.: H. E. Howard, 1990.

Myers, Robert M., ed. *The Children of Pride.* New Haven, Ct.: Yale University Press, 1972.

Nolan, Alan T. *Lee Considered: General Robert E. Lee and Civil War History.* Chapel Hill: University of North Carolina Press, 1991.

Peyton, J. Lewis. *History of Augusta County.* Staunton, Va.: Yost and Son, 1882.

Pollard, E. A. *Life of Jefferson Davis.* Philadelphia: National Publishing Co., 1896.

———. *The Lost Cause.* New York: E. B. Treat & Co., 1866.

Putnam, Sally. *In Richmond during the Confederacy.* New York: G. W. Carleton and Co., 1963.

Ranklin, Thomas M. *Stonewall Jackson's Romney Campaign.* Lynchburg, Va.: H. E. Howard, Inc., 1994.

———. *37th Virginia Infantry.* Lynchburg, Va.: H. E. Howard, Inc., 1987.

Reidenbaugh, Lowell. *27th Virginia Infantry.* Lynchburg, Va.: H. E. Howard, Inc., 1993.

———. *33rd Virginia Infantry.* Lynchburg, Va.: H. E. Howard, Inc., 1987.

Robertson, James I., Jr. *4th Virginia Infantry.* Lynchburg, Va.: H. E. Howard, Inc., 1985.

———. *The Stonewall Brigade.* Baton Rouge: Louisiana State University Press, 1963.

Rowland, Dunbar, ed. *Jefferson Davis: Constitutionalist.* Jackson, Miss.: Mississippi Department of Archives and History, 1923.

Royster, Charles. *The Destructive War.* New York: Alfred A. Knopf, 1991.

Schuricht, Hermann. *History of the German Element in Virginia.* Baltimore: Theo. Kroh & Sons, 1898.

Sears, Stephen W. *To the Gates of Richmond.* New York: Ticknor & Fields, 1992.

Se Cheverall, J. *Journal History of the 29th Ohio.* Privately printed. Cleveland, 1883.

Simpson, Harold B. *Hood's Texas Brigade: Lee's Grenadier Guard.* Dallas: Alcor Publishing, 1983.

Smith, Abram P. *History of the 76th New York Infantry.* Syracuse: Smith & Miles, 1867.

Strickler, Harry M. A *Short History of Page County.* Richmond: Dietz Press, 1952.

Strother, David. *A Virginia Yankee in the Civil War: Diaries of David Strother.* Edited by Cecil D. Eby. Chapel Hill: University of North Carolina Press, 1961.

Summers, Festus P. *The Baltimore and Ohio in the Civil War.* New York: G. P. Putnam's Sons, 1939.

Svenson, Peter. *Battlefield.* Boston: Faber and Faber, 1992.

Thomas, Emory M. *The Confederate State of Richmond.* Austin: University of Texas Press, 1971.

Virginia Central Railroad Co. "Twenty-sixth Annual Report, 1866." Richmond, Virginia, 1861.

Virginia State Government. Militia Laws. Richmond, 1855.

Warner, Ezra. *Generals in Gray.* Baton Rouge: Louisiana State University Press, 1959.

Wayland, John W. *The German Element of the Shenandoah Valley of Virginia.* Charlottesville, Va.: Michie Co., 1907.

———. *History of Rockingham County.* Dayton, Va.: Ruebush-Elkins Co., 1912.

———. *History of Shenandoah County.* Strasburg, Va.: Shenandoah Publishing House, 1927.

———. *Stonewall Jackson's Way.* Staunton, Va.: McClure Co., 1940.

———. *Twenty-five Chapters on the Shenandoah Valley.* Strasburg, Va.: Shenandoah Publishing House, Inc., 1957.

———. *Virginia Valley Records.* Strasburg, Va.: Shenandoah Publishing House, 1930.

Williams, Kenneth P. *Lincoln Finds a General.* 5 vols. New York: Macmillan, 1949.

Wood, George L. *History of the 7th Ohio.* New York: J. Miller, 1865; reprint ed., Louisville, Ky.: Lost Cause Press, 1958.

NEWSPAPERS

Americus, Georgia, *Sumter Republican,* 1862.
Atlanta, Georgia, *Intelligencer,* 1862.
Augusta, Georgia, *Daily Constitutionalist,* 1862.
Boston, Massachusetts, *Daily Advertiser,* 1862.
Charlotte, North Carolina, *Whig,* 1862.
Edinburg, Virginia, *Sentinel,* 1990.
Harrisburg, Pennsylvania, *Daily Telegraph,* 1862.
Harrisonburg, Virginia, *Rockingham Register,* 1862.
Lynchburg, Virginia, *Daily Republican,* 1862.
Macon, Georgia, *Daily Telegraph,* 1862.
Memphis, Tennessee, *Daily Appeal,* 1862.
Mobile, Alabama, *Daily Advertiser and Register,* 1862.
New Orleans, Louisiana, *Daily True Delta,* 1861.
New York, New York, *Herald,* 1862.
New York, New York, *Times,* 1862.
Opelousas, Louisiana, *Courier,* 1862.
Philadelphia, Pennsylvania, *Inquirer,* 1862.
Richmond, Virginia, *Daily Dispatch,* 1861 and 1862.
Richmond, Virginia, *Enquirer,* 1862.
Richmond, Virginia, *Whig,* 1861 and 1862.
Washington, D.C., *Daily National Intelligencer,* 1862.
Washington, D.C., *Evening Star,* 1862.
Washington, D.C., *National Republican,* 1862.
Washington, D.C., *Sunday Morning Chronicle,* 1862.
Winchester, Virginia, *Daily Republican,* 1861 and 1862.
Winchester, Virginia, *Virginian,* 1860.

PERIODICAL ARTICLES

Anderson, Carter. "Train Running for the Confederacy," *Locomotive Engineering,* July 1892.

Bean, William G., ed. "The Valley Campaign of 1862 as Revealed in Letters of Sandie Pendleton," *Virginia Magazine of History and Biography,* 78, no. 3 (July 1970).

Bearss, Edwin C. "War Comes to the Chesapeake and Ohio Canal," *West Virginia History,* 28, no. 4 (October 1966).

Bierne, R. R., ed. "Three War Letters," *Maryland Historical Magazine,* 40, no. 4 (December 1945).

Billman, Calvin J., ed. "Joseph M. Ellison: War Letters (1862)," *Collections of the Georgia Historical Society,* 48, 1964.

Boyd, Caspar. "Caspar W. Boyd, Co. I, 15th Ala. Infantry, C.S.A. A Casualty of the Battle of Cross Keys, Virginia. His Last Letters Written Home," *Alabama Historical Quarterly,* 23 (1961).

Burnett, E. C., ed. "Letters of Barnett Hardeman Cody and Others, 1861–64," *Georgia Historical Quarterly,* 23, no. 4 (December 1939).

Graham, Martin F., and Donald L. Canney. "Port Republic, Virginia: Stonewall Jackson's Narrow Escape. Including the Battles of Cross Keys and Port Republic," *Blue and Gray Magazine,* 2, no. 3 (January 1985).

Hopkins, C. A. Porter, ed. "An Extract from the Journal of Mrs. Hugh H. Lee of Winchester, Va.," *Maryland Historical Magazine,* 53, no. 4 (December 1958).

Krick, Robert K. "The Army of Northern Virginia's Most Notorious Court Martial: Jackson vs. Garnett," *Blue and Gray Magazine,* 3, no. 6 (July 1986).

Kurtz, George. "Account of the Valley Campaign of 1862," *Winchester-Frederick County Historical Society Papers,* 3, 1955.

Lang, Walter P., Jr., J. Frank Hennessee, and William E. Bush, Jr. "Jackson's Valley Campaign and the Operational Level of War," *Parameters* (Winter 1985).

Luvass, Jay. "Lee and the Operational Art: The Right Place, the Right Time," *Parameters* (Autumn 1992).

Montague, Ludwell Lee. "Substance of the Army of the Valley," *Military Affairs,* 12, no. 4 (Winter 1948).

Moore, C. Leon. "Personal Narrative," *Confederate Veteran Magazine,* vol. 22, p. 511.

Scott, W. W., ed. "Diary of Capt. H. W. Wingfield," *Bulletin of the Virginia State Library,* 16, nos. 2 and 3 (July 1927).

INDEX